Khaled Alawadi

RETHINKING SUBURBS: MORPHOLOGICAL AND NETWORK ANALYSIS REVIEW

CONTRIBUTORS

Research Team Members:

Principal Investigator
Dr. Khaled Alawadi

Senior Researchers
Dr. Ngoc Nguyen Hong
Asim Khanal
Nour Al Khaja

Students: Research Assistants
Hind Alameri
Eiman Alrubaei
Azhar El Doudin
Mahmoud Abu Ali
Rahma Magdi Abelghani
Mariam Alkaabi
Sara Alhinai
Abrar Aletaywi
Mariam Alhadhrami
Abdallah Mouselly
Rawan Sohdy Abdelfatteh
Esma Mohamed Vall

ACKNOWLEDGEMENTS

There were many individuals and agencies whose generous support was influential to the realization of this book. I would first like to thank the agencies that graciously shared data and records with us, including the ***Department of Municipalities and Transport (DMT), Abu Dhabi Spatial Data Infrastructure (AD-SDI), and Dubai Municipality (DM)*** for spatial data on Abu Dhabi's and Dubai's urbanized areas respectively. My sincere and very special thanks go to Senior Researchers– Dr. Ngoc Nguyen Hong, Nour Mohamad AlKhaja, and Asim Khanal, who made the most significant contributions of all researchers who participated in the project. They worked with me side by side for about 3 years to produce this book. Their massive efforts throughout the process, which started in September 2019, have been remarkable, valuable, and greatly appreciated. Their involvement in creating the research content and preparing/reviewing several hundred maps have been instrumental to this project, and words are not enough to acknowledge their critical involvement and contribution. Their dedication and patience in carrying out the various tasks connected to the research have been outstanding. I also offer special thanks to Dr. Hong and Asim for their significant contribution to the text and analysis of maps; and to Nour for her hands-on approach in supervising and auditing the analysis work-flow, generating the data visuals and maps.

My greatest appreciation and thanks also go to my Research Assistants/Students in the Sustainable Critical Infrastructure program at Khalifa University. Their research and contributions have been essential and have included the study of diverse sites and landscapes across Abu Dhabi and Dubai. Students' involvement enabled us to carry out the research work smoothly. Their work entailed spending several hours in selected sites (for example, West Island, Dubai Creek, Al Satwa, Baniyas, etc.), observing people's interactions with the physical environment, and taking hundreds of pictures. Hind Alameri, Eiman Alrubaei, Azhar El Doudin, Mahmoud Abu Ali, Rahma Abelghani Magdy, Mariam Alkaabi, Sara Alhinai, Rawan Sohdy Abdelfatteh, Abrar Aletaywi, Abdallah Mouselly, Esma Mohamed Vall, and Mariam Alhadhrami ran several iterations of urban network analyses, and produced maps of various neighborhoods in Abu Dhabi and Dubai. The elaborate task of preparing and finalizing more than two thousand maps was prepared and conducted by the aforementioned students throughout the project duration. The analysis and mapping process required a thorough knowledge of several software, tireless working ethics and team coordination; and I consider myself truly fortunate to have such a prolific group of students contributing to the project. The contributions of these students helped the research team to expedite the extensive mapping and network analysis required for this book. With their involvement and massive effort, ***Rethinking Suburbs: Morphological and Network Analysis Review*** became real.

Many people have collaborated on this project, and I very much appreciate their contributions, including the graphic designers and the entire team at Slash. Special thanks go to Nuno Abreu, Jorge Abreu, Anna Manolatos, Nour Al Khateeb and Nada Al Khateeb for their creative work and coordination. Their continued effort, coordination, dedication, support, and organization have been remarkable throughout all stages of publication. With their involvement, ***Rethinking Suburbs: Morphological and Network Analysis Review*** became tangible. I would also like to acknowledge Khalifa University, for providing facilities, equipment, space, and support during the research and production stages of the project. I would like to thank Khalifa University's Office of Research Services, Labs, Procurement, Facilities, and Finance staff, whose contributions and support were beyond imagination. Special thanks also go to Dr. Tom Skarpas, Civil Infrastructure and Environmental Engineering Department Chair, who greatly supported our research activities. Khalifa University has been my professional home, and none of this would have been possible if Khalifa University hadn't offered the internal funding/grant, time and facilities required to carry out this research project.

Sincerely,
Khaled Alawadi

07 DISCUSSION

08 IMPLICATIONS FOR PRACTICE

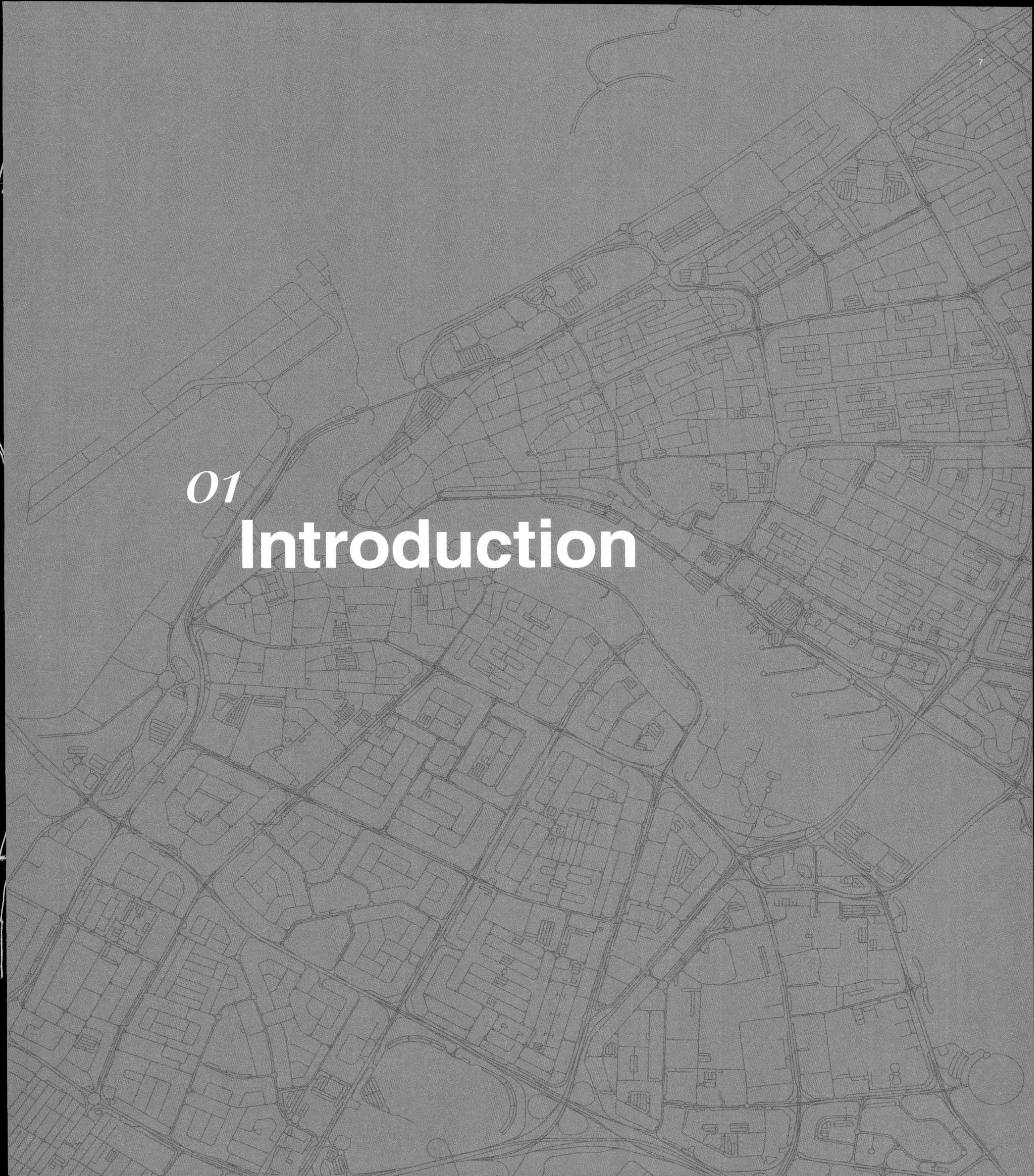

01 Introduction

Cities have been the centers of culture, commerce, politics, and scientific achievement since antiquity (Leon 2008). However, urbanization became a global phenomenon only in the second half of the 20th century (Davis 1995). In general, cities have existed as a collection of urban villages (Gan 1962); London (Hall 1989) and Los Angeles (Jencks 1993) exemplify this pattern. It is argued that the prominent urbanists of the 20th century, such as Olmstead, Geddes, Howard, Burnham, Sitte, Wagner, and Unwin, considered the city a "thing that could be engineered successfully in such a way as to control, contain, modify or enhance social processes" (Harvey 1996, p.50). This line of thought set a path for either a mechanistic approach to urban form, such as that of Le Corbusier's Radiant City, which largely disregarded the surrounding sites and their history, or the more organic approach of Frank Lloyd Wright's Broadacre City, which has been labeled as anti-urban by some critics (Alofsin 2011; Leon 2014). However, viewing cities as stagnant things may marginalize our sense of urbanization as a process (Harvey 1996). Urbanization can be defined as a multi-dimensional process by which land is converted into urban places through the agglomeration of human population (Seto, Parnell, and Elmqvist 2013). In this vein, this book features significant sections elaborating the history of two case-study cities —Abu Dhabi and Dubai— and how different economic, social, and political factors led to the formation of their built environments which we witness today.

Compared with traditional urban neighborhoods, suburbs inhibit sociability and neighborliness (Jacobs 1961; Mumford 1961; Sennett 1977; Gehl 2011, 2013), lack appealing forms and an effective physical language that would promote interaction (Jacobs 1961; Sennett 1977; Gehl 2011, 2013), and promote automobile dependence and environmental degradation (Farr 2008; Condon 2010; Beatley and Newman 2012). By contrast, urban scholars have long admired the forms, patterns, and visual experience of the fine-grain quotidian landscapes that modern and postmodern planning eradicated (Jacobs 1961; Sennett 1977; Gehl 2011, 2013). Although there is a broad consensus among scholars about the definition of urbanization as a process, academic discourse has often focused only on cities as research subjects (Angelo and Wachsmuth 2015). And within cities, inner urban areas have been major sites of consideration for place-making strategies such as densification, pedestrian connectivity enhancement, revitalization, TOD development, landscaping, and other urban design interventions. For example, theories of sustainable urban forms such as the "compact city", which became popular in academic and policy-making circles in the 1990s (Neuman 2005), only focused on inner urban areas. This agenda concurrently depicted suburbs as undesirable and wasteful places (Williams, Joynt, and Hopkins 2010) and as ground zero of many of the social and environmental problems cities face (Williams, Burton, and Jenks 2000). Low-density suburban development has long been a "niche subject" within the urban design literature (Berger and Kotkin 2018, p.12), but scholars have agreed on its deleterious consequences. Lewis Mumford (1975), for example, called suburbs "anti-city" and described the process of massive suburbanization as missing the dynamism of city life and the sociability of central neighborhoods. He said that suburbs allow for the creation of "an encapsulated life" in which inhabitants are prisoners of their automobiles and houses, leading to the disappearance of community and neighborliness, fine-grained street patterns, pedestrian-oriented streets, and mixed uses (Mumford 1961, p.512). Jane Jacobs, Jan Gehl, and Richard Sennett condemned suburbia as desperately ineffectual and particularly inadequate at promoting human interaction. Suburbs and strategies for making them better places have been either largely ignored in the literature (Breheny 1996; Stretton 1996), or discussed negatively. For instance, suburbs have been defined as secondary to urban areas (McNeur 2014), and Batty, Besussi, and Chin (2003) compared suburbs with cancer to describe their uncontrollable growth. These kinds of debates over suburbanization have focused on vilifying suburbs while simultaneously spectacularizing downtown revival. Katie Williams and Pierre Filion are among the scholars who argue that this approach is problematic. However, retrofitting suburbia has become part of the new agenda for some compaction promoters, who argue that, through Transit Oriented Development, suburbs can be intensified or become small cities in themselves, like urban villages (Williams et al. 2010). Most housing stock exists in suburbs; thus, planners and policy makers must consider suburbs not as problematic but as "part of the solution to creating sustainable areas" (Williams et al. 2010, p.106). Williams, Joynt, and Hopkins (2010, p.109) further argue that "suburban areas will be a site of major change" that planners should consider when dealing with pertinent issues such as sustainable development.

Soaring, sprawling, and extravagant suburban growth is a phenomenon that is not unique to the Gulf region or the UAE. Poor accessibility and almost non-existent walking trips in low- density suburbs are topics of global debate among urban scholars and professionals. North American suburbs are associated with poor pedestrian accessibility because their physical features create long walking distances, encourage indirect walking routes, and decrease the number of necessities reachable through walking (Southworth and Ben-Joseph 1997). Similarly, residents of Canadian and Australian suburban developments rely on their cars to reach to destinations within their own neighborhoods because of circuitous street layouts, a lack of sidewalks, and long travel distances (Owen et al. 2007). Kotkin (2010) has labeled the process of suburbanization inevitable and inescapable, as it is taking place in almost all large cities around the world. Thus, suburbanization is considered to be the unavoidable part of the urban transformation process.

Cities have been the centers of culture, commerce, politics and scientific achievement since antiquity.
Leon, D. A. (2008)

Low-density suburbs have proliferated around the world. In the United States, 69 percent of the population now lives in suburbs (Cox 2017). In *The Human City: Urbanism for the Rest*, Joel Kotkin observed that suburban development has spread out and become the urban model that dominates our cities; he argued that dispersed and fragmented low-density developments have become a reality across many regions worldwide. Based on Kotkin's (2016) observations, the glamour and appeal of suburbs have become pervasive and prevalent around the world. In Tokyo, the population flow to suburbs began with the expansion of the rail system and is also attributed to the extreme cost of housing in central Tokyo. Since the 1960s, more than 90 percent of Tokyo's urban development has been on the periphery (Kotkin 2016, p.153). Similarly, in Australia, despite policies and regulations designed to promote densification and compact developments, massive suburban growth has dominated the large cities, which became less dense between 2006 and 2011. About 90 percent of Australians surveyed indicated a preference for owning a property in low- density suburbs (Kotkin 2016, p.154). In Canada, two-thirds of the population lives in suburban locations on the outskirts of cities, and 69 percent of suburban residents own property. Between 2006 and 2011, about 95 percent of the development of Canada's 33 metropolitan areas took place in the suburbs and exurbs (Kotkin 2016, p.154), leading David Gordon, the director of the School of Urban and Regional Planning at Queen's University, to say, "There's a heck of a lot more happening on the edge" [Gordon and Shirokoff 2014, as cited in Kotkin (2016, p.154)]. Similar shifts took place in Europe: a survey of 24 large European cities found that suburban areas had grown to have 60 percent more residents in 2011 than in 2006. In Madrid, for example, suburbs grew 450 percent between 1971 and 2011, compared to only 5 percent growth in the core area (pp.154–55). And the situation is no different in the UAE: low-density suburbs make up a substantial portion of the UAE's cities. As Kotkin (2016) has pointed out, "This dispersion is the common reality, more or less, for almost all large cities in the world" (p.6).

In the UAE, more than 50 percent of Abu Dhabi's land and 40 percent of Dubai's urban area has been developed into low-density suburbs for citizens (Alawadi and Benkraouda 2017). This proliferation has created a "splintering urbanism" (Graham and Marvin 2002)—a disconnect between physicality, environmental stewardship, and humanity (Kotkin 2016, p.6). In these segregated, disconnected, low-density suburbs, social interaction, street-level spontaneity, connectivity, and accessibility are lost or sidelined. How, then, should these sidelined priorities be reintegrated into urban design? How do we mitigate the problems of massive suburban development in designing new suburbs? Many recent works have advocated for restructuring suburban design by bringing back some of the old urban design ideals, such as density, diversity, accessibility and connectivity (Duany and Plater-Zyberk 1994; Glaeser 2012; Montgomery 2013; Speck 2013; Chakrabarti 2013). The urban transformation of the UAE, particularly the rapid growth occurring in Dubai and Abu Dhabi (See Figure 1), have been of interest to various scholars around the globe. Their histories reveal an ongoing paradox: an ambition to provide a better quality of life for their citizens combined with a simultaneous appetite to become a global city. Both cities emerged from a desolate desert landscape and evolved through several phases of urban growth: slow expansion, compact development, suburbanization, and globalization (Elsheshtawy 2004; Alawadi et al. 2018). The growth in these cities became a model signifying urban dominance and primacy in the Gulf region. Both Dubai and Abu Dhabi urbanized in record time through the construction of endless suburbs and mega projects (Alawadi 2014; Alawadi and Dooling 2016). For instance, urban change in Dubai has been called the epitome of dramatic transformation and "the most ambitious physical engineering change" in all of Asia (Yeung 2011, p.71). In a mere couple of decades, Dubai transformed from a small fishing village to a major regional hub (Elsheshtawy 2004; Alawadi 2019). Dubai's model of urban development has been called "entrepreneurial modernism" (Ramos 2010, p.162). Under the influence of neoliberalism, Dubai has been developed to include large-scale transportation infrastructure, landmark architecture, and suburban sprawl as cornerstones (Alawadi 2018). This type of development ignores some social externalities for city dwellers and significantly restricts pedestrian accessibility. According to Elsheshtawy (2004), some of Dubai's iconic landmark buildings are located "far away from the city and designed to be primarily accessible by car" (p. 973). Elsheshtawy (2008) adds that most of the city's urban development aims to serve high-income groups through mega developments (p. 973). Furthermore, due to the peculiarity of the UAE's politics and population, native citizens are a minority in their own country and have their own, dedicated and subsidized neighborhoods, commonly known as national housing.

The growth in these cities became a model signifying urban dominance and primacy in the Gulf region.

Like Dubai, Abu Dhabi is a city with a prominent branding strategy (Ponzini 2011) that includes several iconic projects, such as the Louvre and Sheikh Zayed National Museum, designed by "starchitects" such as Jean Nouvel and Norman Foster (Hazime 2011). Abu Dhabi has been described as a modern city that has numerous configurations of highways and indiscernible spaces (Kansara 2016). Since 2007, Abu Dhabi has incorporated the Vancouver model intensively by utilizing its extensive coastline for beachfront developments and public spaces (Khirfan, Momani and Jaffer 2013). Vancouver's practices were imported to Abu Dhabi to strengthen its identity as the capital of the UAE. A Canadian team, led by Larry Beasley, helped the city build its master plan and develop a vision, Plan Capital 2030, to guide the city's growth and development. The transfer of knowledge and skills from Vancouver's planners helped change the city's approach from "build it and they will come" to aligning with international best-practice bench-

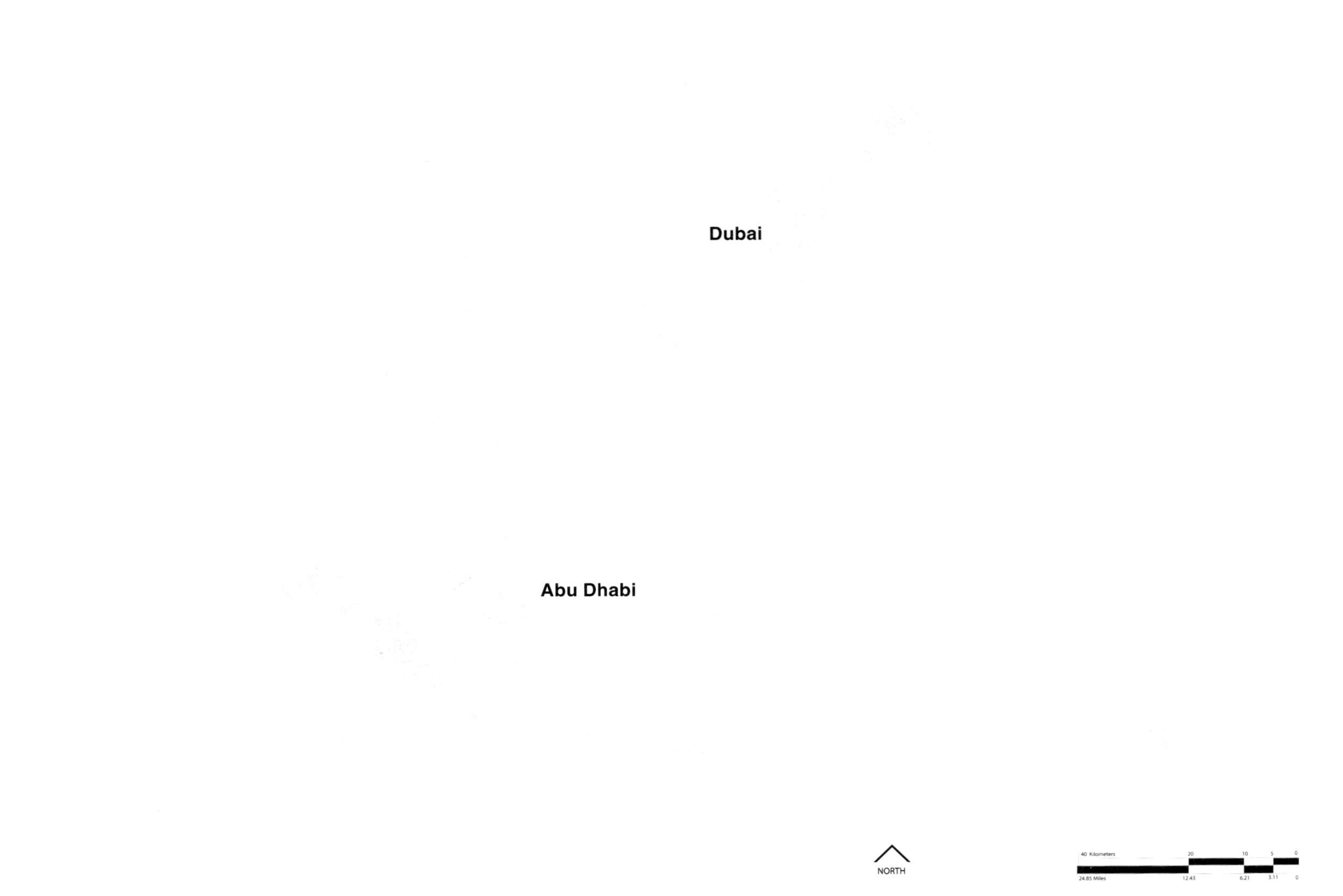

FIG. 1
Map showing the extent of Dubai and Abu Dhabi

marks (Khirfan and Jaffer 2014, p. 493). A notable contribution of the Vancouver team was running the newly established planning regulatory commission, the Urban Planning Council (UPC). This was the first time such a commission had been established in the UAE. UPC was formalized in 2007 and was assigned the task of authorizing and maintaining all new urban development in line with the city's strategic vision (Khirfan and Jaffer 2014). One of the UPC's landmark achievements was the introduction of the Estidama regulation, a local adaptation of the Leadership in Energy and Environmental Design (LEED) and LEED- Neighborhood Design (LEED-ND) frameworks (Khirfan and Jaffer 2014). However, in 2017, the UPC merged with the Department of Municipal Affairs to form the Department of Urban Planning and Municipalities (DPM). Then, in 2019, DPM and the Department of Transport (DOT) were merged to form the Department of Municipalities and Transport (DMT). Although there are similarities between Abu Dhabi's and Dubai's suburbanization, particularly in national housing and city branding that reflects global ambitions, the two cities differ in terms of urban history, population, cultural orientation, territorial extent, and pace of development (Davidson 2007; Elsheshtawy 2008; Ponzini 2011).

This book showcases a total of six different neighborhoods as case studies—six from Abu Dhabi, three in this book and another three are available online via Figshare, and seven from Dubai, three in this book and another four are also available online via Figshare—that were developed during different growth periods. It is widely accepted that the layout of streets plays a crucial role in setting the standards for other urban form elements such as block size, plot size, sidewalk width, etc. and that street layout is difficult to alter once built (Alawadi, Khaleel and Benkraouda 2020). Moreover, both streets and alley networks can help in meeting multiple sustainability objectives related to environment and public health-streets by promoting efficient transportation and alleys by improving walkability. This book explores the street connectivity and accessibility of Abu Dhabi and Dubai at the neighborhood and city scales. Two parameters of street network analysis—efficiency and centrality—are calculated. Efficiency is evaluated in terms of directness, because network designs that provide short and direct access between origins and destinations are more efficient. Centrality is evaluated using graph theory metrics that enable the identification of high- and low-accessibility locations within networks. Research has shown that network centrality metrics are useful for capturing location advantage, a significant factor for land use distribution. An understanding of centrality and its impacts makes it possible to plan land uses that bring destinations closer to residences, an important factor in environmental, economic, and social sustainability. Ultimately, the book provides policy and design strategies to promote more efficient street infrastructure and land use systems at the local (neighborhood) and global (city) scales. The guidebook includes design and policy recommendations in written and graphical formats that address both scales of analysis. The aim is to provide a scientifically grounded resource for redesigning streets and land use systems to serve the needs of 21st century cities, whose residents demand direct, convenient, and straightforward transportation to their desired destinations. In particular, this book addresses the following core questions: 1. How do the morphological attributes of the neighborhoods change in Abu Dhabi and Dubai throughout their urban evolution? 2. Are Abu Dhabi's and Dubai's neighborhood street networks designed to promote efficiency and centrality, toward the goal of overall efficiency, at the local and global scales? 3. How can we design and plan neighborhoods in which non-motorized mobility is a viable and efficient alternative? 4. Which locations in the network are most central and conducive to development or consolidation as activity hubs if driving distances and the global scale are considered? 5. Do existing neighborhood designs integrate with one another to form coherent and accessible urban environments? If not, how could they be retrofitted to make their street systems and urban fabrics more efficient and integrated? How can additional growth be planned and designed to efficiently connect to the existing city? The questions posed above are answered by conducting morphological mapping in ArcGIS followed by the use of the Urban Network Analysis (UNA) tool in the Rhinoceros 3D software. The UNA tool computes centrality metrics such as Reach, Gravity and Betweenness, as well as efficiency metrics such as Straightness.

The obtained results for studied neighborhoods are compared to gather insights, because each neighborhood has its own unique street layout and land use system built during a particular growth period. The local-scale analysis is conducted at three radii—400, 800, and 1,600 meters—and the global scale analysis is conducted at two radii—3 and 6 kilometers. Intra-neighborhood efficiency and centrality is determined from the local, neighborhood- scale analysis, while the global, city-scale analysis reveals how different neighborhoods are integrated or connected with one another. The global-scale analysis shows a neighborhood's level of connectivity with areas beyond the neighborhood's boundary. Underlying the book's research questions is the conviction that good urban design must be integrated across multiple scales (e.g., region, city, district, neighborhood, and site). In asking how the physical designs of different neighborhoods in both cities have responded to regional frameworks, these questions focus attention interconnectedness between different scales). The morphology, network efficiency, and connectivity of neighborhoods in Abu Dhabi and Dubai are analyzed as a means for exploring the implications of physical design attributes for city-wide planning.

The book consists of eight chapters. Chapter one discusses the concepts of cities, urbanization, and suburbanization, as well as contemporary debates about suburbanization worldwide and its contextualization in the UAE. The chapter also introduces the particular research questions being explored and describes the study's methodology in brief. Chapter two begins with an account of the history of urban planning in Abu Dhabi and Dubai. It also introduces the planning urban form of the two cities. Major events, decisions, and planning interventions that influenced or significantly altered the urban form are also elaborated. Chapter three offers an in-depth discussion of Abu Dhabi's urban form and planning approaches during its different growth periods. Chapter four presents Dubai's urban form and planning approaches during its growth periods. Chapter five introduces the dual and primal approaches of network analysis and Multiple Centrality Assessment (MCA). It presents the theoretical foundations of Multiple Centrality Assessment and the UNA (Urban Network Analysis) tool, and it also discusses the study's scales of analysis, network analysis scenarios, and UNA metrics in detail.

Chapter six showcases morphological and UNA maps for selected neighborhoods in Abu Dhabi (*West Island*, *Baniyas*, *Mouhamad Bin Zayed City*) and Dubai (*Dubai Creek*, *Al Satwa*, *Al Warqa*). The chapter also provides global-scale analysis for selected samples. Additional studied neighborhoods from both cities can be found via this link: https://doi.org/10.6084/m9.figshare.21939626.v1. Morphological data such as street density, total street length, number of street intersections, street intersection density, alley density, total alley length, number of alley intersections, alley intersection density, and plot density are analyzed. The results of Reach, Gravity, Straightness and Betweenness analyses are given for radii of 400, 800, and 1,600 meters. Global-scale UNA maps showcase the results of comparable analyses at radii of 3 and 6 kilometers. In all analyses except the city (global-scale) analysis, alleys are taken into consideration in addition to the usual practice of analyzing the street network. Chapter seven starts with a summary of the findings obtained from the maps shown in Chapter six. It also features a discussion that compares the cities of Abu Dhabi and Dubai in terms of efficiency and centrality at the sample and neighborhood scales. The final chapter, Chapter eight, starts with a discussion of the relevance of studying Abu Dhabi and Dubai and the contribution this study can make to the urban planning scholarship. Also discussed are lessons and takeaway for sustainable urban planning and design practice as relates to street design and land use systems in neighborhoods. This chapter also provides final remarks regarding the impact of morphological attributes on the efficiency and centrality of the two cities. The chapter compiles in graphical form the physical design ideals drawn from the morphological mapping and urban network analyses of both cities.

References

Angelo, H., & Wachsmuth, D. (2015). Urbanizing Urban Political Ecology: A Critique of Methodological Cityism. International Journal of Urban and Regional Research, 39 (1), 16-27.

Alawadi, K. (2018). Whatever happened to Dubai's public spaces? International Journal of Middle East Studies, 50(3), 562–567.

Alawadi, Khaled. "A return to the old landscape? Balancing physical planning ideals and cultural constraints in Dubai's residential neighborhoods." Journal of Housing and the Built Environment 34 (2019): 235-263.

Alawadi, Khaled, and Ouafa Benkraouda. "The debate over neighborhood density in Dubai: Between theory and practicality." Journal of Planning Education and Research 39, no. 1 (2019): 18-34.

Alawadi, Khaled, Sahar Khaleel, and Ouafa Benkraouda. "Design and planning for accessibility: Lessons from Abu Dhabi and Dubai's neighborhoods." Journal of Housing and the Built Environment 36 (2021): 487-520.

Alofsin, Anthony. "Broadacre City—Ideal and Nemesis." American Art 25, no. 2 (2011): 21-25.

Batty, Michael, Elena Besussi, and Nancy Chin. "Traffic, urban growth and suburban sprawl." (2003).

Beatley, Timothy, and Peter Newman. Green urbanism down under: Learning from sustainable communities in Australia. Island Press, 2012.

Berger, Alan, and Joel Kotkin, eds. Infinite suburbia. Chronicle Books, 2018.

Breheny, Michael. "Centrists, decentrists and compromisers: views on the future of urban form." The compact city: A sustainable urban form (1996): 13-35.

Chakrabarti, Vishaan. "Vishaan Chakrabarti:" A Country of Cities"." (2013).

Cox, W. (2017). Measuring US urban cores and suburbs. In Infnite Suburbia (pp. 196–206). New York: Princeton Architectural Press.

Davidson, Christopher. "The emirates of Abu Dhabi and Dubai: Contrasting roles in the international system." Asian Affairs 38, no. 1 (2007): 33-48.

Davis, Kingsley. "The origin and growth of urbanization in the world." American Journal of Sociology 60, no. 5 (1955): 429-437.

Douglas, Farr. "Sustainable urbanism: urban design with nature." Hoboken, NJ Wiley (2008).

Duany, Andres, and Elizabeth Plater-Zyberk. "The neighborhood, the district and the corridor." The new urbanism: Toward an architecture of community (1994): 17-20.

Elsheshtawy, Yasser, ed. Planning middle eastern cities: an urban kaleidoscope. Routledge, 2004.

Elsheshtawy, Yasser. "Cities of sand and fog: Abu Dhabi's global ambitions." The evolving Arab city: Tradition, modernity and urban development (2008): 258-304.

Gan, H. (1962). The urban villagers: Group and class in the life of Italian Americans.

Gehl, Jan. "Life between buildings." (2011).

Gehl, Jan. Cities for people. Island press, 2013.

Glaeser, Edward. "Triumph of the city: How our greatest invention makes us richer, smarter, greener, healthier, and happier." New York, NY: Penguin Books. doi 10 (2013): 1726-3247.

Gordon, David LA, and Isaac Shirokoff. "Suburban nation? Population growth in Canadian suburbs, 2006-2011." Proceedings of the 6th Council for Canadian Urbanism (CanU6) summit: Cities at the Edge, Toronto, Ont (2014): 18-20.

Graham, Steve, and Simon Marvin. Splintering urbanism: networked infrastructures, technological mobilities and the urban condition. Routledge, 2002.

Hazime, Hanan. "From city branding to e-brands in developing countries: An approach to Qatar and Abu Dhabi." African Journal of Business Management 5, no. 12 (2011).

Hall, P. (2001). Global city-regions in the twenty-first century. Global city-regions: Trends, theory, policy, 59-77.

Jacobs, Jane. "Jane jacobs." The Death and Life of Great American Cities 21, no. 1 (1961).

Jencks, Charles. "Heteropolis: Los Angeles, the riots and the strange beauty of hetero-architecture." (No Title) (1993).

Kansara, T. "Transitional zone design in the desert Environment of Abu Dhabi: Vernacular vs. modern." Sustainable Cities and Society 23 (2016): 59-67.

Khirfan, Luna, Bessma Momani, and Zahra Jaffer. "Whose authority? Exporting Canadian urban planning expertise to Jordan and Abu Dhabi." Geoforum 50 (2013): 1-9.

Khirfan, Luna, and Zahra Jaffer. "Sustainable urbanism in Abu Dhabi: transferring the vancouver model." Journal of Urban Affairs 36, no. 3 (2014): 482-502.

Kotkin, Joel. The human city: Urbanism for the rest of us. Agate Publishing, 2016.

Leon, D. A. (2008). Cities, urbanization and health. International Journal of Epidemiology, Volume 37, Issue 1, February 2008, Pages 4–8, https://doi.org/10.1093/ije/dym271

Leon, J. K. What Broadacre City can teach us. (2014). Retrieved from https://www.metropolismag.com/cities/what-broadacre-city-can-teach-us/

McNeur, Catherine. Taming Manhattan: Environmental battles in the antebellum city. Harvard University Press, 2014.

Montgomery, Charles. Happy city: Transforming our lives through urban design. Penguin UK, 2013.

Mumford, Lewis. The city in history: Its origins, its transformations, and its prospects. Vol. 67. Houghton Mifflin Harcourt, 1961.

Neuman, Michael. "The compact city fallacy." Journal of planning education and research 25, no. 1 (2005): 11-26.

Owen, Neville, Ester Cerin, Eva Leslie, Neil Coffee, Lawrence D. Frank, Adrian E. Bauman, Graeme Hugo, Brian E. Saelens, and James F. Sallis. "Neighborhood walkability and the walking behavior of Australian adults." American journal of preventive medicine 33, no. 5 (2007): 387-395.

Ponzini, Davide. "Large scale development projects and star architecture in the absence of democratic politics: The case of Abu Dhabi, UAE." Cities 28, no. 3 (2011): 251-259.

Sennett, Richard, ed. The Psychology of society: an anthology. Vol. 234. Vintage Books USA, 1977.

Seto, Karen C., Susan Parnell, and Thomas Elmqvist. "A global outlook on urbanization." Urbanization, biodiversity and ecosystem services:

challenges and opportunities: a global assessment (2013): 1-12.
Speck, Jeff. "Walkable City: How Downtown Can Save America, One Step at a Time Nova York: North Point Press, 312 p. ISBN 978-0865477728." Documents d'Anàlisi Geogràfica 61, no. 2 (2015): 437.
Ramos, Stephen J. Dubai amplified: the engineering of a port geography. Routledge, 2016.
Stretton, Hugh. "Density, efficiency and equality in Australian cities." The compact city: A sustainable urban form (1996): 45-52.
Williams, Katie, Mike Jenks, Michael Jenks, and Elizabeth Burton, eds. Achieving sustainable urban form. Taylor & Francis, 2000.
Williams, Katie, Jennifer LR Joynt, and Diane Hopkins. "Adapting to climate change in the compact city: the suburban challenge." Built Environment 36, no. 1 (2010): 105-115.
Yeung, Yue-man. "Rethinking Asian cities and urbanization: four transformations in four decades." Asian Geographer 28, no. 1 (2011): 65-83.

02

Planning History and City Form

Abu Dhabi

Introduction

Abu Dhabi is the capital of the United Arab Emirates (UAE), which is composed of seven *sheikhdoms*. It has the shape of an elongated triangle and occupies the south-western part of the UAE (See Figure 1). With the majority of the nation's hydrocarbon reserves (i.e., 95 percent of the UAE's oil reserves and 92 percent of its natural gas reserves (Kapur 2010), it is the wealthiest emirate. It is also the largest emirate, with 87 percent of the UAE's landmass, and its capital city region is spread over approximately 760 square kilometers. The population of Abu Dhabi city was approximately 1.7 million in 2015 (SCAD 2016). It is the second-most populated city in the UAE after Dubai. The local and expatriate population ratio stands at 1:4: 80 percent of the total population are expatriates, and remaining 20 percent are Emiratis (SCAD, 2016).

Planning History

The urban planning and design principles applied in Abu Dhabi resemble the ideas discussed in the International Congresses for Modern Architecture (CIAM) of the 1920s and 30s, of which Le Corbusier is the most famous proponent (Southworth & Ben-Joseph 1997, p. 71). Eventually, Le Corbusier published *The Athens Charter*, which was a heavily edited version of the dialogue that occurred during (CIAM) meetings. *The Athens Charter* became the most impactful document resulting from (CIAM) discussions and promoted three main principles: (a) the use of high-rise buildings in urban areas, (b) multi-lane and multi-level road networks, and (c) the concept of the functional city. Functionalism is generally considered identical to early-20th-century European modernism, but it has older precedents and much wider cultural references. Functionalist ideas can be found as early as 70 BC in the writings of the Roman writer Vitruvius, which were mentioned in 15th century Florence by Leon Battista Alberti. In 19th century, Pugin in England and Eugene-Emmanuel Viollet-le-Duc, Henri Labrouste, and Viollet-le-Duc in France asserted that every element constructed should have a function (Peter 1994). Similarly, Cornelis Van Eesteren, a Dutch architect and the president of (CIAM) from 1930 to 1947 (Somer 2007), argued that factories, ports, and recreation spaces are the functional elements of cities. He further asserted that these elements could be organized in tandem with housing through the development of efficient transportation. Drawing on Van Eesteren's approach, (CIAM 4) published its agreed-upon four functions of the city: dwelling, work, transportation, and recreation (Mumford 2019).

In 1896 the Chicago-based architect Louis H. Sullivan had written a more coherent statement regarding functionalism, which simply read "Form Follows Function" (Twombly 1988, p.111). In other words, when the purpose of a building, block, or neighborhood is known, the form can be derived from it. The concept of functional city emphasized the relationship between dwellings and open space and indicated the importance of zoning ordinances to improve the supply of open space and tackle the problems of poor sanitation, pollution, and overcrowding. It also recommended separating residential localities from heavy-traffic corridors. The (CIAM) plan also hinted at the benefits of mixed-use developments by highlighting locational mismatches between workplaces and residences and the resulting problems of long commutes and rush-hour traffic jams. In this way, the plan emphasized zoning and segregation between uses and income classes. Moreover, it argued for locating industrial areas in close proximity to major transport routes and using multi-level crossings and expressways to reorganize traffic flow according to different speeds (Gold 1998). Even though Le Corbusier had published his *Radiant City Plan* in 1930, he published the book *Radiant City* in 1934 after the 1933 conference. So it may be assumed that the street typology for the *Functional City* is similar to that of the *Radiant City*, which features linear streets on a grid network with superblocks of 366 m × 183 m (1200 ft × 600 ft) and 183 m² (600 ft²) (Corbusier 1967). Moreover, F. R. S. Yorke and Marcel Breuer, two proponents of the British Modern Movement, which had been influenced by (CIAM), prepared a plan for the *Garden City of the Future*. This plan presented no prototype of urban form and did not articulate any direct relationship between the street layout and land use (Gold 1998).

The functionalism promoted by Le Corbusier's *Athens Charter* became dominant in the post–World War II USA and also appeared elsewhere around the world. The epitome of this style was Brasilia, which was planned in 1956, around the same time that the first plan for Abu Dhabi was being conceived. Various planned cities—namely Baghdad, Iraq (1958); Islamabad, Pakistan (1960); and Riyadh, Saudi Arabia (1968)— coincide temporally with the planning of Abu Dhabi. These cities were built to feature the characteristic grids of wide arterials roads that define superblocks, along with land use arrangements which align with neighborhood unit principles (Middleton 2009). The main streets were designed in a grid system to allow for future urban growth. In Baghdad, neighborhood planning units (NPUs) have identical street layouts but different building densities, building types, and land uses; each design configuration was based on social segregation (Pyla 2013). For instance, the lower classes had a higher mix of building types and land uses planned around open spaces that created interactive social hubs, called "gossip squares" (Kyriazis, Almehairi, and Al Seri 2017). Other NPUs were planned to be self-sufficient for a mix of different income groups with a wider variety of land uses (Pyla 2013). The plans for Baghdad and Riyadh intended to encourage pedestrian movement inside the NPU by limiting vehicle access to only major streets or highways. However,

FIG. 1
Aerial photo for the city of Abu Dhabi (Esri & USGS, 2021)

these cities exclusively pedestrian networks eventually accommodated automobiles after they became widespread in the late 1960s. Similarly, the plan for Islamabad included a central core with an open-ended axis network to allow for future urban expansion. The NPU's for Islamabad were planned to be 2 km^2, like those of Baghdad and Riyadh. Each NPU in these three cities included parks, schools, and shops and was designed to be self-sustaining. Residential units had a designated area in the NPU that was separated from other land uses, and a mosque was placed at the core (Alawadi et al. 2021).

The common thread between the aforementioned cities and Abu Dhabi is their common reliance on grid systems and their adoption of the planning principle of the NPU. On a local scale, land uses follow a fixed arrangement, and on a global scale, their aggregation is adaptable to future growth, thereby assisting in organized and structured city growth. Abu Dhabi has managed the demands of its rapid growth using a set strategy of superblocks. Beginning in the late 1960s, urban development has been carried out by demarcating large swaths of lands or superblocks along evenly spaced arterial roads (Abdo and Batzel 2011; Alawadi 2018; Alawadi and Benkraouda 2018). More specifically, rectangular superblocks of approximately 900 m × 600 m were developed as neighborhood units, inspired by American planner Clarence Perry, who first introduced the "Neighborhood Unit Plan" in 1929 (Mehaffy, Porta, & Romice 2015; Perry 1939; Patricios 2002). The existing planning approach focuses on the architecture of the community and does not extend beyond the neighborhood scale, which means that it ignores the processes of urbanization, regionalism, and integration of different areas over time.

The discovery of oil proved to be only one of the main drivers of Abu Dhabi's development. The evolution of Abu Dhabi's built landscape has also been greatly affected by other factors, especially shifts in governance and planning paradigms. Since the commercialization of oil and the subsequent economic boom of the 1970s, Abu Dhabi has provided extensive infrastructure, land subsidies, jobs, and services for its native population (Crot 2013). The subsidization of land, energy, and water is a deep-rooted part of the relationship between the government and citizens. This understanding has guided the central housing policy of national housing within Abu Dhabi and its sister *Emirates*. Every UAE citizen receives a generous government subsidy to purchase a new, move-in-ready house or a land parcel of at least 1000 m^2 with a no-interest mortgage (Alawadi 2017a). This practice is considered a method of wealth sharing and a necessary right of citizenship. Abu Dhabi's urban landscape has since been steered by this socio-political phenomenon (Cugurullo 2015). Currently, these subsidized, low-density, single-use neighborhoods occupy a staggering 50 percent of the urbanized land in Abu Dhabi (Alawadi and Benkrouda 2018).

National housing has received a significant amount of attention from the government and leadership, not only in the emirate of Abu Dhabi but in all seven *sheikhdoms*. Abu Dhabi's built landscape and policy agenda makes national housing as a special priority. This policy has contributed to "demand-oriented planning" (Bagaeen 2007 p.175) that prioritizes the building of "comfort zones" for citizens (Acuto 2010, p.280). In 1998, *Sheikh Zayed's* legendary note to one of the UAE's Federal Council members said, "I swear by God Almighty that I don't understand how there are [UAE citizens] in apartment buildings who are still renting ... How is it possible that they are living in rented apartments?" (Cited in Sultan Al Qassemi 2010, p.195). More recently, a government official stated, "The Government wants locals to have a high standard of living. We are not compromising on quality for the locals" (cited in Gillet 2009). Likewise, in March 2017, the general manager of the then Urban Planning Council (now the Department of Municipalities and Transport) announced a plan for more than fifty thousand homes for Emiratis over the next twenty years.

City Growth and Form

Abu Dhabi has transformed profoundly, from a barren semi-island settlement in the 1960s to a global metropolis consisting of high-rise condominiums and marble-fronted architecture in the new millennium (See Figure 2). Abu Dhabi's urban development is generally divided into five growth periods (Elsheshtawy 2008): Pre-1961, 1961–1966, 1966–1988, 1988–2004 and 2004–present. However, with regard to residential landscape, three growth phases are identified: the Inception Period (1966–1975), the Dispersion Period (1975–2007), and the Redemption Period (2007–2017) (Alawadi and Benkraouda 2018); the Dispersion Period resumed in 2017, when the Urban Planning Council (UPC) ceased to exist as an independent agency. This classification was based on morphological attributes of neighborhoods. Each growth phase represents a peculiar morphological period that is different from other periods. Morphological periods are definite periods of time that can be distinguished by their repetitive use of similar street patterns, land use systems, or building densities (Whitehand et al., 2014).

Abu Dhabi's urban development was limited to small settlements until 1961. The built environment was influenced by climate, culture, religion, and governance. *Sheikh Shakhbout Bin Sultan Al Nahyan* had ruled Abu Dhabi since 1928. In 1958, during his rule, oil was discovered; however, only a handful of developments occurred to improve living conditions (Elsheshtawy 2008). It is believed that *Sheikh Shakhbout* wanted to maintain the existing tribal and Bedouin society without much modernization. As a result, the city's development remained modest until 1966. The ruler was also hesitant to spend on large and expensive infrastructure projects, which can be deduced from his having said, "This is Paris! We don't want a Paris in Abu Dhabi!" (Cited in Trench, 1994). Until 1965, Abu Dhabi's landscape showed no signs of modernity and was completely lacking in communication, electricity, and water services. In 1962, the Department of Abu Dhabi Municipality and Town Planning was established to respond to the growing transient population affiliated with the oil companies. *Sheikh Shakhbout* commissioned the British consultancy firm *Halcrow* to develop a plan for Abu Dhabi city. The target population was set at 100,000 with the first phase designed to accommodate 25,000 people.

When *Sheikh Zayed Bin Sultan Al Nahyan* became the ruler of Abu Dhabi in 1966, the transformation of Abu Dhabi began. *Sheikh Zayed* is also known as the founding father of the UAE and 'the man behind Abu Dhabi's master plan' (Ghazal, 2013). He welcomed foreign expertise in the development of Abu Dhabi. He ordered the re-evaluation of *Halcrow's* plan because he disagreed with it. The existing plans were not modular and projected the image of an oil city only, making it incompatible with *Sheikh Zayed's* vision for Abu Dhabi. Abu Dhabi's superblock-based development plan originated during this time period, when British architect John Elliot's *ARABICON* plan introduced a modular system of interconnected superblocks (Abdo & Batzel 2011) which established a grid layout. *Sheikh Zayed* appreciated the design due to its route directness and simplicity. The plan fulfilled his expectations as it matched his vision of urbanizing the city and enhancing living conditions through housing and easy access to daily destinations (Reizs, 2013). The legacy of Elliot's plan continued even when the planning director changed from Katsuhiko Takahashi to Abdulrahman Makhlouf. The modularity of the plan was retained, and the superblock model became the blueprint for neighborhood planning in Abu Dhabi. In 1967, the first national houses were also designed by John Elliott and his firm. The size of the first-ever granted plots in Abu Dhabi were 7.4 m^2 (80 ft^2) and featured surrounding walls 6 m high. These dimensions and other specifications were set by *Sheikh Zayed* himself, and the technical drawings were prepared accordingly. *Al Bateen*, then a fishing village, became one of the first sites where the subsidized plots were laid out (Elsheshtawy 2019). In the beginning, Abu Dhabi's national housing was influenced by everyday urbanism and community needs; designs combined neighborhood self-sufficiency with integration into the rest of the city and enabled privacy while facilitating visiting among neighbors (Alawadi and Benkraouda 2018).

The modularity of the plan was retained, and the superblock model became the blueprint for neighborhood planning in Abu Dhabi.

Katsuhiko Takahashi was the second town planner based in Abu Dhabi; he arrived in 1967. Takahashi was appointed the chief town planner for Abu Dhabi Municipality. He elaborated the *ARABICON* plans and gave detailed designs for the administrative and commercial buildings (Samarrai, 2016). He is also credited with laying out wide roads, parks, and corniches in Abu Dhabi (Zacharias, 2018). The implementation differed from what Takahashi has proposed, but his plan became a reference point for subsequent planning efforts, especially with regard to land use planning that facilitated mixed-use developments. By 1968, the urbanized area had grown to 272 hectares from 54 hectares in 1958 (ADM 2003). It is said that after working with Takahashi, *Sheikh Zayed* wanted an Arab city planner with whom he could communicate directly without any translators. Dr. Abdul Rahman Makhlouf, who was already actively working in the Gulf region, was chosen to become the Director of Abu Dhabi's Town Planning Department from 1968 to 1976. He first arrived in Abu Dhabi in October 1968 as an expert at the UN Technical Support Office in the Middle East. He was also put in charge of the national housing program. He acknowledged the challenges this program faced and voiced great admiration for Shiekh Zayed's enthusiasm:

"I was supposed to plan the city in the deserts. It was a tall task. Few could have imagined the eventual shape that this land was going to take in future. It had to be a miracle. History shows that towns take hundreds of years to take shape. But the approach of *Sheikh Zayed* changed all that. He made history by leading this phenomenal development in such a short span of time. During the eight years that I worked with *Sheikh Zayed*, I saw him personally supervising the implementation of the plans." – Dr. Abdul Rahman Makhlouf (Abdul Aziz 2007).Abu Dhabi underwent another wave of massive urbanism from 1974 to 1979 due to the soaring oil prices (Hume 2008). This continued until the late 1980s. In 1988, The Master Directive Plan for Abu Dhabi and its Environs (MDP) was introduced by Atkins, a British firm. (MDP) was divided into four five-year phases from 1990 to 2010. The plan followed the legacy of *ARABICON* by continuing the use of superblocks. The only difference was that the new superblocks had wider rights of way, larger plot sizes, and discontinuous street designs, resembling "fragmented parallels" (Southworth & Owens 1993; Scoppa, Bawazir, and Alawadi 2018). The MDP was introduced to manage uncontrolled development, enhance the efficiency of the urban land-use system, formalize community planning, and address the housing needs of both citizens and non-citizens. The plan recommended a development pattern which featured single-family dwellings spread across an automobile-oriented landscape with rigidly separated land uses (Bani Hashim 2016). Subsequently, it led to unprecedented suburbanization in the mainland, thereby challenging the city's physical and environmental sustainability (Crot 2013).

Sheikh Zayed Bin Sultan Al Nahyan was a highly influential leader who was actively engaged in the development process. During *Sheikh Zayed's* rule, the built environment of Abu Dhabi underwent an extraordinary evolution. His vision transformed the Emirate "from rags to riches" (Al Fahim 1995) in less than 30 years by endorsing massive development plans focused on housing and infrastructure. Thus, his death in 2004 marked a turning point for Abu Dhabi's development. The city experienced another building boom which was not driven by oil wealth. *Sheikh Zayed's* successors envisaged Abu Dhabi's transformation into a regional and global hub (Cugurullo 2013). This goal was pursued through public-private partnerships driven by "flexible accumulation of capital" (Hoyland 2001, p.28), along with new regulations allowing foreign investment and land ownership, which had not been allowed during *Sheikh Zayed's* time. Openness towards Western economic models and investment plans created a new urban landscape in Abu Dhabi (Ponzini 2011). Private developers started to become more dominant in the urban development process. Large swaths of islands were developed into cultural districts, new commercial business districts (CBDs), tourist zones with theme parks, and mixed-use beachfront communities, towers and gated communities to host the skilled expatriate population.

A longstanding regulation limiting landownership in Abu Dhabi to citizens as well as residents changed, and people from other *Emirates* and expatriates were allowed to own real estate, although the expatriate population could only own properties in designated zones such as Reem Island, Saadiyat Island, Yas Island, and other enclaves near the Abu International Airport. In an effort to manifest these changes in a formalized way, the Urban Planning Council (UPC) was created in 2007 to manage and control the *Emirate's* first strategic plan addressing the city's government, economy, and culture (Alawadi and Benkraouda 2017). A new plan named Plan Capital 2030 was put forward after Larry Beasley was appointed the special advisor to *Sheikh Mohammed bin Zayed Al Nahyan* and the government of Abu Dhabi on all land planning in the *Emirate*. Planning ideals that had been implemented in Vancouver and focused on sustainable high-rise development were an inspiration for Abu Dhabi's growth ambitions (McCann 2011). It is said that the Crown Prince of Abu Dhabi personally initiated contact with Larry Beasley in 2006. Beasley had just retired from his position as a Director of Planning in Vancouver in British Columbia, Canada, and he was approached due to Vancouver's successful restructuring, revitalization, and sustainability planning (Grant 2009; McCann 2011). During a keynote speech at the *CanU Symposium* in Montreal in 2010, Larry Beasley recalled how he was recruited:

> *Our work [in Vancouver] has gotten a fair amount of attention [...]. And I think because of that, not because of me personally, but because of that, I got this email one day, and it was from this minister, and so I thought it was that, you know that spam one, which says 'I am a minister from the south' [...] and so I just deleted it. And about a week later, I got a second email, and there was something about it that made me open it. And the rest, for me, is history. (Khirfan and Jaffer 2012, p.12) .*

Beasley was nicknamed "the crown prince of the new Vancouver" (Bula 2008) and is considered the founding father of Vancouverism (Bani Hashim 2011) for his successful tenure as the "Director of Planning for the city of Vancouver". Influenced by principles of *New Urbanism* and *Smart Growth*, Beasley recommended a sustainable trajectory to avoid the Dubai model, which had received massive criticism from urban studies scholars (Alawadi and Benkraouda 2018). However, in 2017, (UPC) was merged with the Department of Municipal Affairs to form the Department of Urban Planning and Municipalities (DPM). Shortly thereafter, in 2019, (DPM) and the Department of Transport (DOT) were merged to form the Department of Municipalities and Transport (DMT) to plan, oversee and regulate Abu Dhabi's urban and transport development (DMT, 2020). Since the demise in 2017 of the only government agency focused solely on urban planning, the Dispersion Period has resumed in Abu Dhabi. Currently, Abu Dhabi's urban development is dictated by the national housing scheme and the mixed-use developments that appear primarily on the islands.

Openness towards Western economic models and investment plans created a new urban landscape in Abu Dhabi.
Ponzini, (2011).

FIG. 2

Progression of Abu Dhabi's urban growth

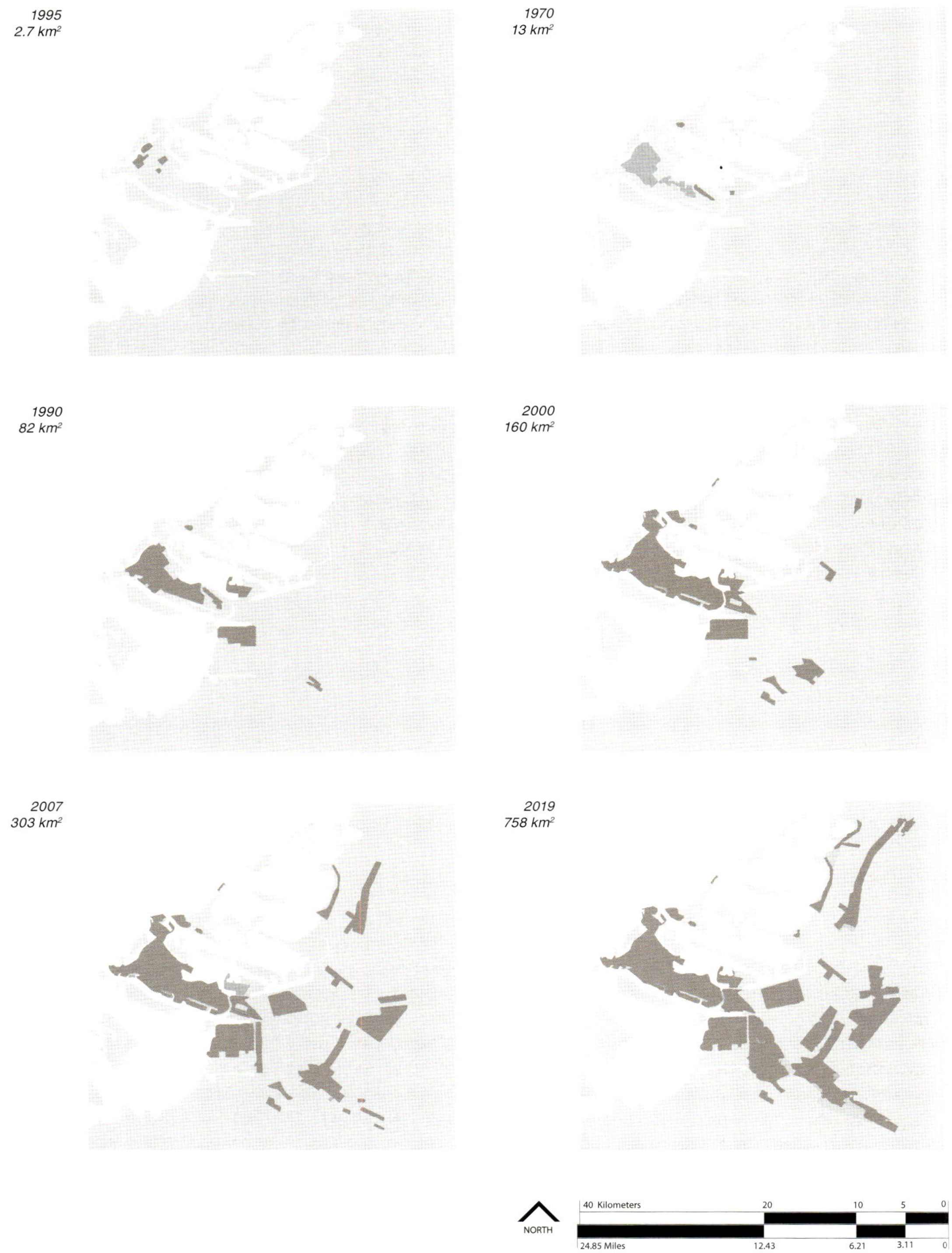

Dubai

Introduction

Dubai is the most populated emirate in the UAE with 3.19 million people (DSC 2018), and 85 percent of the total population are expatriates (worldpopulationreview.com 2021). It is the second-biggest emirate after Abu Dhabi in terms of landmass. The city of Dubai occupies approximately 870 km^2 (See Figure 3). Dubai has received more recognition than any other city in the GCC for pioneering its own version of urbanism (Alawadi 2016) particularly characterized by bigness.

Planning History

Although the national housing scheme and the oil boom affected Dubai's urban development trajectory similarly to other emirates, its planning approach differs from that of Abu Dhabi and other *sheikhdoms*. For several years, Dubai raced to construct the tallest, the biggest, and the most dazzling urban spectacles. In the recent past, Dubai's image of Dubai has highlighted its array of skyscrapers and never-before-seen spectacular structures (Alawadi 2018). Consequently, it became the epitome of the over-the-top style called 'bigness' (Koolhaas and Mau 1995; Sorkin 2009). It is a place that went through *instant urbanism* (Bagaeen 2007) and that features "the largest architectural experiment in progress" (Katodrytis 2007) and the "Guggenheim effect" (Elsheshtawy 2009). Through Dubai's prominent corporate-state nexus (Kanna 2005), the city's planning system has been prioritizing branding over contextual relevance (Al-Kodmany, Ali and Zhang 2013).

This corporate-state nexus, sometimes described as a "neo-patrimonial" system of governance, has endorsed, sponsored, and guided Dubai's rapid increase in scale. The interests of the government and big developers are tightly connected, and decision-making power is concentrated among a small group of business elites and politically powerful tribes. Dubai is "a spatial expression of economic strategy" (Pacione 2005, p.264) that results from the mutual profiteering alignment of the state and the private sector. In this "hybrid form of government, the public and private melt together without clear-cut boundaries" (Acuto 2014, p.1737). Since the core members of the government and prominent tribal allies "have key positions in both public decision making and in the management of private companies", the distinction between public and private sectors is non-existent (Ponzini 2011, p.254). Decisions are made by this network of government officials and powerful tribe leaders who oversee the city's economic and urban development through state-owned private firms that position the government as both a public and a private entity. This kind of urban governance has favored economic returns over social and environmental concerns, thereby creating undesirable morphological problems in the city's built environment (Alawadi and Dooling, 2016).

The planning system in Dubai and the broader region supports separating national from non-national residential districts. The allotment of land for housing is delineated between the housing needs of nationals and expatriates (Dubai Municipality 1995). This practice has created strict lines of geographic segregation between members of various nationalities and especially between nationals and expatriates (Elsheshtawy 2009). The residential enclaves of expatriates are primarily constructed and controlled by the private sector, whereas citizens' housing is regulated and subsidized by the government (Pacione 2005). Like Abu Dhabi and other emirates, Dubai gives every citizen's household a government subsidy composed of a land parcel (minimum size 929 m^2) with a no-interest mortgage or a new, move-in-ready house. These subsidized, low-density, single-use neighborhoods occupy a staggering 38 percent of Dubai's urbanized land (Alawadi, 2017b).

City Growth and Form

The urban form of Dubai has been altered in a record time through several growth phases (See Figure 4). The first stage, extending from 1900 to 1955, is characterized by slow growth due to constrained economic activity (Elsheshtawy 2004). Dubai evolved from a single cluster (i.e., *Al Fahidi*) to a group of housing clusters located in proximity to one another. This occurred due to the arrival of traders from India and Iran during the pearl boom (Al-Sayegh 1998). After World War II, dense, organic, vernacular forms were adopted to respond to climatic and social needs (Katodrytis 2015). Houses were made of coral stone and palm fronds. Government-subsidized housing for citizens had not yet been introduced.

The second stage of growth, from 1955 to 1970, also witnessed restrained development activity (Gabriel 1987), because oil had been discovered but not yet commercialized. This was the period when the first transient population, mainly construction workers, arrived. It was deemed necessary to isolate housing for these low-wage workers, because integrating a large number of single men into existing communities was considered inappropriate (Pacione 2005). In 1959, when Dubai was still a British protectorate, the British Political Agent at the time introduced Dubai's ruler to John R. Harris, who quickly gained the trust of the ruler, *Sheikh Rashid*, and became the town's de facto planner. Harris was a British architect who lacked planning experience (Alawadi and Dooling 2016). Prior to his appointment as the planner of Dubai, his major achievement had been winning the Royal Institute of British Architects' international competition for the design and supervision of Doha's new State Hospital in 195.

FIG. 3
Aerial photo for the city of Dubai (Esri & USGS, 2021)

Vernacular forms continued to dominate Dubai's urban landscape until 1960 (Katodrytis 2015), when Harris produced Dubai's first master plan. This plan proposed a basic layout of streets that divided the city into large subdivisions or superblocks. Each division was geometrically different from all the others. The plan also introduced zoning and land use systems to guide the growth process. The master plan's strategy and implementation indicated strong central control over urban development: the plans were discussed and approved generally by *Sheikh Rashid*, in autonomy (Katodrytis and Mitchell 2015). As the ruler, *Sheikh Rashid* had the right to grant lands in particular areas and reserve lands in other areas, which enabled him to control the urban pattern. This was another factor that shaped the built landscape starting in the 1960s (Pacione 2005), because it was more feasible to build farther outside the city, where people did not have claims to the land, than to develop the central areas by buying out land-owners. Meanwhile, urban development also intensified in the old neighborhoods around the creek. Nevertheless, the urban fabric remained highly connected and relatively compact, as automobile ownership was still rare. The modernist road network plan developed by Harris was the main influence on the morphology of many communities around and near Dubai Creek, including *Al Karama*, *Al Murraqabat*, *Al Mankhool*, *Al Hamriya*, *Umm Hurair*, *Al Muteena*, *Al Murar*, and *Al Baraha*. These neighborhoods differ from organic communities because Harris's master plan, following Western planning practices of the time, attempted to organize further development into a modern, ring-radial metropolitan form centered on the creek and configured the new parts of the city using organized, orthogonal lines. A well-known example of this pattern is *Al Karama*, which was developed as a low-income public housing district for expatriates in the late 1960s and early 1970s (Elsheshtawy 2013). The discovery of oil in 1966 led to a boom in construction that attracted a large number of low-wage workers. Consequently, exclusive settlement areas for low-wage workers were constructed because their assimilation into existing neighborhoods was deemed inappropriate, as most laborers were single men. Constructing laborer housing was a quick way to house the workers and also spatially segregate them in peripheral areas such as Rashid Colony in *Al Ghusais* Industrial Area, *Al Quoz* Industrial Area, and Sonapur in *Al Muhaisnah*. These neighborhoods usually feature a series of repetitive five-storey buildings on identical residential blocks. In 1968, the government began implementing the "national housing scheme", which instituted a large-scale housing program for citizens (Al-Ittihad 1973, July 19). For instance, *Shabiyaat* was developed as low-cost housing arranged compactly in the urban fabric. Neighborhoods such as *Al Satwa*, *Al Rashidiya*, *Al Badaa*, and *Al Jaffaliya* were also planned under the national housing provision.

Dubai's housing landscape changed forever after the widespread application of the welfare policy that grants subsidized plots to its citizens.

Dubai's housing landscape changed forever after the widespread application of the welfare policy that grants subsidized plots to its citizens. This policy, in combination with the commercialization of oil, facilitated suburban growth and sprawl (Alawadi 2017b; Alawadi and Benkraouda 2018), and Dubai underwent its third growth period, which emphasized "planned suburban growth", from 1970 to the 1990s. In 1971, Harris created a plan inspired by modernist city planning principles. His plan featured ring roads around the city core and major arterial networks connecting the core to low-density suburbs (Seccombe and Lawless 1987; Pacione 2005). During this period, new residential typologies resembling post-World War II North American suburbs started to emerge. These types of neighborhoods were characterized by large land divisions with interrupted parallel, looping, curving, and fragmented street layouts. Previously uninhabited areas such as *Jumeirah* and *Al Jaffaliya* were assimilated into the urban landscape. In 1979, many infrastructural projects, including the Dubai International Airport, the World Trade Centre, and the *Jebel Ali* Port and Free Zone, broke the ring-radial structure and the limits outlined in Harris's second master plan. Until this time, Dubai's urban development was centered on Creek, but the pathway of development changed and followed the south-west axis from the World Trade Centre to the *Jebel Ali*. Harris's plan has contributed to and institutionalized the process of suburban growth and eventually created a sprawling, repetitive landscape featuring segregated dormitory communities on the fringes of the city (Dubai Municipality 1995). Starting in the 1980s, these neighborhoods became more prone to sprawl: local neighborhoods expanded in scale and stretched massively along the Gulf shore (Velegrinis and Katodrytis 2015).

In the 1990s, Dubai began to prioritize its efforts to build a global image and capitalize on its strengths as a trading hub and a potential global transit point. However, attracting international trade and commerce was not a new endeavor for Dubai. For centuries, Dubai has been the link connecting different regions for trade. As Lawrence Potter (2009) notes:

> *The Gulf has always been a key international trade route connecting the Middle East to India, East Africa, Southeast Asia, and China. Its orientation was outward, toward the Indian Ocean, and its society reflected this. A cosmopolitan, mercantile, and tolerant society developed here, which thrived in spite of the lack of local resources. The mobility of these people and their assets differed markedly from that of the oasis-based agricultural peasant societies that arose in the interior of neighboring states (p. 1).*

Dubai has always, even in its earliest stages, capitalized on its prime location on a trade route and applied suitable measures, such as becoming a "free port" in 1904 by abolishing customs duty, creating favorable conditions for merchants to relocate from the Persian coast in the 1920s, improving port facilities and trade by dredging the creek in 1955, and developing the port at *Jebel Ali* in 1976 (Pacione 2005; Davidson 2008; Katodrytis and Mitchell 2015). Since the 1990s, however, systematic efforts to become a global city began in a full-fledged way. This fourth period of growth, known as the Bigness era (Alawadi 2018), stretched from the mid-1990s to 2008 and focused on economic diversification (Davidso 2008), privatization of projects (Machado 2006), construction of tourism and high-end residential compounds (Bloch 2010), and scaling up the speed and built outcome of projects (Elsheshtawy 2010). "Bigness" (Koolhaas and Mau, 1995) is defined as upmarket urbanism that comprises "star architecture", and spectacular mega-projects (Ponzini 2011), all of which are over-scaled and privatized (Machado 2006; Acuto 2010). This model of urbanism embraces economic tolerance (Pacione 2005, p. 256) and 'bigness'. The Bigness era turned Dubai into a large site for urban experiments (Katodrytis 2007). The domination of the corporate-state nexus (Kanna 2005) reached its culmination during this era, and the branding of places was prioritized over their contextual significance (Al-Kodmany, Ali, and Zhang 2013). As planned, during this period, flourishing commercial activities attracted and retained numerous knowledge workers and businesspeople. These incoming migrants had a wider variety of skills and backgrounds than those who had arrived in the early migration waves of the 1970s (Kathiravelu 2016). Consequently, the housing needs of the new migrant population were met by new urban typologies featuring towers, gated communities, and island communities (Alawadi, Khanal, and Almulla 2018). However, the dominant residential housing pattern was still suburban single-family dwellings; this planned suburban growth still continued in the background and is ongoing today.

In 2008, the economic recession brought the booming years of Dubai to a standstill. The period from 2008 to 2013 is known as the period of demolish-rebuild (Alawadi 2014). Construction activity slowed down, and various economic sectors suffered a massive crisis (Bloch 2010). The scale and speed of development were impacted severely. Dubai began to pursue a more modest approach to urbanism focused on fine-grained, mixed-use development (Alawadi 2014). Old communities such as Al Satwa were demolished to construct mixed-use developments. This process of supplanting old neighborhoods with new glittery venues was carried out through the market- and profit-driven endeavors of Dubai-based developers. In a similar vein, parts of *Al Wasl*, *Al Safa*, and *Jumeirah*, along with a thriving park, were occupied to construct Business Bay Canal. These high-end constructions compelled many families who had resided in those old neighborhoods for generations to move out unwillingly (Alawadi 2014). Thus, this period can be labelled the period of gentrification in Dubai. However, national housing did not witness any significant transformation.

In 2014, Dubai won the bid to organize Expo 2020 (shifted to 2021 due to the ongoing pandemic). This rekindled a path to economic recovery (Alawadi and Dooling 2016). This period of recovery spanned from 2014 to 2020, when the COVID-19 pandemic hit the world and destabilized many sectors. The recovery period brought the revival of "bigness" including speculative projects and large-scale developments (Ponzini 2011) such as the Dubai Harbour Creek, which houses the Calatrava Tower. In this period also, national housing forms and programs continued in the desert landscape on a massive scale without being challenged or contested (Alawadi and Benkraouda 2017). The size of granted lands increased by 20 percent compared with earlier periods. The design and planning of residential neighborhoods

The recovery period brought the revival of 'bigness' including speculative projects and large-scale developments.
Ponzini, (2011).

are stuck where they were 30 years ago, as no new interventions or physical ideals have been applied in newer versions of national neighborhoods. Fragmented and low-density neighborhoods with dispersed and homogeneous forms and land use systems continue to dominate (Alawadi 2019). Thus, the national housing and bigness projects are dictating urban development in Dubai. While the national housing scheme is firmly established by the unofficial treaty between citizens and the government, Bigness is backed by the neopatrimonial system, which prioritizes profits and economy over other aspects of development. As this book focuses on street connectivity and accessibility in national housing districts, recommending an alternative to Bigness is beyond its scope.

FIG. 4
Progression of Dubai's urban growth

References

Abdo, Rudayna, and Geoffrey M. Batzel. "Planning the modern Arab city: The case of Abu Dhabi." Reconsidering Jane Jacobs (2011): 105-118.

Acuto, Michele. "High-rise Dubai urban entrepreneurialism and the technology of symbolic power." Cities 27, no. 4 (2010): 272-284.

Acuto, Michele. "D ubai in the 'Middle'." International Journal of Urban and Regional Research 38, no. 5 (2014): 1732-1748.

Kyriazis, A., Almehairi, A., & Al Seri, I. (2002). The morphology of Abu Dhabi's superblocks: a modernist vision. Urban Morphology, 1, 21-32.

Ahmed Abdul Azizi. March 10, 2007. Khaleejtimes. https://www.khaleejtimes.com/nation/general/the-master-planner-of-abu-dhabi-al-ain

Al-Sayegh, Fatma. "Merchants' role in a changing society: the case of Dubai, 1900–90." Middle Eastern Studies 34, no. 1 (1998): 87-102.

Alawadi, Khaled. "Urban redevelopment trauma: The story of a Dubai neighbourhood." Built Environment 40, no. 3 (2014): 357-375.

Alawadi, Khaled, and Sarah Dooling. "Challenges and opportunities for participatory planning approaches within Dubai's urban context." Journal of Urbanism: International Research on Placemaking and Urban Sustainability 9, no. 3 (2016): 276-301.

Alawadi, Khaled. "Place attachment as a motivation for community preservation: The demise of an old, bustling, Dubai community." Urban Studies 54, no. 13 (2017): 2973-2997.

Alawadi, Khaled. "Rethinking Dubai's urbanism: Generating sustainable form-based urban design strategies for an integrated neighborhood." Cities 60 (2017): 353-366.

Alawadi, Khaled. "Whatever happened to Dubai's public spaces?." International Journal of Middle East Studies 50, no. 3 (2018): 562-567.

Alawadi, Khaled, and Ouafa Benkraouda. "What happened to Abu Dhabi's urbanism? The question of regional integration." Journal of Urban Design 23, no. 3 (2018): 367-394.

Alawadi, Khaled, Asim Khanal, and Ahmed Almulla. "Land, urban form, and politics: a study on Dubai's housing landscape and rental affordability." Cities 81 (2018): 115-130.

Alawadi, Khaled. "A return to the old landscape? Balancing physical planning ideals and cultural constraints in Dubai's residential neighborhoods." Journal of Housing and the Built Environment 34 (2019): 235-263.

Alawadi, Khaled, and Ouafa Benkraouda. "The debate over neighborhood density in Dubai: Between theory and practicality." Journal of Planning Education and Research 39, no. 1 (2019): 18-34.

Alawadi, Khaled, Ngoc Hong Nguyen, Eiman Alrubaei, and Martin Scoppa. "Streets, density, and the superblock: neighborhood planning units and street connectivity in Abu Dhabi." Journal of Urbanism: International Research on Placemaking and Urban Sustainability (2021): 1-28.

Al Fahim, Mohammed. "From rags to riches." Dubai, UAE: London Centre of Arab Studies (1995).

Alawadi, Khaled, and Ouafa Benkraouda. "The debate over neighborhood density in Dubai: Between theory and practicality." Journal of Planning Education and Research 39, no. 1 (2019): 18-34.

Al-Kodmany, Kheir, Mir M. Ali, and Tingwei Zhang. "Importing urban giants: re-imaging Shanghai and Dubai with skyscrapers." ArchNet-IJAR: International Journal of Architectural Research 7, no. 2 (2013): 22.

Anna Zacharias. April 4, 2018. The national news. https://www.thenationalnews.com/uae/sheikh-abdullah-honours-family-of-the-japanese-architect-who-designed-abu-dhabi-1.718806

Bagaeen, Samer. "Brand Dubai: The instant city; or the instantly recognizable city." International Planning Studies 12, no. 2 (2007): 173-197.

Bani Hashim, A. R. (2011). "Vancouverism in Abu Dhabi: Recreating an Urban Utopia." In Traditional Dwellings and Settlements Review, Working Paper Series v.232, 79–97.

Bani Hashim, Alamira Reem. "The history of planning residential neighborhoods in Abu Dhabi." Transformation: The Emirati National Housing (2016): 58-77.

Bloch, Robin. "Dubai's long goodbye." International Journal of Urban and Regional Research 34, no. 4 (2010): 943-951.

Bula, F. (2008). "Larry Beasley's Simple Plan." Vancouver Magazine, December 1. Accessed April 4, 2021. https://www.vanmag.com/news_and_features/Larry_Beasleys_simple_plan

Corbusier, Le. The radiant city: Elements of a doctrine of urbanism to be used as the basis of our machine-age civilization. Orion Press, 1967.

Cugurullo, Federico. "How to build a sandcastle: An analysis of the genesis and development of Masdar City." Journal of Urban Technology 20, no. 1 (2013): 23-37.

Cugurullo, Federico. "Urban eco-modernisation and the policy context of new eco-city projects: Where Masdar City fails and why." Urban Studies 53, no. 11 (2016): 2417-2433.

Crot, Laurence. "Planning for sustainability in non-democratic polities: The case of Masdar City." Urban Studies 50, no. 13 (2013): 2809-2825.

Davidson, Christopher M. Dubai: The vulnerability of success. Columbia University Press, 2008.

DMT- Department of Municipalities and Transport Abu Dhabi. (2020). www.dmt.gov.ae

Dubai As it used to be (n.d.). John Harris – Dubai's Master Planner 1960-70s. Last accessed. 15.08.2021. Available from: http://dubaiasitusedtobe.net/JohnHarrisMasterPlanner.shtml

Municipality, Dubai. "Structure Plan for the Dubai Urban Area (1993–2012)." A Report prepared by Parsons Harland Bartholomew & Associates, Inc (1995).

Dubai Statistics Center, (2019). Population by Gender – Emirate of Dubai. Last accessed. 15.04.2020. Available from: https://www.dsc.gov.ae/en-us/Themes/Pages/Population-andVital-Statistics.aspx?Theme=42.

Elsheshtawy, Yasser, ed. Planning middle eastern cities: an urban kaleidoscope. Routledge, 2004.

Elsheshtawy, Yasser. "Transitory sites: mapping Dubai's 'forgotten'urban spaces." International Journal of Urban and Regional Research 32, no. 4 (2008): 968-988.

Elsheshtawy, Y. "Arabian tabula rasa: Culture, hegemony and the new Middle East." New Geographies 1 (2009): 98-109.

Elsheshtawy, Yasser. "Little space, big space: everyday urbanism in Dubai." Brown J. World Aff. 17 (2010): 53.

Elsheshtawy, Yasser. Dubai: Behind an urban spectacle. Routledge, 2009.

Elsheshtawy, Yasser. "The Emirati Sha 'bī house: on transformations, adaptation and modernist imaginaries." Arabian Humanities. Revue internationale d'archéologie et de sciences sociales sur la péninsule Arabique/International Journal of Archaeology and Social Sciences in the Arabian Peninsula 11 (2019).

Esri & USGS. (2021). World Imagery. Map Viewer. Retrieved November 10, 2021, from https://www.arcgis.com/apps/mapviewer/index.html?layers=10df2279f9684e4a9f6a7f08febac2a9.

Gabriel, E. F. (1987). The Dubai Handbook. Ahrensburg: Institute for Applied Economic Geography.

Ghazal, R. (2013). "The Man behind Abu Dhabi's Master Plan." The National, Accessed 11 November. https://www.thenational.ae/uae/heritage/the-man-behind-abu-dhabis-masterplan#page3

Gillet, N. "Abu Dhabi plans to build 17,000 villas for Emiratis." In The National, vol. 25. 2009.

Gold, John R. "Creating the Charter of Athens: CIAM and the functional city, 1933-43." The Town Planning Review (1998): 225-247.

Grant, Jill L. "Theory and practice in planning the suburbs: Challenges to implementing new urbanism, smart growth, and sustainability principles." Planning Theory & Practice 10, no. 1 (2009): 11-33.

Hoyland, R. (2001). Arabia and the Arabs. London: Routledge.

Hume, Jessica. 2008. "A Modern City Revives Its Old Heart." The National: 2. Accessed July 30. https://www.thenational.ae/news/a-modern-city-revives-its-old-heart

Jenks, Mike, Daniel Kozak, and Pattaranan Takkanon. World cities and urban form: fragmented, polycentric, sustainable?. Routledge, 2013.

Kanna, Ahmed. "The" state philosophical" in the" land without philosophy": Shopping malls, interior cities, and the image of utopia in Dubai." Traditional Dwellings and Settlements Review (2005): 59-73.

Kanna, Ahmed. Dubai, the city as corporation. U of Minnesota Press, 2011.

Kapur, Shuchita. "Abu Dhabi's oil reserves to last another 150 years." Link: https://goo. gl/5LWLFF (2010).

Kathiravelu, Laavanya. Migrant Dubai: Low wage workers and the construction of a global city. Springer, 2016.

Katodrytis, G. (2007). The Dubai experiment. Al-Manakh Gulf Survey (pp. 38–47). Amsterdam: Stichting Archis.

Katodrytis, George. "Performative urbanism: An emerging model of the Gulf." Architectural Design 85, no. 1 (2015): 120-127.

Katodrytis, George, and Kevin Mitchell, eds. UAE and the Gulf: architecture and urbanism now. John Wiley & Sons, 2015.

Khirfan, Luna, and Zahra Jaffer. "Canadian Planning Knowledge in the Middle East: Transferring Toronto to Amman and Vancouver to Abu Dhabi." Canadian Journal of Urban Research 21, no. 1 (2012): 1-28.

Koolhaas, R., & Mau, B. (1995). SMLXL. New York: Ed. Monacelli.

Kyriazis, Apostolos, Ahmed Almehairi, and Ibrahim Al Seri. "The morphology of Abu Dhabi's superblocks: a modernist vision." Urban Morphology 1 (2002): 21-32.

Machado, Rodolfo. "Dubai is not yet." Harvard Design Magazine 25 (2006): 97-103.

McCann, Eugene. "Urban policy mobilities and global circuits of knowledge: Toward a research agenda." Annals of the Association of American Geographers 101, no. 1 (2011): 107-130.

Mehaffy, Michael W., Sergio Porta, and Ombretta Romice. "The "neighborhood unit" on trial: A case study in the impacts of urban morphology." Journal of Urbanism: International Research on Placemaking and Urban Sustainability 8, no. 2 (2015): 199-217.

Middleton, Jennie. "'Stepping in time': walking, time, and space in the city." Environment and planning A 41, no. 8 (2009): 1943-1961.

Montgomery, Charles. Happy city: Transforming our lives through urban design. Penguin UK, 2013.

Mumford, Eric. "CIAM and its outcomes." Urban Planning 4, no. 3 (2019): 291-298.

Pacione, Michael. "Dubai: City Profile." Cities 22, no. 3 (2005): 255-65.

Patricios, Nicholas N. "The neighborhood concept: A retrospective of physical design and social interaction." Journal of Architectural and Planning Research (2002): 70-90.

Perry, Clarence. ""The Neighborhood Unit": from The Regional Plan of New York and its Environs (1929)." In The City Reader, pp. 557-569. Routledge, 2020.

Peter, J. (1994), The Oral History of Modern Architecture, New York, Abrams. PUGIN, A. W. N. (1841), The True Principles of Pointed or Christian Architecture, London.

Ponzini, Davide. "Large scale development projects and star architecture in the absence of democratic politics: The case of Abu Dhabi, UAE." Cities 28, no. 3 (2011): 251-259.

Potter, Lawrence G., ed. The Persian Gulf in History. New York: Palgrave Macmillan, 2009.

Pyla, Panayiota. "Gossip on the Doxiadis 'Gossip Square': unpacking the histories of an unglamorous public space." Architectural Histories 1, no. 1 (2013).

Ramos, Stephen J. Dubai amplified: the engineering of a port geography. Routledge, 2016.

Reisz, Todd. "Plans the earth swallows: An interview with Abdulrahman Makhlouf." Portal 9, no. 2 (2013): 1-17.

Samarrai, K. (2016). The evolution of Abu Dhabi City's urbanization and the sustainability challenge. In Shaping Cities; Emerging models of planning practice.

SCAD. (2016). Statistical Yearbook of Abu Dhabi 2016: Abu Dhabi Statistics Centre. (2016, October 8). Accessed June 21, 2020. https://www.scad.ae/en/Pages/ThemesReleases.aspx?ThemeID=4

Scoppa, Martin, Khawla Bawazir, and Khaled Alawadi. "Straddling boundaries in superblock cities. Assessing local and global network connectivity using cases from Abu Dhabi, UAE." Transportation Research Part A: Policy and Practice 130 (2019): 770-782.

Seccombe, Ian, and Richard Lawless. "Work camps and company towns: settlement patterns and the Gulf oil industry." (1987).

Somer, Cornelis Jacob. "De functionele stad: De CIAM en Cornelis van Eesteren, 1928-1960." (2007).

Sorkin, Michael. "Connect the dots: Dubai, labor, urbanism, sustainability, and the education of architects." Architectural Record 197, no. 8 (2009).

Southworth, M., and E. Ben-Joseph. "Streets and the Shaping of Cities and Towns." (1997).

Southworth, Michael, and Peter M. Owens. "The evolving metropolis: Studies of community, neighborhood, and street form at the urban edge." Journal of the American Planning Association 59, no. 3 (1993): 271-287.

Sultan Al Qassemi, S. (2010). "Sheikh Zayed." In Al Manakh Continued, edited by T. Reisz, 195. Amsterdam: Stichting Archis.

Trench, Richard. "Arabian Gulf cities: Doha, Abu Dhabi, Dubai and Sharjah." (1994).

Twombly, R. (1988). Louis Sullivan: The Public Papers, Chicago, University of Chicago Press.

Velegrinis, Steven, and George Katodrytis. "Drawing on sand: cities in the making." Architectural Design 85, no. 1 (2015): 72-79.

Whitehand, J. W. R., Kai Gu, Michael P. Conzen, and Susan M. Whitehand. "The typological process and the morphological period: a cross-cultural assessment." Environment and Planning B: Planning and Design 41, no. 3 (2014): 512-533.

World Population Review, (2021). Dubai Population 2021. Last accessed. 15.09.2021. Available from: https://worldpopulationreview.com/world-cities/dubai-population.

03

Growth Phases of Abu Dhabi's Neighborhoods

Evolution of Neighborhoods

This chapter introduces Abu Dhabi's urban form and how the city evolved throughout its urban growth phases. It also discusses each period's urban development trend and the various factors affecting it. Alawadi and Benkraouda (2018) divided the urban development of Abu Dhabi into three periods (See Figure 1). The first period, named the Inception period, lasted from 1967 to 1975. This period exemplified diversity, close-knit neighborhoods, sensitivity to the environment, and integration of neighborhoods with the rest of the city fabric. The second period, the Dispersion period, occurred from 1975 to 2007 and was characterized by fragmentation, massive expansion, parcel inflation, and neighborhoods' segregation from the existing urban fabric. The third period, the Redemption period, began in 2007 and was characterized by nostalgic historicism, densification, parcel deflation, and sparse regional integration. It ended in 2017 when the Urban Planning Council (UPC) and the Department of Municipal Affairs were merged to create the Department of Urban Planning and Municipalities (DPM). Then, in 2019, the Department of Municipalities and Transport (DMT) was formed by the merger of DPM and the Department of Transport (DOT). Since 2017, the Dispersion phase has been revived and continues to the present day.

The urban structure of Abu Dhabi is based on three different forms, namely mega developments, national housing, and fine-grain urbanism. National housing and large-scale developments in the islands have primarily shaped Abu Dhabi's urban growth. The national housing program is deep-rooted in the government's policy as a means of sharing wealth with citizens, while the island developments are the manifestations of Abu Dhabi's economic ambitions. The mega-developments occurring on the islands are outside the scope of this book.

Inception Period (1966–1975)

The ascension of *Sheikh Zayed* in 1966 marks the beginning of the Inception era. He envisioned the transformation of Abu Dhabi from scattered settlements into a modern city. In 1967, John Elliott, Abu Dhabi's first official planner, was recruited from Scandinavia, where he had been working with municipalities on progressive, people-empowered town planning (Wimsatt 2010). *Sheikh Zayed* and Elliot bonded over their appreciation of route directness and simplicity in design (Alawadi and Benkraouda 2018). After several discussions and meetings with *Sheikh Zayed*, Elliott introduced the *ARABICON* Plan, which featured a grid of rectangular superblocks, each with dimensions of 900 m x 600 m and right of ways (ROWs) of 15–18m separated by arterials (Abdo and Batzel 2011). During this period, plots of 25 m^2 (Elsheshtawy 2016) or 25 x 20 m with minimum setbacks were common, with a plot density of 12 plots/ha. The plots were separated by alleys to maintain family privacy. Originally, each superblock was designed as a self-sustaining neighborhood unit capable for growth and expansion (Alawadi and Benkraouda 2018). However, the design of the superblocks took different forms at different times, producing a mix of superblocks, each designed and filled differently (See Figures 2 and 3). This variation occurred due to the involvement of three different planners over a span of seven years. Some blocks are made up of mixed-use high-rise or mid-rise buildings integrated with single-family homes, often located at the block center. Other blocks are zoned entirely for high-rises and mid-rises or are developed primarily as single-family dwellings.

After Elliott's departure, Katushiko Takahashi led the town's planning department. Under the influence of modernist and international planning principles, he continued to design superblocks and generated a land use

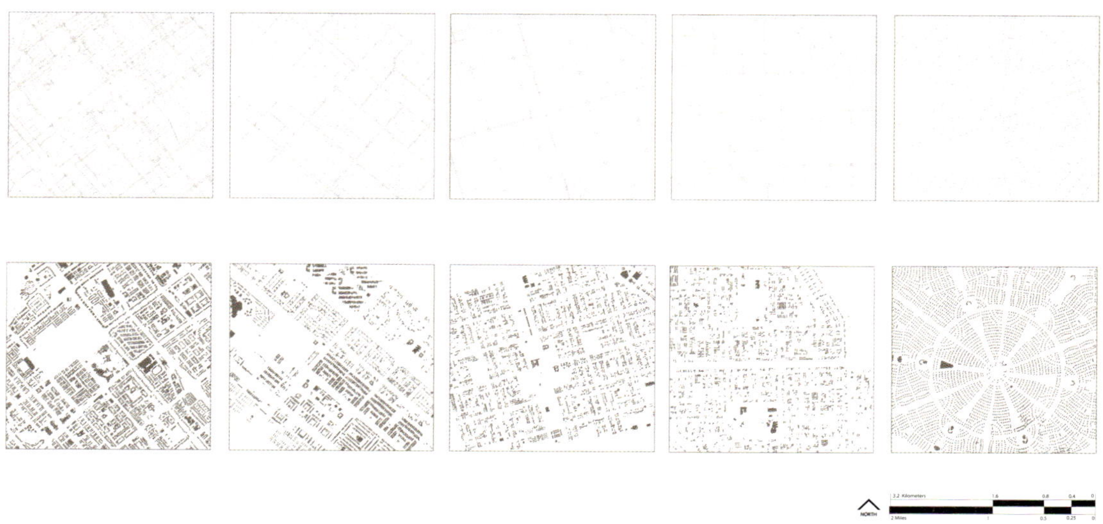

FIG. 1

Evolution of street patterns and density of Abu Dhabi. Earlier neighborhoods featured higher density and more interconnected systems, while newer ones adopted lower densities and broken, disconnected, and fragmented street systems. In the redemption period, Abu Dhabi redeemed itself and adopted a higher density levels and more interconnected pattern in a radial form.

plan and a zoning system for Abu Dhabi (Reisz 2013). According to his planning strategy, each superblock is a mixed-income neighborhood with towers placed in the peripheries (Abdo and Batzel, 2011). Abdelrahman Makhlouf succeeded Takahashi and was assigned as the General Director of the Department of Town Planning in 1968. He confirmed the *ARABICON* plan and tried to use NPU principles to design the details of the superblocks. Later, he was also put in charge of the national housing program. The size and scale of Makhlouf's superblocks promoted a close-knit community that retained the traditional community structure (Menoret 2014) through the use of NPUs. The NPU concept has a long history in urban planning and design scholarship and practice (Rohe 2009; Brody 2010). It emerged in the 1900s as a reaction to the industrial revolution, when the sense of community was dwindling (Lloyd Lawhon 2009; Meenakshi 2011). In 1929, Clarence Arthur Perry proposed planning neighborhood units; his proposal focused heavily on form-based planning approaches (i.e., the size of the NPU, its boundaries, the internal street system, and the distribution of land uses [Perry, 1939]). By the end of the 1940s, the NPU concept became one of the most important topics discussed by scholars and professionals (Stein 1945; Mumford 1954) (See Figure 4). Perry's concept was carried forward with variations by other planners, such as Stein (1945), Andres Duany and Elizabeth Plater-Zyberk (2001), and Douglas Farr (2008). Makhlouf was influenced by planned cities where NPUs were used, such as Baghdad, Islamabad, and Riyadh (Kyriazis, Almehairi, and Al Seri 2017). The key difference between Abu Dhabi's NPUs and those in the other cities was the size of each NPU. Makhlouf's NPU had an approximate dimension of 600 m x 900 m, while Doxiadis's NPU for Baghdad, Islamabad, and Riyadh had a dimension of 2 km x 2 km (Hashim 2018). The NPUs in Abu Dhabi also have a different shape from those in Riyadh, Baghdad, and Islamabad. While Riyadh, Baghdad, and Islamabad adopted large, square NPUs, Abu Dhabi planned for smaller, rectangular NPUs.

Makhlouf's vision aimed to represent Abu Dhabi as a socially oriented city. He envisioned the NPU as a 'social unit' that would include public and semi-private open spaces to promote social inclusion and community life. His NPU had a street system with culs-de-sac surrounded by a set of seven housing units that were near one another but far enough from other housing groups to ensure privacy and security. He advocated for a pedestrian-friendly NPU that would place all land uses, including mosques and schools, near dwellings. Consequently, the superblocks designed during his tenure have all necessary services within walking distance (Alawadi and Benkraouda 2018).

The designed neighborhoods in the Inception Period are characterized by density, orientation to the local culture, diversity, and a pedestrian-friendly layout. This started with Elliott's planning approach, which "evolved around the social needs of people" (Elliott, cited in Wimsatt 2010), and it was continued by successive planners, particularly Makhlouf, who firmly established the "social unit" concept through NPUs. After Makhlouf became involved in the planning of Abu Dhabi, the original, rectangular 900m x 600m NPU became a signature urban pattern that guided Abu Dhabi's neighborhood planning (Kyriazis, Almehairi, and Al Seri 2017). Daily services and amenities were distributed throughout the neighborhoods to promote social interaction among people of different communities. The most essential needs were made available within the neighborhoods' boundaries to provide for self-sufficiency, proximity, and accessibility. The neighborhoods in this period were also designed to connect to future developments through their system of overlapping landscapes, mixed-use borders, and grid networks. By incorporating ideas associated with regional planning, their design supported urban expansion beyond the neighborhoods' boundaries (Alawadi and Benkraouda 2018).

Like the rulers of Dubai and other emirates in the UAE, the rulers of Abu Dhabi decided to share the nation's wealth with their citizens by granting them free land through what is formally known as the national housing scheme. Some have labelled this scheme a wise governance strategy and an act of kindness. However, it is a debatable practice because it promotes the separation of the local population from expatriates. The national housing landscape became prominent in the 1970s during the following the Dispersion Period.

The size and scale of Makhlouf's superblocks promoted a close-knit community that retained the traditional community structure.
Menoret, (2014)

FIG. 2
Superblocks in West Island, Abu Dhabi

FIG. 3
Zoomed-in view of the superblocks in West Island, Abu Dhabi

FIG. 4
Global and regional super blocks/NPU's (Esri & USGS, 2021)

Phoenix (1606m x 1580m)

Buenos Aires (900m x 460m)

Brasilia (1463m x 1437m)

Islamabad (1907m x 1738m)

Baghdad (553m x 416m)

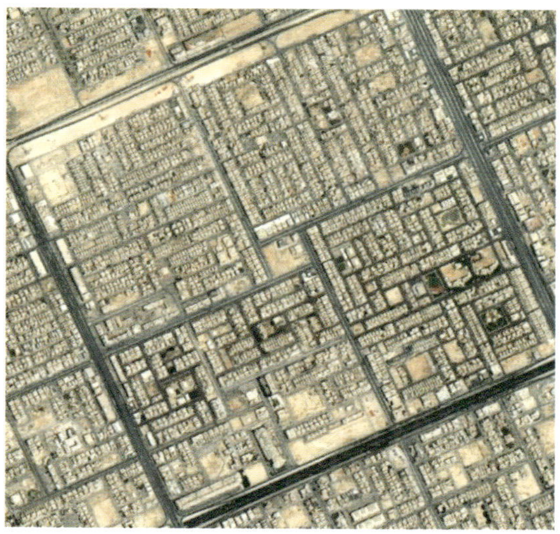
Riyadh (2000m x 1994m)

Dispersion period (1975–2007)

Since 1990, the NPU concept has been used as the building block of neighborhood planning in Abu Dhabi (See Figures 5 and 6). Towards the end of the 1980s, the Abu Dhabi government recognized the need to produce a new, comprehensive master plan to guide the uncontrolled development and improve the efficacy of the urban land-use system. In 1988, Abu Dhabi City Town Planning Department, in collaboration with the United Nations Development Program, hired *W. S. Atkins*, a British engineering consultancy, to prepare Abu Dhabi's first long-term regional plan (Samarai 2016; Elsheshtway 2013). As a result, *The Master Directive Plan for Abu Dhabi and its Environs (*MDP*)* was proposed to comprehensively manage the city's growth from 1990 to 2010. The plan introduced community planning standards and also proposed residential areas for both citizens and non-citizens, thereby addressing the housing needs of different population segments. The plan was rejected, but several of its elements were implemented, including its proposal of expanding development in the mainland and protecting the island from further development pressure, since the island had been 96 percent urbanized by 1985 (ADM 2003). In general, though, regional planning was not an important component of the Atkins plan. Instead, the plan recommended a pattern that favored single-family housing (Ryan 2013) in suburbs and high-rise buildings downtown. Influenced by conventional planning principles in the United States, where "the looping streets and large-scale, homogenous land uses of the newer suburbs represent a different urban pattern than can be found in the older, gridded central area" (Wheeler 2002, p. 271), the Atkins plan introduced a hierarchical system into neighborhood planning, road design, and allocation of community facilities. This approach brought automobile-dependent patterns and land-use segregation to the city (Alawadi and Benkraouda 2018).

Neighborhood design in the Atkins plan completely discarded density, diversity, and connectivity, ideals that had been considered vital during the Inception Period. Planning was instead driven by road infrastructure and large subdivisions and plot sizes. Plot sizes increased throughout this period to reflect citizens' increasing socio-economic status. For instance, plot sizes were 30 m x 45 m and 60 m x 35 m in *Khalifa City*, 45 m x 45 m in Al Bahya, and 45 m x 60 m and 60 m x 60 m in *MBZ City*) (Alawadi and Benkrouda, 2018). Large plot sizes, setbacks, and ROWs ranging from 30 to 80 m resulted in separation between plots and disconnection in the community. Bigger plot sizes increased the land area and scale of communities without concurrent provision for public areas and neighborhood facilities. This form of urbanism echoed post–World War II North American urbanism, which "led to the development of an increasingly controlled and monotonous urban fabric where these areas lack the diversity and character of places that developed incrementally" (Southworth and Owens 1993, p.278). A few exceptions appeared during this period to counter the movement towards isolation. For example, some neighborhoods clustered a group of villas together in one block around a central open space to reflect sensitivity to community needs (e.g., *Al Bahya East*).

The interconnected superblock that helped form a complete neighborhood before the 1970s was swapped for asymmetrical networks composed of large superblocks (usually larger than 1 km^2), broken, curving, and looping streets surrounded by highways and grade-separated interchanges, and a plot density as low as 2 plots per hectare. These design features hinder integration and accessibility. Moreover, the massive expansion of Abu Dhabi's neighborhoods after 1990 led to greater use of NPUs featuring different street layouts and plot densities (See Figure 7). However, the sizes of NPUs and plots inflated to huge scales, which also minimized their ability to connect with the existing urban fabric.

Because of the rigid and segregated nature of the newly built neighborhoods, these communities diminish opportunities for future evolution, adaptability, and integration with the existing city fabric (Alawadi and Benkraouda 2018). The process of suburban growth was institutionalized by the introduction of the national housing program in the 1970s. This subsidy scheme grants a plot of land to every male citizen who is 21 years of age or older. As a result, 55 percent of the total built landscape of Abu Dhabi has been designated for approximately 20 percentof the population. Eventually, these practices created a sprawling and repetitive landscape featuring spatially segregated communities of locals; luxury residential enclaves for white-collar, high-income expatriates; and disconnected blue-collar worker camps.

Because of the rigid and segregated nature of the newly built neighborhoods, these communities diminish opportunities for future evolution, adaptability, and integration with the existing city fabric.
Alawadi and Benkraouda, (2018).

FIG. 5

(Up) West Island, Abu Dhabi, and its mix of superblock designs. (Down) aggregation of identical superblocks in Khalifa City, Abu Dhabi (Esri & USGS, 2021)

FIG. 6

(Up) Khalifa City, how superblocks are used in the development of neighborhoods. (Down) the morphological components of superblocks in Khalifa City.

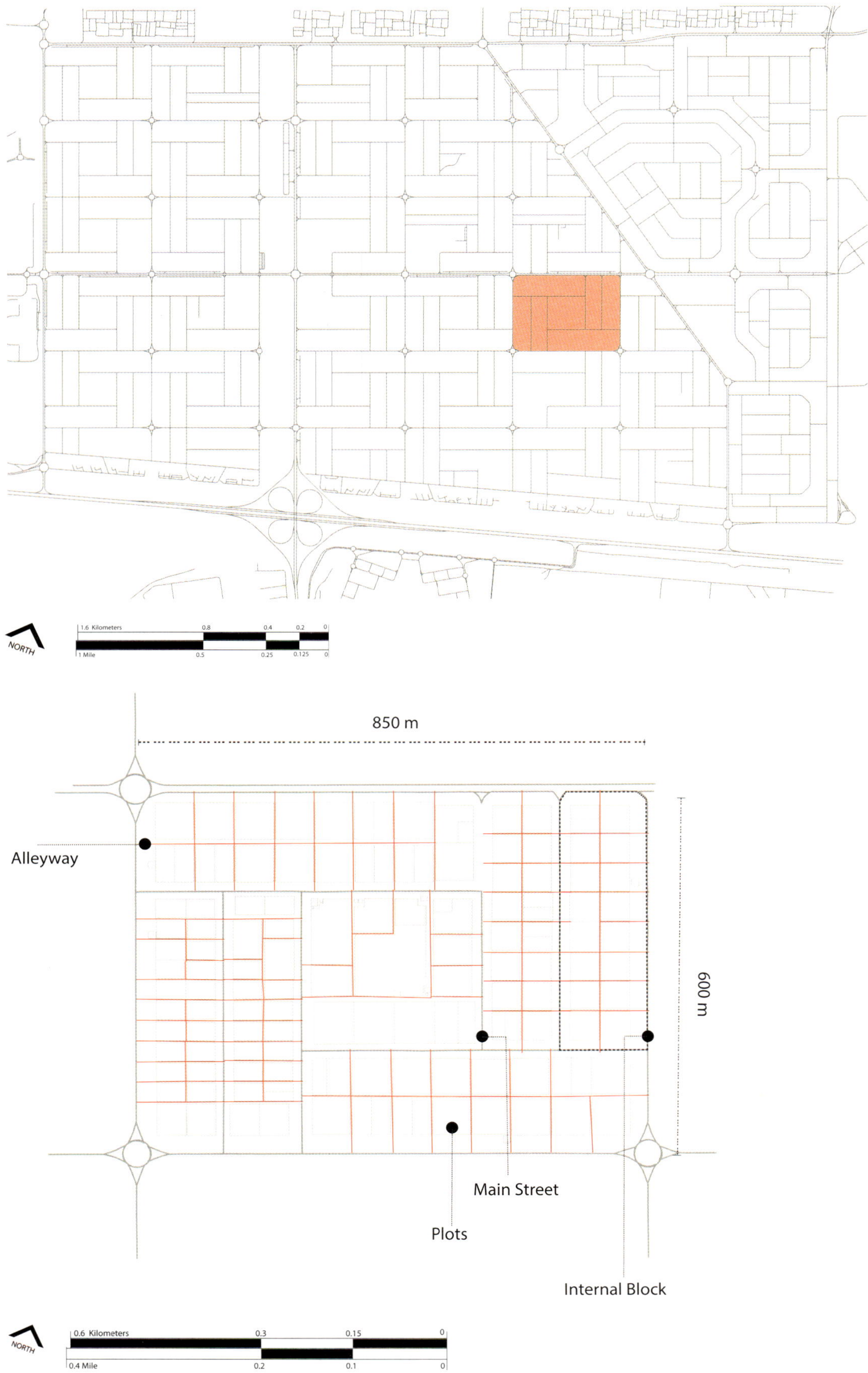

Redemption period (2007-2017)

With the ambition of transforming Abu Dhabi into a regional and global hub, in 2007 the Urban Planning Council (UPC) was established as the new agency in charge of strategy and planning policy for future development. A new plan was deemed necessary to guide Abu Dhabi's growth in the coming decades. This time, the plan was not prepared by an individual expert who arrived from abroad. Instead, several local and international experts, along with government officials from various relevant agencies, gave their input during two charrettes. These sessions were held under the direct supervision of the Crown Prince *Mohammed Bin Zayed Al Nahyan*. In addition, international consultancies, such as *Boston Consulting Group* and *Economic Research Associates*, prepared the demographic projections and economic analysis. (UPC 2007). Both firms estimated that the population of the Abu Dhabi City region would reach 3 million or more by 2030. In November 2013, the UPC updated Plan Abu Dhabi 2030 and revised the population projection for Abu Dhabi City to 2.4 million by 2030 (UPC, 2007). Subsequently, the UPC implemented *Plan Capital 2030* as the city's formal urban structure framework for managing sustainable planning practices serving urban and economic development for the span of 25 years (Alawadi and Benkraouda 2018). This plan differed in scope from the *Atkins* 1990–2010 Comprehensive Master Plan, because it excluded the eastern and the western regions of Abu Dhabi Emirate and focused on the capital city region only. The principles of *Plan Capital 2030* focus on themes such as the identity of Abu Dhabi City as a contemporary Arab capital, its sustainable growth in tandem with the conservation of natural environment, and culturally relevant neighborhood design.

Plan Capital 2030 regulated and formalized planning in Abu Dhabi and thereby had a direct impact on the layout and structure of national housing neighborhoods such as *Yas* and *Al Falah*. These neighborhoods are characterized by unique layouts: *Yas* community's layout was influenced by local traditional principles of urbanism, while *Al Falah's* design was influenced by *New Urbanism* and garden suburbs. In particular, *Yas* community features traditional courtyards and a modern community structure, while *Al Falah* has a radial garden layout and interconnected streets. *Yas* community represents a modern version of courtyard urbanism (ADHA 2014) and a neighborhood system which is locally known as *Al Freej*. *Al Freej*, in the Emirati dialect, refers to a group of houses that surround 100% of the plot with *sikkak*, alleyways that are strategically located to connect neighboring homes, community facilities, and public spaces. This pattern is based on the traditional organization of Emirati settlements and reflects the very great cultural importance of family relationships, daily walking, and daily visits between neighbors (Alawadi and Benkraouda 2018).

The designs adopted higher densities (7 to 19 plots per hectare) by introducing smaller plot sizes of 30 x 35 m and 20 x 25 m, smaller blocks, vernacular forms, open spaces, pedestrian paths, strategic allocation of alleyways, and courtyard-oriented designs. Likewise, *Al Falah's* smaller blocks and radial and interconnected street layouts distinguish it from other suburbs in Abu Dhabi. These neighborhoods resemble *New Urbanist* neighborhoods due to the presence of walkable and interconnected streets, shorter blocks, moderate density, and greater access to public spaces within the neighborhood. However, these communities failed to introduce mixed-use developments that would promote self-sufficiency. *Al Falah* failed to connect the development to the larger city system and adjacent urban fabric, thus restricting its ability to expand contiguously. Similarly, *Yas* was designed as a strictly residential neighborhood without any diversity of uses and in isolation from the regional city plan. Although these neighborhoods were subject to increased control, design standardization, and (UPC) planning guidelines, they were still designed as autonomous built landscapes separated from the larger systems in the city.

To formalize urban planning and design in Abu Dhabi, (UPC) had introduced various new urban planning and design standards, such as the *Public Realm Manual, a Community Facilities Manual, Urban Street Design Standards, and the Estidama Rating System*. The latter is a sustainability rating system that promotes current and future development conditions to fulfill Abu Dhabi's 2030 vision (Alawadi and Benkraouda 2017). This growth period ended when the UPC was assimilated into the newly formed Department of Municipalities and Transport (DMT). UPC's influence automatically plummeted when it ceased operating as an independent agency and became a mere section of the (DMT). Therefore, urban development in Abu Dhabi returned to the Dispersion growth phase in 2017 and remains in this phase today.

In November 2013, the UPC updated Plan Abu Dhabi 2030 and revised the population projection for Abu Dhabi City to 2.4 million by 2030.
UPC, (2007).

FIG. 7

Examples of street networks of ten Abu Dhabi superblocks/NPU's. The areas within the dashed lines are the same for all cases (1000 × 750 m, enclosing 75 ha) and illustrate the size regularity of superblocks.

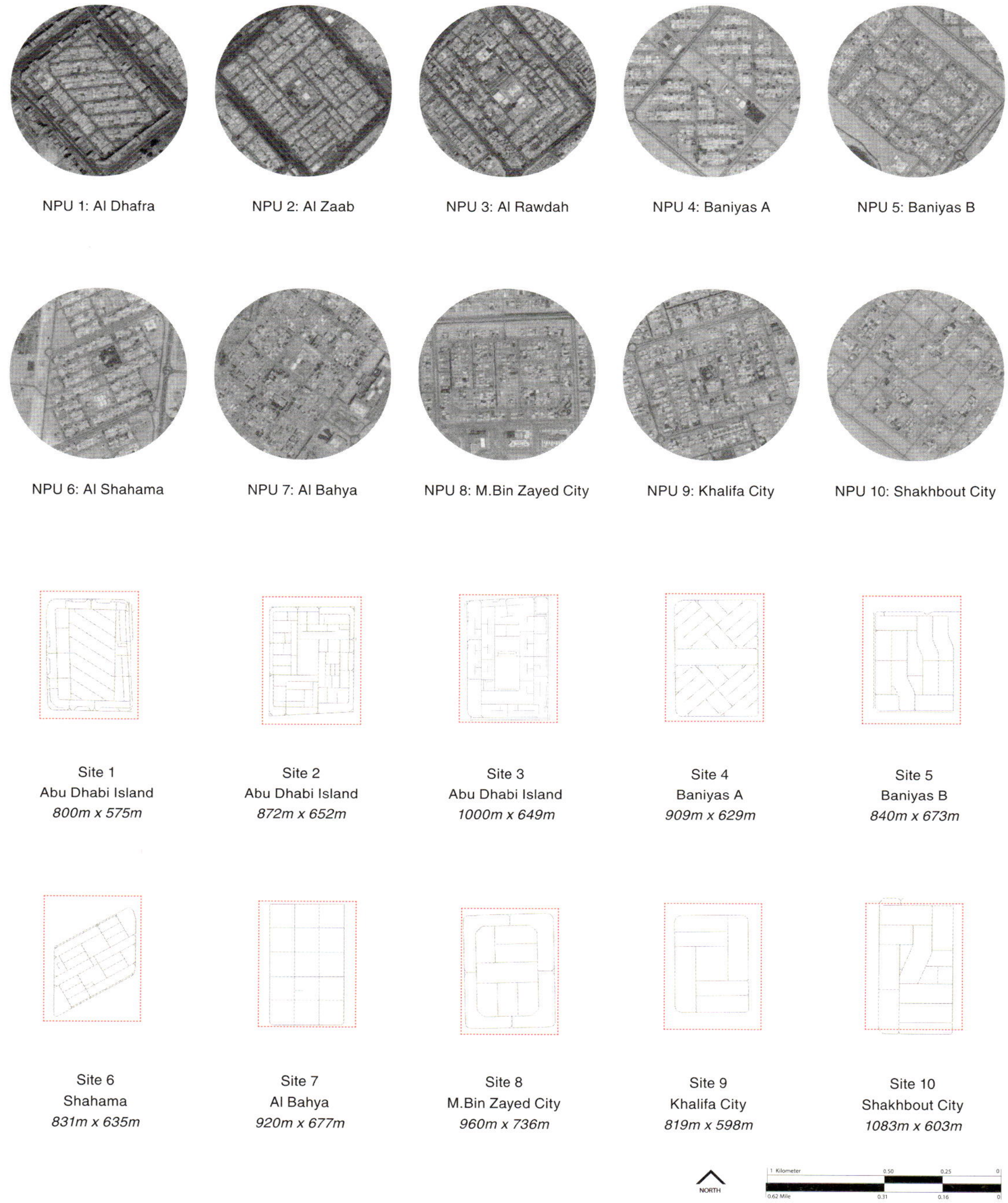

References

Abdo, R., & Batzel, G. M. (2011). Planning the modern Arab city: the case of Abu Dhabi. Reconsidering Jane Jacobs, 105-118.

Abu- Dhabi Urban Planning Council. (2007). Abu Dhabi 2030 Plan.

ADHA. (2014). Abu Dhabi National Housing Guidelines for Integrated Communities: Lessons Learned Report.

ADM. (2003). Abu Dhabi: Dana of the Gulf, Planning and Urban Development (Studies and Research Section). UAE: Abu Dhabi Municipality & Town Planning Department.

Alawadi, K., & Benkraouda, O. (2018). What happened to Abu Dhabi's urbanism? The question of regional integration. Journal of Urban Design, 23(3), 367-394.

Alawadi, K., & Benkraouda, O. (2019). The debate over neighborhood density in Dubai: Between theory and practicality. Journal of Planning Education and Research, 39(1), 18-34.

Brody, J. (2010). The neighbourhood unit concept and the shaping of land planning in the United States 1912–1968. Journal of Urban Design, 18(3), 340-362.

Douglas, F. (2008). Sustainable urbanism: urban design with nature. Hoboken, NJ Wiley,

Duany, A., Plater-Zyberk, E., & Speck, J. (2001). Suburban nation: The rise of sprawl and the decline of the American dream. Macmillan.

Elsheshtawy, Y. (2013). Where the sidewalk ends: Informal Street corner encounters in Dubai. Cities, 31, 382-393.

Elsheshtawy, Y. (2016). Transformation: The Emirati National Housing. Pavilion of the UAE at the 15th Venice Architecture Exhibition, Venice, 28

Esri & USGS. (2021). World Imagery. Map

Viewer. Retrieved November 10, 2021, from https://www.arcgis.com/apps/mapviewer/index.html?layers=10df-2279f9684e4a9f6a7f08febac2a9.

Hashim, A. R. B. 2018. Planning Abu Dhabi: An Urban History. London: Routledge.

Kyriazis, A., Almehairi, A., & Al Seri, I. (2002). The morphology of Abu Dhabi's superblocks: A modernist vision. Urban Morphology, 1, 21-32.

Lloyd Lawhon, L. (2009). The neighborhood unit: physical design or physical determinism? Journal of Planning History, 8(2), 111-132.

Meenakshi, A. (2011). Neighbourhood Unit and its Conceptualization in the Contemporary Urban Context. Institute of Town Planners, India Journal, 8, 81-86.

Ménoret, P. (2014). The Abu Dhabi Guide: Modern Architecture, 1968-1992. FIND (Forming Intersections and Dialogues), NYU Abu Dhabi.

Mumford, L. (1954). The neighborhood and the neighborhood unit. The Town Planning Review, 24(4), 256-270.

Perry, C. (1939). "The Neighborhood Unit": from The Regional Plan of New York and its Environs (1929). The City Reader (pp. 557-569). Routledge.

Reisz, T. (2013). Plans the earth swallows: An interview with Abdulrahman Makhlouf. Portal, 9(2)

Rohe, W. M. (2009). From local to global: One hundred years of neighborhood planning. Journal of the American Planning Association, 75(2), 209-230.

Ryan, B. D. (2013). Whatever happened to "urbanism"? A comparison of premodern, modernist, and HOPE VI morphology in three American cities. Journal of Urban Design, 18(2), 201-219.

Southworth, M., & Owens, P. M. (1993). The evolving metropolis: Studies of community, neighborhood, and street form at the urban edge. Journal of the American Planning Association, 59(3), 271-287.

Stein, C. S. (1945). The city of the Future, a City of Neighborhoods.

Wheeler, S. M. (2002). The new regionalism: Key characteristics of an emerging movement. Journal of the American Planning Association, 68(3), 267-278.

Wimsatt, A. (2010). The houses that John built. Paper presented at the The National, 27.

04

Growth Phases of Dubai's Neighborhoods

Evolution of Neighborhoods

This chapter introduces the urban form of Dubai and describes how it changed during its different growth phases. It also discusses each growth period's urban development trend and the various factors affecting it. The urban development timeline of Dubai has been divided into six distinct growth periods: Necessity (1900–1955), Compact Growth (1955–1970), Planned Suburban Growth (1970–1990), Bigness (1996–2007), Recession (2008–2013), and Post-Expo 2020 Bid (2014–present) (Alawadi 2018). However, with regard to the residential landscape of national housing, only three major growth periods exist: the Necessity or Inception period starting in 1900 and lasting until the early 1960s, the Pre-Dispersion period from the late 1960s to the 1980s, and the Dispersion period from 1980 to the present. Dubai's older neighborhoods, which have organic and compact layouts, were built during the first period, which is characterized by a markedly vernacular style and a dense fabric. The neighborhoods built during the Pre-Dispersion phase feature well-connected gridiron patterns, but towards the end of this phase, less regular patterns and semi-grids began to be adopted. The third phase is characterized by the massive expansion of the city. In this phase, neighborhoods became much bigger with lower density, and streets became fragmented, broken, curving, and looping (See Figure 1).

The Dispersion period coincides with the era of Bigness, which began in the 1990s and lasted until the economic downturn of 2008. A plethora of spectacular architectural feats were achieved or begun during this time, including *Burj Al Arab* and *Burj Khalifa*, to name two. This kind of entrepreneurial urban development led by the neo-patrimonial system turned Dubai into a testing bed for experimental projects. Megaprojects such as *Burj Khalifa* and *Burj Al Arab* spatially express an economic diversification strategy focused on attracting and retaining tourists, investors, and entrepreneurs. Some scholars argue that this kind of urban growth trajectory leads to differential economic growth and ultimately socio-spatial polarization and conflict (Pacione 2005). After 2008, the intensity of high-end construction plummeted until 2013; however, inner core areas such as *Sha'biyat Al Defaa'*, *Sha'biyat al Shorta*, and parts of *Al Satwa* were demolished to build mixed-use developments (See Figures 2 and 3). In 2014, real estate developments again began to soar until Dubai won its Expo 2020 bid (Alawadi 2017). Bigness-related developments are beyond the scope of this book.

Inception Period (1900–1955)

It is unlikely that urban form in this era was guided by any master plan or planning principle. From ancient times, Dubai had been a sparsely settled town due to its harsh climate and desert environment, but it was permanently established due to its creek, which may have offered defensive advantages, and its strategic location along a trade route, which is a typical beginning for organic cities. When Dubai eventually became a permanent settlement, residential quarters grew organically in clusters to serve the purposes of privacy and collective tribal security, not unlike pre-industrial fishing villages elsewhere in the world. The internal parts of each enclave were connected by narrow walkways that were intended for pedestrians and domestic animals and used to transport goods and drinking water (Elsheshtawy 2004). The housing stock in Dubai was composed of *barasti* houses, vernacular architecture with palm frond roofing and wall structures built of clay and corral fragments. This type of architecture was porous, which meant that wind could pass through it to cool the house, and was climatically responsive (Gabriel 1987; Harris 1994; Pacione 2005). Affluent families and tribal leaders lived in houses with wind towers made of coral stone, a vernacular architecture imported from Persia, present-day Iran (Katodrytis and Mitchell 2015). The zoning ordinances of 1971 allowed the construction of mixed-use, ground-plus-three buildings. Thus, many residents opted to demolish their

FIG. 1

Evolution of street patterns and density of Dubai. Earlier neighborhoods featured higher density and more interconnected systems, while newer ones adopted lower density levels with broken, disconnected, and fragmented street systems.

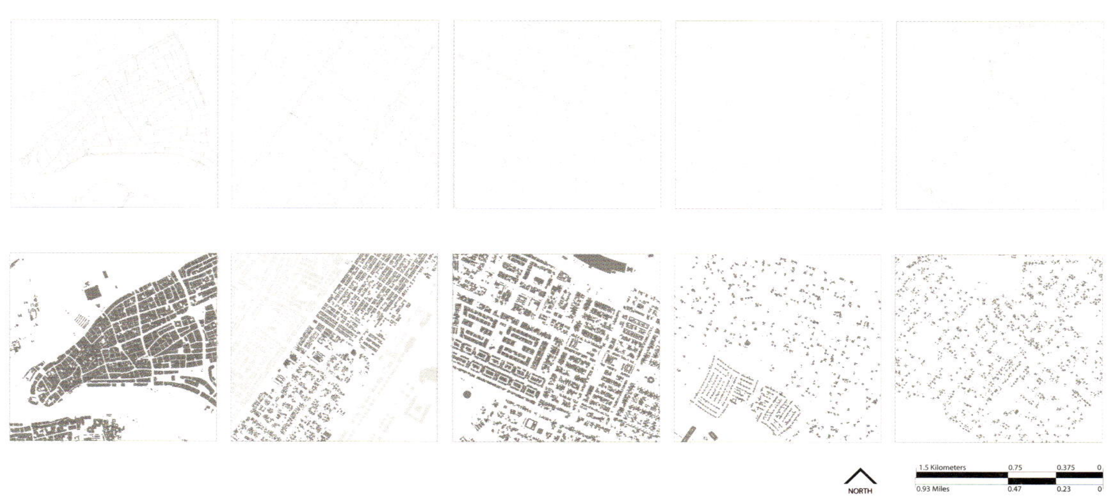

old homes and construct new buildings that maximized plot coverage for financial gain. However, streets and alleys retained their organic pattern (Alawadi, Khanal, and Almulla 2018), even though land uses changed notably.

The cultural value for privacy and the climatic need for natural ventilation and shading shaped the winding, narrow alleyways and led to the proliferation of the courtyard house. Hence, the effort to fulfill social needs in compliance with the demands of nature, the environment, and the climate resulted in the formation of a somewhat dense cityscape with inward-looking structures; similarities can be found in the historical parts of Gulf cities such as Al-Manama, Doha, and Muscat, as well as the '*Kasbah*' of Algiers (Heard-Bey, 1982, p. 260). Dubai's unique location along the important British trade route to India—which arguably fueled its settlement—led to the creation of a polycentric urban structure, undoubtedly laying the foundation for future growth trajectories.

The immigration of people from surrounding regions who, like the natives, were accustomed to living in close communities and tribes, resulted in a segregated urban form, aided by the creek, which created a natural barrier. While these clusters were in close proximity to one another, they were, for reasons of tribal and cultural privacy, distinctly segregated and separated based on origin (Ramos, 2010). This practice of segregation can be claimed as the foundation for separating locals and expatriates, white-collar and blue-collar workers, and high-income and low-income foreigners. The national housing landscape is the present-day manifestation of this practice. It is indisputably an act of kindness and wise governance to share the nation's wealth with the citizens; however, the mode of implementation promotes separation between the local population and expatriates. Some locals deem this kind of segregation necessary to preserve Emirati culture (Alawadi and Benkraouda 2017), while some authors have labelled it an exclusionary urban practice (Khalaf, 2006; Elsheshtawy 2008; Crot 2013). It is challenging to alter this practice, because if locals' incentives are threatened, public opposition might arise (Cugurullo 2015).

Pre-Dispersion Period (1960–1980)

In 1959, *Sheikh Rashid* commissioned John R. Harris to prepare Dubai's first urban master plan. Harris proposed a master plan in 1960 which was modest and suited the small town's needs and pre-oil resources at the time. It called for the provision of a road system; zoning of the town into areas marked for industry, commerce, and public buildings; areas for new residential quarters, and the creation of a new town center (Elsheshtawy 2004; Pacione 2005). The 1960 plan introduced zoning regulations, and growth expanded beyond the existing organic fabric and used the creek as an axis (Ramos 2010). Government land-use policy has played a highly influential role in shaping the city's built landscape, and land ownership laws were first introduced in 1960 and adopted from Sudan.

Urban growth in this phase was characterized by a relatively compact layout, as the small population and pre-oil finances limited the need for expansion.

FIG. 2
Demolition of Sha'biyat Al Shorta

FIG. 3
Demolition of Sha'biyat Al Shorta

The introduction of a new road system allowed the city to grow beyond its original core (See Figure 4) yet remain dense and connected, as many people did not own automobiles; therefore territorial expansion was limited (Pacione 2005). This has some parallel with the 'street car suburbs' of North American towns in the early 20th century; in the North American context, technological advancement allowed the city to expand beyond its traditional core but remain highly connected and relatively compact, as city dwellers still needed to live within walking distance of the streetcars (Condon 2012). A comparable phenomenon happened in Dubai, albeit with differing technologies: Dubai achieved technological prowess in the form of increased automobile ownership (Pacione 2005) as the city expanded beyond its traditional core but remained relatively compact in design because the majority of the population still met their daily needs by foot, even by 1971 (Reisz 2015).

Most North American cities that were structured during the street car era feature a compact grid made up of relatively small, square blocks (Morris 1994). Landowners, speculators, and cable car companies found this pattern easy to lay out and subdivide into marketable parcels, and "today, this pattern helps to create an intimate, highly walkable downtown" (Wheeler 2003, p. 319). The same assessment is applicable to Dubai's historical core (Elsheshtawy, 2008).

When the government implemented the National Housing Scheme in 1968 and started exporting oil in 1969, a new master plan was deemed necessary. In 1971, Harris prepared a second master plan for Dubai to accommodate the national housing and utilize the vast oil revenues at the emirate's disposal. The new plan clearly represented modernist planning principles and called for ring roads around the city core and a radial street network to the low-density suburbs (Pacione 2005; Seccombe and Lawless 1987). It also made provisions for major infrastructure and mobility development (Elsheshtawy 2004; Gabriel 1987; Ramos 2010), including an international airport and Rashid port.

Although, the Creek remained the main node of development, zoning regulations changed along with a significant rise in the urban area designated for construction (Rubio 2019). Harris's second master plan allowed for deteriorating traditional single-family dwelling units to be replaced by higher, mixed-use structures. As a result, the neighborhoods of *Deira* and *Bur Dubai* now contain some of the highest population densities in the city (Katodrytis and Mitchell 2015). The plan also included new expansion areas along the coast towards both the north-east and the south-west. Neighborhoods such as *Al Satwa* (1968), *Al Rashidiya* (1969), and *Al Jaffaliya* (1970) were established that resembled the traditional urban fabric. These traditional, local neighborhoods, also known as '*Shabiyaat*', are dense, diverse, and relatively pedestrian-oriented because of high street connectivity, massive alleyway systems, and legible layouts that make them easy to perceive and understand (Alawadi 2016) (See Figure 5). These communities featured gridded, semi-gridded, and fragmented and looping street networks; smaller plots; and a setback requirement of three meters (ten feet) separating the plots. For instance, *Al Satwa*, *Al Rashidiya*, and *Al Jaffaliya* have average plot length of 15m × 15 m, 18m × 18m, and 18m × 25m respectively. However, the newer part of Al Satwa featured larger plots of 30 m × 35 m. Also, the perfect grid was changed to looping and broken streets when this adjacent area was developed, thereby reducing the density from 20 plots per hectare to less than ten plots per hectare. Moreover, the land use mix in some neighborhoods, such as *Al Satwa* and *Al Badaa*, is polycentric, while Al Jaffaliya has a centralized land use system. This period also marked the beginning of locals moving out from the neighborhoods around Dubai Creek and the simultaneous dismantling of the human-scale city to create an automobile-oriented city (Rubio 2019). However, a number of factors set the course for the sprawling phase of Dispersion, including difficulties acquiring land in the old areas, lack of properly defined borders with neighboring sheikhdoms (Reisz 2015), and the development aspirations of the ruler.

Dispersion period (1980–present)

A break in Dubai's morphology began in 1974 with the location choice for the new World Trade Centre facility, which deviated from the master plan and was considered 'the outskirts' of the city (Ramos, 2010). Harris's plans overprescribed land-use, spatial regulation, and limitation. Moreover, the new growth corridor towards Jebel Ali marked 'the end of any serious pretentions toward even loosely coordinating an emirate-wide master plan, although many such plans were commissioned after Jebel Ali was completed' (Ramos, 2010, p. 130). Thus, sprawl began in Dubai with a new elongated south-west axis parallel to the coast. It completely supplanted the historical compact growth axis of the creek.

Starting in the early 1980s, locals were granted larger plots of 929–1393 square meters (10,000–15,000 ft^2) in newly developed communities located along the southwest growth axis. These newer neighborhoods resembled post–World War II North American suburbs: they consisting of single-use, single-family, detached houses; were made up of large super blocks; fragmented, parallel networks; and looping streets; and were surrounded by multi-lane highways (Alawadi, Khanal, and Almulla 2018). The density of the communities planned in the 1980s and early 1990s was seven plots per hectare, and the average plot length was 30 m × 45 m. This was when the plot sizes for national housing peaked, with plots as large as 1,393 m^2. *Al Barsha*, *Nadd Al Hamar* , *Al Warqa* Second, *Nadd Al Sheba* Foruth, and *Al Mizhar* First are examples of these low-density, sprawling neighborhoods with larger and more dispersed plots. For example, *Al Warqa* Second and *Al Mizhar* First feature plots of 45 m × 30 m and 30 m × 35 m respectively. After 2000, plot density increased slightly to 10 plots per hectare to accommodate more locals and to save land for future generations. Plot size decreased to 929 m^2, with an average lot configuration of 30 m^2. *Al Quoz* II and *Al Barsha* South are examples of neighborhoods that were built with slightly higher density. Furthermore, the street layouts in these neighborhoods are either looping and fragmented or fragmented parallels (with culs-de-sac in some cases). The street layouts in these newer suburbs are the same as those of previous suburbs. The land use system in all neighborhoods of Dispersion period is centralized. This period significantly changed the demographics of old neighborhoods as more and more citizens abandoned the central neighborhoods for larger plots in the suburbs. The older housing stock still belonged to the locals, who rented them to lower- and middle-class residents. The city landscape that had previously been dominated by mixed-use urban neighborhoods turned into a mosaic of residential suburban neighborhoods.

Economic affluence, technological advancements, and land-use policies were three factors that contributed to suburban growth (AlShafieei 1997); these same factors had contributed to suburban growth in North America some thirty years previously. The introduction of the national housing program, around the end of the Inception phase, contributed to and institutionalized the process of suburban growth and its eventual result: a sprawling, repetitive landscape. National housing simultaneously created segregated dormitory communities on the fringes of the city (Dubai Urban Area Structure Plan 1995). Single-family, national neighborhoods are the dominant outcome of this period. They are characterized by asymmetrical street systems made of large super blocks, curves, and looping streets surrounded by multi-lane highways (Alawadi 2016). These neighborhoods are generally single-use, single-family detached houses, and as the plot sizes grew (up to 1,393 m^2 at their peak in the early 1990s), so did the neighborhoods and their monotony (Alawadi 2016).

The city landscape that had previously been dominated by mixed-use urban neighborhoods turned into a mosaic of residential suburban neighborhoods.

FIG. 4
Dubai's creek area, where the organic pattern expanded later into a more regular and planned grid.

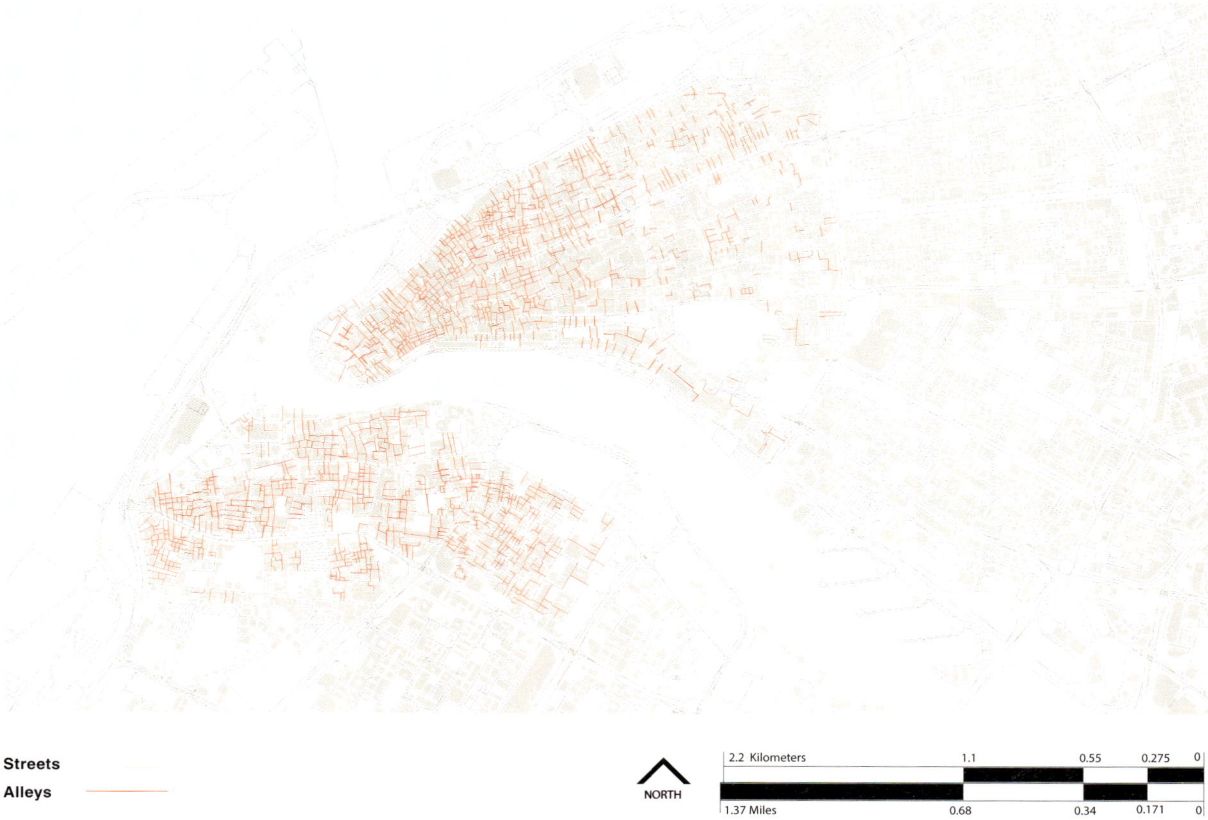

FIG. 5
Map showing Al Satwa neighbourhood (2008 footprints) which is dense, diverse, and relatively pedestrian-oriented because of it's high street connectivity, massive alleyway systems, and legible layouts that make them easy to perceive and understand.

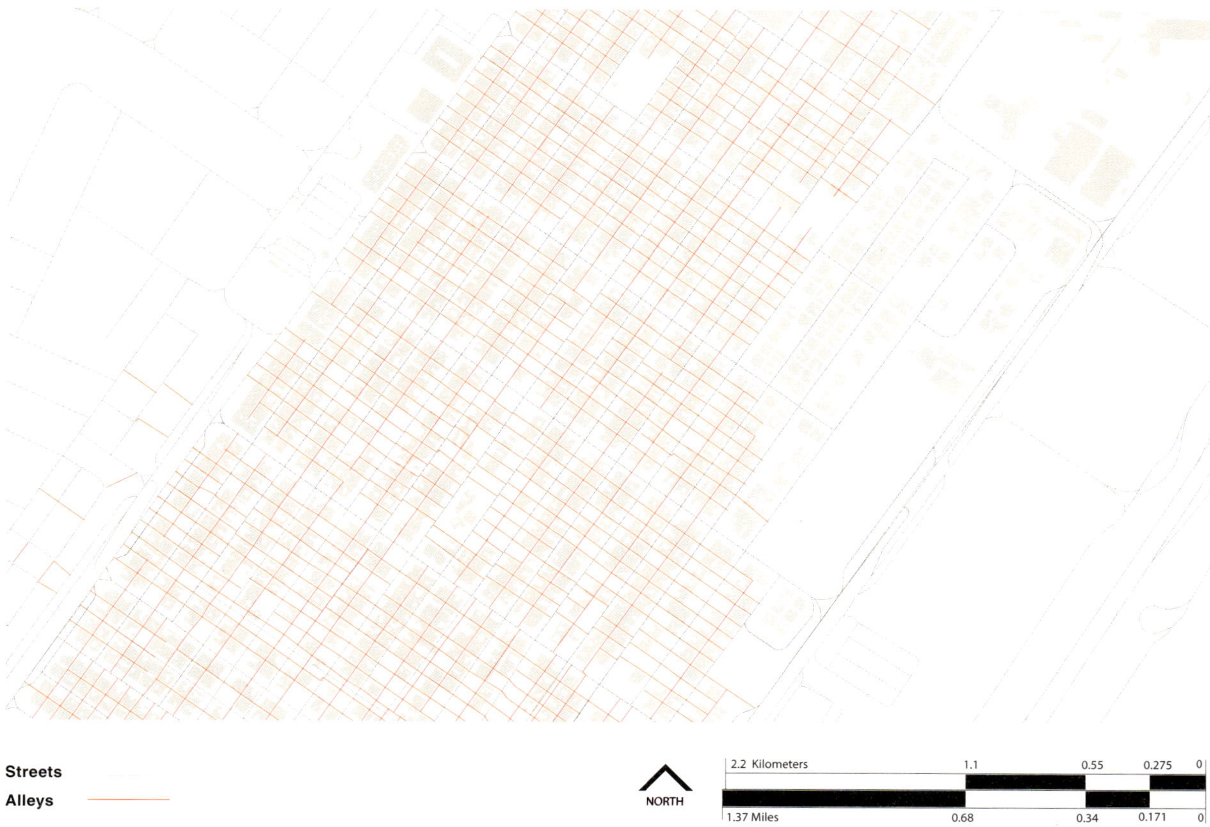

References

Alawadi, K. (2017). Rethinking Dubai's urbanism: Generating sustainable form-based urban design strategies for an integrated neighborhood. Cities, 60, 353-366.

Alawadi, K. (2018). Whatever happened to Dubai's public spaces? International Journal of Middle East Studies, 50(3), 562-567.

Alawadi, K., & Benkraouda, O. (2019). The Debate over Neighborhood Density in Dubai: Between Theory and Practicality. Journal of Planning Education and Research, 39(1), 18-34. https://10.1177/0739456X17720490

Alawadi, K., & Dooling, S. (2016). Challenges and opportunities for participatory planning approaches within Dubai's urban context. Journal of Urbanism: International Research on Placemaking and Urban Sustainability, 9(3), 276-301.

Alawadi, K., Khanal, A., & Almulla, A. (2018). Land, urban form, and politics: A study on Dubai's housing landscape and rental affordability. Cities, 81, 115-130.

Alshafiei, S. A. (1997). The spatial implications of urban land policies in Dubai city.

Condon, P. M. (2012). Seven rules for sustainable communities: Design strategies for the post carbon world. Island Press.

Crot, L. (2013). Planning for sustainability in non-democratic politics: The case of Masdar City. Urban Studies, 50(13), 2809-2825.

Cugurullo, F. (2016). Urban eco-modernisation and the policy context of new eco-city projects: Where Masdar City fails and why. Urban Studies, 53(11), 2417-2433.

Elsheshtawy, Y. (2004). Planning middle eastern cities: an urban kaleidoscope. Routledge.

Elsheshtawy, Y. (2008). Transitory sites: mapping Dubai›s 'forgotten'urban spaces. International Journal of Urban and Regional Research, 32(4), 968-988.

Gabriel, E. F. 1987. The Dubai Handbook. Ahrensburg: Institute for Applied Economic Geography.

Heard-Bey, F. (1982). From Trucial States to United Arab Emirates. A Society in Transition.New York.

Katodrytis, G., & Mitchell, K. (2015). UAE and the Gulf: Architecture and Urbanism Now. John Wiley & Sons.

Khalaf, S. (2006). The evolution of the Gulf city type, oil, and globalization. Globalization and the Gulf (pp. 254-275). Routledge.

Morris, A. (1994). History of urban form: Before the industrial revolutions (444 pages). Harlow, England: Pearson Education & Prentice Hall.

Pacione, M. (2005). Dubai. Cities, 22(3), 255-265.

Plan, S. (1995). Structure Plan for the Dubai Urban Area 1993-2012. Consultant: Parsons-Harland Bertolomew &Associates, Inc.Client: Dubai Municipality Planning & Survey Department, Dubai.

Ramos, S. J. 2010. Dubai Amplified: The Engineering of a Port Geography. Farnham, Surrey, England: Ashgate

Rubio, R.G. (2019). "Building Dubai, the legacy of John Harris". In Eds. Della Torre, Stefano, & Sessa, Valentina. Quanto e come conta l'esperienza per l'affidamento dei lavori sui beni culturali. Accessed on 11th June 2021: https://www.researchgate.net/publication/350919559_Building_Dubai_the_legacy_of_John_Harris

Seccombe, I., & Lawless, R. (1987a). Work camps and company towns: settlement patterns and the Gulf oil industry.

Seccombe, I., & Lawless, R. (1987b). Work camps and company towns: settlement patterns and the Gulf oil industry.

Wheeler, S. M. (2003). The evolution of urban form in Portland and Toronto: Implications for sustainability planning. Local Environment, 8(3), 317-336.

05

Urban Network Metrics and Analysis

Introduction to Dual and Primal Approaches

Hillier and Hanson (1989) and Hillier et al. (1993) studied urban form using the mathematical perspective of configurational analysis. By focusing on the topology of street networks, *Space Syntax* research reveals a city's hidden patterns of social activity and movement (Hillier and Hanson 1989). In the late 1990s, scholars such as Nikos Salingaros (1998) and Batty and Longley (1994) advocated and promoted these kinds of evidence-based research in urban planning; both offer a detailed, mathematical approach to studying street network configurations and the distribution of land uses. Hillier's space syntax has been adopted by various urban morphological studies. The most critical measure in *Space Syntax* is integration, "which measures the mean depth of every other line in the system from each line in turn, relativized with respect to how deep they could possibly be with that number of lines" (Hillier et al. 1993, p. 35). Methodologically, space syntax analyses use graphs to quantify several street network configuration variables and measure topological relationships between different locations in the network.

In the mid-2000s, Sergio Porta and colleagues provided another concept and method of analyzing street networks called *Multiple Centrality Assessment* (MCA). Porta's MCA uses the primal approach of network computation, unlike the dual approach used by Hillier for space syntax. Dual graphs treat street segments as nodes (i.e., a single point represents a line) and treat intersections as links between the nodes, reversing the standard logic of transportation models. In the primal approach, network intersections or settlements are treated as nodes, and streets or relationships are treated as links (Porta et al. 2006). Like *Space Syntax*, MCA quantifies street network configuration using various variables, such as Reach, Gravity, Straightness, Betweenness, and Information centralities. However, MCA differs significantly from space syntax in one key way: it employs a graph representation of street patterns that includes their geometrical distance. The analyses and results presented in this book follows the primal approach of MCA through the application of the Urban Network Analysis (UNA) tool. The UNA tool is a plug-in developed jointly by MIT and the City Form Lab at Singapore University of Technology & Design, and it can be installed as a plug-in on ArcGIS and Rhino software.

Multiple Centrality Assessment (MCA)

The analyses presented in this book use the primal approach of MCA for several reasons. First, MCA closely follows topology as well as distance, which means that the analysis includes both the lengths and the geometrical properties of the street network. By contrast, space syntax ignores the physical length of the network. Instead of street lengths, *Space Syntax* uses the concept of depth—a measure of steps taken as one turns from one street to the next street. By focusing on topological step distance and ignoring real distance, the space syntax approach makes the perception of cities more abstract (Porta et al. 2006). According to Porta et al. (2006) and Ratti (2004), MCA should be preferred for configurational analysis because it is "more realistic". They argue that metric distance is considered one of the main properties of the built environment in various fields, including urban planning, transportation planning, urban design, and geography, and that MCA respects its importance by integrating metric distance into its calculations (Porta et al. 2006).

According to Porta et al. (2006) and Ratti (2004), MCA should be preferred for configurational analysis because it is 'more realistic'.

Moreover, MCA can incorporate buildings and plots into the analysis, adding another real dimension of the urban structure. While *Space Syntax* addresses only two network elements—intersections and street segments (Porta et al. 2006)—MCA adds a third, buildings/plots, to be used as the spatial unit of analysis for all measures (Sevtsuk and Mekonnen 2012). MCA also makes it possible to include buildings and land use distribution as analytic variables (Porta et al. 2006; Sevtsuk and Ratti 2010). Furthermore, unlike *Space Syntax*, MCA is readily calculated using Geographic Information System (GIS) software. This means that MCA can readily be calculated using existing maps and data, such as the street centerlines maps which planners typically use and which commonly appear in urban cadastral geodatabases (Sevtsuk and Mekonnen 2012). The findings presented in this book are particularly based on the formulas of MCA metrics put forward by Sevtsuk and Mekonnen (2012). They introduced some new network indices, such as Reach and Gravity, to complement the previous works by Turner (2001), Porta et al. (2005), and Capier (2011) and also incorporated additional metrics, such as Straightness and Betweenness, into their UNA tool. This particular methodology is used because it is theoretically grounded in the concept of MCA and a user-friendly tool that is available for free.

UNA has proven to be relatively more accurate and reliable than density-based assessments, particularly in its ability to efficiently, mathematically, and graphically reflect the centralities of different street layouts (Porta et al. 2006; Dill 2004; Moudon 1997). Density measures such as street density, intersection density, and block density are widely used in both research and practice. These metrics became popular due their relatively simple calculation process and ease of implementation in regulatory exercises (Handy et al., 2003; Marshall & Garrick 2012; Stangl & Guinn 2011). However, density-based methods do not always accurately depict the situation on the ground: some studies have found that these methods can obtain similar findings (e.g., efficiency and centrality) for very different network systems (Peponis et al. 2008). Moreover, it is claimed that measures of density are susceptible to being manipulated, or "gamed", to meet established standards, even when connectivity is low (Stangl & Guinn 2011). Also, these metrics tend to be unreliable and inconsistent because they are affected by the size and shape of the study area (Knight & Marshall 2015). Furthermore, since these metrics are unable to address route length and directness—two critical factors affecting the decision to walk—they would provide little insight into each network design's potential for walkability. The aforementioned shortcomings, especially the unreliable nature of density metrics in computing the connectivity of different street layouts, make them unsuitable for this book, which analyses the different networks of thirteen neighborhoods in Abu Dhabi and Dubai. Therefore, the analyses conducted for this book use a methodology that combines morphological mapping and MCA.

Application of Multiple Centrality Assessment

In this book, the street connectivity levels of Abu Dhabi and Dubai are analyzed at the neighborhood (local) and city (global) scales. The book focuses on two parameters of street network analysis: efficiency and centrality. Efficiency is evaluated in terms of directness by computing the Straightness metric. This metric identifies efficient network designs as those that provide short and direct access between origins and destinations. Likewise, centrality is evaluated using graph theory metrics such as Reach, Gravity, and Betweenness. However, the Betweenness metric is not calculated at global scales due to the high computation requirements which are beyond the available computation capacity at our disposal. These metrics enable the identification of high- and low-accessibility locations within networks. Research has shown that network centrality metrics are useful for capturing location advantage, a significant factor for land use distribution. An understanding of centrality and its impacts makes it possible to plan land uses that bring destinations closer to residences, an important factor in environmental, economic, and social sustainability. This book attempts to offer scientifically grounded strategies and policies that will enable various stakeholders to design more sustainable street systems and land uses.

A set of questions have been answered in order to arrive at suitable recommendations:

1. How do the morphological attributes of the neighborhoods in Abu Dhabi and Dubai change throughout their urban evolution? This question is answered through conventional mapping using GIS data and layers to determine plot density, street intersection density, street density, alley density, alley intersection density, total network length, street length, alley length and right-of-way (ROWs).
2. Are Abu Dhabi's and Dubai's neighborhood street networks designed to promote efficiency and centrality toward the goal of overall efficiency at the local and global scales? This question is answered by calculating metrics such as Straightness to determine route directness and Reach, Betweenness (at the local scale only), and Gravity to determine the centrality of the street networks in all chosen neighborhoods.
3. How can we design and plan neighborhoods in which non-motorized mobility is a viable and efficient alternative? This question is answered by comparing the obtained results for studied neighborhoods, each with its own unique street layout and land use system. More specifically, metrics such as Reach, Straightness, Gravity, and Betweenness (at the local scale only) are compared for the selected neighborhoods, and morphological attributes such as plot density, land use distribution, and street layout will be determined.
4. Which locations in the network are more central and conducive to development or consolidation as activity hubs if driving distances and the global scale are considered? This question is answered by conducting a global-scale analysis of driving distances. The global-scale analysis uses three-km and six-km as radii corresponding to different driving durations. Since the global-scale analysis focuses on driving distances, alleys are not taken into consideration. This analysis reveals how different neighborhoods are integrated with one another via street networks. It shows connectivity and centrality levels beyond the neighborhood boundary.
5. Do existing neighborhood designs integrate with one another to form coherent and accessible urban environments? If not, how could they be retrofitted to make their street systems and urban fabrics more efficient and integrated? How can additional growth be planned and designed to efficiently connect to the existing city? These questions are answered by the results of global-scale analyses that reveals inter-neighborhood efficiency and centrality.

In asking how the physical designs of different neighborhoods in both cities have responded to regional frameworks, these questions focus attention interconnectedness between different scales). The global-scale morphology, network efficiency, and centrality of neighborhoods in Abu Dhabi and Dubai are explored to understand the implications of their physical design attributes for city-wide planning. Regional integration and multi-scale connectivity yield good urbanism (Elsheshtawy 2009); therefore, global-scale analysis can assist in future city building and growth.

Researchers have used an array of approaches to measure efficiency and centrality. There is no one best approach; different purposes and contexts demand different methods (Handy and Niemeier 1997). Among MCA's metrics, Straightness calculates efficiency, which reflects directness and connectivity to destinations, while Reach, Gravity, and Betweenness calculate centrality, which identifies more and less accessible areas. Straightness addresses a network's geometry and shape, which, along with land use, are the characteristics that most strongly influence efficiency.

Specifically, Straightness (Vragovic et al. 2005) measures the extent to which the shortest paths from a node of interest to all other nodes in the system resemble straight Euclidian paths. Efficiency of connection between two nodes or buildings increases when the shortest path between them deviates less from the virtual straight line connecting them (Scellato et al. 2006). The analysis of Straightness was designed to test the straightness of different street network layouts regardless of any effects that different types of land use might have on efficiency. Therefore, Straightness provides important information about route directness and street connectivity that speaks to the relative ease of pedestrian movement. With the Reach and Gravity metrics, smaller plot sizes, shorter block lengths, and permeable street layouts increase the number of reachable plots within a fixed search radius. The Betweenness metric, on the other hand, depends primarily on street morphology and the proximity of attractive destinations from the segment being studied.

Various scholars have preferred MCA to space syntax because MCA better reflects a city's morphological nature, including both the topological and physical lengths of networks (Batty 2004; Porta and Latora 2007; Ratti 2004). For example, Chang-Deok Kang (2015) used MCA's indices of Gravity, Betweenness, Straightness, and Closeness to compare the effects of different land uses on pedestrian accessibility. His work corroborates the argument that urban form, street configuration, and land use density together determine walkability. Kang's work focused on global (city-scale) analysis and aimed to explore (1) the effects of different types of land use on pedestrian accessibility and (2) the different impacts those aspects of the built environment have on accessibility. Kang's (2016) investigation of different centrality and accessibility indices found that some economic sectors had the benefit of more favorable conditions for accessibility than other sectors, but that accessibility nevertheless mostly depended on street configuration and walking environments. Similarly, Kang (2018) introduced a model named 'S+5D', where S stands for street configuration and 5D includes walking density, land use diversity, design (i.e., safety and amenity), distance to transit, and destination accessibility. This model was used to quantify pedestrian accessibility.

Various scholars have preferred MCA to space syntax because MCA better reflects a city's morphological nature, including both the topological and physical lengths of networks. (Batty 2004; Porta and Latora 2007; Ratti 2004).

Morphological Mapping and Network Analysis

In this book, 'centrality' is interpreted as the cumulative effect of metrics such as Reach, Gravity, and Betweenness, and 'efficiency' is defined as a function of Straightness. In order to provide a greater understanding of the urban structure, this book uses a conventional mapping technique with UNA's mathematical approach. To map neighborhoods' evolution, aerial photos and geospatial data were obtained from Dubai Municipality (DM 2015) and Abu Dhabi Spatial Data Infrastructure (ADSDI 2015). The morphological analysis was carried out using these aerial photos and GIS layers and focused on neighborhoods' street layouts and land uses and sizes. This book treats networks as a combination of streets and alleys. Computed information on network layouts included street intersection density, street density, street design, alley density, alley intersection density, and ROWs. Densities are generally measured by dividing the physical parameter under scrutiny (i.e., streets in the case of street density) by unit of area (Peponis et al. 2007). In this book, all metric units are used—for example, hectare for area and kilometer for length. Consequently, street and alley densities have units of kilometer per hectare (km/ha), and intersection densities are calculated as the number of intersections per unit area. Building and land-use data include neighborhood area, plot sizes, plot dimensions, plot density, building density, residential and non-residential uses (daily uses), and system of land-use distribution. Obtained GIS data from stakeholders does not include alleys. Therefore, alleyway networks for all studied neighborhoods have been digitized. Aerial image analysis completed through site visits allowed our team to trace and digitize the existing alleyway networks in the studied neighborhoods of both Abu Dhabi and Dubai. Alleyways are critical components of a non-motorized transport network. Thus, this book incorporates the alley network into its analysis together with the street networks. The digitized alleyway data can be easily integrated into the stakeholders' existing GIS database. The updated GIS database can then be used for future spatial analysis to obtain accurate results.

The morphological maps and GIS data were further used as inputs (base maps) to Rhinoceros 3D (Rhino) for Urban Network Analysis (UNA) and as a database for interpreting simulation results. For the network analysis, the researchers used Urban Network Analysis (UNA), a toolbox created by the City Form Lab at the Singapore University of Technology and Design in collaboration with MIT. This toolbox is used as a plugin into either GIS or Rhino to conduct graphical and mathematical network analysis in order to describe the spatial patterns of urban areas. UNA is used to both visually and mathematically understand efficiency and centrality in different neighborhood forms that originated in different morphological periods or growth phases. Morphological periods are time spans characterized by a repetitive use of similar street patterns, land use systems, or building densities reproduced over a certain amount of time until they are replaced (Whitehand et al. 2014).

Selection of Neighborhoods and Samples

In this book, the time periods or growth phases are taken from previous studies (Alawadi and Benkraouda 2018; Alawadi, Alameri and Scoppa 2020), while neighborhoods are chosen to ensure an objective comparison of cases: from each city, contemporaneous neighborhoods are selected (i.e., neighborhoods that started and completed their development during the same periods). Six neighborhoods from Abu Dhabi and seven neighborhoods from Dubai, have been selected. The Abu Dhabi neighborhoods are *West Island*, *Baniyas*, *Khalifa City*, *Al Bahya*, *MBZ City*, and *Al Falah* (See Figure 1); the Dubai neighborhoods are *Dubai Creek*, *Al Satwa*, *Al Rashidiya*, *Al Quoz*, *Jumeirah*, *Al Warqa*, and *Al Barsha* (See Figure 2). This print provides detailed analysis of three neighborhoods from Abu Dhabi (*West Island*, *Baniyas*, and *MBZ City*) and three neighborhoods from Dubai (*Dubai Creek*, *Al Satwa*, and *Al Warqa*). Additional neighbrhoods can be found via this link: https://doi.org/10.6084/m9.figshare.21939626.v1. For comprehensive list of all the neighborhoods refer to Table 1. Furthermore, a total of twenty-six samples (12 from Abu Dhabi and 14 from Dubai) have been analyzed. Two samples were taken from each neighborhood, with the exception of *Jumeriah*, where three samples were taken, and *Al Quoz*, where only one sample was taken. Square-shaped samples of one square mile have been selected and analyzed to facilitate a realistic comparison of different neighborhoods. The most representative areas of each neighborhood in terms of street network, plot size, land use, etc. were chosen as samples (See Figure 3). Various studies have previously used square-shaped samples to: (1) analyze urban form and make comparisons across different cities (Jacobs 1995; Southworth and Owens 1993), (2) correlate pedestrian volumes with site design (Moudon et al. 1997), (3) compare cities' urban evolution (Wheeler 2003), and (4) compare the built landscapes of multiple metropolitan regions (Wheeler 2008). A neighborhood area that falls between 1 km^2 and 2 km^2 is deemed appropriate for analysis. This size is large enough to understand the effects of morphological attributes on residents' lives, behavior, and movement patterns (Wheeler 2015). Moudon and Hess (2000) studied urban form within this range (1–2 km^2). They used areas of one square mile to analyze and compare the progression and change of suburban landscapes. Likewise, Cardillo et al. (2006) used areas of one square mile to compare the structural properties of urban street patterns in different cities around the world. Inside each square-mile area, the process of morphological mapping and UNA (Urban Network Analysis) is repeated to obtain sample scale maps.

The sample area is extended to include a buffer of 0.25 mile (roughly equivalent to 400 meters) in each direction for greater accuracy (See Figure 4). Street networks are continuous in reality, and when analyses are carried out within an artificially bounded study area, network elements and events that occur beyond the boundary are ignored (Gil 2017). This ignorance leads to a bias called edge effect, because the analytic algorithms are fundamentally relational. Edge effect influences the nodes on or adjacent to the study area's boundary and all other nodes in the network (Barthélemy 2011). The reliability of any network analysis is deemed questionable if the edge effect is not considered (Ratti 2004). The most effective way to address this problem is to extend the network with a buffer around the study area (Hillier et al. 1993). Thus, the sample area is extended beyond its boundary by approximately 0.25 mile in each direction.

City	Morphological Period	Neighborhood	Period	Area (in hectares)	Street Layout
Abu Dhabi	Inception	West Island	1968-1975	3,200	Interconnected small blocks
	Dispersion	Baniyas	1970s	1,918	Looping and fragmented
		Khalifa City	1990-2010	1,992	Looping and fragmented
		Al Bahya	1995-2005	817	Looping and fragmented
		MBZ City	2000-2010	5,071	Looping and fragmented
	Redemption	Al Falah	2010-Present	2,024	Interconnected
Dubai	Inception	Dubai Creek	1950-1970	467	Compact organic
	Pre-Dispersion	Al Satwa	1968-1974	266	Interconnected small blocks
		Al Rashidiya	1969-1977	387	Looping and fragmented
	Dispersion	Jumeirah	1975-1995	933	Looping and fragmented
		Al Quoz	1976-1977	351	Looping and fragmented
		Al Warqa	2001	1,608	Curvilinear blocks, looping and fragmented
		Al Barsha	1992-1994	1,526	Looping, fragmented with culs-de-sac

TABLE. 1
Table showing chronological order of neighborhoods evolvement in Dubai and Abu Dhabi

4
1
3
5
2

FIG. 1

Map showing the extent of Abu Dhabi and the locations of the selected neighborhoods for this analysis:

1. West Island
2. Baniyas
3. Khalifa City
4. Al Bahya
5. MBZ City
6. Al Falah

The analysis of the following neighborhoods (Khalifa City, Al Bahya, Al Falah) is available via the following link: https://doi.org/10.6084/m9.figshare.21939626.v1

1
4
2
5
7
NORTH

FIG. 2

Map showing the extent of Dubai and the locations of the selected neighborhoods for this analysis:

1. Dubai Creek
2. Al Satwa
3. Al Rashidiya
4. Jumeirah
5. Al Quoz
6. Al Warqa
7. Al Barsha

The analysis of the following neighborhoods (Al Rashidiya, Jumeirah,Al Quoz,Al Barsha) is available via the following link: https://doi.org/10.6084/m9.figshare.21939626.v1

FIG. 3
Selected samples from neighborhoods: Abu Dhabi (top) and Dubai (bottom)

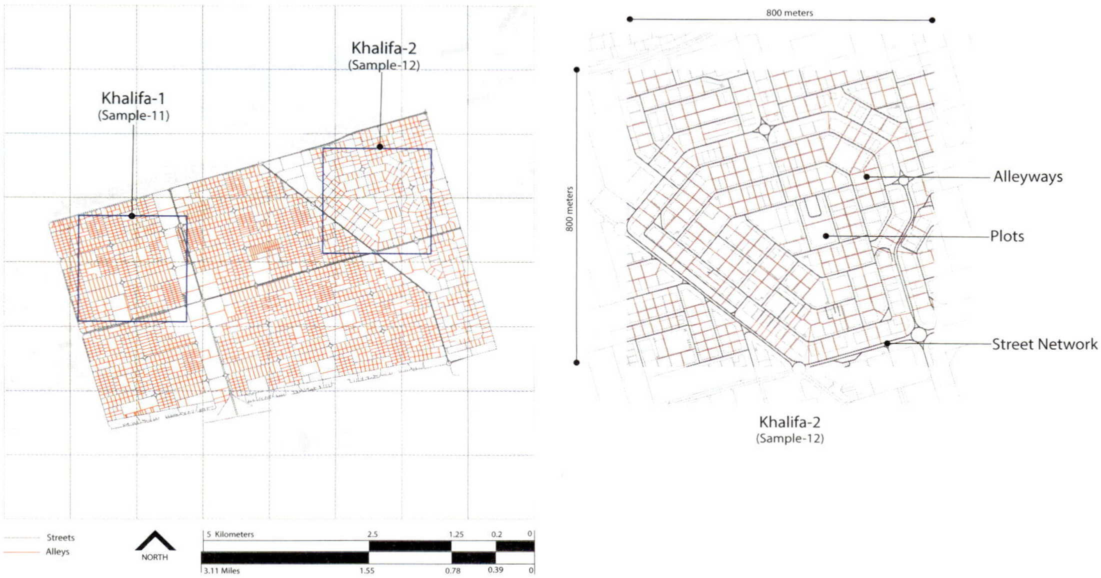

FIG. 4

Diagram showing samples taken from Khalifa City. The sample area is extended to include a buffer of 0.25 mile (roughly equivalent to 400 meters) in each direction for greater accuracy.

Scales of Analysis

This book presents three scales of analysis: city scale, neighborhood scale, and sample scale. Broadly, the UNA tool classifies these analyses into two categories: global scale analysis and local scale analysis. Street network analysis requires the consideration of distances as main criteria for understanding efficiency and centrality. In other words, distance thresholds are key to understanding a network's performance and ability to connect places using different means of mobility. At the local scale, the focus is on which destinations can be accessed by residents on foot (See Figure 5). Accepted distances for pedestrian travel correspond to five-, ten-, and twenty-minute walks, which equate to 400, 800, and 1,600 meters (Dill 2004; Ewing, Cervero 2001; Lee Moudon 2006; Weinstein et al. 2008.). Local-scale analyses of urban street networks serve an important function: they provide the necessary information for understanding how different street network designs support the formation of well-integrated neighborhoods. Integrated neighborhoods maximize the number of destinations that are accessible through a short and direct walk and feature pedestrian routes that support the formation of local activity centers, which reduce automobile trips to more distant ones. The distance thresholds of 400, 800, and 1,600 meters address the UAE's climate context: hot months require shorter distances, while cooler months allow for longer distances.

The use of a 400 m, 800 m, and 1,600 m search radii also addresses a primary shortfall of one of the centrality measures: Straightness (Dill 2004; Stangl 2012). Straightness's measure of the ratio of straight-line distance to route distance (or its inverse) is useful as a direct measure of ease of movement. However, Straightness is more sensitive for shorter distances and less sensitive for longer distances. The lack of objectivity for studying neighborhoods is exacerbated by the fact that metrics such as Reach, Gravity, Straightness, and Betweenness vary from one neighborhood to another: "The larger the study area, the [better] the straightness measure" if all morphological metrics such as plot sizes, densities, and block sizes are held constant. Straightness's higher sensitivity to shorter areas than to longer ones is particularly relevant for this study of neighborhoods. Because longer network paths tend to resemble straight lines more closely than shorter network paths, the larger the neighborhood, the better its Straightness values are. By applying a limiting search radius of 400 m, 800 m, and 1,600 m in every neighborhood, this study prevents the testing of long routes and reduces the impact of the measure's bias toward larger neighborhoods. Overall, while the study's inclusion of neighborhoods of various sizes presents potential analytic challenges, this variation is important for the study's larger purpose of using the analysis of detailed and finer scales to understand larger, more general trends in neighborhood design across morphological periods.

Global-scale analyses (three-and-six km) evaluate street networks' ability to create integrated systems that facilitate movement and interactions, bringing together and bridging together the many buildings and places that make up the city (See Figure 6). This global outlook has been important in creating a better understanding of the association between, on one hand, the location and strength of central places in the urban street network and, on the other, areas of intense non-residential activity, particularly economic activity related to retail and service businesses (Hillier 1999a; Porta et al., 2009; Porta et al. 2012; Wang 2011; Wang et al. 2014; Sevtsuk 2014; Scoppa and Peponis 2015). The study of the global scale, including the identification of centralities using network centrality metrics, serves important purposes in planning. First, it allows for the identification of loca-

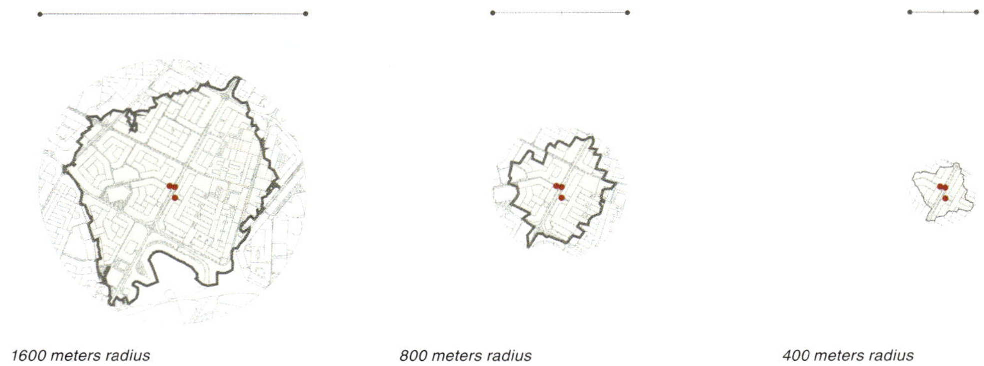

FIG. 5
Accepted distances for pedestrian travel, 400, 800, and 1,600 meters

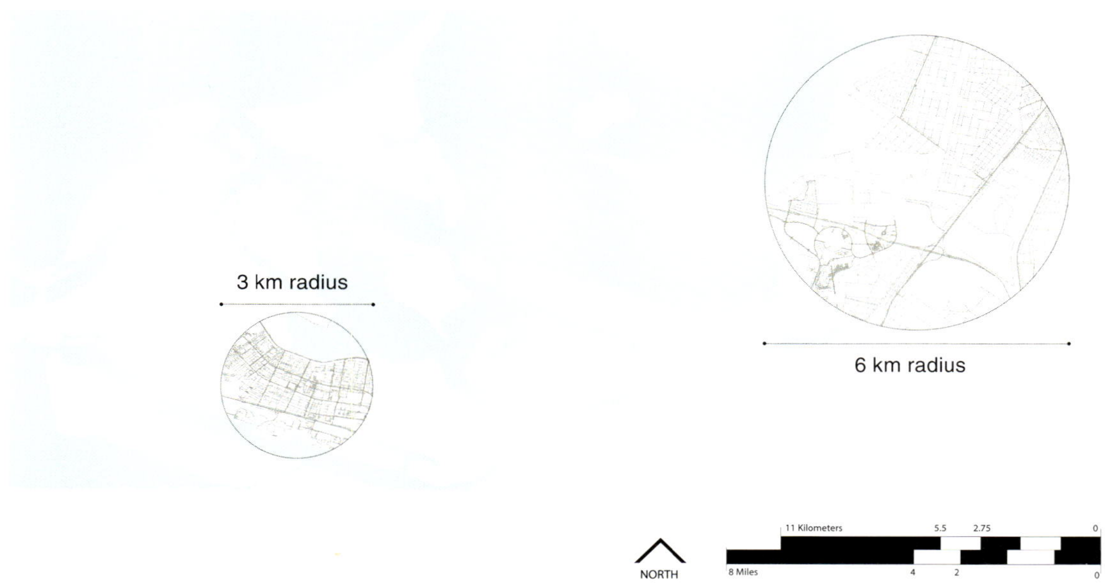

FIG. 6
Map showing some selected zones in the city of Abu Dhabi for global scale for two different radii 3km and 6 km

tion advantages that operate at a larger scale than that of the individual neighborhood. In this project, distance thresholds of three-and-six km enable the evaluation of how different neighborhoods' street systems work together to create centralities that transcend their boundaries. Identifying the locations of these higher-order centralities will provide valuable insights for city planning, particularly in terms of addressing the key urban sustainability objectives of increasing built density and land use diversity. Spatially locating these higher-order centers within the street networks of Dubai and Abu Dhabi will permit the identification of areas that have the potential to develop into denser activity areas due to their advantage in commanding larger pools of users who reside within the specified distance thresholds. In addition, this scale of analysis provides a foundation for studying the impact of centrality on new additions to the street network brought about by the development of new neighborhoods). In other words, it will be possible to evaluate whether existing centers become stronger, weaker, or shift spatially as new neighborhoods are built and connected to the existing street system (Hillier et al. 2009; Chiaradia et al. 2009). Both cities consist of three global-scale study areas: one with a three km radius and two with a six km radius. The three km radius has been found to be suitable for the older neighborhoods, namely *Dubai Creek* in Dubai and *West Island* in Abu Dhabi, while the six km radius has been appropriate for the newer neighborhoods or suburbs in both cities. The use of these two radii makes it possible to accommodate the differing scales of urban form prevalent in the older and newer neighborhoods of Abu Dhabi and Dubai.

In this way, unlike manuals that focus on the street scale, this guidebook discusses design strategies at various scales, from the local (400, 800, and 1,600 meters) to the citywide or global. It offers plans for street and land-use design at multiple scales, from a bird's eye view to granulated detail, to illustrate the role of scale in shaping efficient communities and cities. This emphasis on scale stems from Calthorpe and Fulton (2001), who shed light on how physical planning at different scales can be synthesized. Movements such as *New Urbanism*, *Smart Growth*, *Transit Oriented Development*, and other physical design ideals emphasize that "good urban design must be integrated across" multiple scales (e.g., regional, city, district, neighborhood, and site scales) to achieve regional goals and needs (Talen and Ellis 2002; Wheeler 2002, p. 273). These movements have led Neuman (2000, p. 115) to state, 'We are witnessing a rebirth of physical design, both in practice and the academy'.

Network Analysis Scenarios

In this guidebook, except for the global-scale analysis, all calculations at neighborhood and sample scales have been conducted in reference to two scenarios – Scenario 1 where only streets are taken, and Scenario 2 where both streets and alleys are taken into analysis (See Figure 7). The global-scale analysis is applicable mainly for motorized travel only, and not for pedestrians, especially in hot, arid zones; thus, the inclusion of alleys is redundant. The two aforementioned scenarios at the neighborhood and sample scales explore alternative network systems such as alleys and their role in improving efficiency and centrality. Street networks, once built, cannot be changed easily because such change involves complicated processes such as land acquisition, compensation to private land owners, displacement of residents, reorientation of utility lines, and nuisance to surrounding inhabitants during construction. Thus, an understanding of a complementary network of alleys and their potential to improve pedestrian movement is critical. Alleys are "enigmatic, liminal spaces whose identity is blurred" (Wolch et al. 2010, p. 2874). The etymological meaning of alleys provides insight into their functions: "alley" is a contraction of the Latin word ambulare, meaning "to walk." Alleyways are critical but often forgotten components of urban form (Alawadi et al. 2021). The incorporation of pedestrian-friendly alleys can make for a better-connected network and lead to substantial improved conditions for pedestrians (Alawadi, Alameri, and Scoppa 2020; Alawadi et al. 2021). The common presence of alleys in both cities' neighborhoods also indicates their importance in network design. Thus, the neighborhood and sample scale analyses shown in this book are carried out in two scenarios: with and without alleys.

FIG. 7

Network scenarios - Scenario 1: Streets only (left), and Scenario 2: Streets + alleys (right)

Urban Network Analysis (UNA) Metrics

In light of the growing consensus in urban planning and design scholarship about the importance of physical design across scales, UNA metrics provide a reliable, convenient, and less data-intensive way[1], compared with other metrics, to quantify the characteristics of the built environment. For instance, the Reach measure counts the number of surrounding plots each plot reaches within a given search radius on the network. The Reach metric $Reach[i]^r$ of a node i in a graph G at a search radius r describes the number of other nodes in G that are reachable from i at a shortest-path distance of r or less. It is defined as follows:

$$Reach\,[i]^{\,r} = \sum_{j \in G-\{i\}, d[i,j] \leq r} W[j]$$

In the above equation, $d[i,j]$ is the shortest-path distance between nodes i and j in G, and W[j] is the weight of a destination node j. The weights can represent various characteristics of the destination buildings, such as their size, the number of employees they contain, the number of residents they accommodate, etc. Figure 8 visualizes the Reach metric.

In this book, the attractiveness of a destination (the weight factor) in both Reach and Gravity is set by default to count, meaning that all plots have the same opportunity to create trips. To indicate a place's attractiveness as a destination, the UNA tool offers an option to weight specific attributes, such as population density, building capacity, brand recognition, number of jobs, building area and height, building use, and indoor or outdoor location. Each building or land plot can be described by a set of numerical attributes that connect the building in the graph with its real characteristics in the built environment (Sevtsuk and Mekonnen 2012). The weight factor creates a wide range of options for analyzing spatial connections between buildings and networks. Appropriate assignment of weights, however, requires thorough investigation of the destinations under study, which becomes challenging when the analysis addresses a large set of case studies and land uses. One alternative might be to adopt a "fixed" attribute for weighting the different daily uses—for example, weighting all destinations by the destination's 'area', or size. However, this approach raises obstacles of reliability, because assigning a destination weight to describe the attractiveness of a destination is subjective if it is not based on accurate data obtained from site investigation and surveys. Due to the lack of previous studies that conducted resident surveys and the challenges associated with obtaining such data in the UAE, this book uses plot counts as weights. In addition, uniformly using area as a weight of attractiveness would confound types of destinations: a big hypermarket that sells a variety of goods would get the same weight as a large furniture shop that has the same area but attracts fewer and different customers.

Thus, for the sake of efficiency, this book does not assign weights to destinations and instead retains the default attribute of plot counts as the main computed attribute. Leaving buildings or plots unweighted places some limitations on the nuance of the outcome but simplifies the analysis. Because our focus is the morphological parameters of neighborhoods, our analysis keeps the attractiveness of land-use destinations constant (unweighted) in all cases and focuses solely on differences of efficiency and centrality that are purely attributable to morphological parameters.

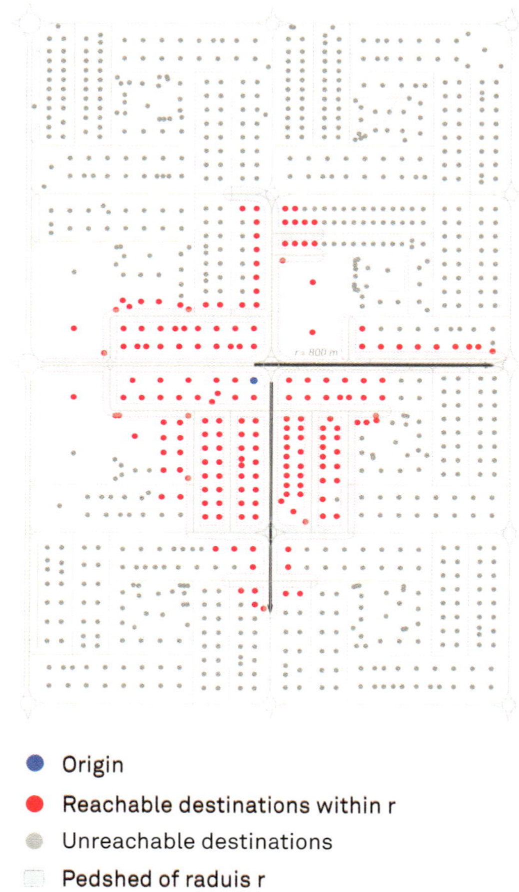

FIG. 8
Diagram explaining Reach metric

1 *Only street centerlines and plots are required to gain general insights, thus making these metrics less data-intensive than others.*

The Gravity metric was first introduced by Hansen (1959), and it is one of the most widely used spatial accessibility measures in transportation research. The Gravity metric additionally factors in the spatial impedance required to reach the destinations, unlike the Reach metric, which simply counts the number of destinations around each building within a given radius. In essence, Gravity measures the appeal of traveling to a destination by taking into account both the destination's overall attractiveness and the difficulty of getting to it. In mathematical terms, Gravity is the weight or attractiveness of the destination divided by the distance from the origin to the destination. The larger the distance from an origin to a destination, the higher the 'friction', which reduces the appeal of walking to the destination. The Gravity metric $Gravity[i]^r$ of a node i in graph G at a radius r is based on the intuition that centrality is inversely proportional to the shortest-path distance between i and each of the other nodes in G that are reachable from i within a geodesic distance r. It is defined as follows:

$$Gravity\ [i]^{\ r} = \sum_{j \in G-\{i\}, d[i,j] \leq r} W[j]^{\alpha} / e^{\beta . d[i,j]}$$

FIG. 9
Diagram explaining Gravity metric

In the above equation, β is the exponent that controls the effect of distance decay on each shortest path between and i and j. The exponent that regulates distance decay is determined by the assumed mode of travel—for example, walking, cycling, driving, or transit. Beta values that are higher (closer to 1) indicate stronger aversion to walking (Sevtsuk et al. 2016). If beta is set to zero, then no distance effect is applied and Gravity becomes equivalent to Reach. Figure 9 illustrates how the Gravity metric works. The beta value of 0.004 used in this book was determined based on a recommendation made in a previous study of walking as a mode of transportation in Singapore—a city with a hot and humid climate (Handy and Niemeier 1997; Kang 2016; Kalvo and Sevtsuk 2017) that is comparable to the climate of Abu Dhabi and Dubai. Reach does not account for walking time and impedance in relation to the number of accessible destinations and has also been criticized for treating all opportunities equally.

The set-up and calibration of gravity-based spatial models are complex and demanding tasks, because distance's effect on attraction is affected by numerous variables, such as seasonal variations, daily walking patterns, age, gender, population behavior, and other factors. The equation used by UNA can be understood as a way to better represent reality because, whereas Reach cannot address these complications, the Gravity equation factors distance decay into its measurement of centrality. In other words, while the concept of Gravity can be more rigorously specified, its use in this book is merely oriented at refining the information provided by Reach.

The Betweenness of a plot can be defined as the fraction of shortest paths between pairs of other plots in the network that pass by the plot (Freeman 1977). If cases when more than one shortest path is found between two plots (which is common in the case of grid networks), then each of the equidistant paths is given equal weight such that the weights sum to 1. The Betweenness metric, $Betweenness\ [i]^{\ r,dr}$, of a building i in graph G estimates the number of times i lies on shortest paths between pairs of other reachable nodes in G that lie within the network radius r (Freeman 1977). It is defined as follows:

$$Betweenness\ [i]^{\ r,dr} = \sum_{j,k \in G-\{i\}, d[j,k] \leq r.dr} \frac{n_{j,k}[i]}{n_{j,k}} . W[j] . \frac{1}{e^{\beta . d[j,k]}}$$

In the above equation, n_{jk} is the number of shortest paths from building j to building k in G, and $n_{jk}[i]$ is the subset of these paths that pass through i, with j and k lying within radius r from i. Sevtsuk and Mekonnen (2012) defined Betweenness as the metric that estimates the potential for passersby at different locations of the network.

TABLE. 2
Table showing head/tail classification or head/tail breaks (Jiang, 2014; 2016) to define high, medium, and low Betweenness values

Radius\Betweenness	Very Low	Low	Medium	High	Very High
400 m	N/A	<865	865–6,702	6,703–32,203	>32,203
800 m	<2,540	2,540–11,517	11,518–20,478	20,479–59,383	>59,383
1,600 m	<73,683	73,683–123,568	123,569–179,444	179,445–251,415	>251,415

In this book, we have used head/tail classification or head/tail breaks (Jiang 2014; 2016) to define high, medium, and low Betweenness values, because the Betweenness values resemble a power-law distribution. For each local radius (i.e., 400, 800, and 1,600 m), separate head/tail breaks are computed. Figure 10 illustrates the Betweenness metric and Table 2 indicates the Betweenness values this study considers low, medium, high, and very high for each radius.

The Straightness metric showcases the extent to which the shortest paths from a plot of interest to all other accessible nodes within a search radius in the network resemble straight Euclidean distances. In other words, the Straightness metric reveals the positive deviations in travel distances that result from the geometric constraints of the street network in comparison to straight-line distances (Sevtsuk and Mekonnen 2012). The Straightness metric, $Straightness[i]^r$, of a building i in a graph G illustrates how closely the shortest network distances between i and other buildings in G that are reachable within radius r resemble Euclidean distances (Vragovic, Louis et al. 2005; Porta et al., 2005). It is defined as follows:

$$Straightness\ [i]^r = \sum_{j \in G-\{i\}; d[i,j] \leq r} \frac{\delta\ [i,j]\ .W[j]}{d\ [i,j]}$$

In the above equation, $\delta[i\ ,j]$ is the as-the-crow-flies distance between nodes i and j, and $d[i\ ,\ j]$ the shortest network distance between the same buildings. As a ratio between the Euclidian distance and the geodesic distance from each location i to the surrounding locations j, Straightness can only be estimated if impedance is measured in units of linear distance (e.g., kilometers), not units of time (e.g., minutes) or topology (e.g., turns). Straightness gives information about efficiency of the networks regardless of any effects that land uses might have on route directness and connectivity (Alawadi, Khaleel, and Benkraouda 2020). Figure 11 illustrates the Straightness metric.

In this book, Normalized Straightness is used to facilitate the comparison of straightness results across different neighborhoods. The raw Straightness value for each plot is divided by the corresponding Reach value to obtain a normalized Straightness value. In all analyses, normalized Straightness values range from zero to one, where zero represents total absence of straightness due to zero reachable plots and one represents the maximum straightness. In this book, we have used criterion-reference classification to define high, medium, and low Normalized Straightness values.

This approach is based on percentiles and standard deviations. In other words, Normalized Straightness values lower than 0.25 are labelled low, those from 0.26 to 0.74 are labelled medium, and those above 0.75 are considered high.

$$Normalized\ Straightness\ [i]^r = Straightness\ [i]^r / Reach\ [i]^r$$

In the previous equation, the Straightness value of a building i is divided by the Reach value of the same building i from other buildings that are reachable within radius r.

For all metrics, connections between all possible origins and destinations within the noted distance thresholds are evaluated by UNA according to the aforementioned formulas. Specifically, all plots are designated as origins and destinations simultaneously. The obtained results are then exported to MS Excel, where they are prepared for further processing on ArcGIS. Only relevant information is kept, such that the UNA results or the values for each plot or street segment (in the case of Betweenness) can be integrated with the corresponding shapefiles in GIS. After the integration of UNA results, maps can be color-coded in GIS to identify high- and low-accessibility areas, efficient street layouts, or highly used thoroughfares. These computations reveal the general performances of different neighborhoods' street designs. The aim is to quantify different network designs' ability to provide a well-integrated neighborhood environment where all possible destinations (both residential and non-residential) can be accessed through short and direct routes.

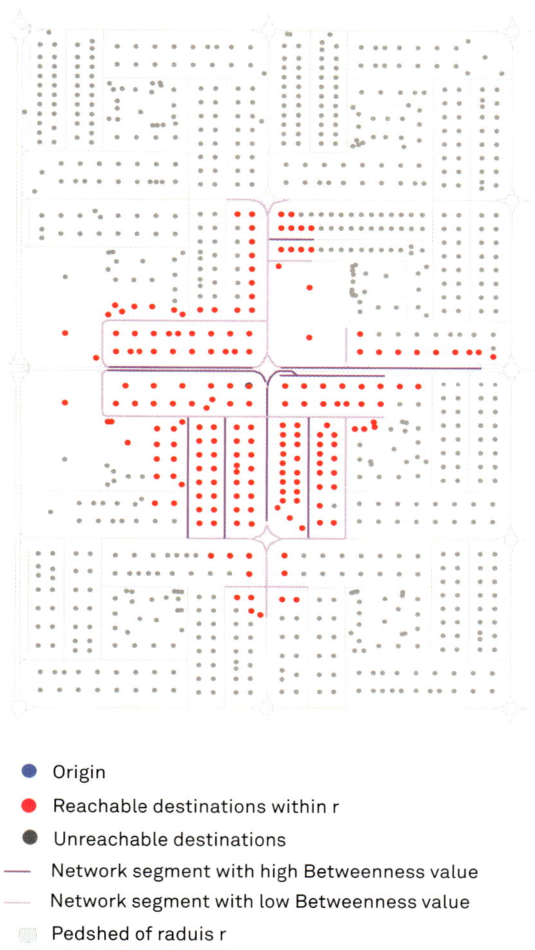

FIG. 10
Diagram explaining Betweenness metric

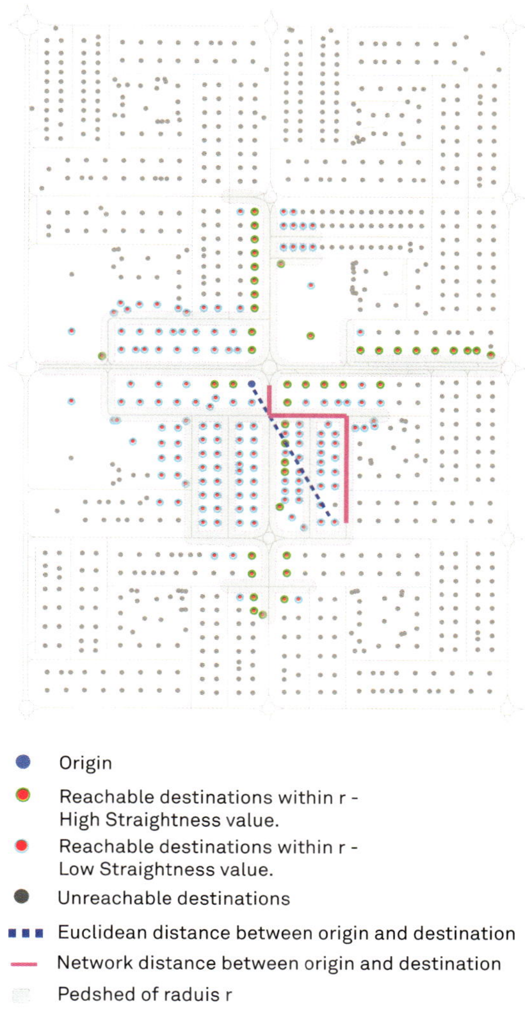

FIG. 11
Diagram explaining Straightness metric

References

Alawadi, Khaled, Asim Khanal, Azhar Doudin, and Rahma Abdelghani. "Revisiting transit-oriented development: Alleys as critical walking infrastructure." Transport Policy 100 (2021): 187-202.

Barthélemy, Marc. "Spatial networks." Physics reports 499, no. 1-3 (2011): 1-101.

Batty, Michael. "A new theory of space syntax." (2004).

Batty, Michael, and Paul A. Longley. Fractal cities: a geometry of form and function. Academic press, 1994.

Calthorpe, Peter, and William Fulton. "The Regional City.-Washington, Covelo." (2001).

Cardillo, A., Scellato, S., Latora, V., & Porta, S. (2006). Structural properties of planar graphs of urban street patterns. Physical Review E, 73(6), 066107.

Carr, C. M. H., and J. W. R. Whitehand. Twentieth-century suburbs: a morphological approach. Routledge, 2014.

Dill, Jennifer. "Measuring network connectivity for bicycling and walking. Presented at the 83rd Annual Meeting of the Transportation Research Board, Washington, DC January 11-15, 2004." (2004).

Elsheshtawy, Yasser. Dubai: Behind an urban spectacle. Routledge, 2009.

Ewing, Reid, and Robert Cervero. "Travel and the built environment: a synthesis." Transportation research record 1780, no. 1 (2001): 87-114.

Freeman, Linton C. "A set of measures of centrality based on betweenness." Sociometry (1977): 35-41.

Gil, Jorge. "Street network analysis "edge effects": Examining the sensitivity of centrality measures to boundary conditions." Environment and Planning B: Urban Analytics and City Science 44, no. 5 (2017): 819-836.

Handy, Susan L., and Debbie A. Niemeier. "Measuring accessibility: an exploration of issues and alternatives." Environment and planning A 29, no. 7 (1997): 1175-1194.

Handy, Susan, Robert G. Paterson, and Kent Butler. "Planning for street connectivity." Getting from here to there. American Planning Association, Planning Advisory Service (Planning Advisory Service report, no. 515), Chicago (2003).

Hansen, Walter G. "How accessibility shapes land use." Journal of the American Institute of planners 25, no. 2 (1959): 73-76.

Hillier, Bill. "Centrality as a process: accounting for attraction inequalities in deformed grids." Urban design international 4, no. 3-4 (1999): 107-127.

Hillier, Bill, and Julienne Hanson. The social logic of space. Cambridge university press, 1989.

Hillier, Bill, Alan Penn, Julienne Hanson, Tadeusz Grajewski, and Jianming Xu. "Natural movement: or, configuration and attraction in urban pedestrian movement." Environment and Planning B: planning and design 20, no. 1 (1993): 29-66.

Jacobs, Allan B. "Great streets: Monument avenue, richmond, virginia." (1993).

Jiang, Bin, and Junjun Yin. "Ht-index for quantifying the fractal or scaling structure of geographic features." Annals of the Association of American Geographers 104, no. 3 (2014): 530-540.

Jiang, Bin. "Head/tail breaks for visualization of city structure and dynamics." European handbook of crowdsourced geographic information 169 (2016).

Sevtsuk, Andres, and Raul Kalvo. "Patronage of urban commercial clusters: A network-based extension of the Huff model for balancing location and size." Environment and Planning B: Urban Analytics and City Science 45, no. 3 (2018): 508-528.

Kang, Chang-Deok. "The effects of spatial accessibility and centrality to land use on walking in Seoul, Korea." Cities 46 (2015): 94-103.

Kang, Chang-Deok. "Spatial access to pedestrians and retail sales in Seoul, Korea." Habitat international 57 (2016): 110-120.

Kang, Chang-Deok. "The S+ 5Ds: Spatial access to pedestrian environments and walking in Seoul, Korea." Cities 77 (2018): 130-141.

Knight, Paul L., and Wesley E. Marshall. "The metrics of street network connectivity: their inconsistencies." Journal of Urbanism: International Research on Placemaking and Urban Sustainability 8, no. 3 (2015): 241-259.

Marshall, Wesley E., and Norman W. Garrick. "Community design and how much we drive." Journal of Transport and Land Use 5, no. 2 (2012): 5-20.

Moudon, Anne Vernez. "Urban morphology as an emerging interdisciplinary field." Urban morphology 1, no. 1 (1997): 3-10.

Moudon, Anne Vernez, Paul M. Hess, Mary Catherine Snyder, and Kiril Stanilov. "Effects of site design on pedestrian travel in mixed-use, medium-density environments." Transportation Research Record 1578, no. 1 (1997): 48-55.

Moudon, Anne Vernez, and Paul Mitchell Hess. "Suburban clusters: The nucleation of multifamily housing in suburban areas of the Central Puget Sound." Journal of the American Planning Association 66, no. 3 (2000): 243-264.

Moudon, Anne Vernez, Chanam Lee, Allen D. Cheadle, Cheza Garvin, Donna Johnson, Thomas L. Schmid, Robert D. Weathers, and Lin Lin. "Operational definitions of walkable neighborhood: theoretical and empirical insights." Journal of physical activity and health 3, no. s1 (2006): S99-S117.

Peponis, John, Douglas Allen, Steve French, Martin Scoppa, and Jason Brown. "Street connectivity and urban density." In 6th International Space Syntax Symposium, pp. 1-12. Istanbul: Citeseer, 2007.

Peponis, John, Sonit Bafna, and Zongyu Zhang. "The connectivity of streets: reach and directional distance." Environment and Planning B: Planning and Design 35, no. 5 (2008): 881-901.

Porta, Sergio, Paolo Crucitti, and Vito Latora. "The network analysis of urban streets: a primal approach." Environment and Planning B: planning and design 33, no. 5 (2006): 705-725.

Porta, Sergio, and Vito Latora. "11 Multiple centrality assessment: mapping centrality in networks of urban spaces." Urban Sustainability Through Environmental Design: Approaches to Time-People-Place Responsive Urban Spaces (2007): 101.

Porta, Sergio, and John Luciano Renne. "Linking urban design to sustainability: formal indicators of social urban sustainability field research in Perth, Western Australia." Urban Design International 10 (2005): 51-64.

Porta, Sergio, Emanuele Strano, Valentino Iacoviello, Roberto Messora, Vito Latora, Alessio Cardillo, Fahui Wang, and Salvatore Scellato. "Street centrality and densities of retail and services in Bologna, Italy." Environment and Planning B: Planning and design 36, no. 3 (2009): 450-465..

Ratti, Carlo. "Space syntax: some inconsistencies." Environment and planning B: Planning and design 31, no. 4 (2004): 487-499.

Salingaros, Nikos A. "A scientific basis for creating architectural forms." Journal of Architectural and Planning Research (1998): 283-293.

Scellato, Salvatore, Alessio Cardillo, Vito Latora, and Sergio Porta. "The backbone of a city." The European Physical Journal B-Condensed Matter and Complex Systems 50 (2006): 221-225.

Sevtsuk, Andres, Raul Kalvo, and Onur Ekmekci. "Pedestrian accessibility in grid layouts: the role of block, plot and street dimensions." Urban Morphology 20, no. 2 (2016): 89-106.

Sevtsuk, Andres, and Michael Mekonnen. "Urban network analysis." Revue internationale de géomatique–n 287 (2012): 305.

Sevtsuk, Andres, and Carlo Ratti. "Does urban mobility have a daily routine? Learning from the aggregate data of mobile networks." Journal of Urban Technology 17, no. 1 (2010): 41-60.

Southworth, Michael, and Peter M. Owens. "The evolving metropolis: Studies of community, neighborhood, and street form at the urban edge." Journal of the American Planning Association 59, no. 3 (1993): 271-287.

Stangl, Paul. "The pedestrian route directness test: A new level-of-service model." Urban Design International 17 (2012): 228-238.

Stangl, Paul, and Jeffery M. Guinn. "Neighborhood design, connectivity assessment and obstruction." Urban Design International 16 (2011): 285-296.

Talen, Emily, and Cliff Ellis. "Beyond relativism: Reclaiming the search for good city form." Journal of Planning Education and Research 22, no. 1 (2002): 36-49.

Turner, Alasdair. "Depthmap: a program to perform visibility graph analysis." In Proceedings of the 3rd international symposium on space syntax, vol. 31, pp. 31-12. 2001.

Vragović, I., E. Louis, and Albert Díaz-Guilera. "Efficiency of informational transfer in regular and complex networks." Physical Review E 71, no. 3 (2005): 036122.

Wheeler, Stephen M. "The new regionalism: Key characteristics of an emerging movement." Journal of the American Planning Association 68, no. 3 (2002): 267-278.

Wolch, Jennifer, Josh Newell, Mona Seymour, Hilary Bradbury Huang, Kim Reynolds, and Jennifer Mapes. "The forgotten and the future: Reclaiming back alleys for a sustainable city." Environment and Planning A 42, no. 12 (2010): 2874-2896.

06 Results of Analysis

KHALIFA CITY
WEST ISLAND
MBZ CITY

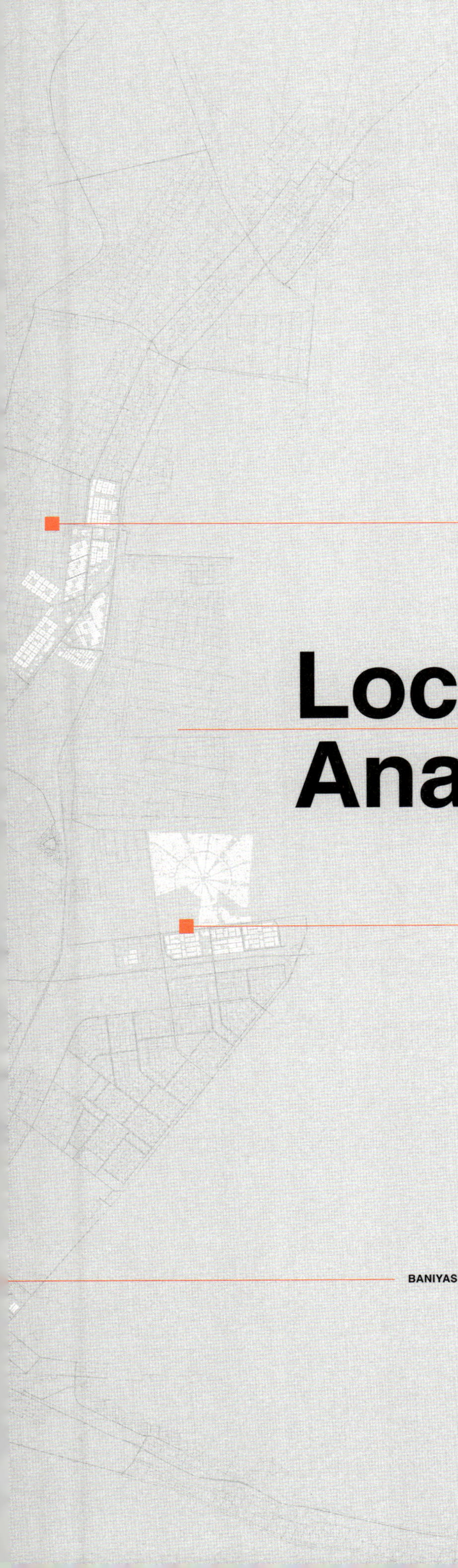

Local Scale Analysis

Abu Dhabi

West Island

West Island

FIG. 1
West Island skyline

FIG. 2
Street view showing internal streets within a superblock

FIG. 3
A photo montage with different views of West Island

FIG. 4
Aerial image showing West Island (Esri & USGS, 2021)

Morphological Analysis:

Neighborhood Scale

Residential= 7,511 Plots
Non-residential= 2,725 Plots

Plots/Buildings:

- Total area = 3,476.99 Hectares
- Total plots = 10,235 Plots
- Total buildings = 12,607 Buildings
- Average plot density = 2.94 Plots/Hectare
- Average building density = 3.62 Buildings/Hectare
- Average plot area = 0.49 Hectare
- Average population density = 177.93 Population/ Hectare

FIG. 5.1
Residential/ non-residential classification

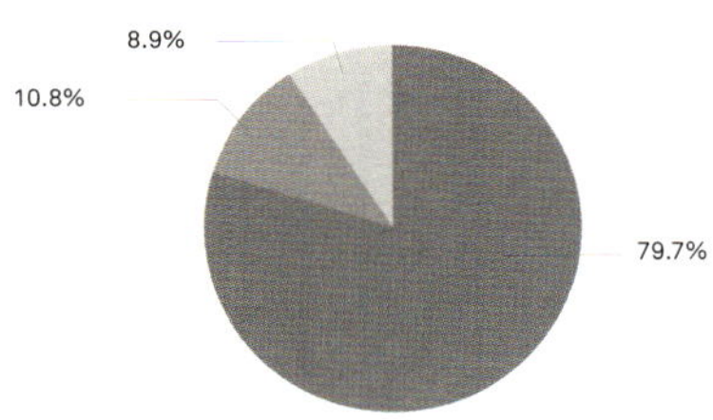

Low-rise (1-4) = 10,051 Buildings
Mid-rise (4-10)= 362 Buildings
High-rise (+10)= 1,132 Buildings

FIG. 5.2
Buildings height classification

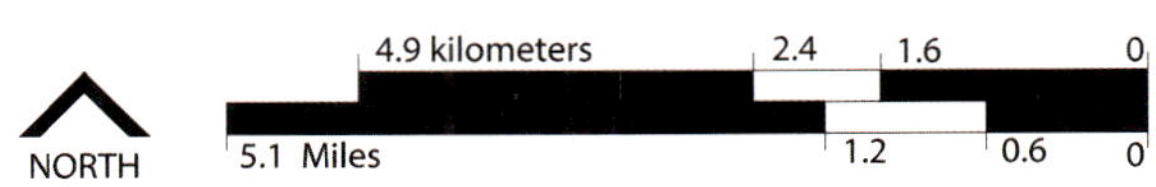

FIG. 5.3

Population density

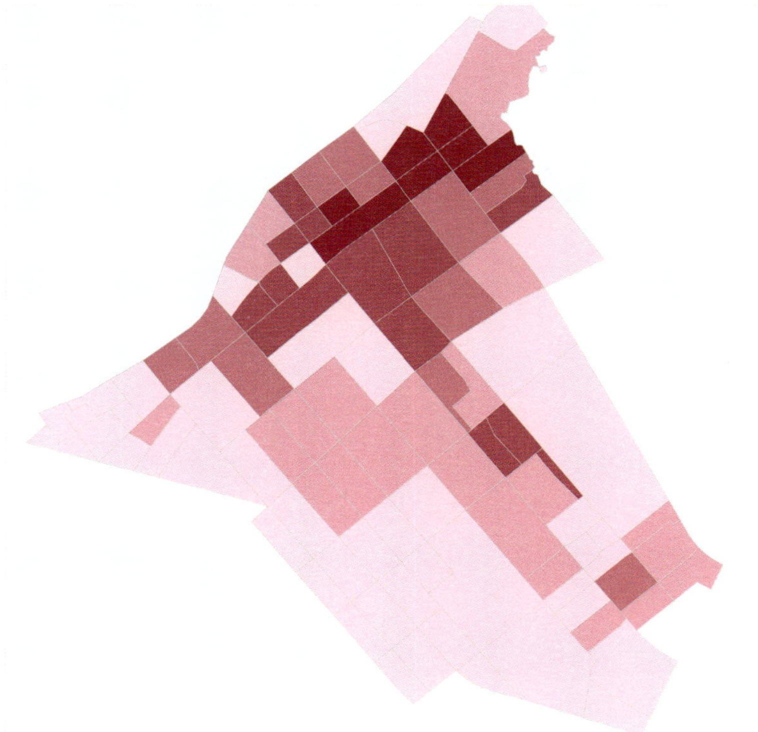

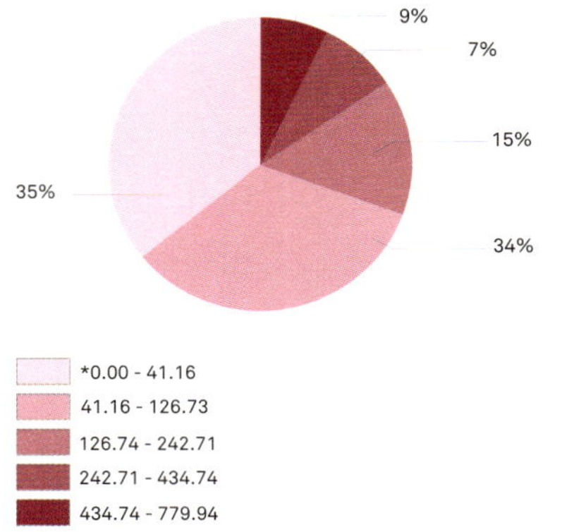

*Population per hectare.

FIG. 5.4

Land use classification

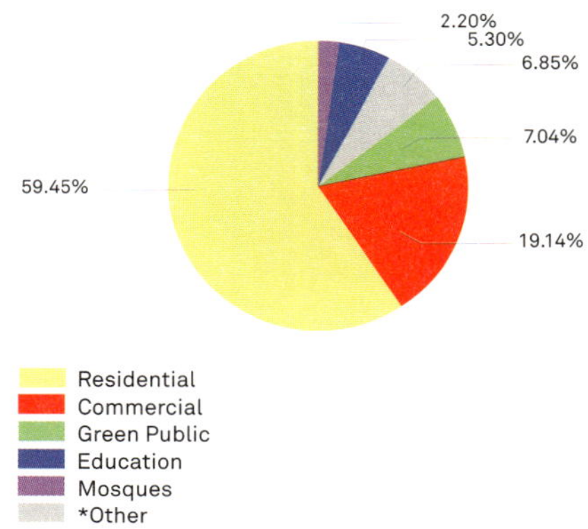

* Other land uses include: Health Care, Municipal/Goverment Facilities, Beaches, Public Library, Community Center, Utilities, Wedding hall, and Graveyard.

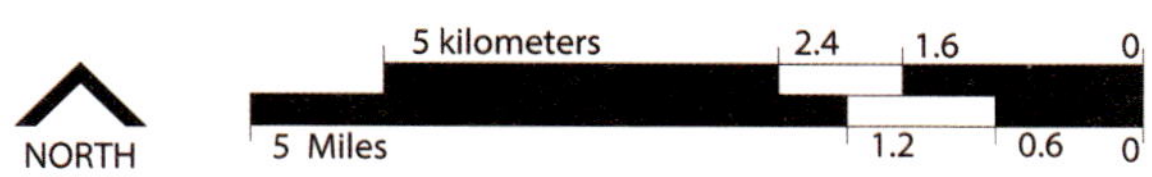

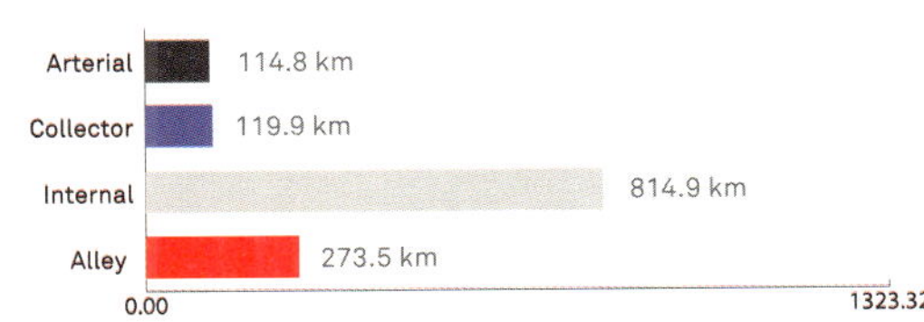

FIG. 5.5

Map showing network classification in the West Island

Streets:

- Street length = 1,049.6 km
- Street density = 0.40 km/Hectare
- Street intersections = 8,762 Intersections
- Street intersection density = 2.52 Intersections /Hectare

Alleys:

- Alley length = 273.5 km
- Alley density = 0.15 km/Hectare
- Alley intersections = 1,791 Intersections
- Alley intersection density = 0.52 Intersections/Hectare

FIG. 6
Map showing West Island, with the location of the selected samples. Each sample has an area of 1 square mile.

Morphological Analysis:

Sample Scale — Sample 01

Residential= 818 Plots
Non-residential= 199 Plots

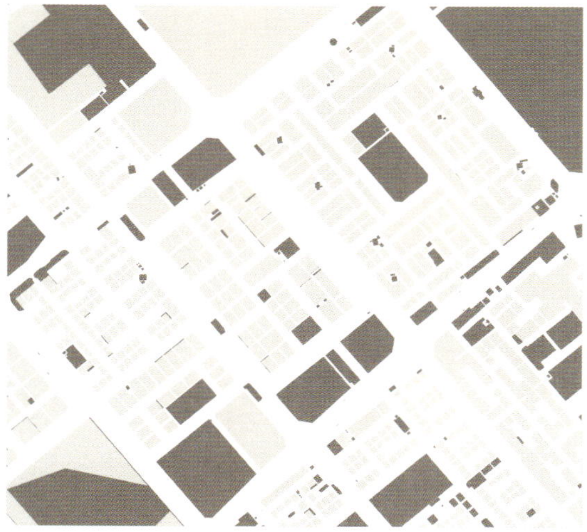

FIG. 7.1
Residential/non-residential classification

Plots/Buildings:

- Total area = 256 Hectares
- Total plots = 1,017 Plots
- Total buildings = 2,573 Buildings
- Average plot area = 0.20 Hectare
- Average plot density = 3.97 Plots/Hectare

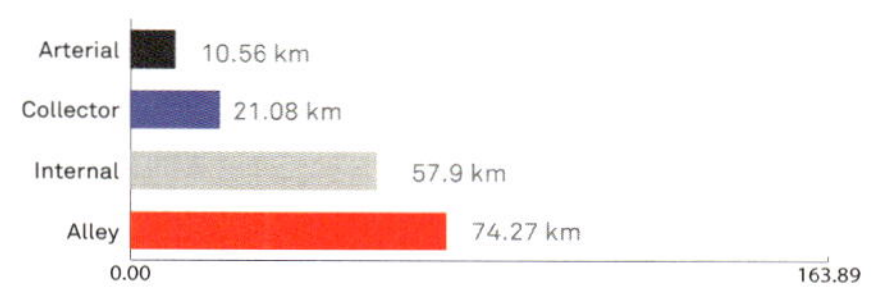

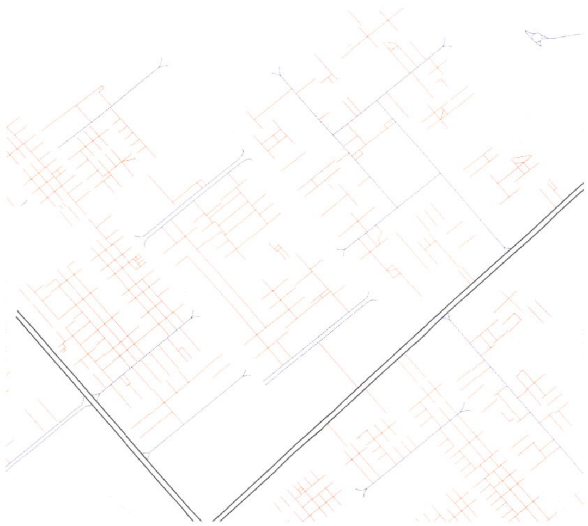

FIG. 7.2
Network classification

Streets:

- Street length = 89.62 km
- Street density = 0.35 km/Hectare
- Street intersections = 776 Intersections
- Street intersection density = 3.03 Intersections/Hectare

Alleys:

- Alley length = 74.27 km
- Alley density = 0.29 km/Hectare
- Alley intersections = 291 Intersections
- Alley intersection density = 1.14 Intersections/Hectare

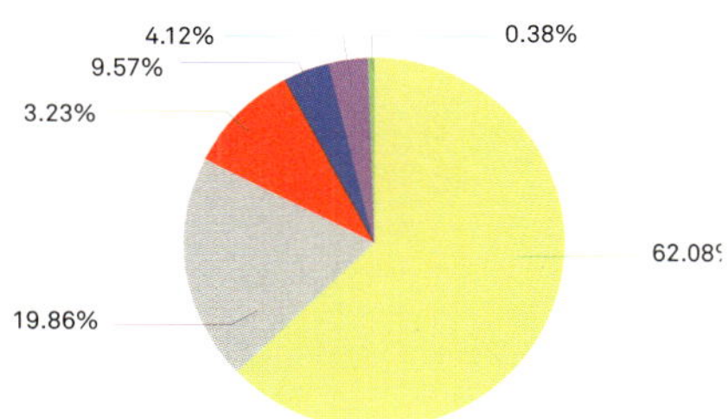

Residential
Commercial\Mixed Use
Education
Green Public
Mosques
*Other

FIG. 7.3
Land use classification

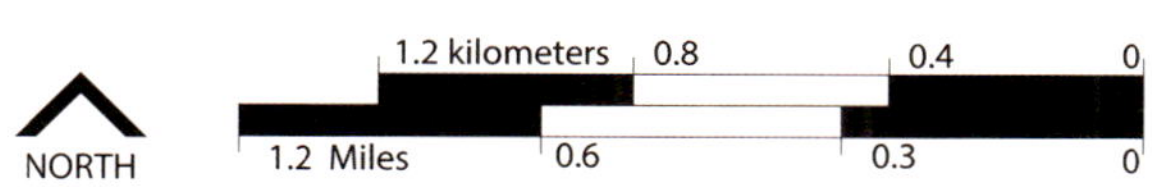

Sample Scale — Sample 02

FIG. 8.1
Residential/non-residential classification

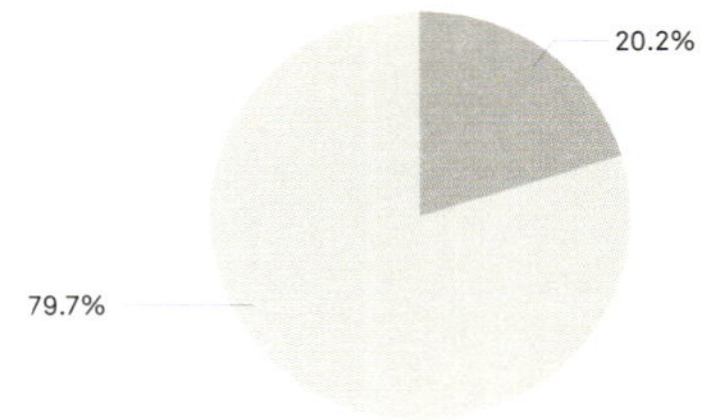

Non-Residential\Mixed Use= 877 Plots
Residential= 223 Plots

Plots/Buildings:

- Total area = 256 Hectares
- Total plots = 807 Plots
- Total buildings = 1,349 Buildings
- Average plot density = 3.15 Plots/Hectare
- Average plot area = 0.17 Hectare

FIG. 8.2
Network classification

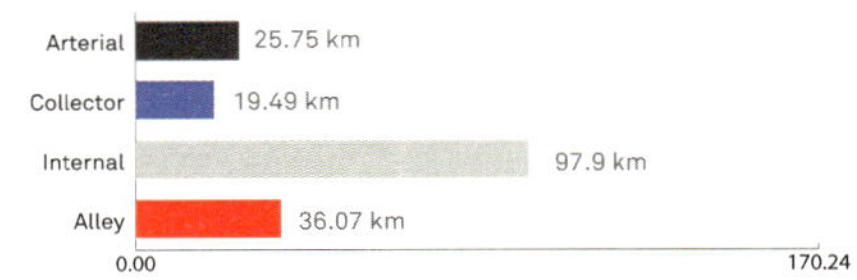

Streets:

- Street length = 134.17 km
- Street density = 0.52 km/Hectare
- Street intersections = 1,439 Intersections
- Street intersection density = 5.62 Intersections/Hectare

Alleys:

- Alley length = 36.07 km
- Alley density = 0.14 km/Hectare
- Alley intersections = 233 Intersections
- Alley intersection density = 0.91 Intersection/Hectare

FIG. 8.3
Land use classification

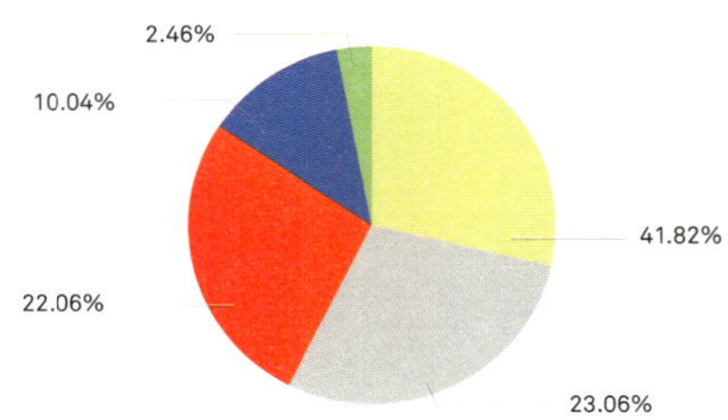

Residential
Commercial\Mixed Use
Education
Green Public
Mosques
*Other

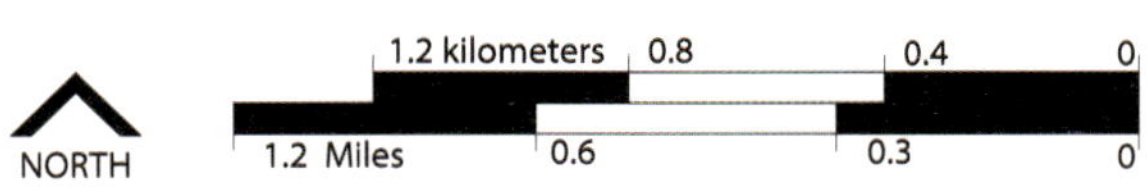

Centrality Analysis: Neighborhood Scale

Scenario 1: Streets Only — 400 m Radius

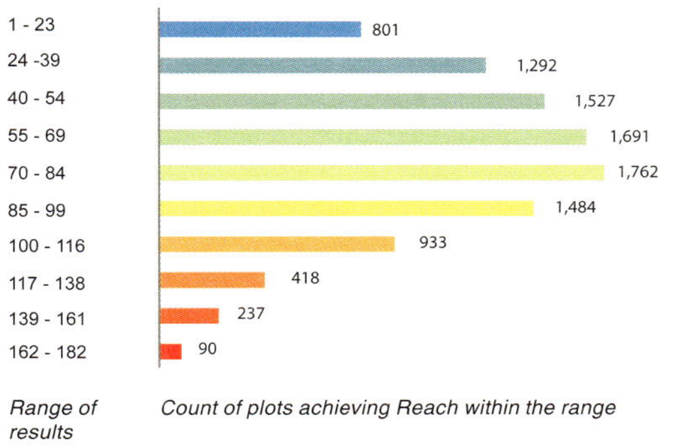

The warmer colors (i.e., greenish-yellow to red) represent a Reach value of 70 or more, while the cooler colors (i.e., light green to dark blue) correspond to Reach values of less than 70. The majority of plots (i.e., 5,311 out of 10,235), corresponding to 52% of all plots, have Reach values of less than 70. Among the categories shown in the legend, 17% of all plots can reach 70 to 84 other plots within 5 minutes of walking. On average, each plot in West Island AD can access at least 69 plots within a distance of 400 m.

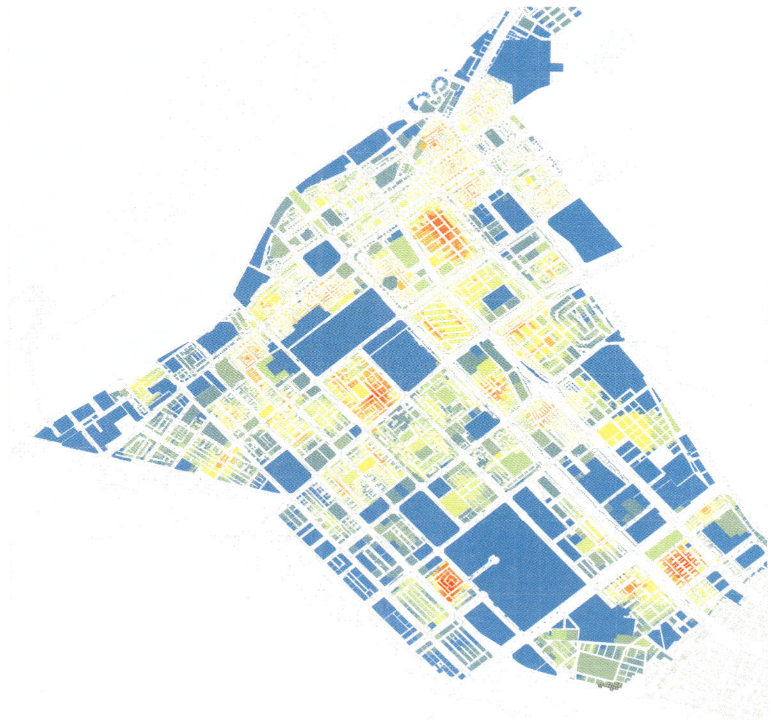

FIG. 9.1
Reach

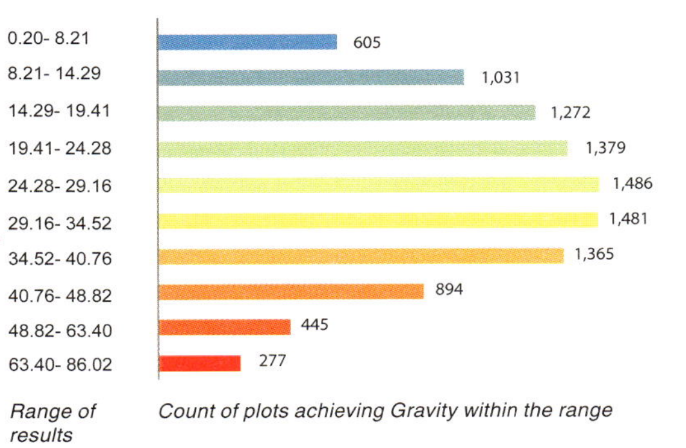

The warmer colors (i.e., greenish-yellow to red) represent Gravity values greater than 24.27, while the cooler colors (i.e., light green to dark blue) correspond to a Gravity value of 24.27 or less. Fifty-six percent of all plots (i.e., 5,773 out of 10,235) have Gravity values of less than 29.16. Among the categories shown in the legend, 1,486 plots, or 15% of all plots, can reach 24.28 to 29.16 plots, making this the most common range; this range is illustrated by greenish-yellow on the map. On average, at a radius of 400 m, each plot can reach 28 other plots when spatial impedance or distance decay effect is taken into consideration.

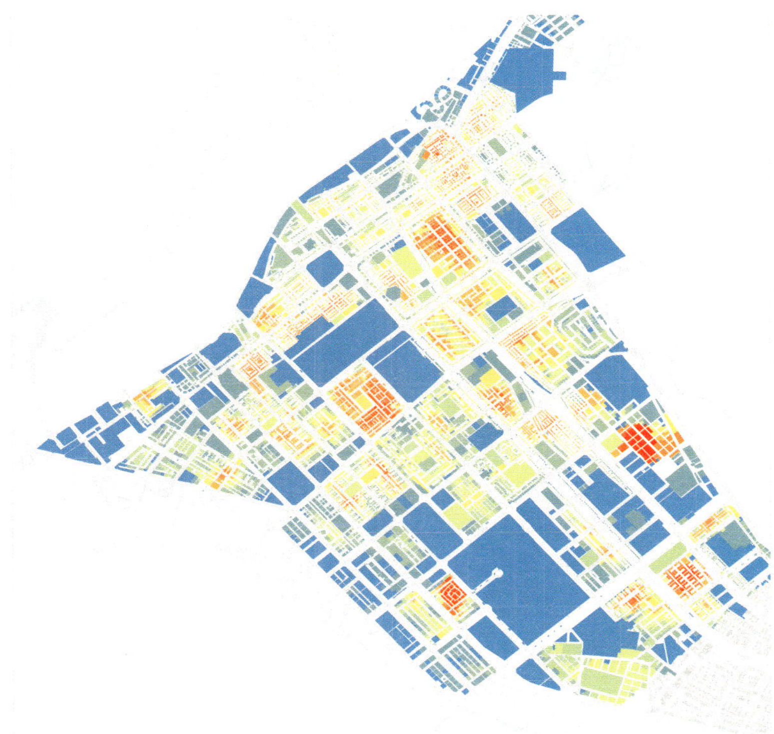

FIG. 9.2
Gravity

Scenario 1: Streets Only — 400 m Radius

FIG. 9.3
Betweenness

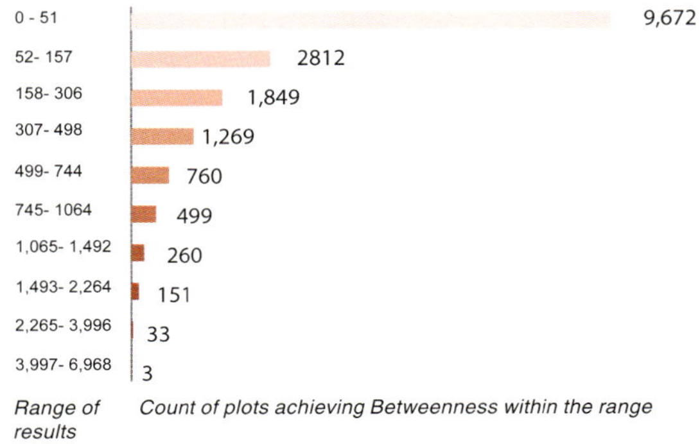

The majority of segments, corresponding to 96% (i.e., 16,589 out of 17,308 segments), have low Betweenness values ranging from 0 to 864. Among the categories shown in the legend, 9,672 segments have values in the range of 0 to 52, making this the most common range; this range is represented by the lightest brown on the map. In West Island, the mid-range Betweenness values—those between 865 and 6,702—are obtained by 718 segments, which is 4% of all segments. Only one segment has a high level of Betweenness (higher than 6,702), corresponding to only 0.01% of all segments. Ten percent of the segments have Betweenness values higher than 498. The average Betweenness value in West Island is 165 (smaller than 865), while the median is 28, indicating low Betweenness at a 400 m radius.

FIG. 9.4
Straightness

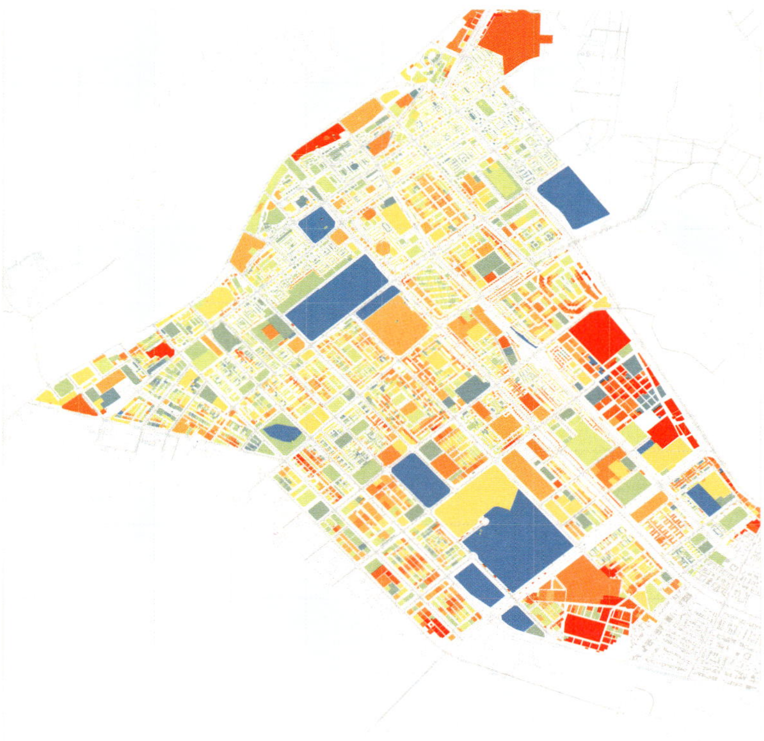

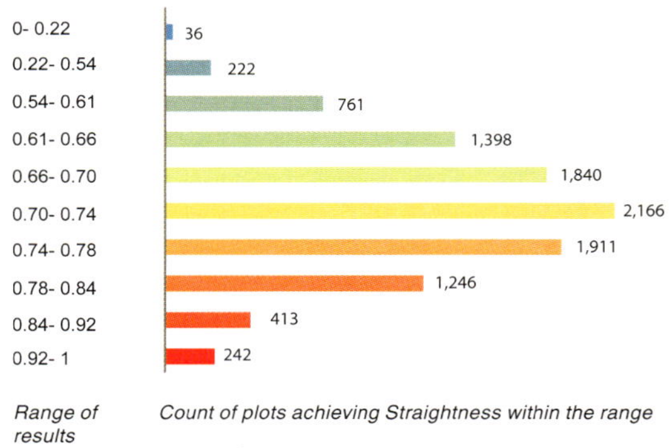

The light orange to red colors represent Straightness values higher than 0.73, while light blue to dark blue correspond to Straightness values lower than 0.54. The majority of plots, corresponding to 58% (or 5,917 out of 10,235 plots) have Straightness values ranging from 0.66 to 0.78. Among the categories shown in the legend, 2,166 plots have values in the range of 0.70 to 0.74, making this the most common range; this range is represented by yellow on the map. The average Straightness value of plots in West Island is 0.72 at a radius of 400 m, which means that their paths to other plots are 72% as straight as a straight line.

Scenario 1: Streets Only — 800 m Radius

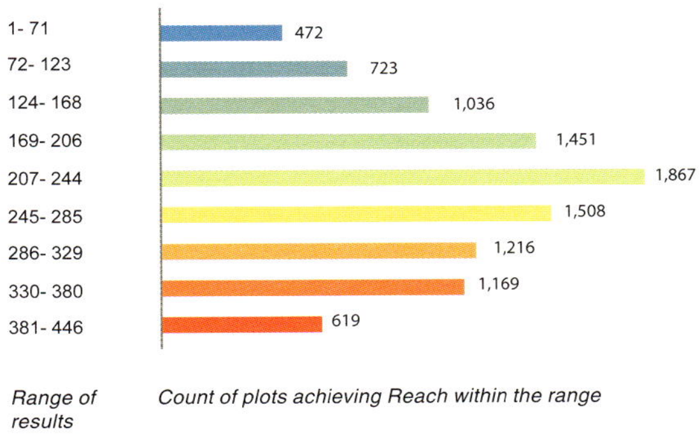

The warmer colors (i.e., greenish-yellow to red) represent a Reach value of 207 or more, while the cooler colors (i.e., light green to dark blue) correspond to a Reach value of 206 or less. The majority of plots (i.e., 5,549 out of 10,235), corresponding to 54%, have Reach values of less than 245. Among the categories shown in the legend, 18% of plots can reach 207 to 244 other plots within 10 minutes of walking. On average, each plot in West Island AD can access at least 240 plots within a distance of 800 m.

FIG. 10.1
Reach

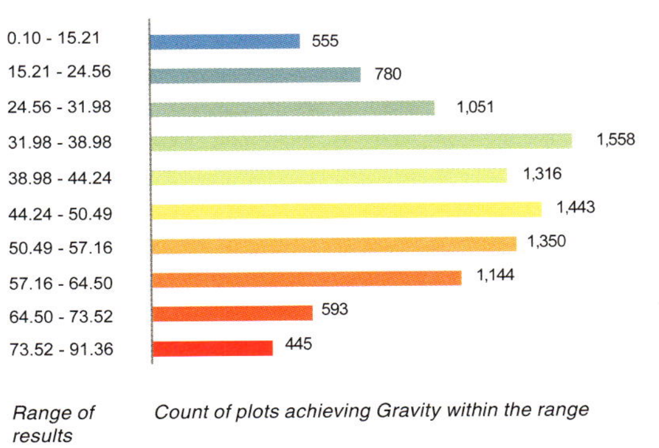

The warmer colors (i.e., greenish-yellow to red) represent Gravity values of more than 38.97, while the cooler colors (i.e., light green to dark blue) correspond to Gravity values of less than 38.98. Fifty-one percent of plots (i.e., 5,260 out of 10,235) have Gravity values of less than 44.24. Among the categories shown in the legend, 1,558 plots, or 15% of plots, can reach 31.98 to 38.98 other plots, making this the most common range; this range is represented by light green on the map. On average, at an 800 m radius, each plot can reach 44 other plots when spatial impedance or distance decay effect is taken into consideration.

FIG. 10.2
Gravity

Scenario 1: Streets Only — 800 m Radius

FIG. 10.3
Betweenness

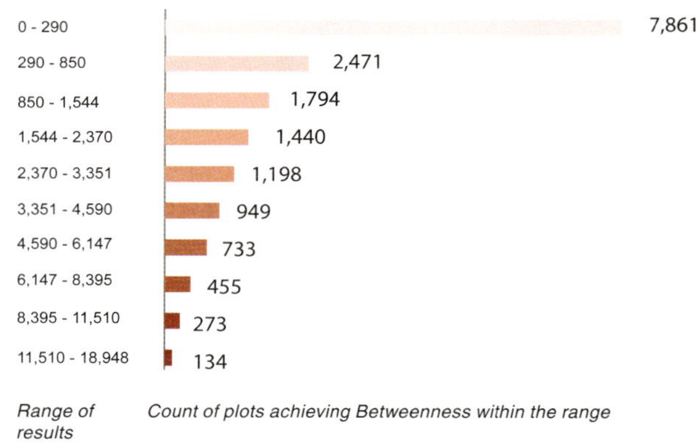

The majority of segments, corresponding to 80% (i.e., 13,826 out of 17,308 segments), have very low Betweenness values in the range of 0–2,539. Among the categories shown in the legend, 7,861 segments have values in the range of 0 to 290, making this the most common range; this range is represented by the lightest brown on the map. All the low Betweenness values ranging from 2,540 to 11,510 are obtained by 3,349 segments, which is 19% of all segments. Only 134, or 0.8% of the segments, have mid-range Betweenness values; these range from 11,518 to 20,478. The average Betweenness value in West Island is 1,456 (smaller than 2,540), and the median is 432, indicating very low Betweenness at an 800 m radius.

FIG. 10.4
Straightness

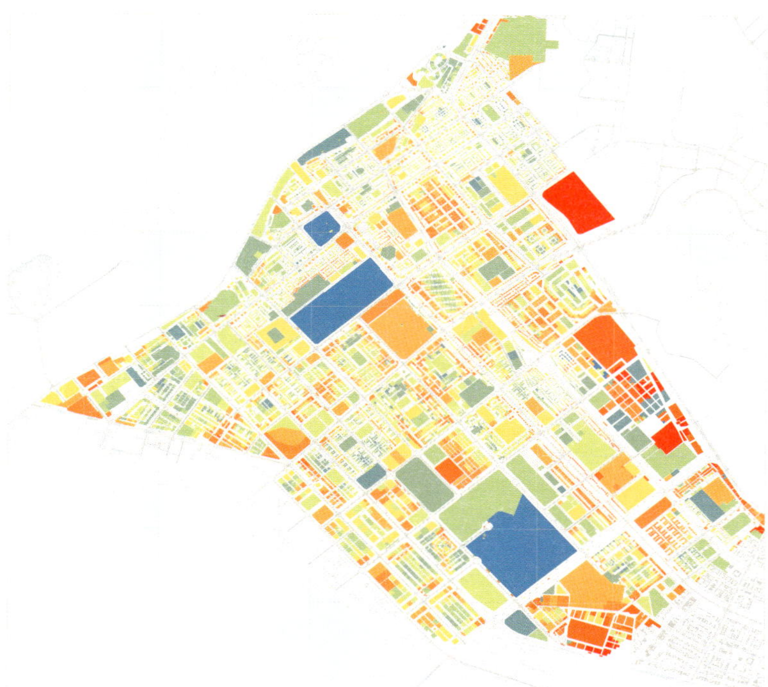

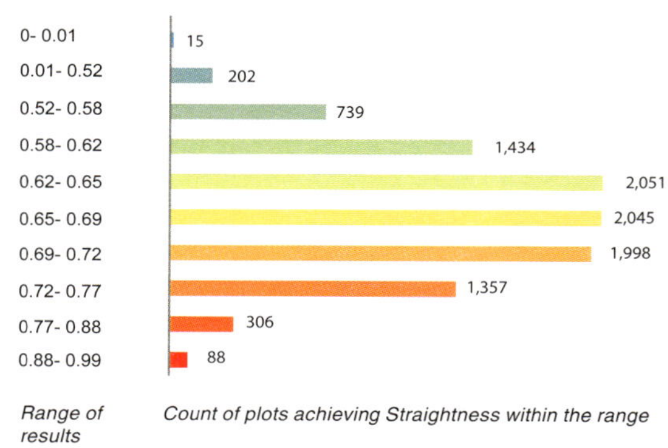

The light orange to red colors represent Straightness values higher than 0.68, while light blue to dark blue correspond to Straightness values lower than 0.58. The majority of plots, corresponding to 60% (or 6,094 out of 10,235 plots) have Straightness values ranging from 0.63 to 0.73. Among the categories shown in the legend, 2,051 plots have values in the range of 0.62 to 0.65, making this the most common range; this range is represented by greenish-yellow on the map. The average Straightness value of plots in West Island is 0.67 at an 800 m radius, which means that their paths to other plots are 67% as straight as a straight line.

Scenario 1: Streets Only — 1,600 m Radius

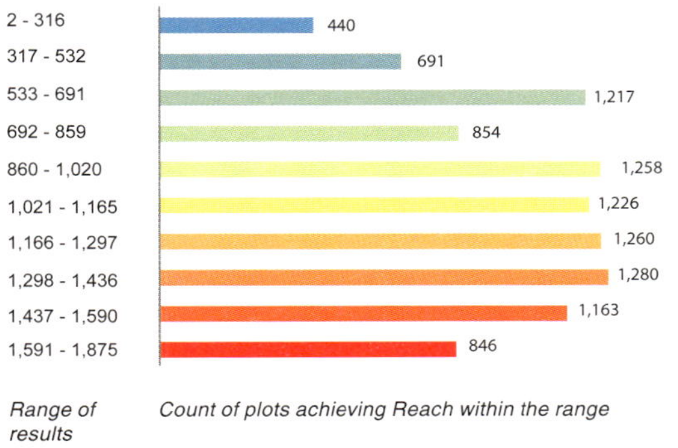

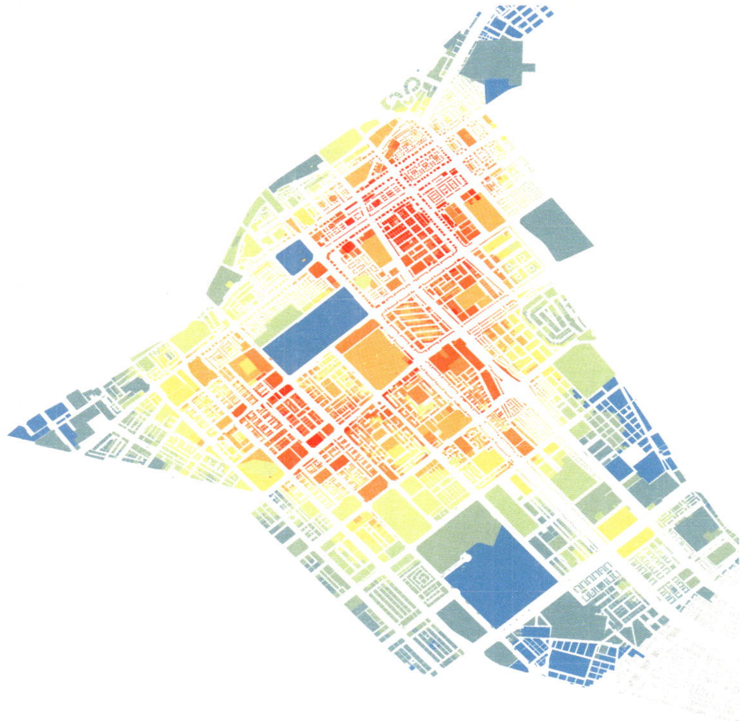

FIG. 11.1
Reach

The warmer colors (i.e., greenish-yellow to red) represent Reach values greater than 859, while the cooler colors (i.e., light green to dark blue) correspond to Reach values lower than 860. The majority of plots (i.e., 5,686 out of 10,235), corresponding to 56%, have Reach values of less than 1,166. Among the categories shown in the legend, 13% of plots can reach 1,298 to 1,436 other plots within 20 minutes of walking. On average, each plot in West Island AD can access at least 1,056 plots within a distance of 1,600 m.

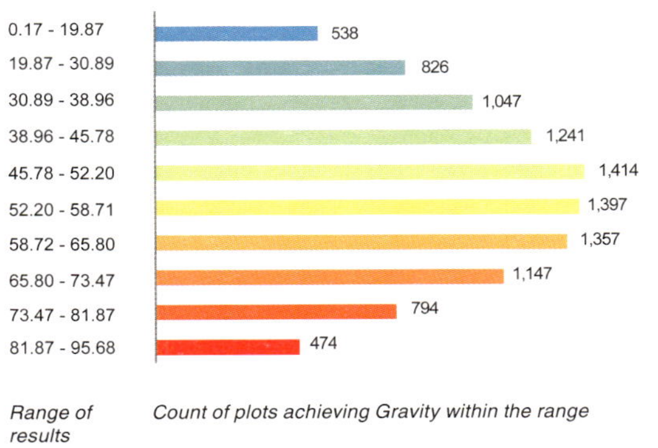

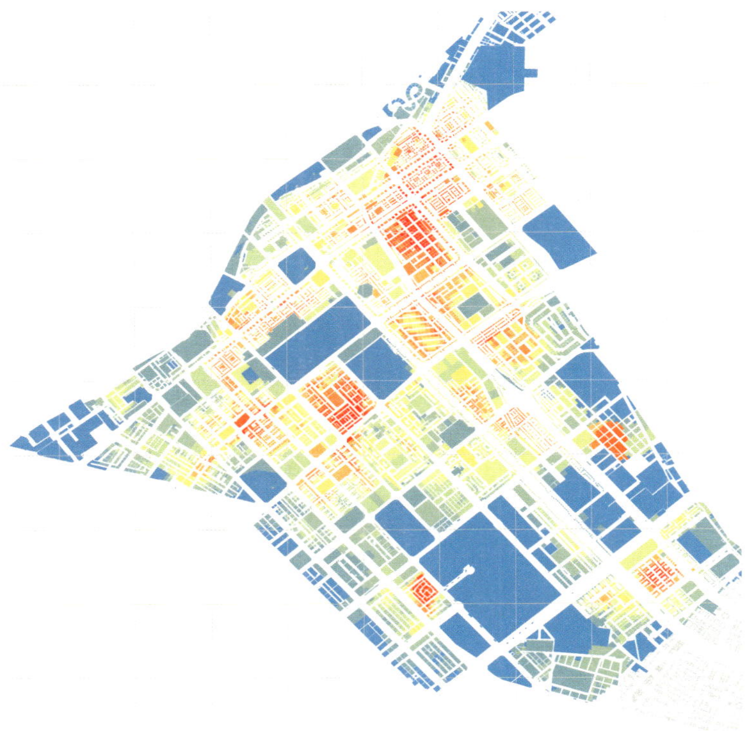

FIG. 11.2
Gravity

The warmer colors (i.e., greenish-yellow to red) represent Gravity values greater than 45.77, while the cooler colors (i.e., light green to dark blue) correspond to Gravity values lower than 45.78. Sixty-three percent of all plots (i.e., 6,463 out of 10,235) have Gravity values lower than 58.72. Among the categories shown in the legend, 1,414 plots, or 14% of all plots, can reach 45.78 to 52.20 plots, making this the most common range; this range is represented by greenish-yellow on the map. On average, at a 1,600 m radius, each plot can reach 52 other plots when spatial impedance or distance decay effect is taken into consideration.

Scenario 1: Streets Only — 1,600 m Radius

FIG. 11.3
Betweenness

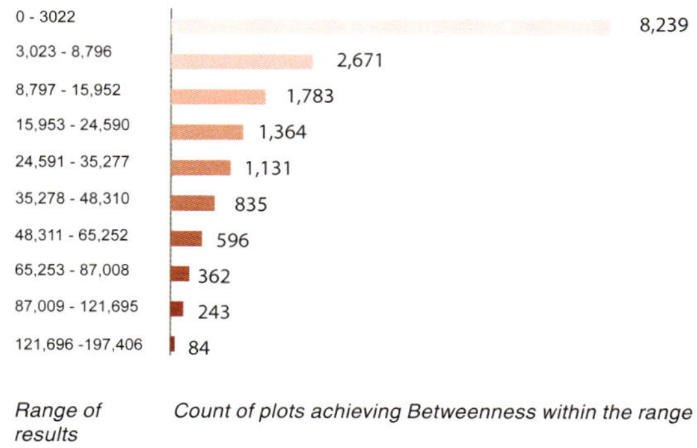

The majority of segments, corresponding to 97% (i.e., 16,780 out of 17,308 segments), have very low Betweenness values in the range of 0 to 73,682. Among the categories shown in the legend, 8,239 segments have values in the range of 0 to 3,023, making this the most common range; this range is represented by the lightest brown on the map. Low Betweenness values ranging from 73,683 to 123,568 are obtained by 448 segments, which is 3% of all segments. The m-d-range Betweenness values ranging from 123,569 to 179,444 are obtained by only 71 segments, which is 0.4% of the total segments. Nine segments have high Betweenness values (higher than 179,444 but less than 251,416). The average Betweenness value in West Island is 13,480 (smaller than 73,683), and the median is 3,649, indicating very low levels of Betweenness at a 1,600m radius.

FIG. 11.4
Straightness

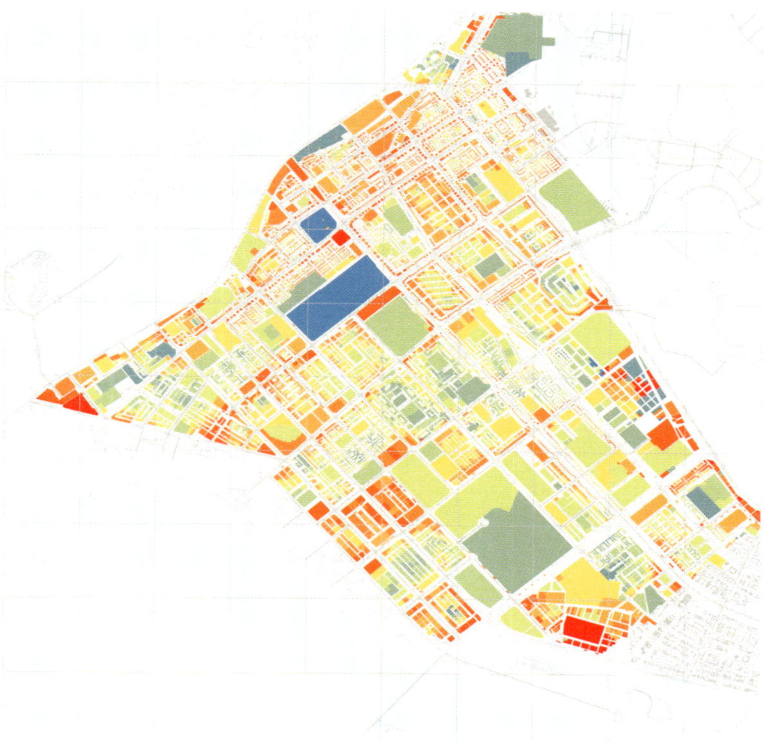

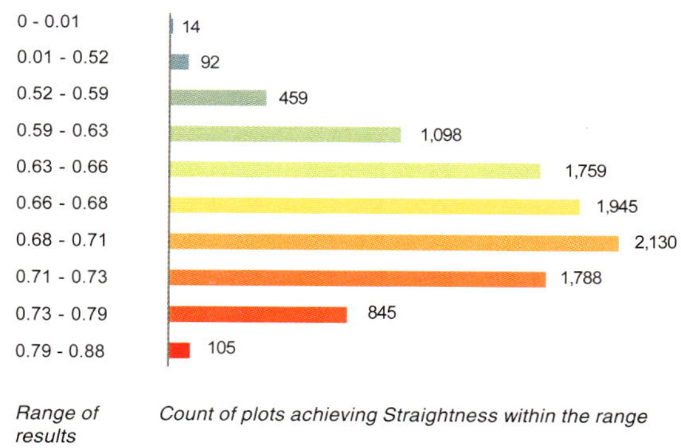

The warmer colors (greenish-yellow to red) represent Straightness values greater than 0.62, while the cooler colors (light green to dark blue) correspond to Straightness values lower than 0.63. The majority of plots, corresponding to 57% (or 5,834 out of 10,235 plots), have Straightness values ranging from 0.63 to 0.71. Among the categories shown in the legend, 2,130 plots have values in the range of 0.68 to 0.71, making this the most common range; this range is represented by orange on the map. At a 1,600 m radius, the average Straightness value of plots in West Island is 0.68, which means that their paths to other plots are 68% as straight as a straight line.

Centrality Analysis: Neighborhood Scale

Scenario 2: Streets + Alleys — 400 m Radius

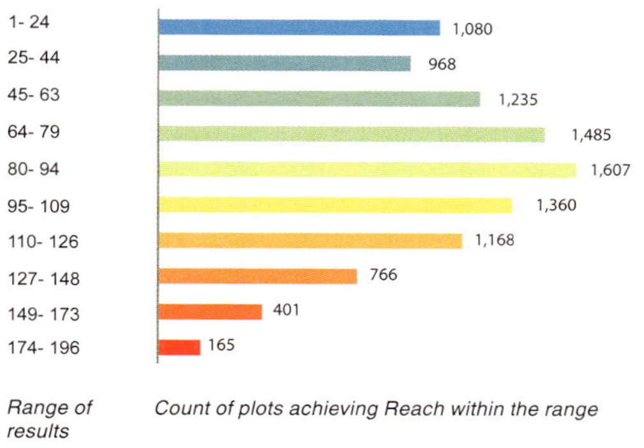

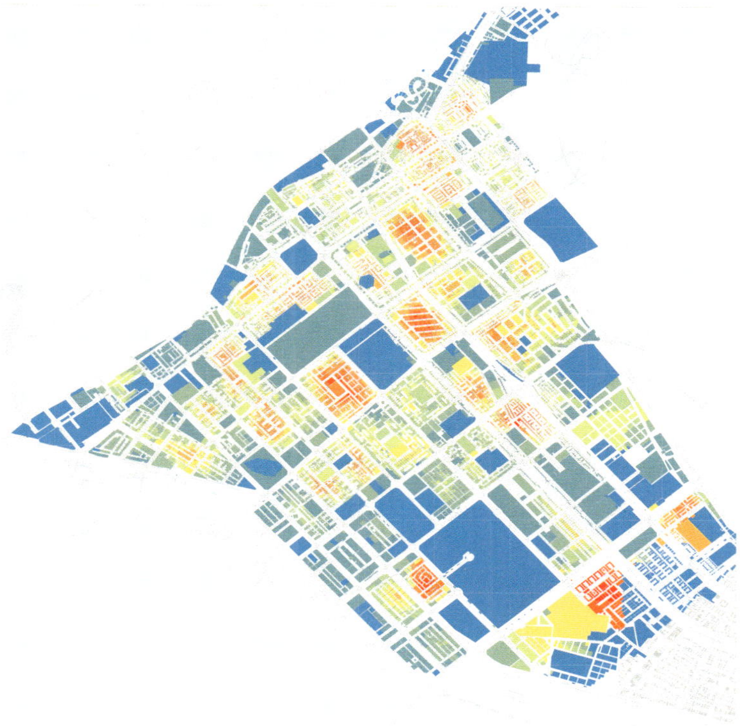

FIG. 12.1
Reach

The warmer colors (i.e., greenish-yellow to red) represent a Reach value of 80 or more, while the cooler colors (i.e., light green to dark blue) correspond to a Reach value of 79 or less. The majority of plots (i.e., 6,375 out of 10,235), corresponding to 62%, have Reach values of less than 95. Among the categories shown in the legend, 16% of the total plots can reach 80 to 94 other plots within 5 minutes of walking. On average, each plot in West Island AD can access at least 86 plots within a distance of 400 m.

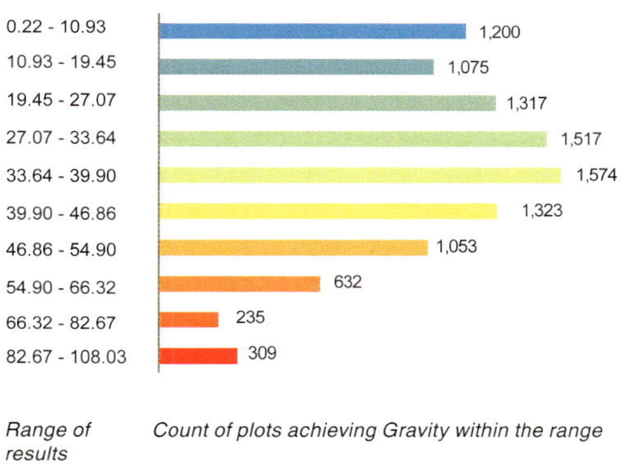

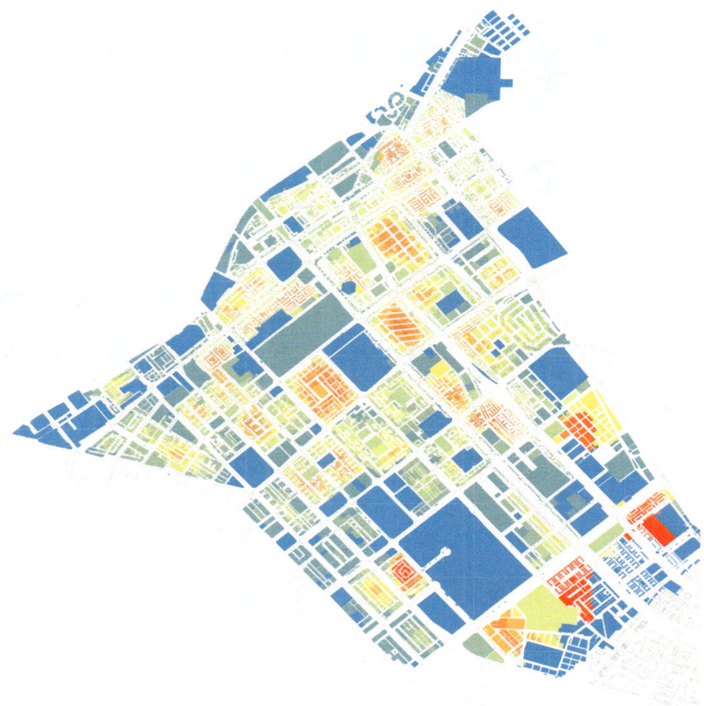

FIG. 12.2
Gravity

The warmer colors (i.e., greenish-yellow to red) represent Gravity values of more than 33.63, while the cooler colors (i.e., light green to dark blue) correspond to a Gravity value of 33.63 or less. Sixty-five percent of all plots (i.e., 6,683 out of 10,235) have Gravity values of less than 39.90. Among the categories shown in the legend, 1,574 plots, or 15% of the total plots, can reach 33.64 to 39.90 plots, making this the most common range; this range is represented by greenish-yellow on the map. On average, at a 400 m radius, each plot can reach 36 other plots when spatial impedance or distance decay effect is taken into consideration.

Scenario 2: Streets + Alleys — 400 m Radius

FIG. 12.3
Betweenness

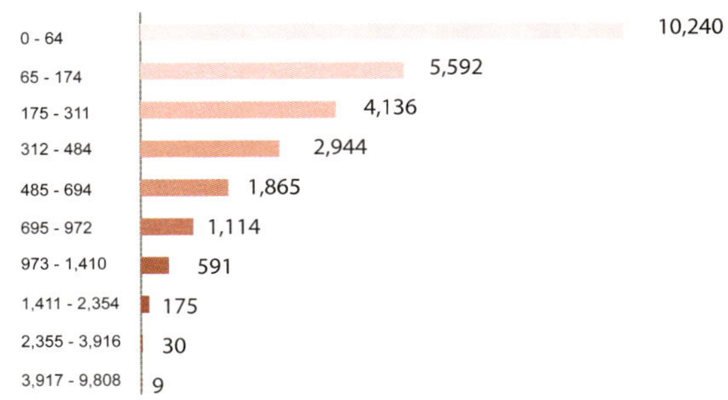

The majority of segments, corresponding to 96% (i.e., 25,555 out of 26,696 segments), have low Betweenness values, ranging from 0 to 864. Among the categories shown in the legend, 10,240 segments have values in the range of 0 to 65, making this the most common range; this range is represented by the lightest brown on the map. Mid-range Betweenness values between 865 and 6,702 are obtained by 1,140 segments, which is 4% of the total segments. The average Betweenness value in West Island is 226 (smaller than 865), and the median is 120, indicating low levels of Betweenness at a 400 m radius.

FIG. 12.4
Straightness

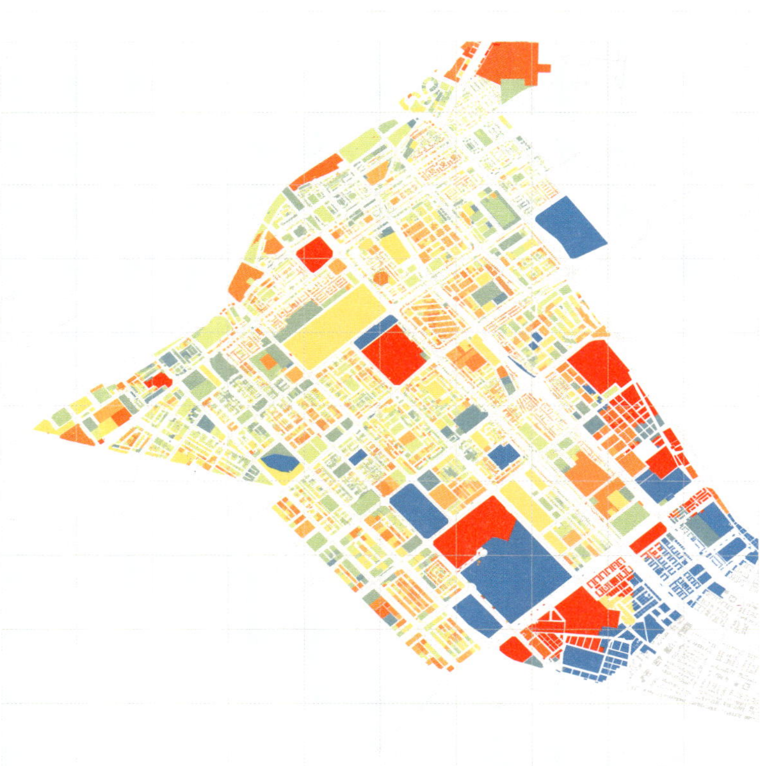

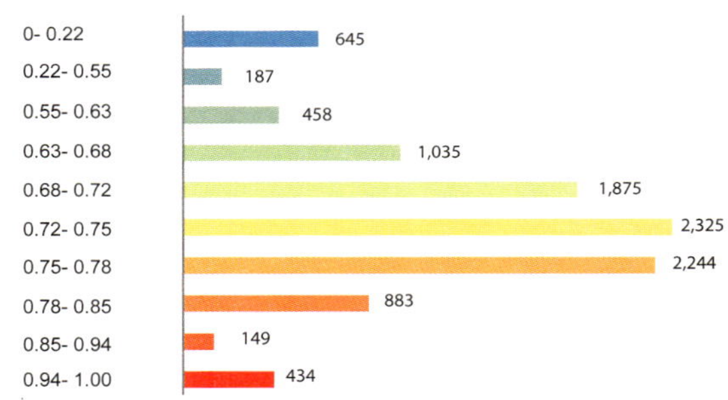

The warmer colors (greenish-yellow to red) represent Straightness values higher than 0.67, while the cooler colors (light green to dark blue) correspond to Straightness values lower than 0.68. The majority of plots, corresponding to 73% (or 7,479 out of 10,235 plots), have Straightness values ranging from 0.64 to 0.78. Among the categories shown in the legend, 2,325 plots have values in the range of 0.72 to 0.75, making this the most common range; this range is represented by yellow on the map. The average Straightness value of plots in West Island is 0.69 at a 400 m radius, which means that their paths to other plots are 69% as straight as a straight line.

Scenario 2: Streets + Alleys — 800 m Radius

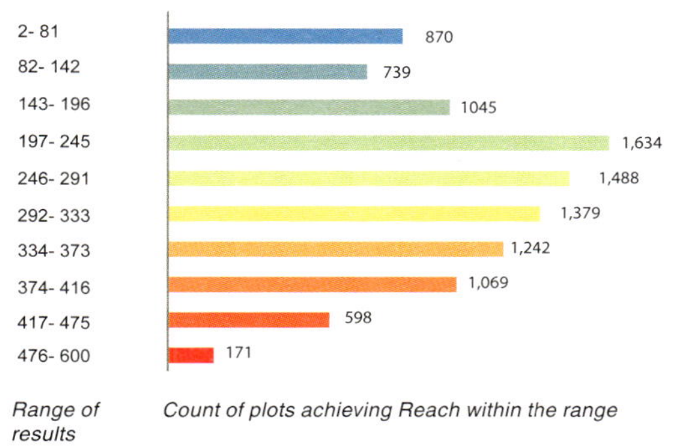

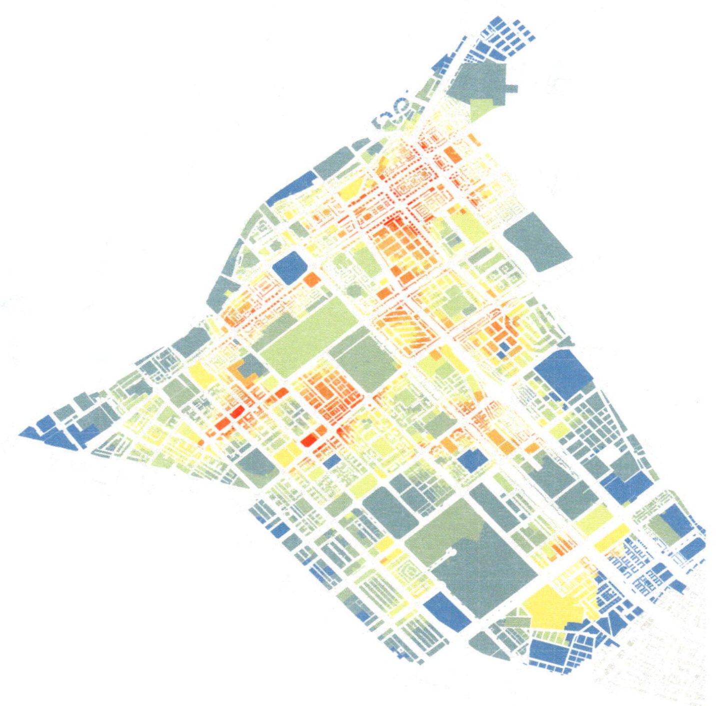

FIG. 13.1
Reach

The warmer colors (i.e., greenish-yellow to red) represent a Reach value of 246 or more, while the cooler colors (i.e., light green to dark blue) correspond to a Reach value of 245 or less. The majority of plots (i.e., 5,776 out of 10,235), corresponding to 56% of all plots, have Reach values of less than 292. Among the categories shown in the legend, 16% of plots can reach 197 to 245 other plots within 10 minutes of walking. On average, each plot in West Island AD can access at least 279 plots within a distance of 800 m.

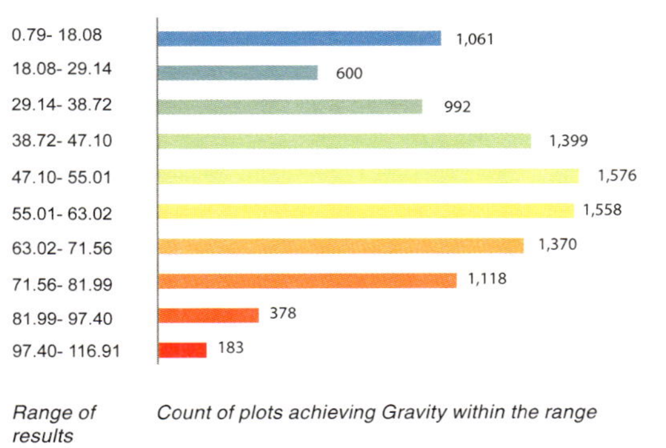

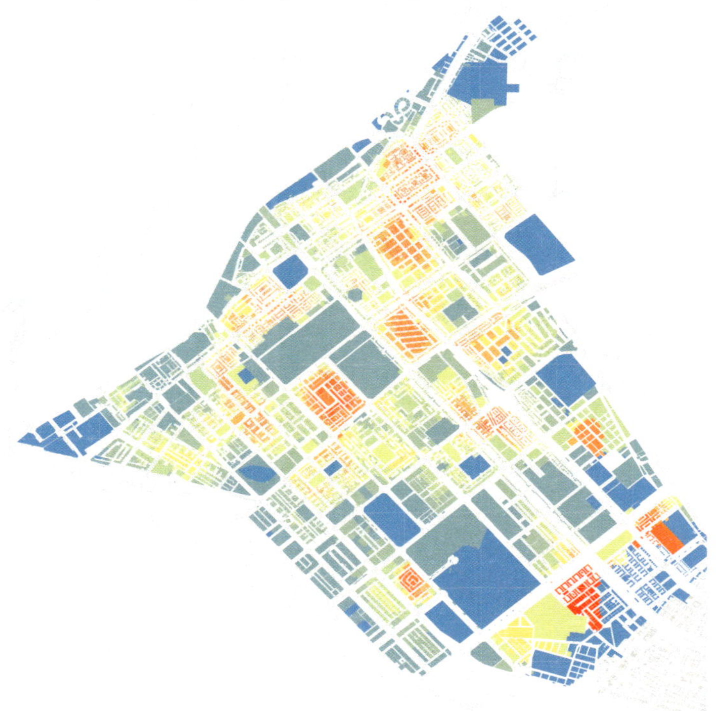

FIG. 13.2
Gravity

The warmer colors (i.e., greenish-yellow to red) represent Gravity values of more than 47.09, while the cooler colors (i.e., light green to dark blue) correspond to Gravity values of less than 47.10. Fifty-five percent of all plots (i.e., 5,628 out of 10,235) have Gravity values lower than 55.01. Among the categories shown in the legend, 1,576 plots, or 15% of all plots, can reach 47.10–55.01 plots, making this the most common range; this range is represented by greenish-yellow on the map. On average, at an 800 m radius, each plot can reach 54 other plots when spatial impedance and distance decay are taken into consideration.

Scenario 2: Streets + Alleys — 800 m Radius

FIG. 13.3
Betweenness

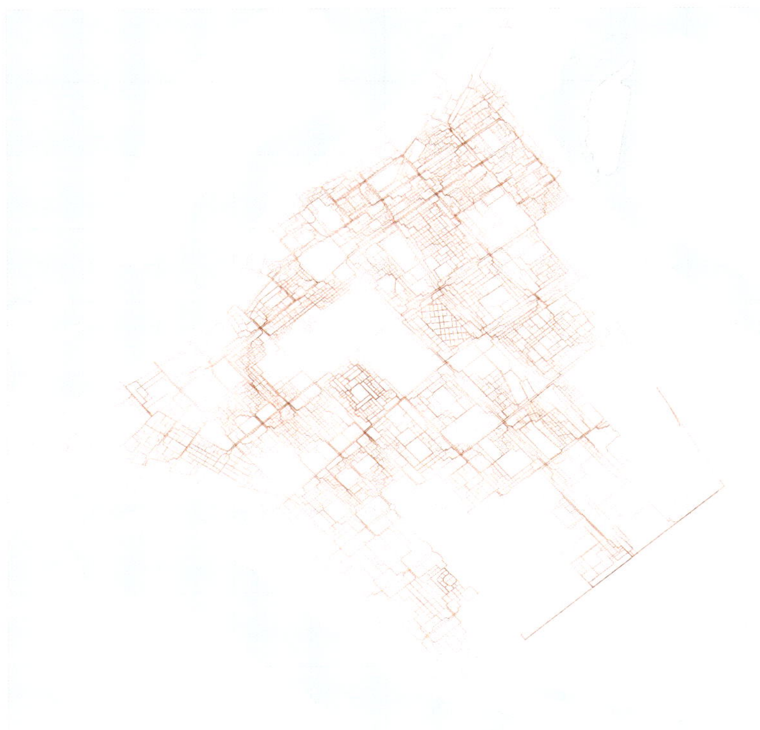

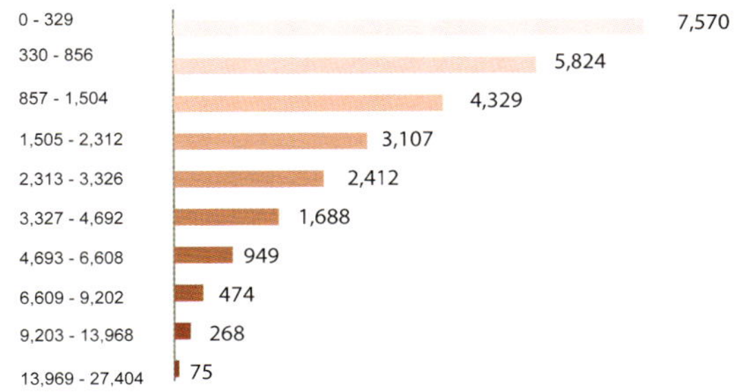

Range of results *Count of plots achieving Betweenness within the range*

The majority of segments, corresponding to 81% (i.e., 21,523 out of 26,696 segments), have very low Betweenness values in the 0–2,539 range. Among the categories shown in the legend, 7,570 have values in the range of 0 to 330, making this the most common range; this range is represented by the lightest brown on the map. Low Betweenness values ranging from 2,540 to 11,432 are obtained by 5,021 segments, which is 19% of all segments. Mid-range Betweenness values ranging from 11,518 to 20,478 are obtained by 146 segments, which is only 0.6% of the total segments. Only six segments have high Betweenness values in the range of 20,479 to 59,383 corresponding to only 0.02% of total segments. The average Betweenness value in West Island is 1,543 (smaller than 2,540), while the median is 850, indicating very low Betweenness at an 800 m radius.

FIG. 13.4
Straightness

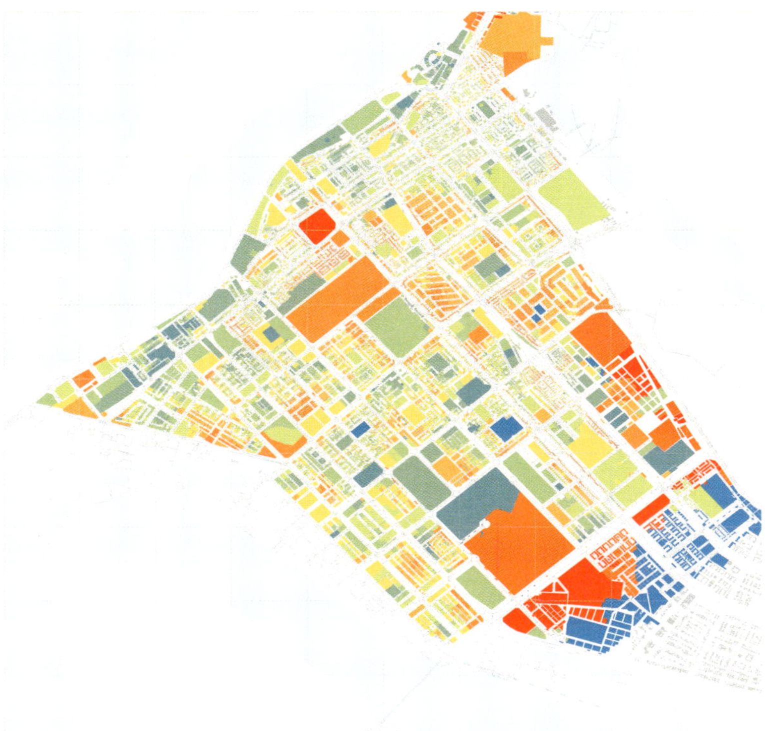

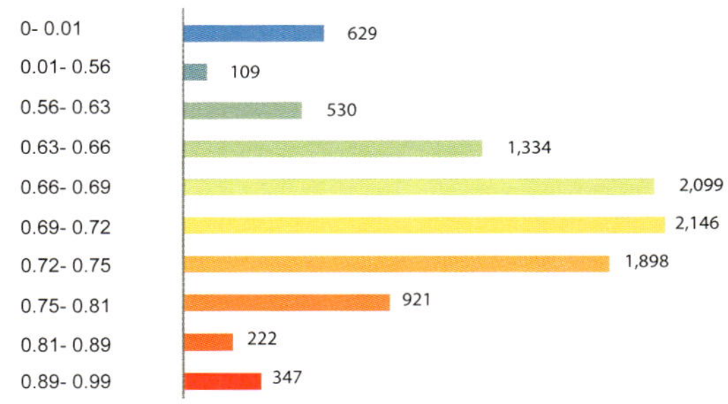

Range of results *Count of plots achieving Straightness within the range*

The warmer colors (greenish-yellow to red) represent Straightness values higher than 0.65, while the cooler colors (light green to dark blue) correspond to Straightness values lower than 0.66. The majority of plots, corresponding to 55% (or 5,579 out of 10,235 plots), have Straightness values ranging from 0.63 to 0.73. Among the categories shown in the legend, 2,146 plots have values in the range of 0.69 to 0.72, making this the most common range; this range is represented by yellow on the map. The average Straightness value of plots in West Island is 0.67 at an 800 m radius, which means that their paths to other plots are 67% as straight as a straight line.

Scenario 2: Streets + Alleys — 1,600 m Radius

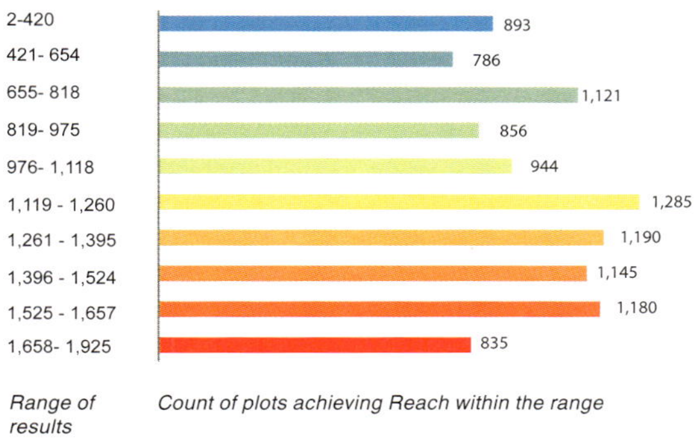

The warmer colors (i.e., greenish-yellow to red) represent a Reach value of 976 or more, while the cooler colors (i.e., light green to dark blue) correspond to a Reach value of 975 or less. The majority of plots (i.e., 5,635 out of 10,235), corresponding to 55% of all plots, have Reach values of more than 1,118. Among the categories shown in the legend, 13% of plots can reach 1,119–1,260 other plots within 20 minutes of walking. On average, each plot in West Island AD can access at least 1,167 plots within a distance of 1,600 m.

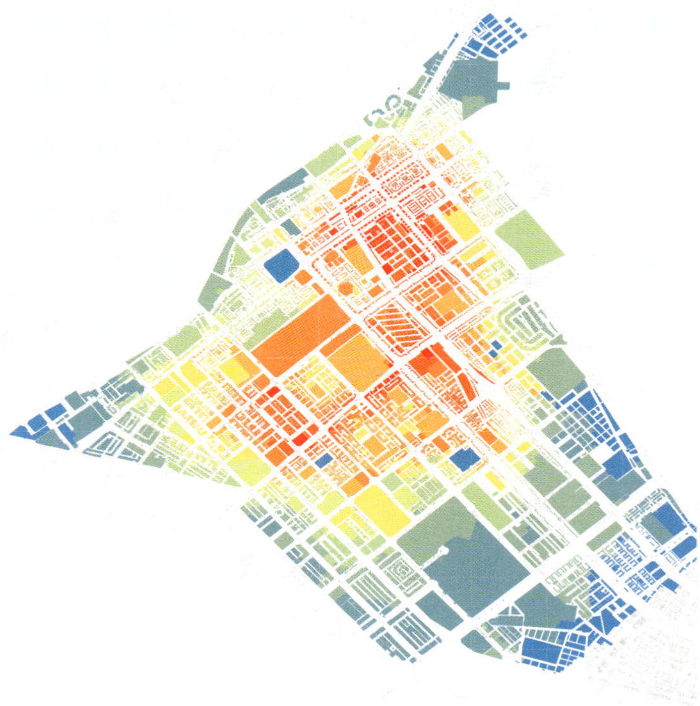

FIG. 14.1
Reach

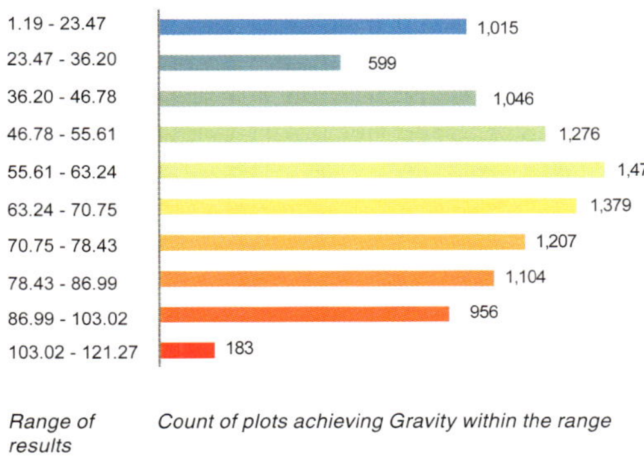

The warmer colors (i.e., greenish-yellow to red) represent Gravity values of more than 55.60, while the cooler colors (i.e., light green to dark blue) correspond to Gravity values of less than 55.61. Sixty-six percent of all plots (i.e., 6,785 out of 10,235) have Gravity values of less than 70.75. Among the categories shown in the legend, 1,470 plots, or 14% of all plots, can reach 55.61–63.24 other plots, making this the most common range; this range; this range is represented by greenish-yellow on the map. On average, at a 1,600 m radius, each plot can reach 63 other plots when spatial impedance or distance decay effect is taken into consideration.

FIG. 14.2
Gravity

Scenario 2: Streets + Alleys — 1,600 m Radius

FIG. 14.3
Betweenness

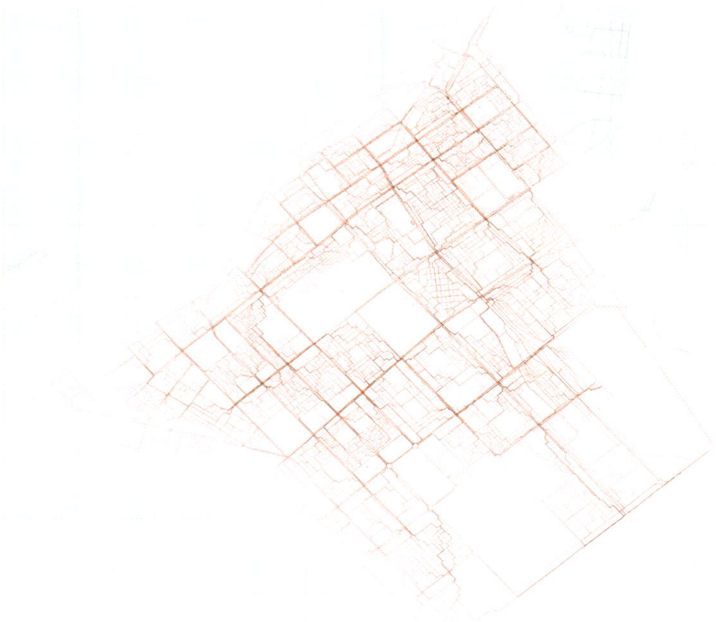

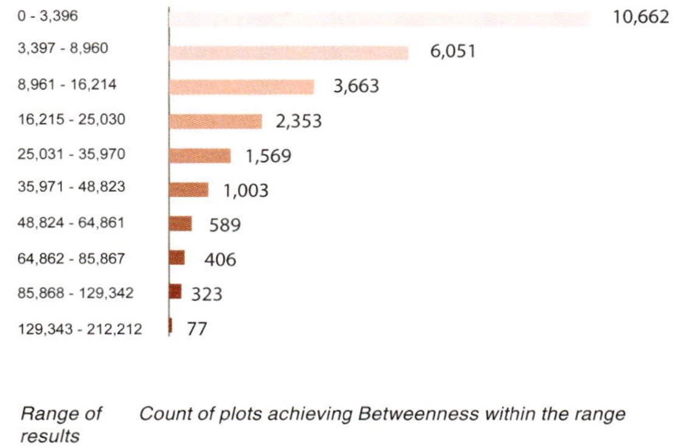

The majority of segments, corresponding to 98% (i.e., 26,100 out of 26,696 segments), have very low Betweenness values in the 0–73,682 range. Among the categories shown in the legend, 10,662 segments have values in the range of 0 to 3,397, making this the most common range; this range is represented by the lightest brown on the map. Low Betweenness values ranging from 73,683 to 123,568 are obtained by 506 segments, which is 2% of all segments. Mid-range Betweenness values ranging from 123,569 to 179,444 are obtained by only 74 segments, which is 0.3% of the total segments. Sixteen segments have high Betweenness values (higher than 179,444). The average Betweenness value in West Island is 12,594 (smaller than 73,683), and the median is 5,206, indicating very low levels of Betweenness at a 1,600 m radius.

FIG. 14.4
Straightness

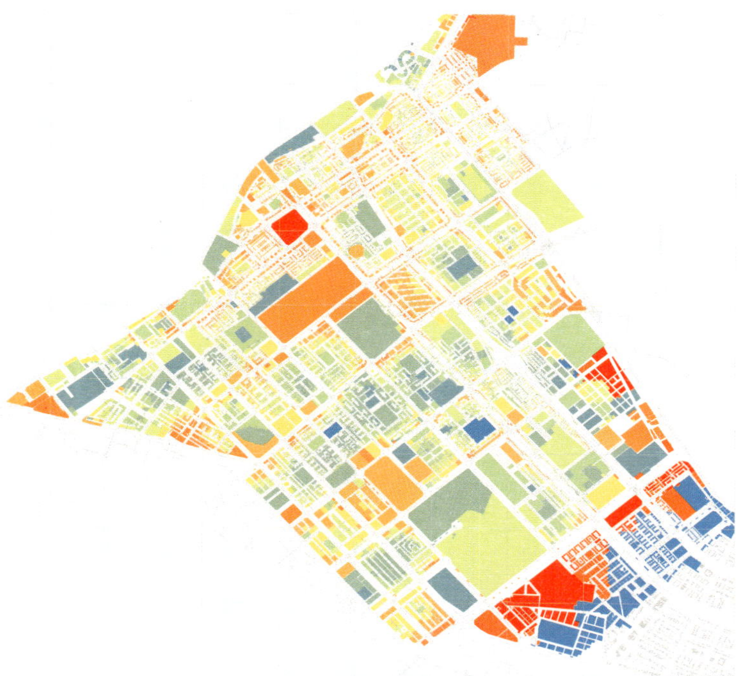

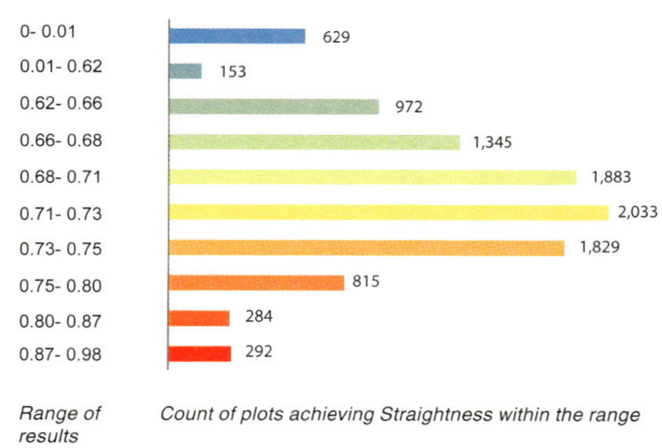

The warmer colors (greenish-yellow to red) represent Straightness values greater than 0.67, while the cooler colors (light green to dark blue) correspond to Straightness values lower than 0.68. The majority of plots, corresponding to 56% (or 5,745 out of 10,235 plots), have Straightness values ranging from 0.69 to 0.76. Among the categories shown in the legend, 2,033 plots have values in the range of 0.71 to 0.73, making this the most common range; this range is represented by yellow on the map. The average Straightness value of plots in West Island is 0.67 at a 1,600 m radius, which means that their paths to other plots are 67% as straight as a straight line.

Centrality Analysis

Sample Scale — Sample 01

FIG. 15.1

Reach

Scenario 1: Streets only

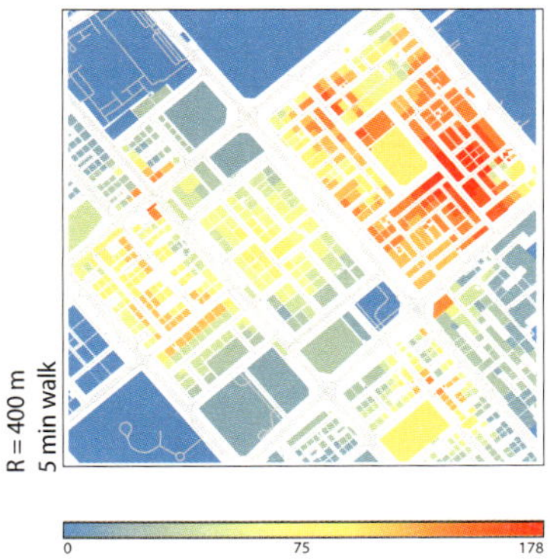

Reach (Radius = 400 m)

The maximum number of plots that can be reached within 5 min walking distance is 178 plots. The average Reach of the sample is 75 plots.

Summary of Reach results
Minimum: 0
Maximum: 178
Mean: 75
Median: 76

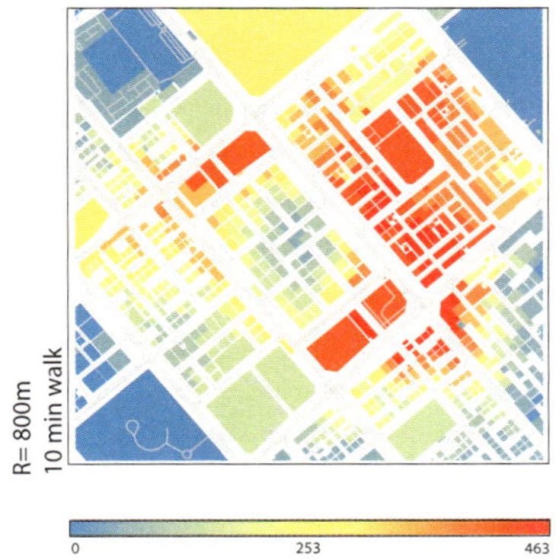

Reach (Radius = 800 m)

The maximum number of plots that can be reached within 10 min walking distance is 463 plots. The average Reach of the sample is 253 plots.

Summary of Reach results
Minimum: 0
Maximum: 463
Mean: 253
Median: 256

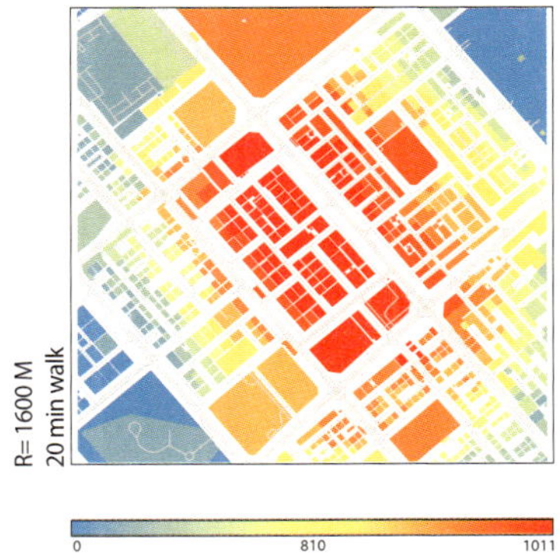

Reach (Radius = 1600 m)

The maximum number of plots that can be reached within 20 min walking distance is 1,011 plots. The average Reach of the sample is 810 plots.

Summary of Reach results
Minimum: 0
Maximum: 1 ,011
Mean: 810
Median: 821

FIG. 15.2

Reach

Scenario 2: Streets + Alleys

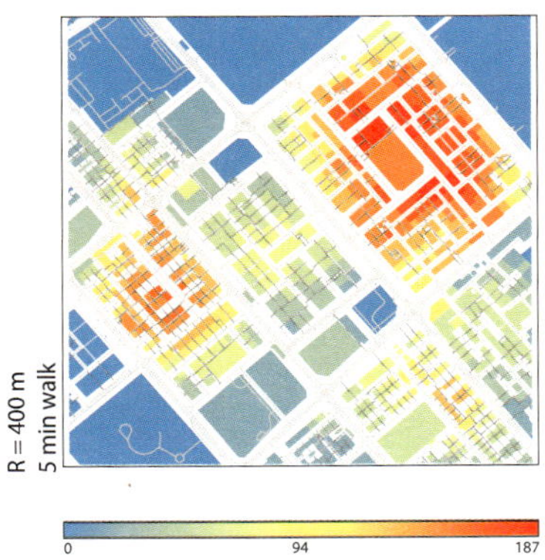

Reach (Radius = 400 m)

The maximum number of plots that can be reached within 5 min walking distance is 187 plots. The average Reach of the sample is 94 plots.

Summary of Reach results
Minimum: 0
Maximum: 187
Mean: 94
Median: 94

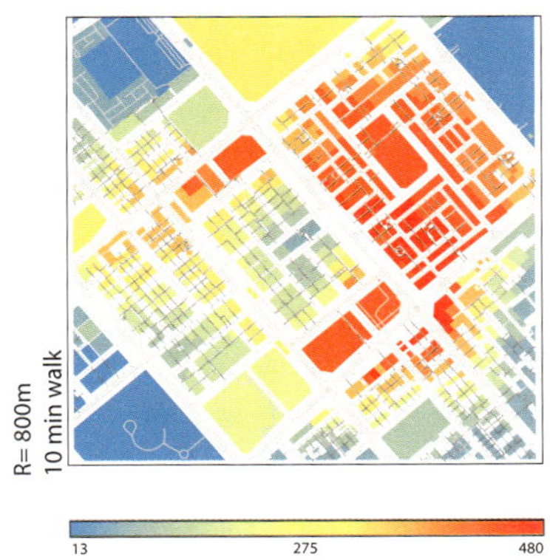

Reach (Radius = 800 m)

The maximum number of plots that can be reached within 10 min walking distance is 480 plots. The average Reach of the sample is 275 plots.

Summary of Reach results
Minimum: 13
Maximum: 480
Mean: 275
Median: 280

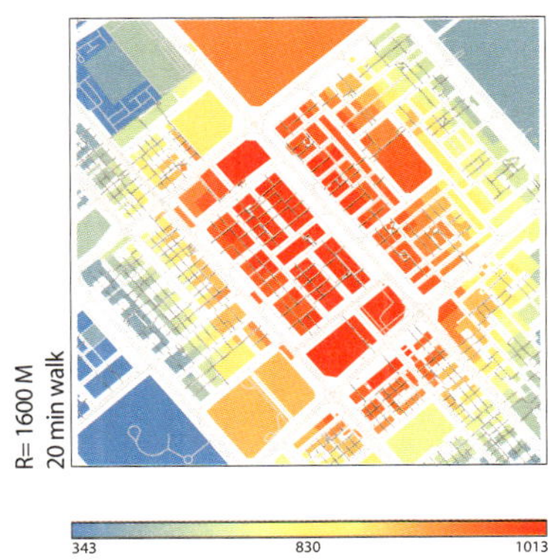

Reach (Radius = 1600 m)

The maximum number of plots that can be reached within 20 min walking distance is 1013 plots. The average Reach of the sample is 830 plots.

Summary of Reach results
Minimum: 343
Maximum: 1013
Mean: 830
Median: 840

At a 400 m radius, the plots with high Reach values ranging from 108 to 178 concentrate in one corner of the NPU—an area with an interlocking street pattern. At an 800 m radius, plots with high Reach values also appear on the other side of the NPU. For example, Reach values vary from 253 to 463 in plots adjacent to the arterial street. At a 1,600 m radius, all plots within the centrally located NPU have high Reach values. With the introduction of alleys, at a 400 m radius, the concentration of high Reach values becomes stronger and clearer around the central area of the same NPUs that have interlocking street patterns. At an 800 m radius, most plots with high Reach values are seen around the central area with values ranging from 275 to 480. As in the scenario without alleys, at a 1,600 m radius, plots with high Reach values are seen in the NPU with fragmented patterns with values ranging from 830 to 1013.

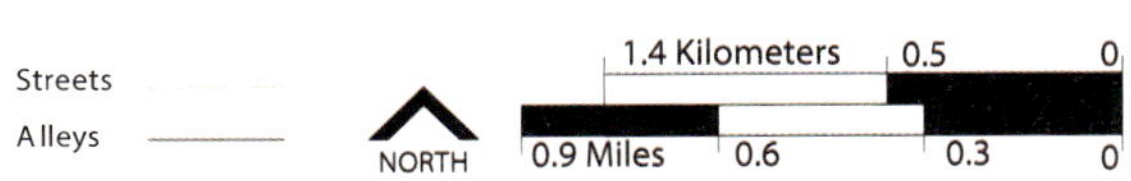

Sample Scale — Sample 01

FIG. 15.3
Gravity
Scenario 1: Streets only

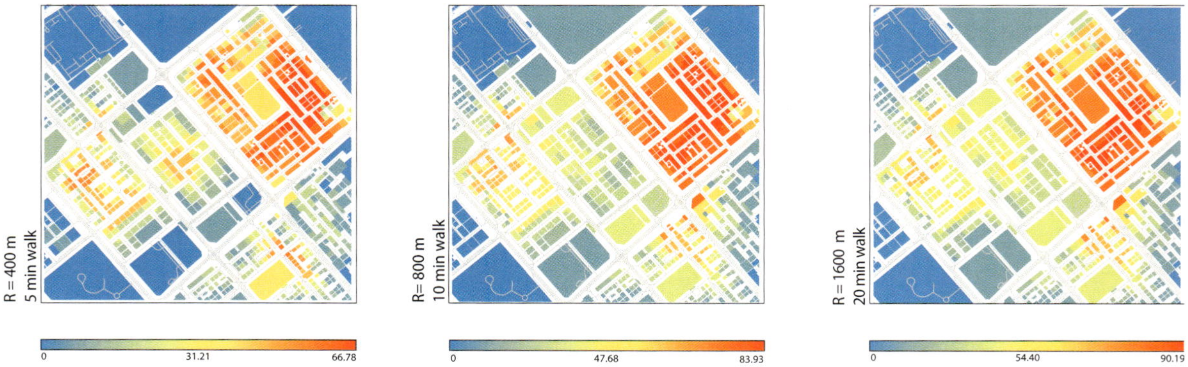

Gravity (Radius = 400 m)
The maximum number of plots that can be reached within 5 min walking distance with the distance decay effect is 66.78 66.78 plots. The average Gravity of the sample is 31.21 plots.

Summary of Gravity results
Minimum: 0
Maximum: 66.8
Mean: 31.21
Median: 30.44

Gravity (Radius = 800 m)
The maximum number of plots that can be reached within 10 min walking distance with the distance decay effect is 83.93 plots. The average Gravity of the sample is 47.68 plots.

Summary of Gravity results
Minimum: 0
Maximum: 83.93
Mean: 47.68
Median: 47.12

Gravity (Radius = 1600 m)
The maximum number of plots that can be reached within 20 min walking distance with the distance decay effect is 90.19 plots. The average Gravity of the sample is 54.40 plots.

Summary of Gravity results
Minimum: 0
Maximum: 90.19
Mean: 54.40
Median: 53.53

FIG. 15.4
Gravity
Scenario 2: Streets + Alleys

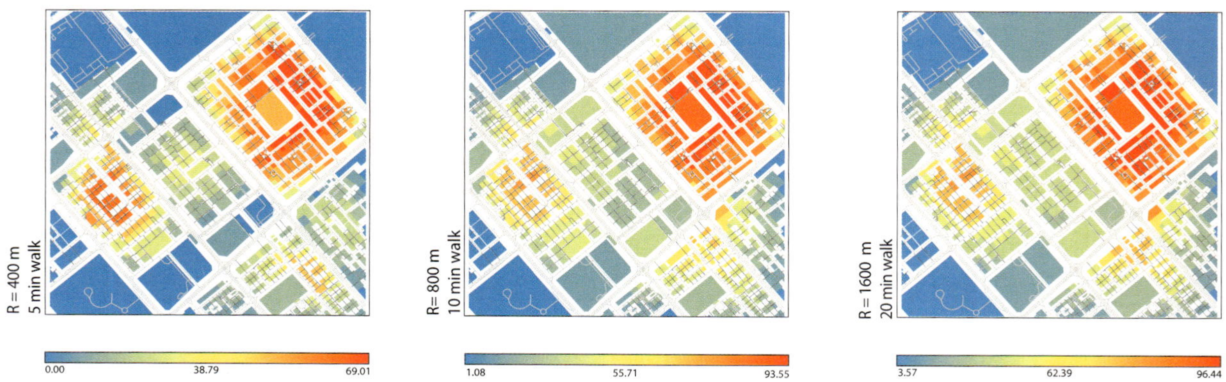

Gravity (Radius = 400 m)
The maximum number of plots that can be reached within 5 min walking distance with the distance decay effect is 69.01 plots. The average Gravity of the sample is 38.79 plots.

Summary of Gravity results
Minimum: 0.00
Maximum: 69.01
Mean: 38.79
Median: 38.53

Gravity (Radius = 800 m)
The maximum number of plots that can be reached within 10 min walking distance with the distance decay effect is 93.55 plots. The average Gravity of the sample is 55.71 plots.

Summary of Gravity results
Minimum: 1.08
Maximum: 93.55
Mean: 55.71
Median: 55.22

Gravity (Radius = 1600 m)
The maximum number of plots that can be reached within 20 min walking distance with the distance decay effect is 96.44 plots. The average Gravity of the sample is 62.39 plots.

Summary of Gravity results
Minimum: 3.57
Maximum: 96.44
Mean: 62.39
Median: 61.92

At a 400 m radius, the NPU with the interlocking pattern consists of plots with high Gravity values ranging from 31.21 to 66.78. At 800 m and 1,600 m radii, high Gravity values are found within the biggest NPU, where the values range from 47.68 to 90.19. When alley networks are included in the analysis, the clustering of plots with high Gravity values becomes clearer. At a 400 m radius, the concentration of high Gravity values becomes stronger and clearer around the areas where the interlocking street pattern is present. The distribution of Gravity values does not change notably across the three different radii; however, with the inclusion of alleys, the values slightly improve at all radii.

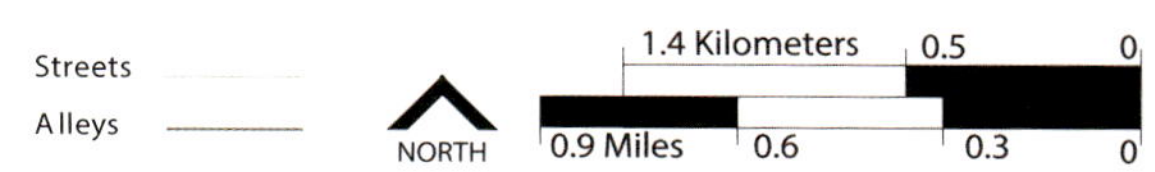

FIG. 15.5

Straightness

Scenario 1: Streets only

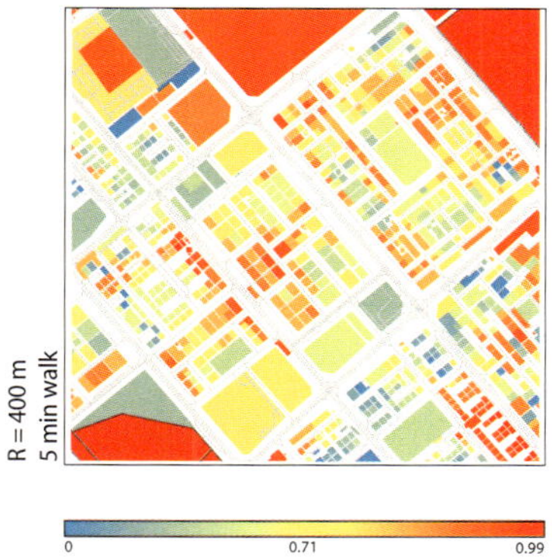

Straightness (Normalized Values, Radius= 400 m)
Plots withing 5 min walking distance have access to streets with an average Straightness value of 0.71.

Summary of Straightness results
Minimum: 0
Maximum: 0.99
Mean: 0.71
Median: 0.71

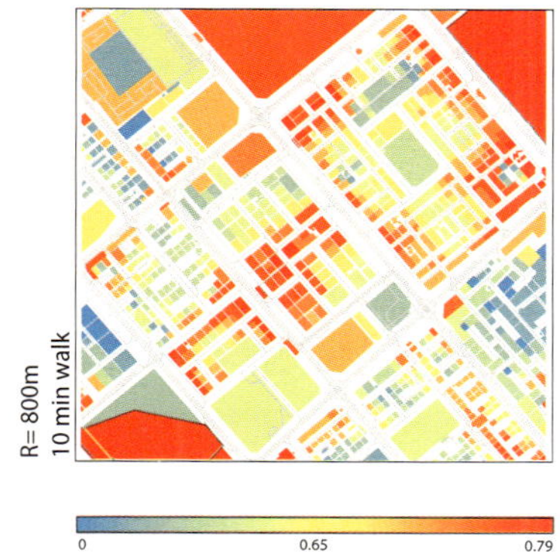

Straightness (Normalized Values, Radius= 800 m)
Plots withing 10 min walking distance have access to streets with an average Straightness value of 0.65.

Summary of Straightness results
Minimum: 0
Maximum: 0.79
Mean: 0.65
Median: 0.65

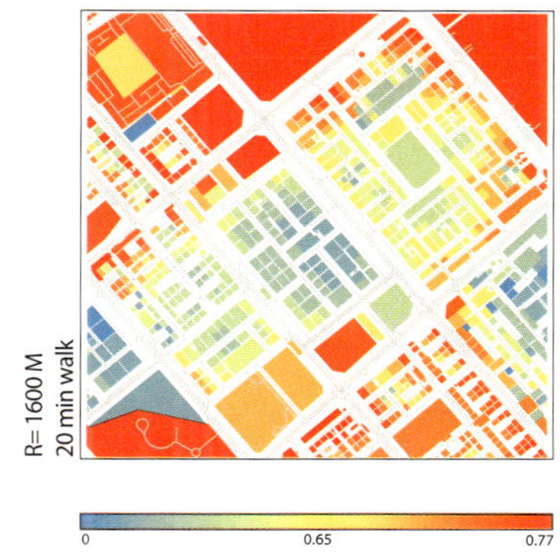

Straightness (Normalized Values, Radius= 1600 m)
Plots withing 20 min walking distance have access to streets with an average Straightness value of 0.65.

Summary of Straightness results
Minimum: 0
Maximum: 0.77
Mean: 0.65
Median: 0.65

FIG. 15.6

Straightness

Scenario 2: Streets + Alleys

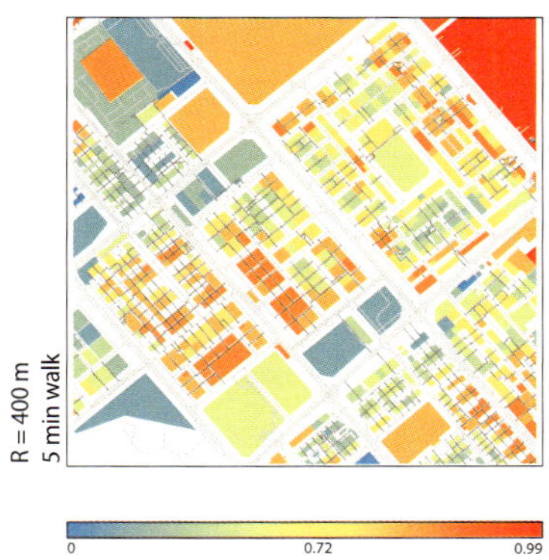

Straightness (Normalized Values, Radius= 400 m)
Plots withing 5 min walking distance have access to streets with an average Straightness value of 0.72.

Summary of Straightness results
Minimum: 0.47
Maximum: 0.99
Mean: 0.72
Median: 0.72

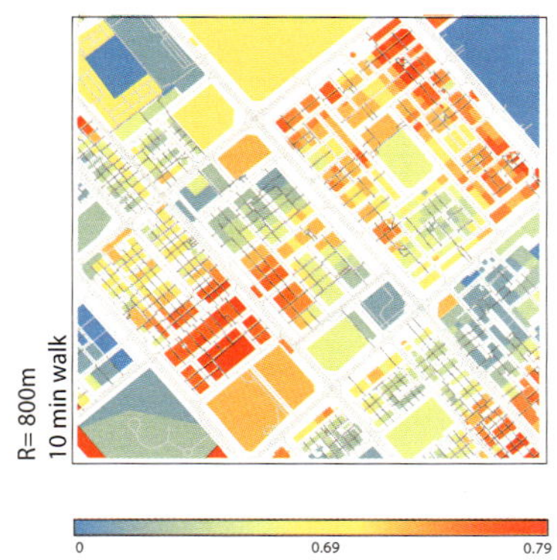

Straightness (Normalized Values, Radius= 800 m)
Plots withing 10 min walking distance have access to streets with an average Straightness value of 0.69.

Summary of Straightness results
Minimum: 0
Maximum: 0.79
Mean: 0.69
Median: 0.70

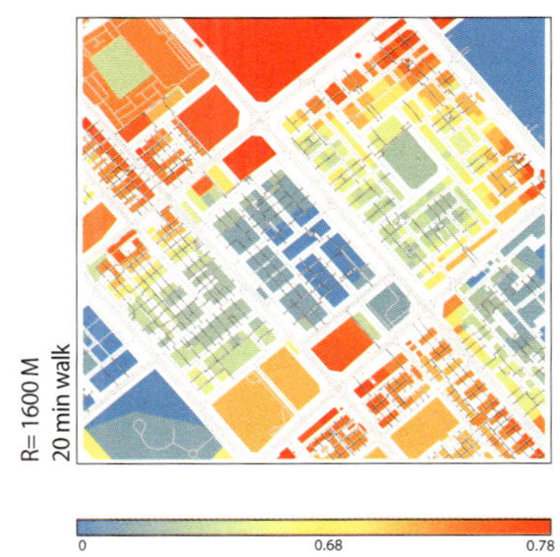

Straightness (Normalized Values, Radius= 1600 m)
Plots withing 20 min walking distance have access to streets with an average Straightness value of 0.68.

Summary of Straightness results
Minimum: 0
Maximum: 0.78
Mean: 0.68
Median: 0.68

At a 400 m radius, high Straightness values (0.75–1) are evenly distributed throughout all NPUs. At 800 m, high Straightness values become concentrated in the central NPUs. At a 1,600 m radius, high values shift from central NPUs to bigger plots on superblocks' corners and NPUs that lie near the edges of the sample. This is due to the presence of arterial streets that yield high Straightness values ranging from 0.75 to 0.77. With the introduction of alleys, at 400 m, the NPU with the interlocking street pattern contains the majority of plots with high Straightness values (ranging from 0.75 to 0.99). At 800 m, values become even higher within the central NPUs, but are also high along the edge of the biggest NPU. At a 1,600 m radius, plots with high Straightness values concentrate near the edges of the sample. The Straightness values slightly improve at all radii when alleys are taken into consideration.

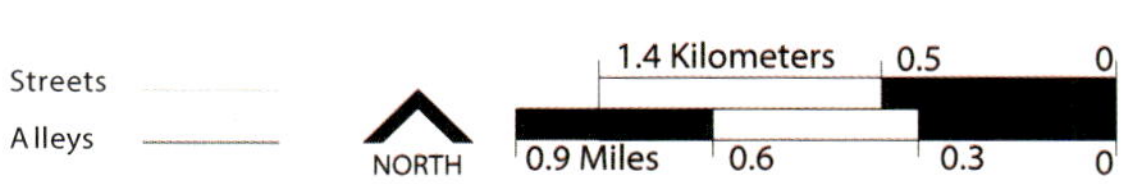

Sample Scale — Sample 02

FIG. 16.1

Reach

Scenario 1: Streets only

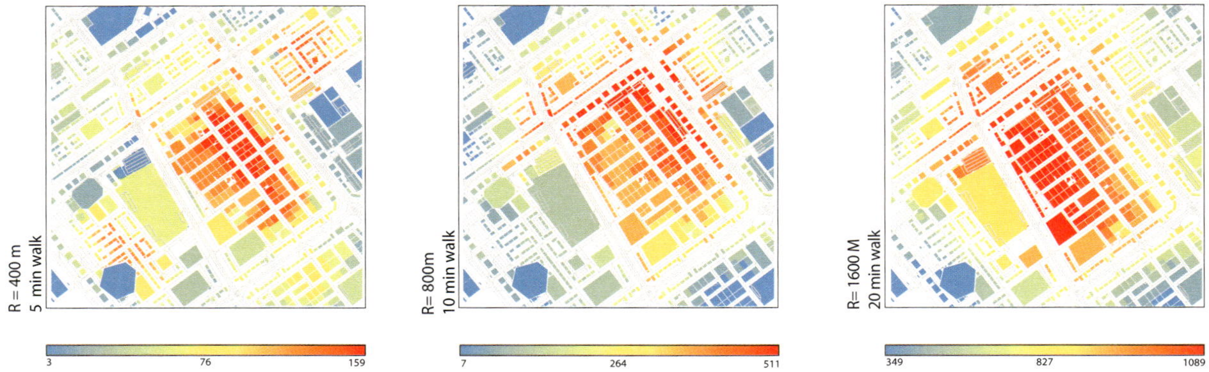

Reach (Radius = 400 m)

The maximum number of plots that can be reached within 5 min walking distance is 159 plots. The average Reach of the sample is 76 plots.

Summary of Reach results
Minimum: 3
Maximum: 159
Mean: 76
Median: 76

Reach (Radius = 800 m)

The maximum number of plots that can be reached within 10 min walking distance is 511 plots. The average Reach of the sample is 264 plots.

Summary of Reach results
Minimum: 7
Maximum: 511
Mean: 264
Median: 261

Reach (Radius = 1600 m)

The maximum number of plots that can be reached within 20 min walking distance is 1,089 plots. The average Reach of the sample is 827 plots.

Summary of Reach results
Minimum: 349
Maximum: 1 ,089
Mean: 827
Median: 822

FIG. 16.2

Reach

Scenario 2: Streets + Alleys

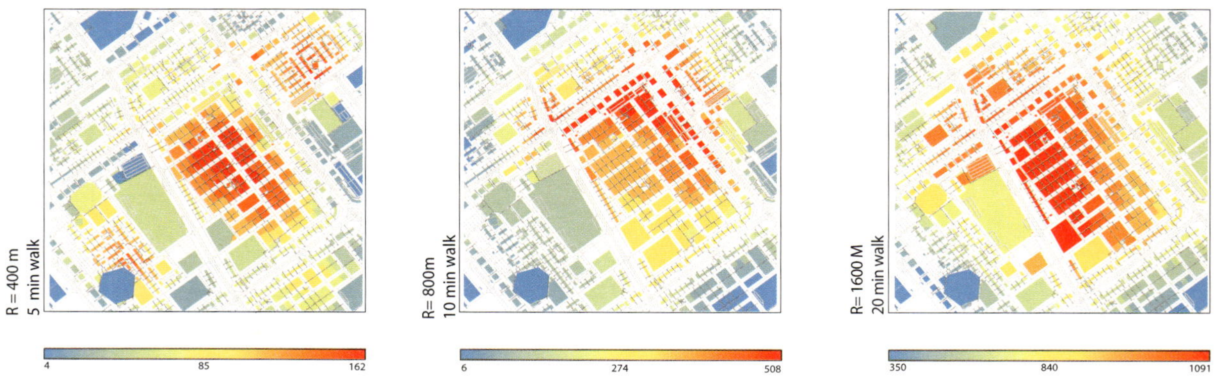

Reach (Radius = 400 m)

The maximum number of plots that can be reached within 5 min walking distance is 162 plots. The average Reach of the sample is 85 plots.

Summary of Reach results
Minimum: 4
Maximum: 162
Mean: 85
Median: 85

Reach (Radius = 800 m)

The maximum number of plots that can be reached within 10 min walking distance is 508 plots. The average Reach of the sample is 274 plots.

Summary of Reach results
Minimum: 6
Maximum: 508
Mean: 274
Median: 272

Reach (Radius = 1600 m)

The maximum number of plots that can be reached within 20 min walking distance is 1,091 plots. The average Reach of the sample is 840 plots.

Summary of Reach results
Minimum: 350
Maximum: 1 ,091
Mean: 840
Median: 837

At a 400 m radius, the plots with high Reach values ranging from 76 to 159 concentrate towards the center of the biggest NPU that has an interconnected grid pattern. At an 800 m radius, a significant number of plots with high Reach values appears on the upper edges of the biggest NPU. For example, Reach values vary from 264 to 511 in plots adjacent to the arterial street at the top. At a 1,600 m radius, high Reach values shift towards the arterial street on the left, but within the same NPU. With the introduction of alleys, at 400 m and 1,600 m, slight improvements can be seen for all plots: the highest Reach value increases from 159 to 162 and from 1089 to 1091, respectively. At an 800 m radius, by contrast, Reach values decrease for some plots, and the highest Reach value also drops from 511 to 508.

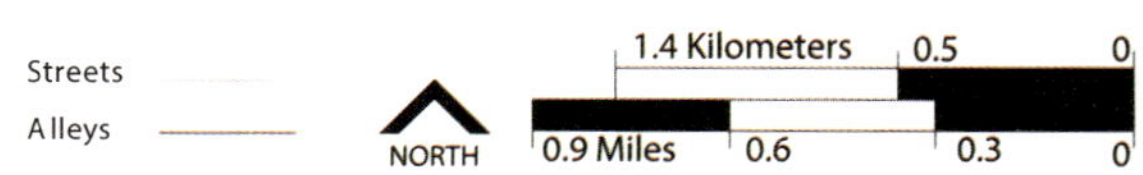

FIG. 16.3
Gravity
Scenario 1: Streets only

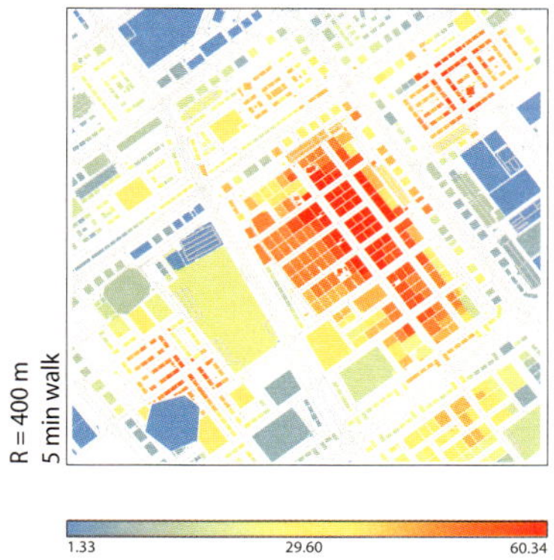

Gravity (Radius = 400 m)
The maximum number of plots that can be reached within 5 min walking distance with the distance decay effect is 60.34 plots. The average Gravity of the sample is 29.60 plots.

Summary of Reach results
Minimum: 1.34
Maximum: 60.34
Mean: 29.60
Median: 29.41

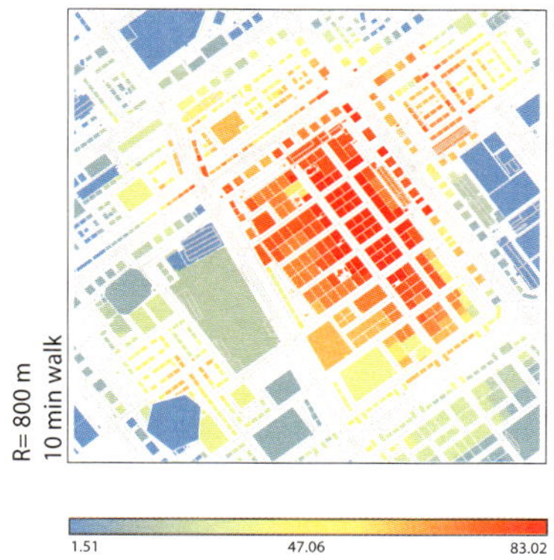

Gravity (Radius = 800 m)
The maximum number of plots that can be reached within 10 min walking distance with the distance decay effect is 83.02 plots. The average Gravity of the sample is 47.06 plots.

Summary of Reach results
Minimum: 1.51
Maximum: 83.02
Mean: 47.06
Median: 47.23

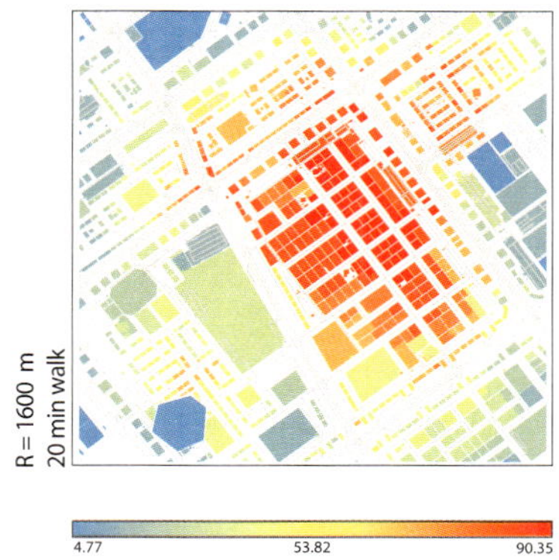

Gravity (Radius = 1600 m)
The maximum number of plots that can be reached within 20 min walking distance with the distance decay effect is 90.35 plots. The average Gravity of the sample is 53.82 plots.

Summary of Reach results
Minimum: 4.77
Maximum: 90.35
Mean: 53.82
Median: 53.47

FIG. 16.4
Gravity
Scenario 2: Streets + Alleys

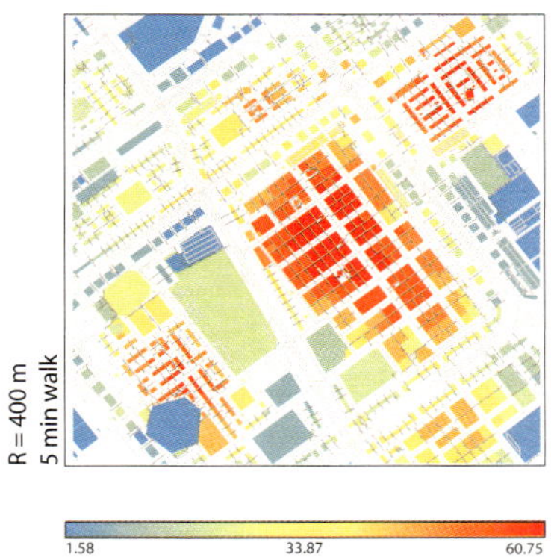

Gravity (Radius = 400 m)
The maximum number of plots that can be reached within 5 min walking distance with the distance decay effect is 60.75 plots. The average Gravity of the sample is 33.87 plots.

Summary of Gravity results
Minimum: 1.58
Maximum: 60.75
Mean: 33.87
Median: 33.62

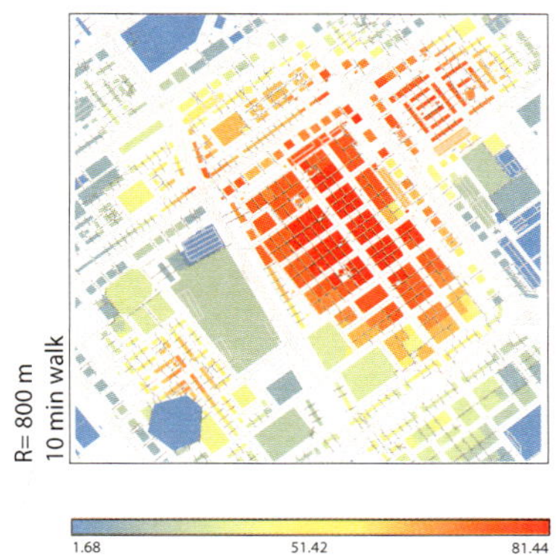

Gravity (Radius = 800 m)
The maximum number of plots that can be reached within 10 min walking distance with the distance decay effect is 81.44 plots. The average Gravity of the sample is 51.42 plots.

Summary of Gravity results
Minimum: 1.68
Maximum: 81.44
Mean: 51.42
Median: 52.23

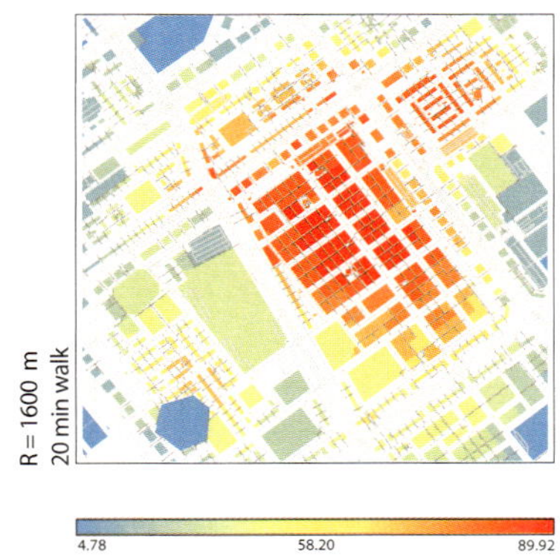

Gravity (Radius = 1600 m)
The maximum number of plots that can be reached within 20 min walking distance with the distance decay effect is 89.92 plots. The average Gravity of the sample is 58.20 plots.

Summary of Gravity results
Minimum: 4.78
Maximum: 89.92
Mean: 58.20
Median: 58.99

At a 400 m radius, the biggest NPU with a grid-like pattern consists of plots with high Gravity values ranging from 29.60 to 60.34. At 800 m and 1,600 m radii, high Gravity values are still found within the biggest NPU, where they range from 47.06 to 90.35. With the introduction of alleys, at a 400 m radius, high Gravity values become even more concentrated in the smaller NPU near the top-right corner and also cluster in the biggest NPU at the center. The clustering of plots with high Gravity values becomes clearer. The distribution of Gravity values does not change notably across the three different radii; however, with the inclusion of alleys, the values slightly improve for most plots.

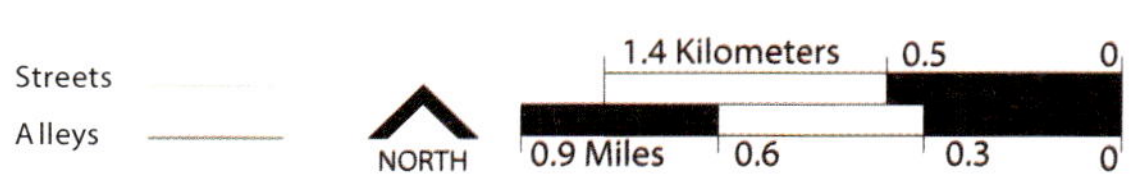

Sample Scale — Sample 02

FIG. 16.5
Straightness
Scenario 1: Streets only

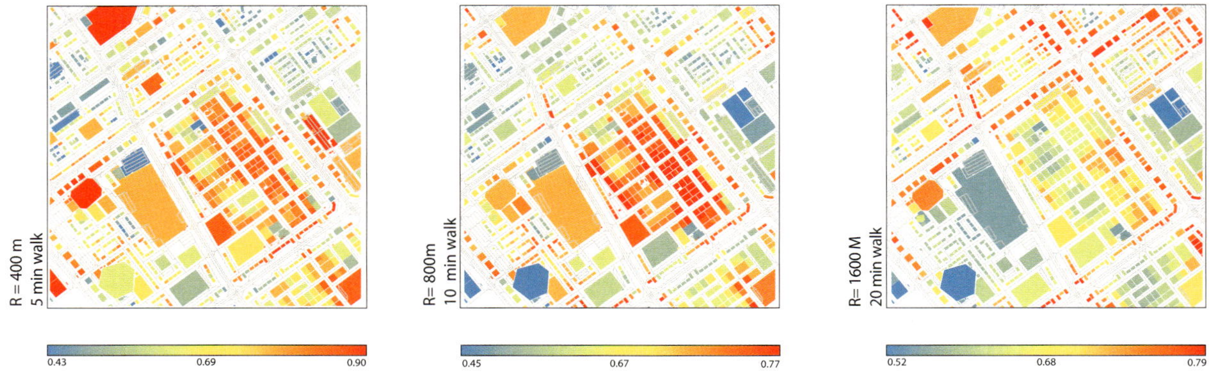

Straightness (Normalized Values, Radius= 400 m)
Plots withing 5 min walking distance have access to streets with an average Straightness value of 0.69.

Summary of Straightness results
Minimum: 0.43
Maximum: 0.90
Mean: 0.69
Median: 0.70

Straightness (Normalized Values, Radius= 800 m)
Plots withing 10 min walking distance have access to streets with an average Straightness value of 0.67.

Summary of Straightness results
Minimum: 0.45
Maximum: 0.77
Mean: 0.67
Median: 0.67

Straightness (Normalized Values, Radius= 1600 m)
Plots withing 20 min walking distance have access to streets with an average Straightness value of 0.68.

Summary of Straightness results
Minimum: 0.52
Maximum: 0.79
Mean: 0.68
Median: 0.68

FIG. 16.6
Straightness
Scenario 2: Streets + Alleys

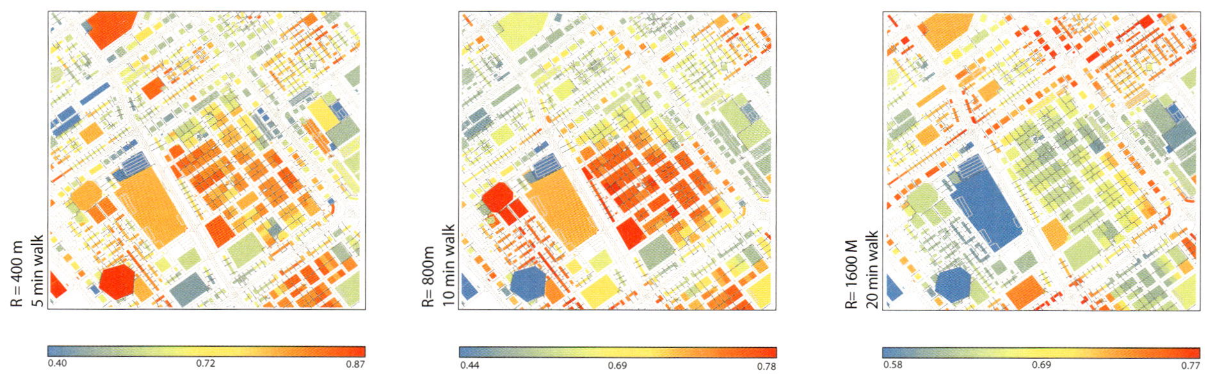

Straightness (Normalized Values, Radius= 400 m)
Plots withing 5 min walking distance have access to streets with an average Straightness value of 0.72.

Summary of Straightness results
Minimum: 0.40
Maximum: 0.87
Mean: 0.72
Median: 0.73

Straightness (Normalized Values, Radius= 800 m)
Plots withing 10 min walking distance have access to streets with an average Straightness value of 0.69.

Summary of Straightness results
Minimum: 0.44
Maximum: 0.78
Mean: 0.69
Median: 0.70

Straightness (Normalized Values, Radius= 1600 m)
Plots withing 20 min walking distance have access to streets with an average Straightness value of 0.69.

Summary of Straightness results
Minimum: 0.58
Maximum: 0.77
Mean: 0.69
Median: 0.69

At a 400 m radius, high Straightness values ranging from 0.75 to 0.90 cluster in the grid-shaped blocks within the centrally located NPU, and also appear in few big plots adjacent to arterial streets. At 800 m, Straightness values become even higher in the central NPU only. At a 1,600 m radius, high values completely shift from the central NPU to some plots lying adjacent to the arterial streets. At higher radii, the location of arterial streets generally yields high Straightness values. With the introduction of alleys, at 400 m, high Straightness values (ranging from 0.76 to 0.87) are more evenly spread within the central NPU. At 800 m, values become even higher within the central NPU, but also increase in other NPUs located on the left and bottom of the central NPU. At 1,600 m, high Straightness values concentrate in plots lying along the arterial streets.

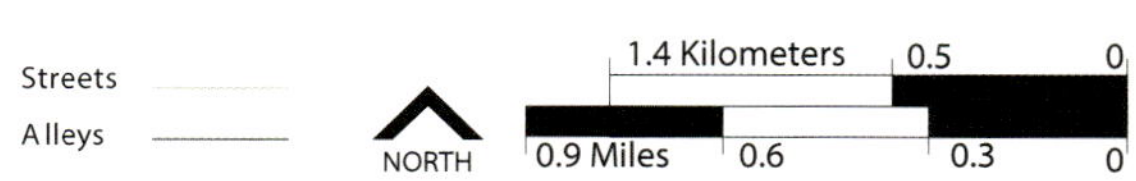

Summary of Centrality Results

Neighborhood

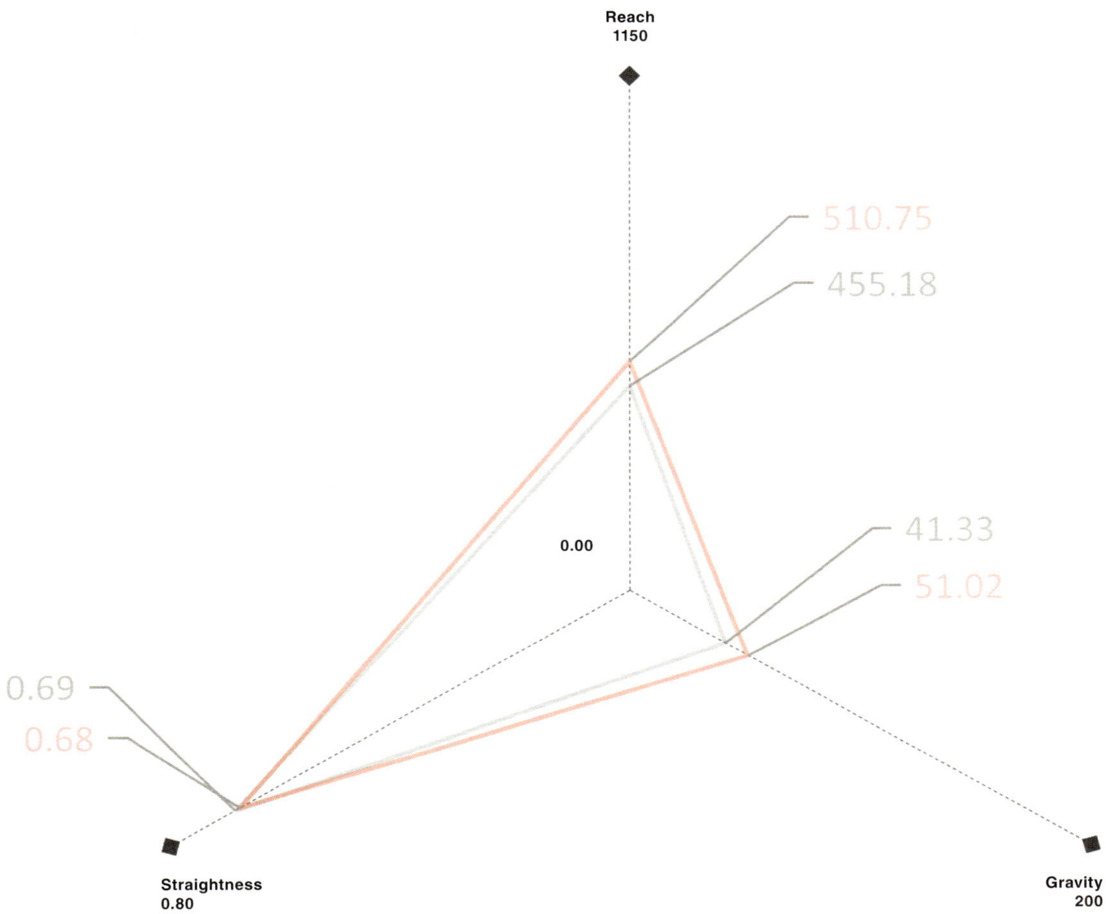

FIG. 17
Spider graphs showing the contribution of alleyways to the averages of 400m, 800m, and 1600m scales of Reach, Gravity and Straightness

Sample 01

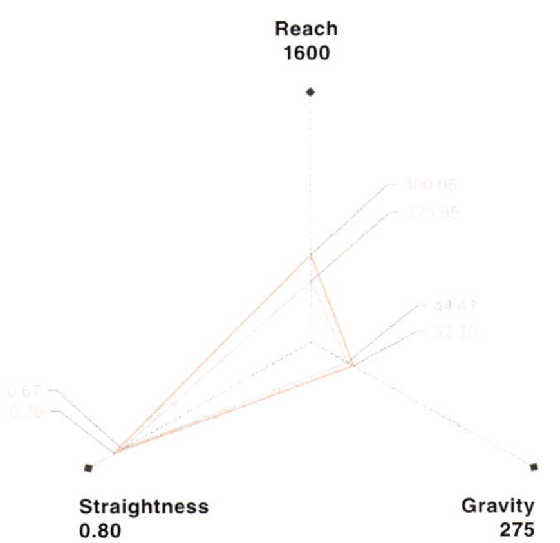

Sample 02

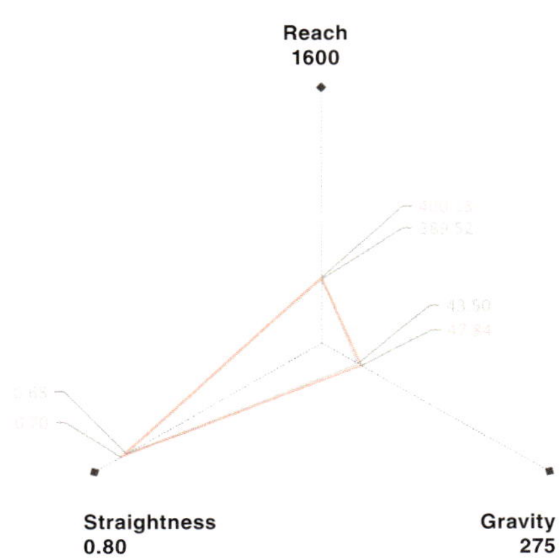

Neighborhood Scale

FIG. 18

Histograms showing the distribution of centrality values (Reach, Gravity, and Straightness) among plots with and without alleys at three different scales 400m, 800m, and 1600m. The X axis is for the centrality metric values, while the Y axis is for the percentage of plots achieving a centrality value denoted on the X axis.

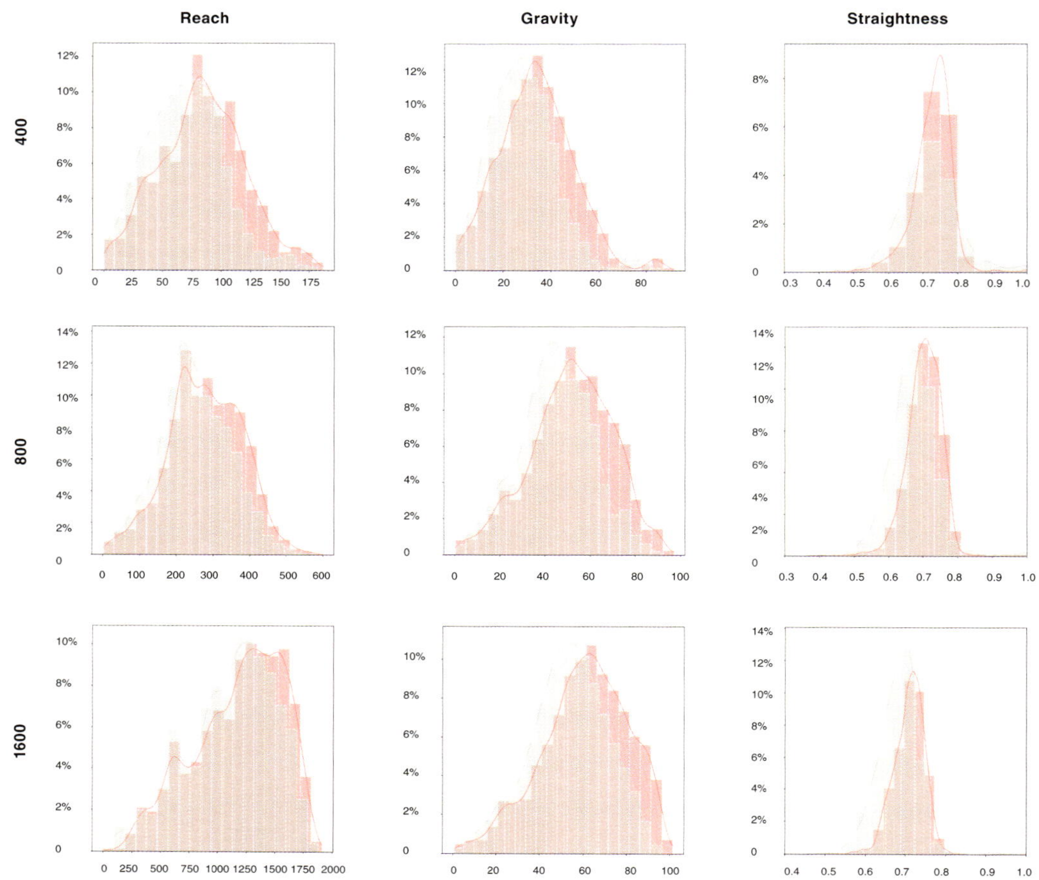

TABLE. 1

Neighborhood scale centrality values

UNA		Radius	Min	Max	Avg
Scenario 1: Streets Only	Reach	400	1	182	69
		800	1	582	240
		1600	2	1875	1056
	Gravity	400	0.21	86.03	28.19
		800	0.11	91.36	43.77
		1600	0.17	95.69	52.03
	Straightness	400	0.00	1.00	0.72
		800	0.00	1.00	0.67
		1600	0.00	0.88	0.68

UNA		Radius	Min	Max	Avg
Scenario 2: Streets + Alleys	Reach	400	1	198	68
		800	2	709	279
		1600	2	2707	1166
	Gravity	400	0.23	73.21	36.35
		800	0.73	111.84	53.81
		1600	1.19	125.00	62.88
	Straightness	400	0.00	0.98	0.69
		800	0.00	0.90	0.67
		1600	0.00	0.78	0.67

Sample Scale — Sample 01

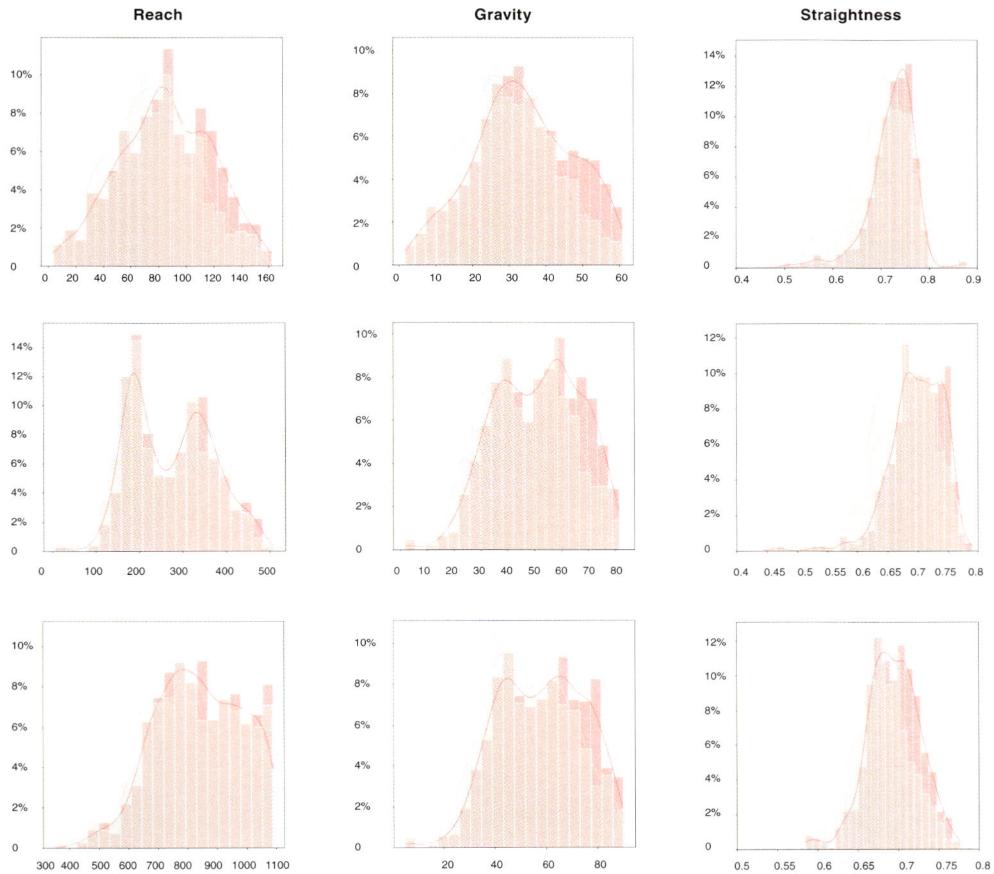

FIG. 19

Histograms showing the distribution of centrality values (Reach, Gravity, and Straightness) among plots with and without alleys at three different scales 400m, 800m, and 1600m. The X axis is for the centrality metric values, while the Y axis is for the percentage of plots achieving a centrality value denoted on the X axis.

UNA		Radius	Min	Max	Avg
Scenario 1: Streets Only	Reach	400	0	178	75
		800	0	463	254
		1600	0	1011	811
	Gravity	400	0.00	66.79	31.22
		800	0.00	83.93	47.68
		1600	0.00	90.19	54.40
	Straightness	400	0.00	1.00	0.71
		800	0.00	0.79	0.65
		1600	0.00	0.78	0.66

UNA		Radius	Min	Max	Avg
Scenario 2: Streets + Alleys	Reach	400	0	187	94
		800	13	480	275
		1600	343	1013	831
	Gravity	400	0.00	69.02	38.79
		800	1.08	93.55	55.72
		1600	3.57	96.45	62.39
	Straightness	400	0.00	1.00	0.72
		800	0.00	0.79	0.70
		1600	0.00	0.79	0.69

TABLE. 2

Sample 01 centrality values

Sample Scale — Sample 02

FIG. 20
Histograms showing the distribution of centrality values (Reach, Gravity, and Straightness) among plots with and without alleys at three different scales 400m, 800m, and 1600m.The X axis is for the centrality metric values, while the Y axis is for the percentage of plots achieving a centrality value denoted on the X axis.

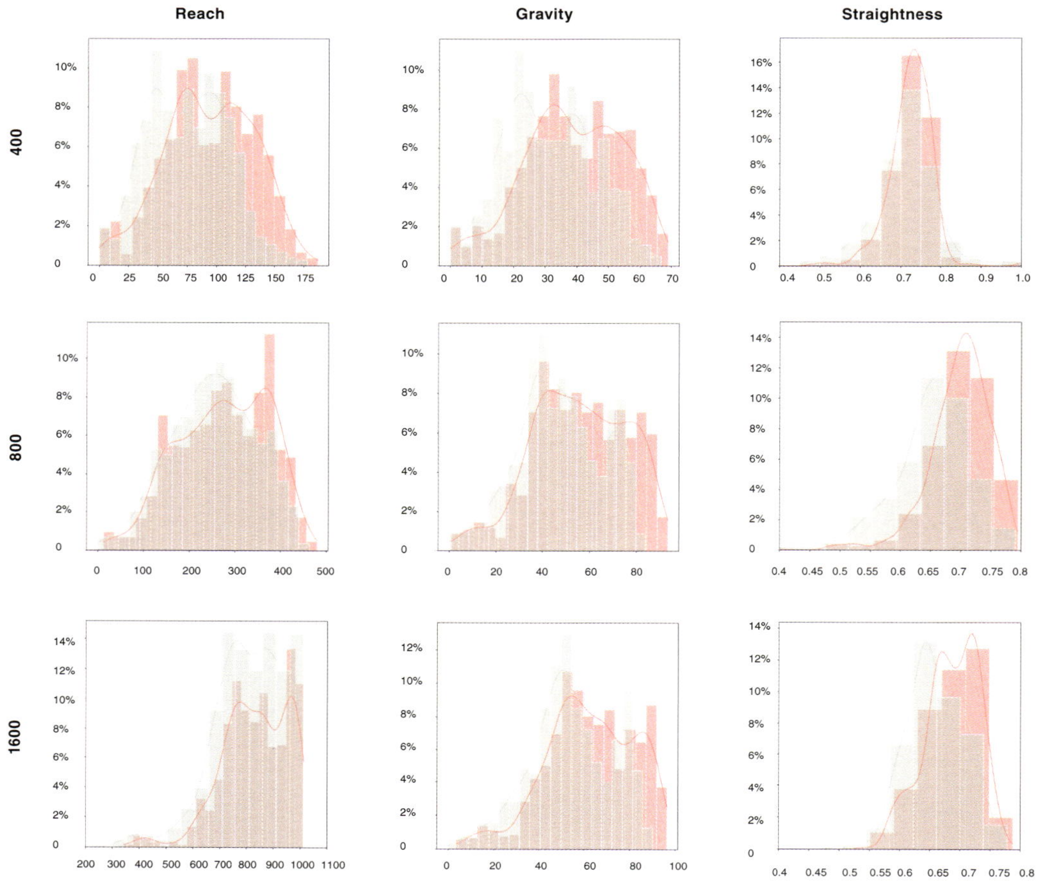

TABLE. 3
Sample 02 centrality values

UNA		Radius	Min	Max	Avg
Scenario 1: Streets Only	Reach	400	3	159	76
		800	7	511	265
		1600	349	1089	828
	Gravity	400	1.33	60.35	29.60
		800	1.52	83.02	47.06
		1600	4.77	90.36	53.83
	Straightness	400	0.44	0.90	0.70
		800	0.46	0.78	0.67
		1600	0.52	0.79	0.68

UNA		Radius	Min	Max	Avg
Scenario 2: Streets + Alleys	Reach	400	4	162	85
		800	6	508	275
		1600	350	1091	840
	Gravity	400	1.59	60.75	33.87
		800	1.68	81.44	51.43
		1600	4.78	89.93	58.21
	Straightness	400	0.40	0.88	0.72
		800	0.44	0.79	0.69
		1600	0.58	0.78	0.69

Baniyas

Baniyas

FIG. 1
Baniyas skyline

FIG. 2
Everyday urbanism in Baniyas

FIG. 3
A photo montage with different views of Baniyas

FIG. 4
Aerial image showing Baniyas (Esri & USGS, 2021)

Morphological Analysis

Neighborhood Scale

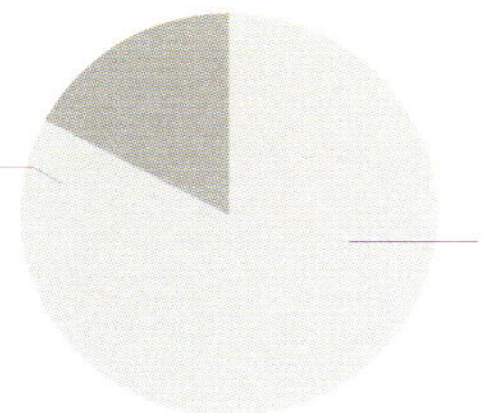

Residential= 5,248 Plots
Non-residential= 1,072 Plots

Plots/Buildings:

- Total area = 2,215 Hectares
- Total plots = 5,347 Plots
- Total buildings = 10,124 Buildings
- Average plot density = 2.41 Plots/Hectare
- Average building density = 4.57 Buildings/Hectare
- Average plot area = 0.17 Hectare
- Average population density = 18.57 Population/Hectare

FIG. 5.1
Residential/ non-residential classification

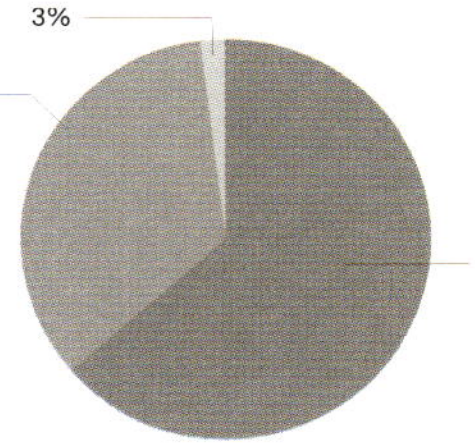

Low-rise (1-4) = 6,460 Buildings
Mid-rise (4-10)= 3,495 Buildings
High-rise (+10)= 169 Buildings

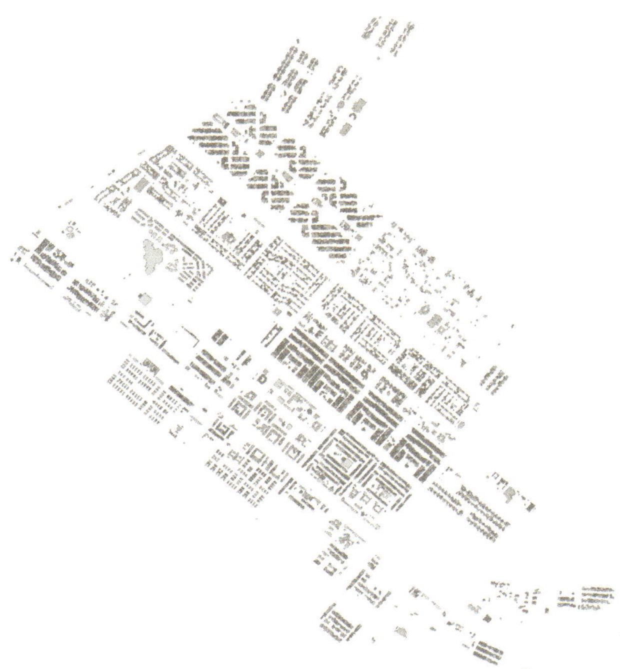

FIG. 5.2
Buildings height classification

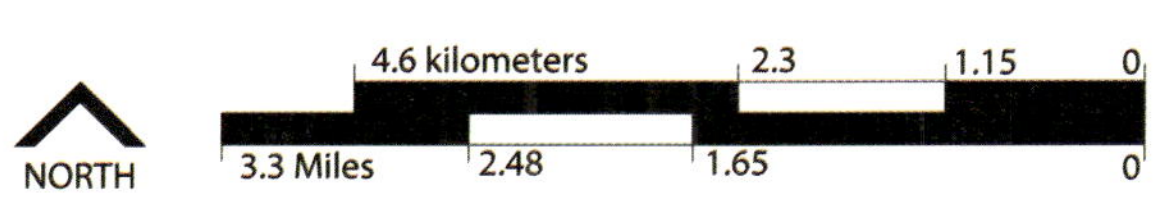

FIG. 5.3
Population density

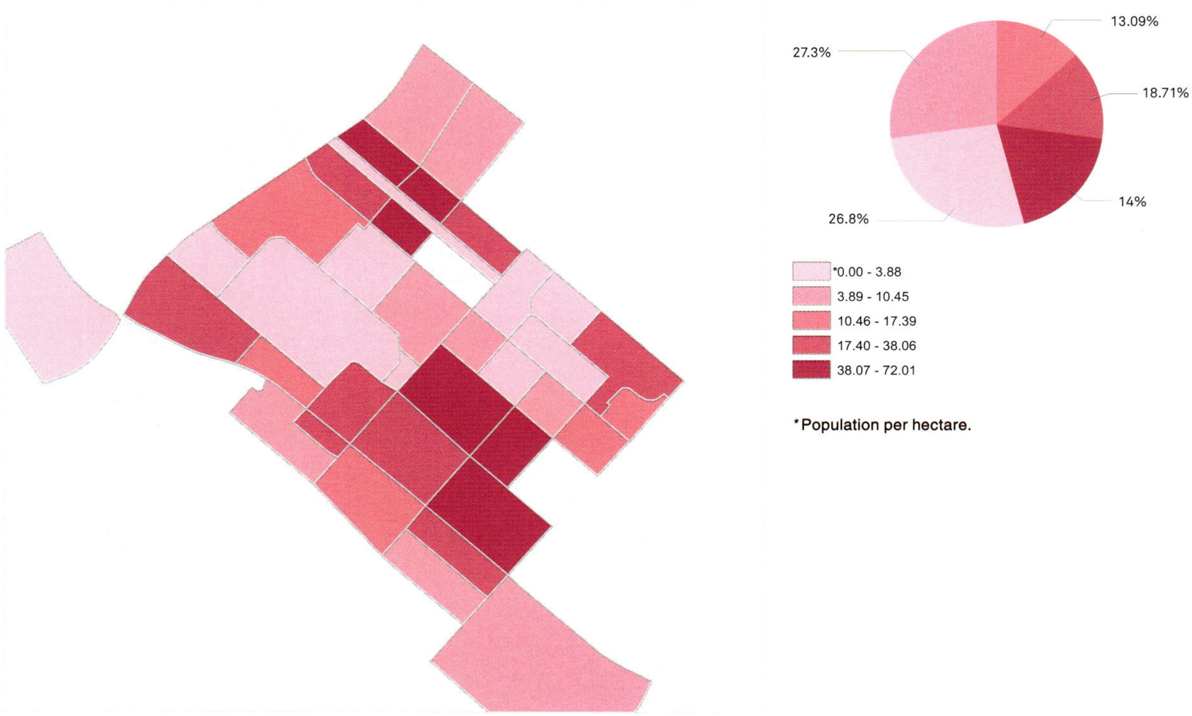

*Population per hectare.

FIG. 5.4
Land use classification

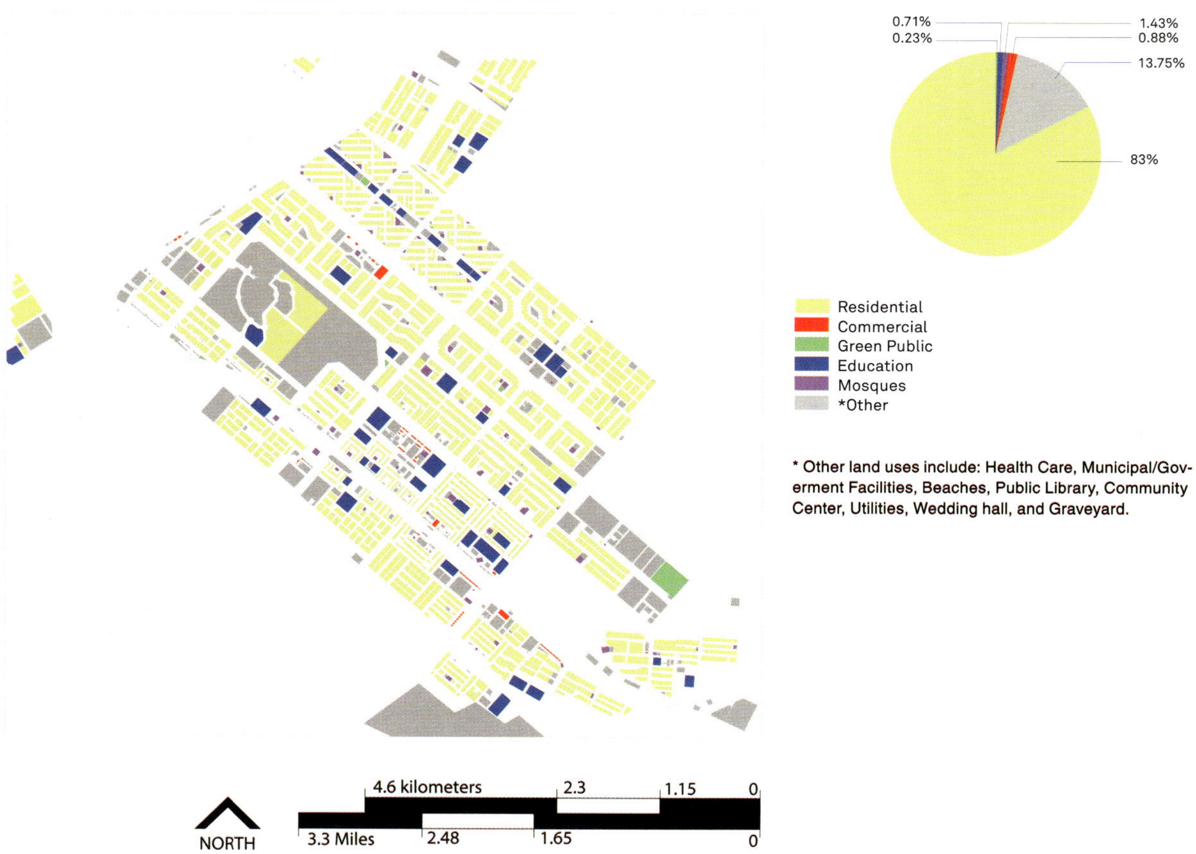

* Other land uses include: Health Care, Municipal/Goverment Facilities, Beaches, Public Library, Community Center, Utilities, Wedding hall, and Graveyard.

FIG. 5.5

Map showing network classification in Baniyas

Streets:

- Street length = 533.04 km
- Street density = 0.24 km/Hectare
- Street intersections = 730 Intersections
- Street intersections density = 0.32 Intersections/Hectare

Alleys:

- Alley length = 223.69 km
- Alley density = 0.10 km/Hectare
- Alley intersections = 1,373 Intersections
- Alley intersections density = 0.61 Intersections/Hectare

FIG. 6
Map showing Baniyas, with the location of the selected samples. Each sample has an area of 1 square mile.

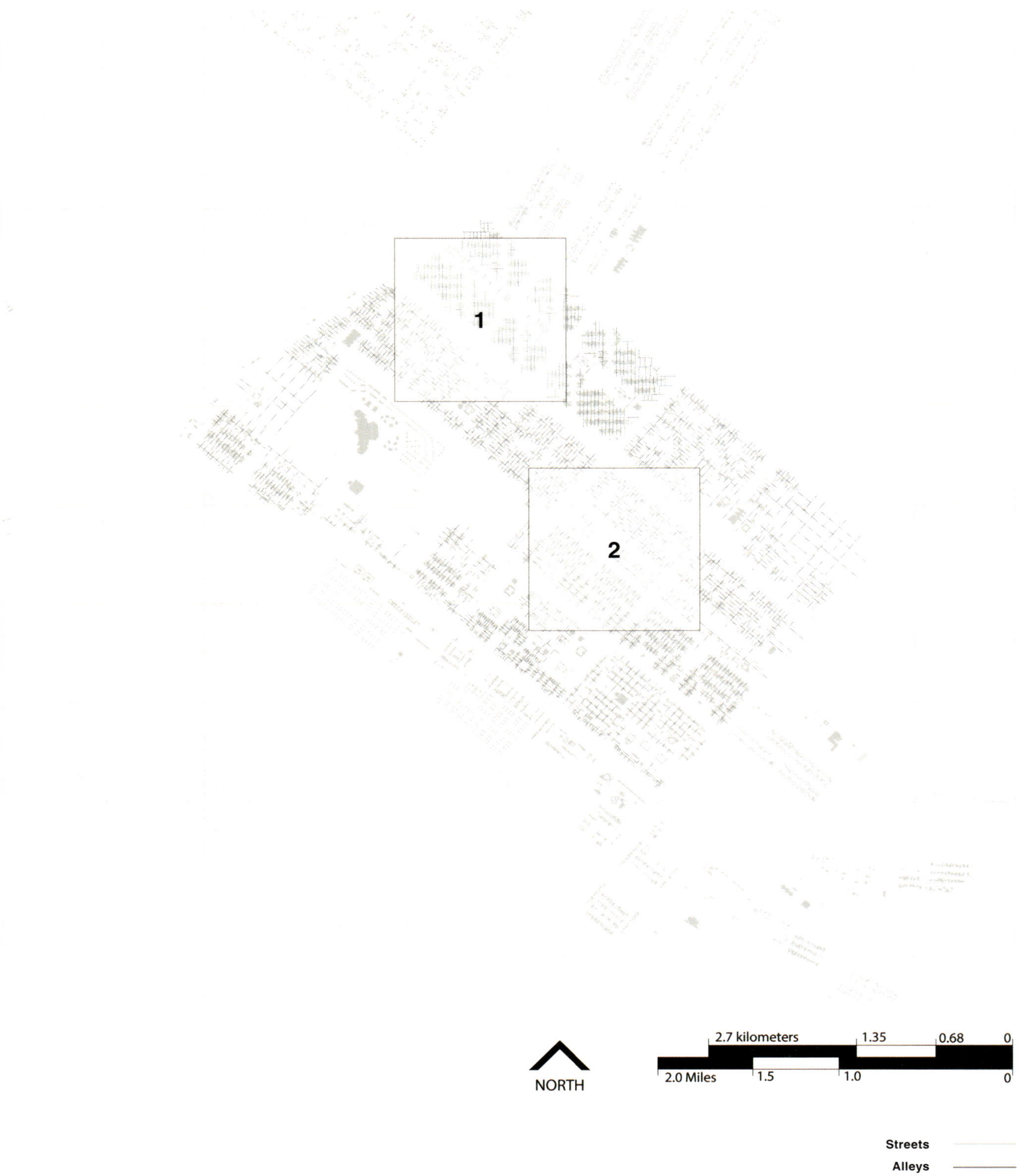

Morphological Analysis

Sample Scale — Sample 01

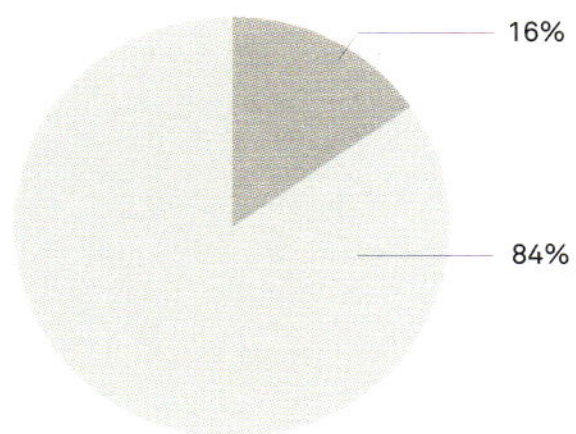

Residential= 684 Plots
Non-residential= 123 Plots

Plots/Buildings:

- Total area = 256 Hectares
- Total plots = 807 Plots
- Total buildings = 1,101 Buildings
- Average plot area = 0.24 Hectare
- Average plot density = 3.15 Plots/Hectare

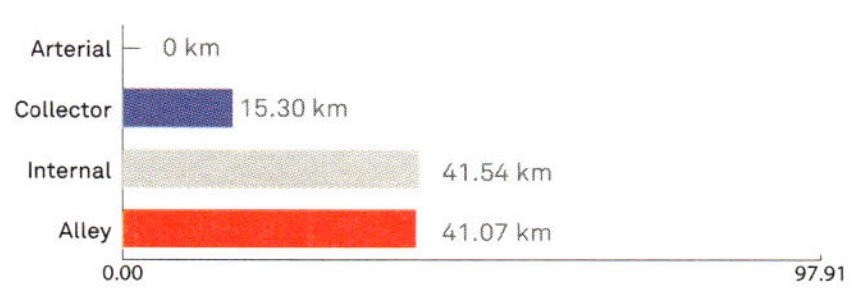

Streets:

- Street length = 56.37 km
- Street density = 0.02 km/Hectare
- Street intersections = 462 Intersections
- Street intersections density = 3.03 Intersections/Hectare

Alleys:

- Alley length = 41.07 km
- Alley density = 0.16 km/Hectare
- Alley intersections = 127 Intersections
- Alley intersections density = 0.49 Intersections/Hectare

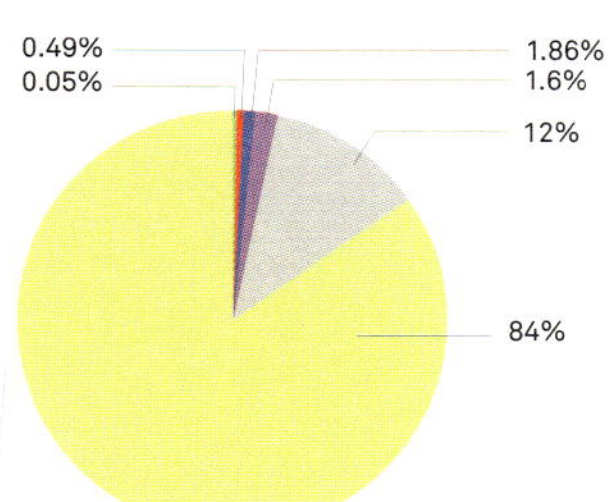

Residential
Commercial
Green Public
Education
Mosques
*Other

FIG. 7.1
Residential/non-residential classification

FIG. 7.2
Network classification

FIG. 7.3
Land use classification

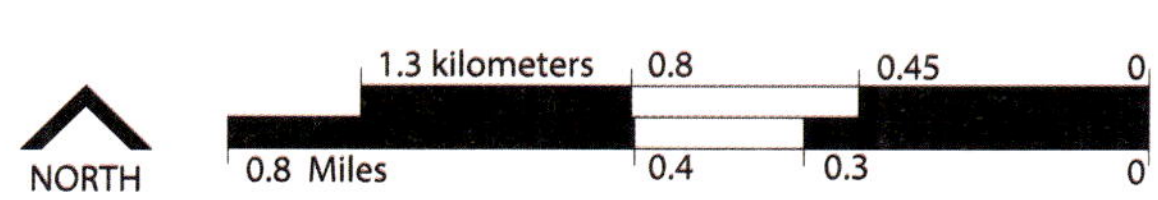

Sample Scale — Sample 02

FIG. 8.1
Residential/non-residential classification

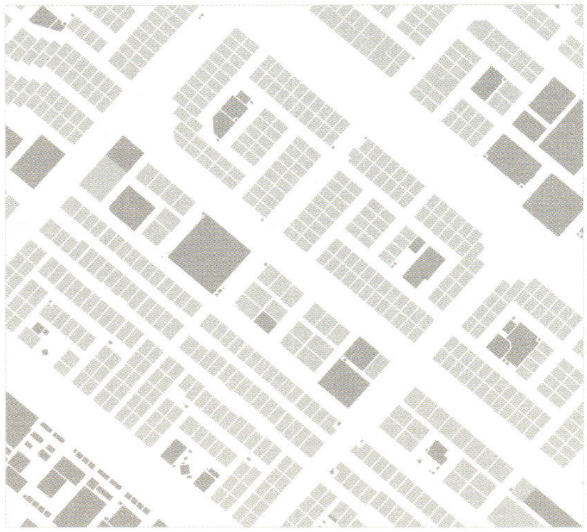

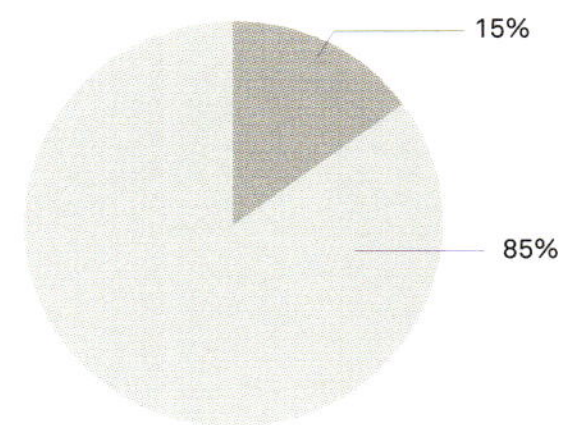

Residential= 751 Plots
Non-residential= 130 Plots

Plots/Buildings:

- Total area = 256 Hectares
- Total plots = 881 Plots
- Total buildings = 1,106 Buildings
- Average plot area = 0.24 Hectare
- Average plot density = 3.44 Plots/Hectare

FIG. 8.2
Network classification

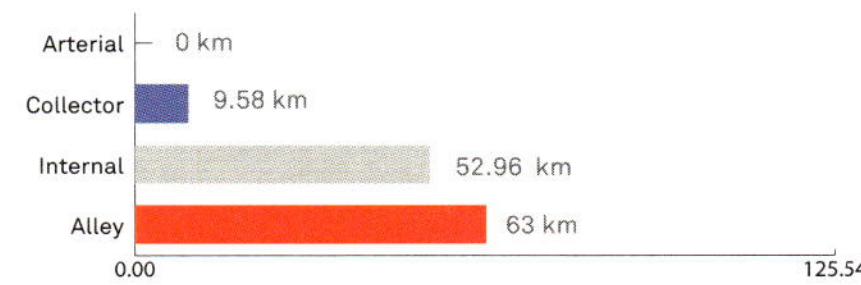

Streets:

- Street length = 62.54 km
- Street density = 0.20 km/Hectare
- Street intersections = 407 Intersections
- Street intersections density = 1.58 Intersections/Hectare

Alleys:

- Alley length = 63 km
- Alley density = 0.24 km/Hectare
- Alley intersections = 250 Intersections
- Alley intersections density = 0.97 Intersections/Hectare

FIG. 8.3
Land use classification

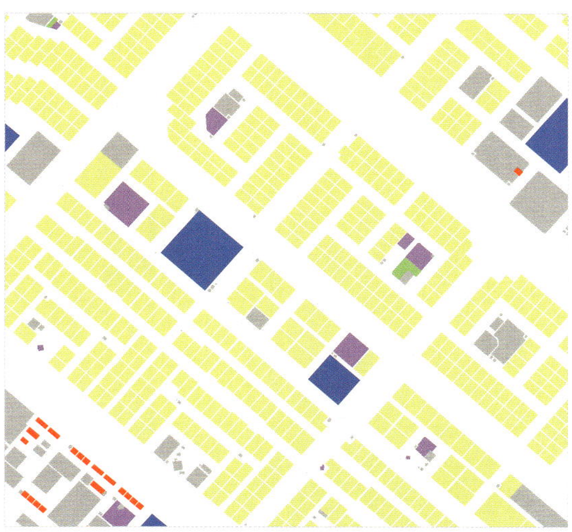

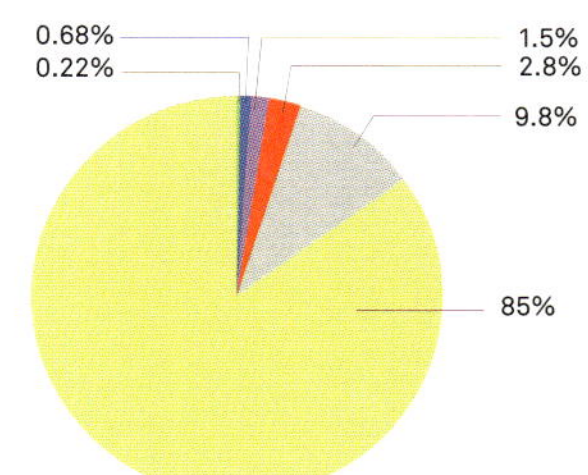

Residential
Commercial
Green Public
Education
Mosques
*Other

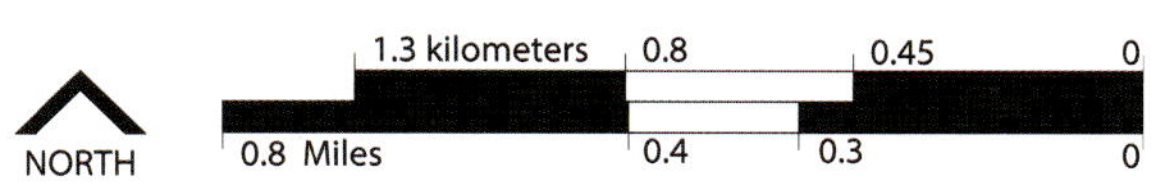

Centrality Analysis: Neighborhood Scale

Scenario 1: Streets only — 400 m Radius

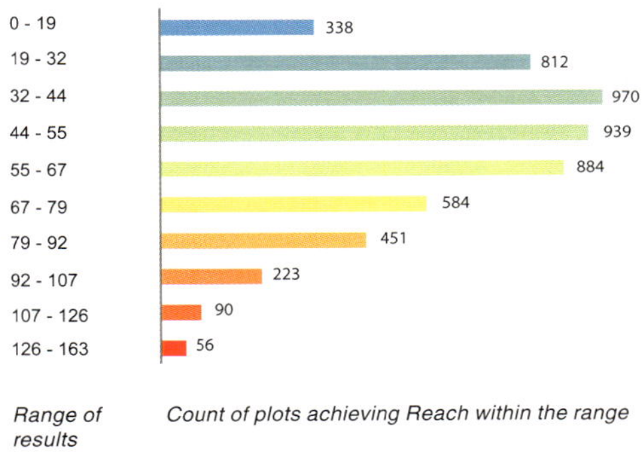

The warmer colors (i.e., greenish-yellow to red) represent a Reach value of 55 or more, while the cooler colors (i.e., light green to dark blue) correspond to a Reach value of 54 or less. The majority of plots (i.e., 3,227 out of 5,347), corresponding to 60% of all plots, have Reach values of more than 43. Among the categories shown in the legend, 18% of all plots can reach 32 to 44 other plots within 5 minutes of walking. On average, each plot in Baniyas can access at least 54 plots within a distance of 400 m.

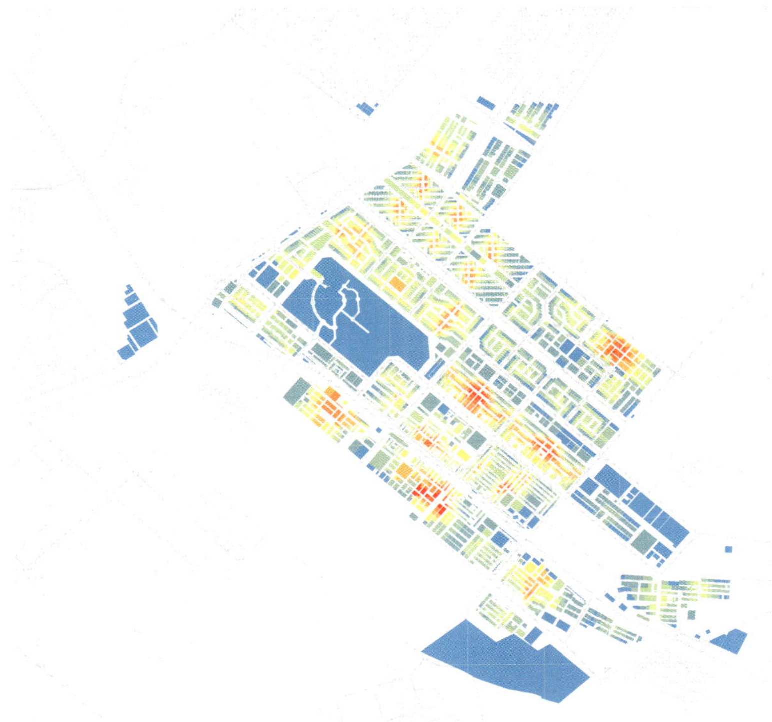

FIG. 9.1
Reach

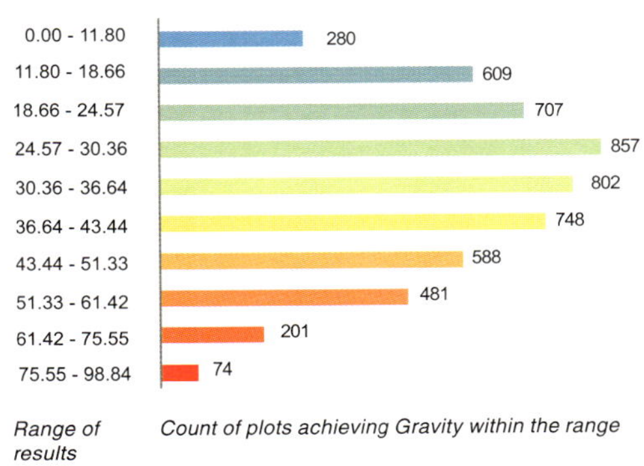

The warmer colors (i.e., greenish-yellow to red) represent Gravity values greater than 30.35, while the cooler colors (i.e., light green to dark blue) correspond to Gravity values lower than 30.36. Sixty-one percent of all plots (i.e., 3,255 out of 5,347) have Gravity values of less than 36.64. Among the categories shown in the legend, 857 plots, or 16% of all plots, can reach 24.57 to 30.36 plots, making this the most common range; this range is represented by light green on the map. On average, at a radius of 400 m, each plot can reach 34 other plots when spatial impedance or distance decay effect is taken into consideration.

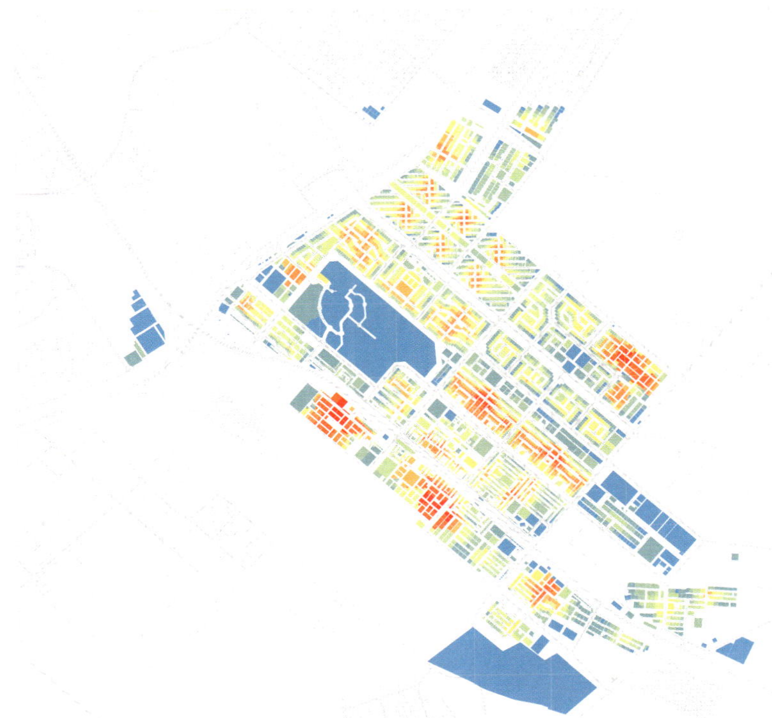

FIG. 9.2
Gravity

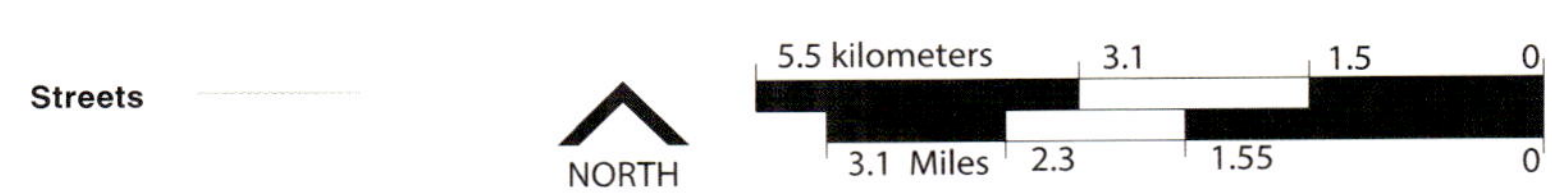

Scenario 1: Streets only — 400 m Radius

FIG. 9.3

Betweenness

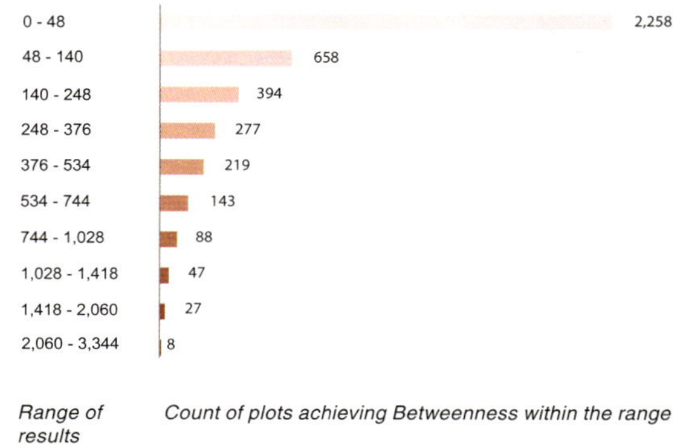

The majority of segments, corresponding to 97% (i.e., 3,991 out of 4,119 segments), have low Betweenness values ranging from 0 to 864. Among the categories shown in the legend, 2,258 segments have values in the range of 0 to 48, making this the most common value range; this range is represented by the lightest brown on the map. Mid-range Betweenness values– those between 865 and 6,702 are obtained by 128 segments, which is 3% of all segments. No segment has a high level of Betweenness values (higher than 6,702). The average Betweenness value in Baniyas is 151 (smaller than 865), while the median is 30, indicating low Betweenness at a 400 m radius.

FIG. 9.4

Straightness

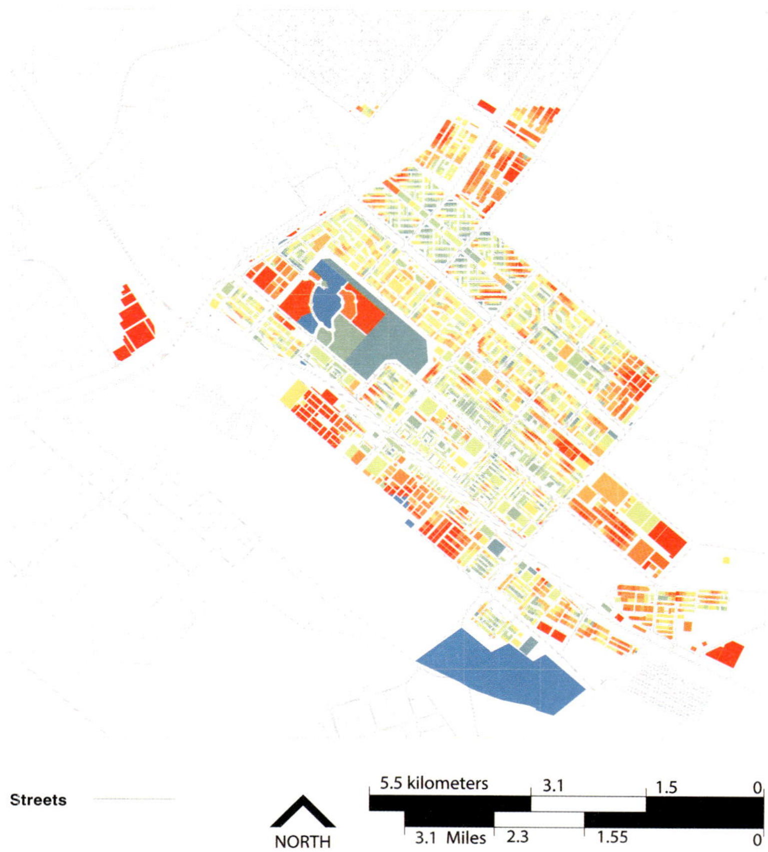

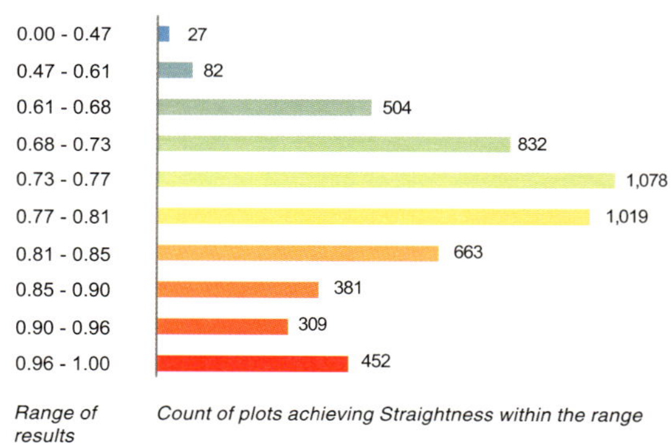

The warmer colors (greenish-yellow to red) represent Straightness values higher then 0.72, while the cooler colors (light green to dark blue) correspond to Straightness values lower than 0.73. The majority of plots, corresponding to 55% (or 2,929 out of 5,347 plots) have Straightness values ranging from 0.68 to 0.81. Among the categories shown in the legend, 1,078 plots have values in the range of 0.73 to 0.77, making this the most common value range; this range is represented by greenish-yellow on the map. The average Straightness value of plots in Baniyas is 0.79 at a radius of 400 m, which means that their paths to other plots are 79% as straight as a straight line.

Scenario 1: Streets only — 800 m Radius

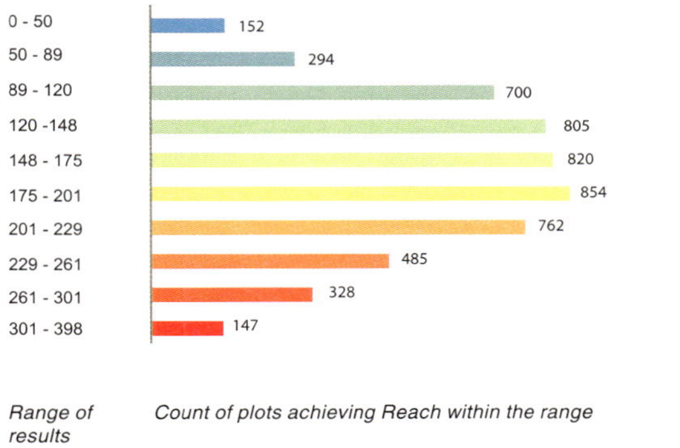

The warmer colors (i.e., greenish-yellow to red) represent a Reach value of 148 or more, while the cooler colors (i.e., light green to dark blue) correspond to a Reach value of 147 or less. Fifty-two percent of all plots (i.e., 2,771 out of 5,347), have Reach values of less than 175. Among the categories shown in the legend, 16% of plots can reach 175 to 201 other plots within 10 minutes of walking. On average, each plot in Baniyas can access at least 173 plots within a distance of 800 m.

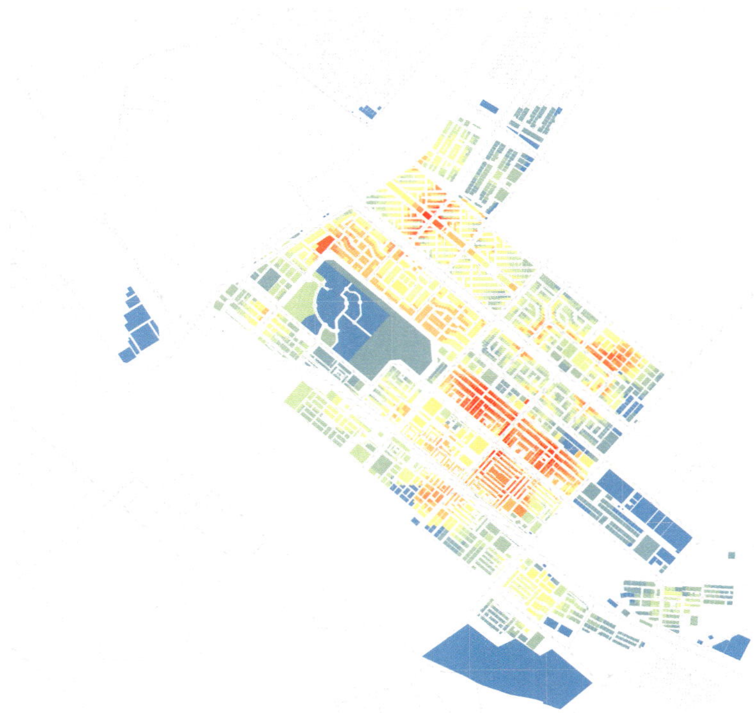

FIG. 10.1
Reach

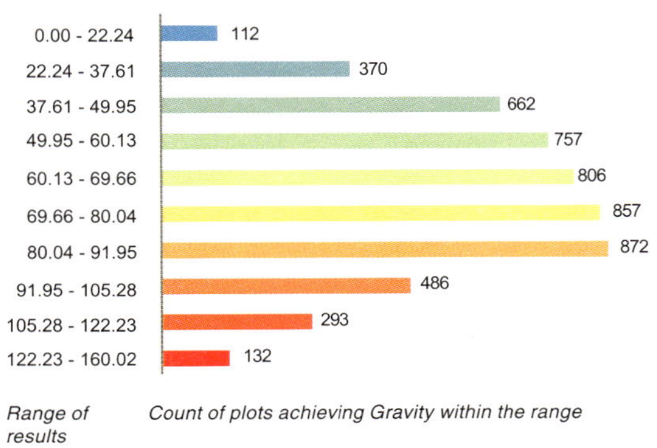

The warmer colors (i.e., greenish-yellow to red) represent Gravity values of more than 60.12, while the cooler colors (i.e., light green to dark blue) correspond to Gravity values of less than 60.13. Fifty-one percent of plots (i.e., 2,707 out of 5,347) have Gravity values of less than 69.66. Among the categories shown in the legend, 872 plots, or 16% of plots, can reach 80.04 to 91.95 other plots, making this the most common range; this range is represented by light orange on the map. On average, at an 800 m radius, each plot can reach 70 other plots when spatial impedance or distance decay effect is taken into consideration.

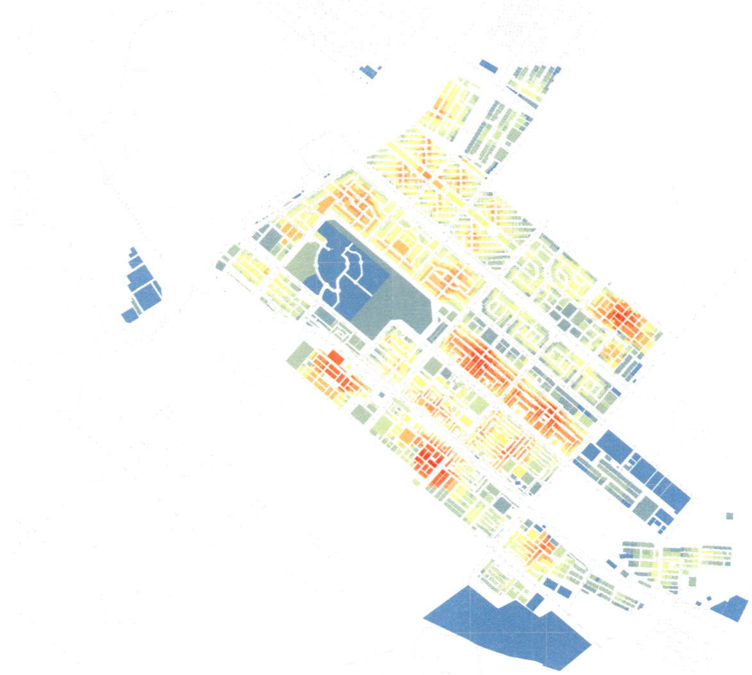

FIG. 10.2
Gravity

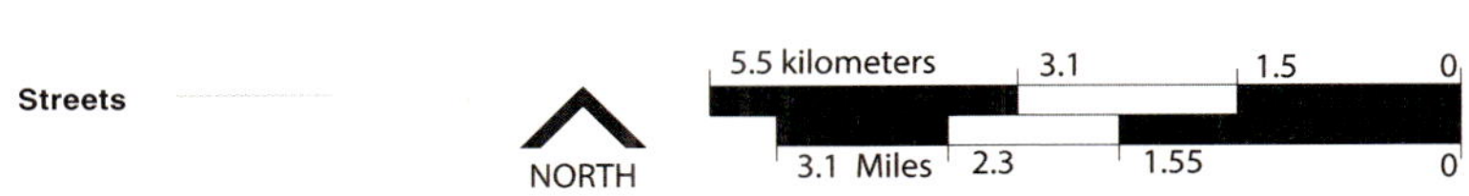

Scenario 1: Streets only — 800 m Radius

FIG. 10.3
Betweenness

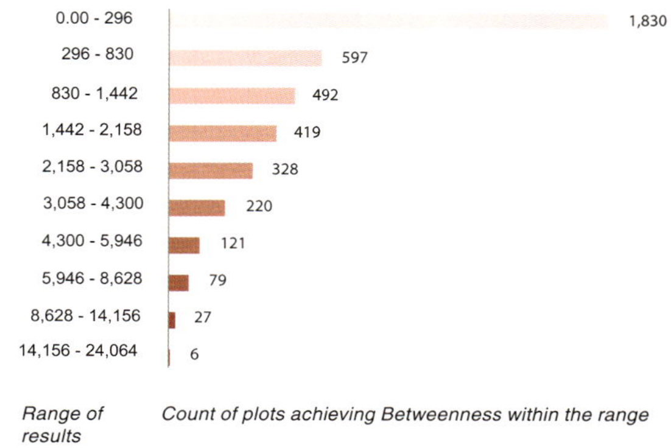

Almost all segments, corresponding to 85% (i.e., 3,504 out of 4,119 segments), have very low Betweenness values in the range of 0–2,539. Among the categories shown in the legend, 1,830 segments have values in the range of 0 to 296, making this the most common value range; this range is represented by the lightest brown on the map. Low Betweenness values ranging from 2,540 to 11,517 are obtained by 601 segments, which is 15% of all segments. Twelve segments obtain mid-range Betweenness values in the range of 11,518 to 20,478, and 2 segments obtain high Betweenness values (20,479–59,383). The average Betweenness value in Baniyas is 1,183 (smaller than 2,540), and the median is 503, indicating very low Betweenness at an 800 m radius.

FIG. 10.4
Straightness

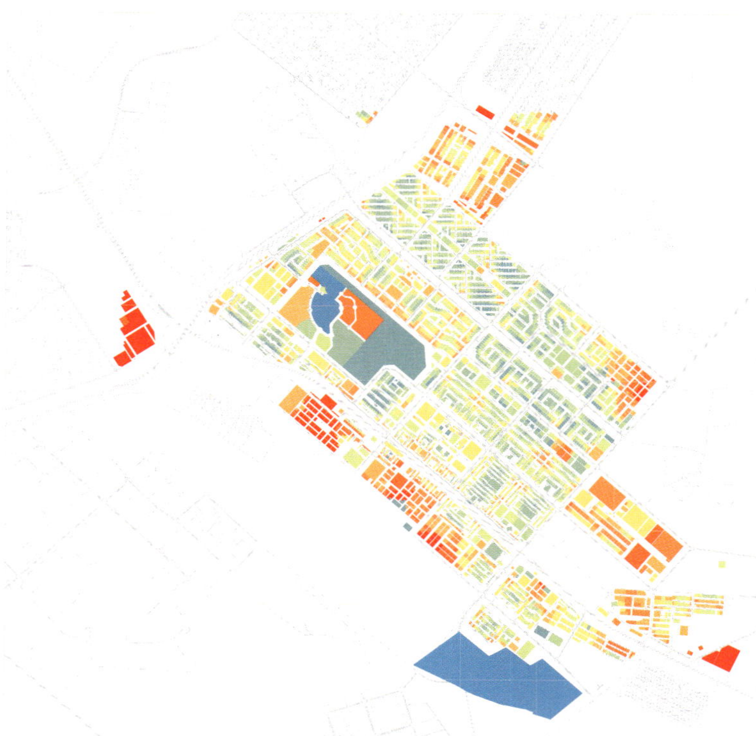

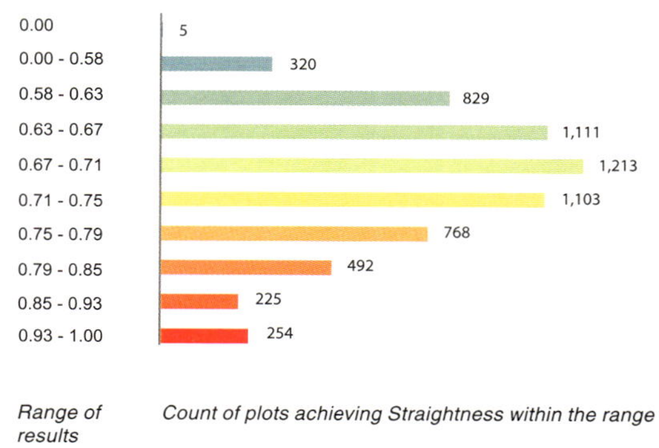

The warmer colors (greenish-yellow to red) represent Straightness values higher than 0.66, while the cooler colors (light green to dark blue) correspond to Straightness values lower than 0.67. The majority of plots, corresponding to 64% (or 3,426 out of 5,347 plots) have Straightness values ranging from 0.63 to 0.75. Among the categories shown in the legend, 1,213 plots have values in the range of 0.67 to 0.71, making this the most common value range; this range is represented by light green on the map. The average Straightness value of plots in Baniyas is 0.71 at an 800 m radius, which means that their paths to other plots are 71% as straight as a straight line.

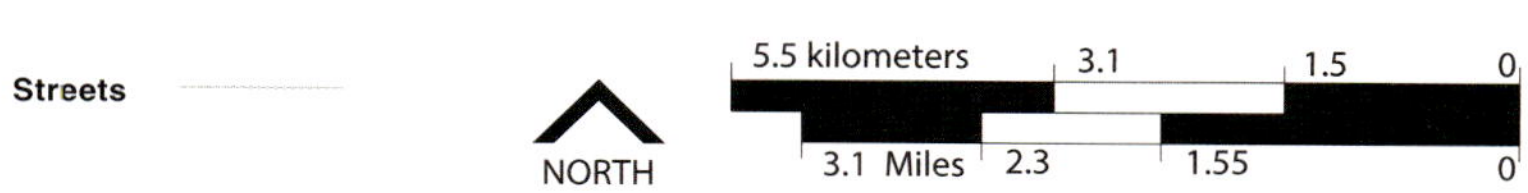

Scenario 1: Streets only — 1,600 m Radius

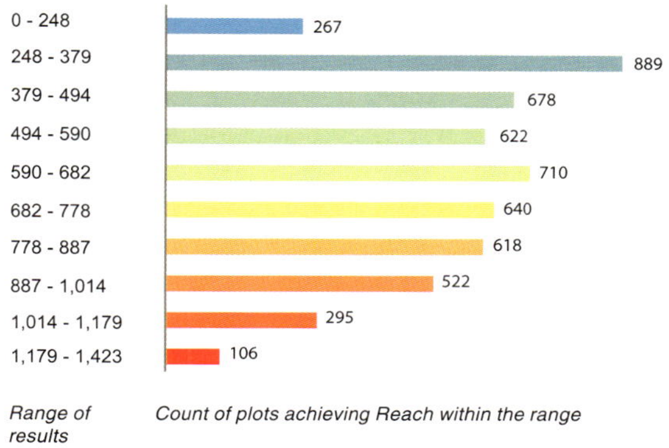

The warmer colors (i.e., greenish-yellow to red) represent Reach values greater than 589, while the cooler colors (i.e., light green to dark blue) correspond to Reach values lower than 590. The majority of plots (i.e., 2,891 out of 5,347), corresponding to 54% of all plots, have Reach values of more than 589. Among the categories shown in the legend, 17% of plots can reach 248 to 379 other plots within 20 minutes of walking. On average, each plot in Baniyas can access at least 626 plots within a distance of 1,600 m.

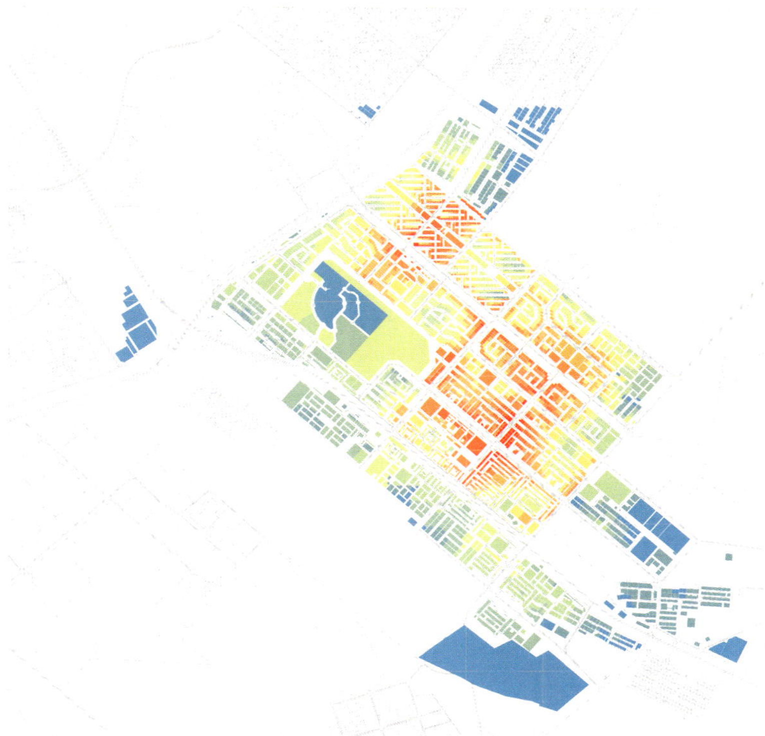

FIG. 11.1
Reach

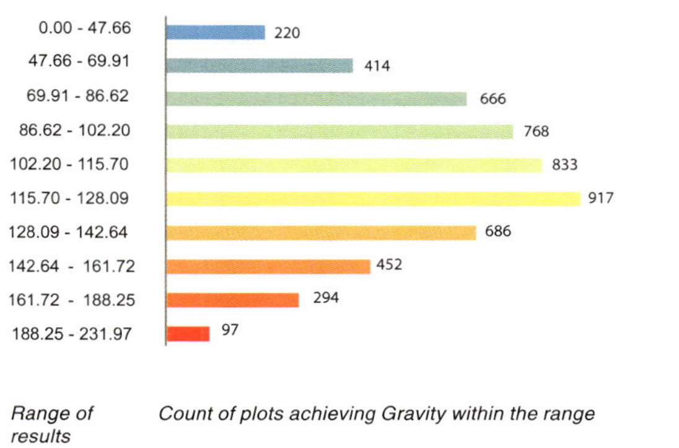

The warmer colors (i.e., greenish-yellow to red) represent Gravity values greater than 102.19, while the cooler colors (i.e., light green to dark blue) correspond to Gravity values lower than 102.20. Fifty-four percent of all plots (i.e., 2,901 out of 5,347) have Gravity values lower than 115.70. Among the categories shown in the legend, 917 plots, or 17% of plots, can reach 115.70 to 128.09 plots, making this the most common range; this range is represented by yellow on the map. On average, each plot can reach 111 other plots when spatial impedance or distance decay effect is taken into consideration.

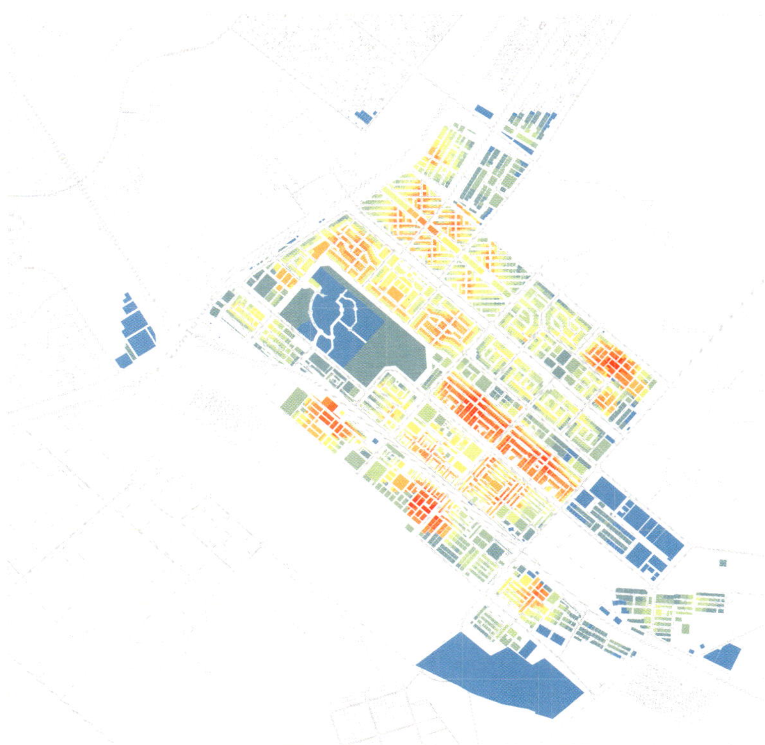

FIG. 11.2
Gravity

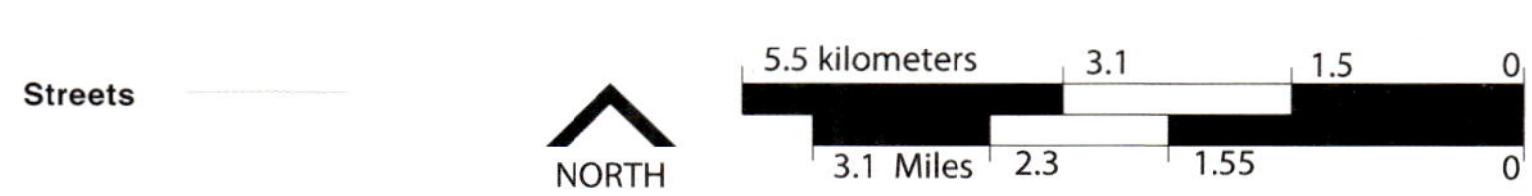

Scenario 1: Streets only — 1,600 m Radius

FIG. 11.3
Betweenness

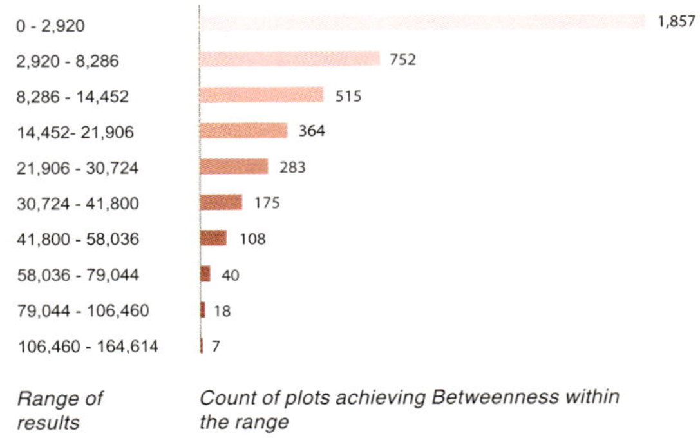

The majority of segments, corresponding to 99% (i.e., 4,083 out of 4,119 segments), have very low Betweenness values in the range of 0 to 73,682. Among the categories shown in the legend, 1,857 segments have values in the range of 0 to 2,920, making this the most common value range; this range is represented by the lightest brown on the map. Low Betweenness values ranging from 73,683 to 123,568 are obtained by 30 segments, which is 0.73% of all segments. Mid-range Betweenness values ranging from 123,569 to 179,444 are obtained by only 6 segments, which is 0.2% of all segments. No segments have high Betweenness values (higher than 179,444). The average Betweenness value in Baniyas is 10,058 (smaller than 73,683), while the median is 3,988, indicating very low Betweenness at a 1,600 m radius.

FIG. 11.4
Straightness

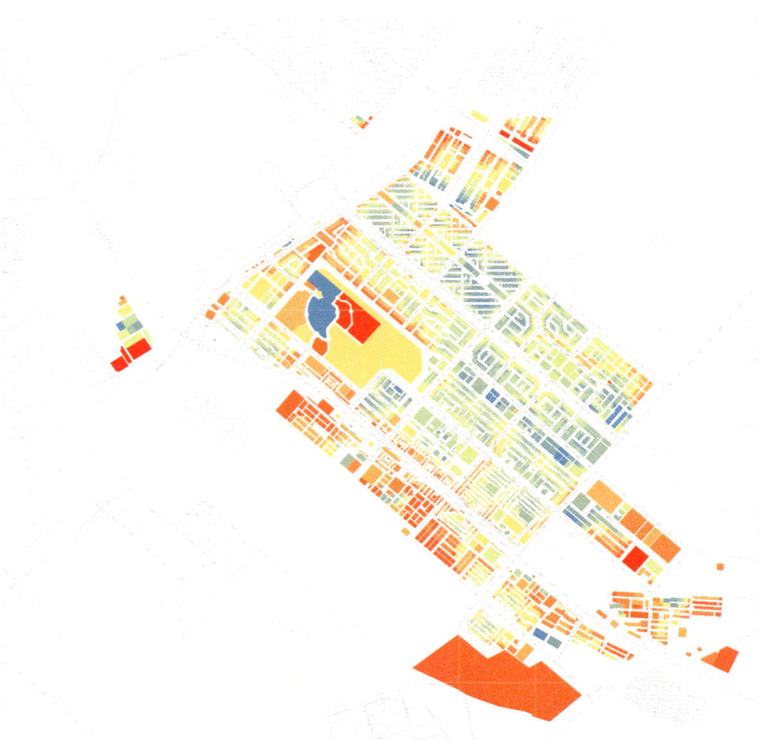

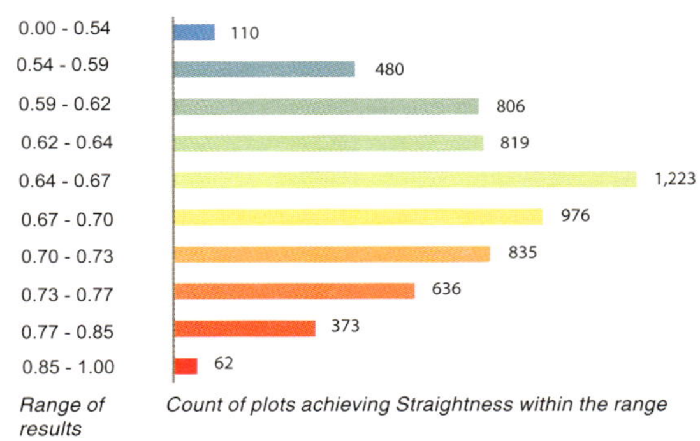

The warmer colors (greenish-yellow to red) represent Straightness values higher than 0.63, while the cooler colors (light green to dark blue) correspond to Straightness values lower than 0.64. The majority of plots, corresponding to 72% (or 3,853 out of 5,347 plots) have Straightness values ranging from 0.62 to 0.73. Among the categories shown in the legend, 1,223= plots have values in the range of 0.64 to 0.67, making this the most common value range; this range is represented by light green on the map. At a 1,600 m radius, the average Straightness value of plots in Baniyas is 0.67, which means that their paths to other plots are 67% as straight as a straight line.

Streets

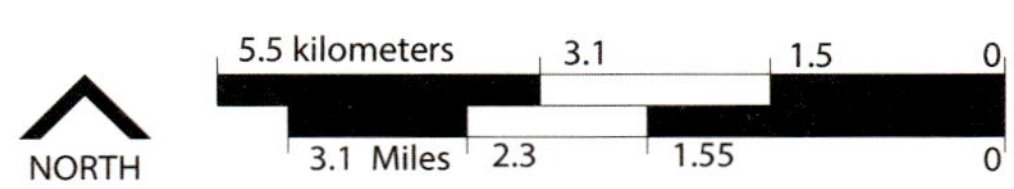

Centrality Analysis: Neighborhood Scale

Scenario 2: Streets + Alleys — 400 m Radius

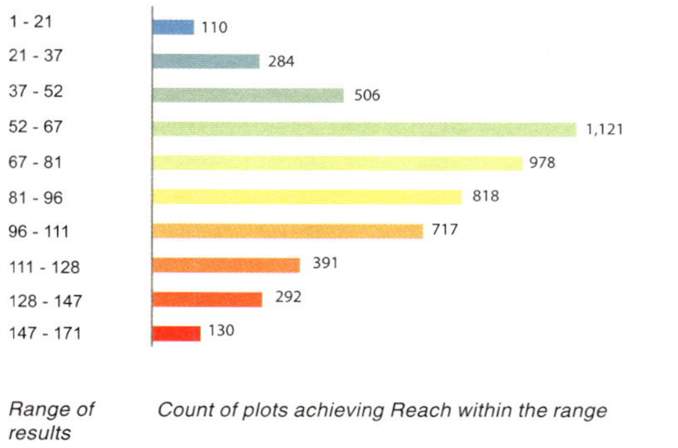

The warmer colors (i.e., greenish-yellow to red) represent a Reach value of 67 or more, while the cooler colors (i.e., light green to dark blue) correspond to a Reach value of 66 or less. Sixty-two percent of all plots (i.e., 3,326 out of 5,347) have Reach values of more than 66. Among the categories shown in the legend, 21% of all plots can reach 52 to 67 other plots within 5 minutes of walking. On average, each plot in Baniyas can access at least 80 plots within a distance of 400 m.

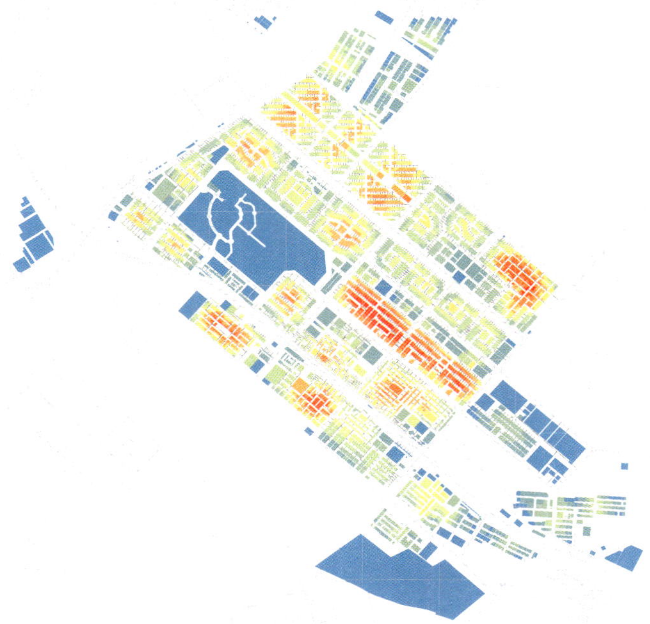

FIG. 12.1
Reach

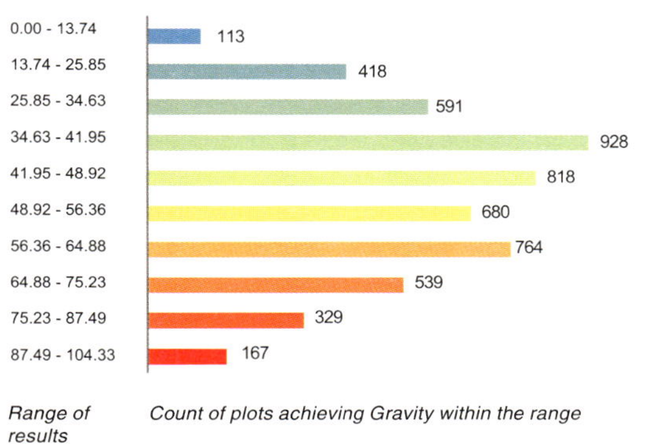

The warmer colors (i.e., greenish-yellow to red) represent Gravity values greater than 41.94, while the cooler colors (i.e., light green to dark blue) correspond to Gravity values lower than 41.95. Fifty-four percent of all plots (i.e., 2,868 out of 5,347) have Gravity values of less than 48.92. Among the categories shown in the legend, 928 plots, or 17% of the total plots, can reach 34.63 to 41.95 plots, making this the most common range; this range is represented by light green on the map. On average, each plot can reach 49 other plots when spatial impedance or distance decay effect is taken into consideration.

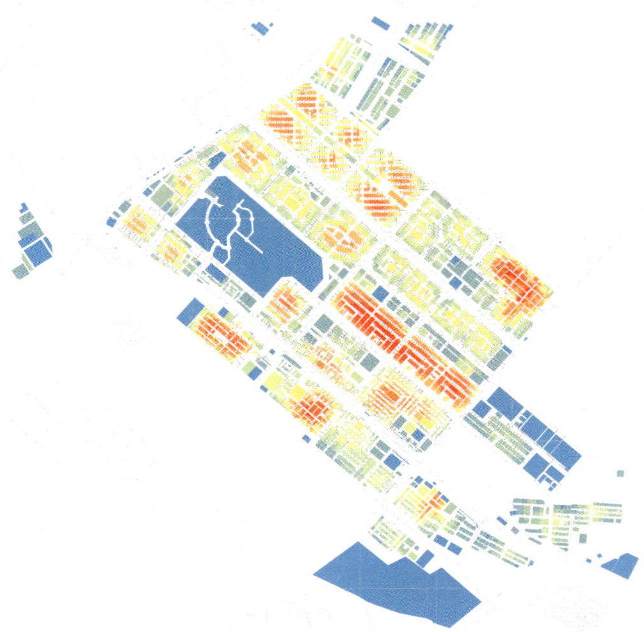

FIG. 12.2
Gravity

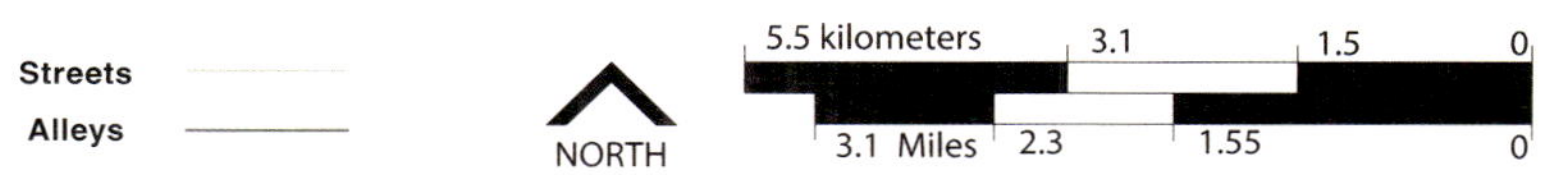

Scenario 2: Streets + Alleys — 400 m Radius

FIG. 12.3
Betweenness

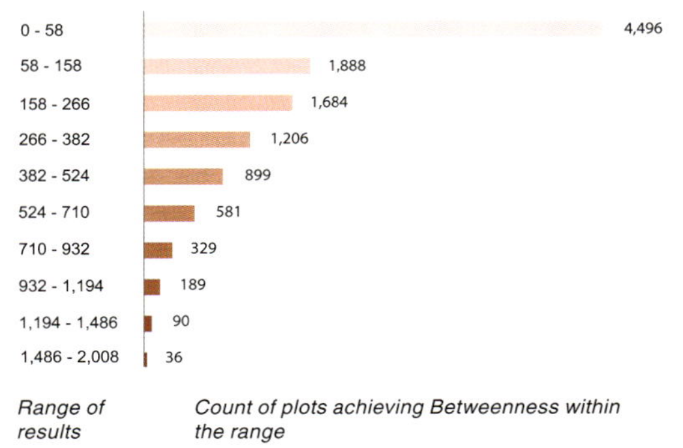

The majority of segments, corresponding to 96% (i.e., 10,996 out of 11,398 segments), have low Betweenness values ranging from 0 to 864. Among the categories shown in the legend, 4,496 segments have values in the range of 0 to 58, making this the most common value range; this range is represented by the lightest brown on the map. Mid-range Betweenness values ranging from 865 to 6,702 are obtained by 402 segments, which is 4% of the total segments. No segments have high Betweenness values (higher than 6,702). The average Betweenness value in Baniyas is 210 (smaller than 865), and the median is 122, indicating low Betweenness at a 400 m radius.

FIG. 12.4
Straightness

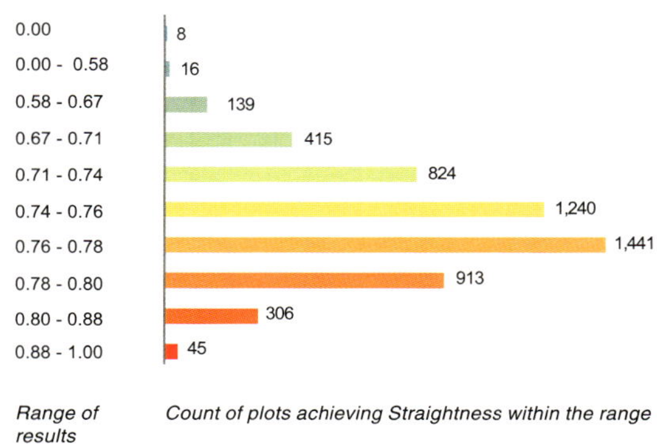

The warmer colors (greenish-yellow to red) represent Straightness values higher than 0.70, while the cooler colors (light green to dark blue) correspond to Straightness values lower than 0.71. The majority of plots, corresponding to 67% (or 3,594 out of 5,347 plots) have Straightness values ranging from 0.74 to 0.80. Among the categories shown in the legend, 1,441 plots have values in the range of 0.76 to 0.78, making this the most common value range; this range is represented by light orange on the map. The average Straightness value of plots in Baniyas is 0.75 at a 400 m radius, which means that their paths to other plots are 75% as straight as a straight line.

Scenario 2: Streets + Alleys — 800 m Radius

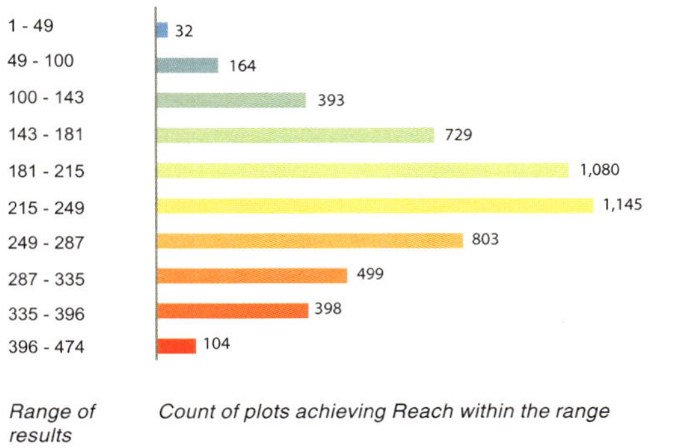

The warmer colors (i.e., greenish-yellow to red) represent a Reach value of 181 or more, while the cooler colors (i.e., light green to dark blue) correspond to a Reach value of 180 or less. The majority of plots (i.e., 2,949 out of 5,347), corresponding to 55% of all plots, have Reach values of more than 214. Among the categories shown in the legend, 21% of the total plots can reach 215 to 249 other plots within 10 minutes of walking. On average, each plot in Baniyas can access at least 228 plots within a distance of 800 m.

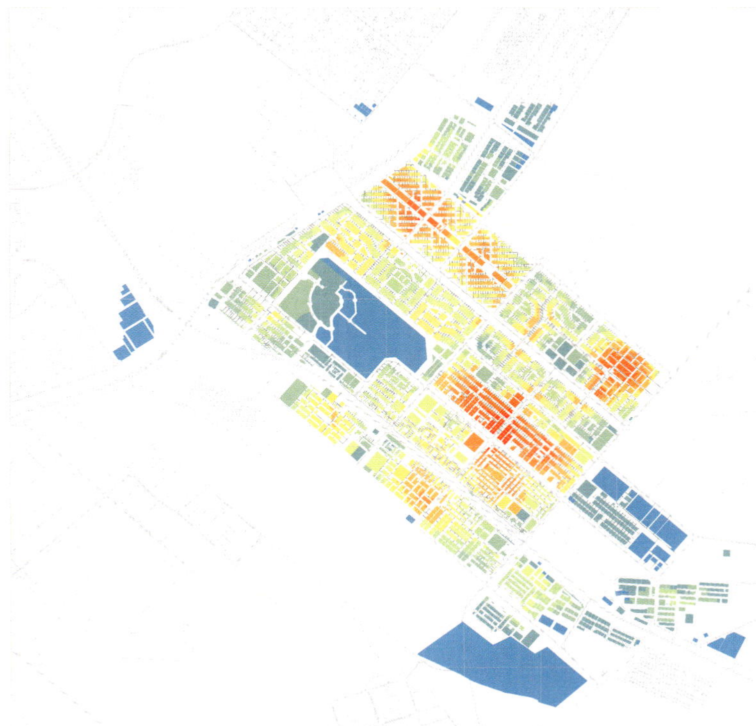

FIG. 13.1
Reach

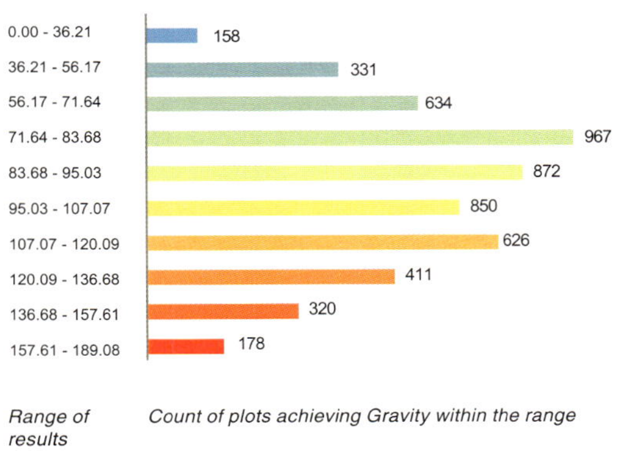

The warmer colors (i.e., greenish-yellow to red) represent Gravity values of more than 83.67, while the cooler colors (i.e., light green to dark blue) correspond to Gravity values of less than 83.68. Fifty-five percent of all plots (i.e., 2,962 out of 5,347) have Gravity values of less than 95.03. Among the categories shown in the legend, 967 plots, or 18% of the total plots, can reach 71.64 to 83.68 plots, making this the most common range; this range is represented by light green on the map. On average, each plot can reach 94 other plots when spatial impedance or distance decay effect is taken into consideration.

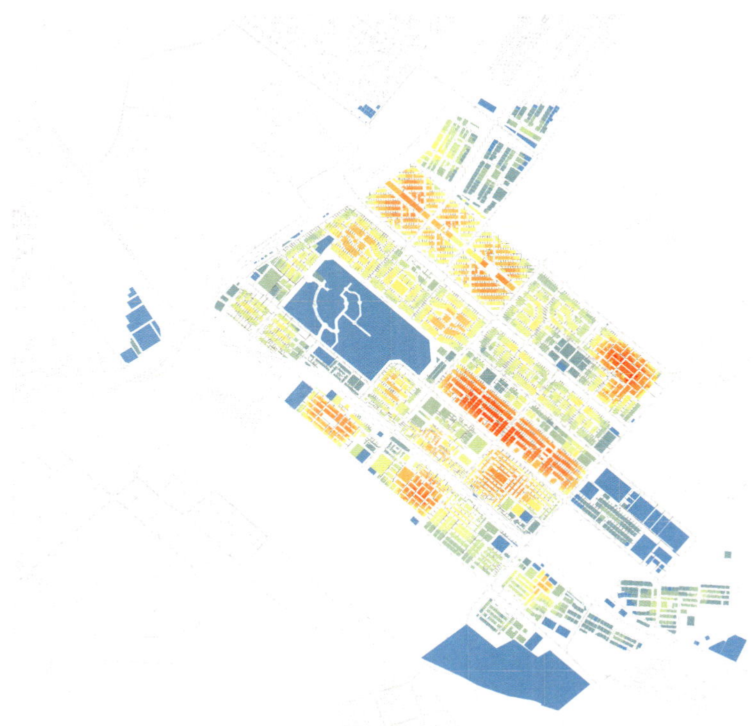

FIG. 13.2
Gravity

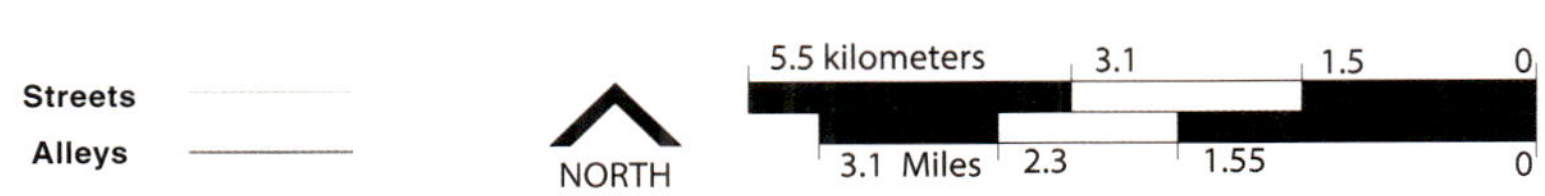

Scenario 2: Streets + Alleys — 800 m Radius

FIG. 13.3
Betweenness

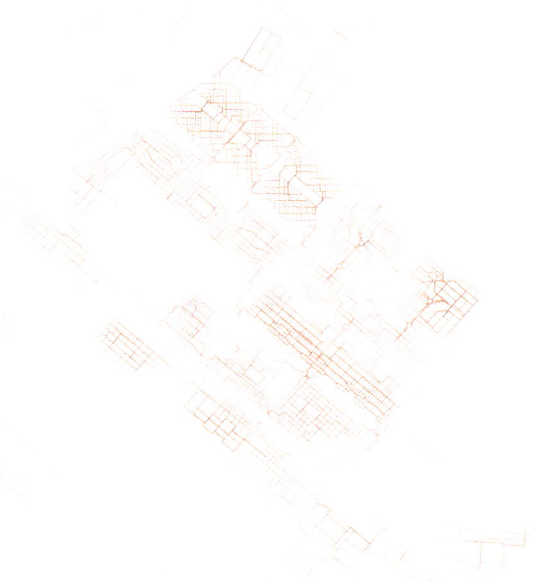

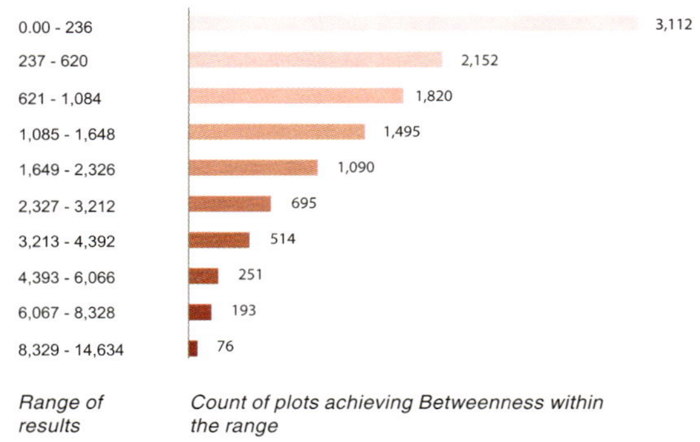

The majority of segments, corresponding to 87% (i.e., 9,904 out of 11,398 segments), have very low Betweenness values ranging from 0 to 2,539. Among the categories shown in the legend, 3,112 segments have values in the range of 0 to 236, making this the most common value range; this range is represented by the lightest brown on the map. Low Betweenness values ranging from 2,540 to 11,517 are obtained by 1,484 segments, which is 13% of all segments. Mid-range Betweenness values ranging from 11,518 to 20,478 are obtained by only 10 segments, which is only 0.1% of the total segments. No segments have high Betweenness values (higher than 20,478). The average Betweenness value in Baniyas is 1,223 (smaller than 2,540), while the median is 710, indicating very low Betweenness at an 800 m radius.

FIG. 13.4
Straightness

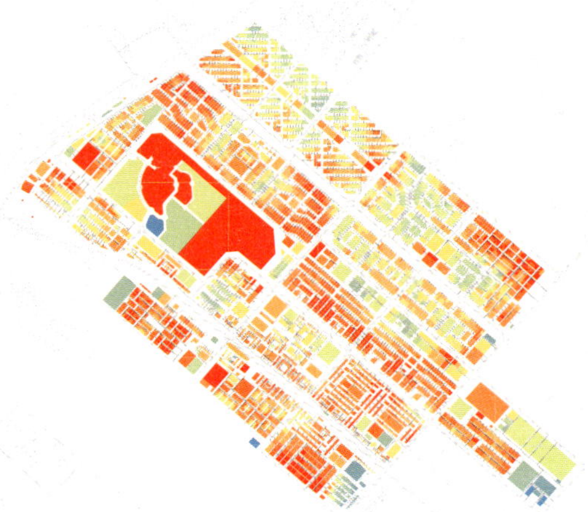

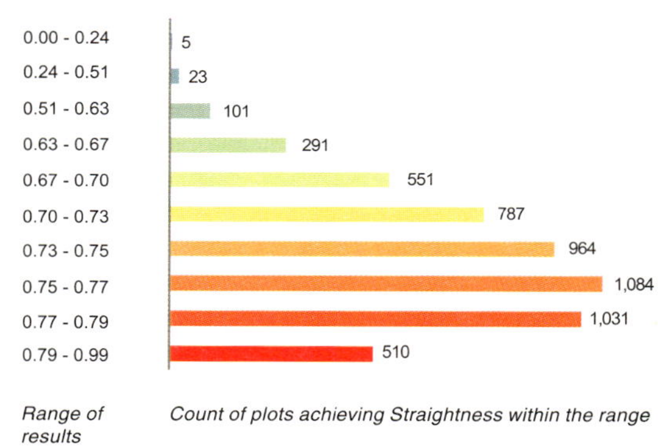

The warmer colors (greenish-yellow to red) represent Straightness values higher than 0.66, while the cooler colors (light green to dark blue) correspond to Straightness values lower than 0.67. The majority of plots, corresponding to 58% (or 3,079 out of 5,347 plots) have Straightness values ranging from 0.73 to 0.79. Among the categories shown in the legend, 1,084 plots have values in the range of 0.75 to 0.77, making this the most common value range; this range is represented by orange on the map. The average Straightness value of plots in Baniyas is 0.74 at an 800 m radius, which means that their paths to other plots are 74% as straight as a straight line.

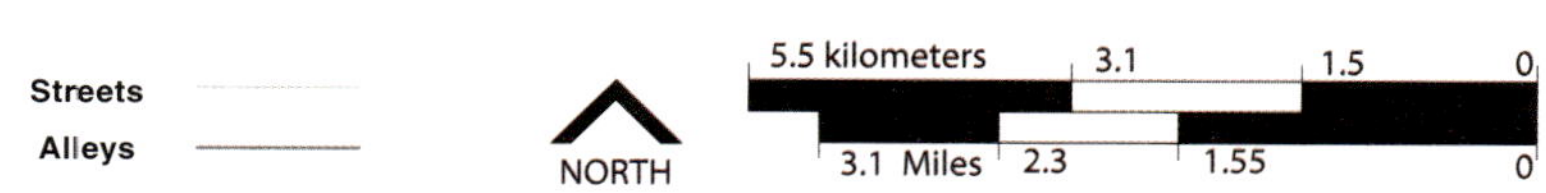

Scenario 2: Streets + Alleys — 1,600 m Radius

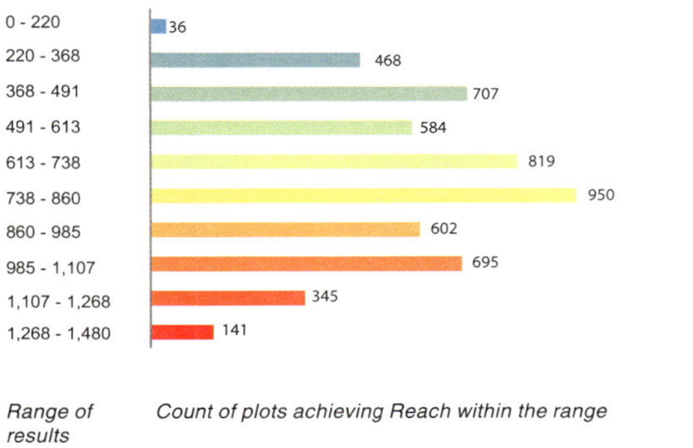

The warmer colors (i.e., greenish-yellow to red) represent a Reach value of 613 or more, while the cooler colors (i.e., light green to dark blue) correspond to a Reach value of 612 or less. The majority of plots (i.e., 2,733 out of 5,347), corresponding to 51% of all plots, have Reach values of more than 737. Among the categories shown in the legend, 18% of plots can reach 738 to 860 other plots within 20 minutes of walking. On average, each plot in Baniyas can access at least 743 plots within a distance of 1,600 m.

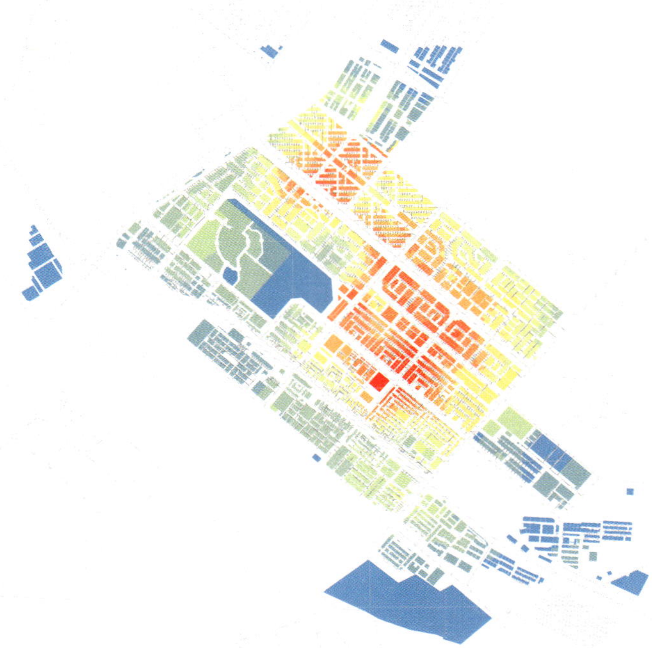

FIG. 14.1
Reach

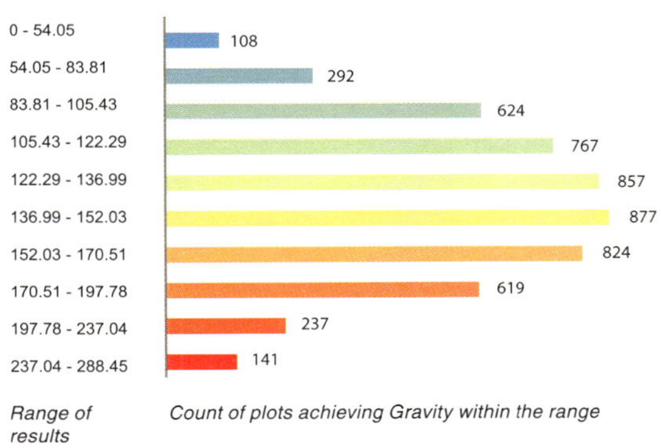

The warmer colors (i.e., greenish-yellow to red) represent Gravity values greater than 83.81, while the cooler colors (i.e., light green to dark blue) correspond to Gravity values lower than 83.81. Sixty-six percent of the total plots (i.e., 3,47 out of 5,347) have Gravity values of more than 122.29. Among the categories shown in the legend, 877 plots, or 16% of all plots, can reach 136.99 to 152.03 plots, making this the most common range; this range is represented by yellow on the map. On average, each plot can reach 138.82 other plots when spatial impedance or distance decay effect is taken into consideration.

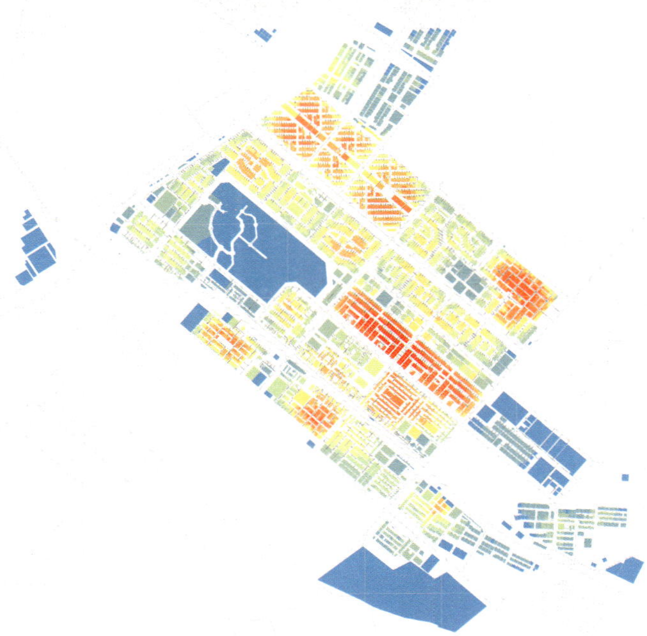

FIG. 14.2
Gravity

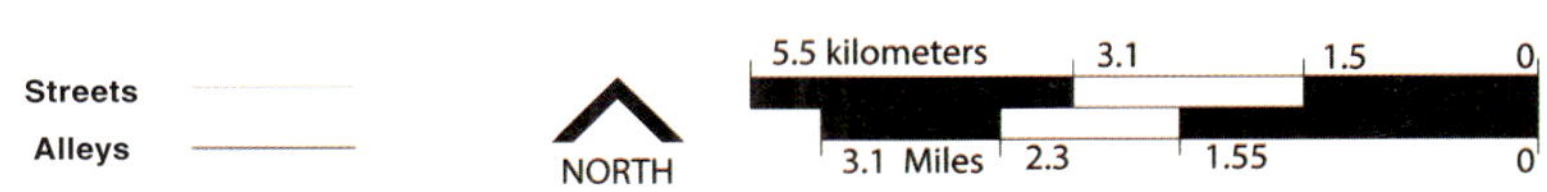

Scenario 2: Streets + Alleys — 1,600 m Radius

FIG. 14.3

Betweenness

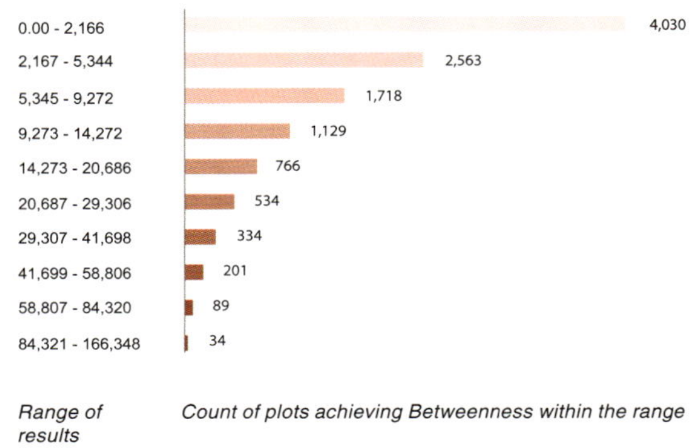

The majority of segments, corresponding to 99.5% (i.e., 11,344 out of 11,398 segments), have very low Betweenness values ranging from 0 to 73,682. Among the categories shown in the legend, 4,030 segments have values in the range of 0 to 2,166, making this the most common value range; this range is represented by the lightest brown on the map. Low Betweenness values ranging from 73,683 to 123,568 are obtained by 48 segments, which is 0.42% of all segments. Mid-range Betweenness values ranging from 123,569 to 179,444 are obtained by only 6 segments, which is 0.1% of the total segments. No segments have high Betweenness values (higher than 179,444). The average Betweenness value in Baniyas is 8,316 (smaller than 73,683), while the median is 3,978, indicating very low Betweenness at a 1,600 m radius.

FIG. 14.4

Straightness

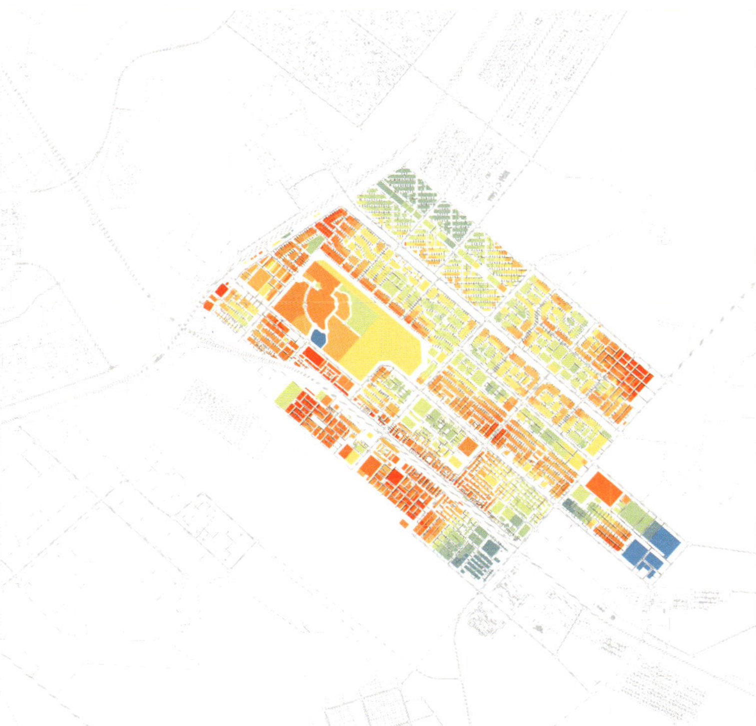

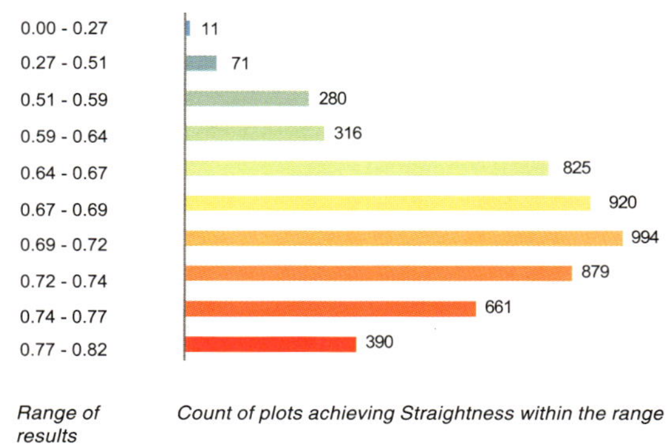

The warmer colors (greenish-yellow to red) represent Straightness values higher than 0.63, while the cooler colors (light green to dark blue) correspond to Straightness values lower than 0.64. The majority of plots, corresponding to 52% (or 2,793 out of 5,347 plots) have Straightness values ranging from 0.67 to 0.74. Among the categories shown in the legend, 994 plots have values in the range of 0.69 to 0.72, making this the most common value range; this range is represented by light orange on the map. At a 1,600 m radius, the average Straightness value of plots in Baniyas is 0.69, which means that their paths to other plots are 69% as straight as a straight line.

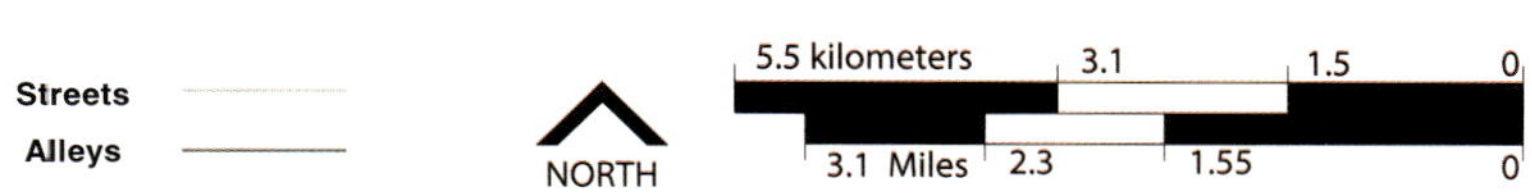

Centrality Analysis: Sample Scale

Sample 01

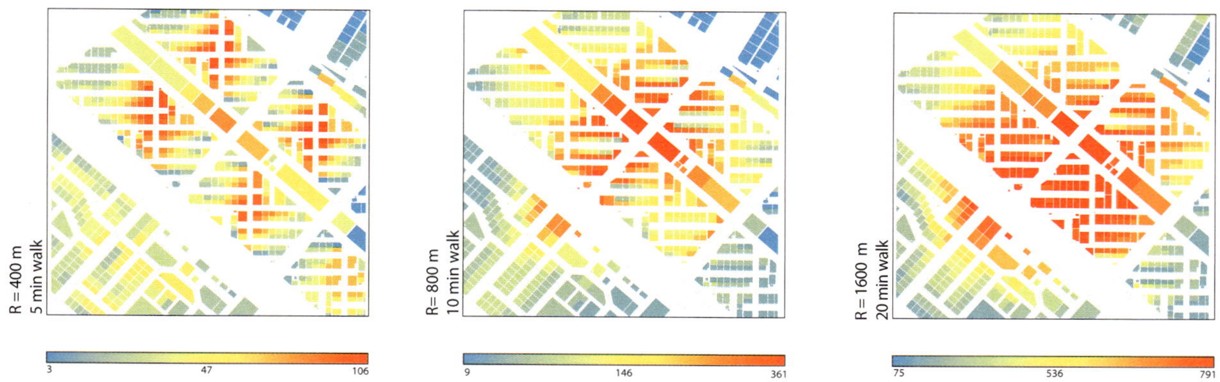

FIG. 15.1
Reach
Scenario 1: Streets only

Reach (Radius = 400 m)
The maximum number of plots that can be reached within 10 min walking distance is 106 plots. The average Reach of the sample is 47plots.

Summary of Reach results
Minimum: 3
Maximum: 106
Mean: 47
Median: 45

Reach (Radius = 800 m)
The maximum number of plots that can be reached within 10 min walking distance is 361plots. The average Reach of the sample is 146 plots.

Summary of Reach results
Minimum: 9
Maximum: 361
Mean: 146
Median: 142

Reach (Radius = 1600 m)
The maximum number of plots that can be reached within 20 min walking distance is 791 plots. The average Reach of the sample is 536 plots.

Summary of Reach results
Minimum: 75
Maximum: 791
Mean: 536
Median: 543

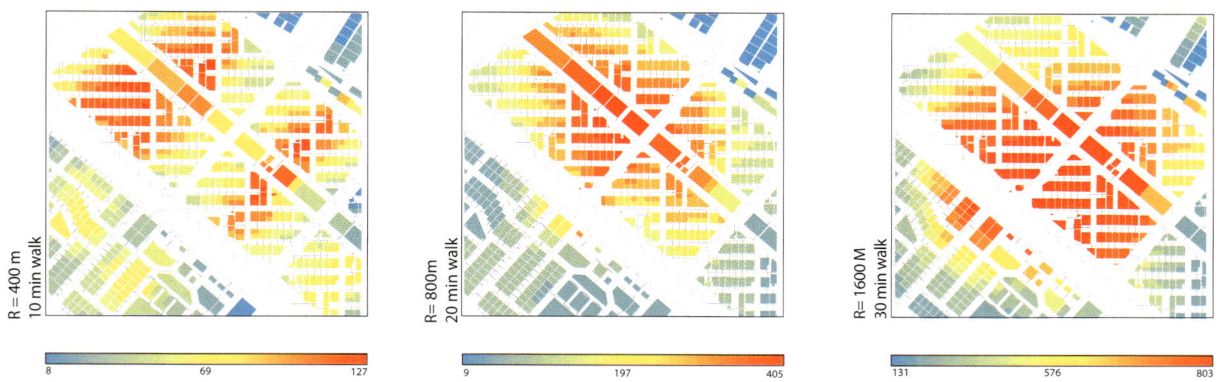

FIG. 15.2
Reach
Scenario 2: Streets + Alleys

Reach (Radius = 400 m)
The maximum number of plots that can be reached within 10 min walking distance is 127 plots. The average Reach of the sample is 69 plots.

Summary of Reach results
Minimum: 8
Maximum: 127
Mean: 69
Median: 69

Reach (Radius = 800 m)
The maximum number of plots that can be reached within 20 min walking distance is 405 plots. The average Reach of the sample is 197 plots.

Summary of Reach results
Minimum: 9
Maximum: 405
Mean: 197
Median: 210

Reach (Radius = 1600 m)
The maximum number of plots that can be reached within 30 min walking distance is 803 plots. The average Reach of the sample is 576 plots.

Summary of Reach results
Minimum: 131
Maximum: 803
Mean: 576
Median: 580

At a 400 m radius, plots with high Reach values ranging from 47 to 106 concentrate in the center of four NPUs lying in the upper half of the sample. At an 800 m radius, plots with high Reach values (ranging from 146 to 361) shift along the arterial street that crosses through those four NPUs. At a 1,600 m radius, Reach values become even higher throughout the four NPUs. With the introduction of alleys, at a 400 m radius, the concentration of high Reach values becomes stronger and clearer around the central area of the four NPUs. At an 800 m radius, most plots with high Reach values are seen within the two NPUs at the top, with values ranging from 197 to 405. At a 1,600 m radius, when alleys are included in the analysis, plots with high Reach values are most prominent in one of the smallest NPUs at the lower corner. Most plots within this small NPU have the highest Reach value of 803.

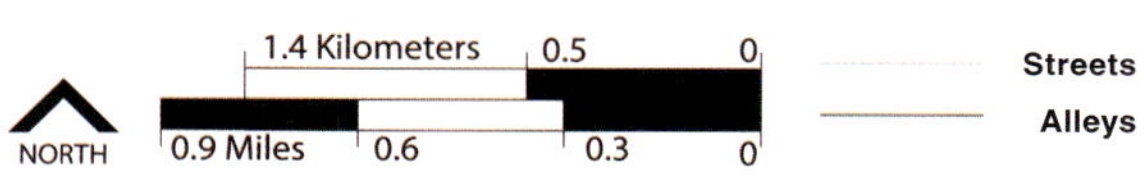

Sample 01

FIG. 15.3
Gravity
Scenario 1: Streets only

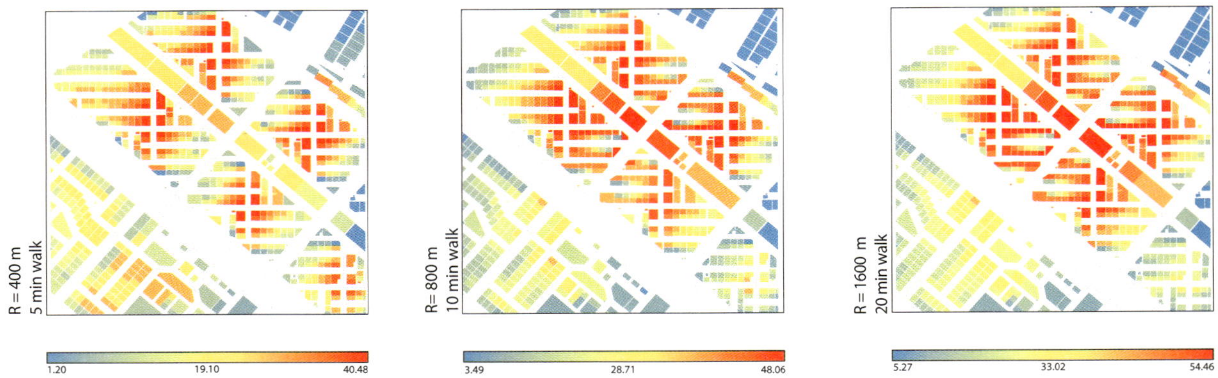

Gravity (Radius = 400 m)
The maximum number of plots that can be reached within 5 min walking distance with the distance decay effect is 40.48 plots. The average Gravity of the sample is 19.10 plots.

Summary of Gravity results
Minimum: 1.20
Maximum: 40.48
Mean: 19.10

Gravity (Radius = 800 m)
The maximum number of plots that can be reached within 10 min walking distance with the distance decay effect is 48.06 plots. The average Gravity of the sample is 28.71 plots.

Summary of Gravity results
Minimum: 3.49
Maximum: 48.06
Mean: 28.71

Gravity (Radius = 1600 m)
The maximum number of plots that can be reached within 20 min walking distance with the distance decay effect is 54.5 plots. The average Gravity of the sample is 33 plots.

Summary of Gravity results
Minimum: 5.27
Maximum: 54.46
Mean: 33.02

FIG. 15.4
Gravity
Scenario 2: Streets + Alleys

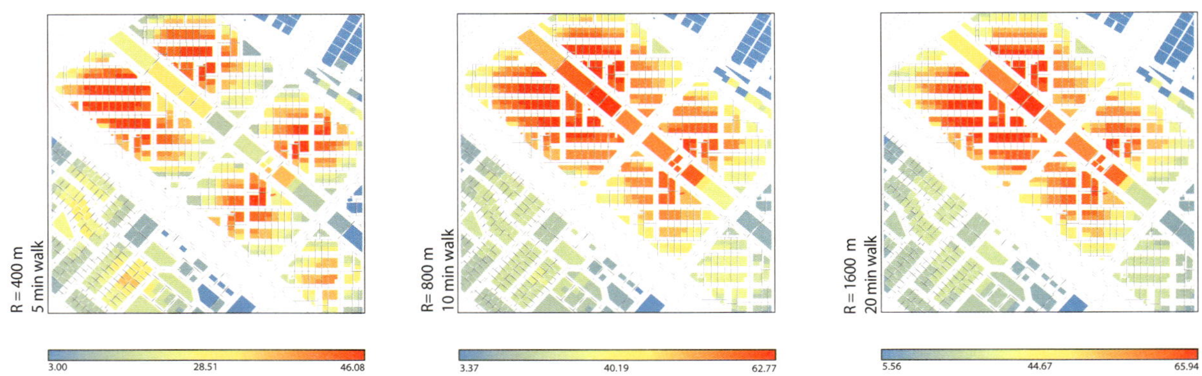

Gravity (Radius = 400 m)
The maximum number of plots that can be reached within 5 min walking distance with the distance decay effect is 46.08 plots. The average Gravity of the sample is 28.51 plots.

Summary of Gravity results
Minimum: 3.00
Maximum: 46.08
Mean: 28.51
Median: 28.81

Gravity (Radius = 800 m)
The maximum number of plots that can be reached within 10 min walking distance with the distance decay effect is 62.8 plots. The average Gravity of the sample is 40.2 plots.

Summary of Gravity results
Minimum: 3.37
Maximum: 62.77
Mean: 40.19
Median: 41.44

Gravity (Radius = 1600 m)
The maximum number of plots that can be reached within 20 min walking distance with the distance decay effect is 65.994 plots. The average Gravity of the sample is 44.67 plots

Summary of Gravity results
Minimum: 5.56
Maximum: 65.94
Mean: 44.67
Median: 46.72

At a 400 m radius, the central parts of five NPUs with linear patterns consist of plots with high Gravity values ranging from 19.10 to 40.50. At 800 m and 1,600 m radii, Gravity values ranging from 28.71 to 54.50 become even more concentrated at the center of the four NPUs and also appear at the center of the mixed-use corridor. Gravity values decrease for the fifth NPU near the bottom right corner of the sample. With the introduction of alleys, at a 400 m radius, the concentration of high Gravity values becomes stronger and clearer, especially for the two larger NPUs located at the top. At 800 m and 1,600 m radii, the larger NPUs at the top become more prominent; the majority of plots have the highest Gravity values of 62.78 and 65.94, respectively.

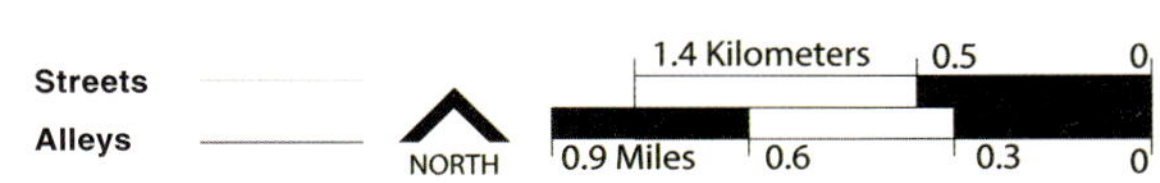

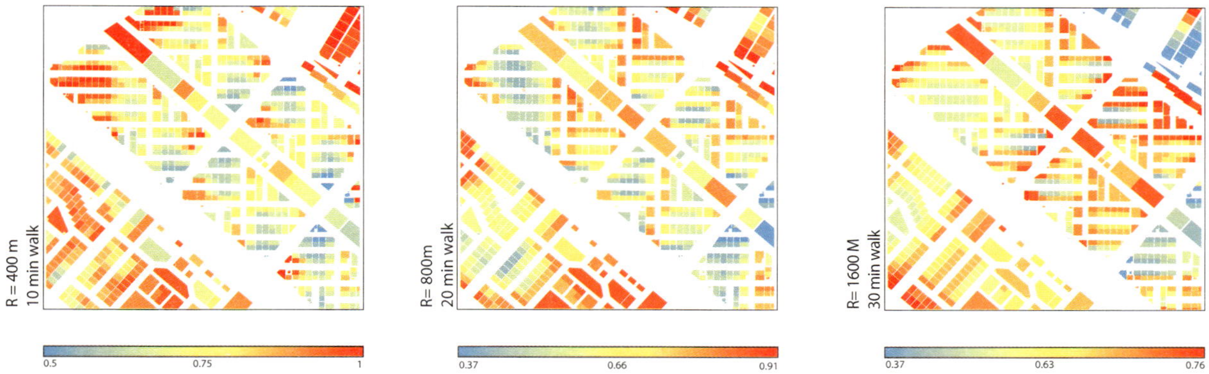

Straightness (Normalized Values, Radius= 400 m)
Plots withing 10 min walking distance have access to streets with an average Straightness value of 0.70.

Summary of Straightness results
Minimum: 0.5
Maximum: 1
Mean: 0.75
Median: 0.75

Straightness (Normalized Values, Radius= 800 m)
Plots withing 20 min walking distance have access to streets with an average Straightness value of 0.70.

Summary of Straightness results
Minimum: 0.37
Maximum: 0.91
Mean: 0.66
Median: 0.66

Straightness (Normalized Values, Radius= 1600 m)
Plots withing 30 min walking distance have access to streets with an average Straightness value of 0.60.

Summary of Straightness results
Minimum: 0.37
Maximum: 0.76
Mean: 0.63
Median: 0.64

FIG. 15.5
Straightness
Scenario 1: Streets only

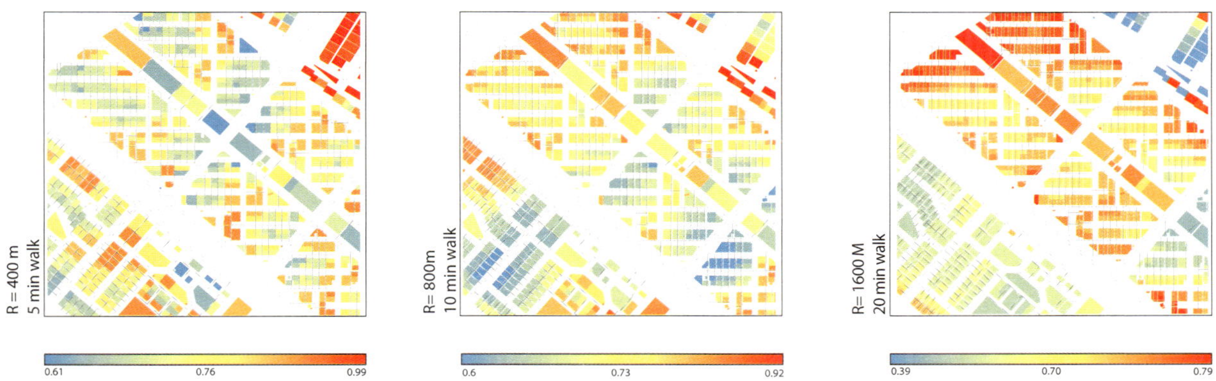

Straightness (Normalized Values, Radius= 400 m)
Plots withing 5 min walking distance have access to streets with an average Straightness value of 0.76.

Summary of Straightness results
Minimum: 0.61
Maximum: 0.99
Mean: 0.76
Median: 0.75

Straightness (Normalized Values, Radius= 800 m)
Plots withing 10 min walking distance have access to streets with an average Straightness value of 0.73.

Summary of Straightness results
Minimum: 0.60
Maximum: 0.92
Mean: 0.73
Median: 0.73

Straightness (Normalized Values, Radius= 1600 m)
Plots withing 20 min walking distance have access to streets with an average Straightness value of 0.70.

Summary of Straightness results
Minimum: 0.39
Maximum: 0.79
Mean: 0.70
Median: 0.71

FIG. 15.6
Straightness
Scenario 2: Streets + Alleys

At a 400 m radius, high Straightness values (0.75 to 1) become prominent in different locations: the NPUs at the bottom of the sample, plots located near the arterial street located at the top right corner, and in the upper parts of the NPUs near top left corner of the sample. At an 800 m radius, high Straightness values concentrate at the center of the five NPUs in the middle. Simultaneously, the intensification of high Straightness values decreases for the NPUs at the bottom and for plots at the top right corner. At a 1,600 m radius, high values ranging from 0.75 to 0.76 mostly accumulate in the two smaller NPUs in the middle. With the introduction of alleys, at 400 m, Straightness values are distributed evenly, with only one visible cluster of high values at the top right corner. At 800 m, the values increase for the two bigger NPUs in the middle while decreasing for other NPUs. At a 1,600 m radius, plots with high Straightness values concentrate near the upper edges of the bigger NPUs at the center of the sample.

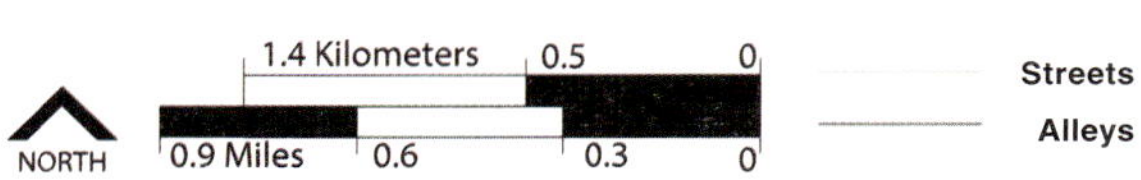

Sample 02

FIG. 16.1
Reach
Scenario 1: Streets only

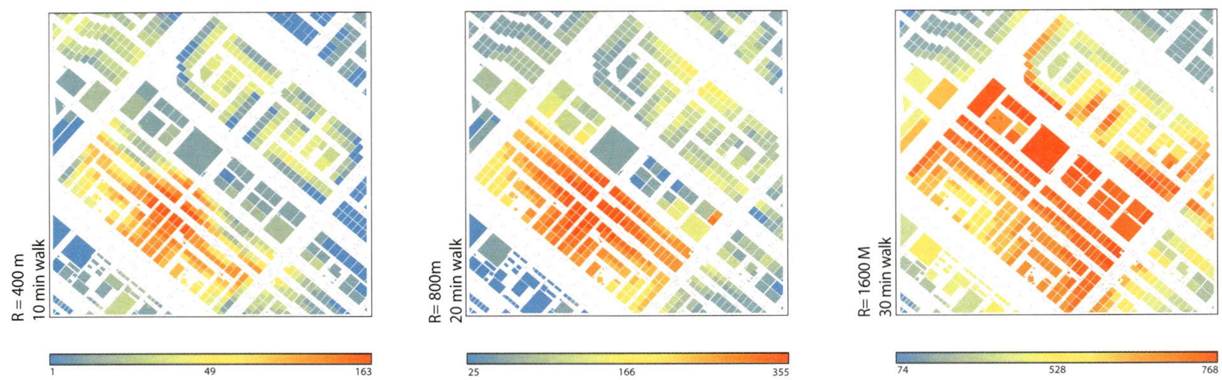

Reach (Radius = 400 m)
The maximum number of plots that can be reached within 10 min walking distance is 163 plots. The average Reach of the sample is 49 plots.

Summary of Reach results
Minimum: 1
Maximum: 163
Mean: 49
Median: 43

Reach (Radius = 800 m)
The maximum number of plots that can be reached within 20 min walking distance is 355 plots. The average Reach of the sample is 166 plots.

Summary of Reach results
Minimum: 25
Maximum: 355
Mean: 166
Median: 132

Reach (Radius = 1600 m)
The maximum number of plots that can be reached within 30 min walking distance is 768 plots. The average Reach of the sample is 528 plots.

Summary of Reach results
Minimum: 74
Maximum: 768
Mean: 528
Median: 561

FIG. 16.2
Reach
Scenario 2: Streets + Alleys

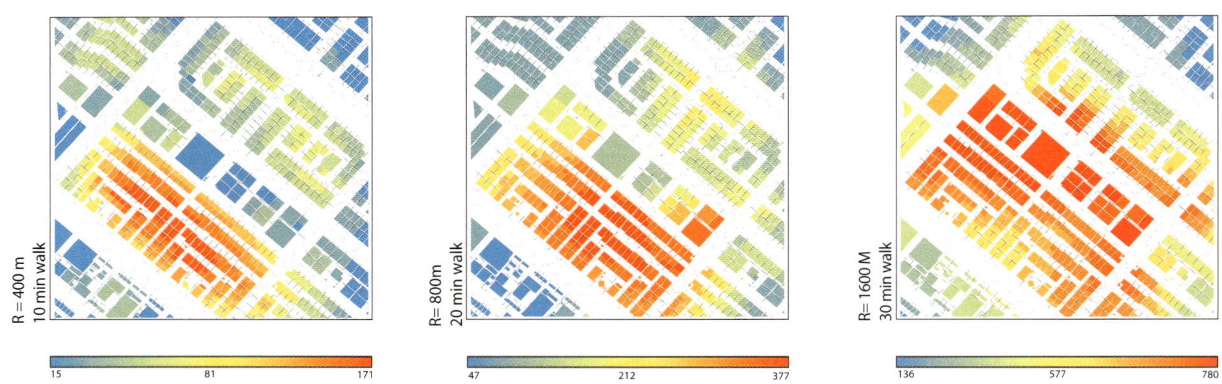

Reach (Radius = 400 m)
The maximum number of plots that can be reached within 10 min walking distance is 171 plots. The average Reach of the sample is 81 plots.

Summary of Reach results
Minimum: 15
Maximum: 171
Mean: 81
Median: 71

Reach (Radius = 800 m)
The maximum number of plots that can be reached within 20 min walking distance is 377 plots. The average Reach of the sample is 212 plots.

Summary of Reach results
Minimum: 47
Maximum: 377
Mean: 212
Median: 203

Reach (Radius = 1600 m)
The maximum number of plots that can be reached within 30 min walking distance is 780 plots. The average Reach of the sample is 577 plots.

Summary of Reach results
Minimum: 136
Maximum: 780
Mean: 577
Median: 622

At a 400 m radius, plots with high Reach values ranging from 49 to 163 concentrate at the center of the NPU located on the lower side of the sample. At an 800 m radius, plots with high Reach values (ranging from 252 to 355) become even more concentrated at the same spot. At a 1,600 m radius, high Reach values are visible throughout the same NPU, and also in few plots of the adjacent NPU that lie along the major corridor. With the introduction of alleys, at a 400 m radius, the concentration of high Reach values becomes stronger and clearer around the central area of the NPU located on the lower side. At an 800 m radius, the location of high Reach values ranging from 212 to 377 does not change. At a 1,600 m radius, when alleys are included in the analysis, the distribution of high Reach values does not alter significantly from previous scenarios. The highest Reach value of 780 is obtained by the bigger-sized plots located at the center of the sample at the major corridor.

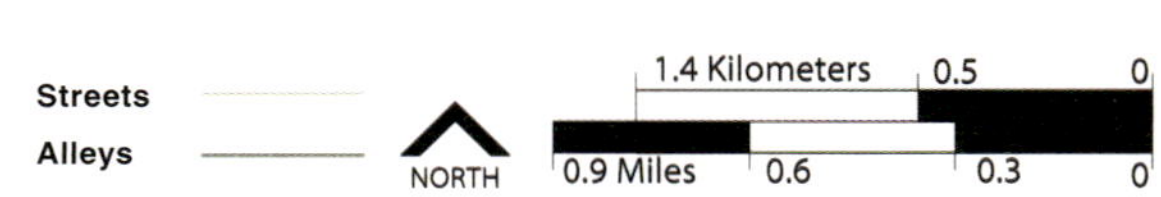

FIG. 16.3
Gravity
Scenario 1: Streets only

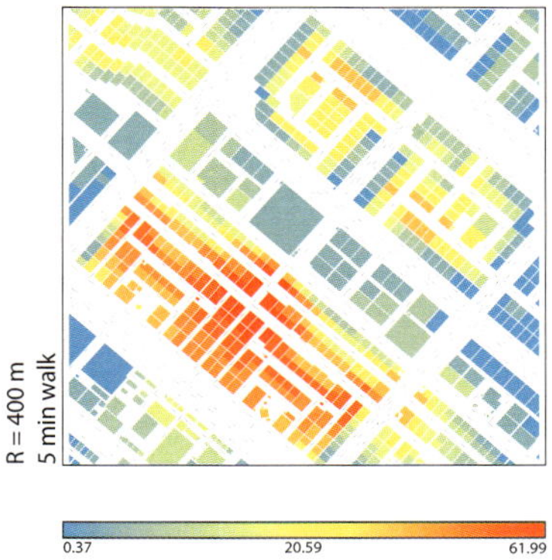

Gravity (Radius = 400 m)
The maximum number of plots that can be reached within 5 min walking distance with the distance decay effect is 61.99 plots. The average Gravity of the sample is 20.59 plots.

Summary of Gravity results
Minimum: 0.37
Maximum: 61.99
Mean: 20.59
Median: 19.14

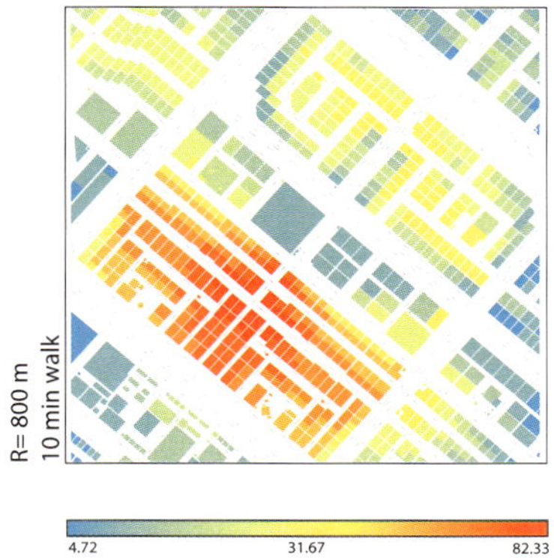

Gravity (Radius = 800 m)
The maximum number of plots that can be reached within 10 min walking distance with the distance decay effect is 82.33 plots. The average Gravity of the sample is 31.67 plots.

Summary of Gravity results
Minimum: 4.72
Maximum: 82.33
Mean: 31.67
Median: 26.65

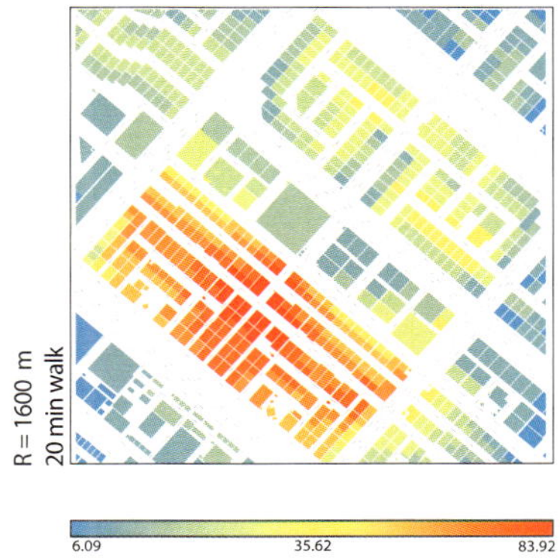

Gravity (Radius = 1600 m)
The maximum number of plots that can be reached within 20 min walking distance with the distance decay effect is 83.92 plots. The average Gravity of the sample is 35.62 plots.

Summary of Gravity results
Minimum: 6.09
Maximum: 83.92
Mean: 35.62
Median: 30.88

FIG. 16.4
Gravity
Scenario 2: Streets + Alleys

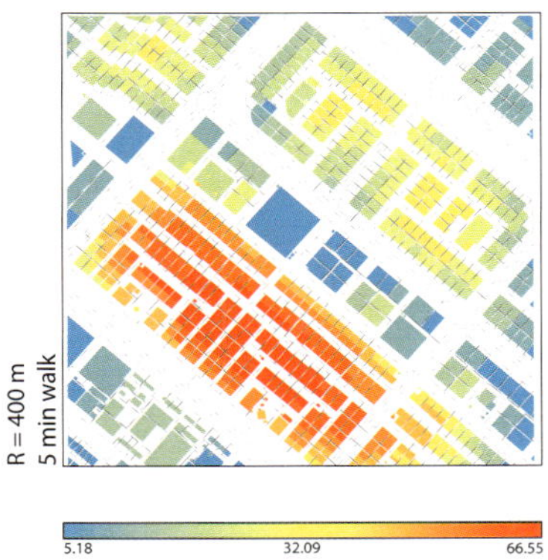

Gravity (Radius = 400 m)
The maximum number of plots that can be reached within 5 min walking distance with the distance decay effect is 66.55 plots. The average Gavity of the sample is 32.09 plots.

Summary of Gravity results
Minimum: 5.18
Maximum: 66.55
Mean: 32.09
Median: 28.87

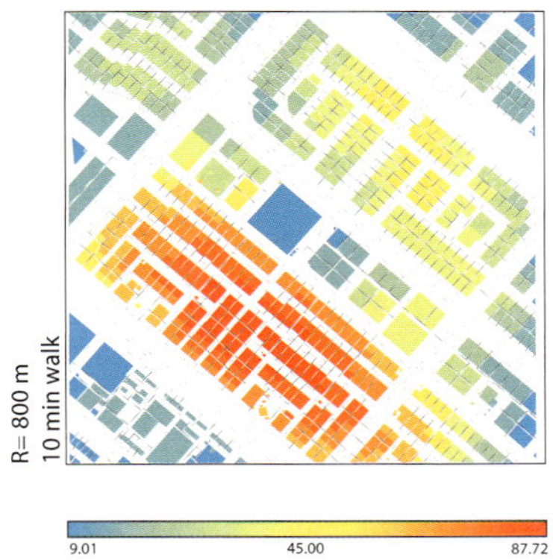

Gravity (Radius = 800 m)
The maximum number of plots that can be reached within 10 min walking distance with the distance decay effect is 87.72 plots. The average Gravity of the sample is 45.00 plots.

Summary of Gravity results
Minimum: 9.01
Maximum: 87.72
Mean: 45.00
Median: 39.88

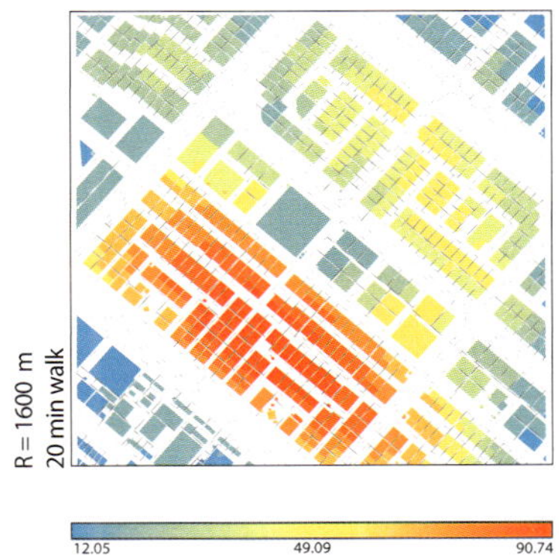

Gravity (Radius = 1600 m)
The maximum number of plots that can be reached within 20 min walking distance with the distance decay effect is 90.74 plots. The average Gravity of the sample is 49.09 plots.

Summary of Gravity results
Minimum: 12.05
Maximum: 90.74
Mean: 49.09
Median: 44.52

At a 400 m radius, the NPU located at the bottom consists of plots with high Gravity values ranging from 20.59 to 61.99. At 800 m and 1,600 m radii, high Gravity values ranging from 31.68 to 83.92 become even more concentrated at the same spots within the NPU. With the introduction of alleys, at a 400 m radius, the concentration of high Gravity values becomes stronger and clearer for the NPU at the bottom, while the values improve for the adjacent NPU at the top. At 800 m and 1,600 m radii, the NPU at the bottom continues to become more prominent: the majority of plots have the highest Gravity values of 87.73 and 90.75, respectively.

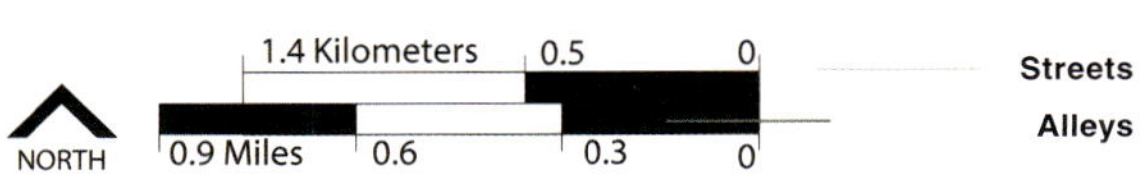

Sample 02

FIG. 16.5
Straightness
Scenario 1: Streets only

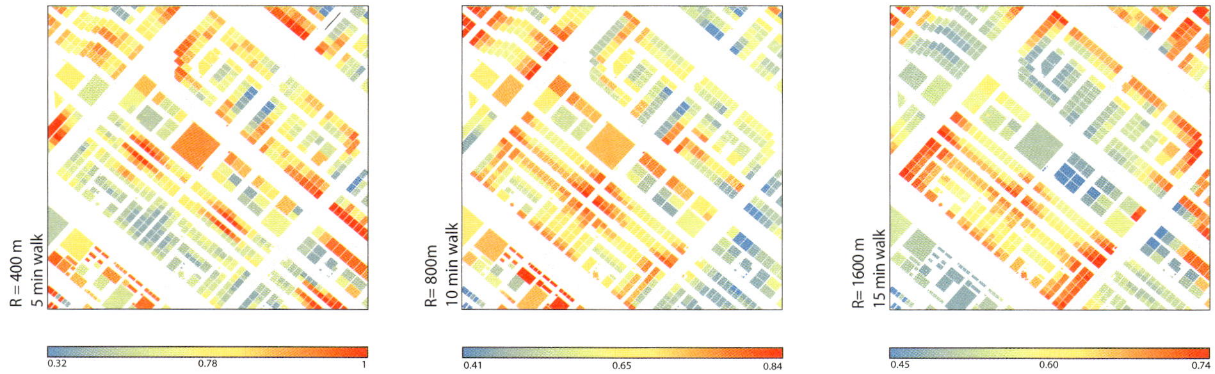

Straightness (Normalized Values, Radius= 400 m)
Plots withing 10 min walking distance have access to streets with an average Straightness value of 0.78.

Summary of Reach results
Minimum: 0.32
Maximum: 1
Mean: 0.78
Median: 0.77

Straightness (Normalized Values, Radius= 800 m)
Plots withing 20 min walking distance have access to streets with an average Straightness value of 0.70.

Summary of Reach results
Minimum: 0.41
Maximum: 0.84
Mean: 0.65
Median: 0.66

Straightness (Normalized Values, Radius= 1600 m)
Plots withing 30 min walking distance have access to streets with an average Straightness value of 0.60.

Summary of Reach results
Minimum: 0.45
Maximum: 0.74
Mean: 0.60
Median: 0.60

FIG. 16.6
Straightness
Scenario 2: Streets + Alleys

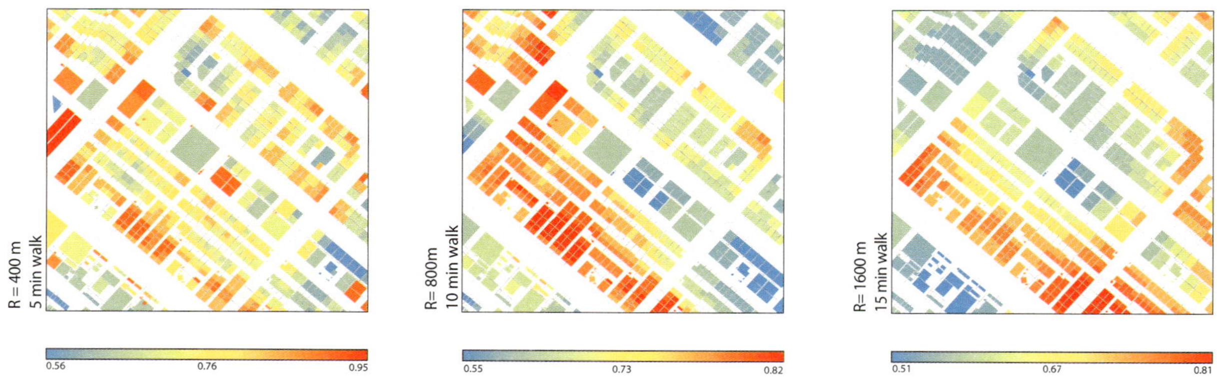

Straightness (Normalized Values, Radius= 400 m)
Plots withing 10 min walking distance have access to streets with an average Straightness value of 0.76.

Summary of Reach results
Minimum: 0.56
Maximum: 0.95
Mean: 0.76
Median: 0.76

Straightness (Normalized Values, Radius= 800 m)
Plots withing 20 min walking distance have access to streets with an average Straightness value of 0.73.

Summary of Reach results
Minimum: 0.55
Maximum: 0.82
Mean: 0.73
Median: 0.75

Straightness (Normalized Values, Radius= 1600 m)
Plots withing 30 min walking distance have access to streets with an average Straightness value of 0.67.

Summary of Reach results
Minimum: 0.51
Maximum: 0.81
Mean: 0.67
Median: 0.68

At a 400 m radius, high Straightness values (0.75 to 1) are obtained by a few centrally located plots within the lower NPU and a few plots lying on the edges of the adjacent NPU at the top. At 800 m, Straightness values become even higher within the lower NPU. Simultaneously, high Straightness values can be witnessed at the top right corner. At a 1,600 m radius, Straightness values decrease for most plots except for a few near the arterial streets. With the introduction of alleys, at 400 m, Straightness values are distributed evenly, with only one visible cluster of high values within the lower NPU. At 800 m, high values are obtained by the plots within the lower NPU which lie near the arterial street. At 1,600 m, Straightness values decrease for most plots while increasing for few plots located near the bottom right corner of the sample.

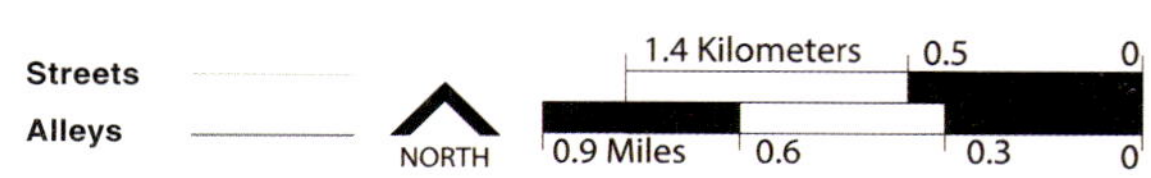

Summary of Centrality Results

Neighborhood

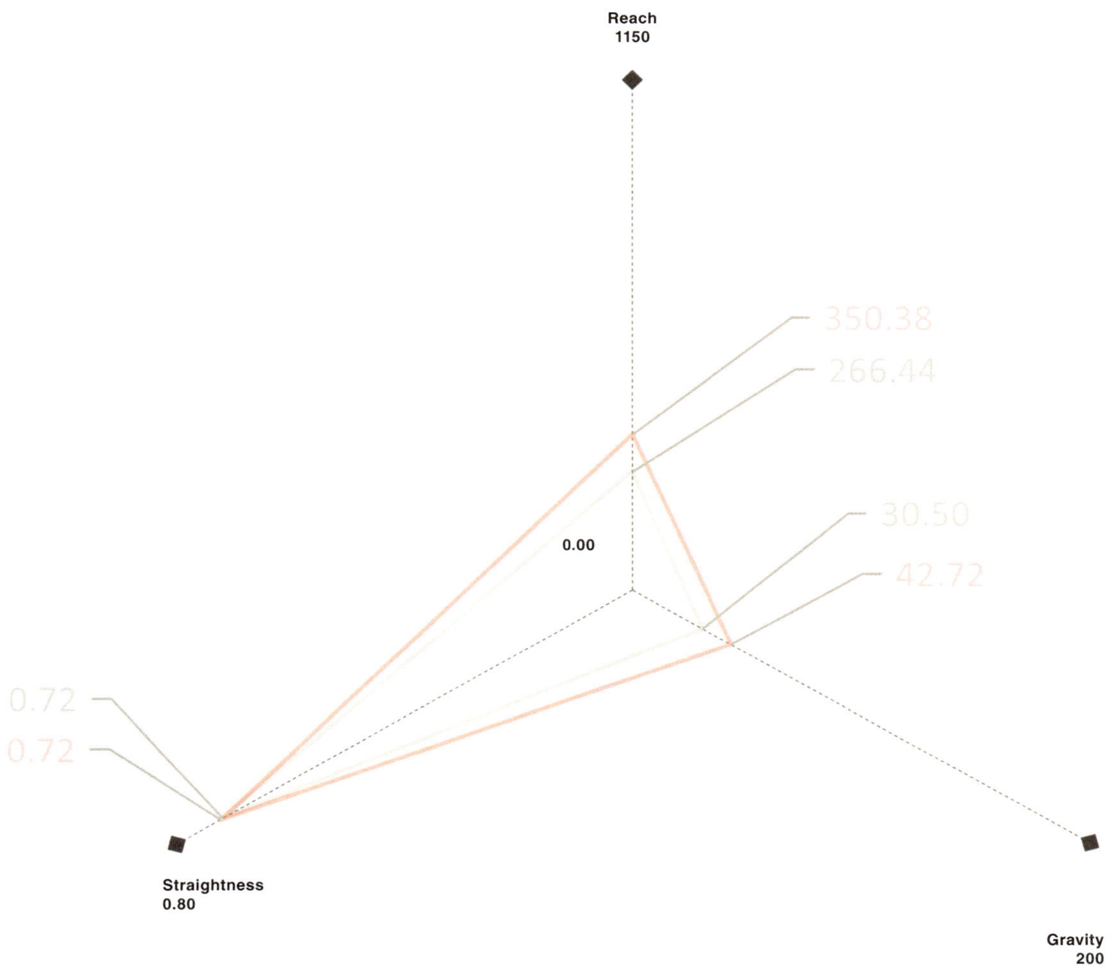

Sample 01

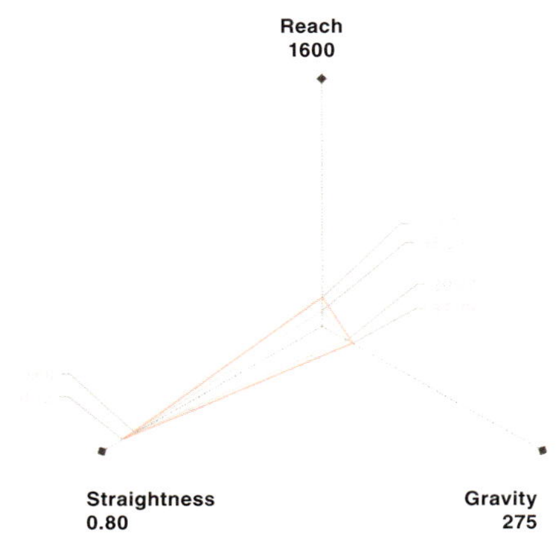

Sample 02

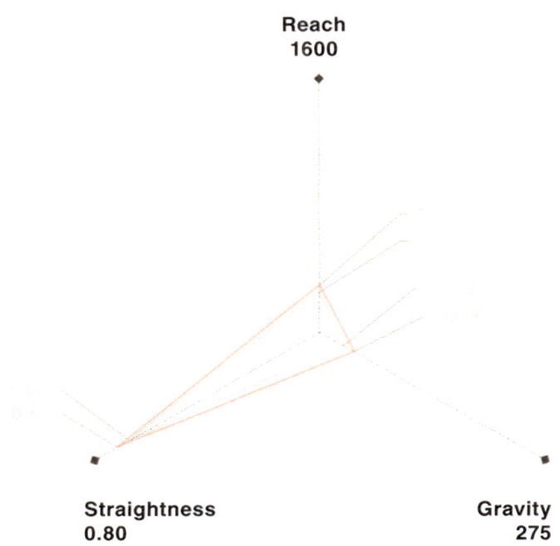

FIG. 17
Spider graphs showing the contribution of alleyways to the averages of 400m, 800m, and 1600m scales of Reach, Gravity and Straightness

Neighborhood Scale

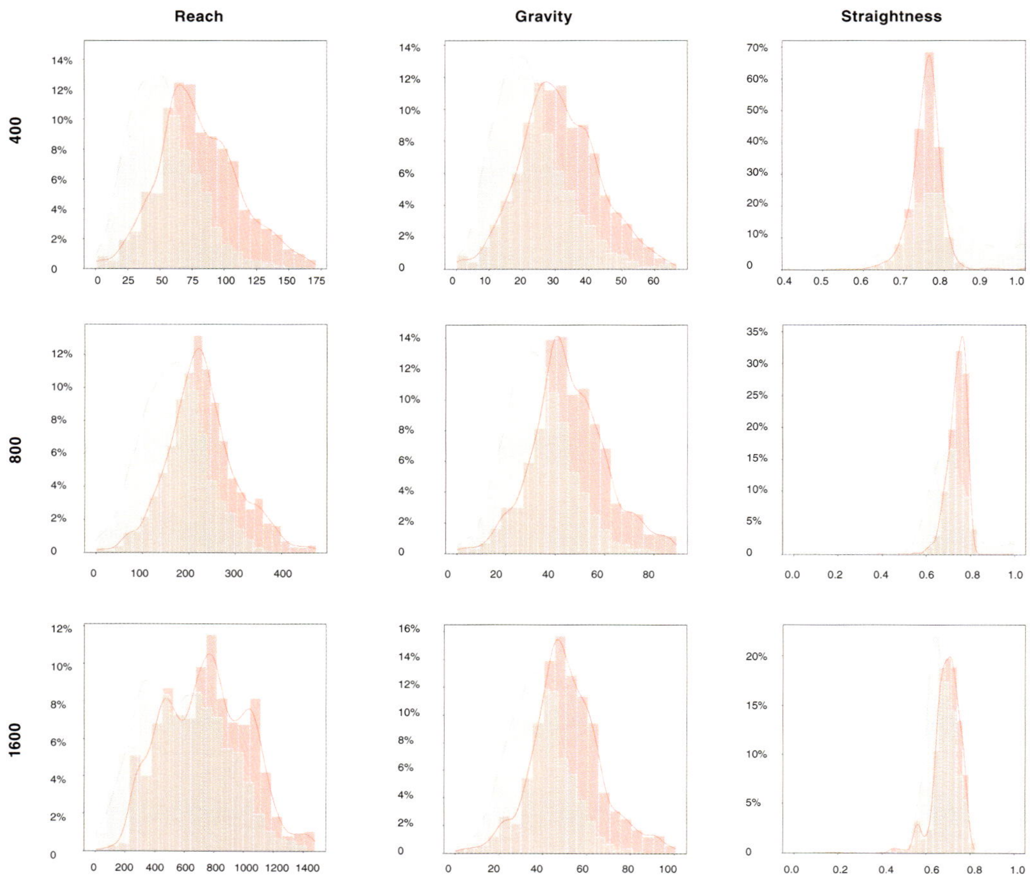

FIG. 18

Histograms showing the distribution of centrality values (Reach, Gravity, and Straightness) among plots with and without alleys at three different scales 400m, 800m, and 1600m. The X axis is for the centrality metric values, while the Y axis is for the percentage of plots achieving a centrality value denoted on the X axis.

TABLE. 1

Neighborhood scale centrality values

UNA		Radius	Min	Max	Avg
Scenario 1: Streets only	Reach	400	0	163	52
		800	0	398	163
		1600	0	1423	584
	Gravity	400	0	64.67	21.95
		800	0	82.37	32.67
		1600	0	84.94	36.87
	Straightness	400	0	1	0.79
		800	0	1	0.71
		1600	0	1	0.67

UNA		Radius	Min	Max	Avg
Scenario 2: Streets + Alleys	Reach	400	1	171	80
		800	1	474	228
		1600	9	1480	743
	Gravity	400	0.21	65.55	31.46
		800	0.23	89.20	45.47
		1600	0.02	100.61	50.96
	Straightness	400	0.00	1.00	0.75
		800	0.00	0.99	0.73
		1600	0.00	0.82	0.69

Sample Scale — Sample 01

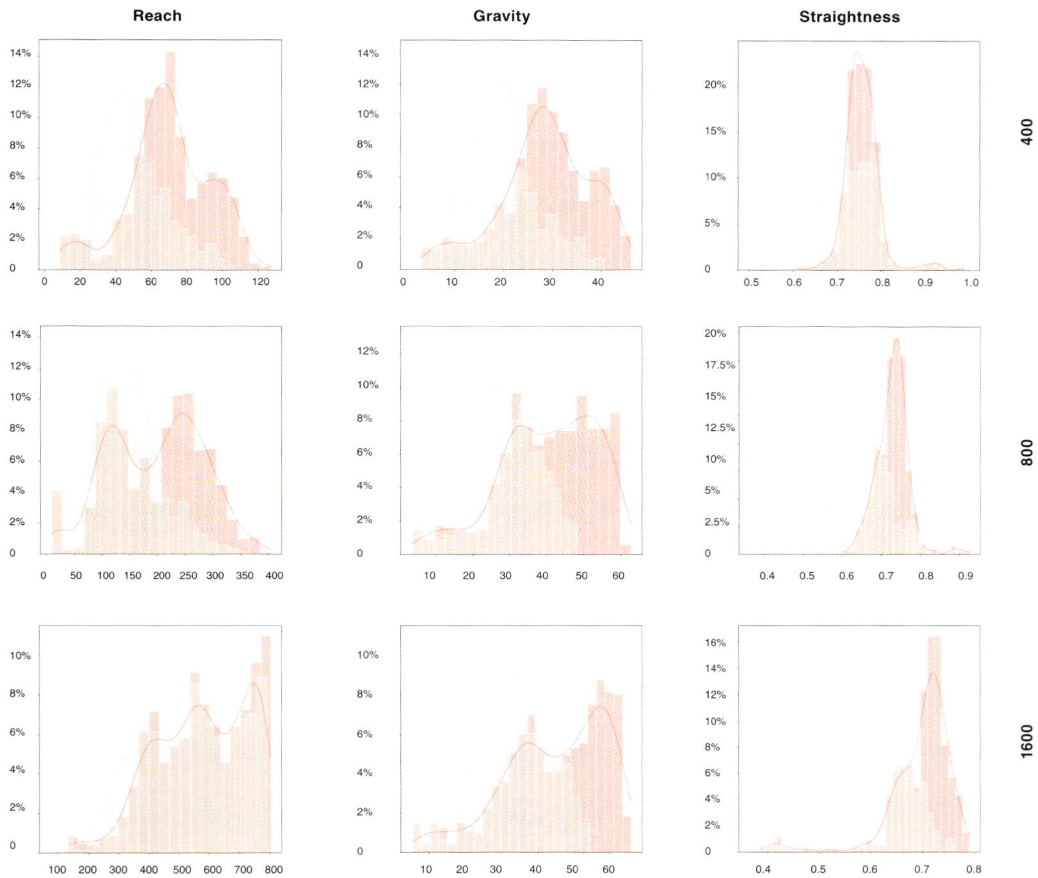

FIG. 19

Histograms showing the distribution of centrality values (Reach, Gravity, and Straightness) among plots with and without alleys at three different scales 400m, 800m, and 1600m. The X axis is for the centrality metric values, while the Y axis is for the percentage of plots achieving a centrality value denoted on the X axis.

Scenario 1: Streets only	UNA	Radius	Min	Max	Avg
	Reach	400	3	106	47
		800	9	361	146
		1600	75	791	536
	Gravity	400	1.20	40.48	19.10
		800	3.49	48.06	28.71
		1600	5.27	54.46	33.02
	Straightness	400	0.50	1.00	0.74
		800	0.36	0.91	0.66
		1600	0.36	0.75	0.63

Scenario 2: Streets + Alleys	UNA	Radius	Min	Max	Avg
	Reach	400	8	127	69
		800	9	405	196
		1600	131	803	576
	Gravity	400	3.00	46.08	28.51
		800	3.37	62.77	40.19
		1600	5.56	65.94	44.67
	Straightness	400	0.60	0.99	0.75
		800	0.60	0.92	0.72
		1600	0.38	0.79	0.69

TABLE. 2

Sample 01 centrality values

Sample Scale — Sample 02

FIG. 20

Histograms showing the distribution of centrality values (Reach, Gravity, and Straightness) among plots with and without alleys at three different scales 400m, 800m, and 1600m. The X axis is for the centrality metric values, while the Y axis is for the percentage of plots achieving a centrality value denoted on the X axis.

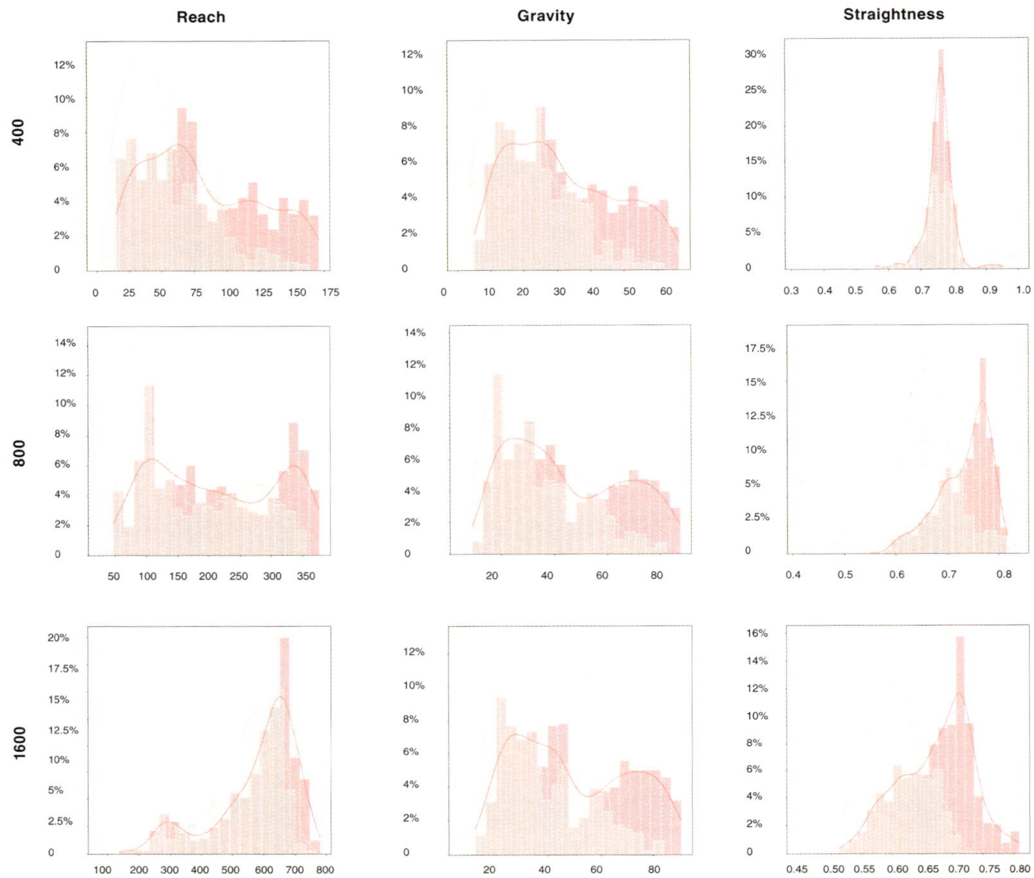

TABLE. 3

Sample 02 centrality values

UNA		Radius	Min	Max	Avg
Scenario 1: Streets only	Reach	400	1	163	49
		800	25	355	165
		1600	74	768	528
	Gravity	400	0.37	61.99	20.59
		800	4.27	82.33	31.67
		1600	6.09	83.92	35.62
	Straightness	400	0.31	0.99	0.77
		800	0.41	0.83	0.65
		1600	0.44	0.74	0.60

UNA		Radius	Min	Max	Avg
Scenario 2: Streets + Alleys	Reach	400	15	171	81
		800	47	377	211
		1600	136	780	577
	Gravity	400	5.18	66.55	32.09
		800	9.01	87.72	45.00
		1600	12.05	90.74	49.09
	Straightness	400	0.55	0.95	0.75
		800	0.55	0.81	0.73
		1600	0.51	0.80	0.67

MBZ City

MBZ City

FIG. 1
A photo representing house façades from MBZ City

FIG. 2
Low residential density in MBZ City

FIG. 3

A photo montage with different views of MBZ City

FIG. 4
Aerial image showing MBZ City (Esri & USGS, 2021)

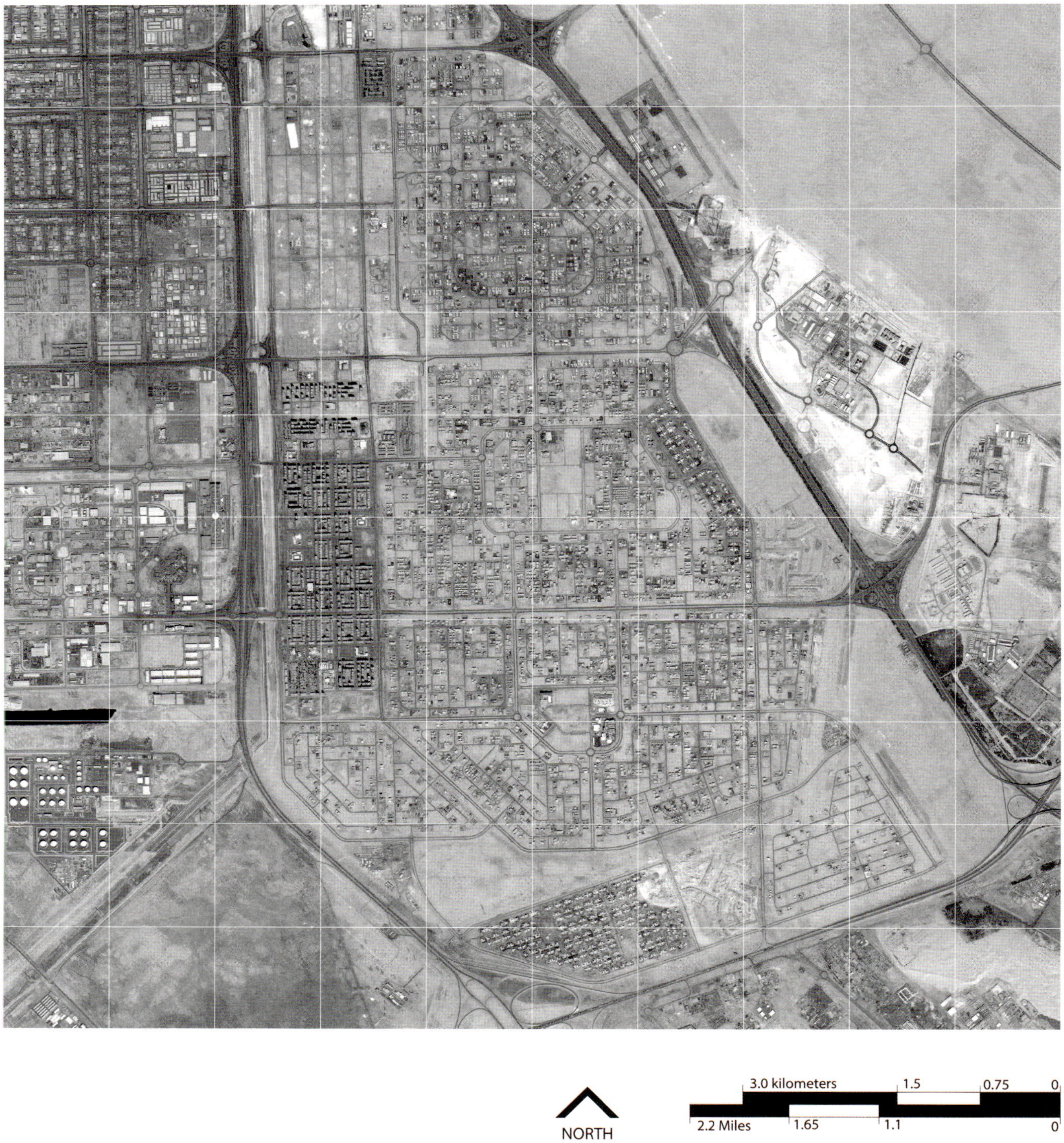

Morphological Analysis

Neighborhood Scale

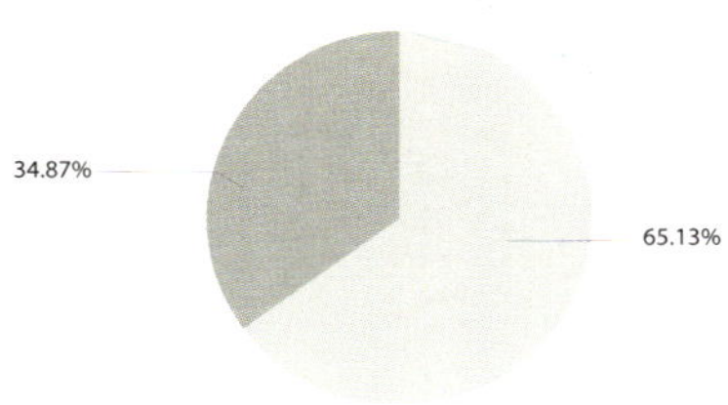

Residential= 5,978 Plots
Non-residential= 3,200 Plots

Plots/Buildings:

- Total area = 5,071 Hectares
- Total plots = 9,178 Plots
- Total buildings = 10,650 Buildings
- Average plot density = 1.81 Plots/Hectare
- Average building density = 2.10 Buildings/Hectare
- Average plot area = 0.58 Hectare
- Average population density = 23.15 Population/Hectare

FIG. 5.1
Residential/ non-residential classification

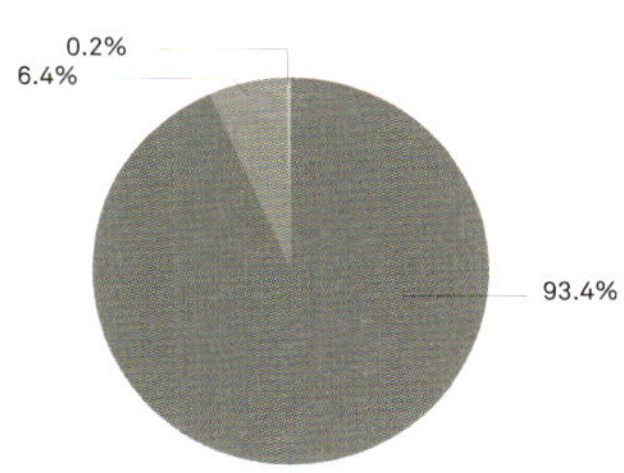

Low rise (1-4) = 9,944 Buildings
Mid rise (4-10)= 685 Buildings
High rise (+10)= 21 Buildings

FIG. 5.2
Buildings height classification

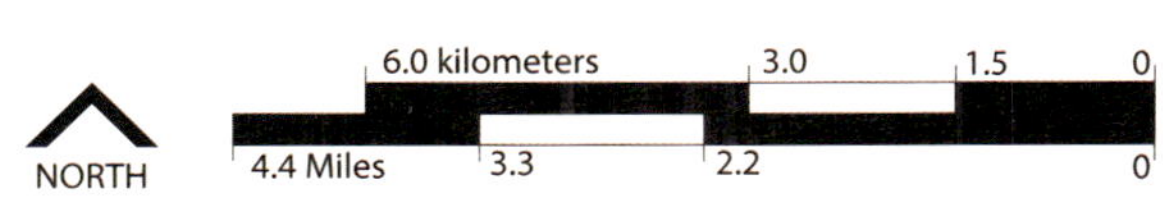

FIG. 5.3

Population density

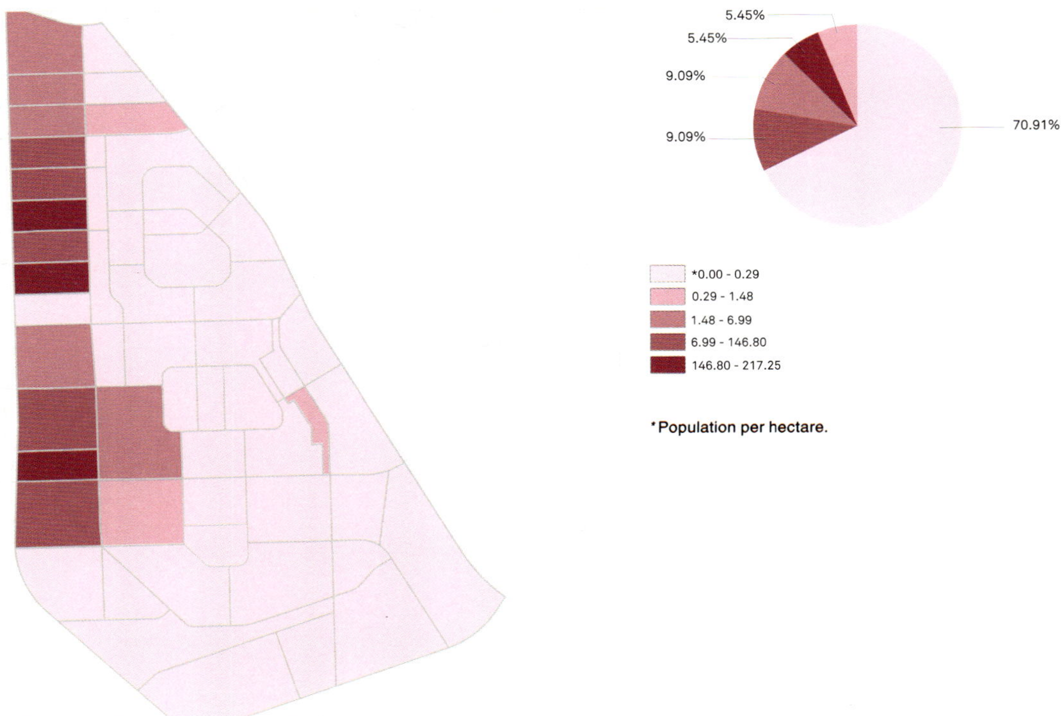

*Population per hectare.

FIG. 5.4

Land use classification

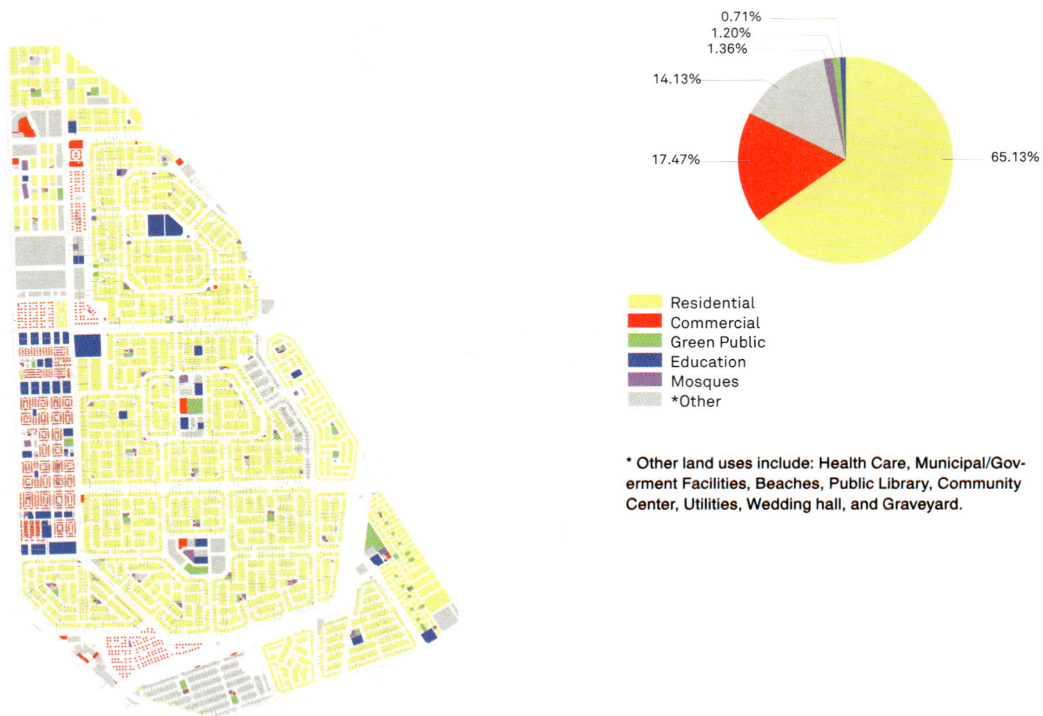

* Other land uses include: Health Care, Municipal/Goverment Facilities, Beaches, Public Library, Community Center, Utilities, Wedding hall, and Graveyard.

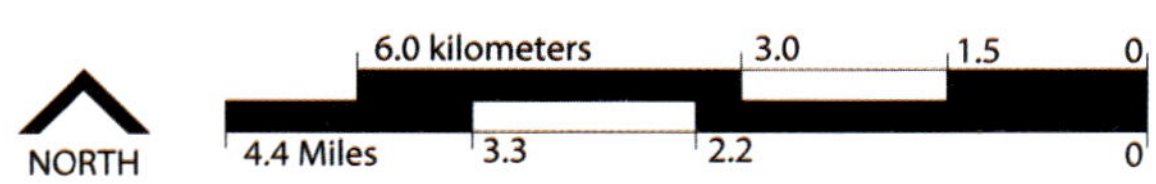

FIG. 5.5

Map showing network classification in MBZ City

Streets:

- Street length = 699.67 km
- Street density = 0.14 km/Hectare
- Street intersections = 3,153 Intersections
- Street intersectiosn density = 0.62 Intersection/Hectare

Alleys:

- Alley length = 446.4 km
- Alley density = 0.09 km/Hectare
- Alley intersections = 2,692 Intersections
- Alley intersections density = 0.53 Intersection/Hectare

FIG. 6
Map showing MBZ City with the location of the selected samples. Each sample has an area of 1 square mile.

Morphological Analysis

Sample Scale — Sample 01

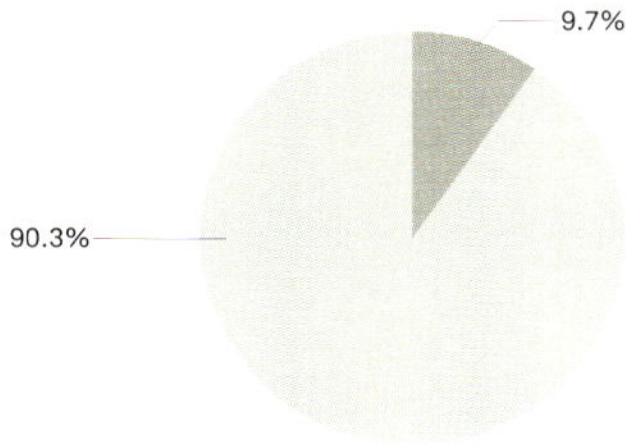

Residential= 485 Plots
Non-residential= 52 Plots

FIG. 7.1
Residential/non-residential classification

Plots/Buildings:

- Total area = 256 Hectares
- Total plots = 537 Plots
- Total buildings = 2,573 Buildings
- Average plot area = 0.56 Hectare
- Average plot density = 2.09 Plots/Hectare

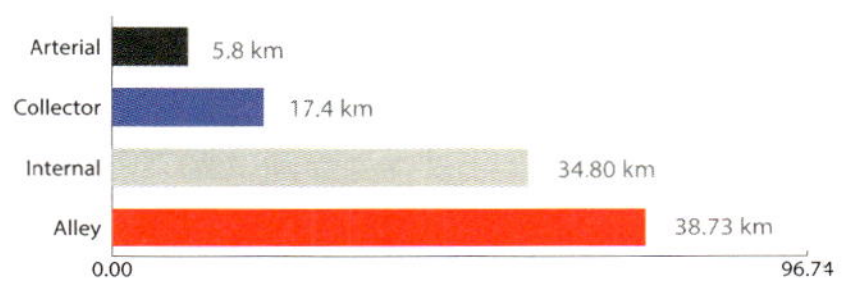

FIG. 7.2
Network classification

Streets:

- Street length= 58 km
- Street density = 0.23 km/Hectare
- Street intersections = 213 Intersections
- Street intersections density = 0.83 Intersection/Hectare

Alleys:

- Alley length = 38.73 km
- Alley density = 0.15 km/Hectare
- Alley intersections = 110 Intersections
- Alley intersections density= 0.43 Intersection/Hectare

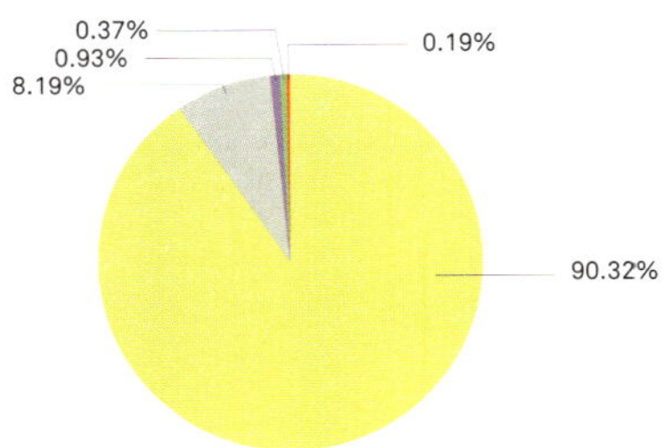

Residential
Commercial
Education
Green Public
Mosques
*Other

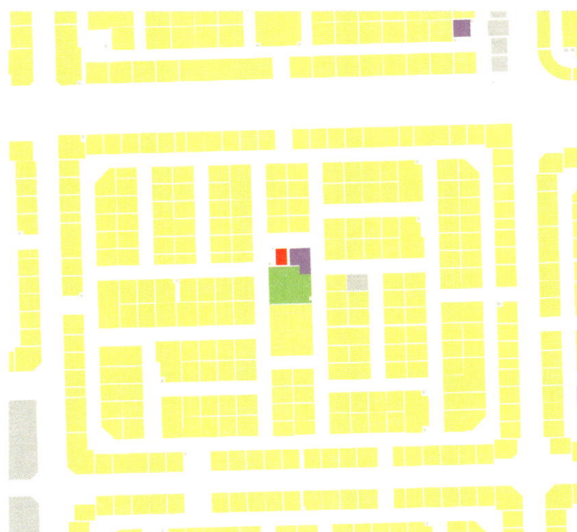

FIG. 7.3
Land use classification

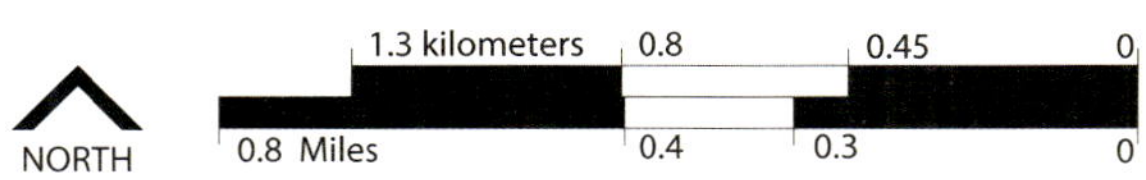

Sample Scale — Sample 02

FIG. 8.1
Residential/non-residential classification

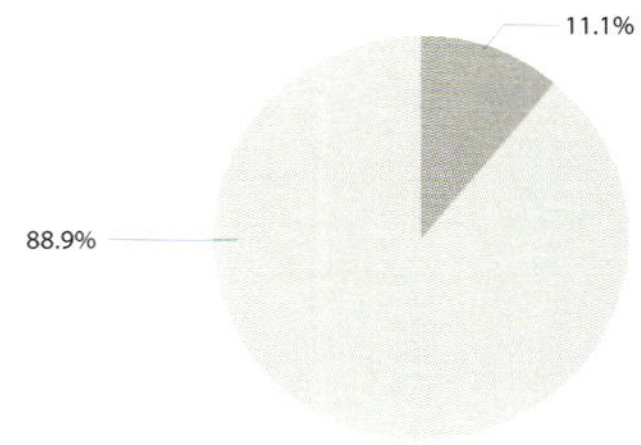

Residential= 473 Plots
Non-residential= 59 Plots

Plots/Buildings:

- Total area = 256 Hectares
- Total plots = 532 Plots
- Total buildings = 1,349 Buildings
- Average plot density = 2.08 Plot,/Hectare
- Average plot area = 0.61 Hectare

FIG. 8.2
Network classification

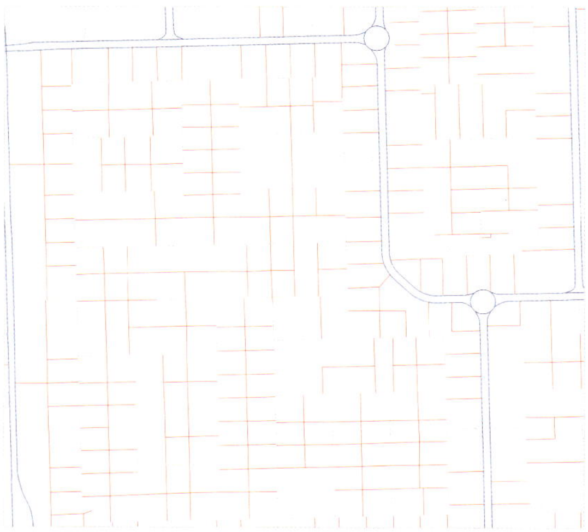

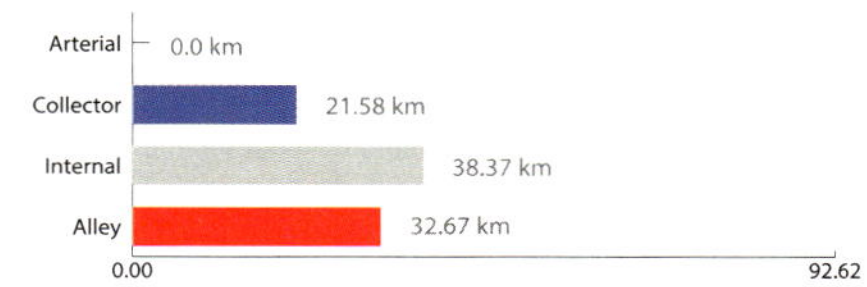

Streets:

- Street length = 59.95 km
- Street density = 0.23 km/Hectare
- Street intersections = 301 Intersection
- Street intersections density = 1.18 Intersection/Hectare

Alleys:

- Alley length = 32.67 km
- Alley density = 0.13 km/Hectare
- Alley intersections = 106 Intersections
- Alley intersections density = 0.41 Intersection/Hectare

FIG. 8.3
Land use classification

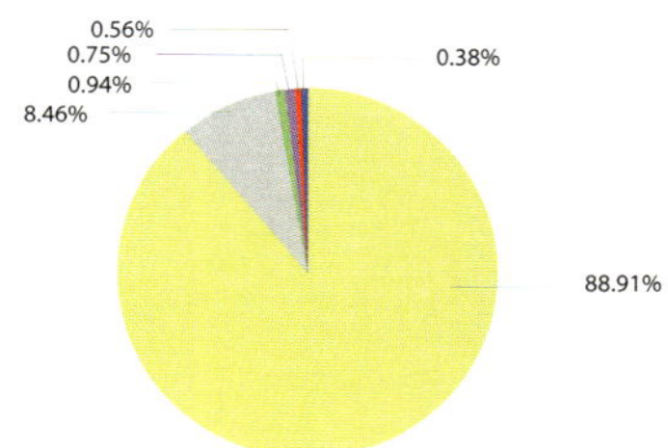

Residential
Commercial
Education
Green Public
Mosques
*Other

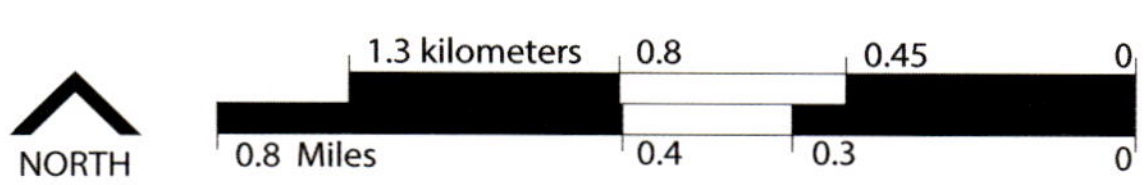

Centrality Analysis: Neighborhood Scale

Scenario 1: Streets only — 400 m Radius

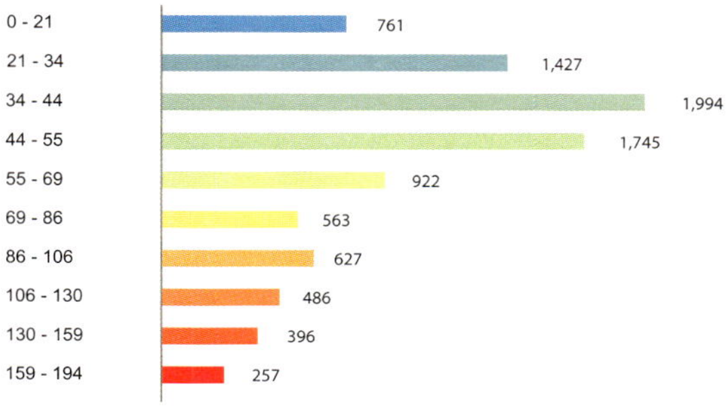

Range of results *Count of plots achieving Reach within the range*

FIG. 9.1
Reach

The warmer colors (i.e., greenish-yellow to red) represent a reach value of 55 or more, while the cooler colors (i.e., light green to dark blue) correspond to a reach value of 54 or less. The majority of plots (i.e., 5,927 out of 9,178), corresponding to 65% of all plots, have reach values of less than 55. Among the categories shown in the legend, about 22% of the total plots can reach 34 to 44 other plots within 5 minutes of walking. On average, each plot in MBZ City can access at least 58 plots within a distance of 400 m.

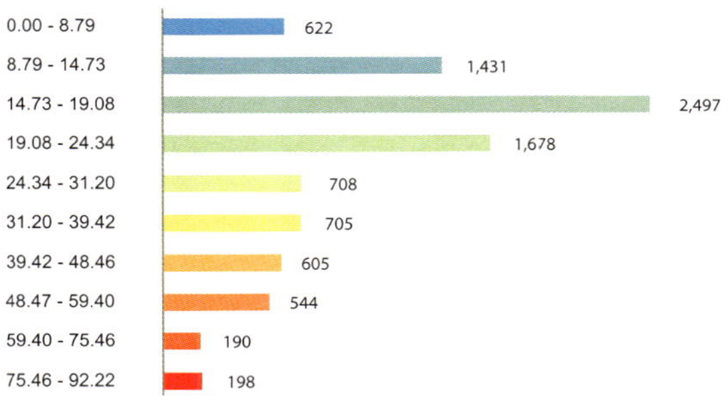

Range of results *Count of plots achieving Gravity within the range*

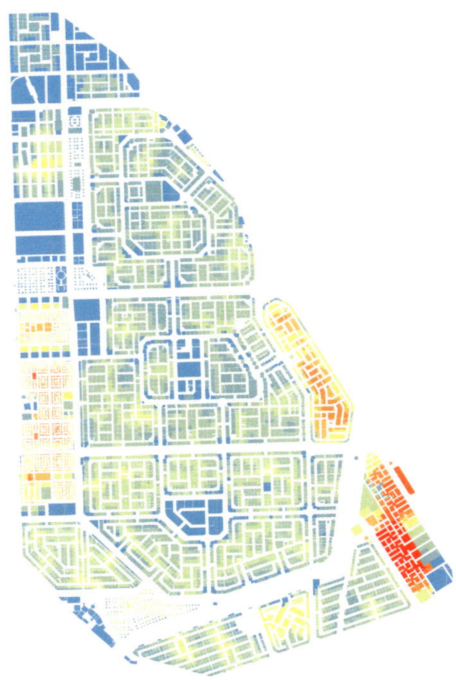

FIG. 9.2
Gravity

The warmer colors (i.e., greenish-yellow to red) represent gravity values greater than 24.33, while the cooler colors (i.e., light green to dark blue) correspond to gravity values lower than 24.34. Fifty percent of all plots (i.e., 4,628 out of 9,178) have gravity values of more than 19.07. Among the categories shown in the legend, 27% of the total plots can reach 14.73 to 19.08 plots, making this the most common value range; this range is represented by bluish-green on the map. On average, each plot can reach 25 other plots when spatial impedance or distance decay effect is taken into consideration.

Streets

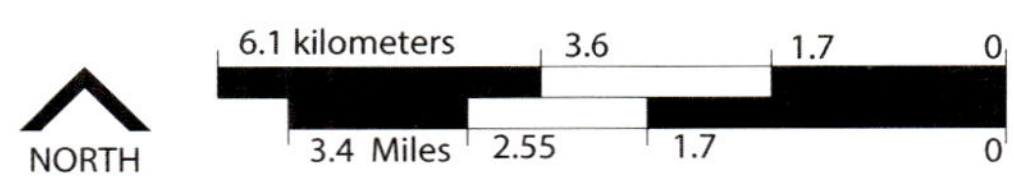

Scenario 1: Streets only — 400 m Radius

FIG. 9.3
Betweenness

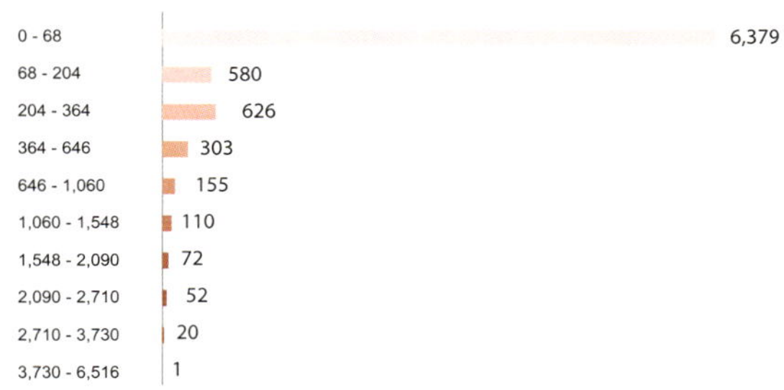

The majority of segments, corresponding to 96% (i.e., 7,979 out of 8,298 segments), have low Betweenness values ranging from 0 to 864. Among the categories shown in the legend, 6,379 segments have values in the range of 0 to 68, making this the most common range; this range is represented by the lightest brown on the map. In MBZ City, mid-range Betweenness values ranging from 865 to 6,702 are obtained by 319 segments, which is 4% of all segments. No segments have high Betweenness values (higher than 32,203). The average Betweenness value in MBZ City is 122 (smaller than 865), while the median is 34, indicating very low Betweenness at a 400 m radius.

FIG. 9.4
Straightness

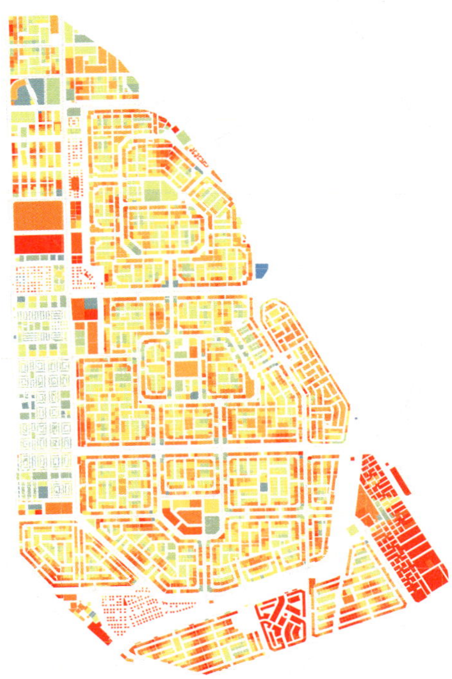

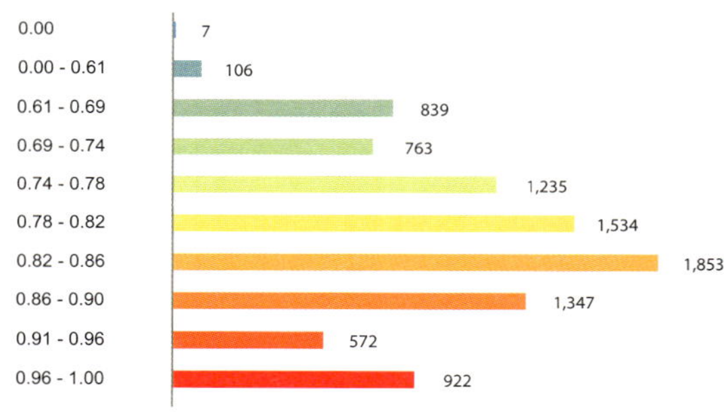

The warmer colors (greenish-yellow to red) represent Straightness values higher than 0.73, while the cooler colors (light green to dark blue) correspond to Straightness values lower than 0.74. The majority of plots, corresponding to 59% (or 5,385 out of 9,178 plots) have Straightness values ranging from 0.69 to 0.86. Among the categories shown in the legend, 1,853 plots have values in the range of 0.82 to 0.86, making this the most common range; this range is represented by light orange on the map. The average Straightness value of plots in MBZ City is 0.82 at a 400 m radius, which means that their paths to other plots are 82% as straight as a straight line.

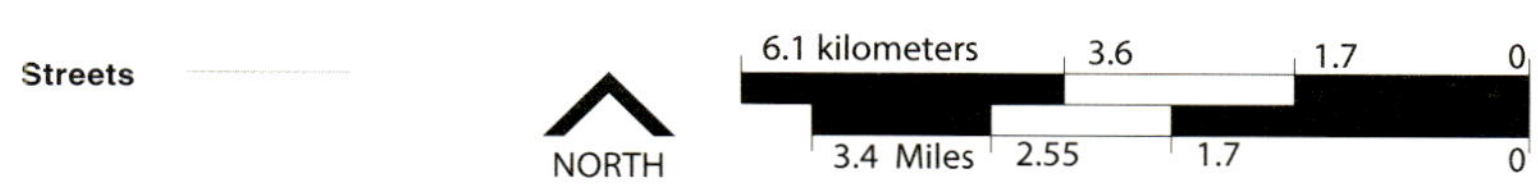

Scenario 1: Streets only — 800 m Radius

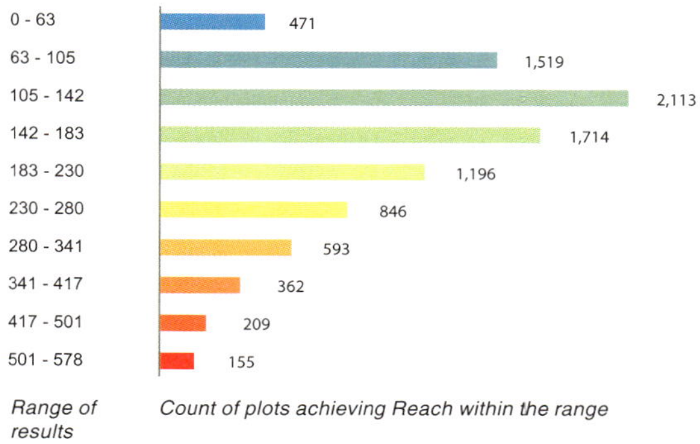

The warmer colors (i.e., greenish-yellow to red) represent a reach value of 183 or more, while the cooler colors (i.e., light green to dark blue) correspond to a reach value of 182 or less. Sixty-three percent of all plots (i.e., 5,817 out of 9,178) have reach values of less than 183. Among the categories shown in the legend, 23% of the total plots can reach 105 to 142 other plots within 10 minutes of walking. On average, each plot in MBZ City can access at least 180 plots within a distance of 800 m.

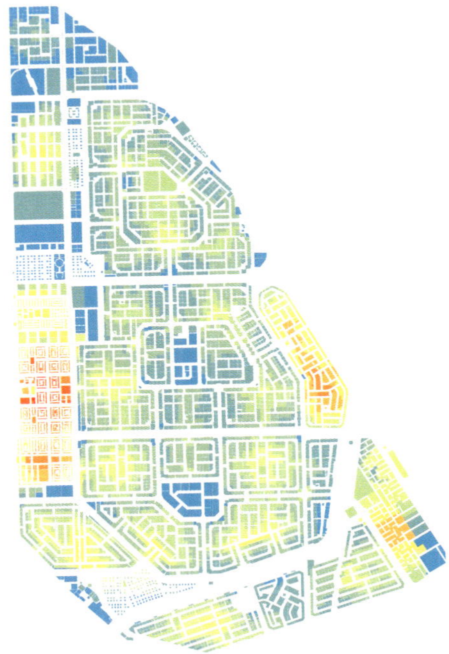

FIG. 10.1
Reach

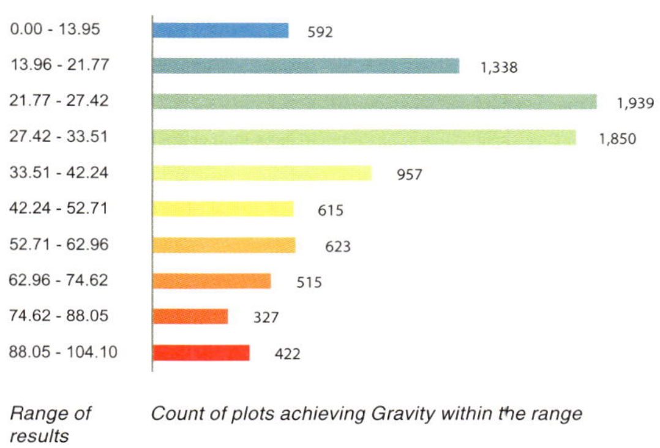

The warmer colors (i.e., greenish-yellow to red) represent gravity values of more than 33.50, while the cooler colors (i.e., light green to dark blue) correspond to gravity values of less than 33.51. About 58% of all plots (i.e., 5,309 out of 9,178) have gravity values of more than 27.41. Among the categories shown in the legend, 21% of the total plots can reach 21.77 to 27.42 plots, making this the most common value range; this range is represented by bluish-green on the map. On average, each plot can reach 37 other plots when spatial impedance or distance decay effect is taken into consideration.

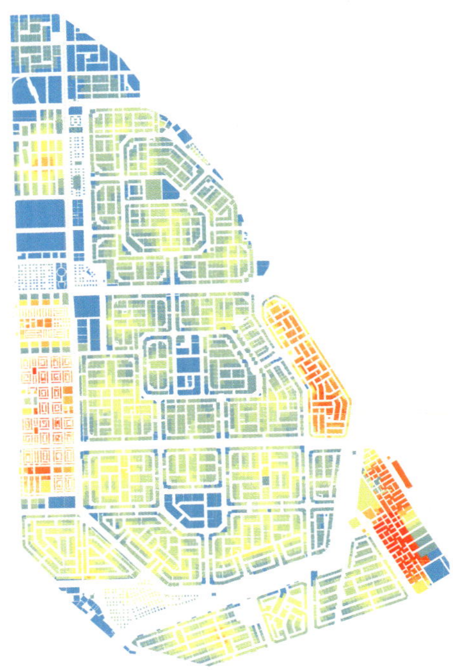

FIG. 10.2
Gravity

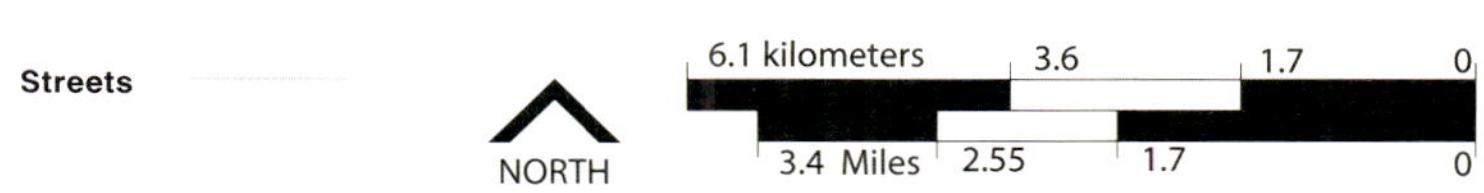

Scenario 1: Streets only — 800 m Radius

FIG. 10.3
Betweenness

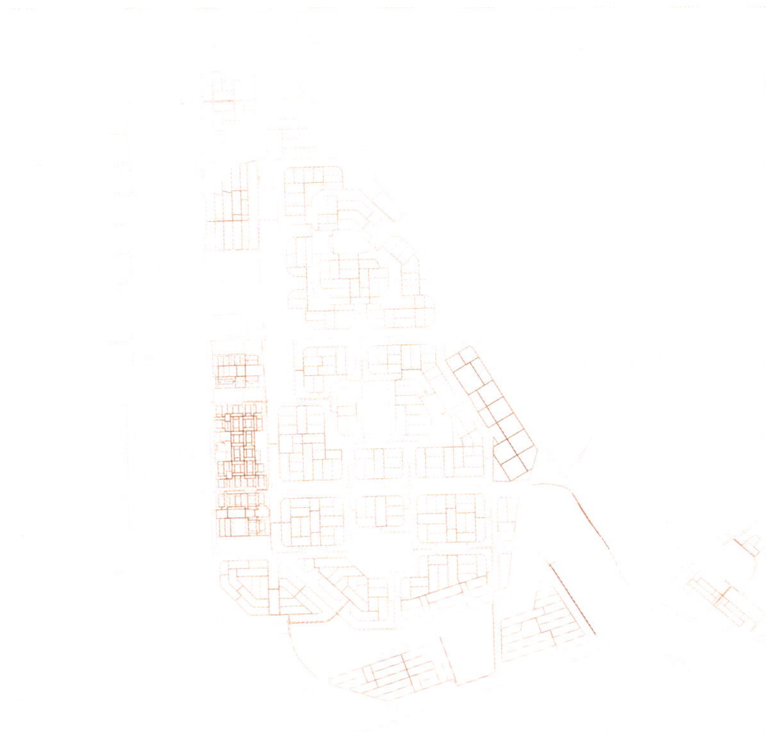

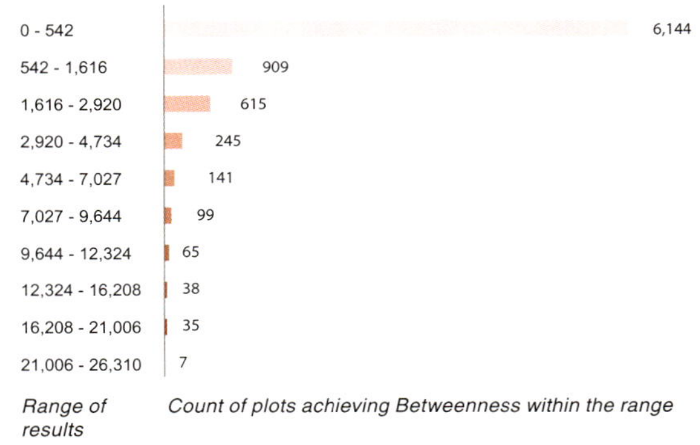

The majority of segments, corresponding to 91% (i.e., 7,536 out of 8,298 segments), have very low Betweenness values ranging from 0 to 2,539. Among the categories shown in the legend, 6,144 segments have values in the range of 0 to 542, making this the most common range; this range is represented by the lightest brown on the map. Low Betweenness values ranging from 2,540 to 11,517 are obtained by 660 segments which is 8% of all segments. Only 93, or 1% of the segments, have mid-range Betweenness values in the range of 11,518 to 20,478. The average Betweenness value in MBZ City is 865 (smaller than 2,539), while the median is 271, indicating very low Betweenness at an 800 m radius.

FIG. 10.4
Straightness

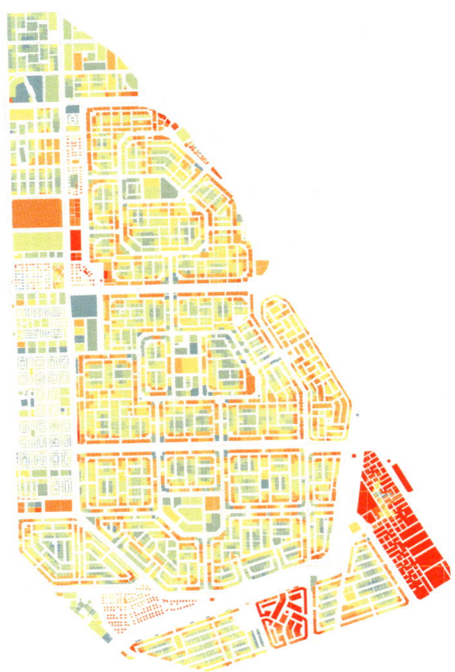

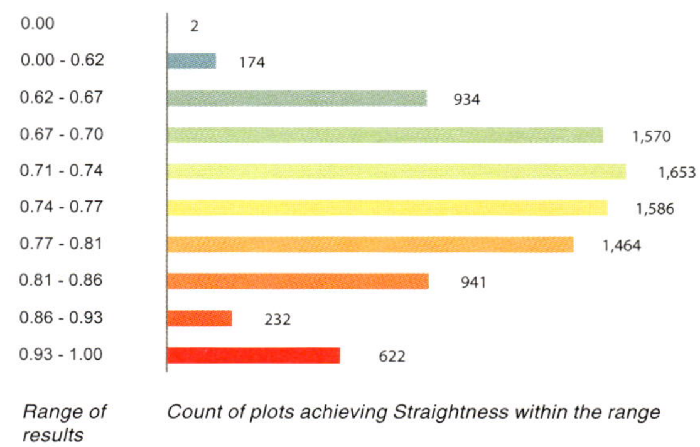

The warmer colors (greenish-yellow to red) represent Straightness values higher than 0.70, while the cooler colors (light green to dark blue) correspond to Straightness values lower than 0.71. The majority of plots, corresponding to 52% (or 4,809 out of 9,178 plots) have Straightness values ranging from 0.67 to 0.77. Among the categories shown in the legend, 1,653 plots have values in the range of 0.71 to 0.74, making this the most common range; this range is represented by greenish-yellow on the map. The average Straightness value of plots in MBZ City is 0.76 at an 800 m radius, which means that their paths to other plots are 76% as straight as a straight line.

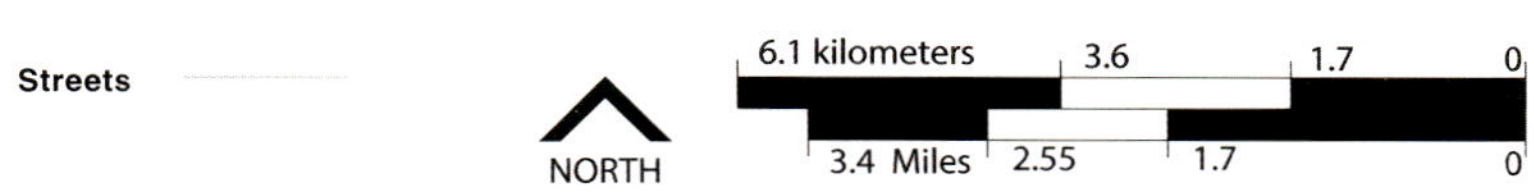

Scenario 1: Streets only — 1,600 m Radius

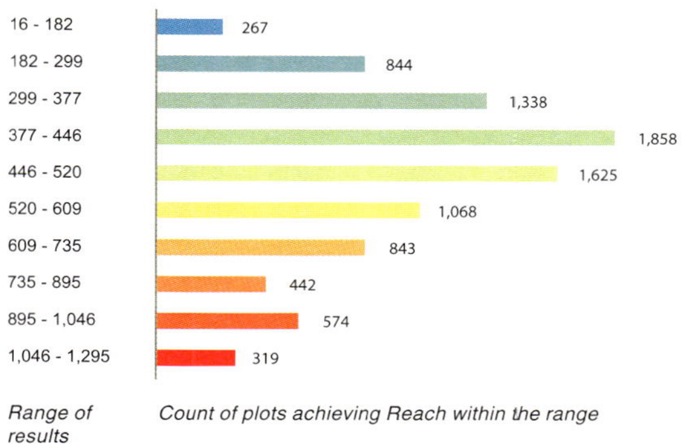

The warmer colors (i.e., greenish-yellow to red) represent reach values of more than 445, while the cooler colors (i.e., light green to dark blue) correspond to Reach values of less than 446. The majority of plots (i.e., 5,932 out of 9,178), corresponding to 65%, have reach values of less than 520. Among the categories shown in the legend, 20% of all plots can reach 377 to 446 other plots within 20 minutes of walking. On average, each plot in MBZ City can access at least 510 plots within a distance of 1,600 m.

FIG.11.1
Reach

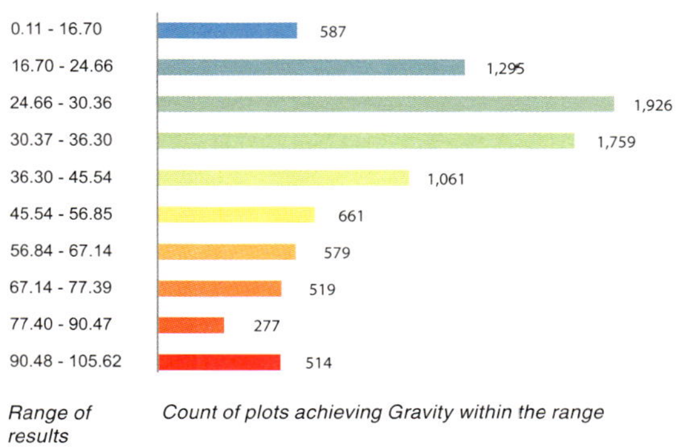

The warmer colors (i.e., greenish-yellow to red) represent gravity values greater than 36.29, while the cooler colors (i.e., light green to dark blue) correspond to gravity values lower than 36.30. Sixty-one percent of all plots (i.e., 5,567 out of 9,178) have gravity values of less than 36.30. Among the categories shown in the legend, 21% of the total plots can reach 24.66 to 30.37 plots, making this the most common value range; this range is represented by bluish-green on the map. On average, each plot can reach 40 other plots when spatial impedance or distance decay effect is taken into consideration.

FIG.11.2
Gravity

Streets

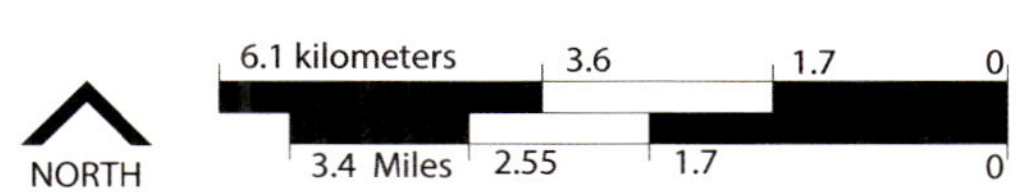

Scenario 1: Streets only — 1,600 m Radius

FIG. 11.3
Betweenness

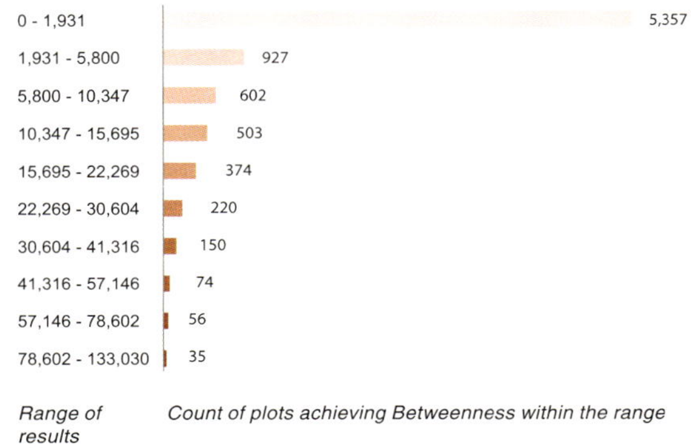

Almost all segments, corresponding to 99% (i.e., 8,252 out of 8,298 segments), have very low Betweenness values ranging from 0 to 73,682. Among the categories shown in the legend, 5,357 segments have values in the range of 0 to 1,931, making this the most common range; this range is represented by the lightest brown on the map. Low Betweenness values ranging from 73,683 to 123,568 are obtained by 45 segments, which is 0.5% of all segments. Mid-range Betweenness values ranging from 123,569 to 179,444 are obtained by only 1 segment, which is 0.01% of all segments. No segments have high Betweenness values (higher than 179,444). The average Betweenness value in MBZ City is 5,295 (smaller than 73,682), while the median is 965, indicating very low Betweenness at a 1,600 m radius.

FIG. 11.4
Straightness

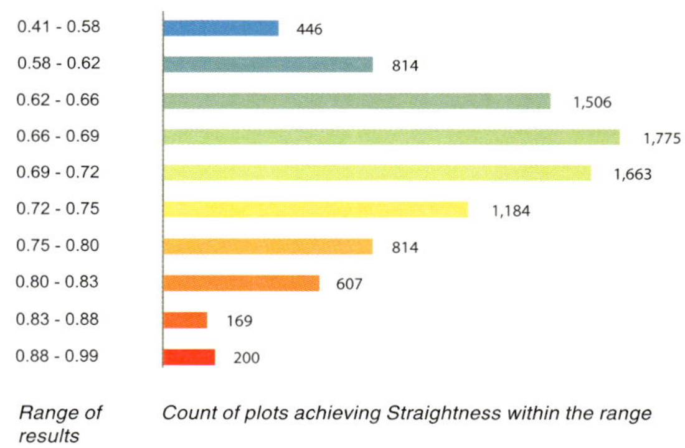

The warmer colors (greenish-yellow to red) represent Straightness values higher than 0.68, while the cooler colors (light green to dark blue) correspond to Straightness values lower than 0.69. The majority of plots, corresponding to 54% (or 4,944 out of 9,178 plots) have Straightness values ranging from 0.62 to 0.72. Among the categories shown in the legend, 1,775 plots have values in the range of 0.66 to 0.69, making this the most common range; this range is represented by light green on the map. The average Straightness value of plots in MBZ City is 0.70 at a 1,600 m radius, which means that their paths to other plots are 70% as straight as a straight line.

Centrality Analysis: Neighborhood Scale

Scenario 2: Streets + Alleys — 400 m Radius

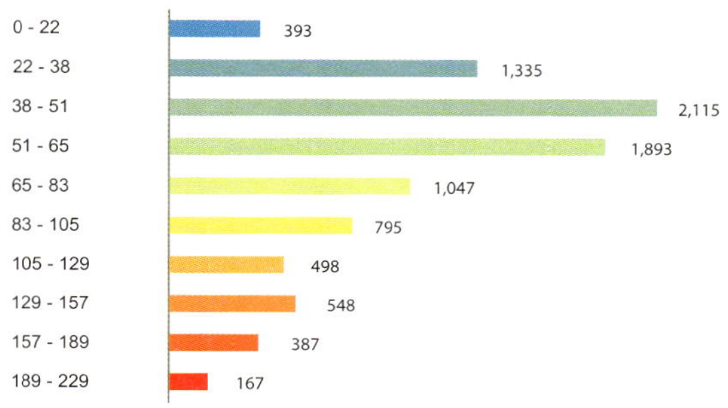

Range of results *Count of plots achieving Reach within the range*

The warmer colors (i.e., greenish-yellow to red) represent a reach value of 65 or more, while the cooler colors (i.e., light green to dark blue) correspond to a reach value of 64 or less. Sixty-two percent of all plots (i.e., 5,736 out of 9,178) have reach values of less than 65. Among the categories shown in the legend, 23% of the total plots can reach 38 to 51 other plots within 5 minutes of walking. On average, each plot in MBZ City can access at least 70 plots within a distance of 400 m.

FIG. 12.1
Reach

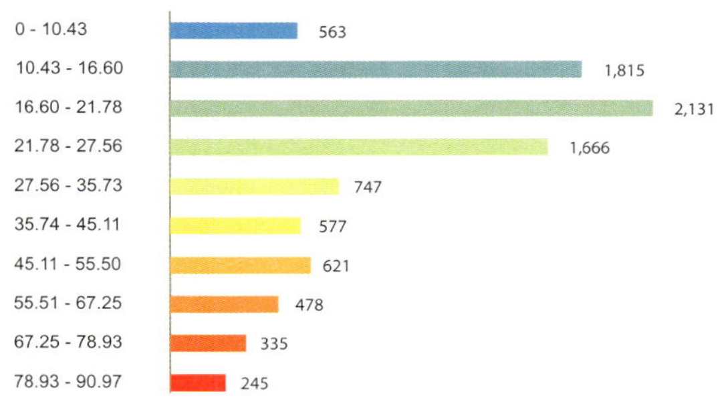

Range of results *Count of plots achieving Gravity within the range*

The warmer colors (i.e., greenish-yellow to red) represent gravity values of more than 27.55, while the cooler colors (i.e., light green to dark blue) correspond to gravity values of less than 27.56. Fifty-one percent of all plots (i.e., 4,669 out of 9,178) have gravity values of more than 21.77. Among the categories shown in the legend, 23% of the total plots can reach 16.60 to 21.78 plots, making this the most common value range; this range is represented by bluish-green on the map. On average, each plot can reach 29 other plots when spatial impedance or distance decay effect is taken into consideration.

FIG. 12.2
Gravity

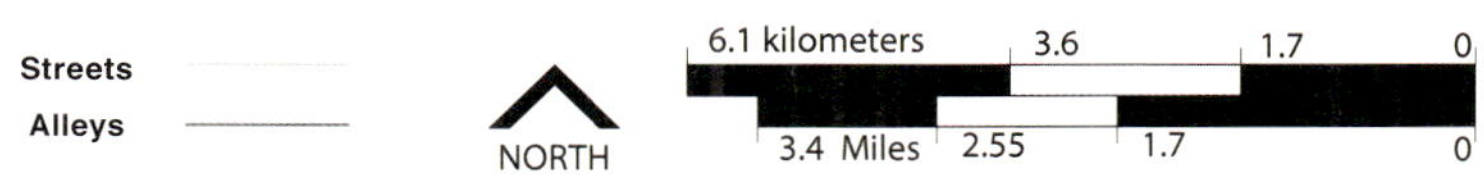

Scenario 2: Streets + Alleys — 400 m Radius

FIG. 12.3
Betweenness

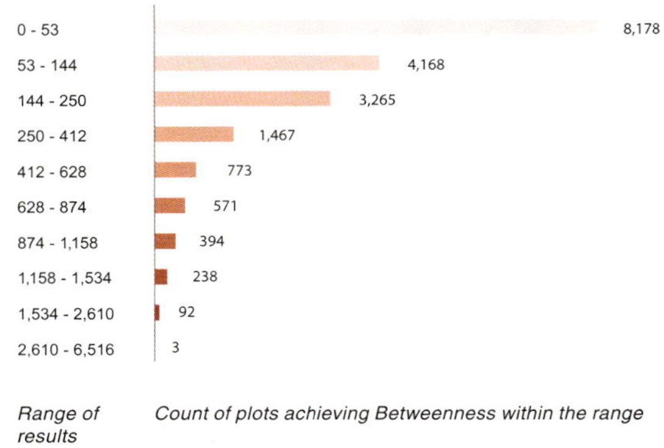

The majority of segments, corresponding to 96% (i.e., 18,406 out of 19,149 segments), have low Betweenness values ranging from 0 to 864. Among the categories shown in the legend, 8,178 segments have values in the range of 0 to 53, making this the most common range; this range is represented by the lightest brown on the map. Mid-range Betweenness values ranging from 865 to 6,702 are obtained by 743 segments, which is 4% of all segments. No segments have high Betweenness value that is higher than 6,703. The average Betweenness value in MBZ City is 170 (smaller than 865), while the median is 84, indicating very low Betweenness at a 400 m radius.

FIG. 12.4
Straightness

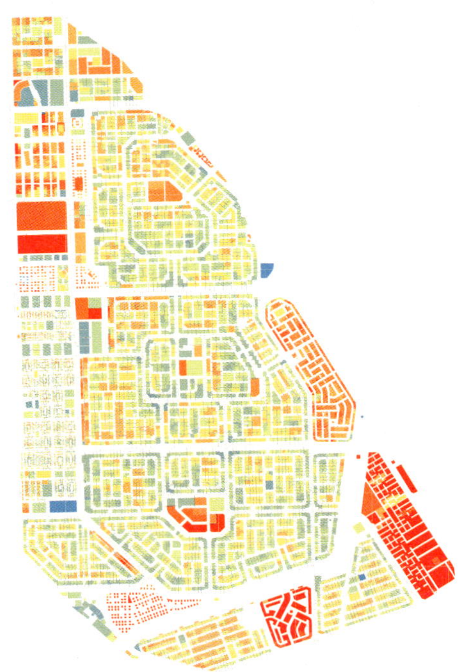

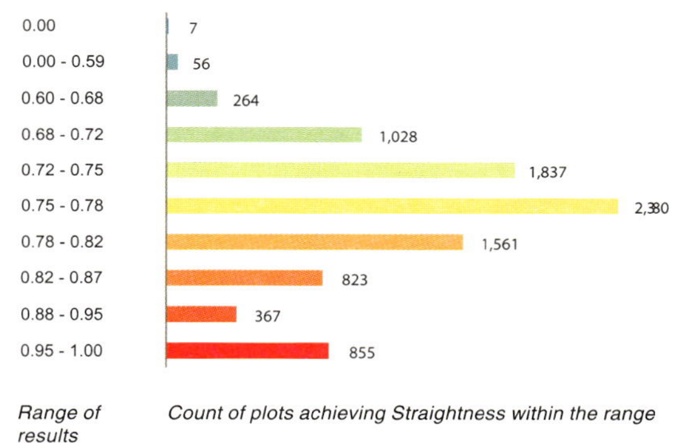

The warmer colors (greenish-yellow to red) represent Straightness values higher than 0.71, while the cooler colors (light green to dark blue) correspond to Straightness values lower than 0.72. The majority of plots, corresponding to 57% (or 5,245 out of 9,178 plots) have Straightness values ranging from 0.68 to 0.78. Among the categories shown in the legend, 2,380 plots have values in the range of 0.75 to 0.78, making this the most common range; this range is represented by yellow on the map. The average Straightness value of plots in MBZ City is 0.79 at a 400 m radius, which means that their paths to other plots are 79% as straight as a straight line.

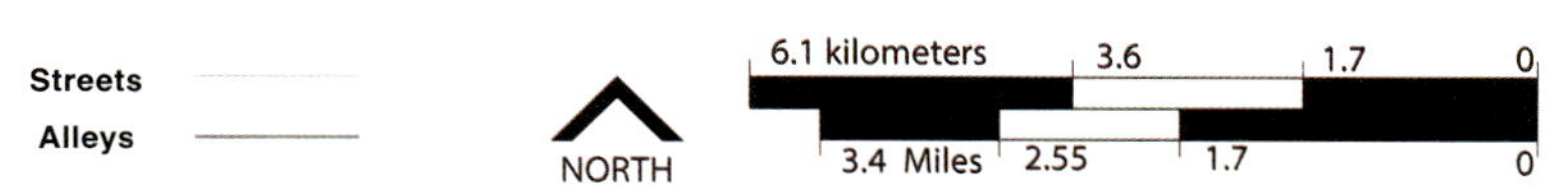

Scenario 2: Streets + Alleys — 800 m Radius

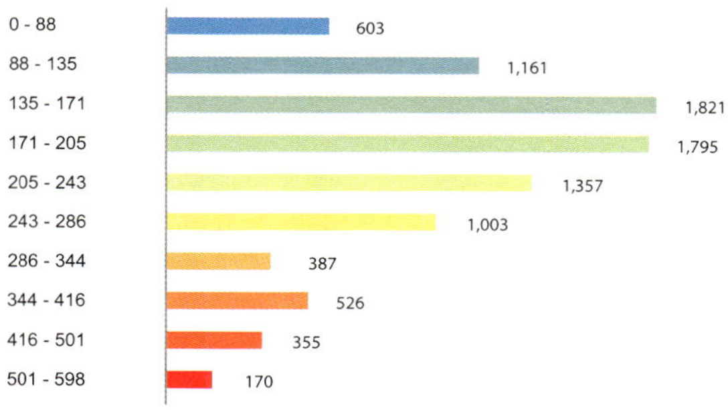

Range of results

Count of plots achieving Reach within the range

FIG. 13.1
Reach

The warmer colors (i.e., greenish-yellow to red) represent a reach value of 205 or more, while the cooler colors (i.e., light green to dark blue) correspond to a reach value of 204 or less. The majority of plots (i.e., 5,380 out of 9,178), corresponding to 59% of all plots, have reach values of less than 205. Among the categories shown in the legend, 20% of the total plots can reach 135 to 170 other plots within 10 minutes of walking. On average, each plot in MBZ City can access at least 210 plots within a distance of 800 m.

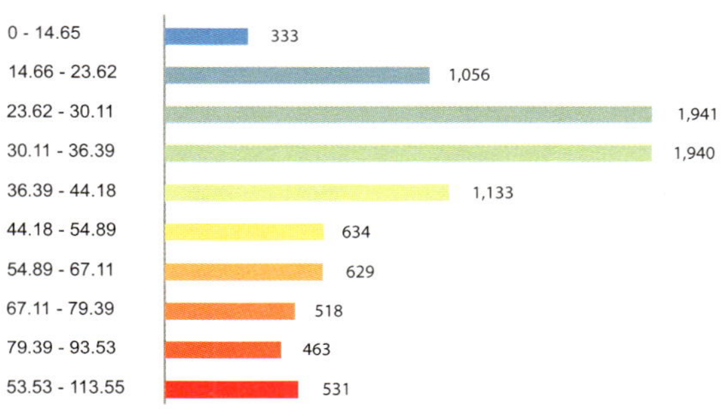

Range of results

Count of plots achieving Gravity within the range

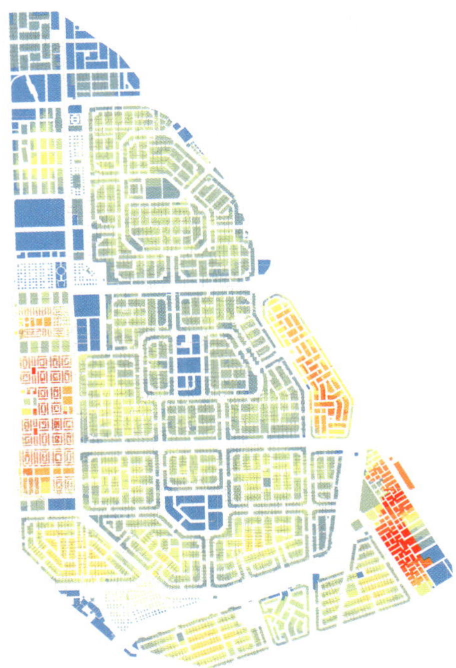

FIG. 13.2
Gravity

The warmer colors (i.e., greenish-yellow to red) represent gravity values greater than 36.38, while the cooler colors (i.e., light green to dark blue) correspond to gravity values lower than 36.39. Fifty-seven percent of all plots (i.e., 5,270 out of 9,178) have gravity values of less than 36.39. Among the categories shown in the legend, 21% of all plots can reach 23.62 to 30.11 plots, making this the most common value range; this range is represented by bluish-green on the map. On average, each plot can reach 42 other plots when spatial impedance or distance decay effect is taken into consideration.

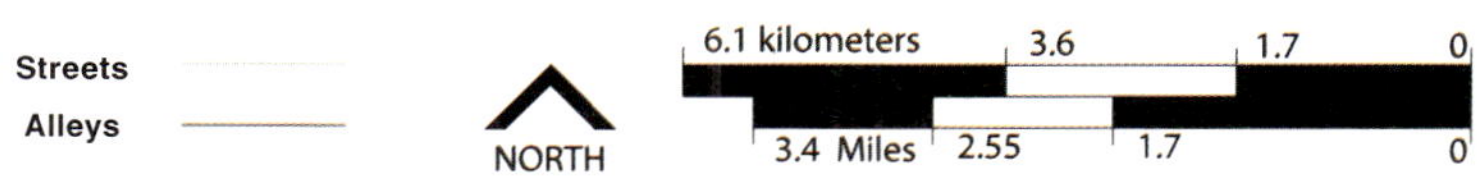

Scenario 2: Streets + Alleys — 800 m Radius

FIG. 13.3
Betweenness

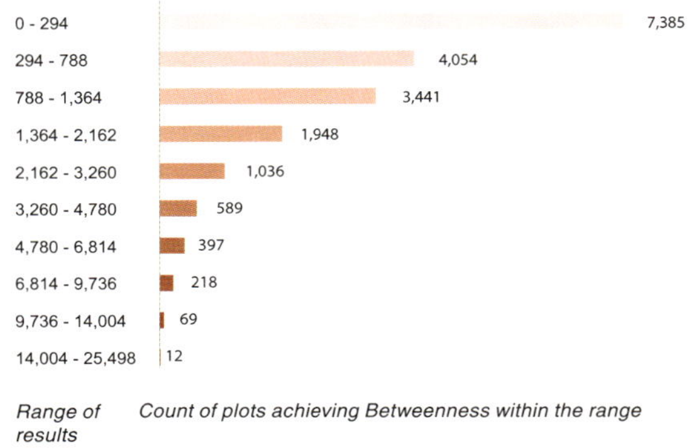

The majority of segments, corresponding to 90% (i.e., 17,268 out of 19,149 segments), have very low Betweenness values ranging from 0 to 2,539. Among the categories shown in the legend, 7,385 segments have values in the range of 0 to 294, making this the most common range; this range is represented by the lightest brown on the map. Low Betweenness values ranging from 2,540 to 11,517 are obtained by 1,836 segments, which is 10% of all segments. Mid-range Betweenness values ranging from 11,517 to 20,478 are obtained by 44 segments, which is only 0.23% of all segments. Only one segment has a high level of Betweenness in ranges of 20,479 to 59,383, corresponding to only 0.01% of all segments. The average Betweenness value in MBZ City is 1,016 (smaller than 2,539), while the median is 552, indicating very low Betweenness at an 800 m radius.

FIG. 13.4
Straightness

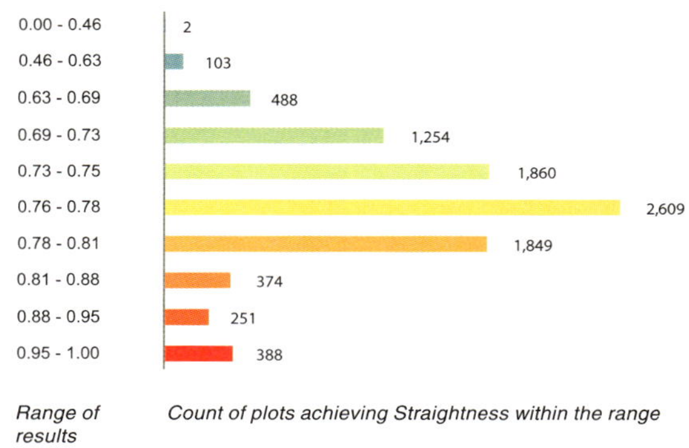

The warmer colors (greenish-yellow to red) represent Straightness values higher than 0.72, while the cooler colors (light green to dark blue) correspond to Straightness values lower than 0.73. The majority of plots, corresponding to 62% (or 5,723 out of 9,178 plots) have Straightness values ranging from 0.69 to 0.78. Among the categories shown in the legend, 2,609 plots have values in the range of 0.76 to 0.78, making this the most common range; this range is represented by yellow on the map. The average Straightness value of plots in MBZ City is 0.77 at an 800 m radius, which means that their paths to other plots are 77% as straight as a straight line.

Scenario 2: Streets + Alleys — 1,600 m Radius

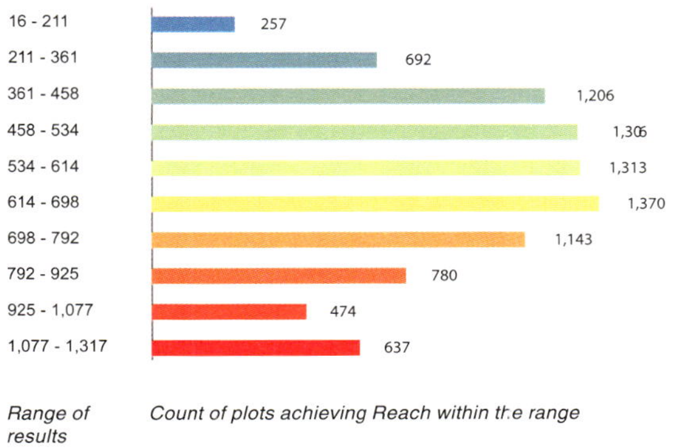

The warmer colors (i.e., greenish-yellow to red) represent a reach value of 534 or more, while the cooler colors (i.e., light green to dark blue) correspond to a reach value of 533 or less. The majority of plots (i.e., 5,717 out of 9,178), corresponding to 62% of all plots, have reach values of more than 533. Among the categories shown in the legend, 15% of all plots can reach 614 to 698 other plots within 20 minutes of walking. On average, each plot in MBZ City can access at least 628 plots within a distance of 1,600 m.

FIG. 14.1
Reach

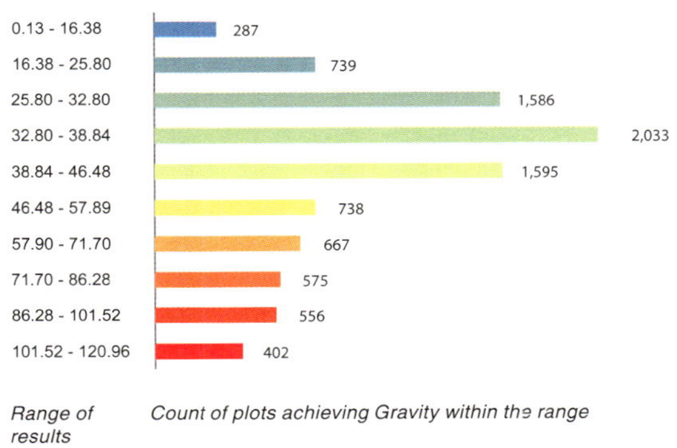

The warmer colors (i.e., greenish-yellow to red) represent gravity values of more than 38.83, while the cooler colors (i.e., light green to dark blue) correspond to gravity values of less than 38.84. About half of all plots (i.e., 4,645 out of 9,178) have gravity values of less than 38.84. Among the categories shown in the legend, 22% of all plots can reach 32.80 to 38.84 plots, making this the most common value range; this range is represented by light green on the map. On average, each plot can reach 47 other plots when spatial impedance or distance decay effect is taken into consideration.

FIG. 14.2
Gravity

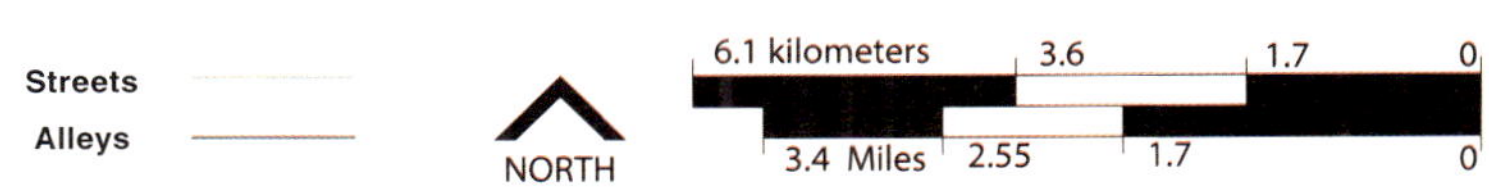

Scenario 2: Streets + Alleys — 1,600 m Radius

FIG. 14.3
Betweenness

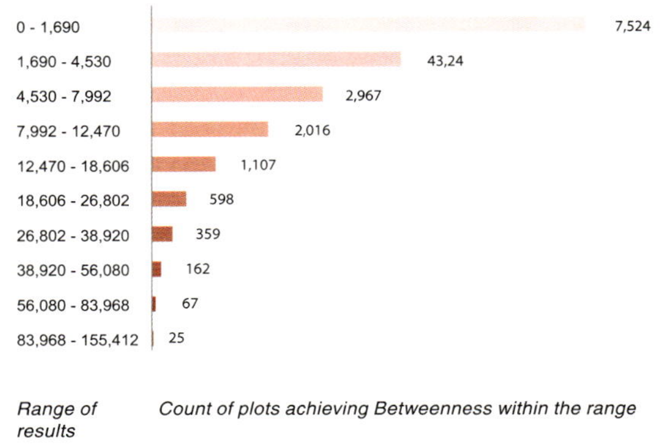

The majority of segments, corresponding to 99.83% (i.e., 19,116 out of 19,149 segments), have very low Betweenness values ranging from 0 to 73,682. Among the categories shown in the legend, 7,524 segments have values in the range of 0 to 1,690, making this the most common range; this range is represented by the lightest brown on the map. Low Betweenness values ranging from 73,683 to 123,568 are obtained by 30 segments, which is 0.16% of all segments. Mid-range Betweenness values ranging from 123,569 to 179,444 are obtained by only 3 segments, which is 0.02% of the total segments. None segment ha high Betweenness values (higher than 179,444). The average Betweenness value in MBZ City is 5,729 (smaller than 73,682), while the median is 2,854, indicating very low Betweenness at a 1,600 m radius.

FIG. 14.4
Straightness

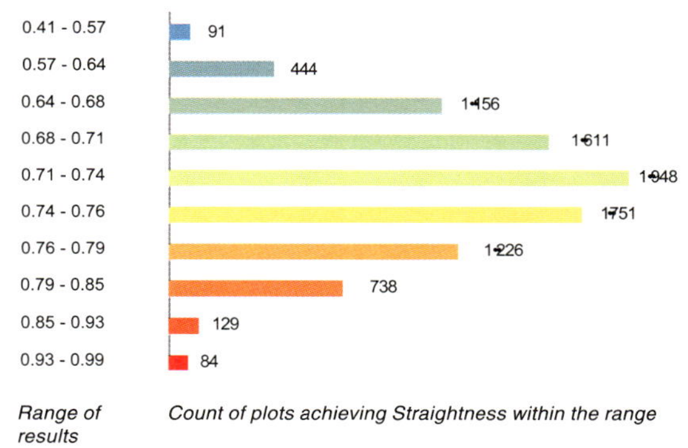

The warmer colors (greenish-yellow to red) represent Straightness values higher than 0.71, while the cooler colors (light green to dark blue) correspond to Straightness values lower than 0.72. The majority of plots, corresponding to 58% (or 5,310 out of 9,178 plots) have Straightness values ranging from 0.69 to 0.77. Among the categories shown in the legend, 1,948 plots have values in the range of 0.71 to 0.74, making this the most common range; this range is represented by greenish-yellow on the map. The average Straightness value of plots in MBZ City is 0.73 at a 1,600 m radius, which means that their paths to other plots are 73% as straight as a straight line.

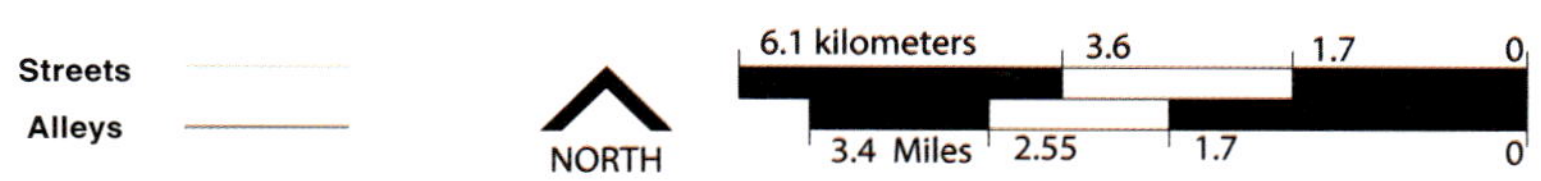

Centrality Analysis: Sample Scale

Sample 01

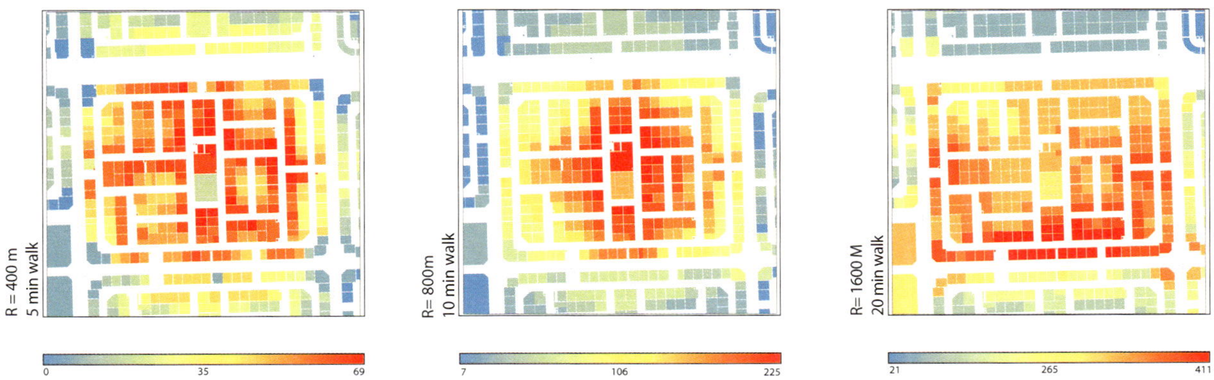

FIG. 15.1
Reach
Scenario 1: Streets only

Reach (Radius = 400 m)
The maximum number of plots that can be reached within 5 min walking distance is 69 plots. The average Reach of the sample is 35 plots.

Summary of Reach results
Minimum: 0
Maximum: 69
Mean: 35
Median: 37

Reach (Radius = 800 m)
The maximum number of plots that can be reached within 10 min walking distance is 225 plots. The average Reach of the sample is 106 plots.

Summary of Reach results
Minimum: 7
Maximum: 225
Mean: 106
Median: 117

Reach (Radius = 1600 m)
The maximum number of plots that can be reached within 20 min walking distance is 411plots. The average Reach of the sample is 265 plots.

Summary of Reach results
Minimum: 21
Maximum: 411
Mean: 265
Median: 326

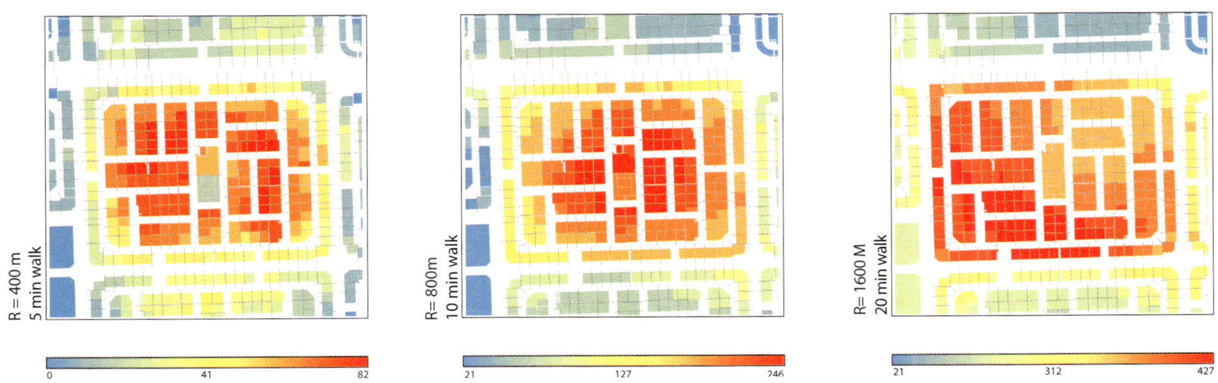

FIG. 15.2
Reach
Scenario 2: Streets + Alleys

Reach (Radius = 400 m)
The maximum number of plots that can be reached within 5 min walking distance is 82 plots. The average Reach of the sample is 41 plots.

Summary of Reach results
Minimum: 0
Maximum: 82
Mean: 41
Median: 38

Reach (Radius = 800 m)
The maximum number of plots that can be reached within 10 min walking distance is 246 plots. The average Reach of the sample is 127 plots.

Summary of Reach results
Minimum: 21
Maximum: 246
Mean: 127
Median: 138

Reach (Radius = 1600 m)
The maximum number of plots that can be reached within 20 min walking distance is 427 plots. The average Reach of the sample is 359 plots.

Summary of Reach results
Minimum: 21
Maximum: 427
Mean: 312
Median: 359

At a 400 m radius, the plots with high Reach values ranging from 35 to 69 lie adjacent to the internal streets within the centrally located NPU. At an 800 m radius, plots with high Reach values (ranging from 106 to 225) significantly appear at the center of the same NPU. At a 1,600 m radius, a great majority of plots within the centrally located NPU have high Reach values ranging from 265 to 411. With the introduction of alleys, at a 400 m radius, the concentration of high Reach values becomes stronger and clearer throughout the centrally located NPU. At 800 m and 1,600 m radii, high Reach values continue to concentrate at same spots with the highest Reach value of 246 and 427 respectively.

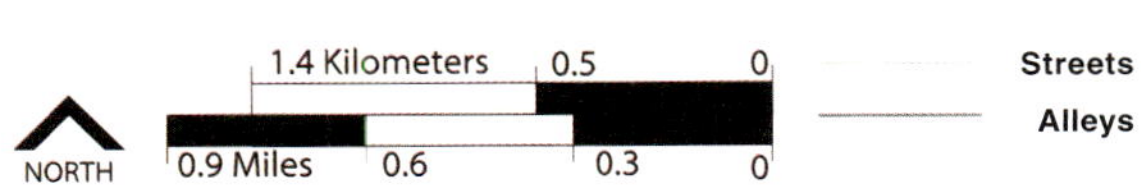

Sample 01

FIG. 15.3
Gravity
Scenario 1: Streets only

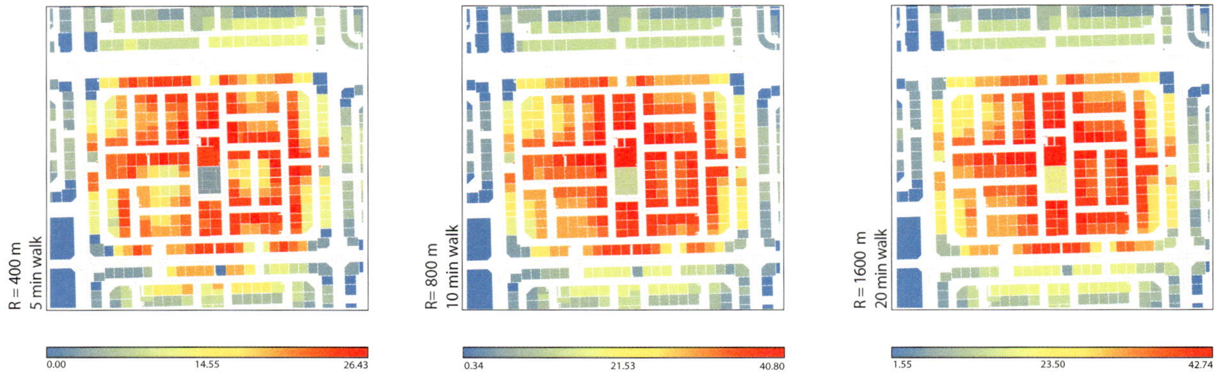

Gravity (Radius = 400 m)
The maximum number of plots that can be reached within 5 min walking distance with the distance decay effect is 26.43 plots. The average Gravity of the sample is 14.55 plots.

Summary of Gravity results
Minimum: 0.00
Maximum: 26.43
Mean: 14.55
Median: 15.51

Gravity (Radius = 800 m)
The maximum number of plots that can be reached within 10 min walking distance with the distance decay effect is 40.80 plots.The average Gravity of the sample is 21.53 plots.

Summary of Gravity results
Minimum: 0.34
Maximum: 40.80
Mean: 21.53
Median: 22.81

Gravity (Radius = 1600 m)
The maximum number of plots that can be reached within 20 min walking distance with the distance decay effect is 42.7 plots. The average Gravity of the sample is 23.5 plots.

Summary of Gravity results
Minimum: 1.6
Maximum: 42.7
Mean: 23.5
Median: 25.4

FIG. 15.4
Gravity
Scenario 2: Streets + Alleys

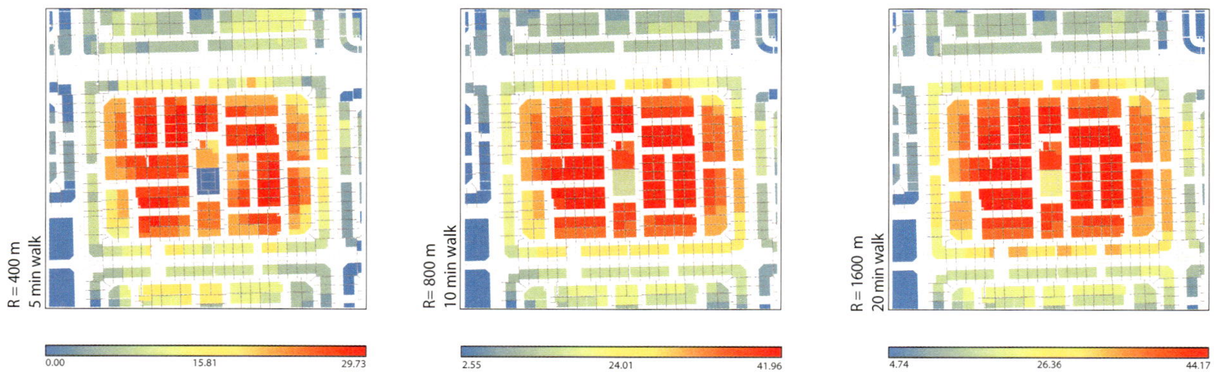

Gravity (Radius = 400 m)
The maximum number of plots that can be reached within 5 min walking distance with the distance decay effect is 29.73 plots.The average Gravity of the sample is 15.81 plots.

Summary of Gravity results
Minimum: 0.00
Maximum: 29.73
Mean: 15.81
Median: 14.89

Gravity (Radius = 800 m)
The maximum number of plots that can be reached within 10 min walking distance with the distance decay effect is 41.96 plots.The average Gravity of the sample is 24.01 plots.

Summary of Gravity results
Minimum: 2.55
Maximum: 41.96
Mean: 24.01
Median: 23.00

Gravity (Radius = 1600 m)
The maximum number of plots that can be reached within 20 min walking distance with the distance decay effect is 44.17 plots.The average Gravity of the sample is 26.36 plots.

Summary of Gravity results
Minimum: 4.74
Maximum: 44.17
Mean: 26.36
Median: 26.13

At a 400 m radius, the plots within the centrally located NPU that lie adjacent to internal streets have high Gravity values ranging from 14.55 to 26.43. At 800 m and 1,600 m radii, high Gravity values concentrate at the center of the same NPU with values ranging from 21.53 to 42.74. With the introduction of alleys, at a 400 m radius, high Gravity values are evenly distributed throughout the centrally located NPU. At 800 m and 1,600 m radii, high Gravity values become even more concentrated at the same spots with the highest values of 41.96 and 44.17 respectively. The distribution of Gravity values does not change notably across three different radii, however with the inclusion of alleys, the values are slightly improved at all radii.

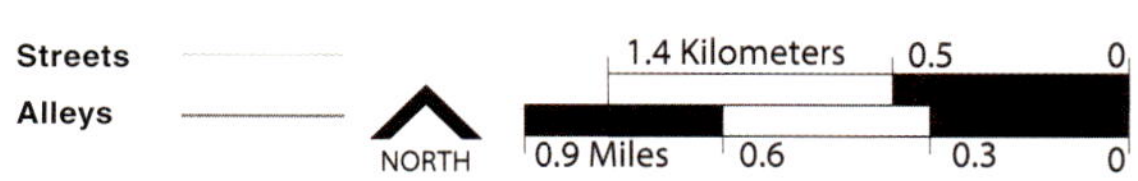

FIG. 15.5

Straightness

Scenario 1: Streets only

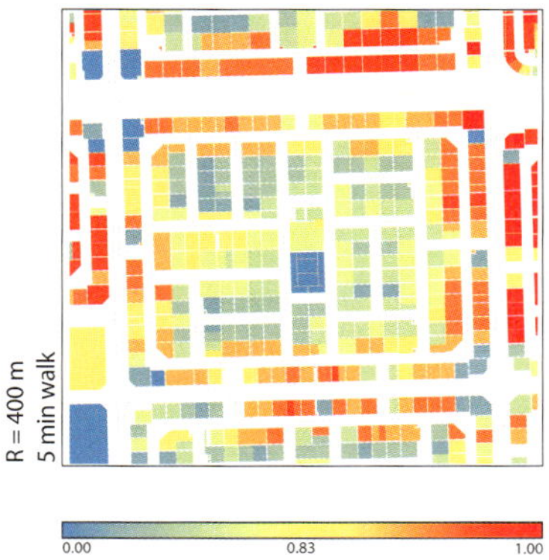

Straightness (Normalized Values, Radius= 400 m)

Plots withing 5 min walking distance have access to streets with an average straightness value of 0.83.

Summary of Reach results
Minimum: 0.00
Maximum: 1.00
Mean: 0.83
Median: 0.83

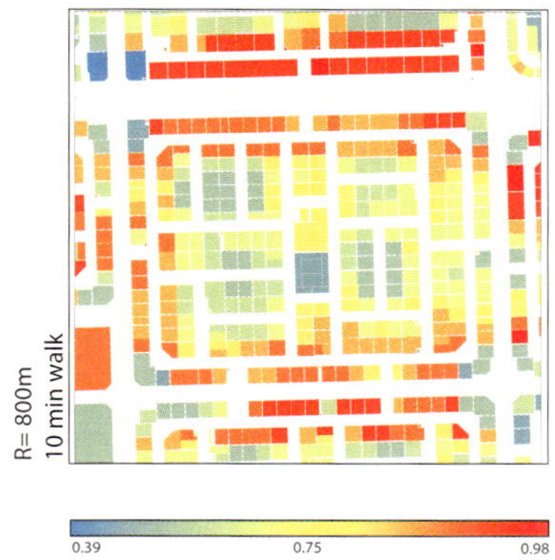

Straightness (Normalized Values, Radius= 800 m)

Plots withing 10 min walking distance have access to streets with an average straightness value of 0.75.

Summary of Reach results
Minimum: 0.39
Maximum: 0.98
Mean: 0.75
Median: 0.75

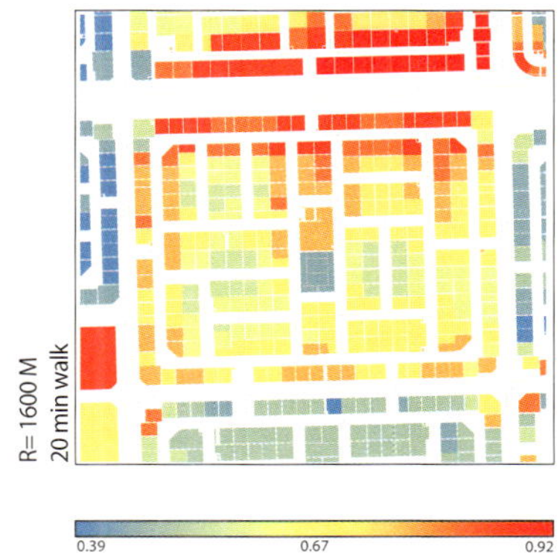

Straightness (Normalized Values, Radius= 1600 m)

Plots withing 20 min walking distance have access to streets with an average straightness value of 0.67.

Summary of Reach results
Minimum: 0.39
Maximum: 0.92
Mean: 0.67
Median: 0.68

FIG. 15.6

Straightness

Scenario 2: Streets + Alleys

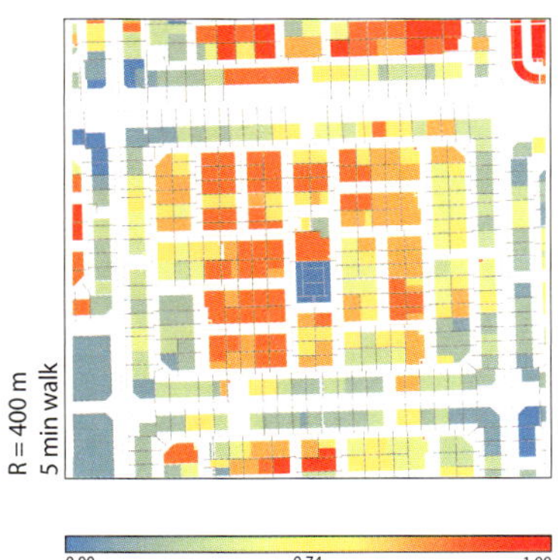

Straightness (Normalized Values, Radius= 400 m)

Plots withing 5 min walking distance have access to streets with an average Straightness value of 0.74.

Summary of Straightness results
Minimum: 0.52
Maximum: 1.00
Mean: 0.74
Median: 0.75

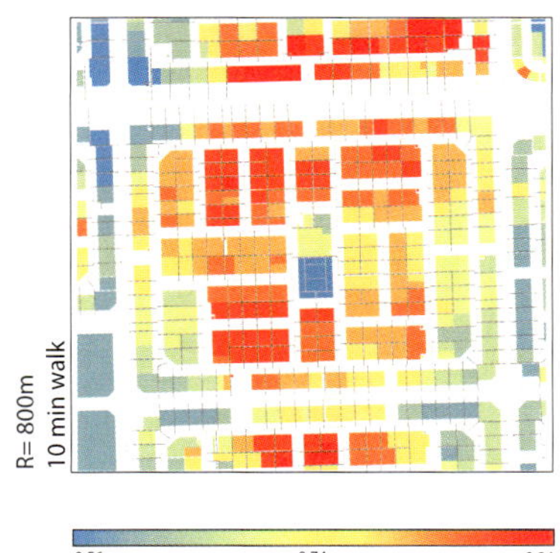

Straightness (Normalized Values, Radius= 800 m)

Plots withing 10 min walking distance have access to streets with an average Straightness value of 0.74.

Summary of Straightness results
Minimum: 0.56
Maximum: 0.84
Mean: 0.74
Median: 0.76

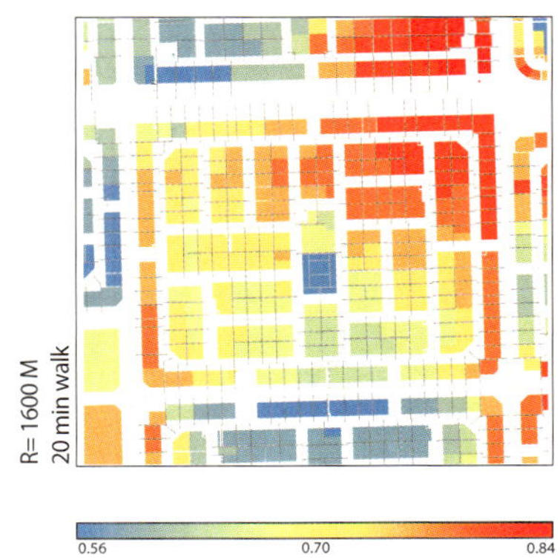

Straightness (Normalized Values, Radius= 1600 m)

Plots withing 20 min walking distance have access to streets with an average Straightness value of 0.70.

Summary of Straightness results
Minimum: 0.56
Maximum: 0.84
Mean: 0.70
Median: 0.71

At a 400 m radius, high Straightness values (0.75 to 1.00) are obtained by plots lying adjacent to arterial streets. At an 800 m radius, high Straightness values continue to appear near the arterial streets. However, Straightness value decreases for a majority of plots. At a 1,600 m radius, Straightness values further decrease for most plots while a sharp reduction can be observed for some plots lying in outer NPUs. With the introduction of alleys, at 400 m, high Straightness values (0.75 to 1.00) shift from the plots adjacent to arterial streets to the plots within the centrally located NPU. Some plots lying in the peripheral NPUs also have high Straightness values. At 800 m, high values become even more concentrated at the same spots. At a 1,600 m radius, high Straightness values concentrate towards the top right corner of the centrally located NPU and the plots opposite to it located in the NPU across the arterial street.

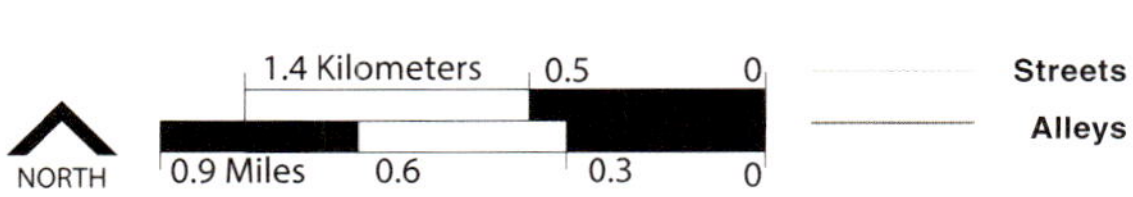

Sample 02

FIG. 16.1

Reach

Scenario 1: Streets only

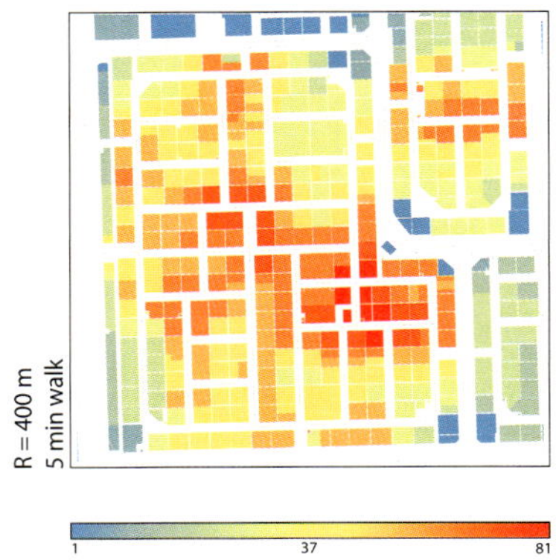

Reach (Radius = 400 m)

The maximum number of plots that can be reached within 5 min walking distance is 81 plots. The average Reach of the sample is 37 plots.

Summary of Reach results
Minimum: 1
Maximum: 81
Mean: 37
Median: 40

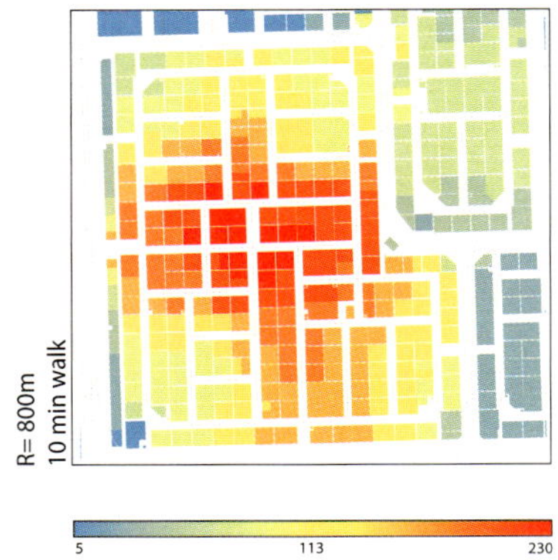

Reach (Radius = 800 m)

The maximum number of plots that can be reached within 10 min walking distance is 230 plots. The average Reach of the sample is 113 plots.

Summary of Reach results
Minimum: 5
Maximum: 230
Mean: 113
Median: 117

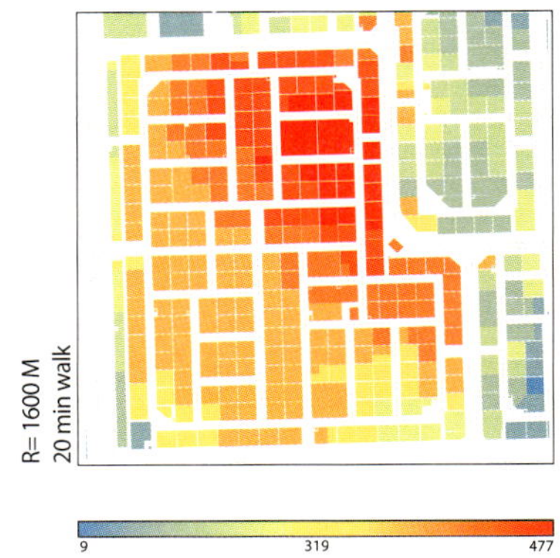

Reach (Radius = 1600 m)

The maximum number of plots that can be reached within 20 min walking distance is 477 plots. The average Reach of the sample is 319 plots.

Summary of Reach results
Minimum: 9
Maximum: 477
Mean: 319
Median: 345

FIG. 16.2

Reach

Scenario 2: Streets + Alleys

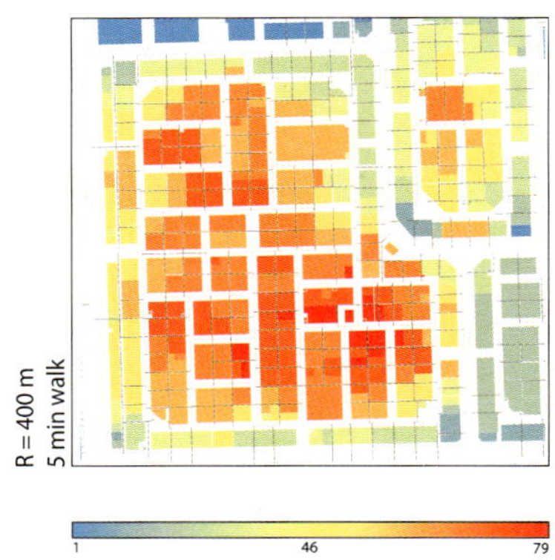

Reach (Radius = 400 m)

The maximum number of plots that can be reached within 5 min walking distance is 79 plots. The average Reach of the sample is 46 plots.

Summary of Reach results
Minimum: 1
Maximum: 79
Mean: 46
Median: 49

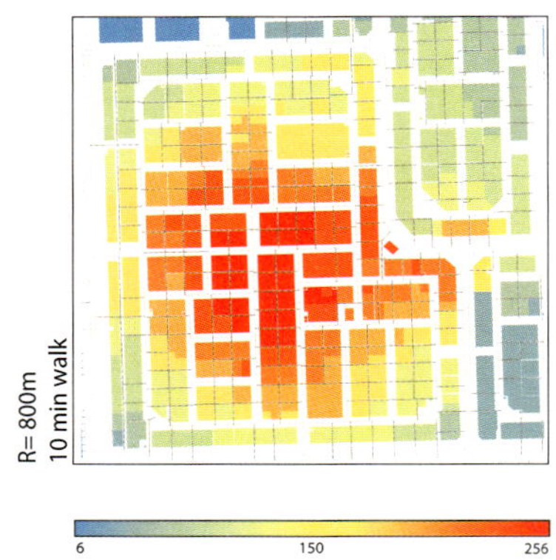

Reach (Radius = 800 m)

The maximum number of plots that can be reached within 10 min walking distance is 256 plots. The average Reach of the sample is 150 plots.

Summary of Reach results
Minimum: 6
Maximum: 256
Mean: 150
Median: 153

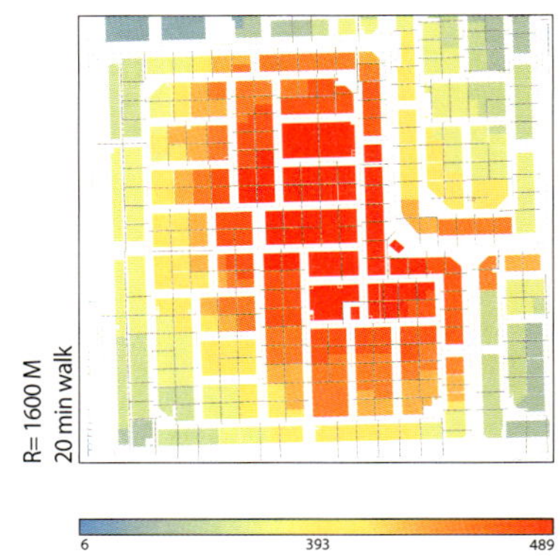

Reach (Radius = 1600 m)

The maximum number of plots that can be reached within 20 min walking distance is 489 plots. The average Reach of the sample is 393 plots.

Summary of Reach results
Minimum: 6
Maximum: 489
Mean: 393
Median: 393

At a 400 m radius, the plots lying adjacent to internal streets within the biggest NPU have high Reach values ranging from 37 to 81. At an 800 m radius, plots with high Reach values ranging from 113 to 230 concentrate at the center of the biggest NPU. At a 1,600 m radius, high Reach values shift towards the top right corner of the same NPU. With the introduction of alleys, at a 400 m radius, the concentration of high Reach values becomes stronger and clearer near the three corners of the biggest NPU. At an 800 m radius, plots with high Reach values lie at the center of the same NPU with values ranging from 150 to 256. Similar to the case without alleys, at a 1,600 m radius, when alleys are included in the analysis, plots with high Reach values shift towards the top right corner of the biggest NPU with the highest Reach value of 489.

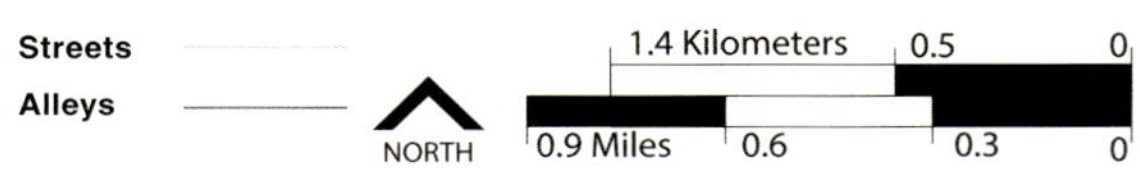

FIG. 16.3

Gravity

Scenario 1: Streets only

R = 400 m
5 min walk

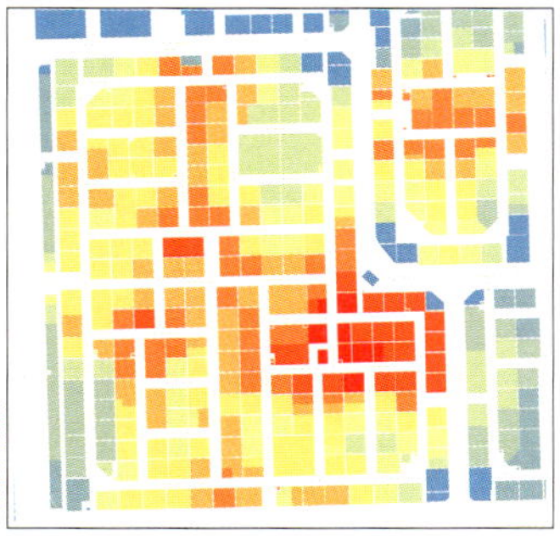

0.20 15.20 30.15

Gravity (Radius = 400 m)

The maximum number of plots that can be reached within 5 min walking distance with the distance decay effect is 30.15 plots. The average Gravity of the sample is 15.20 plots.

Summary of Gravity results
Minimum: 0.20
Maximum: 30.15
Mean: 15.20
Median: 16.21

R = 800 m
10 min walk

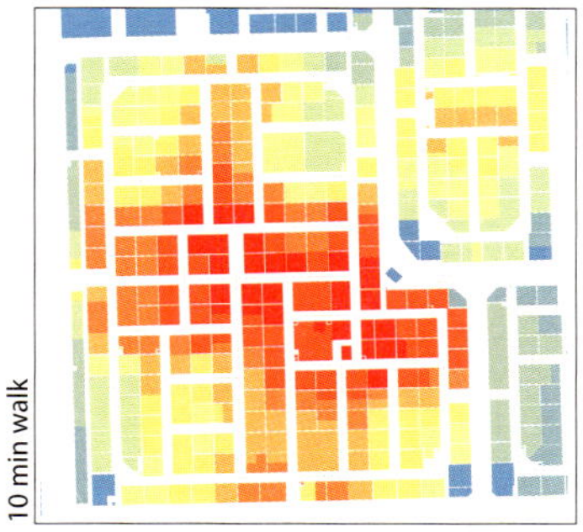

0.87 22.60 37.57

Gravity (Radius = 800 m)

The maximum number of plots that can be reached within 10 min walking distance with the distance decay effect is 37.57 plots. The average Gravity of the sample is 22.60 plots.

Summary of Gravity results
Minimum: 0.87
Maximum: 37.57
Mean: 22.60
Median: 24.35

R = 1600 m
20 min walk

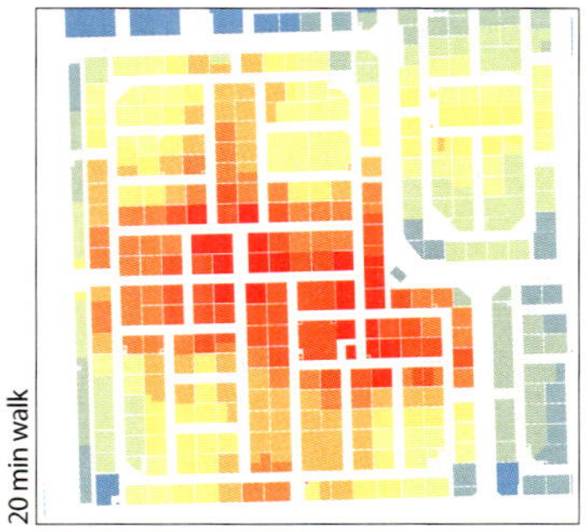

1.68 24.96 40.42

Gravity (Radius = 1600 m)

The maximum number of plots that can be reached within 20 min walking distance with the distance decay effect is 40.42 plots. The average Gravity of the sample is 26.7 plots.

Summary of Gravity results
Minimum: 1.68
Maximum: 40.42
Mean: 24.96
Median: 26.67

FIG. 16.4

Gravity

Scenario 2: Streets + Alleys

R = 400 m
5 min walk

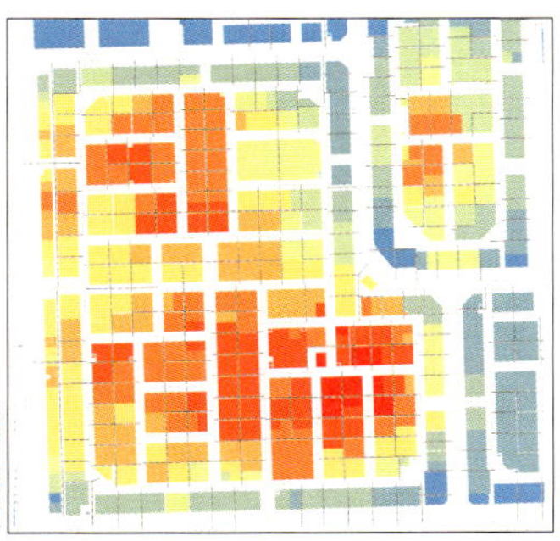

0.27 17.59 27.95

Gravity (Radius = 400 m)

The maximum number of plots that can be reached within 5 min walking distance with the distance decay effect is 27.95 plots. The average Gravity of the sample is 17.59 plots.

Summary of Gravity results
Minimum: 0.27
Maximum: 29.1
Mean: 17.59
Median: 19.3

R = 800 m
10 min walk

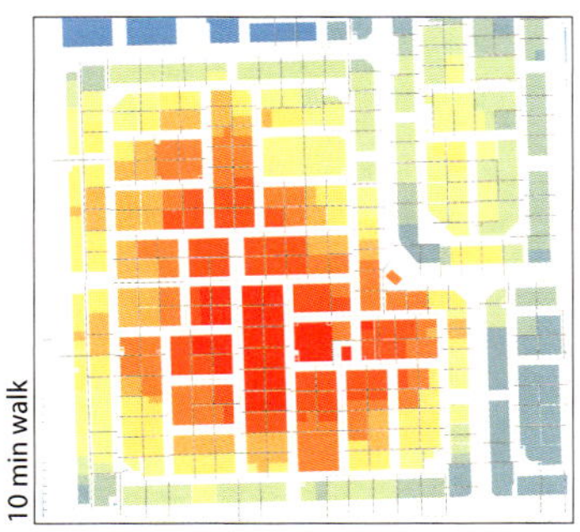

0.73 27.58 42.23

Gravity (Radius = 800 m)

The maximum number of plots that can be reached within 10 min walking distance with the distance decay effect is 43.4 plots. The average Gravity of the sample is 27.6 plots.

Summary of Gravity results
Minimum: 0.7
Maximum: 43.4
Mean: 27.6
Median: 28.9

R = 1600 m
20 min walk

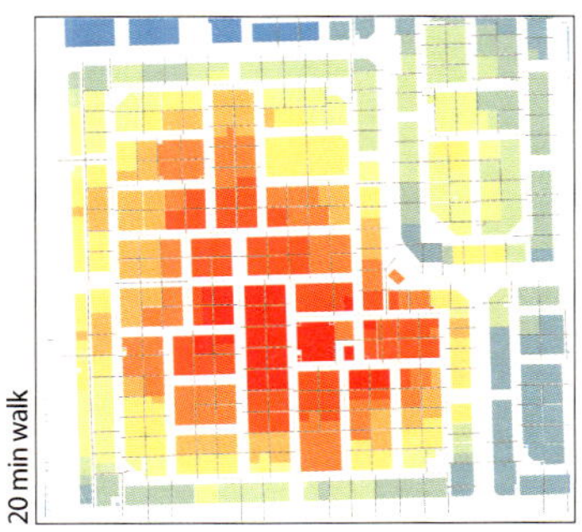

2.18 30.68 45.57

Gravity (Radius = 1600 m)

The maximum number of plots that can be reached within 20 min walking distance with the distance decay effect is 46.9 plots. The average Gravity of the sample is 30.7 plots.

Summary of Gravity results
Minimum: 2.2
Maximum: 46.9
Mean: 30.7
Median: 32

At a 400 m radius, the biggest NPU consists of plots with high Gravity values ranging from 15.20 to 31.15. The highest values are obtained by plots located near the T-intersection of collector streets. At 800 m and 1,600 m radii, high Gravity values are found at and around the center of the biggest NPU where the values range from 22.60 to 42.42. With the introduction of alleys, at a 400 m radius, high Gravity values form two distinct clusters within the biggest NPU. At 800 m and 1,600 m radii, high values form a single cluster within the same NPU. The highest Gravity values of 42.23 and 45.57 are found at the center of the NPU at 800 m and 1,600 m radii respectively. The distribution of Gravity values does not change from 800 m to 1,600 m, however with the inclusion of alleys, the values are slightly improved.

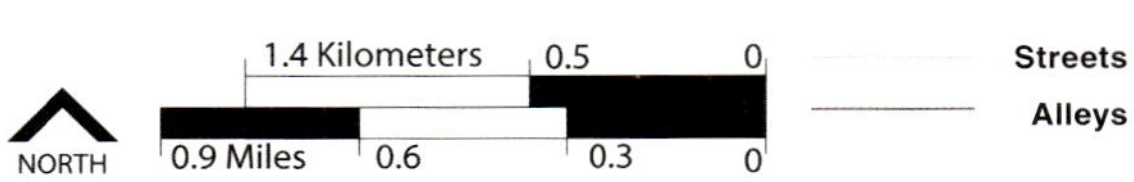

Sample 02

FIG. 16.5
Straightness
Scenario 1: Streets only

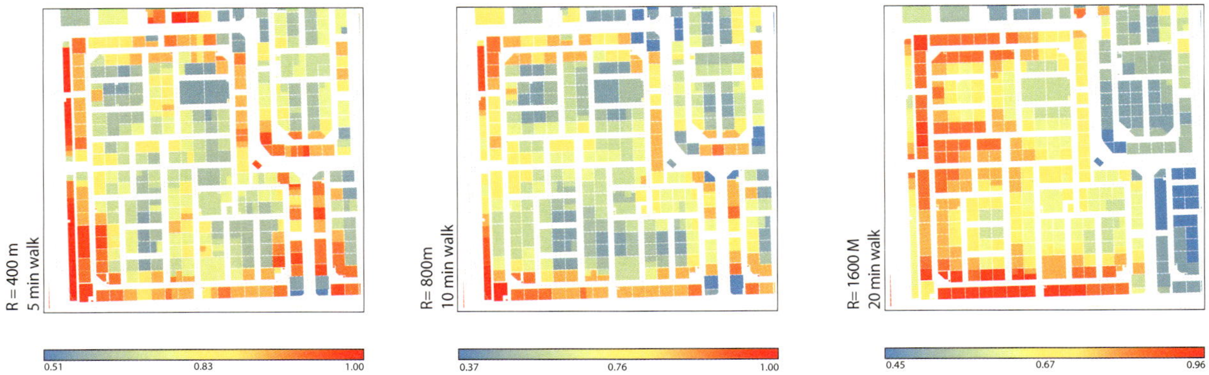

Straightness (Normalized Values, Radius= 400 m)
Plots withing 5 min walking distance have access to streets with an average straightness value of 0.83.

Summary of Reach results
Minimum: 0.51
Maximum: 1.00
Mean: 0.83
Median: 0.83

Straightness (Normalized Values, Radius= 800 m)
Plots withing 10 min walking distance have access to streets with an average straightness value of 0.76.

Summary of Reach results
Minimum: 0.37
Maximum: 1.00
Mean: 0.76
Median: 0.76

Straightness (Normalized Values, Radius= 1600 m)
Plots withing 20 min walking distance have access to streets with an average straightness value of 0.67.

Summary of Reach results
Minimum: 0.45
Maximum: 0.96
Mean: 0.67
Median: 0.68

FIG. 16.6
Straightness
Scenario 2: Streets + Alleys

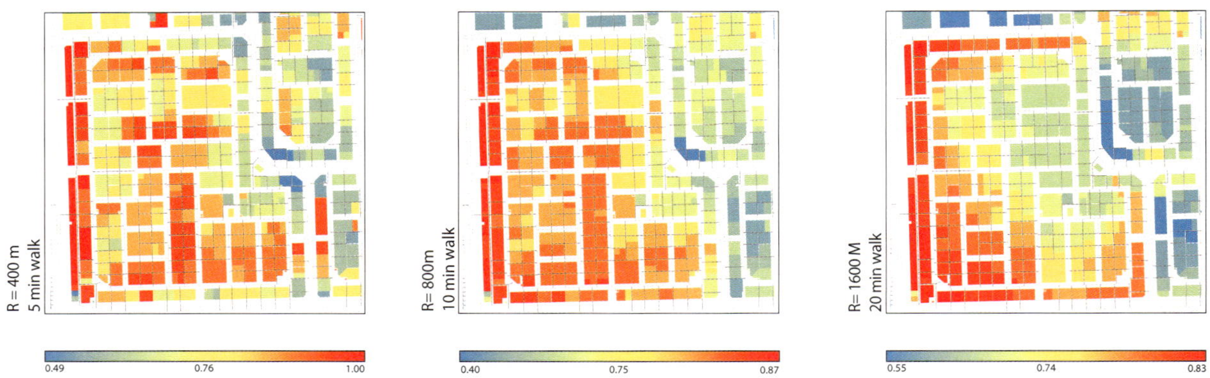

Straightness (Normalized Values, Radius= 400 m)
Plots withing 5 min walking distance have access to streets with an average Straightness value of 0.76.

Summary of Straightness results
Minimum: 0.49
Maximum: 1.00
Mean: 0.76
Median: 0.77

Straightness (Normalized Values, Radius= 800 m)
Plots withing 10 min walking distance have access to streets with an average Straightness value of 0.75.

Summary of Straightness results
Minimum: 0.40
Maximum: 0.87
Mean: 0.75
Median: 0.76

Straightness (Normalized Values, Radius= 1600 m)
Plots withing 20 min walking distance have access to streets with an average Straightness value of 0.74

Summary of Straightness results
Minimum: 0.55
Maximum: 0.83
Mean: 0.74
Median: 0.75

At a 400 m radius, high Straightness values (0.75 to 1.00) are obtained by plots that lie adjacent to arterial and collector streets. At 800 m, Straightness values slightly decrease for a majority of plots, while the distribution of values do not change notably. At a 1,600 m radius, high Straightness values prominently appear on the left side of the biggest NPU, and also form three linear clusters within it. With the introduction of alleys, at 400 m, high Straightness values (0.75 to 1.00) are obtained by plots adjacent to arterial streets, and also by plots lying around the center of the biggest NPU. At 800 m, high values are distributed throughout the biggest NPU. At a 1,600 m radius, Straightness values decreases for a majority of plots, while high values concentrate on the edges of the biggest NPU.

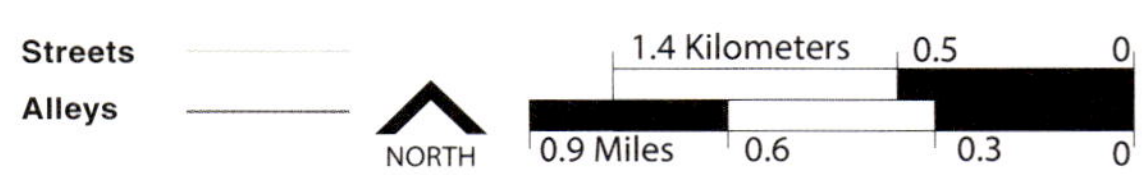

Summary of Centrality Results

Neighborhood

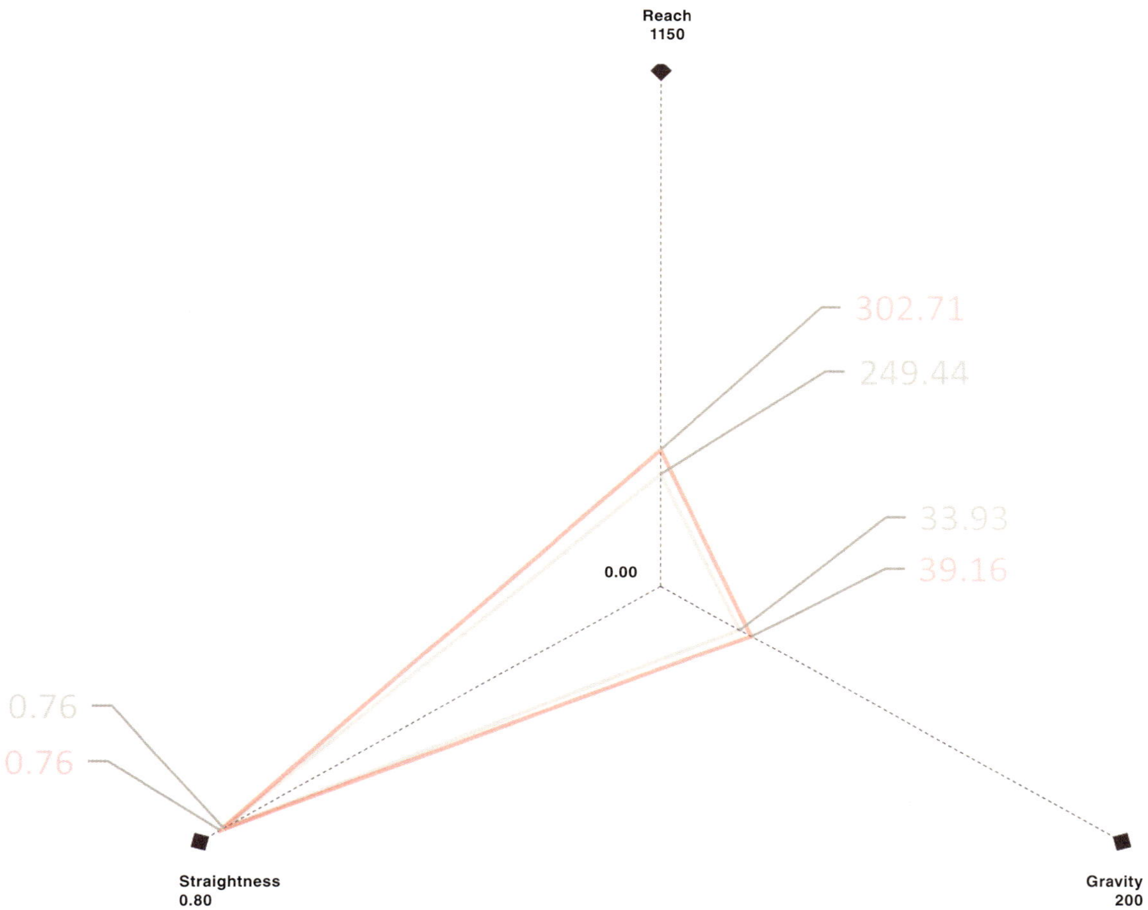

FIG. 17
Spider graphs showing the contribution of alleyways to the averages of 400m, 800m, and 1600m scales of Reach, Gravity and Straightness.

Sample 01

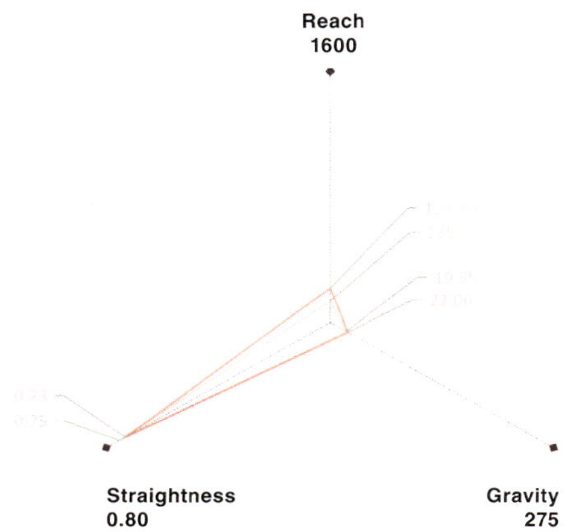

Sample 02

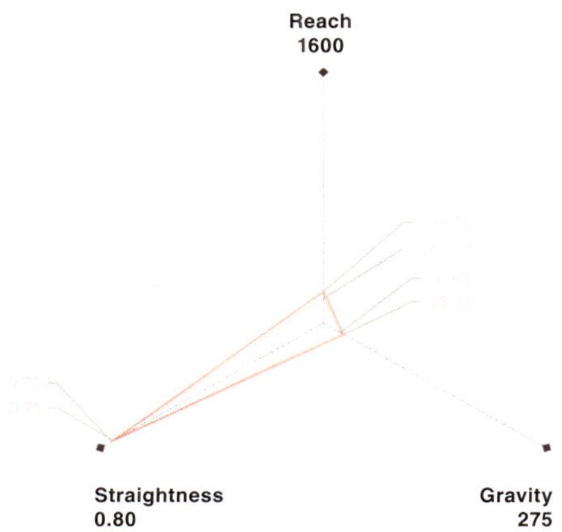

Neighborhood Scale

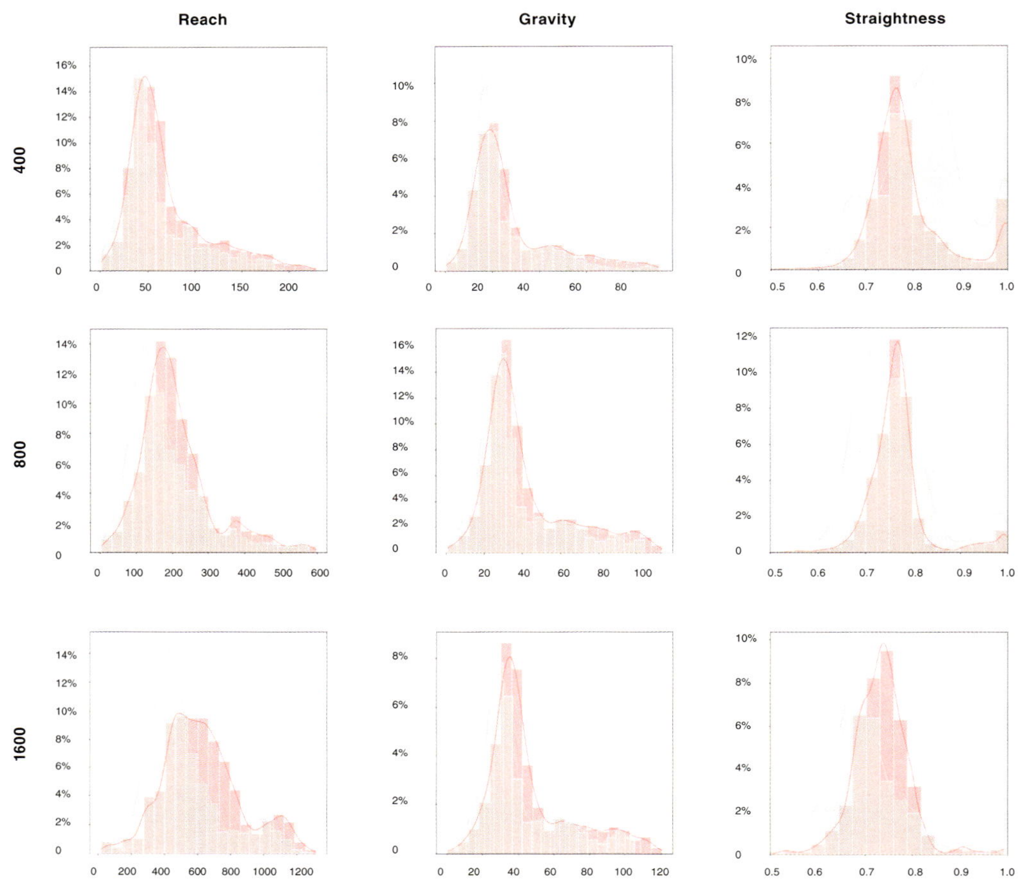

FIG. 18
Histograms showing the distribution of centrality values (Reach, Gravity, and Straightness) among plots with and without alleys at three different scales 400m, 800m, and 1600m. The X axis is for the centrality metric values, while the Y axis is for the percentage of plots achieving a centrality value denoted on the X axis.

TABLE. 1
Neighborhood scale centrality values

UNA		Radius	Min	Max	Avg
Scenario 1: Streets only	Reach	400	1	194	58
		800	4	578	180
		1600	16	1295	510
	Gravity	400	0.21	92.22	24.88
		800	0.40	104.10	36.69
		1600	0.11	105.62	40.24
	Straightness	400	0.00	1.00	0.82
		800	0.00	1.00	0.76
		1600	0.41	0.99	0.70

UNA		Radius	Min	Max	Avg
Scenario 2: Streets + Alleys	Reach	400	1	229	70
		800	4	598	210
		1600	16	1317	628
	Gravity	400	0.21	90.97	28.65
		800	0.84	113.55	42.16
		1600	0.13	120.96	46.68
	Straightness	400	0.00	1.00	0.79
		800	0.00	1.00	0.77
		1600	0.41	0.99	0.73

Sample Scale — Sample 01

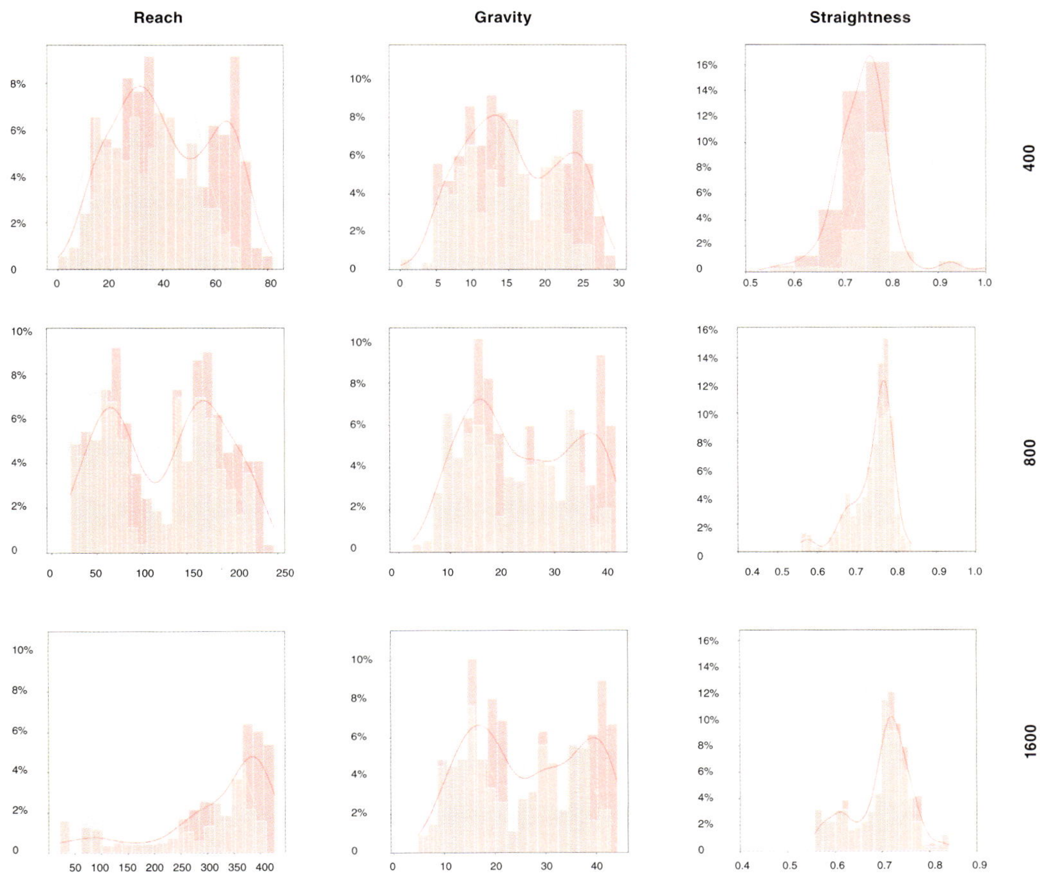

FIG. 19

Histograms showing the distribution of centrality values (Reach, Gravity, and Straightness) among plots with and without alleys at three different scales 400m, 800m, and 1600m. The X axis is for the centrality metric values, while the Y axis is for the percentage of plots achieving a centrality value denoted on the X axis.

Scenario	UNA	Radius	Min	Max	Avg
Scenario 1: Streets only	Reach	400	0	69	34
		800	7	225	106
		1600	21	411	265
	Gravity	400	0.00	26.43	14.55
		800	0.34	40.79	21.53
		1600	1.55	42.74	23.47
	Straightness	400	0.00	1.00	0.83
		800	0.39	0.98	0.75
		1600	0.39	0.92	0.67

Scenario	UNA	Radius	Min	Max	Avg
Scenario 2: Streets + Alleys	Reach	400	0	82	41
		800	21	246	127
		1600	21	427	312
	Gravity	400	0.00	29.73	15.81
		800	2.55	41.96	24.01
		1600	4.74	44.17	26.36
	Straightness	400	0.00	1.00	0.74
		800	0.56	0.84	0.74
		1600	0.56	0.84	0.70

TABLE. 2

Sample 01 centrality values

Sample Scale — Sample 02

FIG. 20

Histograms showing the distribution of centrality values (Reach, Gravity, and Straightness) among plots with and without alleys at three different scales 400m, 800m, and 1600m. The X axis is for the centrality metric values, while the Y axis is for the percentage of plots achieving a centrality value denoted on the X axis.

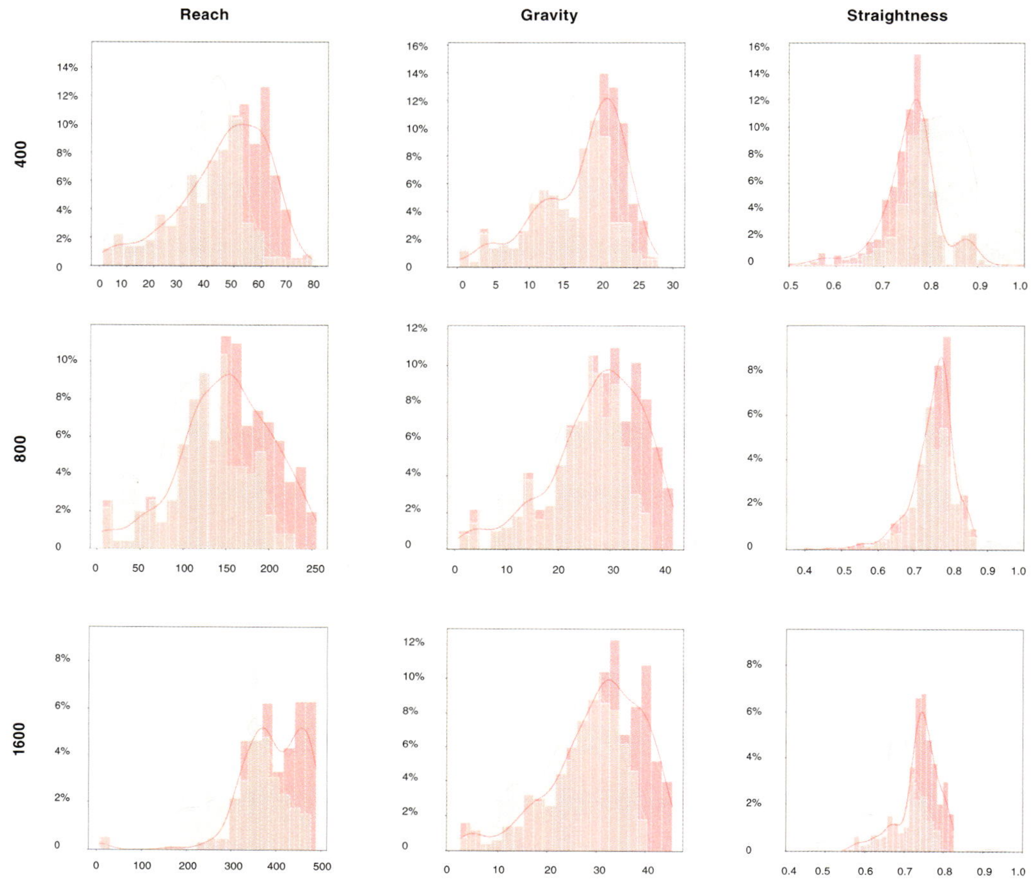

TABLE. 3

Sample 02 centrality values

UNA		Radius	Min	Max	Avg
Scenario 1: Streets only	Reach	400	1	81	37
		800	5	230	113
		1600	9	477	319
	Gravity	400	0.20	30.15	15.18
		800	0.87	37.57	22.60
		1600	1.68	40.42	24.96
	Straightness	400	0.51	1.00	0.83
		800	0.37	1.00	0.76
		1600	0.45	0.96	0.67

UNA		Radius	Min	Max	Avg
Scenario 2: Streets + Alleys	Reach	400	1	79	46
		800	6	256	150
		1600	6	489	393
	Gravity	400	0.27	27.95	17.59
		800	0.73	42.23	27.58
		1600	2.18	45.57	30.68
	Straightness	400	0.49	1.00	0.76
		800	0.40	0.87	0.75
		1600	0.54	0.83	0.74

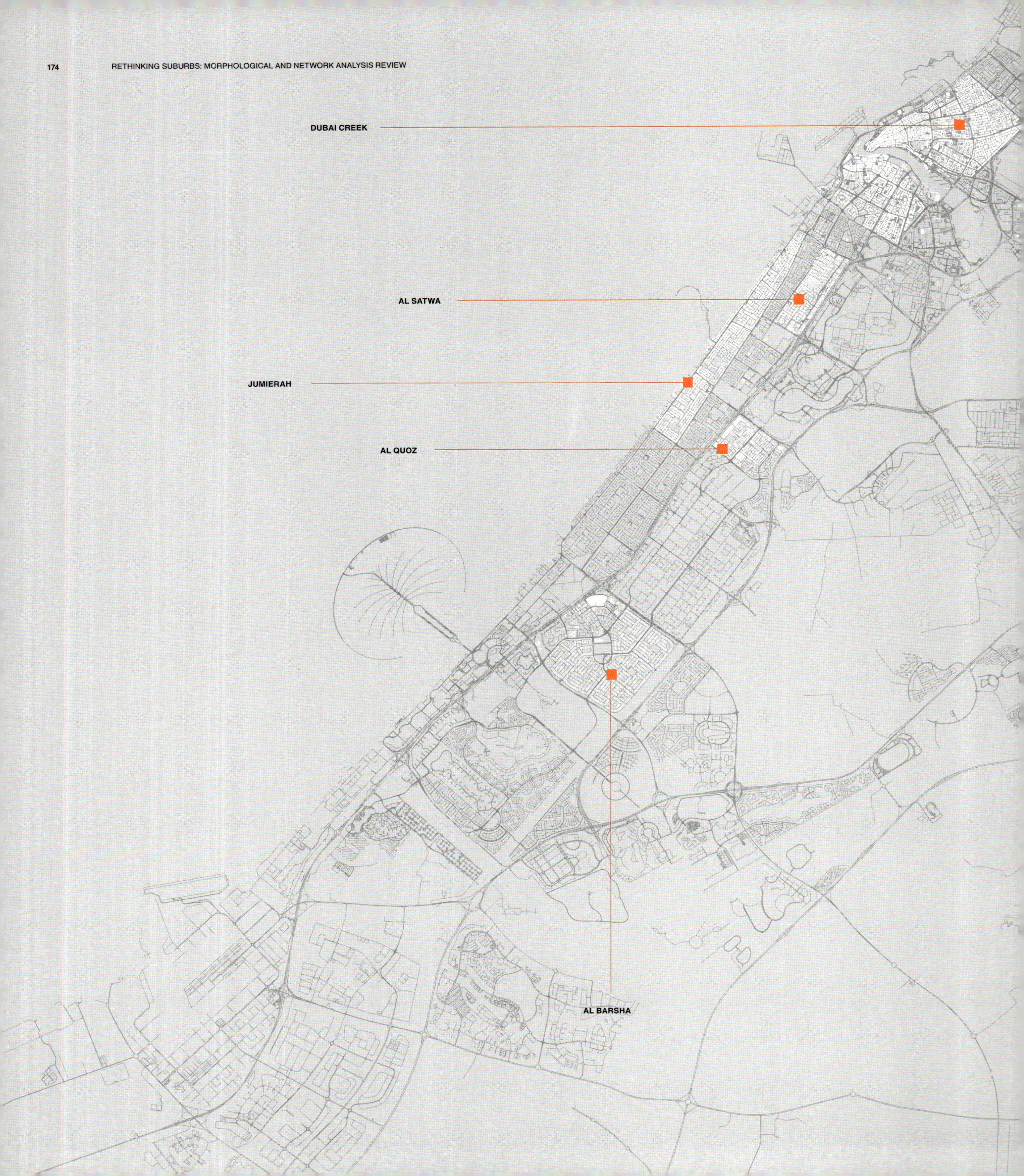
DUBAI CREEK
AL SATWA
JUMIERAH
AL QUOZ
AL BARSHA

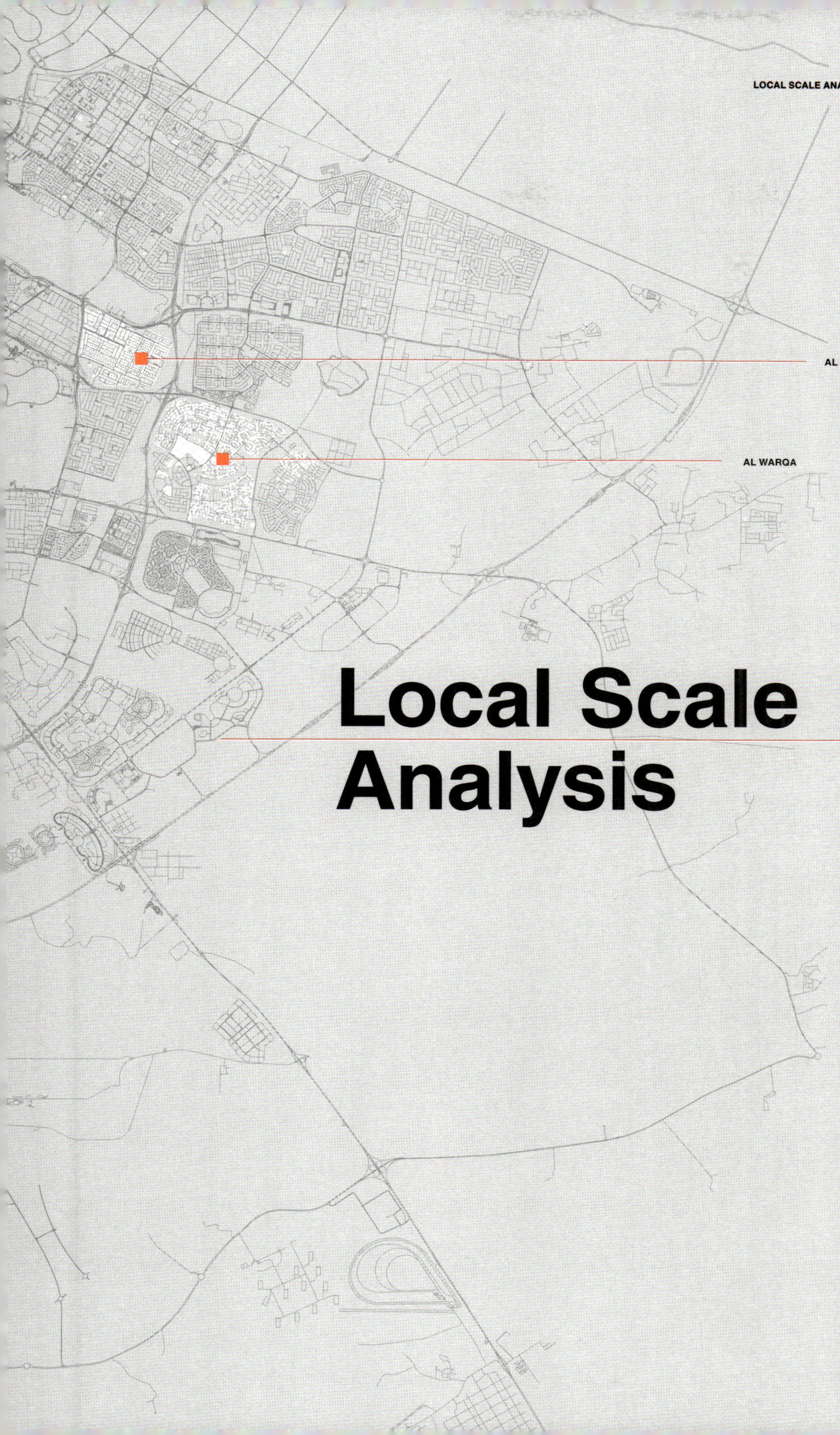

Local Scale Analysis

Dubai

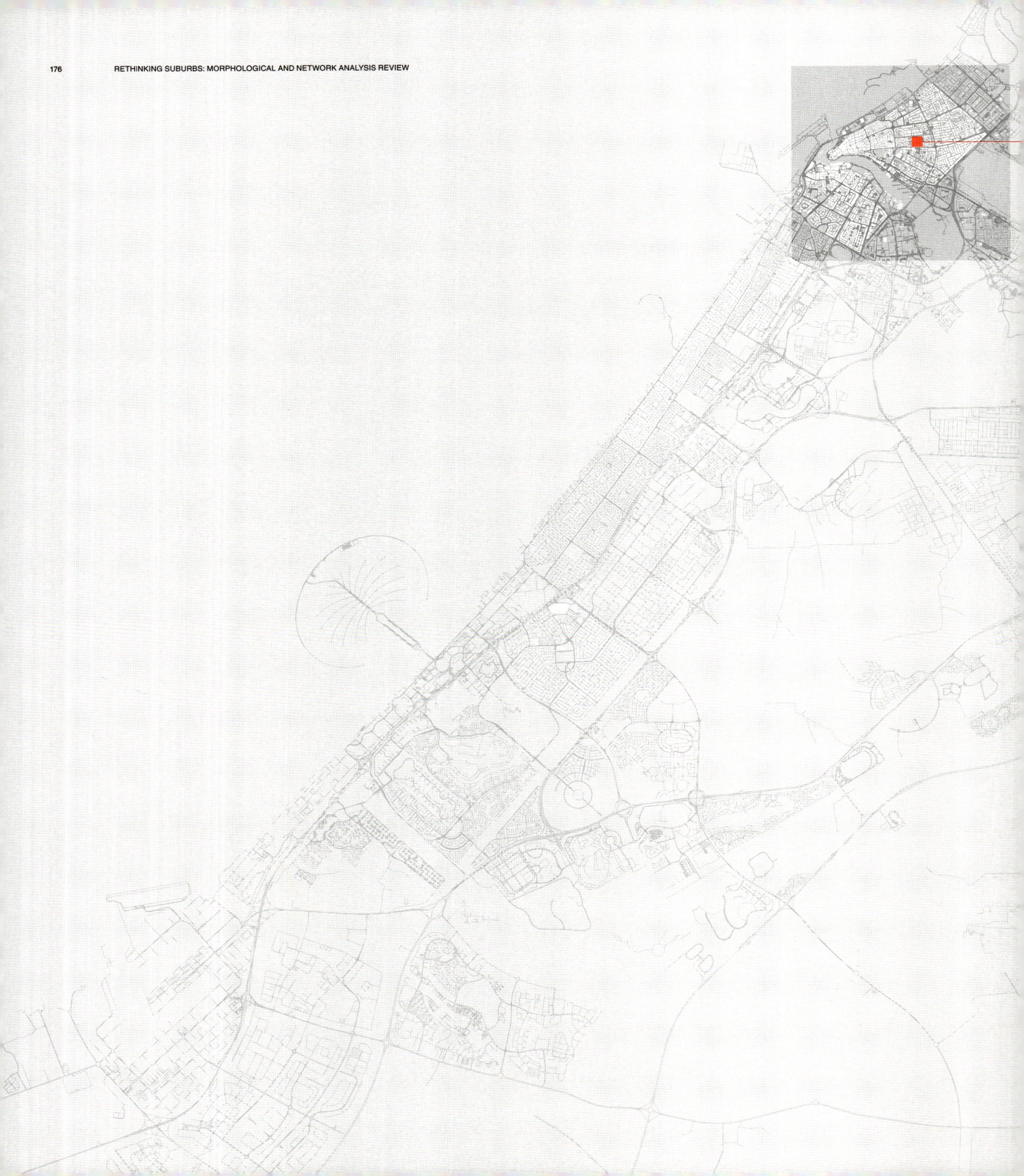

Dubai Creek

Dubai Creek

FIG. 1
Dubai Creek skyline

FIG. 2
Street view showing internal streets in Dubai Creek area

FIG. 3
A photo montage with different views of the Neighborhood

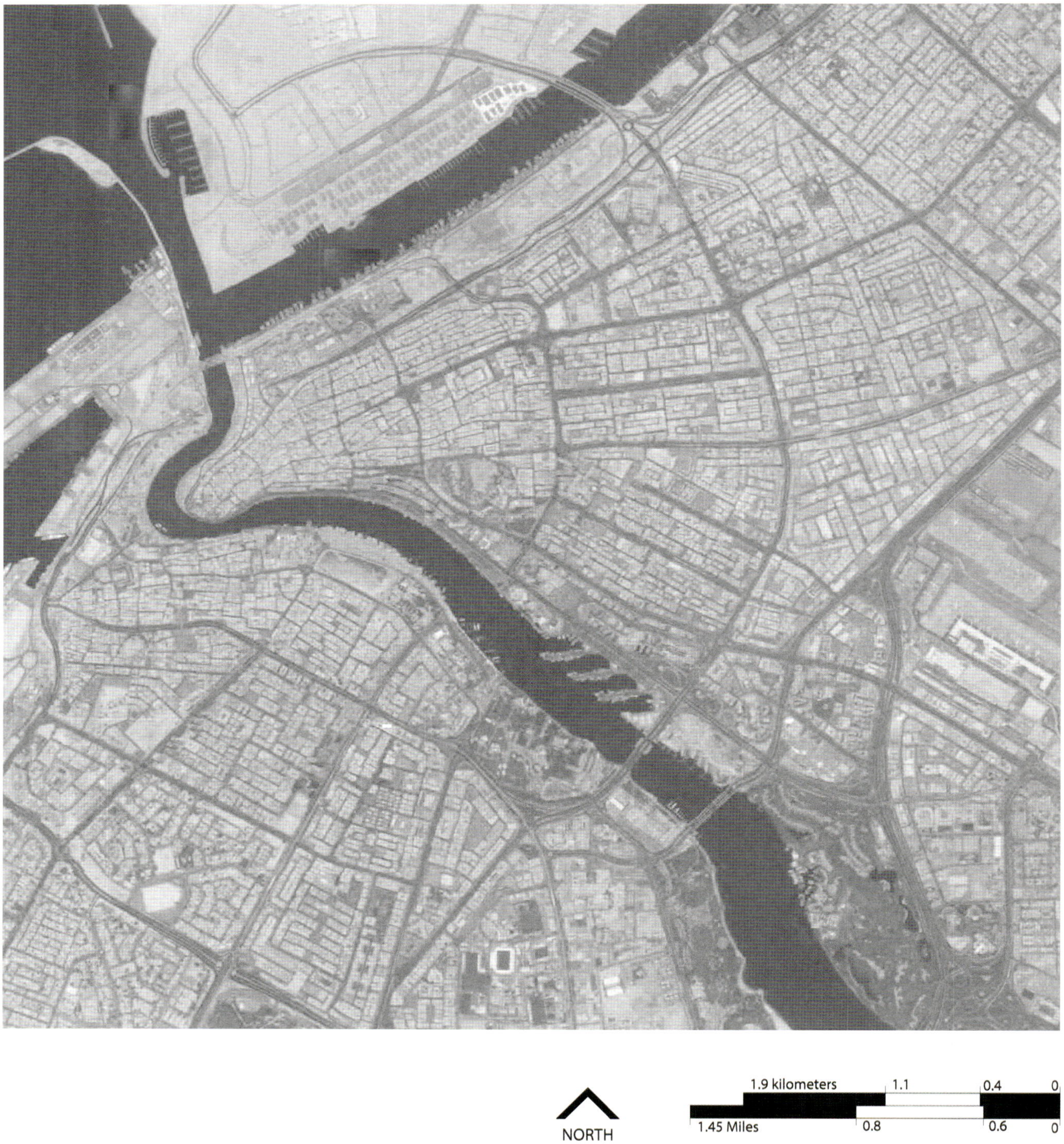

FIG. 4
Aerial image showing Creek (Esri & USGS, 2021)

Morphological Analysis

Neighborhood Scale

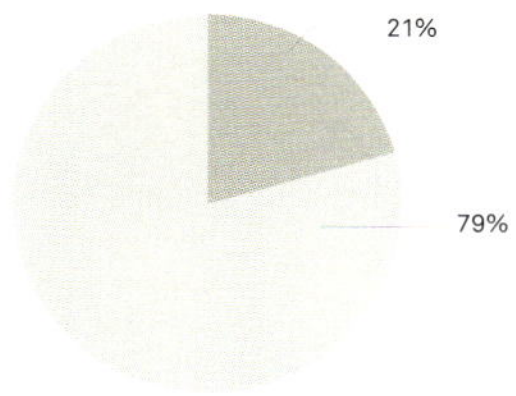

Residential= 11,657 Plots
Non-residential= 2,992 Plots

Plots/Buildings:

- Total area = 2,569 Hectares
- Total plots = 14,649 Plots
- Total buildings = 13,686 Buildings
- Average plot density = 5.70 Plots/Hectare
- Average building density = 5.32 Buildings/Hectare
- Average plot area = 0.11 Hectare
- Average population density = 296.06 Population/Hectare

FIG. 5.1
Residential/ non-residential classification

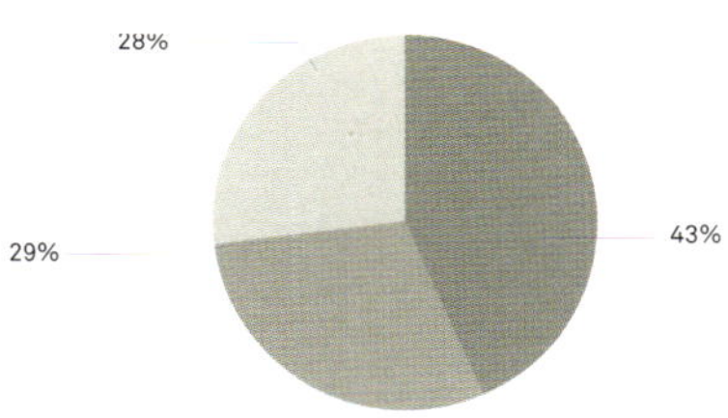

Low-rise (1-4) = 3,662 Buildings
Mid-rise (4-10)= 4,087 Buildings
High-rise (+10)= 5,937 Buildings

FIG. 5.2
Buildings height classification

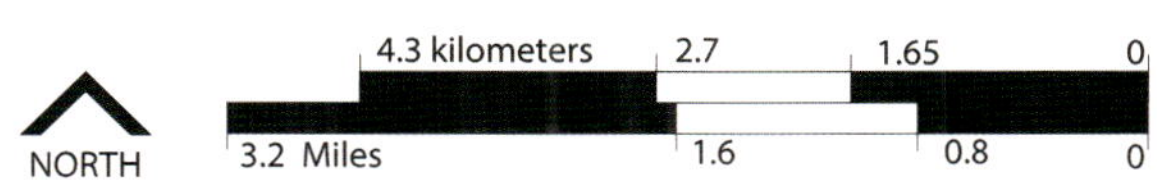

FIG. 5.3
Population density

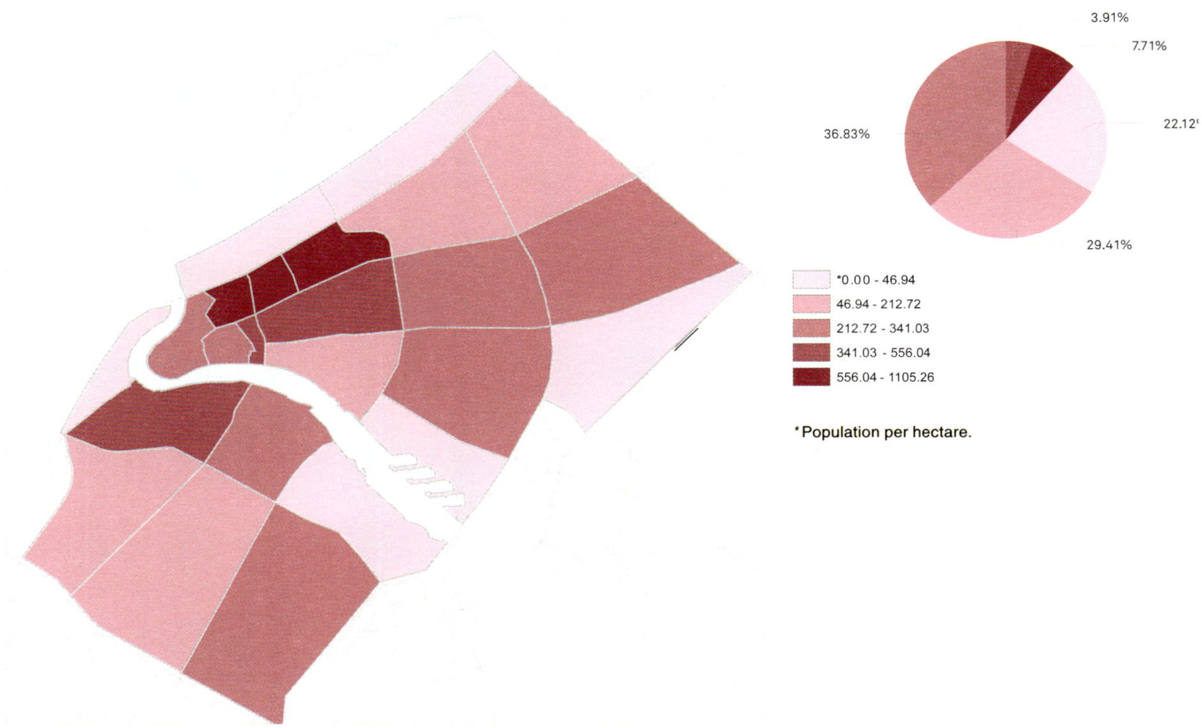

FIG. 5.4
Land use classification

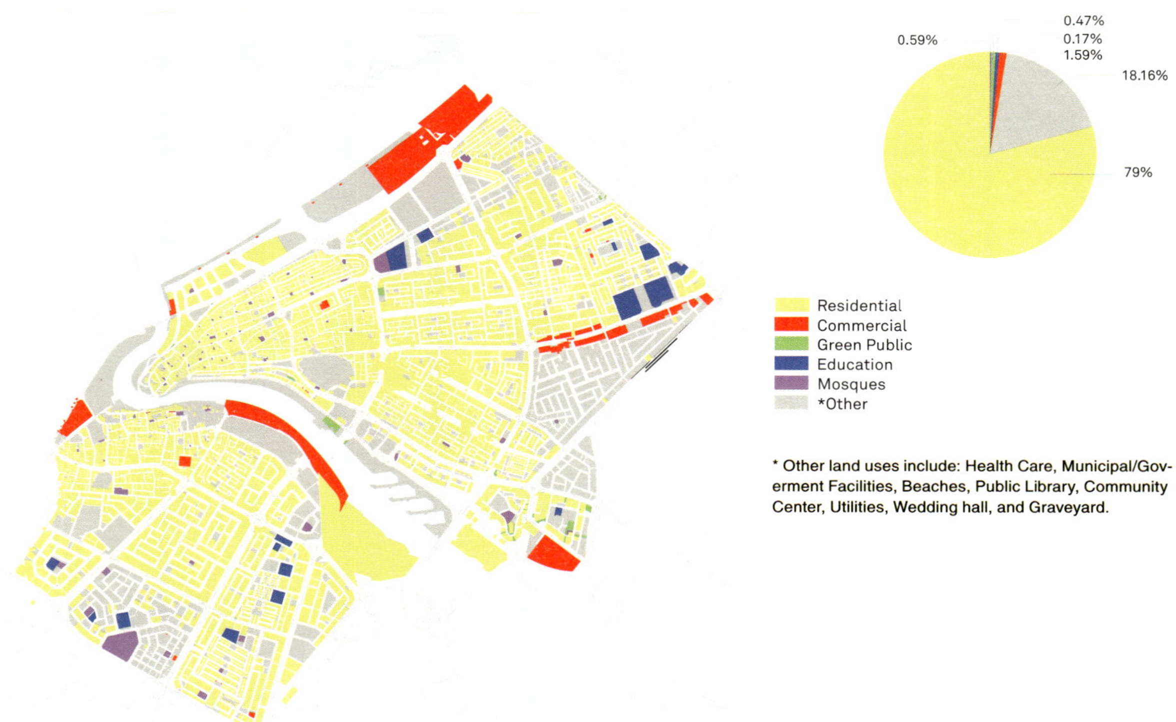

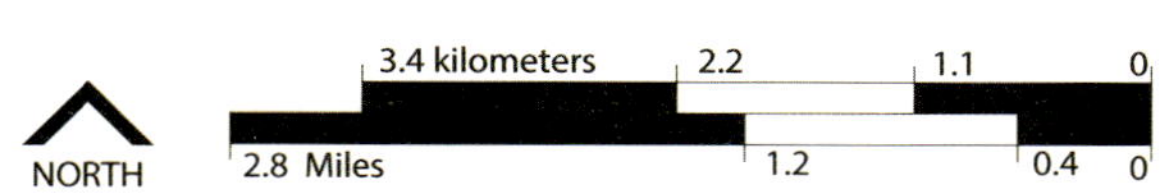

FIG. 5.5
Map showing network classification in Dubai Creek

Streets:

- Street length = 765.23 km
- Street density = 0.29 km/Hectare
- Street intersections = 47,663 Intersections
- Street intersections density = 18.55 Intersections/Hectare

Alleys:

- Alley length = 1,360.2 km
- Alley density = 0.56 km/Hectare
- Alley intersections = 19,337 Intersections
- Alley intersections density = 7.52 Intersections/Hectare

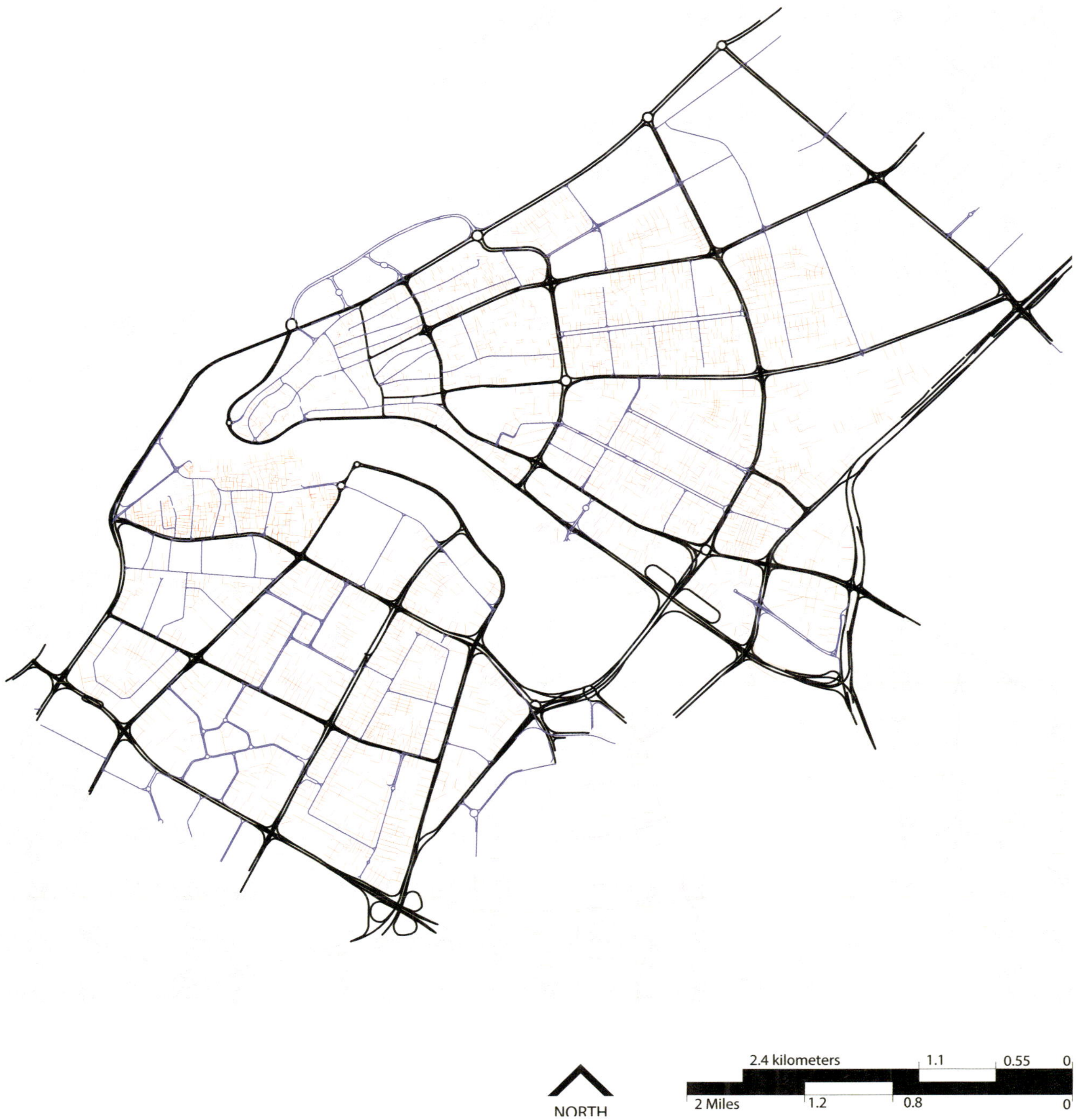

FIG. 6
Map showing Creek with the location of the selected samples. Each sample has an area of 1 square mile.

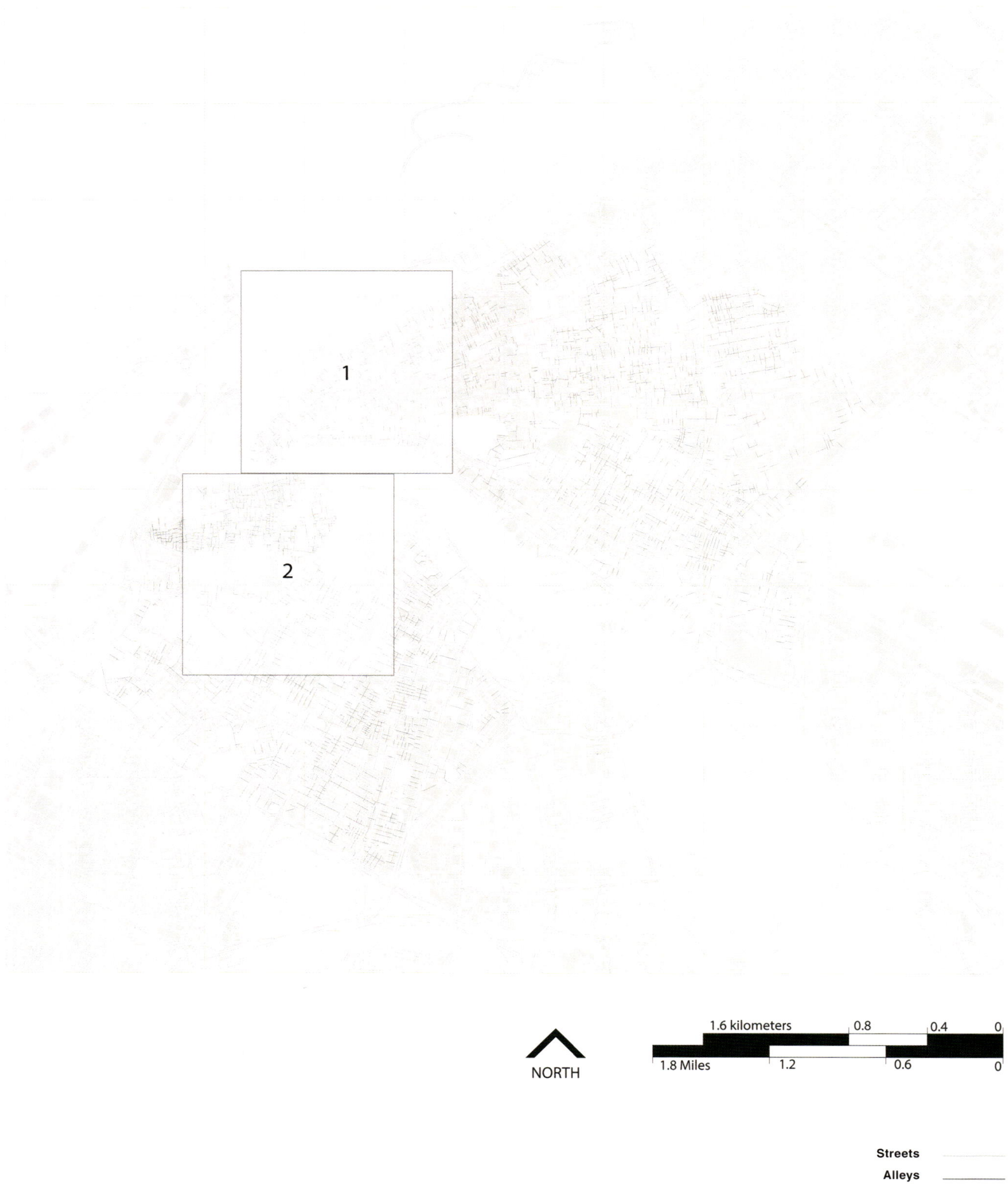

Morphological Analysis

Sample Scale — Sample 01

Residential and Retail= 2,578
Non-residential= 254 Plots

FIG. 7.1
Residential/non-resident al classification

Plots/Buildings:

- Total area = 256 Hectares
- Total plots = 2,832 Plots
- Total buildings = 2,287 Buildings
- Average plot area = 0.07 Hectare
- Average plot density = 11.06 Plots/Hectare

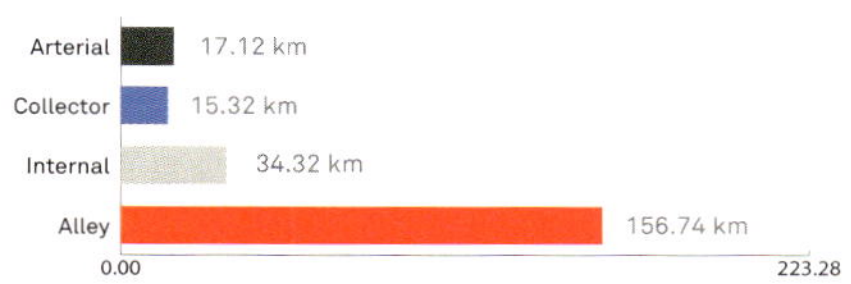

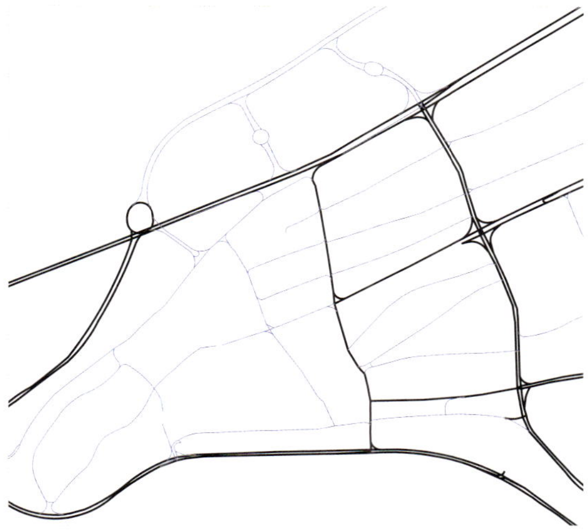

FIG. 7.2
Network classification

Streets:

- Street length = 32.44 km
- Street density = 0.12 km/Hectare
- Street intersections = 634 Intersections
- Street Intersections density = 2.47 Intersections/ Hectare

Alleys:

- Alley length = 156.74 km
- Alley density = 0.61 km/Hectare
- Alley intersections = 570 Intersections
- Alley intersections density = 2.22 Intersections/Hectare

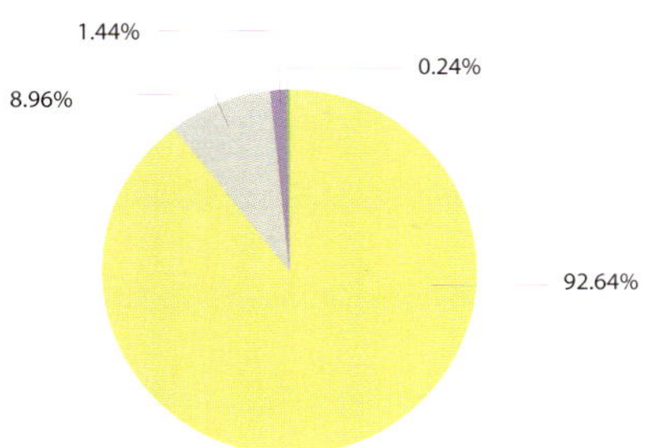

Residential and Retail
*Other
Mosques
Green Public

FIG. 7.3
Land use classification

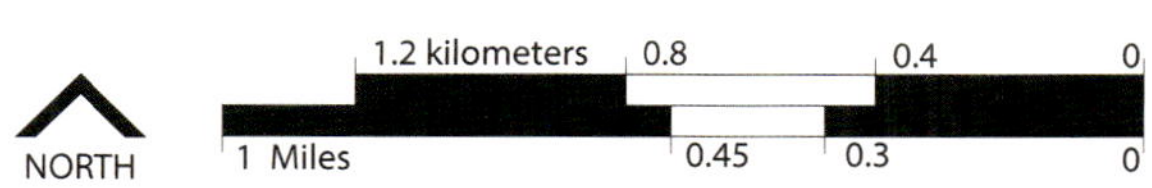

Sample Scale — Sample 02

FIG. 8.1
Residential/non-residential classification

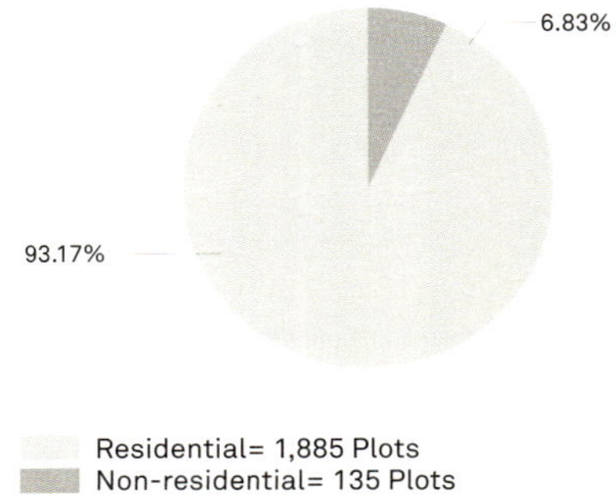

Plots/Buildings:

- Total area = 256 Hectares
- Total plots = 2,020 Plots
- Total buildings = 1,895
- Average plot density = 7.89 Plots/Hectare
- Average plot area = 0.12 Hectare

FIG. 8.2
Network classification

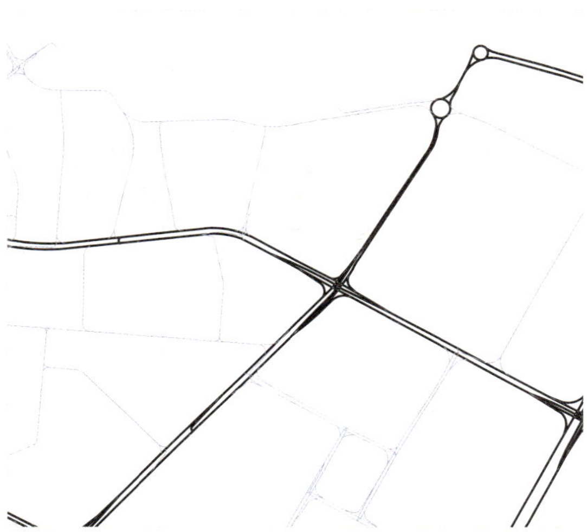

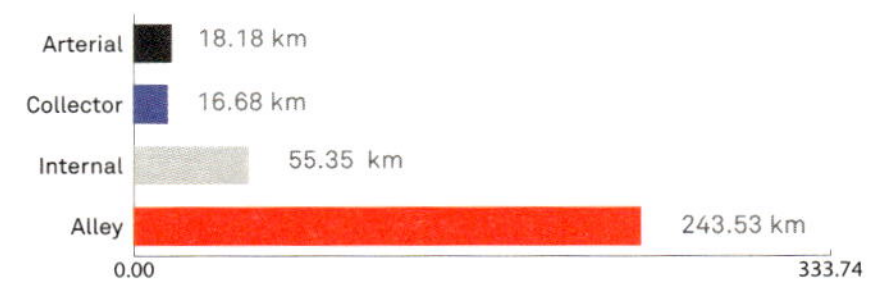

Streets:

- Street length = 90.21 km
- Street density = 0.35 km/Hectare
- Street intersections = 924 Intersections
- Street intersections density = 3.60 Intersection/Hectare

Alleys:

- Alley length = 243.53 km
- Alley density = 0.95 km/Hectare
- Alley intersections = 565 Intersections
- Alley intersections density= 2.20 Intersections/Hectare

FIG. 8.3
Land use classification

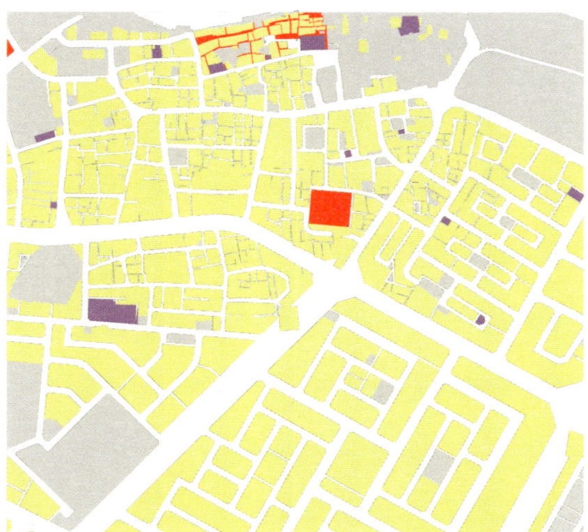

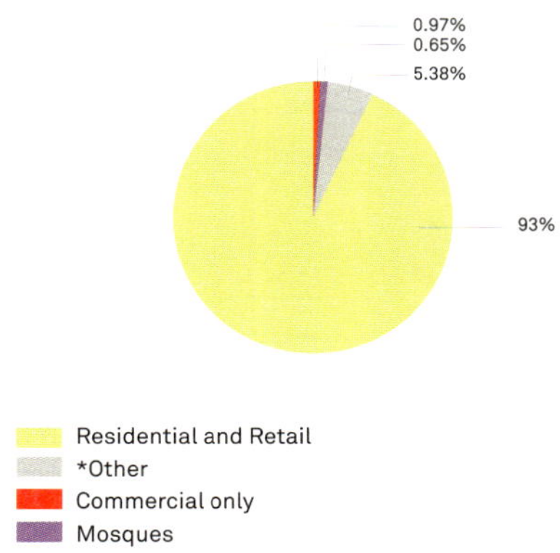

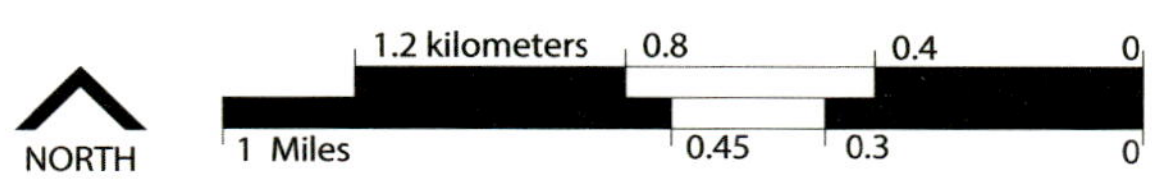

Centrality Analysis: Neighborhood Scale

Scenario 1: Streets only — 400 m Radius

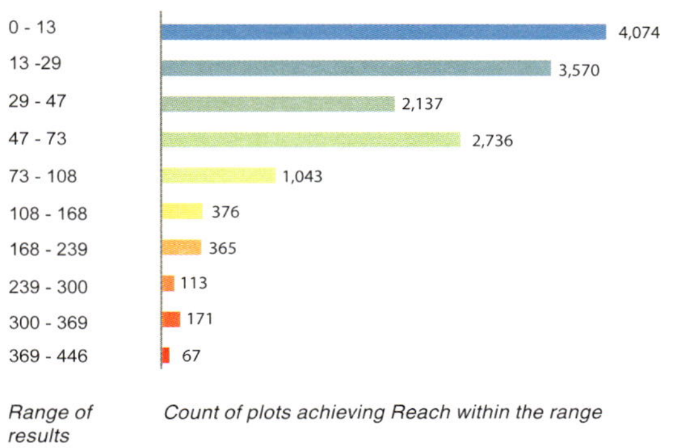

The warmer colors (i.e., greenish-yellow to red) represent a Reach value of 73 or more, while the cooler colors (i.e., light green to dark blue) correspond to a Reach value of 72 or less. The majority of plots (i.e., 9,781 out of 14,652), corresponding to 67% of all plots, have Reach values of less than 73. Among the categories shown in the legend, 28% of the total plots can reach 0 to 13 plots within 5 minutes of walking. On average, each plot in Creek can access at least 312 plots within a distance of 400 m.

FIG. 9.1
Reach

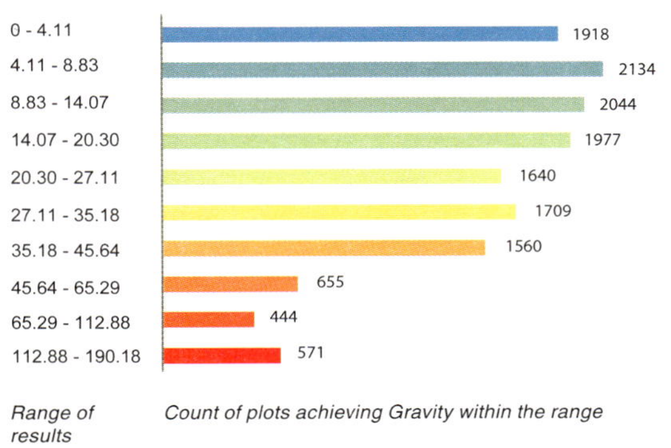

The warmer colors (i.e., greenish-yellow to red) represent Gravity values greater than 45.64, while the cooler colors (i.e., light green to dark blue) correspond to Gravity values lower than 45.64. Forty-one percent of all plots (i.e., 6,096 out of 14,652) have Gravity values of less than 14.07. Among the categories shown in the legend, 4,052 plots, or 27% of the total plots, can reach 0 to 8.83 plots, making this the most common range; this range is represented by dark blue on the map. On average, each plot can reach 26 other plots when spatial impedance or distance decay effect is taken into consideration.

FIG. 9.2
Gravity

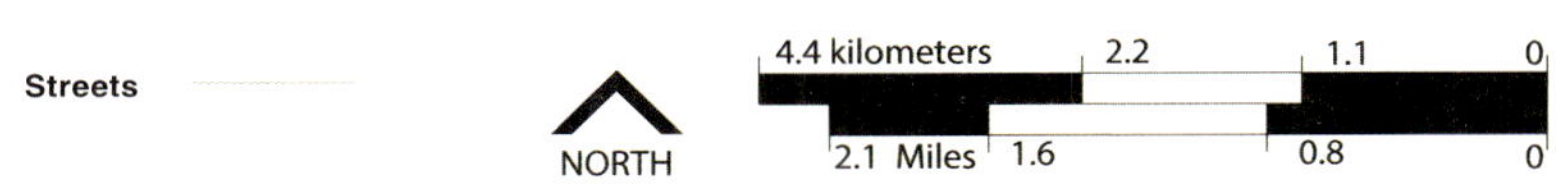

Scenario 1: Streets only — 400 m Radius

FIG. 9.3
Betweenness

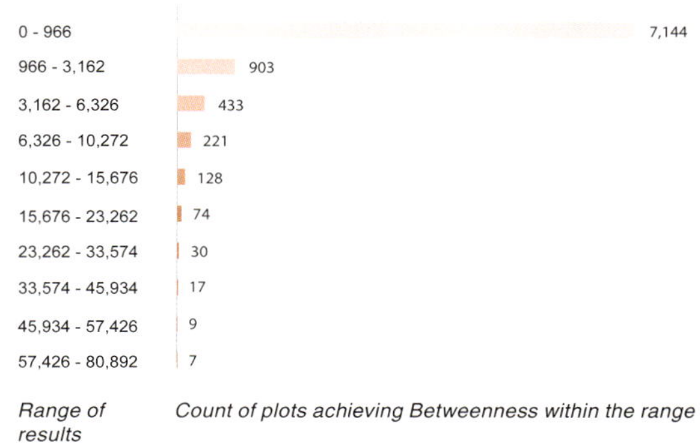

The majority of segments, corresponding to 78% (i.e., 7,038 out of 8,966 segments), have low Betweenness values ranging from 0 to 864. Among the categories shown in the legend, 7,144 segments have values in the range of 0 to 966, making this the most common value range; this range is represented by the lightest brown on the map. Mid-range Betweenness values ranging from 865 to 6,702 are obtained by 1,472 segments, which is 16% of all segments. There are 419 segments that have high Betweenness values (higher than 6,702 but smaller than 32,203) and 37 segments have very high Betweenness values (higher than 32,203). The average Betweenness value in Creek is 1,323 (smaller than 6,703), while the median is 94, indicating low Betweenness at a 400 m radius.

FIG. 9.4
Straightness

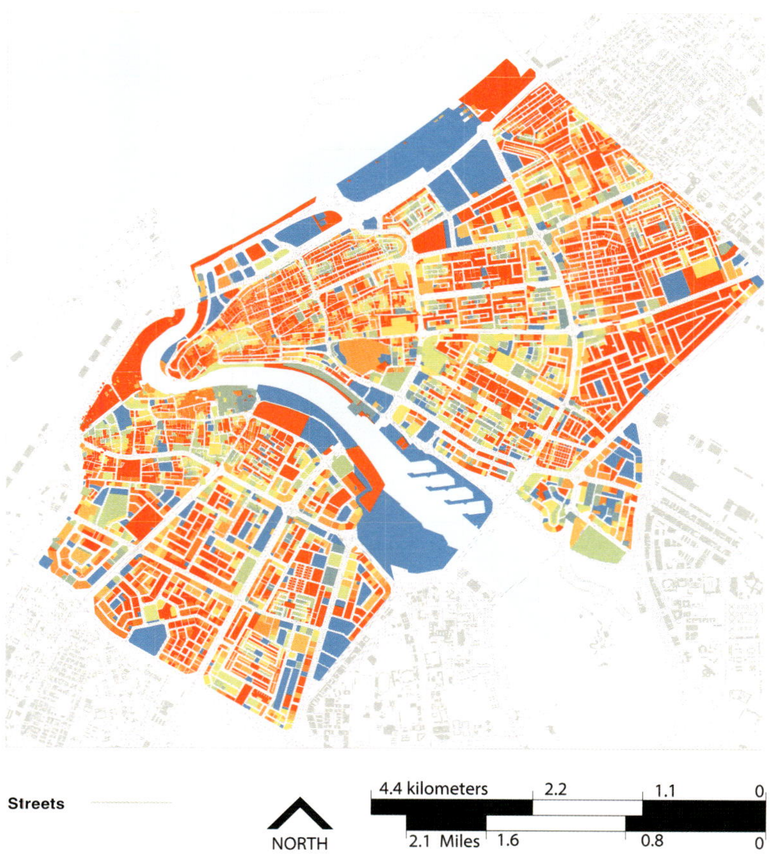

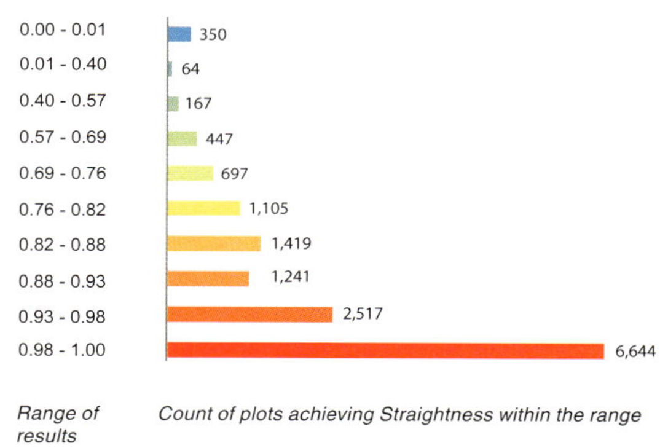

The warmer colors (greenish-yellow to red) represent Straightness values higher than 0.687, while the cooler colors (light green to dark blue) correspond to Straightness values lower than 0.69. The majority of plots, corresponding to 63% (or 9,161 out of 14,652 plots) have Straightness values ranging from 0.93 to 1.00. Among the categories shown in the legend, 6,644 plots have values in the range of 0.98 to 1.00, making this the most common value range; this range is represented by red on the map. On average, at a 400 m radius, all plots in Creek are 90% as straight as a straight line.

Scenario 1: Streets only — 800 m Radius

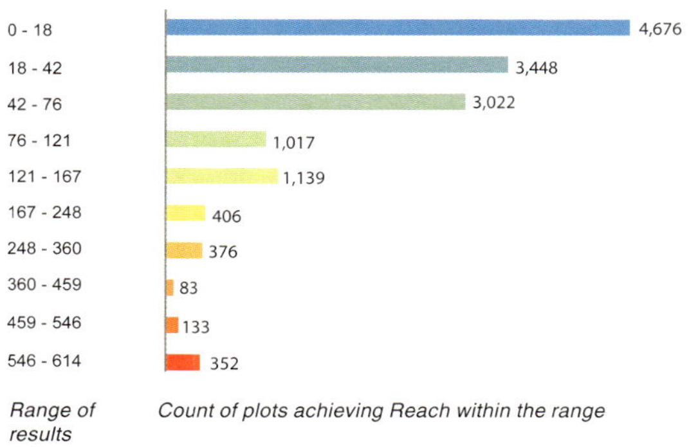

The warmer colors (i.e., greenish-yellow to red) represent a Reach value of 121 or more, while the cooler colors (i.e., light green to dark blue) correspond to a Reach value of 120 or less. A majority of plots (i.e., 8,124 out of 14,652), corresponding to 55% of all plots, have Reach values of less than 42. Among the categories shown in the legend, 32% of the total plots can reach 0 to 18 other plots within 10 minutes of walking. On average, each plot in Creek can access at least 921 plots within a distance of 800 m.

FIG. 10.1
Reach

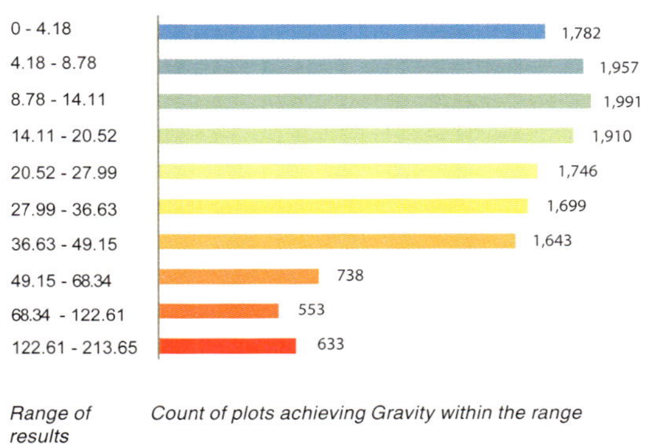

The warmer colors (i.e., greenish-yellow to red) represent Gravity values of more than 36.63, while the cooler colors (i.e., light green to dark blue) correspond to Gravity values of less than 36.63.Sixty-four percent of all plots (i.e., 9,386 out of 14,652) have Gravity values of less than 27.99. Among the categories shown in the legend, 3,739 plots, or 25% of the total plots, can reach 0.00 to 8.78 plots, making this the most common range; this range is represented by dark blue on the map. On average, each plot can reach 29 other plots when spatial impedance or distance decay effect is taken into consideration.

FIG. 10.2
Gravity

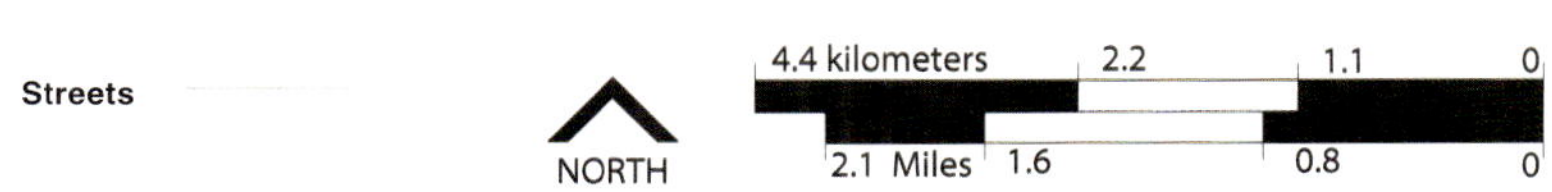

Scenario 1: Streets only — 800 m Radius

FIG. 10.3
Betweenness

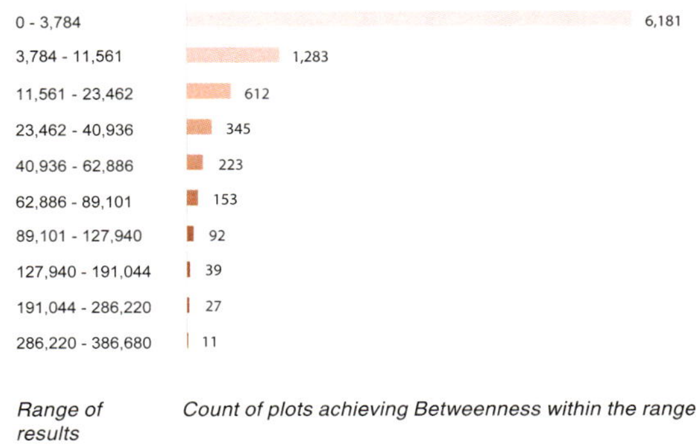

The majority of segments, corresponding to 62% (i.e., 5,592 out of 8,966 segments), have very low Betweenness values ranging from 0 to 2,539. Among the categories shown in the legend, 6,181 segments have values in the range of 0 to 3,784, making this the most common value range; this range is represented by the lightest brown on the map. Low Betweenness values ranging from 2,540 to 11,517 are obtained by 1,868 segments, which is 21% of all segments. Mid-range Betweenness values ranging from 11,518 to 20,478 are obtained by 520 segments, which is 6% of the total segments. There are 637 segments that have high Betweenness values (higher than 20,478 but smaller than 59,384) and 349 segments have very high Betweenness values (higher than 59,383). The average Betweenness value in Creek is 9,240 (smaller than 11,518), while the median is 1,160, indicating low Betweenness at an 800 m radius.

FIG. 10.4
Straightness

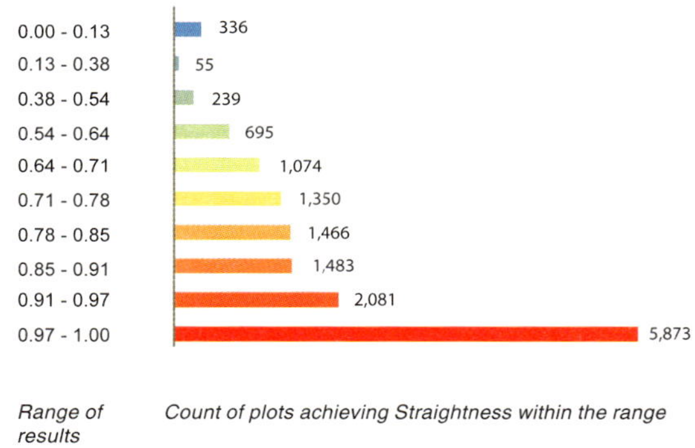

The warmer colors (greenish-yellow to red) represent Straightness values higher than 0.63, while the cooler colors (light green to dark blue) correspond to Straightness values lower than 0.64. The majority of plots, corresponding to 54% (or 7,954 out of 14,652 plots) have Straightness values ranging from 0.91 to 1.00. Among the categories shown in the legend, 5,873 plots have values in the range of 0.97 to 1.00, making this the most common value range; this range is represented by red on the map. On average, at an 800 m radius, all plots in Creek are 86% as straight as a straight line.

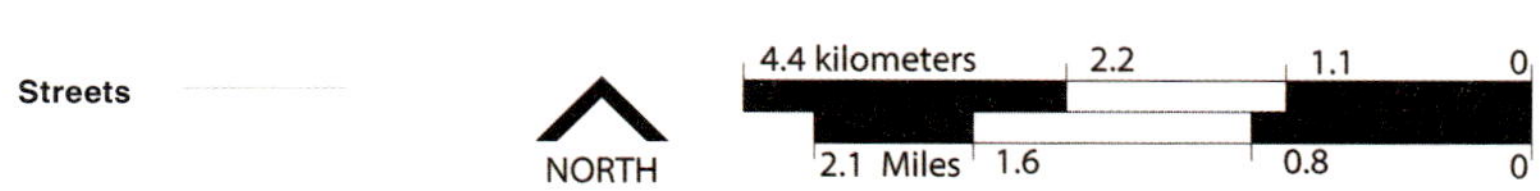

Scenario 1: Streets only — 1,600 m Radius

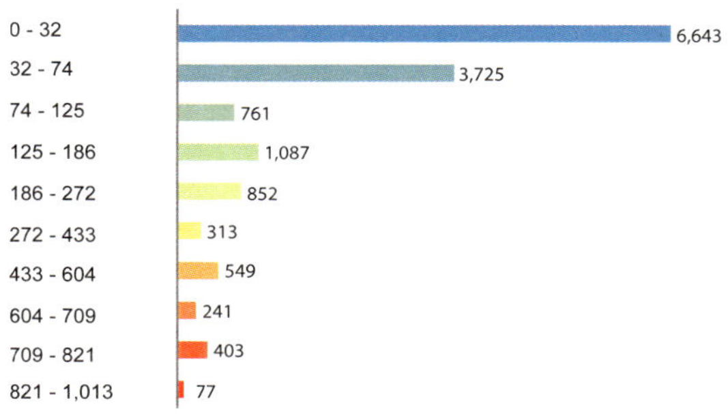

Range of results   *Count of plots achieving Reach within the range*

FIG.11.1
Reach

The warmer colors (i.e., greenish-yellow to red) represent Reach values of more than 185, while the cooler colors (i.e., light green to dark blue) correspond to Reach values of less than 186. The majority of plots (i.e., 8,008 out of 14,652), corresponding to 55% of all plots, have Reach values of more than 31. Among the categories shown in the legend, 45% of the total plots can reach 0 to 32 other plots within 20 minutes of walking. On average, each plot in Creek can access at least 2,118 plots within a distance of 1,600 m.

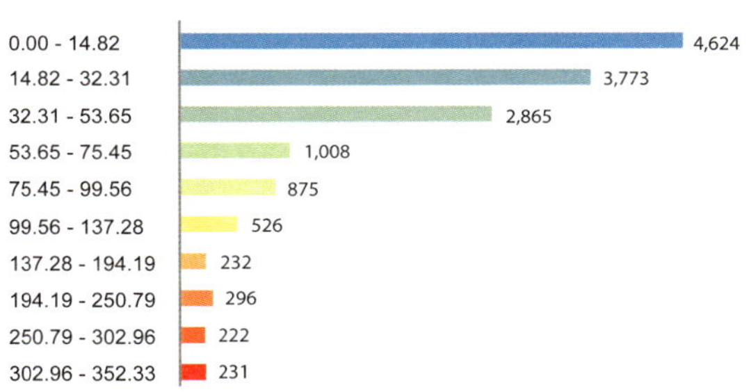

Range of results   *Count of plots achieving Gravity within the range*

FIG.11.2
Gravity

The warmer colors (i.e., greenish-yellow to red) represent Gravity values greater than 75.44, while the cooler colors (i.e., light green to dark blue) correspond to Gravity values lower than 75.45. Fifty-seven percent of all plots (i.e., 8,397 out of 14,652) have Gravity values of less than 32.31. Among the categories shown in the legend, 4,624 plots, or 32% of the total plots, can reach 0.00 to 14.82 plots, making this the most common range; this range is represented by dark blue on the map. On average, each plot can reach 199 other plots when spatial impedance or distance decay effect is taken into consideration.

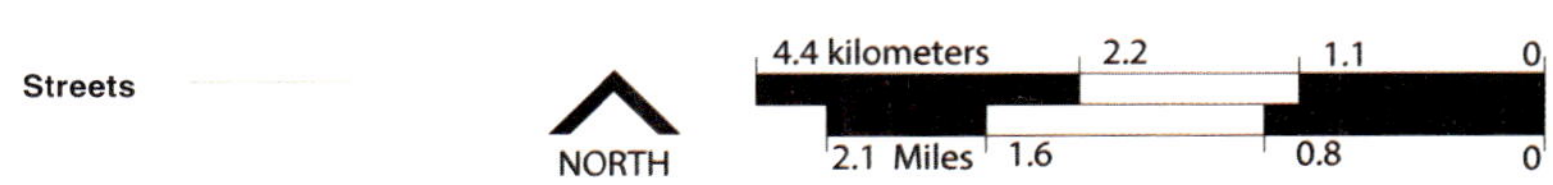

Scenario 1: Streets only — 1,600 m Radius

FIG. 11.3
Betweenness

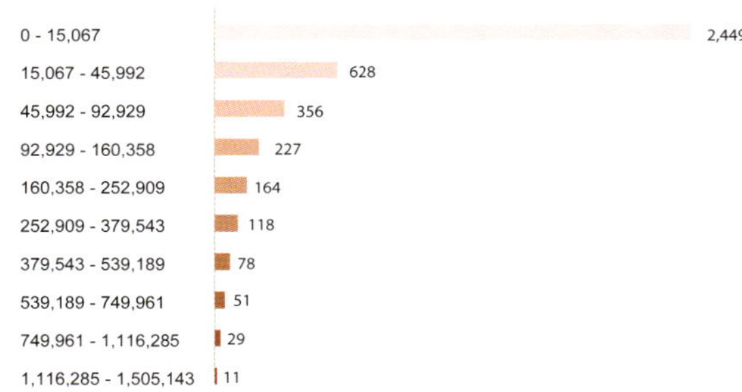

Range of results *Count of plots achieving Betweenness within the range*

The majority of segments, corresponding to 81% (i.e., 3,321 out of 4,111 segments), have very low Betweenness values ranging from 0 to 73,682. Among the categories shown in the legend, 2,449 segments have values in the range of 0 to 15,067, making this the most common value range; this range is represented by light brown on the map. Low Betweenness values ranging from 73,683 to 123,568 are obtained by 238 segments, which is 5.79% of all segments. Mid-range Betweenness values ranging from 123,568 to 179,444 are obtained by 139 segments, which is 3.38% of all segments. One hundred and twenty-three segments have high Betweenness values (from 179,444 to 251,415) and 290 segments have very high Betweenness values (higher than 251,415). The average Betweenness value at a 1,600 m radius in Creek is 61,941 (smaller than 73,683), while the median is 7,864, indicating this neighborhood has very low Betweenness.

FIG. 11.4
Straightness

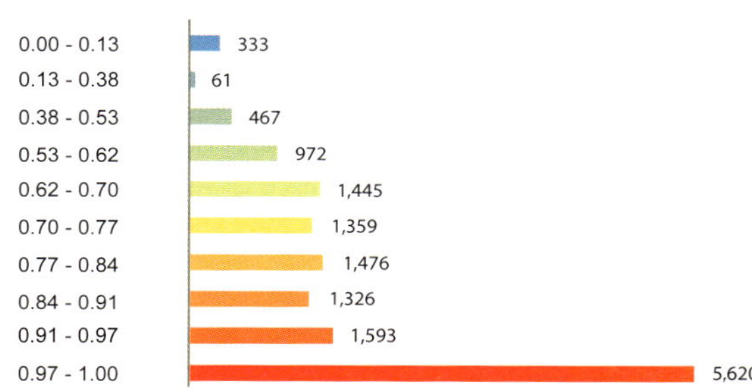

Range of results *Count of plots achieving Straightness within the range*

The warmer colors (greenish-yellow to red) represent Straightness values higher than 0.61, while the cooler colors (light green to dark blue) correspond to Straightness values lower than 0.62. The majority of plots, corresponding to 58% (or 8,539 out of 14,652 plots) have Straightness values ranging from 0.84 to 1.00. Among the categories shown in the legend, 5,620 plots have values in the range of 0.97 to 1.00, making this the most common value range; this range is represented by red on the map. On average, at a 1,600 m radius, all plots in Creek are 84% as straight as a straight line.

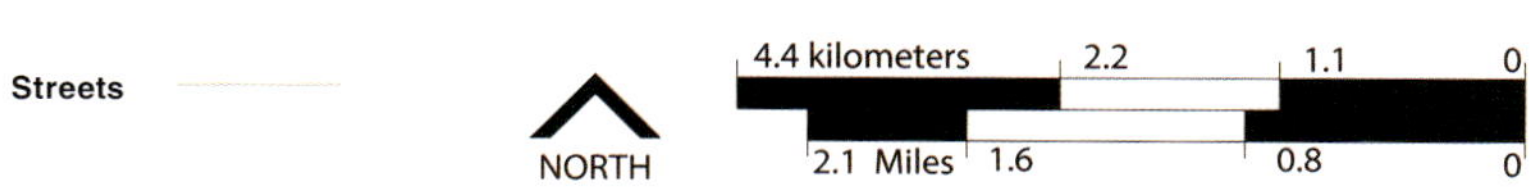

Centrality Analysis: Neighborhood Scale

Scenario 2: Streets + Alleys — 400 m Radius

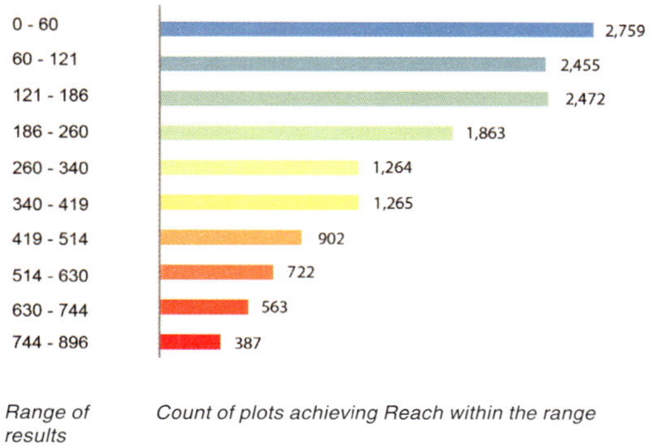

FIG. 12.1
Reach

The warmer colors (i.e., greenish-yellow to red) represent a Reach value of 260 or more, while the cooler colors (i.e., light green to dark blue) correspond to a Reach value of 259 or less. The majority of plots (i.e., 7,686 out of 14,652), corresponding to 52% of all plots, have Reach values of less than 186. Among the categories shown in the legend, 19% of the total plots can reach 0 to 60 other plots within 5 minutes of walking. On average, each plot in Creek can access at least 356 plots within a distance of 400 m.

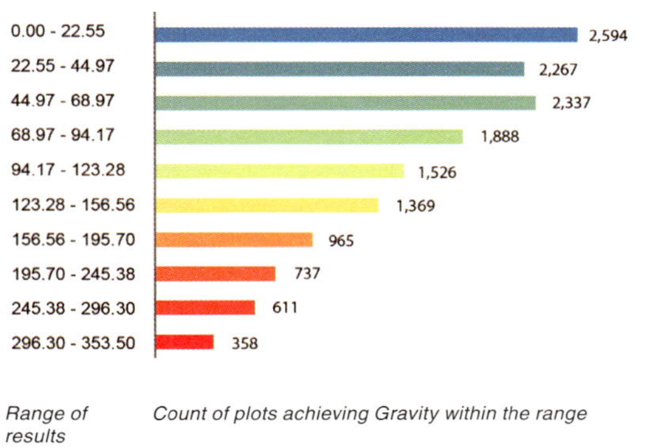

FIG. 12.2
Gravity

The warmer colors (i.e., greenish-yellow to red) represent Gravity values of more than 94.16, while the cooler colors (i.e., light green to dark blue) correspond to Gravity values of less than 94.17. Fifty-one percent of all plots (i.e., 7,454 out of 14,652) have Gravity values of more than 68.96. Among the categories shown in the legend, 2,594 plots, or 18% of the total plots, can reach 0.00 to 22.55 plots, making this the most common range; this range is represented by dark blue on the map. On average, each plot can reach 140 other plots when spatial impedance or distance decay effect is taken into consideration.

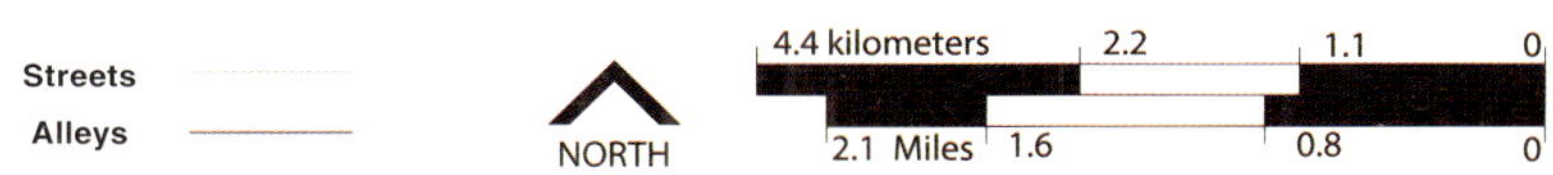

Scenario 2: Streets + Alleys — 400 m Radius

FIG. 12.3
Betweenness

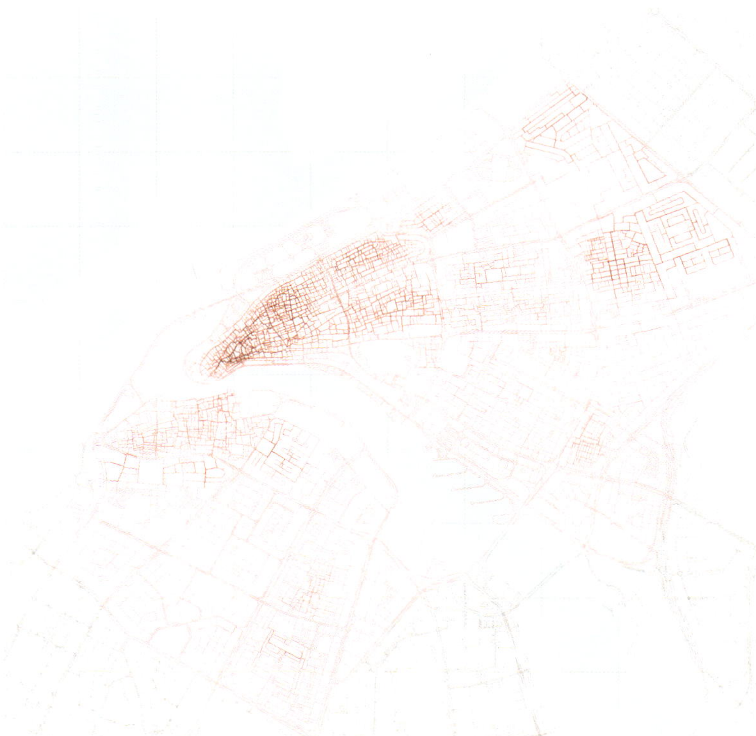

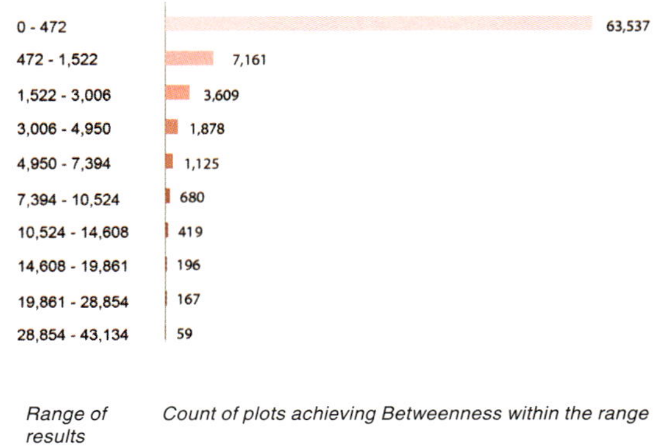

The majority of segments, corresponding to 85% (i.e., 67,392 out of 78,831 segments), have low Betweenness values ranging from 0 to 864. Among the categories shown in the legend, 63,537 segments have values in the range of 0 to 472, making this the most common value range; this range is represented by the lightest brown on the map. Mid-range Betweenness values ranging from 865 to 6,702 are obtained by 9,633 segments, which is 12% of all segments. There are 1,765 segments that have high Betweenness values (higher than 6,702 but smaller than 32,203) and 41 segments have very high Betweenness values (higher than 32,203). The average Betweenness value in Creek is 662 (smaller than 865), while the median is 20, indicating low Betweenness at a 400 m radius.

FIG. 12.4
Straightness

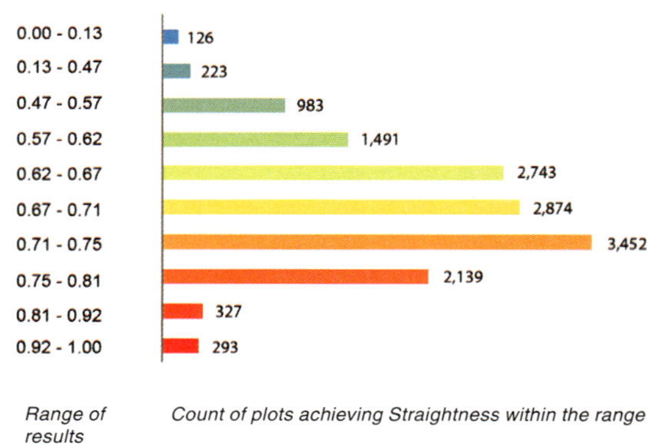

The warmer colors (greenish-yellow to red) represent Straightness values higher than 0.61, while the cooler colors (light green to dark blue) correspond to Straightness values lower than 0.62. The majority of plots, corresponding to 58% (or 8,465 out of 14,652 plots) have Straightness values ranging from 0.67 to 0.81. Among the categories shown in the legend, 3,452 plots have values in the range of 0.71 to 0.75, making this the most common value range; this range is represented by light orange on the map. On average, at a 400 m radius, all plots in Creek are 68% as straight as a straight line.

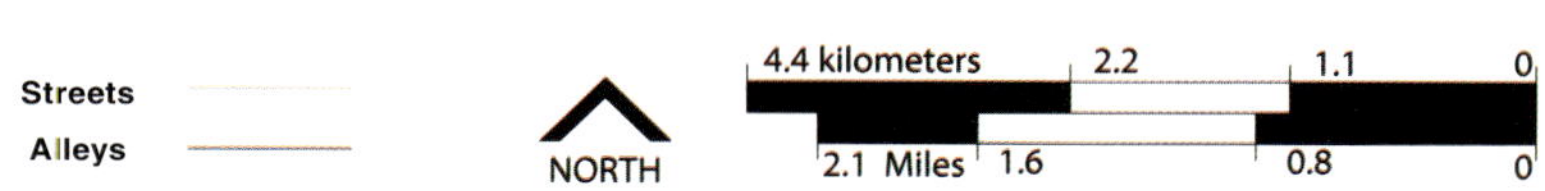

Scenario 2: Streets + Alleys — 800 m Radius

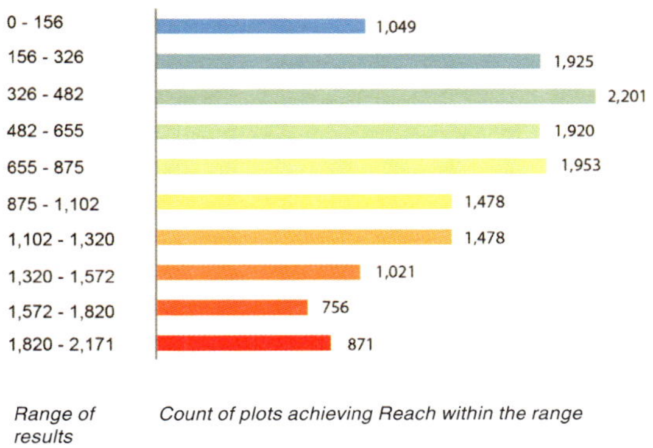

The warmer colors (i.e., greenish-yellow to red) represent a Reach value of 655 or more, while the cooler colors (i.e., light green to dark blue) correspond to a Reach value of 654 or less. The majority of plots (i.e., 7,557 out of 14,651), corresponding to 52% of all plots, have Reach values of more than 654. Among the categories shown in the legend, 15% of the total plots can reach 326 to 482 other plots within 10 minutes of walking. On average, each plot in Creek can access at least 979 plots within a distance of 800 m.

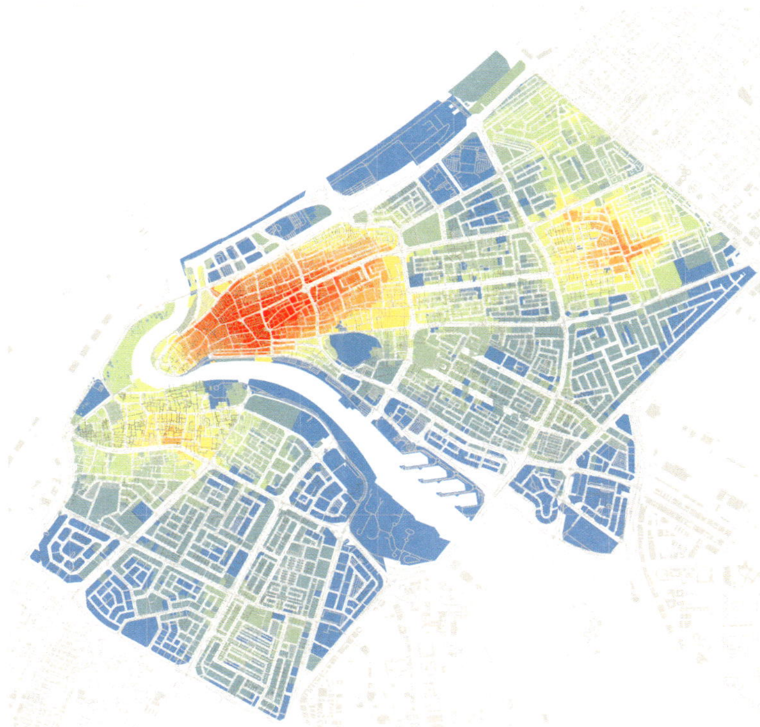

FIG. 13.1
Reach

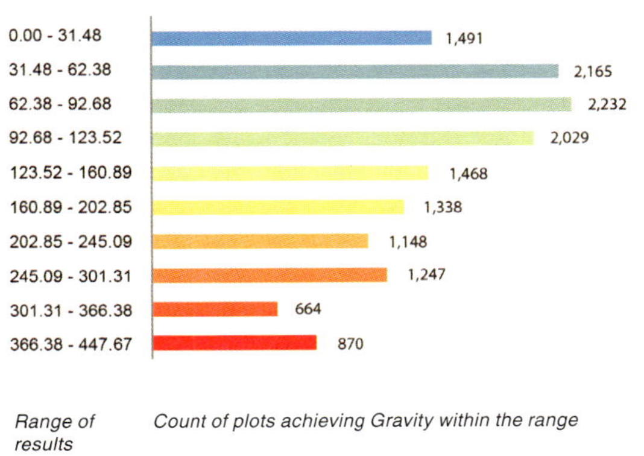

The warmer colors (i.e., greenish-yellow to red) represent Gravity values greater than 123.51, while the cooler colors (i.e., light green to dark blue) correspond to Gravity values lower than 123.52. Fifty-four percent of all plots (i.e., 7,917 out of 14,652) have Gravity values of less than 123.52. Among the categories shown in the legend, 2,232 plots, or 15% of the total plots, can reach 62.38 to 92.68 plots, making this the most common range; this range is represented by bluish-green on the map. On average, each plot can reach 202 other plots when spatial impedance or distance decay effect is taken into consideration.

FIG. 13.2
Gravity

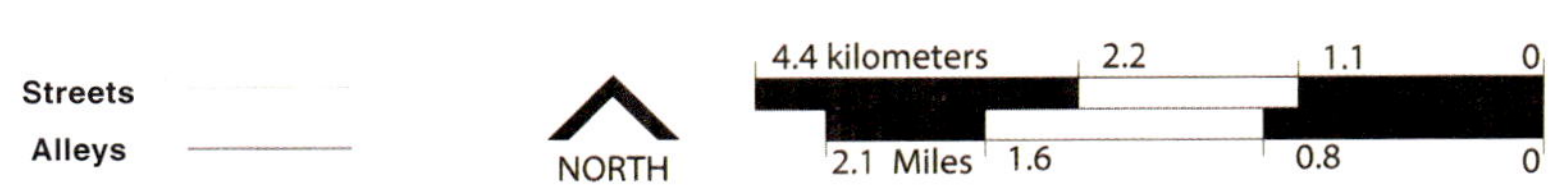

Scenario 2: Streets + Alleys — 800 m Radius

FIG. 13.3

Betweenness

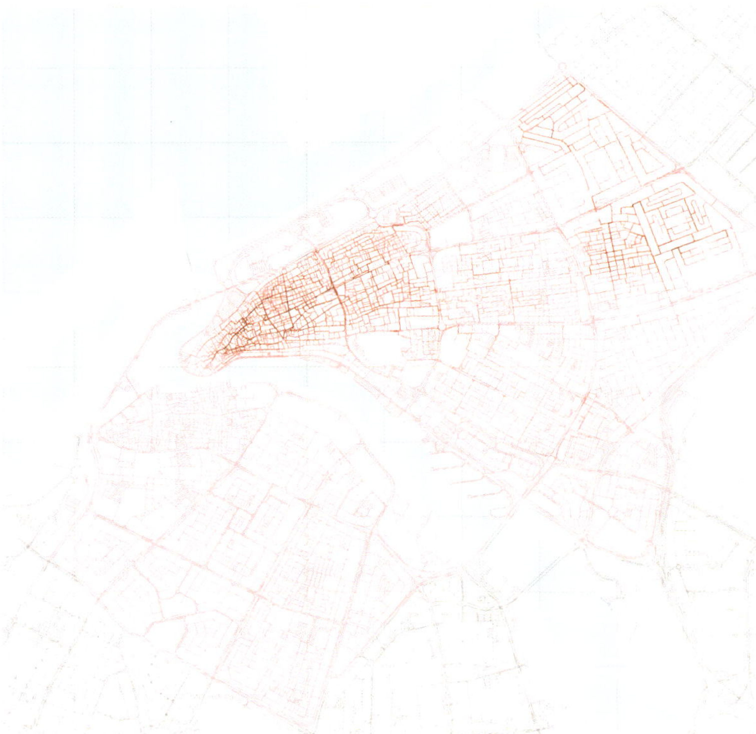

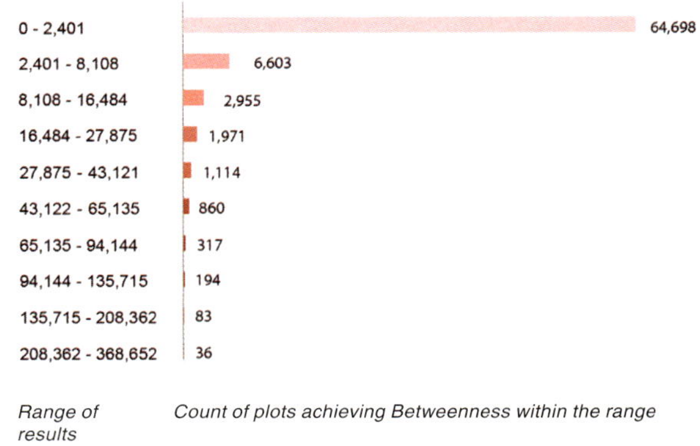

The majority of segments, corresponding to 82% (i.e., 64,962 out of 78,831 segments), have very low Betweenness values ranging from 0 to 2,539. Among the categories shown in the legend, 64,698 segments have values in the range of 0 to 2,401, making this the most common value range; this range is represented by light brown on the map. Low Betweenness values ranging from 2,540 to 11,517 are obtained by 7,937 segments, which is 10% of all segments. Mid-range Betweenness values ranging from 11,518 to 20,478 are obtained by 2,281 segments, which is 3% of the total segments. There are 2,886 segments that have high Betweenness values (higher than 20,478 but smaller than 59,384) and 765 segments have very high Betweenness values (higher than 59,383). The average Betweenness value in Creek is 3,435 (higher than 2,539 but smaller than 11,518), while the median is 0, indicating low Betweenness at an 800 m radius.

FIG. 13.4

Straightness

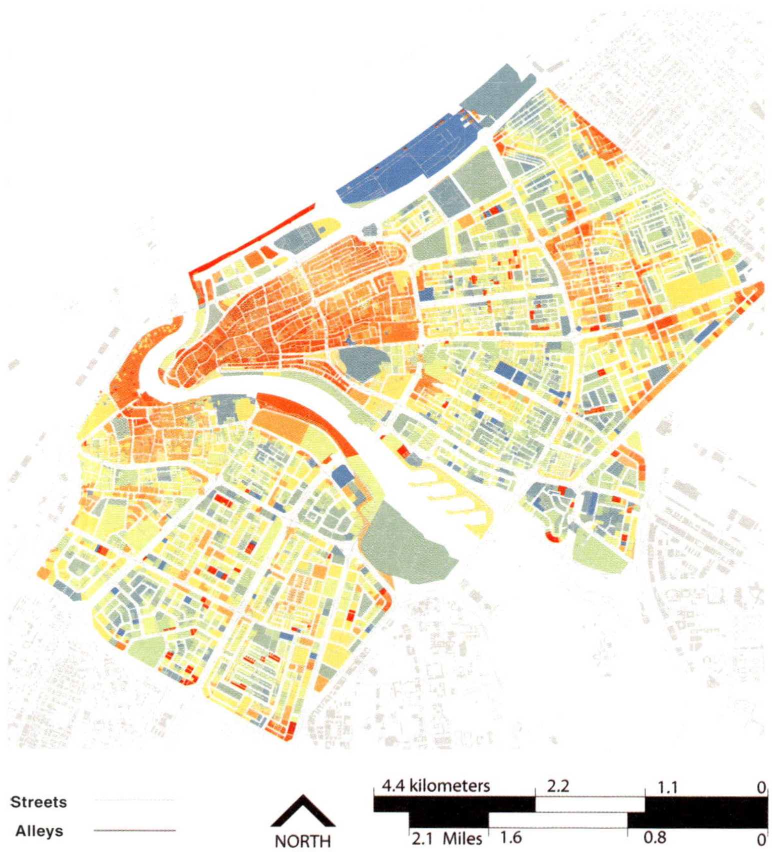

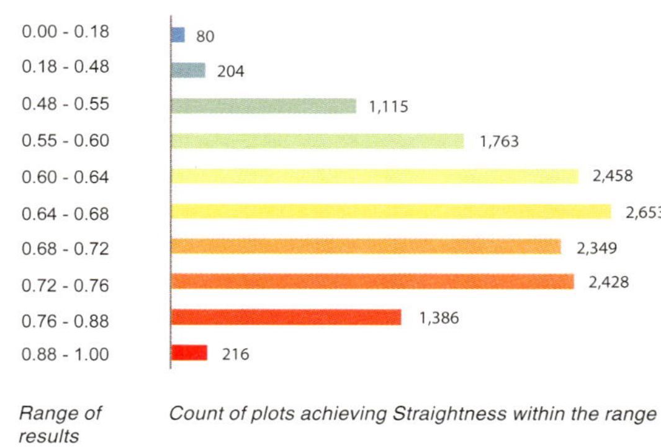

The warmer colors (greenish-yellow to red) represent Straightness values higher than 0.59, while the cooler colors (light green to dark blue) correspond to Straightness values lower than 0.60. The majority of plots, corresponding to 63% (or 9,223 out of 14,652 plots) have Straightness values ranging from 0.55 to 0.72. Among the categories shown in the legend, 2,653 plots have values in the range of 0.64 to 0.68, making this the most common value range; this range is represented by yellow on the map. On average, at an 800 m radius, all plots in Creek are 67% as straight as a straight line.

Scenario 2: Streets + Alleys — 1,600 m Radius

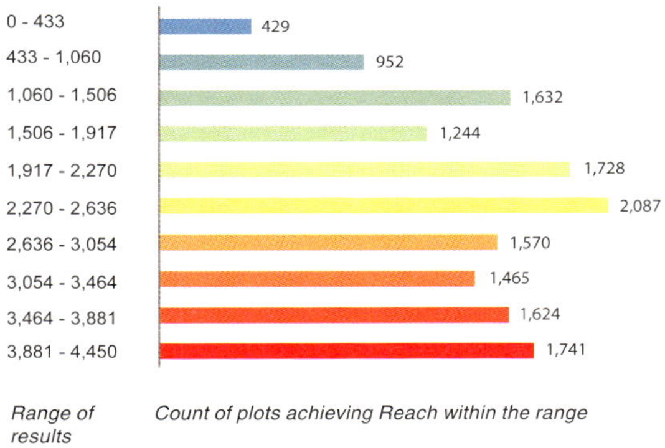

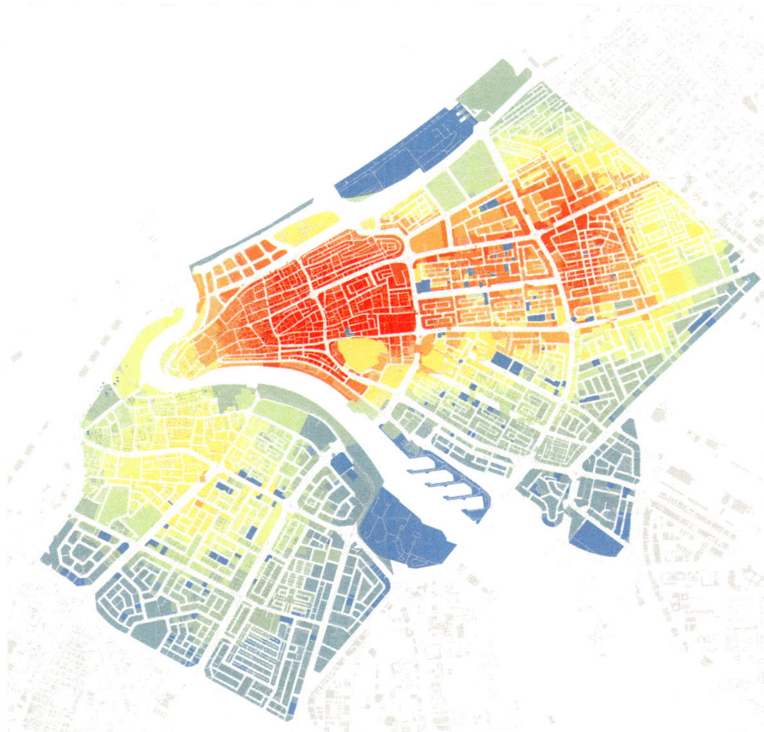

FIG. 14.1
Reach

The warmer colors (i.e., greenish-yellow to red) represent a Reach value of 1,917 or more, while the cooler colors (i.e., light green to dark blue) correspond to a Reach value of 1,916 or less. The majority of plots (i.e., 8,252 out of 14,652), corresponding to 56% of all plots, have Reach values of less than 2,636. Among the categories shown in the legend, 14% of the total plots can reach 2,270 to 2,635 other plots within 20 minutes of walking. On average, each plot in Creek can access at least 2,099 plots within a distance of 1,600 m.

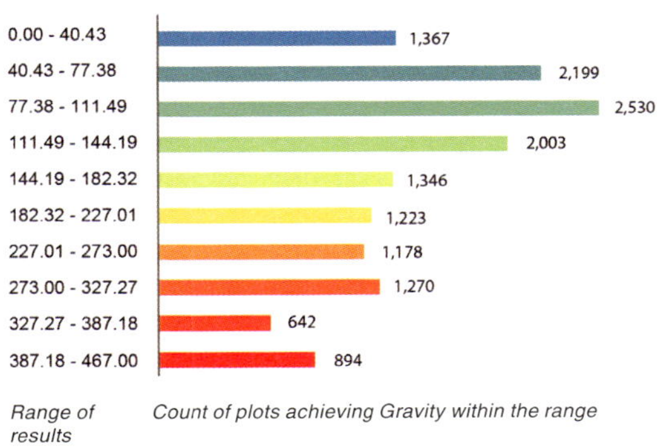

FIG. 14.2
Gravity

The warmer colors (i.e., greenish-yellow to red) represent Gravity values of more than 144.18, while the cooler colors (i.e., light green to dark blue) correspond to Gravity values of less than 144.19. Fifty-five percent of the total plots (i.e., 8,099 out of 14,652) have Gravity values of less than 14.19. Among the categories shown in the legend, 2,530 plots, or 17% of all plots, can reach 77.38 to 111.49 plots, making this the most common range; this range is represented by bluish-green on the map. On average, each plot can reach 217 other plots when spatial impedance or distance decay effect is taken into consideration.

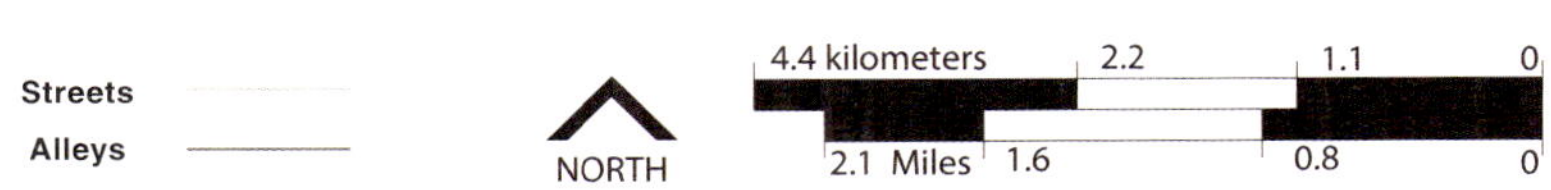

Scenario 2: Streets + Alleys — 1,600 m Radius

FIG. 14.3

Betweenness

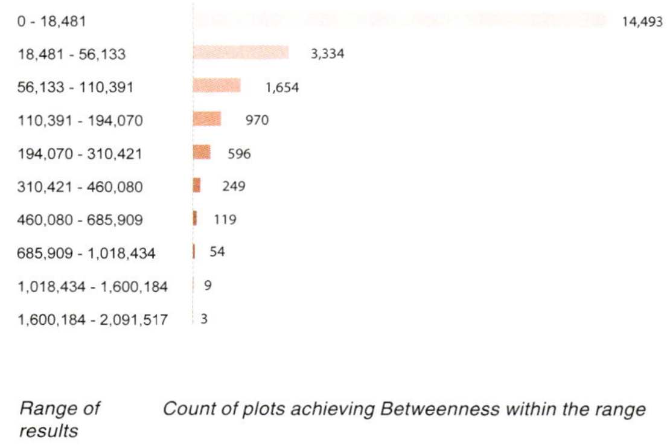

The majority of segments, corresponding to 86% (i.e., 18,508 out of 21,481 segments), have very low Betweenness values ranging from 0 to 73,682. Among the categories shown in the legend, 14,493 segments have values in the range of 0 to 18,481, making this the most common value range; this range is represented by the lightest brown on the map. Low Betweenness values ranging from 73,683 to 123,568 are obtained by 1,230 segments, which is 5.73% of all segments. Mid-range Betweenness values ranging from 123,568 to 179,444 are obtained by 626 segments, which is 2.91% of all segments. Four hundred and thirty-four segments have high Betweenness values (from 179,444 to 251,415) and 683 segments have very high Betweenness values (higher than 251,415). The average Betweenness value at a 1,600 m radius in Creek is 37,432 (smaller than 73,683), while the median is 5,758, indicating this neighborhood has very low Betweenness.

FIG. 14.4

Straightness

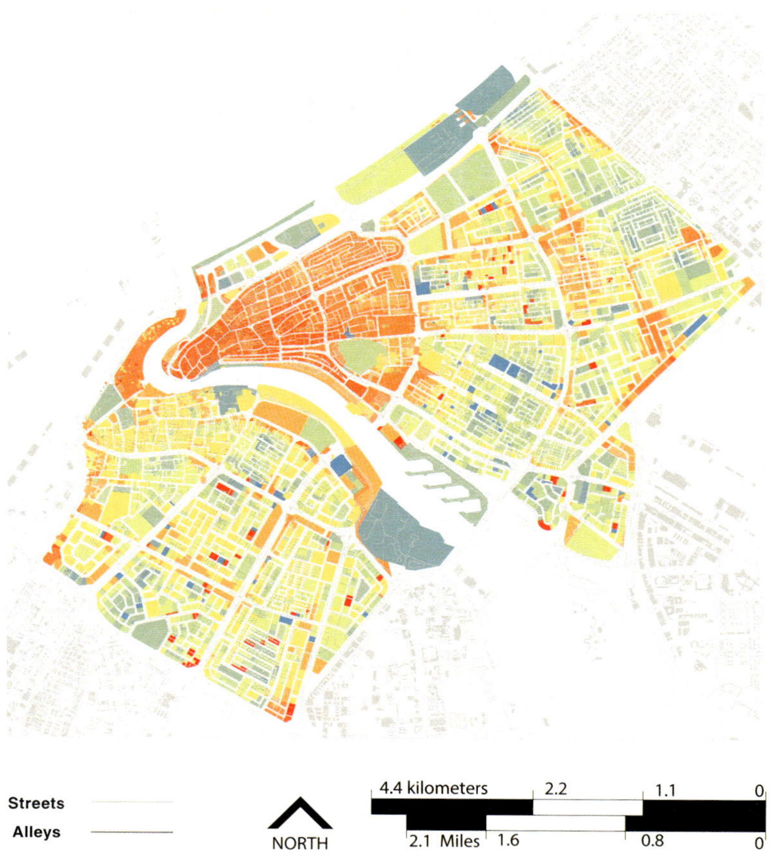

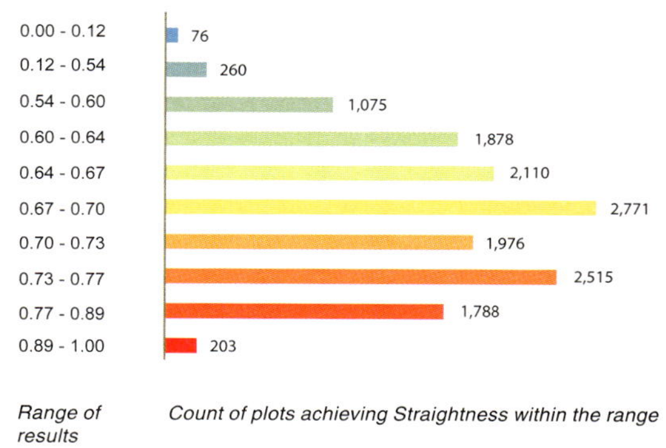

The warmer colors (greenish-yellow to red) represent Straightness values higher than 0.63, while the cooler colors (light green to dark blue) correspond to Straightness values lower than 0.64. The majority of plots, corresponding to 60% (or 8,735 out of 14,652 plots) have Straightness values ranging from 0.60 to 0.72. Among the categories shown in the legend, 2,771 plots have values in the range of 0.67 to 0.70, making this the most common value range; this range is represented by yellow on the map. On average, at a 1,600 m radius, all plots in Creek are 70% as straight as a straight line.

Centrality Analysis: Sample Scale

Sample 01

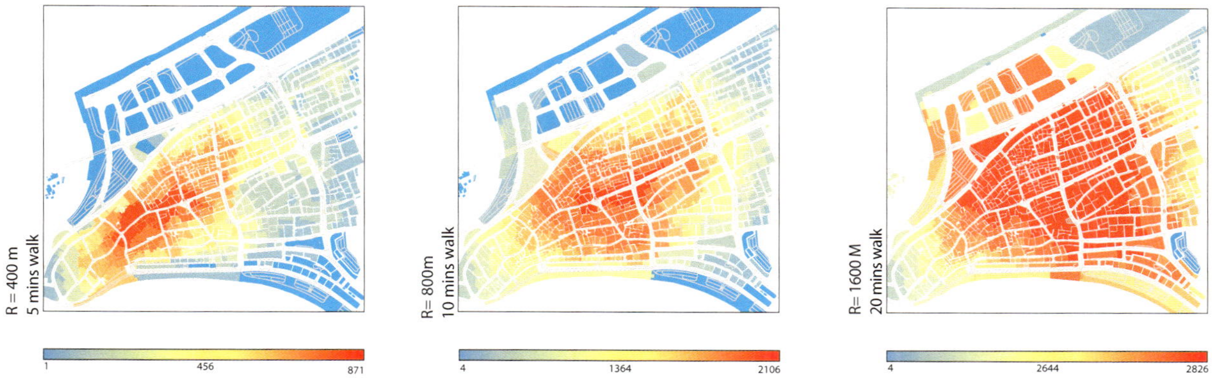

FIG. 15.1

Reach

Scenario 1: Streets only

Reach (Radius = 400 m)

The maximum number of plots that can be reached within 5 minutes walking distance is 871 plots. The average Reach of the sample is 456 plots.

Summary of Reach results
Minimum: 1
Maximum: 871
Mean: 456
Median: 461

Reach (Radius = 800 m)

The maximum number of plots that can be reached within 10 minutes walking distance is 2,106 plots. The average Reach of the sample is 1,364 plots.

Summary of Reach results
Minimum: 4
Maximum: 2,106
Mean: 1,364
Median: 1,477

Reach (Radius = 1600 m)

The maximum number of plots that can be reached within 20 minutes walking distance is 2,826 plots. The average Reach of the sample is 2,644 plots.

Summary of Reach results
Minimum: 4
Maximum: 2,826
Mean: 2,644
Median: 2,756

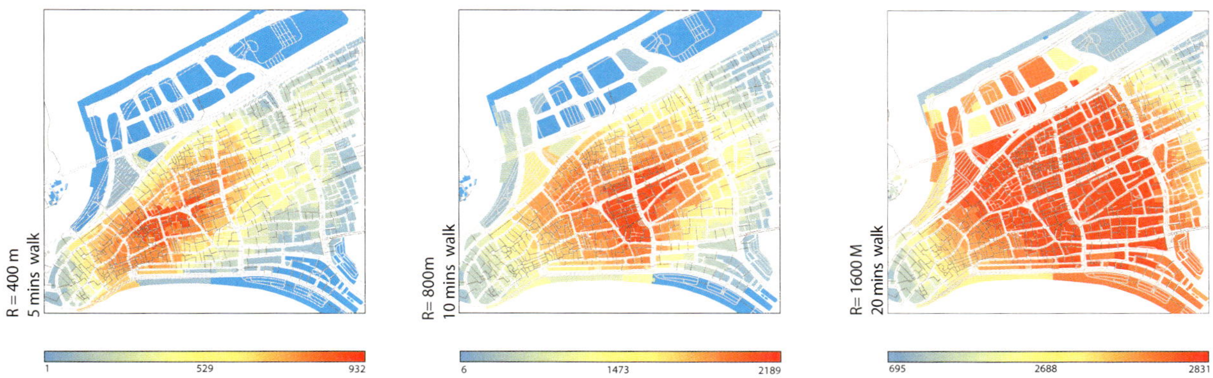

FIG. 15.2

Reach

Scenario 2: Streets + Alleys

Reach (Radius = 400 m)

The maximum number of plots that can be reached within 10 min walking distance is 932 plots. The average Reach of the sample is 529 plots.

Summary of Reach results
Minimum: 1
Maximum: 932
Mean: 529
Median: 548

Reach (Radius = 800 m)

The maximum number of plots that can be reached within 20 min walking distance is 2,189 plots. The average Reach of the sample is 1,473 plots.

Summary of Reach results
Minimum: 6
Maximum: 2 ,189
Mean: 1,473
Median: 1,556

Reach (Radius = 1600 m)

The maximum number of plots that can be reached within 30 min walking distance is 2,831 plots. The average Reach of the sample is 2,688 plots.

Summary of Reach results
Minimum: 695
Maximum: 2, 831
Mean: 2,688
Median: 2,787

At a 400 m radius, high Reach values ranging from 456 to 871 are obtained by plots located near the intersections of internal and collector streets. At an 800 m radius, plots with high Reach values largely appear at the center of the sample. At a 1,600 m radius, a great majority of plots located around the central part of the sample have high Reach values ranging from 2,644 to 2,826. With the introduction of alleys, at a 400 m radius, the concentration of high Reach values becomes stronger and clearer around the intersections of internal and collector streets. The highest Reach value is 932, compared to 871 when alleys are not included. At an 800 m radius, most plots with high Reach values are found at the center, with values ranging from 1,473 to 2,189. At a 1,600 m radius, all plots have Reach values greater than 694, with the highest Reach value of 2,831 obtained by numerous plots located at the center of the sample.

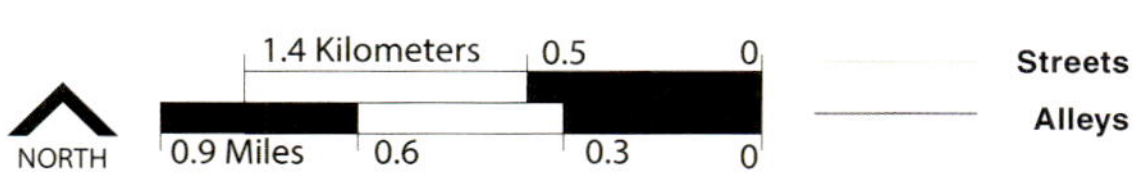

Sample 01

FIG. 15.3
Gravity
Scenario 1: Streets only

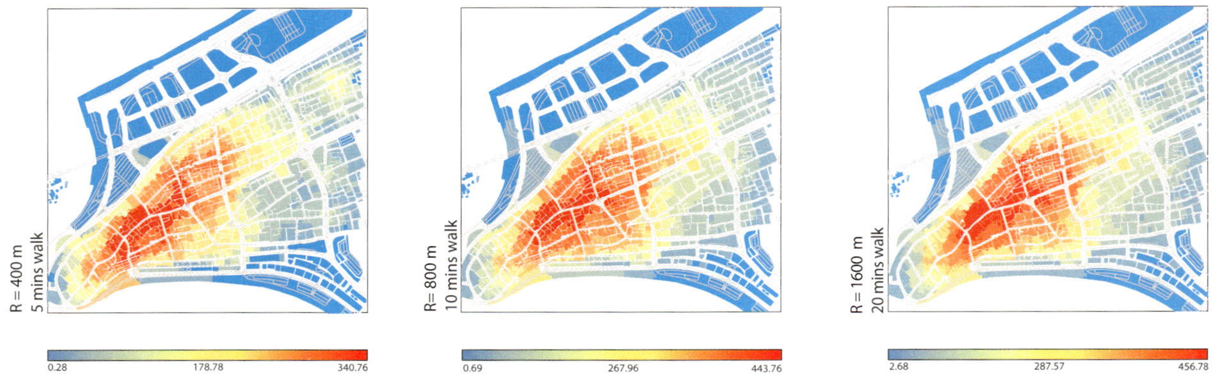

Gravity (Radius = 400 m)
The maximum number of plots that can be reached within 5 minutes walking distance with the distance decay effect is 340.76 plots. The average Gravity of the sample is 178.78 plots.

Summary of Gravity results
Minimum: 0.28
Maximum: 340.76
Mean: 178.78
Median: 179.04

Gravity (Radius = 800 m)
The maximum number of plots that can be reached within 10 minutes walking distance with the distance decay effect is 443.76 plots. The average Gravity of the sample is 267.96 plots.

Summary of Gravity results
Minimum: 0.69
Maximum: 443.76
Mean: 267.96
Median: 282.46

Gravity (Radius = 1600 m)
The maximum number of plots that can be reached within 20 minutes walking distance with the distance decay effect is 456.78 plots. The average Gravity of the sample is 287.57 plots.

Summary of Gravity results
Minimum: 2.68
Maximum: 456.78
Mean: 287.57
Median: 304.41

FIG. 15.4
Gravity
Scenario 2: Streets + Alleys

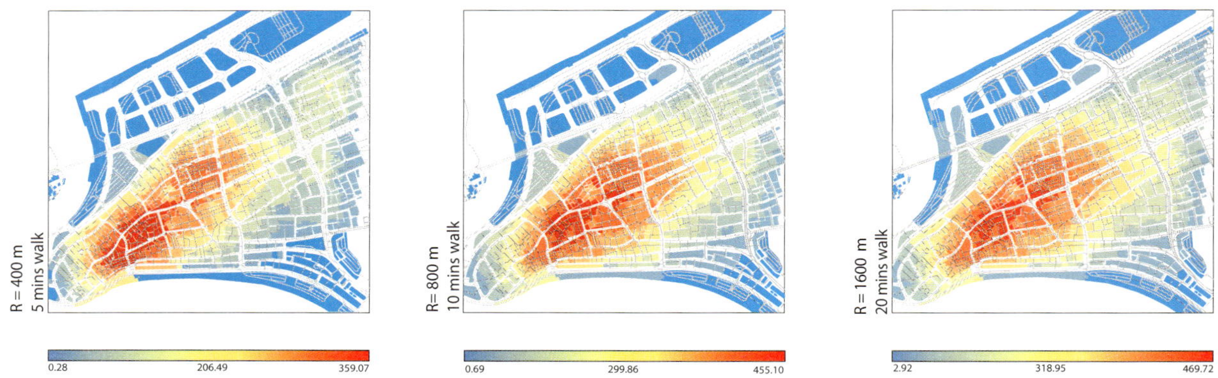

Gravity (Radius = 400 m)
The maximum number of plots that can be reached within 5 minutes walking distance with the distance decay effect is 359.07 plots. The average Gravity of the sample is 206.49 plots.

Summary of Gravity results
Minimum: 0.28
Maximum: 359.07
Mean: 206.49
Median: 207.09

Gravity (Radius = 800 m)
The maximum number of plots that can be reached within 10 minutes walking distance with the distance decay effect is 455.10 plots. The average Gravity of the sample is 299.86 plots.

Summary of Gravity results
Minimum: 0.69
Maximum: 455.10
Mean: 299.86
Median: 321.30

Gravity (Radius = 1600 m)
The maximum number of plots that can be reached within 20 minutes walking distance with the distance decay effect is 469.72 plots. The average Gravity of the sample is 318.95 plots.

Summary of Gravity results
Minimum: 2.92
Maximum: 469.72
Mean: 318.95
Median: 339.33

At a 400 m radius, high Gravity values ranging from 178.78 to 340.76 are obtained by plots located near the intersections of internal and collector streets. At 800 m and 1,600 m radii, Gravity values become even higher at the same spots. As the radius of analysis increases, Gravity values increase for all plots, as is evident from the rising Minimum, Mean, and Maximum values shown above. With the introduction of alleys, at a 400 m radius, high Gravity values concentrate at the same spots near the intersections of internal and collector streets. At 800 m and 1,600 m radii, the distribution of Gravity values does not change. The highest Gravity values of 455.10 and 469.72 at 800 m and 1,600 m respectively are found near intersections of internal and collector streets. The distribution of Gravity values does not notably change when the radius is increased; however, the values improve slightly.

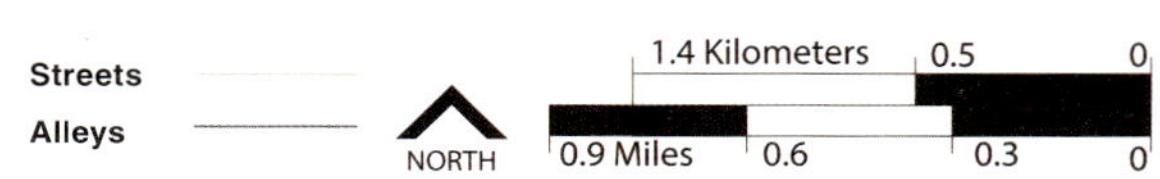

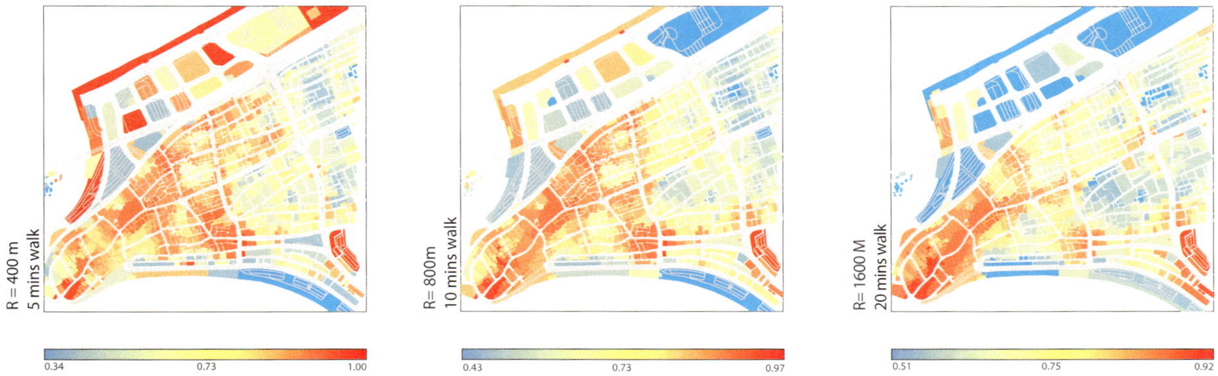

FIG. 15.5
Straightness
Scenario 1: Streets only

Straightness (Normalized Values, Radius= 400 m)
Plots withing 5 minutes walking distance have access to streets with an average straightness value of 0.73.

Summary of results
Minimum: 0.34
Maximum: 1.00
Mean: 0.73
Median: 0.74

Straightness (Normalized Values, Radius= 800 m)
Plots withing 10 minutes walking distance have access to streets with an average straightness value of 0.72.

Summary of results
Minimum: 0.43
Maximum: 0.97
Mean: 0.72
Median: 0.74

Straightness (Normalized Values, Radius= 1600 m)
Plots withing 20 minutes walking distance have access to streets with an average straightness value of 0.75.

Summary of results
Minimum: 0.51
Maximum: 0.92
Mean: 0.75
Median: 0.76

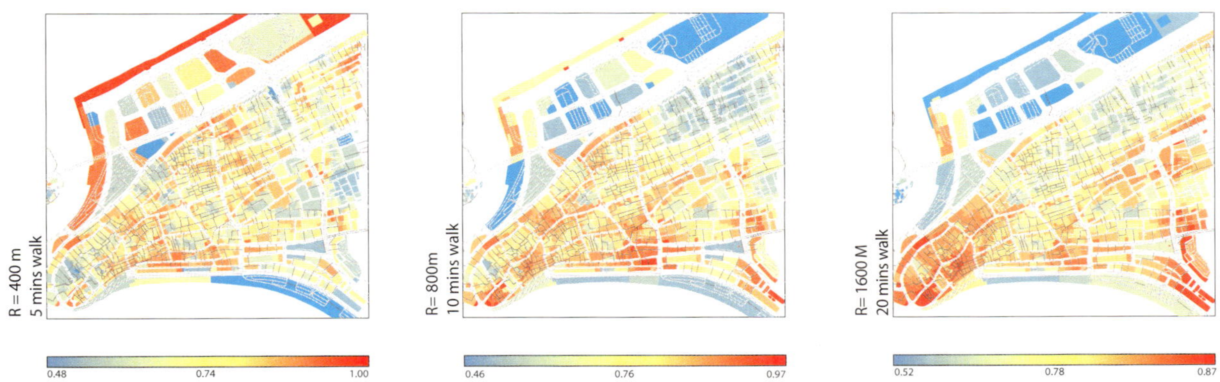

FIG. 15.6
Straightness
Scenario 2: Streets + Alleys

Straightness (Normalized Values, Radius= 400 m)
Plots withing 5 minutes walking distance have access to streets with an average Straightness value of 0.74.

Summary of Straightness results
Minimum: 0.48
Maximum: 1.00
Mean: 0.74
Median: 0.75

Straightness (Normalized Values, Radius= 800 m)
Plots withing 10 minutes walking distance have access to streets with an average Straightness value of 0.76.

Summary of Straightness results
Minimum: 0.46
Maximum: 0.97
Mean: 0.76
Median: 0.77

Straightness (Normalized Values, Radius= 1600 m)
Plots withing 20 minutes walking distance have access to streets with an average Straightness value of 0.79.

Summary of Straightness results
Minimum: 0.52
Maximum: 0.87
Mean: 0.79
Median: 0.79

At a 400 m radius, high Straightness values (0.75 to 1.00) are obtained by plots that lie adjacent to collector and arterial streets. At an 800 m radius, Straightness values increase for low-performing plots, while the distribution of values does not change notably. At a 1,600 m radius, high Straightness values prominently appear near the tip of the Creek located at the bottom left corner of the sample. With the introduction of alleys, at 400 m, high Straightness values (0.75 to 1.00) do not form any cluster and are distributed evenly. At 800 m, high values can be observed near the intersections of internal and collector streets. At 1,600 m, high Straightness values are visible along the arterial street at the bottom and towards the tip of the Creek.

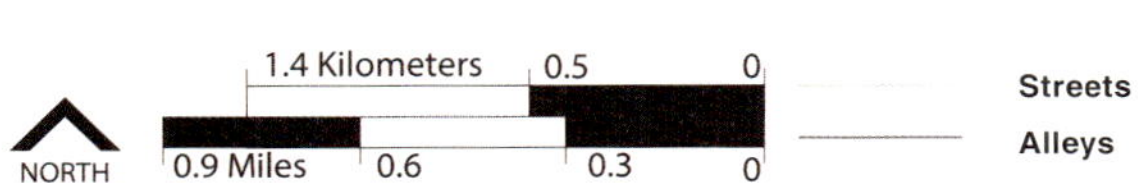

Sample 02

FIG. 16.1
Reach
Scenario 1: Streets only

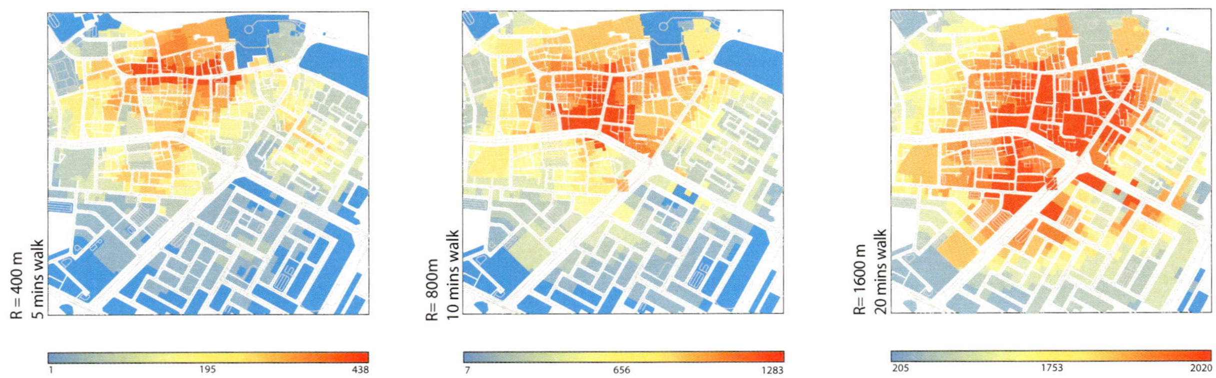

Reach (Radius = 400 m)
The maximum number of plots that can be reached within 5 minutes walking distance is 438 plots. The average Reach of the sample is 195 plots.

Summary of Reach results
Minimum: 1
Maximum: 438
Mean: 195
Median: 195

Reach (Radius = 800 m)
The maximum number of plots that can be reached within 10 minutes walking distance is1,283 plots. The average Reach of the sample is 656 plots.

Summary of Reach results
Minimum: 7
Maximum: 1,283
Mean: 656
Median: 682

Reach (Radius = 1600 m)
The maximum number of plots that can be reached within 20 minutes walking distance is 2,020 plots. The average Reach of the sample is 1,753 plots.

Summary of Reach results
Minimum: 205
Maximum: 2,020
Mean: 1,753
Median: 1,816

FIG. 16.2
Reach
Scenario 2: Streets + Alleys

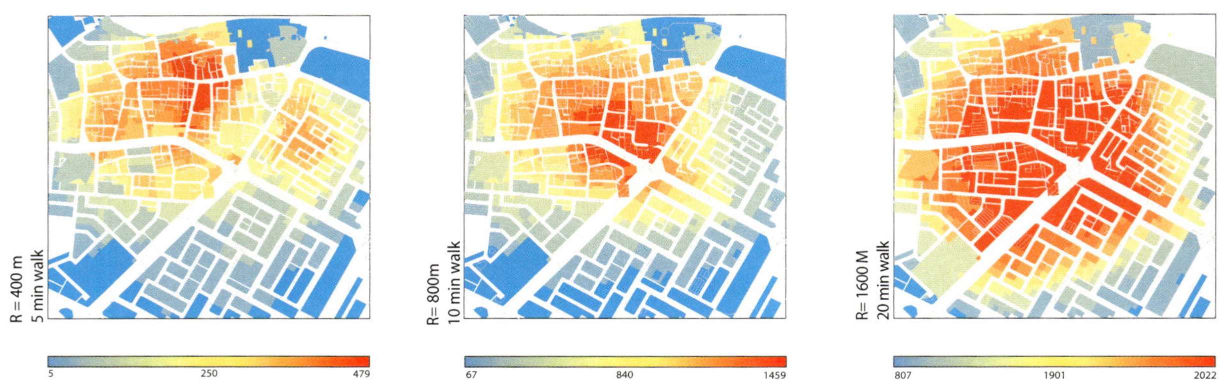

Reach (Radius = 400 m)
The maximum number of plots that can be reached within 10 min walking distance is 479 plots. The average Reach of the sample is 250 plots.

Summary of Reach results
Minimum: 5
Maximum: 479
Mean: 250
Median: 260

Reach (Radius = 800 m)
The maximum number of plots that can be reached within 10 min walking distance is 1,459 plots. The average Reach of the sample is 841 plots.

Summary of Reach results
Minimum: 67
Maximum: 1,459
Mean: 840
Median:864

Reach (Radius = 1600 m)
The maximum number of plots that can be reached within 20 min walking distance is 2,022 plots. The average Reach of the sample is 1,901 plots.

Summary of Reach results
Minimum: 807
Maximum: 2 ,022
Mean: 1,901
Median: 1,964

At a 400 m radius, high Reach values ranging from 195 to 438 are obtained by plots at the top part of the sample, where the streets from a dense, organic pattern. At an 800 m radius, plots with high Reach values become even more concentrated around the same spot. At a 1,600 m radius, high Reach values ranging from 1,753 to 2,020 further concentrate at the same spot and also along the arterial streets that pass through the sample's center. With the introduction of alleys, at a 400 m radius, the concentration of high Reach values becomes stronger and clearer around the organic street section at the top. At an 800 m radius, Reach values are even higher around the same spot, with values ranging from 840 to 1,459. At a 1,600 m radius, all plots have Reach values greater than 806, with the highest Reach value of 2,022 obtained by numerous plots located at and around the center of the sample.

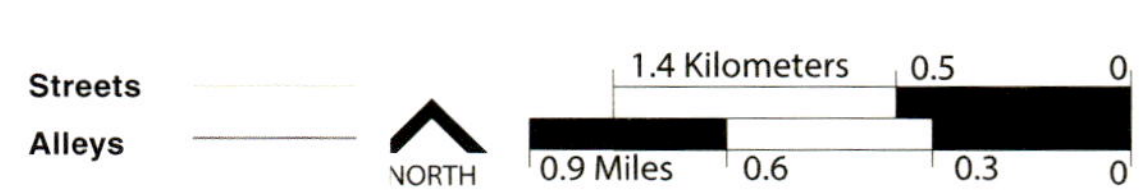

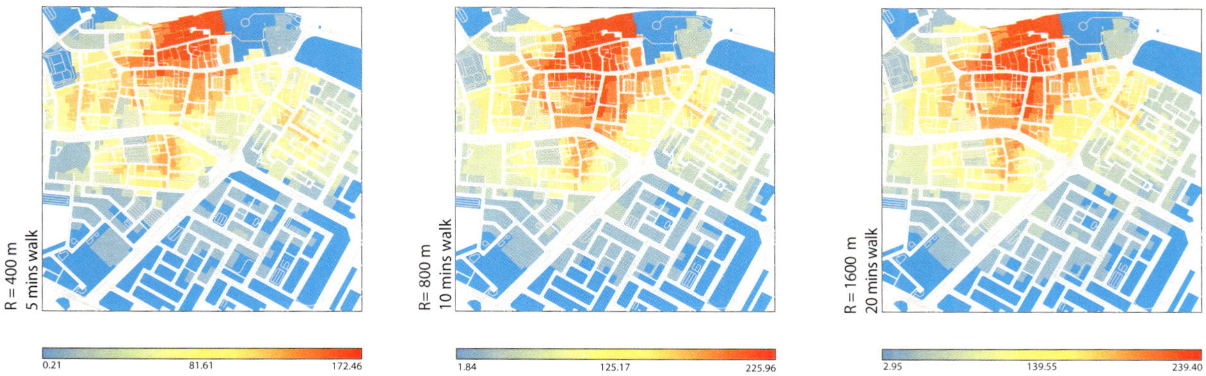

FIG. 16.3
Gravity
Scenario 1: Streets only

Gravity (Radius = 400 m)
The maximum number of plots that can be reached within 5 minutes walking distance with the distance decay effect is 172.46 plots. The average Gravity of the sample is 81.61 plots.

Summary of Gravity results
Minimum: 0.21
Maximum: 172.46
Mean: 81.61
Median: 78.17

Gravity (Radius = 800 m)
The maximum number of plots that can be reached within 10 minutes walking distance with the distance decay effect is 225.96 plots. The average Gravity of the sample is 125.17 plots.

Summary of Gravity results
Minimum: 1.84
Maximum: 225.96
Mean: 125.17
Median: 126.87

Gravity (Radius = 1600 m)
The maximum number of plots that can be reached within 20 minutes walking distance with the distance decay effect is 239.40 plots. The average Gravity of the sample is 139.55 plots.

Summary of Gravity results
Minimum: 2.95
Maximum: 239.40
Mean: 139.55
Median:144.21

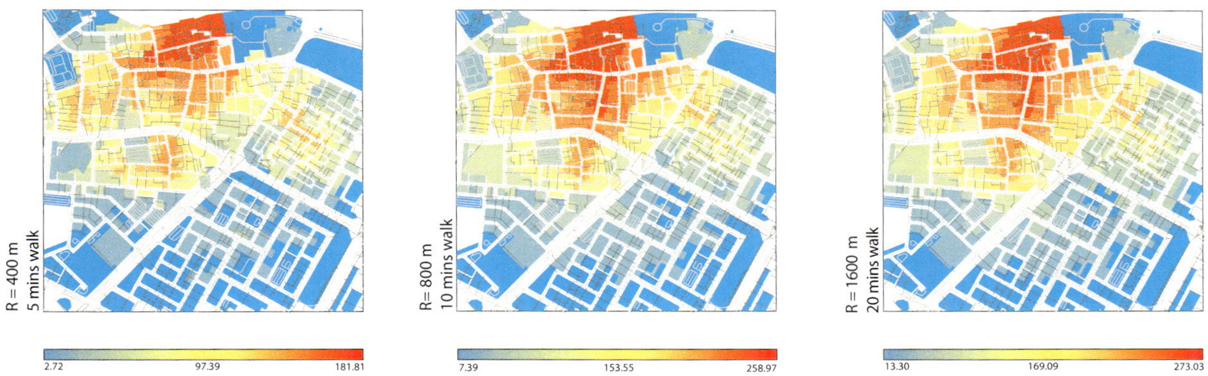

FIG. 16.4
Gravity
Scenario 2: Streets + Alleys

Gravity (Radius = 400 m)
The maximum number of plots that can be reached within 5 minutes walking distance with the distance decay effect is 172.46 plots. The average Gravity of the sample is 81.61 plots.

Summary of Gravity results
Minimum: 2.72
Maximum: 181.81
Mean: 97.39
Median: 104.04

Gravity (Radius = 800 m)
The maximum number of plots that can be reached within 10 minutes walking distance with the distance decay effect is 225.96 plots. The average Gravity of the sample is 125.17 plots.

Summary of Gravity results
Minimum: 7.39
Maximum: 258.97
Mean: 153.55
Median: 162.86

Gravity (Radius = 1600 m)
The maximum number of plots that can be reached within 20 minutes walking distance with the distance decay effect is 239.40 plots. The average Gravity of the sample is 139.55 plots.

Summary of Gravity results
Minimum: 13.30
Maximum: 273.03
Mean: 169.09
Median:178.98

At a 400 m radius, high Gravity values ranging from 81.61 to 172.46 are obtained by plots near the organic street patterns at the top. At 800 m and 1,600 m radii, Gravity values become even higher around the same spot, with values ranging from 125.17 to 239.40. With the introduction of alleys, at a 400 m radius, Gravity values improve for all plots, while high values concentrate at the same spots. At 800 m and 1,600 m radii, high values form a single cluster within the organic section of the sample. The highest Gravity values of 258.97 and 273.03 are found at 800 m and 1,600 m radii, respectively. The distribution of Gravity values does not change significantly from 800 m to 1,600 m; however, the values improve for all plots when the radius increases.

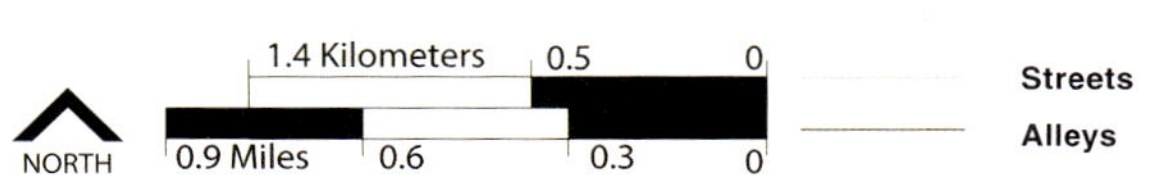

Sample 02

FIG. 16.5

Straightness

Scenario 1: Streets only

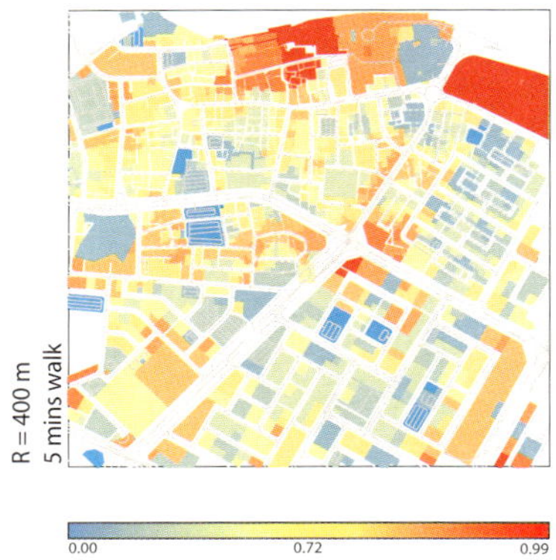

Straightness (Normalized Values, Radius= 400 m)

Plots withing 5 minutes walking distance have access to streets with an average Straightness value of 0.72.

Summary of Straightness results
Minimum: 0.00
Maximum: 0.99
Mean: 0.72
Median: 0.72

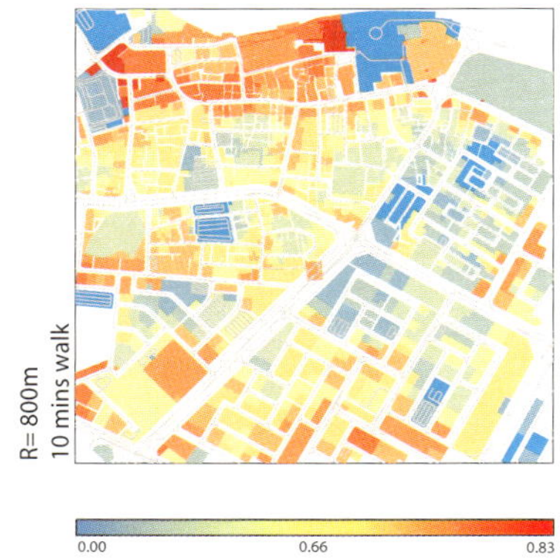

Straightness (Normalized Values, Radius= 800 m)

Plots withing 10 minutes walking distance have access to streets with an average Straightness value of 0.66.

Summary of Straightness results
Minimum: 0.00
Maximum: 0.83
Mean: 0.66
Median: 0.67

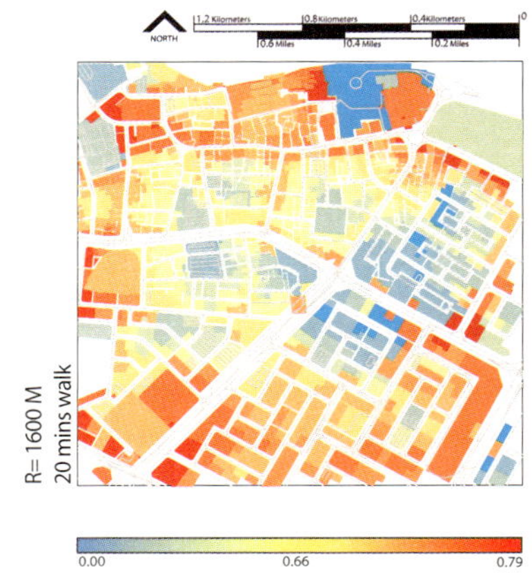

Straightness (Normalized Values, Radius= 1600 m)

Plots withing 20 minutes walking distance have access to streets with an average Straightness value of 0.66.

Summary of Straightness results
Minimum: 0.00
Maximum: 0.79
Mean: 0.66
Median: 0.67

FIG. 16.6

Straightness

Scenario 2: Streets + Alleys

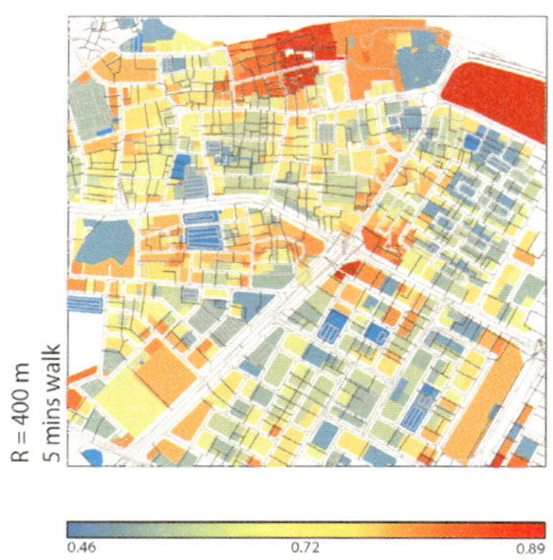

Straightness (Normalized Values, Radius= 400 m)

Plots withing 5 minutes walking distance have access to strets with an average Straightness value of 0.72.

Summary of Straightness results
Minimum: 0.46
Maximum: 0.89
Mean: 0.72
Median: 0.73

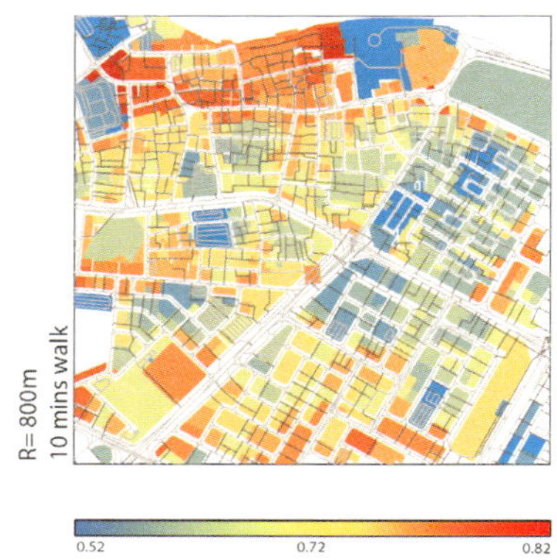

Straightness (Normalized Values, Radius= 800 m)

Plots withing 10 minutes walking distance have access to streets with an average Straightness value of 0.66.

Summary of Straightness results
Minimum: 0.00
Maximum: 0.82
Mean: 0.72
Median: 0.73

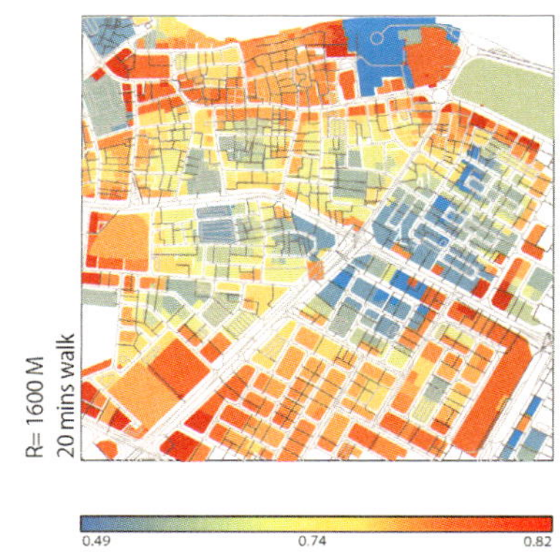

Straightness (Normalized Values, Radius= 1600 m)

Plots withing 20 minutes walking distance have access to streets with an average Straightness value of 0.66.

Summary of Straightness results
Minimum: 0.00
Maximum: 0.82
Mean: 0.74
Median: 0.75

At a 400 m radius, high Straightness values (0.75 to 0.99) form a small cluster on the upper side within the organic section at the top. At 800 m, Straightness values decrease for previously high-performing plots, while the distribution of values does not change notably. This is evident from the decrement of the maximum value, which is 0.99 at 400 m and 0.83 at 800 m. At a 1,600 m radius, high Straightness values prominently appear along the arterial streets at the bottom part of the sample. With the introduction of alleys, at 400 m, high Straightness values (0.75 to 0.89) are distributed evenly compared with the scenario without alleys. At 800 m, high values are also distributed throughout the sample, while the maximum value decreases from 0.89 at 400 m to 0.82. At a 1,600 m radius, high Straightness values can be observed at the bottom half of the sample, where the arterial streets lie.

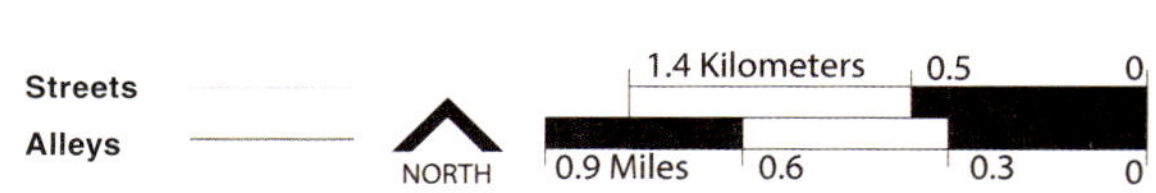

Summary of Centrality Results

Neighborhood

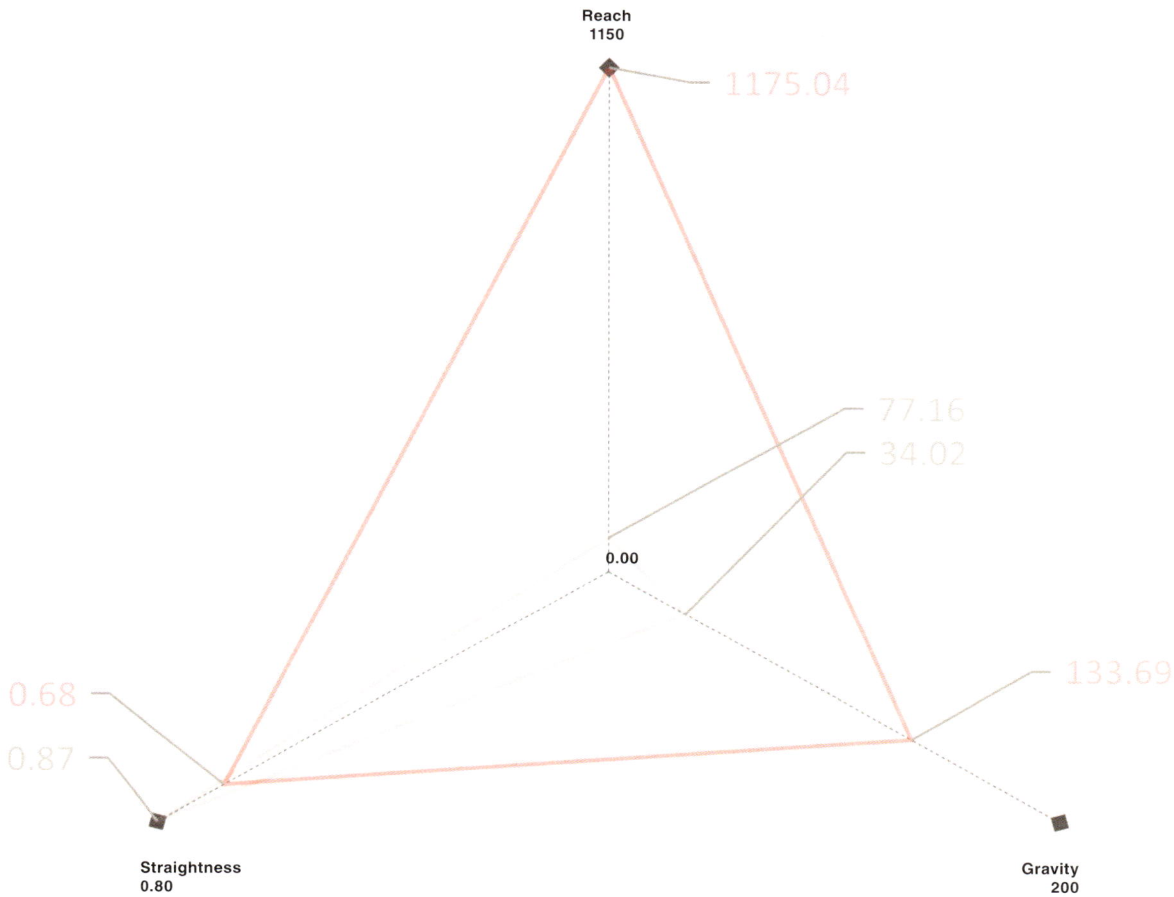

FIG. 17
Spider graphs showing the contribution of alleyways to the averages of 400m, 800m, and 1600m scales of Reach, Gravity and Straightness

Sample 01

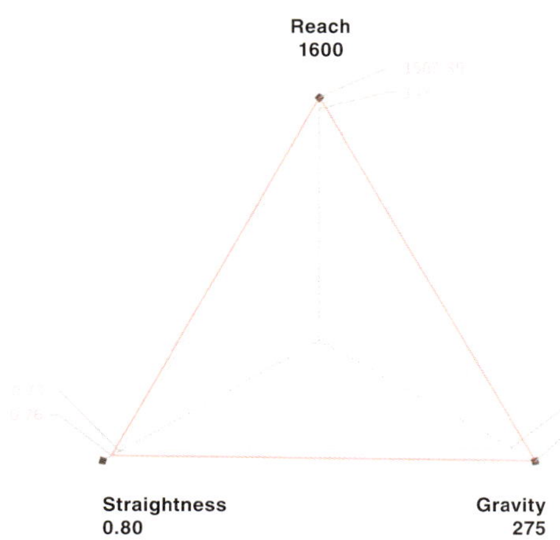

Sample 02

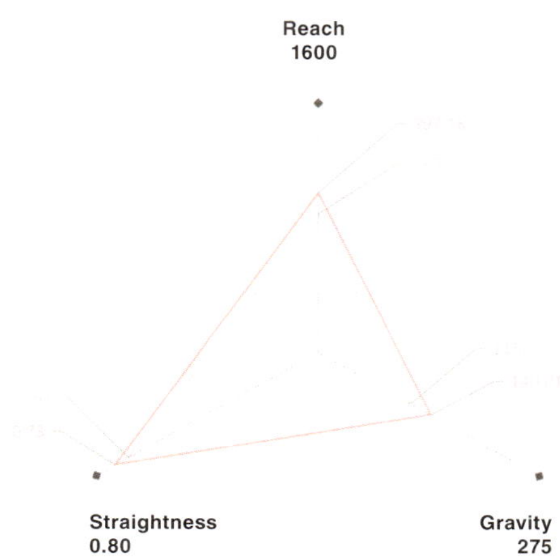

Neighborhood Scale

FIG. 18

Histograms showing the distribution of centrality values (Reach, Gravity, and Straightness) among plots with and without alleys at three different scales 400m, 800m, and 1600m. The X axis is for the centrality metric values, while the Y axis is for the percentage of plots achieving a centrality value denoted on the X axis.

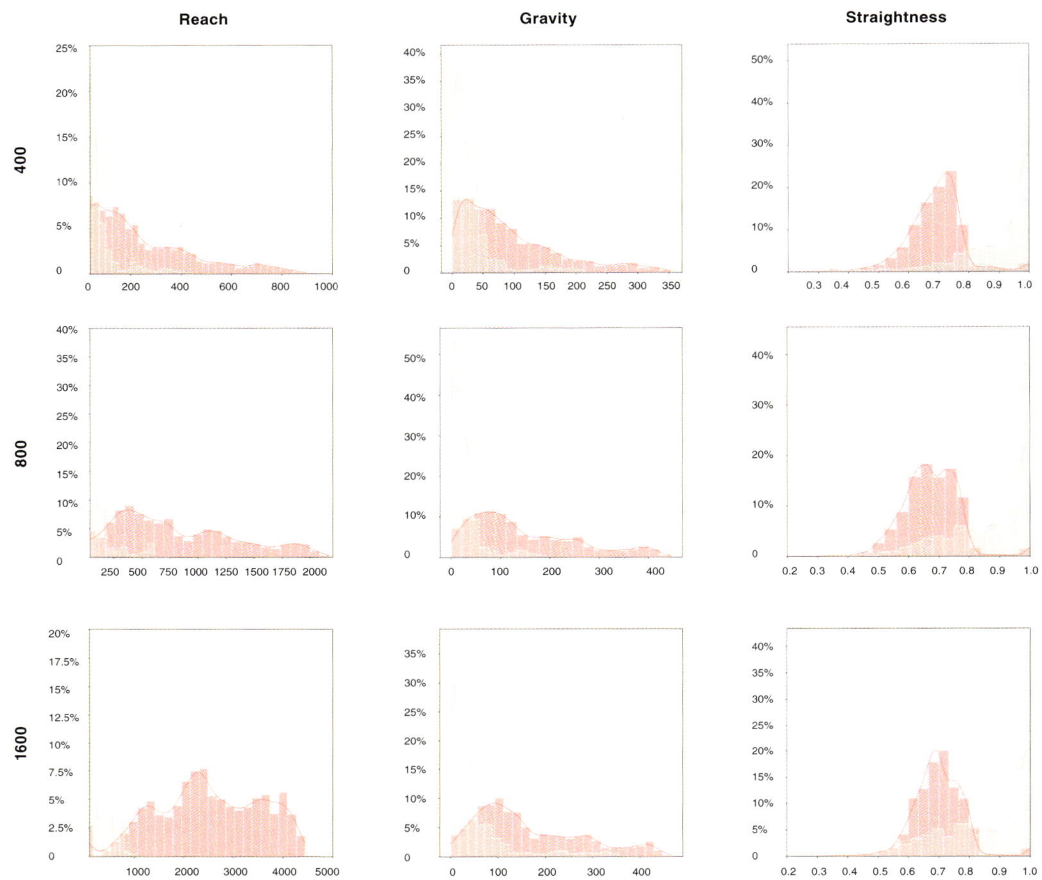

TABLE. 1

Neighborhood scale centrality values

UNA		Radius	Min	Max	Avg
Scenario 1: Streets only	Reach	400	0	446	46
		800	0	614	73
		1600	0	1013	112
	Gravity	400	0.00	214.16	29.47
		800	0.00	193.10	26.08
		1600	0.00	352.33	46.51
	Straightness	400	0.00	1.00	0.90
		800	0.00	1.00	0.86
		1600	0.00	1.00	0.84

UNA		Radius	Min	Max	Avg
Scenario 2: Streets + Alleys	Reach	400	0	896	237
		800	0	2171	797
		1600	0	4450	2491
	Gravity	400	0.00	353.50	92.57
		800	0.00	447.67	145.00
		1600	0.00	467.00	163.51
	Straightness	400	0.00	1.00	0.68
		800	0.00	1.00	0.67
		1600	0.00	1.00	0.70

Sample Scale — Sample 01

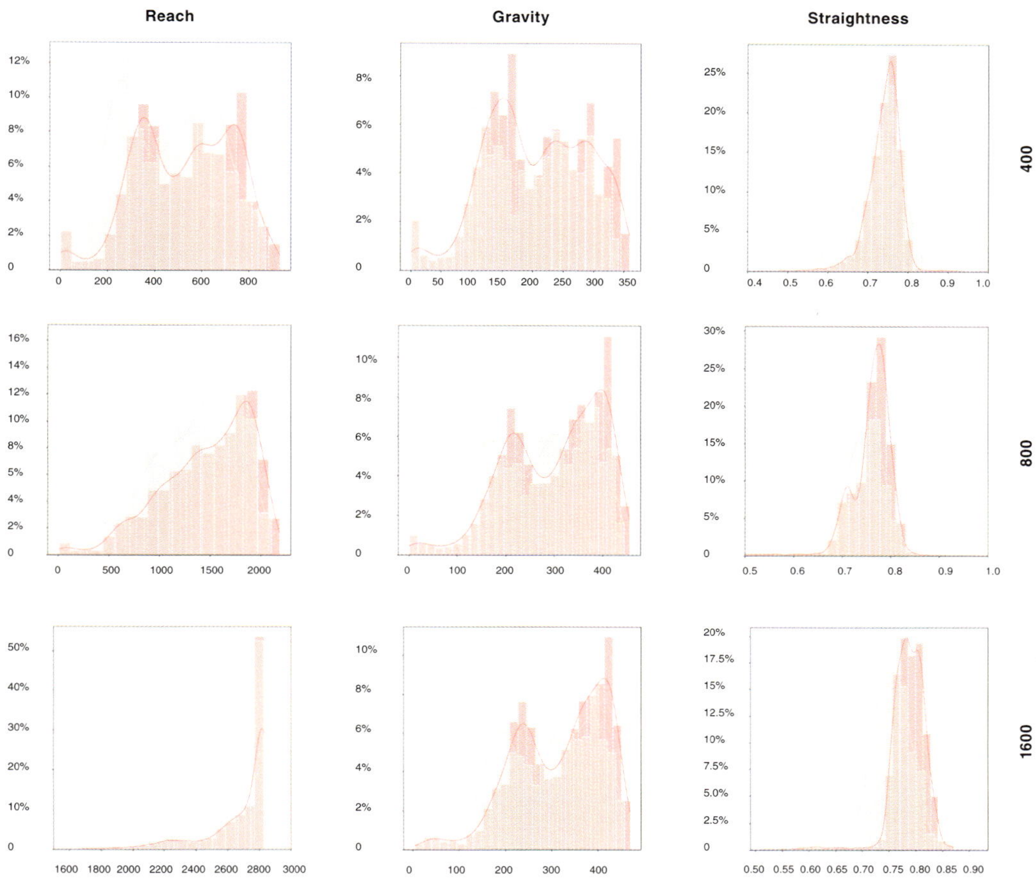

FIG. 19

Histograms showing the distribution of centrality values (Reach, Gravity, and Straightness) among plots with and without alleys at three different scales 400m, 800m, and 1600m. The X axis is for the centrality metric values, while the Y axis is for the percentage of plots achieving a centrality value denoted on the X axis.

UNA		Radius	Min	Max	Avg
Scenario 1: Streets only	Reach	400	1	871	456
		800	4	2106	1364
		1600	4	2826	2644
	Gravity	400	0.28	340.76	178.78
		800	0.69	443.76	267.96
		1600	2.68	456.78	287.57
	Straightness	400	0.34	1.00	0.73
		800	0.43	0.97	0.72
		1600	0.51	0.92	0.75

UNA		Radius	Min	Max	Avg
Scenario 2: Streets + Alleys	Reach	400	1	932	529
		800	6	2189	1473
		1600	695	2831	2688
	Gravity	400	0.28	359.07	206.49
		800	0.69	455.10	299.86
		1600	2.92	469.72	318.95
	Straightness	400	0.48	1.00	0.74
		800	0.46	0.97	0.76
		1600	0.52	0.87	0.79

TABLE. 2

Sample 01 centrality values

Sample Scale — Sample 02

FIG. 20

Histograms showing the distribution of centrality values (Reach, Gravity, and Straightness) among plots with and without alleys at three different scales 400m, 800m, and 1600m. The X axis is for the centrality metric values, while the Y axis is for the percentage of plots achieving a centrality value denoted on the X axis.

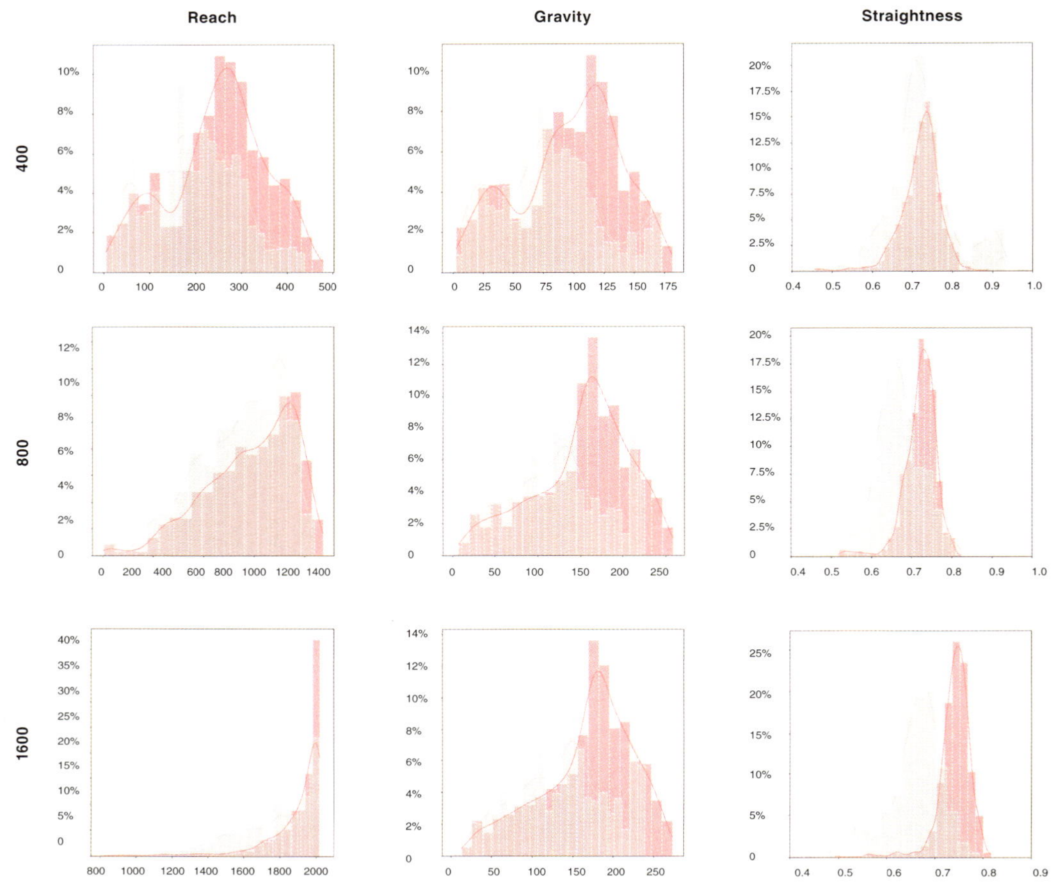

TABLE. 3

Sample 02 centrality values

UNA		Radius	Min	Max	Avg
Scenario 1: Streets only	Reach	400	1	438	195
		800	7	1283	656
		1600	205	2020	1753
	Gravity	400	0.21	172.46	81.61
		800	1.84	225.96	125.17
		1600	2.95	239.40	139.55
	Straightness	400	0.00	0.99	0.72
		800	0.00	0.83	0.66
		1600	0.00	0.79	0.66

UNA		Radius	Min	Max	Avg
Scenario 2: Streets + Alleys	Reach	400	5	479	250
		800	67	1459	841
		1600	807	2022	1901
	Gravity	400	2.72	181.81	97.39
		800	7.39	258.97	153.55
		1600	13.30	273.03	169.09
	Straightness	400	0.46	0.89	0.72
		800	0.52	0.82	0.72
		1600	0.49	0.82	0.74

3
Sikka

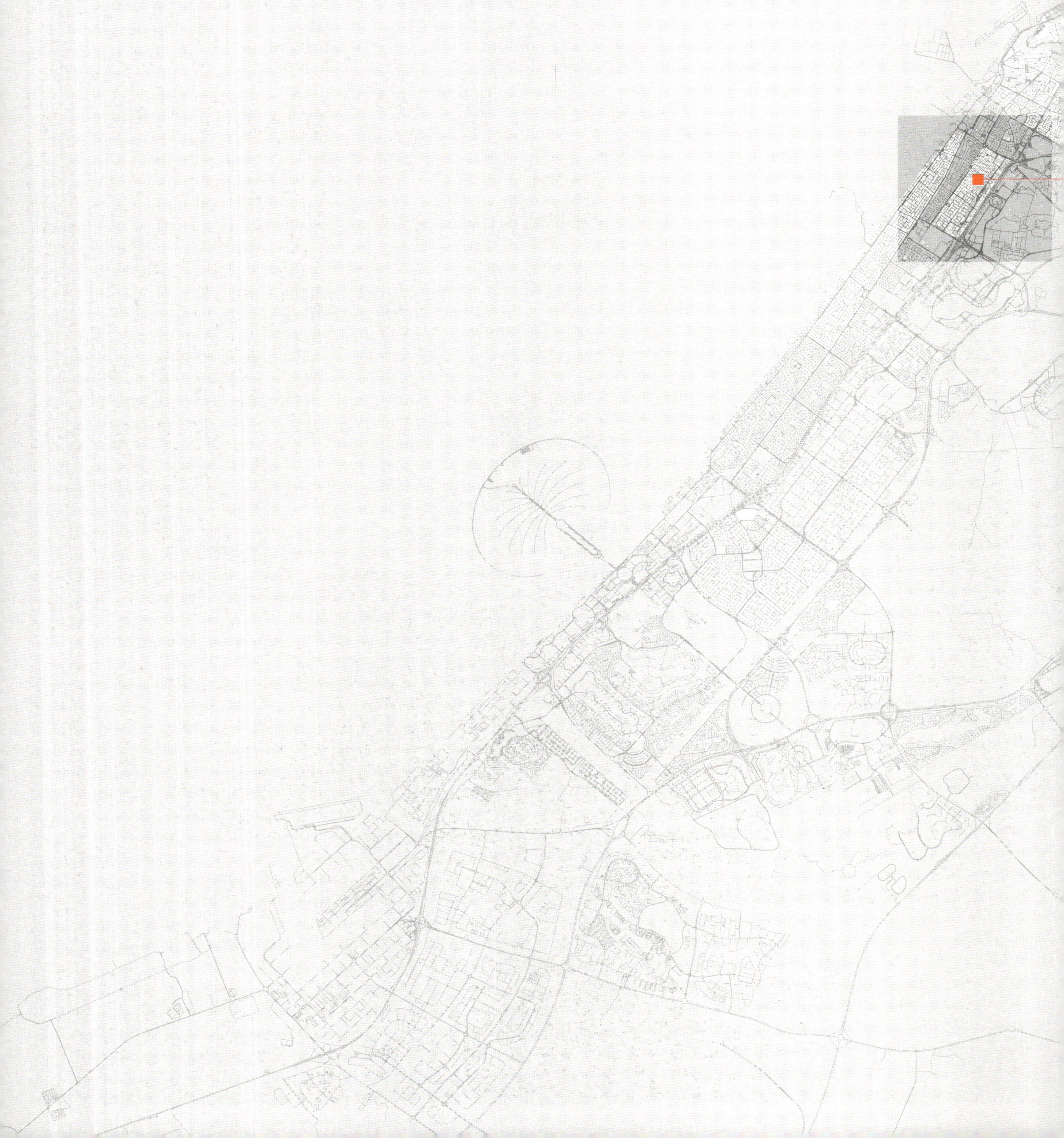

Al Satwa

Al Satwa

FIG. 1
Al Satwa skyline

FIG. 2
View from one of the older blocks in Al Satwa

FIG. 3
A photo montage with different views of Al Satwa

FIG. 4
Aerial image showing Al Satwa (Esri & USGS, 2021)

Morphological Analysis

Neighborhood Scale

Residential= 2,303 Plots
Non-residential= 247 Plots

Plots/Buildings:

- Total area = 266 Hectares
- Total plots = 2,550 Plots
- Total buildings = 3,412 Buildings
- Average plot density = 9.86 Plots/Hectare
- Average building density = 12.83 Buildings/Hectare
- Average plot area = 0.06 Hectare
- Average population density = 118.80 Population/Hectare

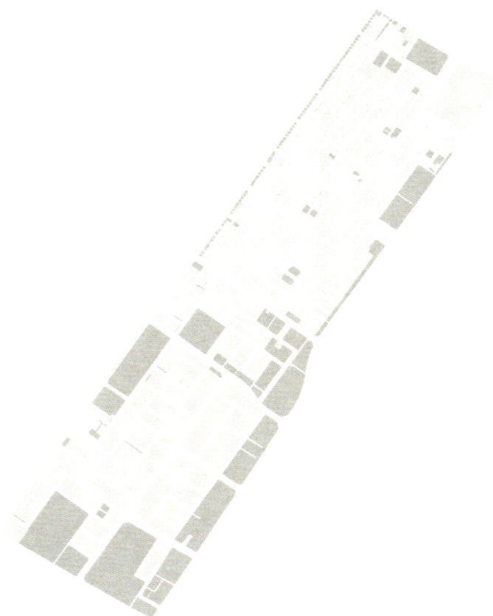

FIG. 5.1
Residential/ non-residential classification

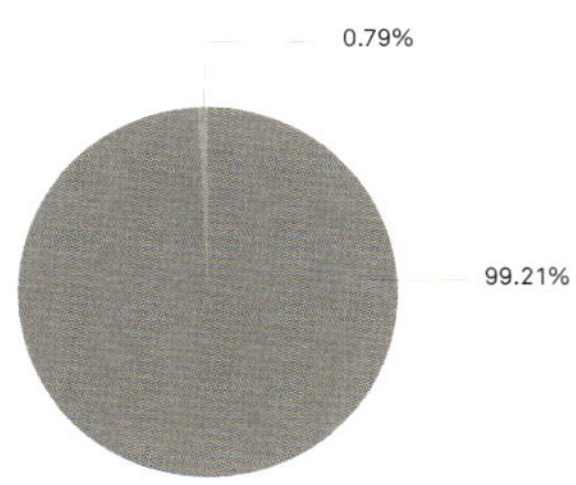

Low-rise (1-4) = 3,384 Buildings
Mid-rise (4-10)= 27 Buildings

FIG. 5.2
Buildings height classification

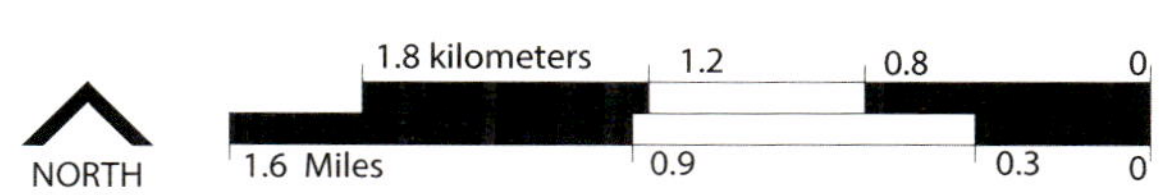

FIG. 5.3

Population density

*Population per hectare.

FIG. 5.4

Land use classification

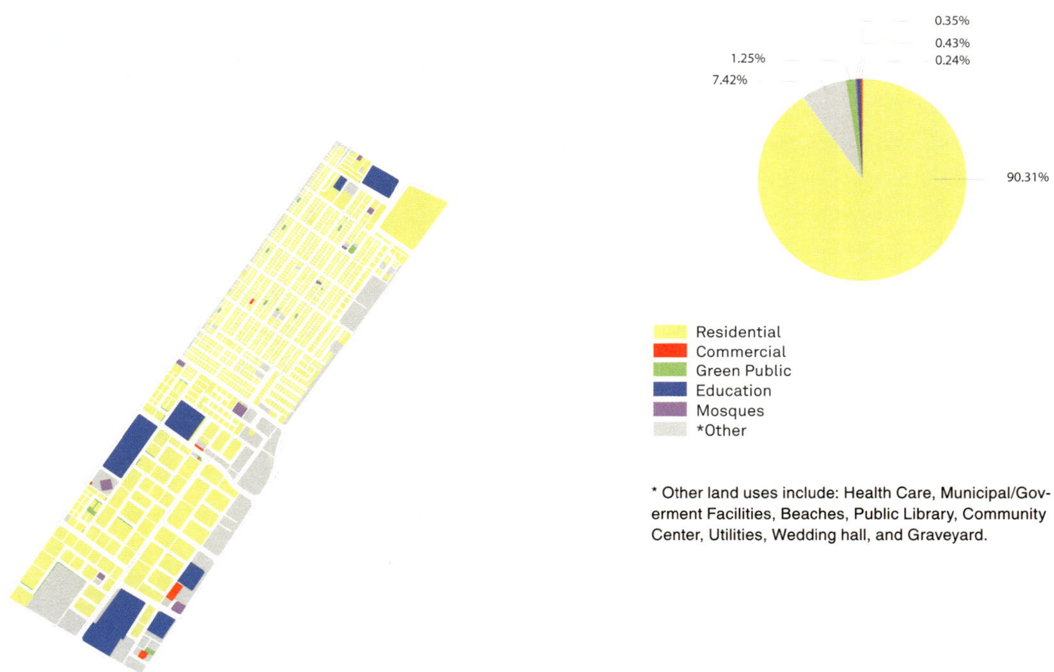

* Other land uses include: Health Care, Municipal/Goverment Facilities, Beaches, Public Library, Community Center, Utilities, Wedding hall, and Graveyard.

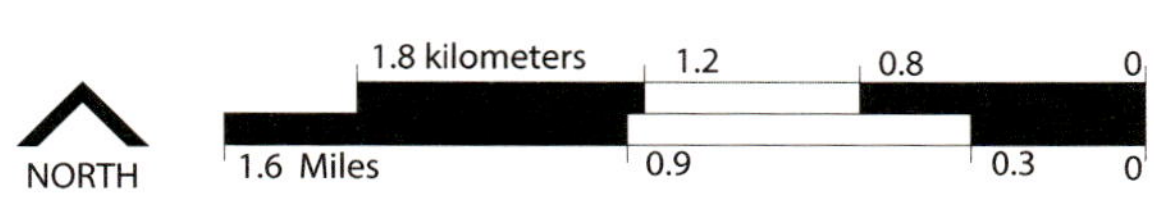

FIG. 5.5
Map showing network classification in Al Satwa

Streets:

- Street length = 51.21 km
- Street density = 0.19 km/Hectare
- Street intersections = 285 Intersections
- Street intersections density = 1.07 Intersections/Hectare

Alleys:

- Alley length = 60.0 km
- Alley density = 0.23 km/Hectare
- Alley intersections = 704 Intersections
- Alley intersections density = 2.65 Intersections/Hectares

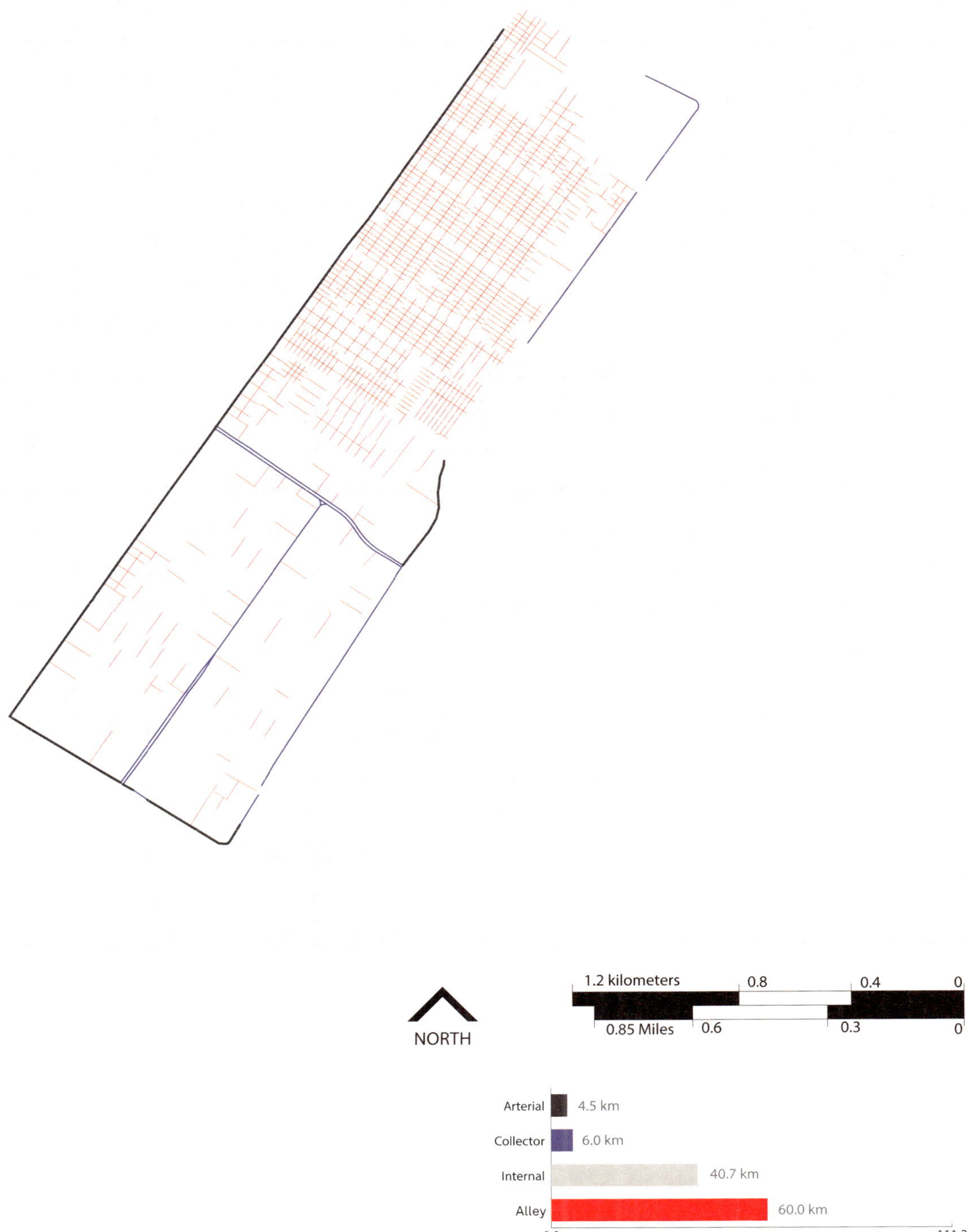

FIG. 6
Map showing Al Satwa with the location of the selected samples. Each sample has an area of 1 square mile.

Morphological Analysis

Sample Scale — Sample 01

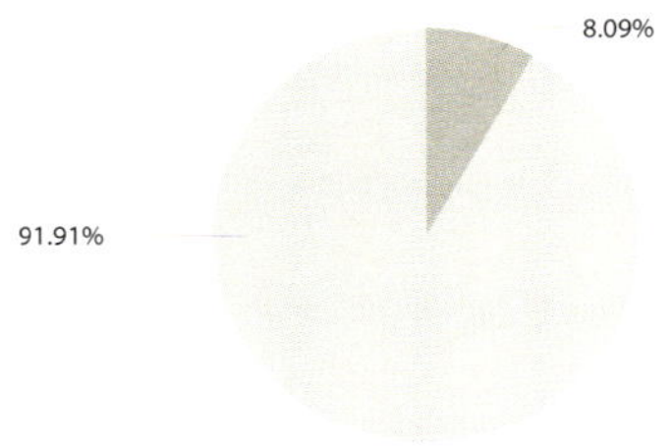

Residential= 1,853 Plots
Non-residential= 163 Plots

Plots/Buildings:

- Total area = 256 Hectares
- Total plots = 2,016 Plots
- Total buildings = 794 Buildings
- Average plot area = 0.03 Hectare
- Average plot density = 7.88 Plots/Hectare

FIG. 7.1
Residential/non-residential classification

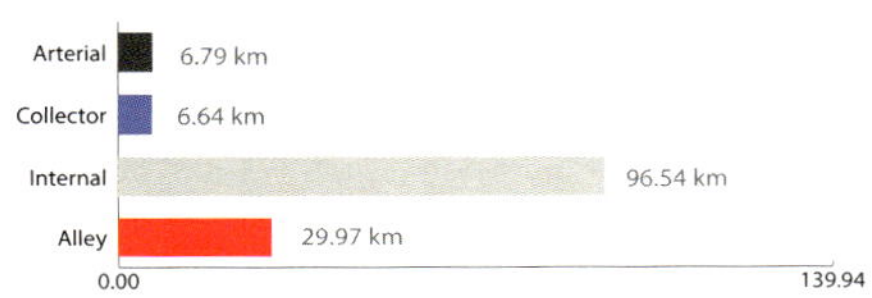

Streets:

- Street length = 106.97 km
- Street density = 0.42 km/Hectare
- Street intersections = 754 Intersections
- Street intersections density = 2.95 Intersections/Hectare

Alleys:

- Alley length = 29.97 km
- Alley density = 0.12 km/Hectare
- Alley intersections = 406 Intersections
- Alley intersections density = 1.59 Intersections/Hectare

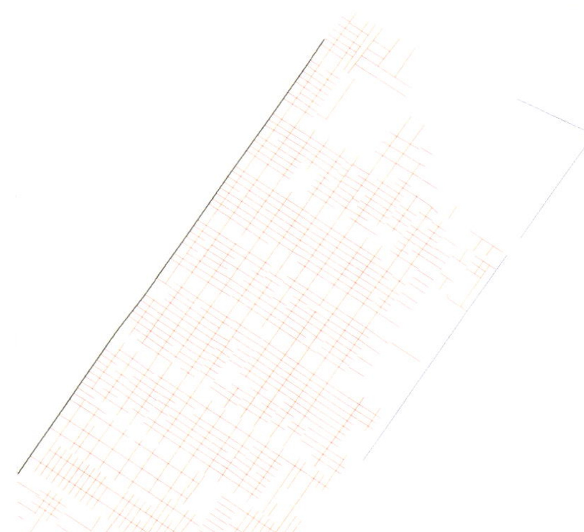

FIG. 7.2
Network classification

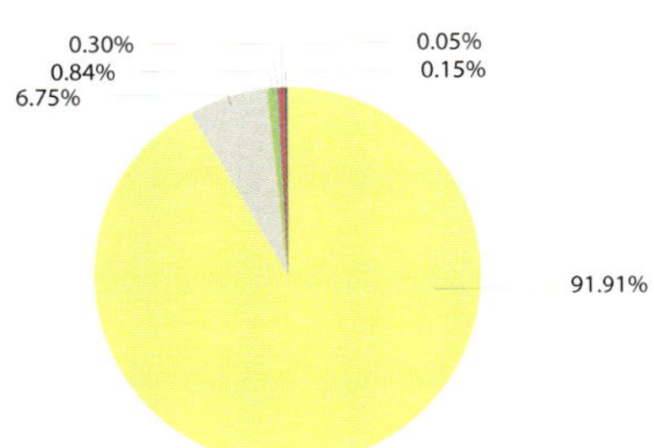

Residential
Commercial
Education
Green Public
Mosques
*Other

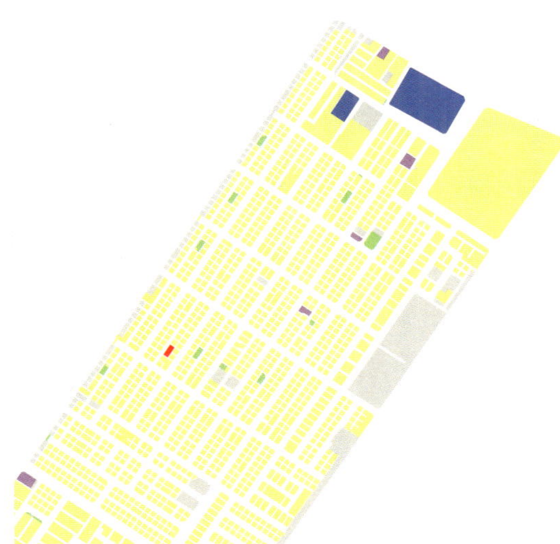

FIG. 7.3
Land use classification

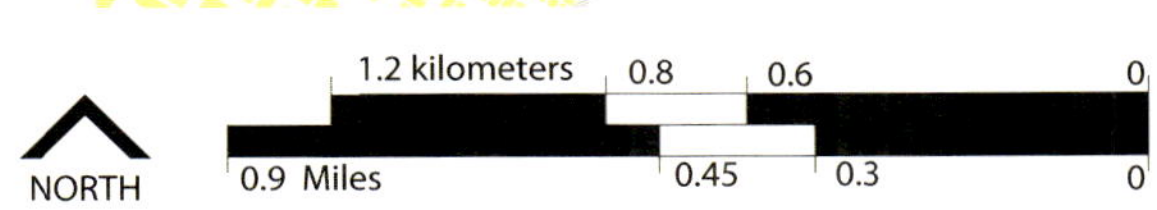

Sample Scale — Sample 02

FIG. 8.1
Residential/non-residential classification

Residential= 605 Plots
Non-residential= 135 Plots

Plots/Buildings:

- Total area = 256 Hectares
- Total plots = 740 Plots
- Total buildings = 1,504 Buildings
- Average plot density = 2.89 Plots/Hectare
- Average plot area = 0.14 Hectare

FIG. 8.2
Network classification

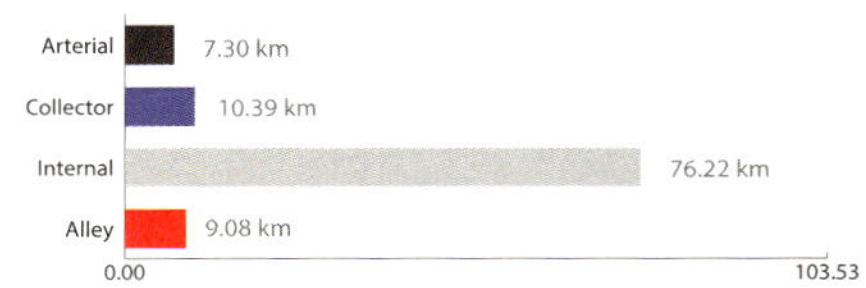

Streets:

- Street length = 94.45 km
- Street density = 0.37 km/Hectare
- Street intersections = 660 Intersections
- Street intersections density= 2.58 Intersections/Hectare

Alleys:

- Alley length = 9.08 km
- Alley density = 0.04 km/Hectare
- Alley intersections = 44 Intersections
- Alley intersections density = 0.17 Intersection/Hectare

FIG. 8.3
Land use classification

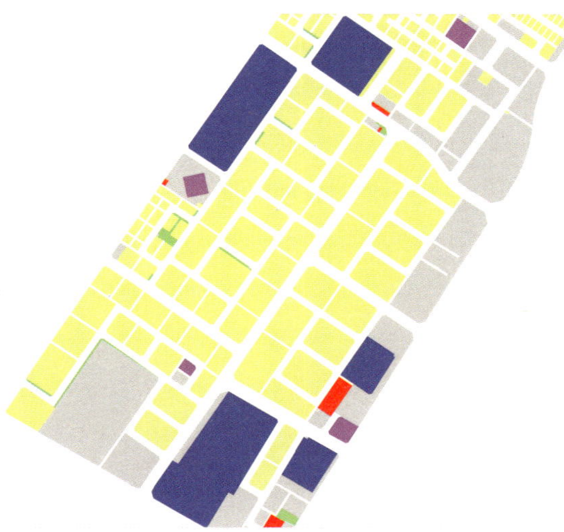

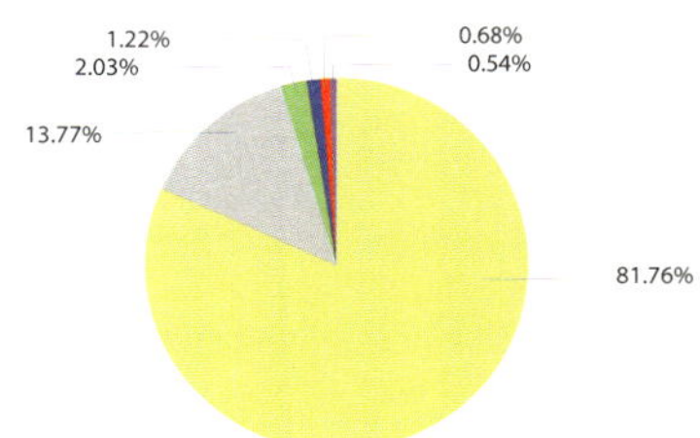

Residential
Commercial
Education
Green Public
Mosques
*Other

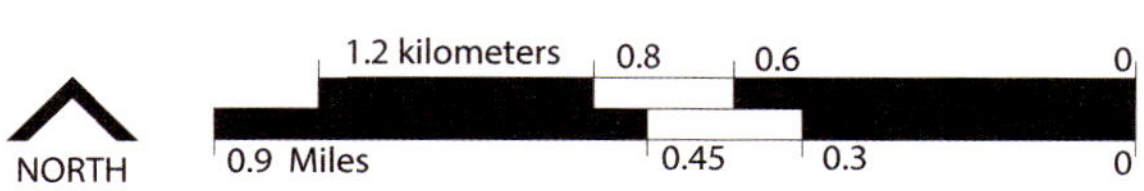

Centrality Analysis: Neighborhood Scale

Scenario 1: Streets only — 400 m Radius

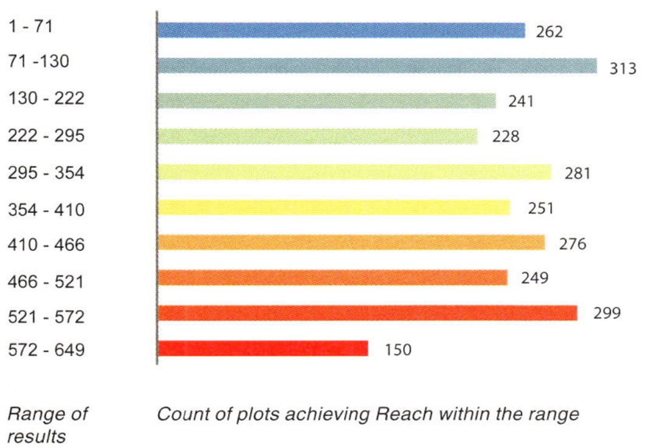

The warmer colors (i.e., greenish-yellow to red) represent a Reach value of 295 or more, while the cooler colors (i.e., light green to dark blue) correspond to a Reach value of 294 or less. The majority of plots (i.e., 1,325 out of 2,550), corresponding to 52% of all plots, have Reach values of less than 354. Among the categories shown in the legend, 12% of the total plots can reach 71 to 130 other plots within 5 minutes of walking. On average, each plot in Al Satwa can access at least 325 plots within a distance of 400 m.

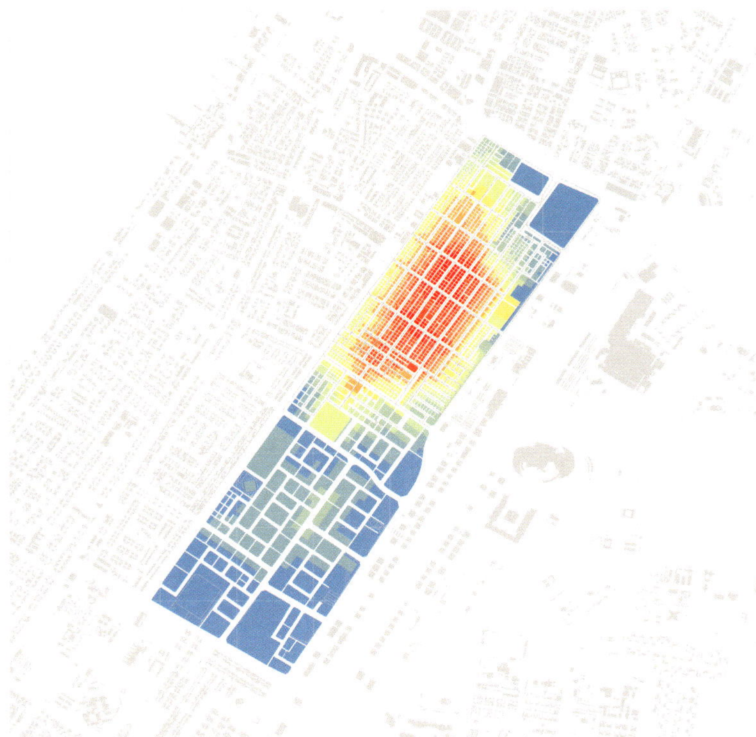

FIG. 9.1
Reach

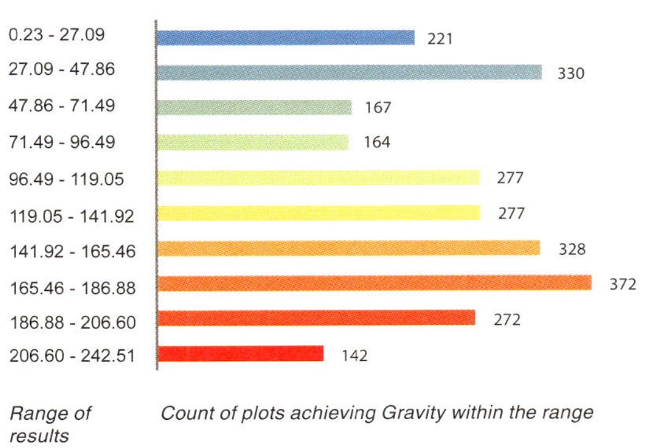

The warmer colors (i.e., greenish-yellow to red) represent Gravity values greater than 96.48, while the cooler colors (i.e., light green to dark blue) correspond to Gravity values lower than 96.49. Fifty-six percent of all plots (i.e., 1,436 out of 2,550) have Gravity values of less than 141.92. Among the categories shown in the legend, 372 plots, or 15% of the total plots, can reach 165.46 to 186.88 plots, making this the most common range; this range is represented by orange on the map. On average, each plot can reach 120 other plots when spatial impedance or distance decay effect is taken into consideration.

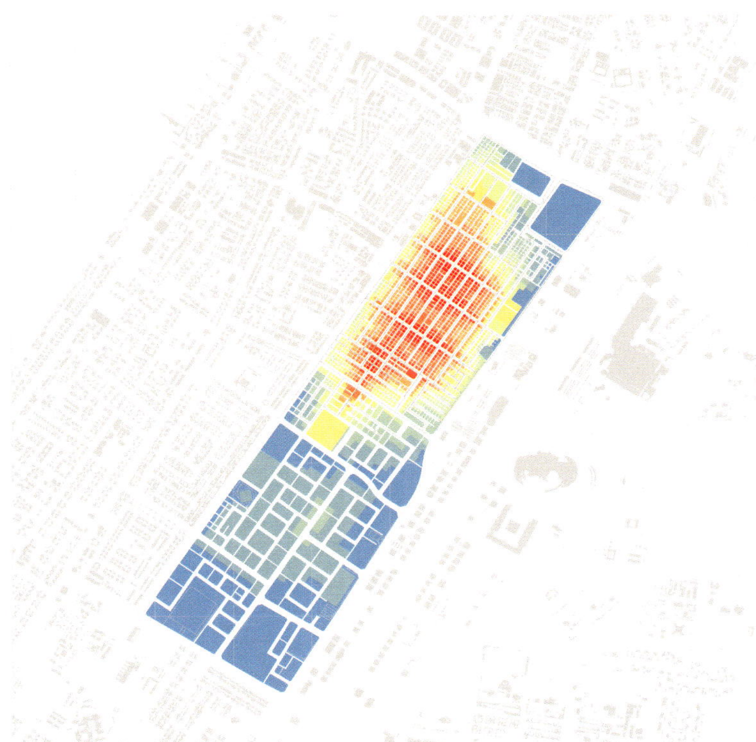

FIG. 9.2
Gravity

Scenario 1: Streets only — 400 m Radius

FIG. 9.3

Betweenness

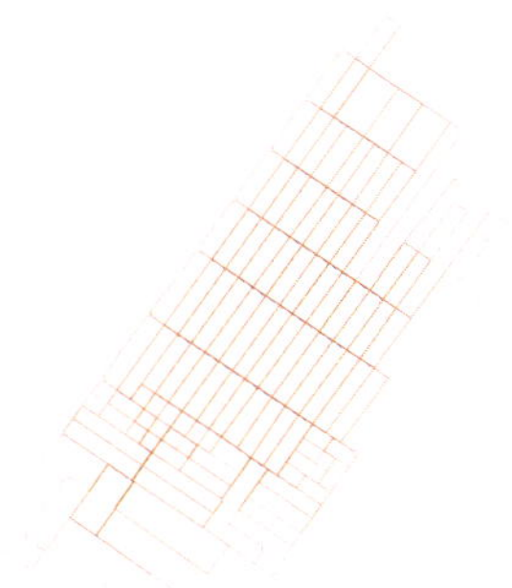

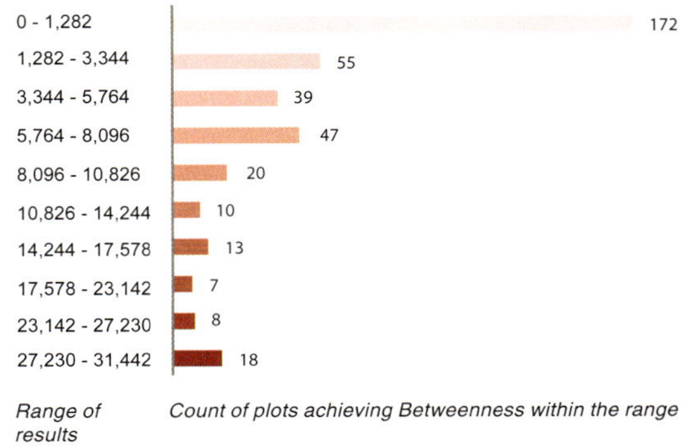

Thirty-four percent of all segments (i.e., 134 out of 389 segments) have mid-range Betweenness values ranging from 865 to 6,702. Among the categories shown in the legend, 172 segments have values in the range of 0 to 1,282, making this the most common value range; this range is represented by the lightest brown on the map. Low Betweenness values ranging from 0 to 864 are obtained by 145 segments, which is 37% of all segments. One hundred and ten segments have high Betweenness values (higher than 6,702 but smaller than 32,203) but no segments have very high Betweenness values (higher than 32,203). The average Betweenness value in Al Satwa is 5,473 (higher than 864 but smaller than 6,703), while the median is 1,860, indicating mid-range Betweenness at a 400 m radius.

FIG. 9.4

Straightness

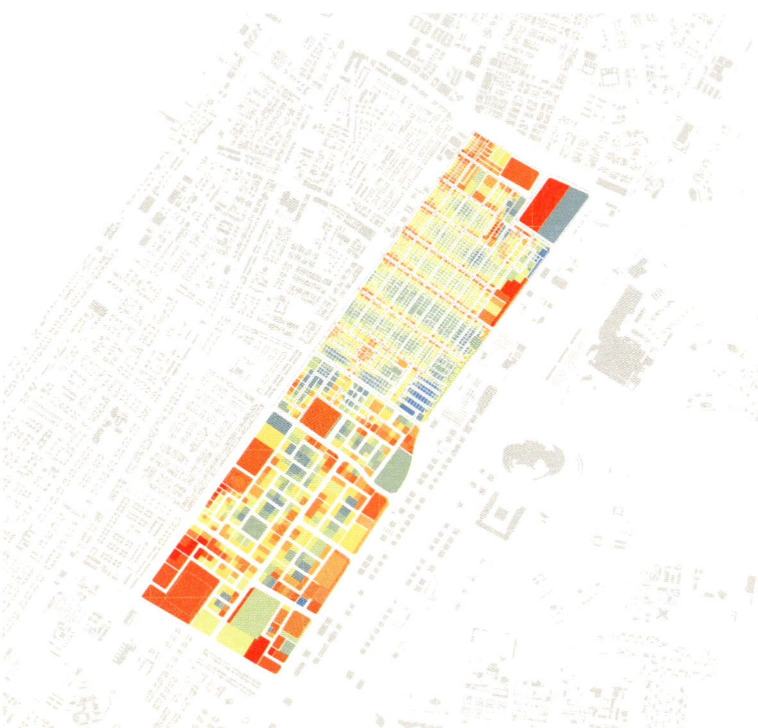

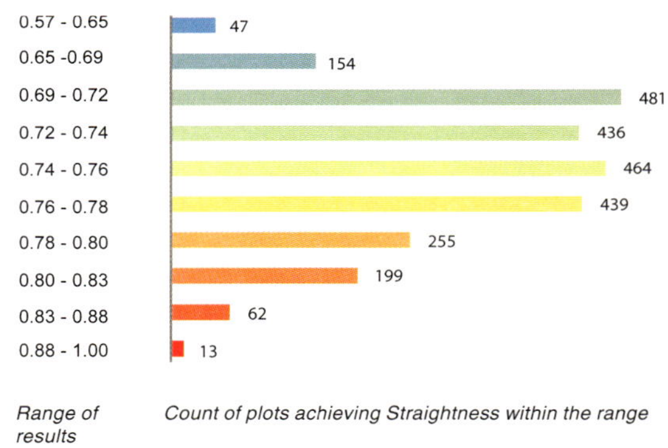

The warmer colors (greenish-yellow to red) represent Straightness values higher than 0.73, while the cooler colors (light green to dark blue) correspond to Straightness values lower than 0.74. The majority of plots, corresponding to 53% (or 1,339 out of 2,550 plots) have Straightness values ranging from 0.72 to 0.78. Among the categories shown in the legend, 481 plots have values in the range of 0.69 to 0.72, making this the most common value range; this range is represented by bluish-green on the map. On average, at a 400 m radius, all plots in Al Satwa are 75% as straight as a straight line.

Scenario 1: Streets only — 800 m Radius

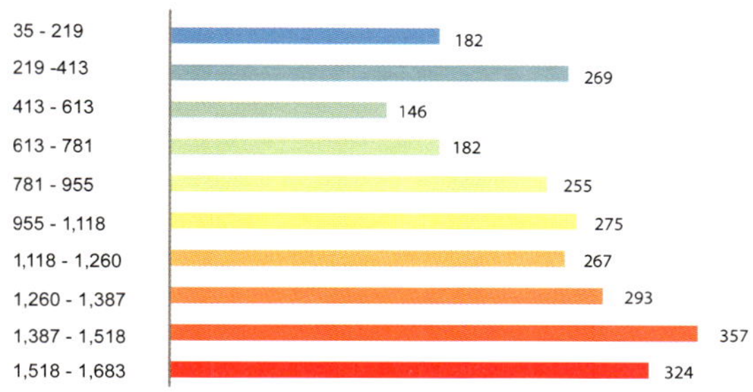

Range of results *Count of plots achieving Reach within the range*

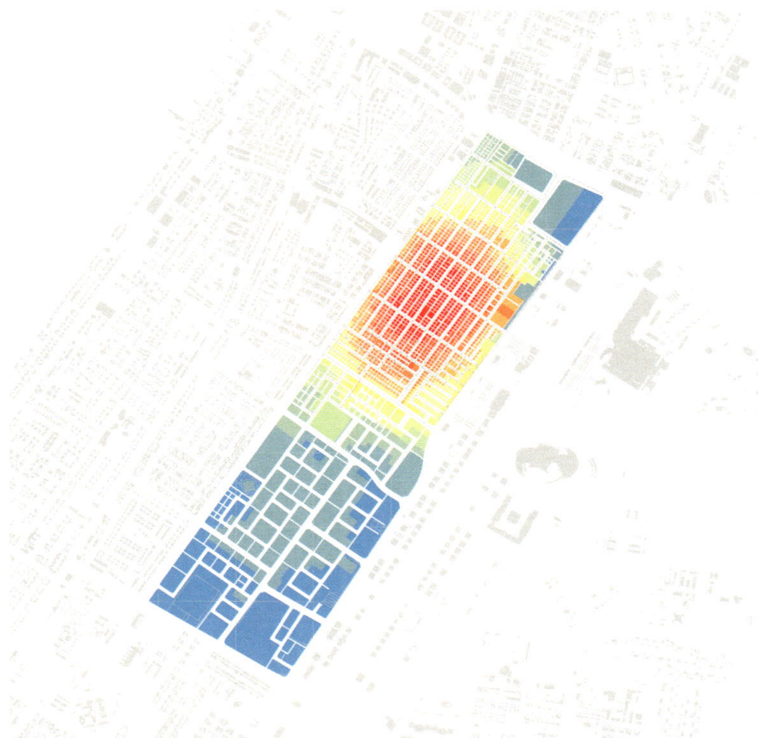

FIG. 10.1
Reach

The warmer colors (i.e., greenish-yellow to red) represent a Reach value of 781 or more, while the cooler colors (i.e., light green to dark blue) correspond to a Reach value of 780 or less. Fifty-one percent of all plots (i.e., 1,309 out of 2,550) have Reach values of less than 1,118. Among the categories shown in the legend, 14% of the total plots can reach 1,387 to 1,518 other plots within 10 minutes of walking. On average, each plot in Al Satwa can access at least 1,003 plots within a distance of 800 m.

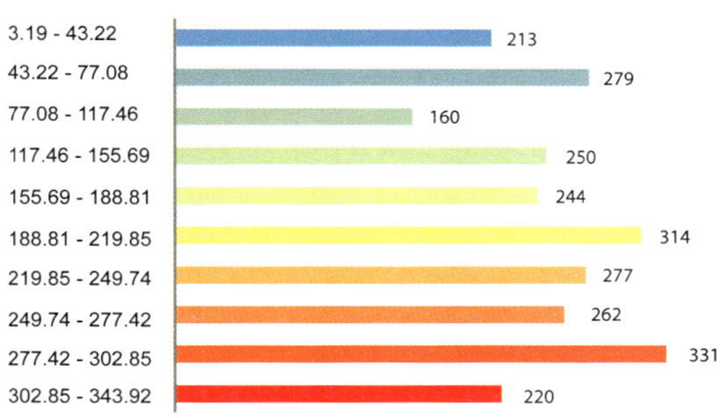

Range of results *Count of plots achieving Gravity within the range*

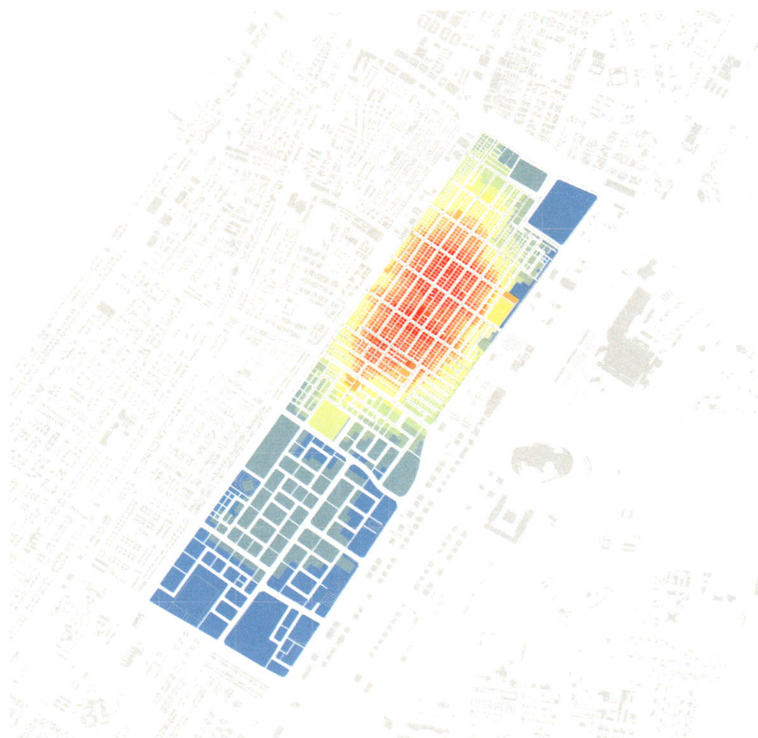

FIG. 10.2
Gravity

The warmer colors (i.e., greenish-yellow to red) represent Gravity values of more than 155.68, while the cooler colors (i.e., light green to dark blue) correspond to Gravity values of less than 155.69. Fifty-seven percent of all plots (i.e., 1,460 out of 2,550) have Gravity values of less than 219.85. Among the categories shown in the legend, 331 plots, or 13% of all plots, can reach 277.42 to 302.85 plots, making this the most common range; this range is represented by dark orange on the map. On average, each plot can reach 188 other plots when spatial impedance or distance decay effect is taken into consideration.

Scenario 1: Streets only — 800 m Radius

FIG. 10.3
Betweenness

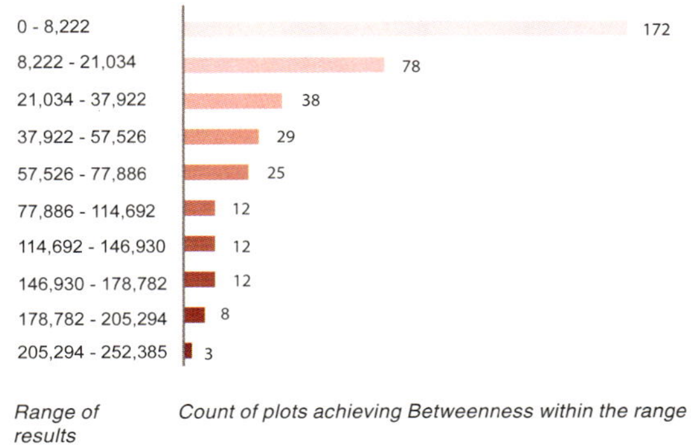

Twenty-nine percent of all segments (i.e., 111 out of 389 segments) have low Betweenness values ranging from 2,540 to 11,517. Among the categories shown in the legend, 172 segments have values in the range of 0 to 8,222, making this the most common value range; this range is represented by the lightest brown on the map. Very low Betweenness values ranging from 0 to 2,539 are obtained by 87 segments, which is 22% of all segments. Mid-range Betweenness values ranging from 11,518 to 20,478 are obtained by 49 segments, which is 13% of the total segments. Seventy segments have high Betweenness values (higher than 20,478 but smaller than 59,384) and 72 segments have very high Betweenness values (higher than 59,383). The average Betweenness value in Al Satwa is 33,321, while the median is 11,206, indicating high Betweenness at an 800 m radius.

FIG. 10.4
Straightness

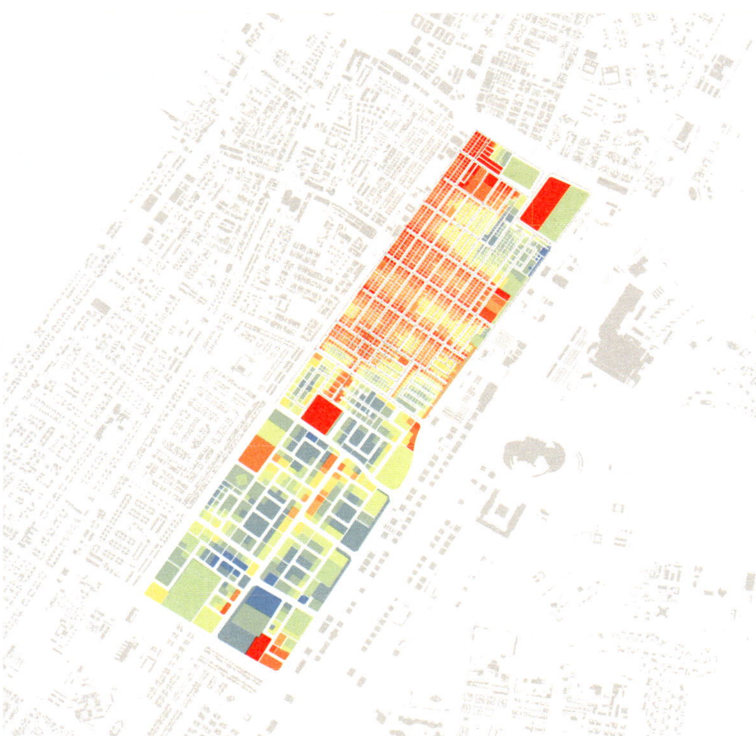

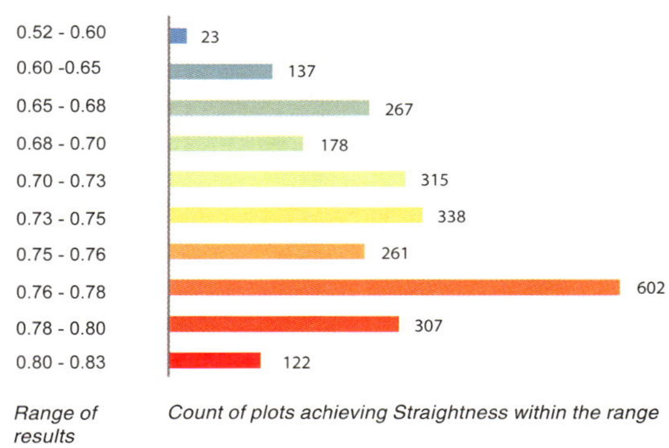

The warmer colors (greenish-yellow to red) represent Straightness values higher than 0.69, while the cooler colors (light green to dark blue) correspond to Straightness values lower than 0.70. The majority of plots, corresponding to 59% (or 1,508 out of 2,550 plots) have Straightness values ranging from 0.73 to 0.80. Among the categories shown in the legend, 602 plots have values in the range of 0.76 to 0.78, making this the most common value range; this range is represented by orange on the map. On average, at an 800 m radius, all plots in Al Satwa are 74% as straight as a straight line.

Scenario 1: Streets only — 1,600 m Radius

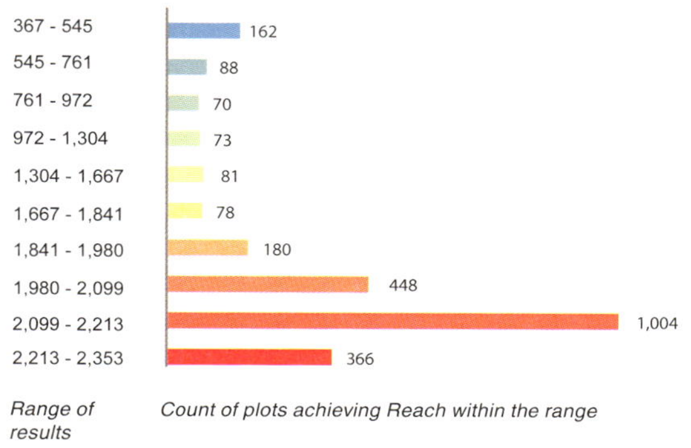

The warmer colors (i.e., greenish-yellow to red) represent Reach values of more than 1,303, while the cooler colors (i.e., light green to dark blue) correspond to Reach values of less than 1,304. The majority of plots (i.e., 1,370 out of 2,550), corresponding to 54% of all plots, have Reach values of more than 2,098. Among the categories shown in the legend, 39% of the total plots can reach 2,099 to 2,213 other plots within 20 minutes of walking. On average, each plot in Al Satwa can access at least 1,878 plots within a distance of 1,600 m.

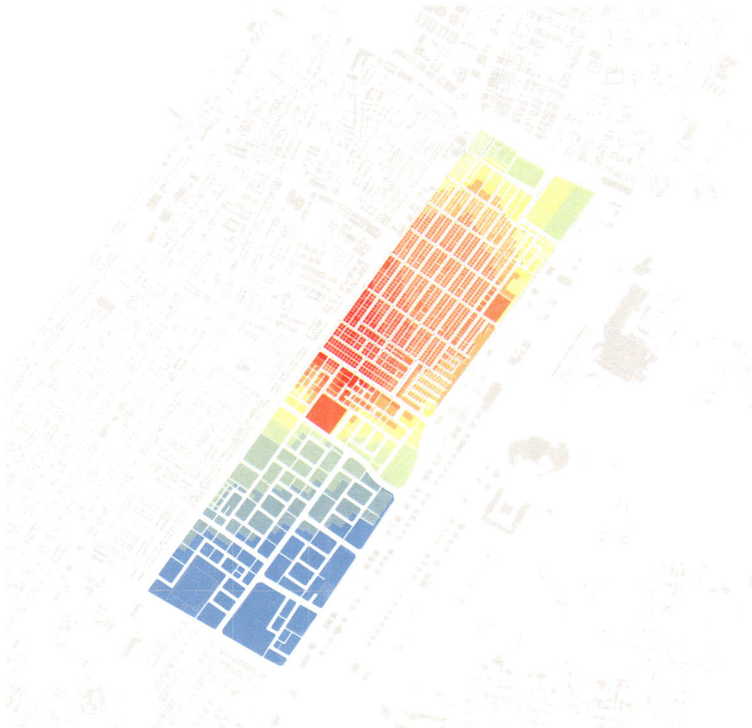

FIG.11.1
Reach

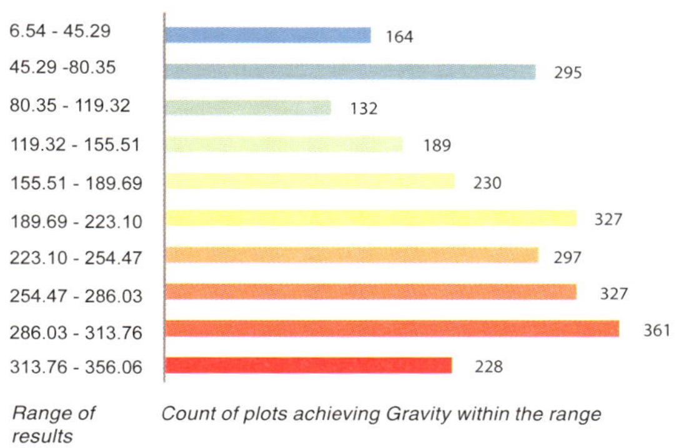

The warmer colors (i.e., greenish-yellow to red) represent Gravity values greater than 155.50, while the cooler colors (i.e., light green to dark blue) correspond to Gravity values lower than 155.51. Fifty-two percent of all plots (i.e., 1,337 out of 2,550) have Gravity values of less than 223.10. Among the categories shown in the legend, 361 plots, or 14% of the total plots, can reach 286.03 to 313.76 plots, making this the most common range; this range is represented by dark orange on the map. On average, each plot can reach 201 other plots when spatial impedance or distance decay effect is taken into consideration.

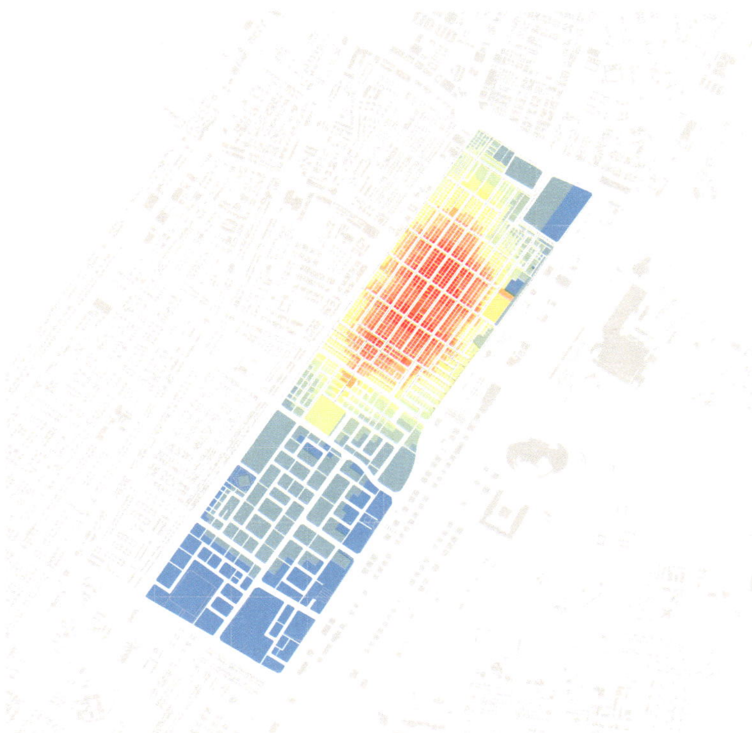

FIG.11.2
Gravity

Streets

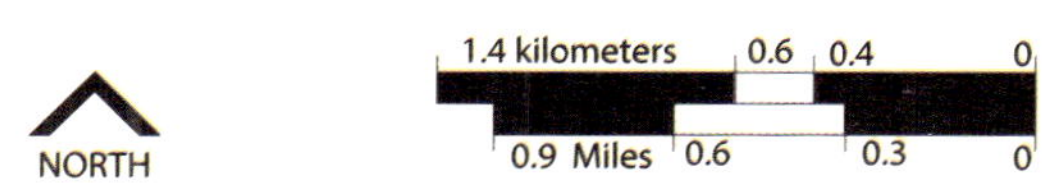

Scenario 1: Streets only — 1,600 m Radius

FIG. 11.3
Betweenness

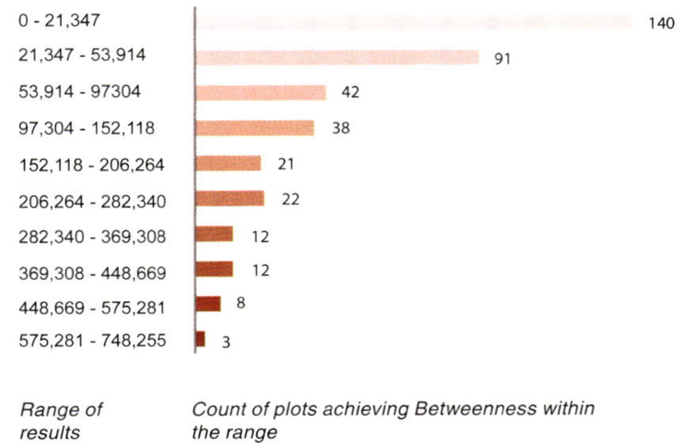

The majority of segments, corresponding to 65% (i.e., 254 out of 389 segments), have very low Betweenness values ranging from 0 to 73,682. Among the categories shown in the legend, 140 segments have values in the range of 0 to 21,347, making this the most common value range; this range is represented by the lightest brown on the map. Low Betweenness values ranging from 73,683 to 123,568 are obtained by 37 segments, which is 10% of all segments. Mid-range Betweenness values ranging from 123,569 to 179,444 are obtained by 30 segments, which is 8% of the total segments. Twenty-seven segments have high Betweenness values (from 179,445 to 251,415) and 41 segments have very high Betweenness values (higher than 251,415). The average Betweenness value in Al Satwa is 94,217 (higher than 73,682 but smaller than 123,569), while the median is 36,412, indicating low Betweenness at a 1,600 m radius.

FIG. 11.4
Straightness

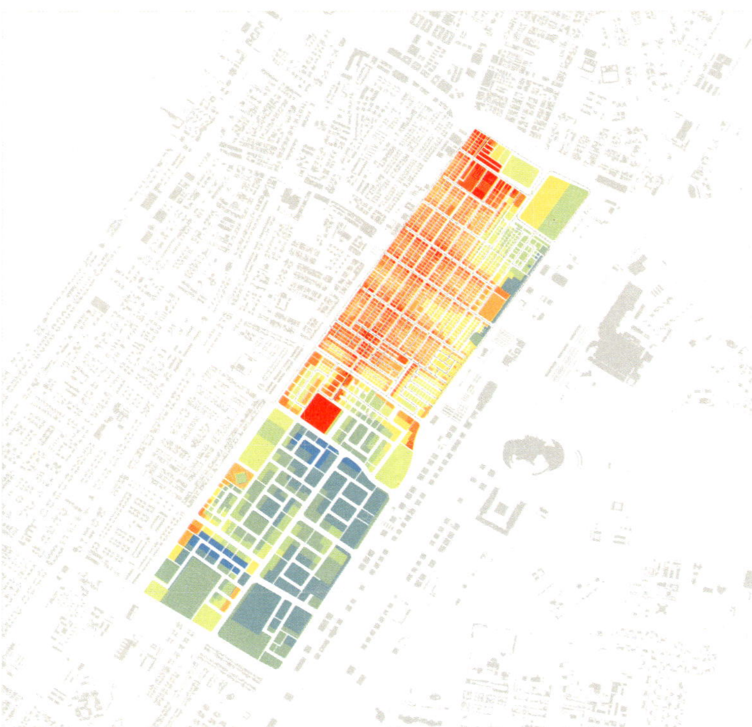

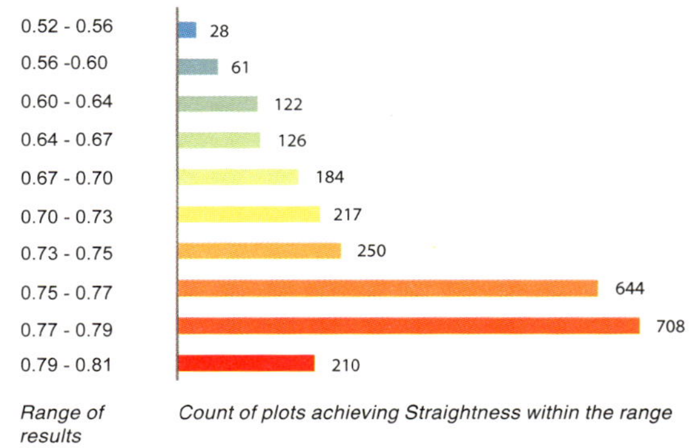

The warmer colors (greenish-yellow to red) represent Straightness values higher than 0.66, while the cooler colors (light green to dark blue) correspond to Straightness values lower than 0.67. The majority of plots, corresponding to 53% (or 1,352 out of 2,550 plots) have Straightness values ranging from 0.75 to 0.79. Among the categories shown in the legend, 708 plots have values in the range of 0.77 to 0.79, making this the most common value range; this range is represented by dark orange on the map. On average, at a 1,600 m radius, all plots in Al Satwa are 74% as straight as a straight line.

Centrality Analysis: Neighborhood Scale

Scenario 2: Streets + Alleys — 400 m Radius

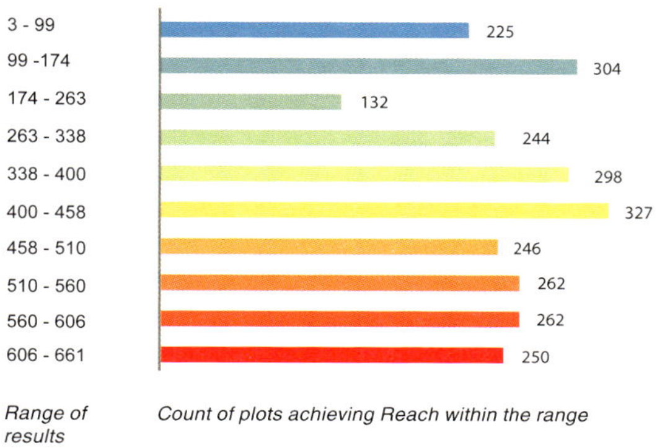

The warmer colors (i.e., greenish-yellow to red) represent a Reach value of 338 or more, while the cooler colors (i.e., light green to dark blue) correspond to a Reach value of 337 or less. Half of the total plots (i.e., 1,530 out of 2,550) have Reach values of less than 458. Among the categories shown in the legend, 13% of all plots can reach 400 to 458 other plots within 5 minutes of walking. On average, each plot in Al Satwa can access at least 385 plots within a distance of 400 m.

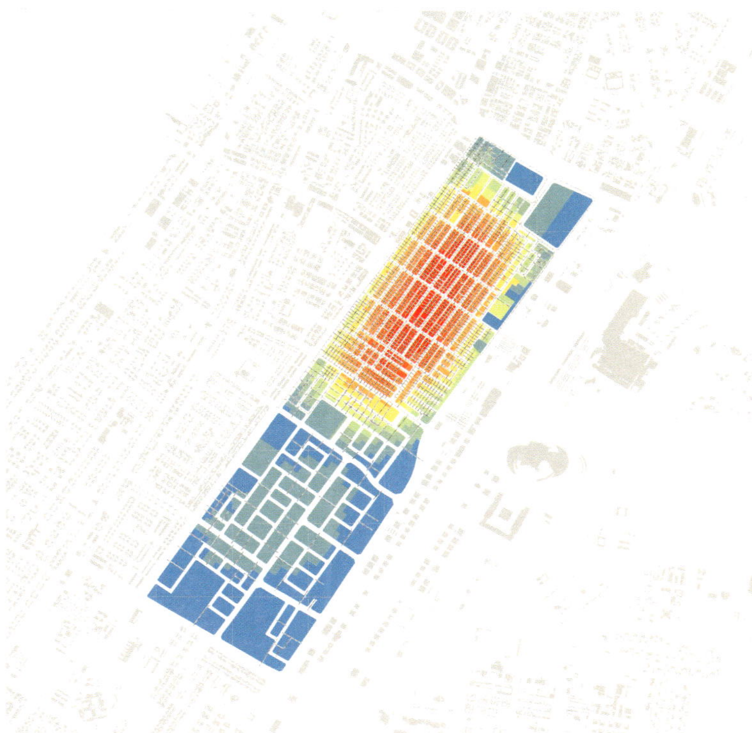

FIG. 12.1
Reach

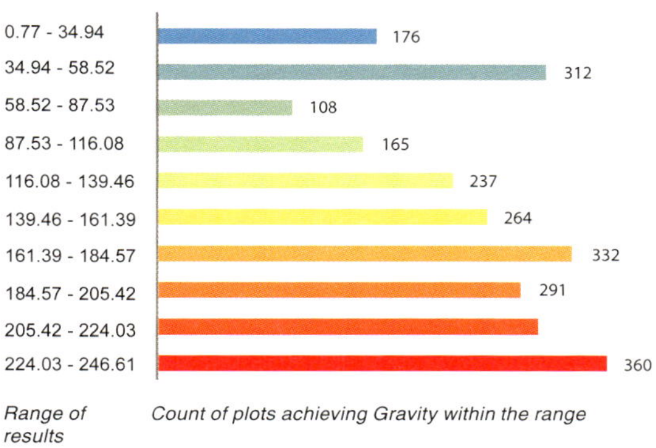

The warmer colors (i.e., greenish-yellow to red) represent Gravity values of more than 116.07, while the cooler colors (i.e., light green to dark blue) correspond to Gravity values of less than 116.08. Fifty-one percent of all plots (i.e., 1,288 out of 2,550) have Gravity values of more than 161.38. Among the categories shown in the legend, 360 plots, or 14% of the total plots, can reach 224.03 to 246.61 plots, making this the most common range; this range is represented by red on the map. On average, each plot can reach 148 other plots when spatial impedance or distance decay effect is taken into consideration.

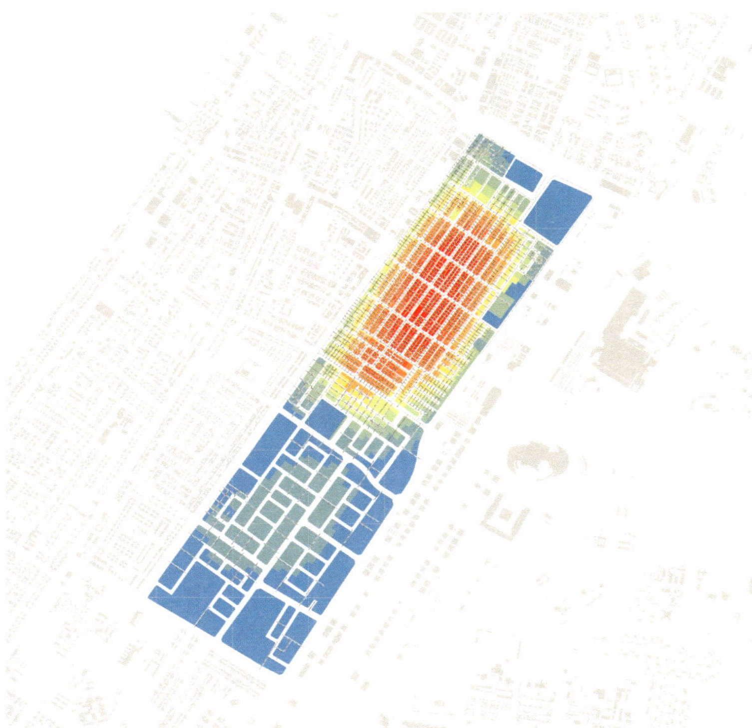

FIG. 12.2
Gravity

Scenario 2: Streets + Alleys — 400 m Radius

FIG. 12.3
Betweenness

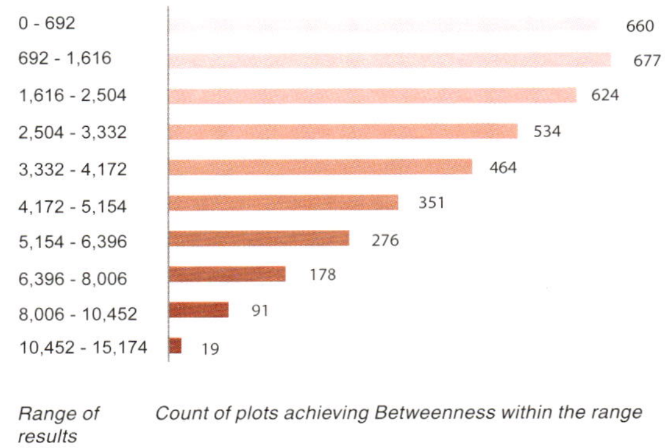

The majority of segments, corresponding to 73% (i.e., 2,845 out of 3,874 segments), have mid-range Betweenness values ranging from 865 to 6,702. Among the categories shown in the legend, 677 segments have values in the range of 692 to 1,616, making this the most common value range; this range is represented by light brown on the map. Low Betweenness values ranging from 0 to 864 are obtained by 780 segments, which is 20% of all segments. Two hundred and forty-nine segments have high Betweenness values (higher than 6,702 but smaller than 32,203) but no segments have very high Betweenness values (higher than 32,203). The average Betweenness value in Al Satwa is 2,850 (higher than 864 but smaller than 6,703), while the median is 2,473, indicating mid-range Betweenness at a 400 m radius.

FIG. 12.4
Straightness

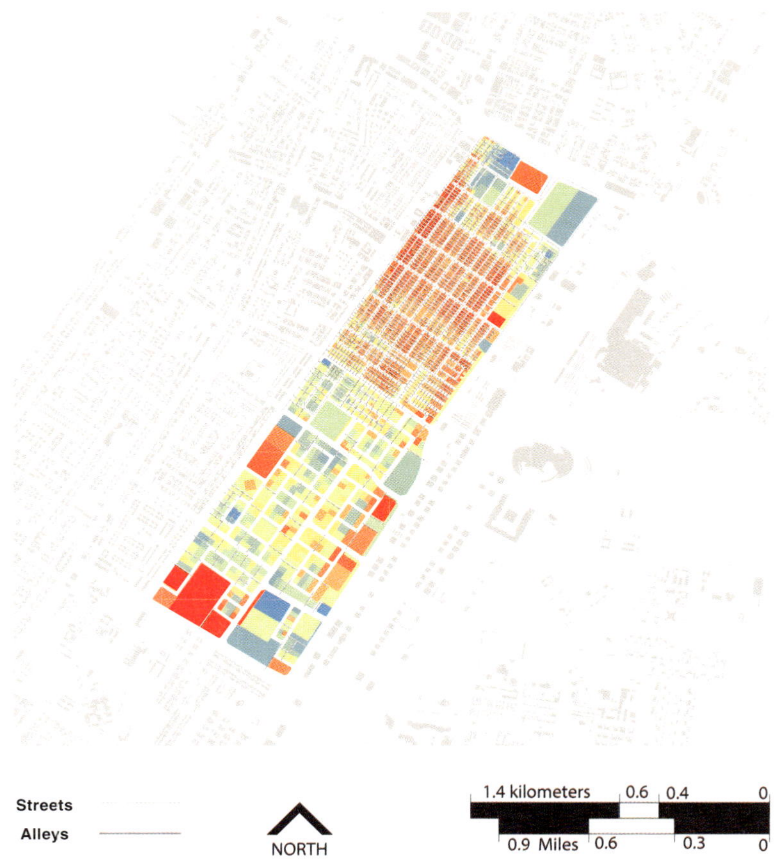

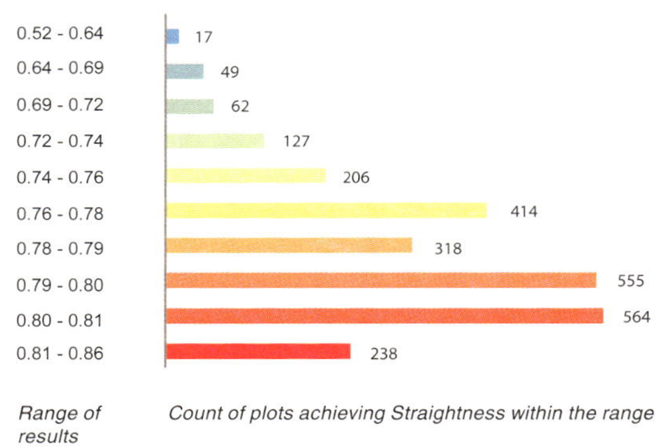

The warmer colors (greenish-yellow to red) represent Straightness values higher than 0.73, while the cooler colors (light green to dark blue) correspond to Straightness values lower than 0.74. The majority of plots, corresponding to 59% (or 1,493 out of 2,550 plots) have Straightness values ranging from 0.74 to 0.80. Among the categories shown in the legend, 564 plots have values in the range of 0.80 to 0.81, making this the most common value range; this range is represented by dark orange on the map. On average, at a 400 m radius, all plots in Al Satwa are 78% as straight as a straight line.

Scenario 2: Streets + Alleys — 800 m Radius

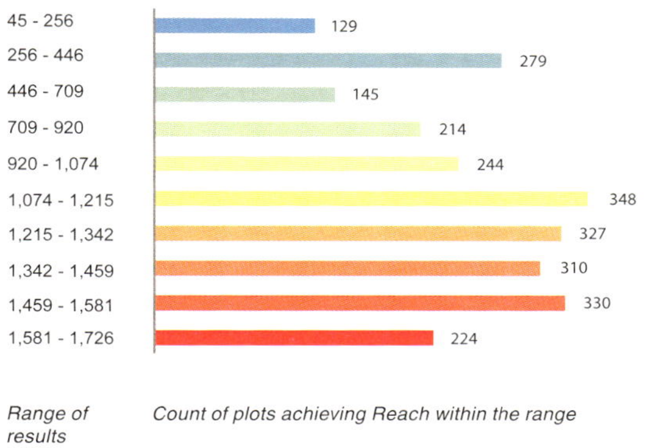

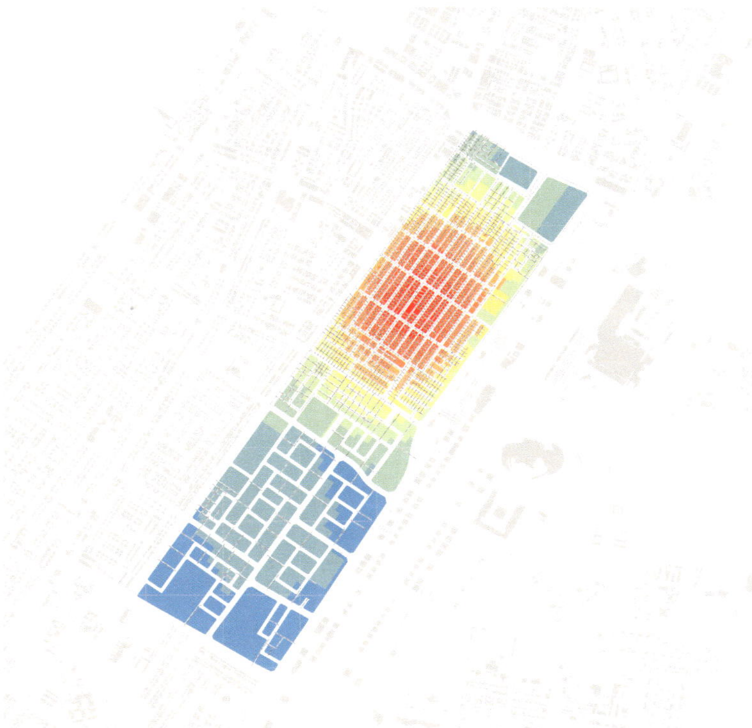

FIG. 13.1
Reach

The warmer colors (i.e., greenish-yellow to red) represent a Reach value of 920 or more, while the cooler colors (i.e., light green to dark blue) correspond to a Reach value of 919 or less. The majority of plots (i.e., 1,359 out of 2,550), corresponding to 53% of all plots, have Reach values of less than 1,215. Among the categories shown in the legend, 14% of the total plots can reach 1,074 to 1,215 other plots within 10 minutes of walking. On average, each plot in Al Satwa can access at least 1,077 plots within a distance of 800 m.

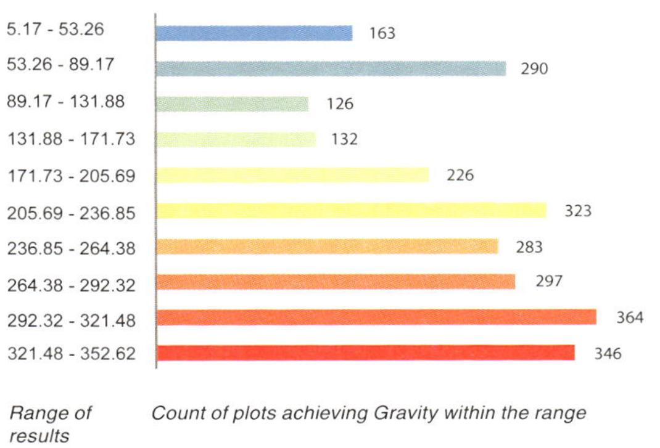

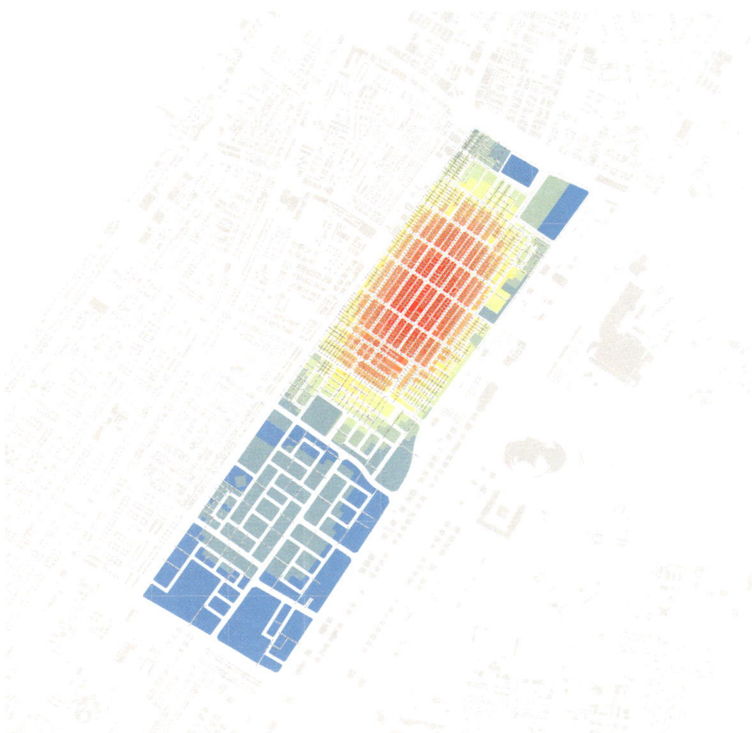

FIG. 13.2
Gravity

The warmer colors (i.e., greenish-yellow to red) represent Gravity values greater than 171.72, while the cooler colors (i.e., light green to dark blue) correspond to Gravity values lower than 171.73. Fifty-one percent of all plots (i.e., 1,290 out of 2,550) have Gravity values of more than 236.84. Among the categories shown in the legend, 364 plots, or 14% of the total plots, can reach 292.32 to 321.48 plots, making this the most common range; this range is represented by dark orange on the map. On average, each plot can reach 218 other plots when spatial impedance or distance decay effect is taken into consideration.

Scenario 2: Streets + Alleys — 800 m Radius

FIG. 13.3

Betweenness

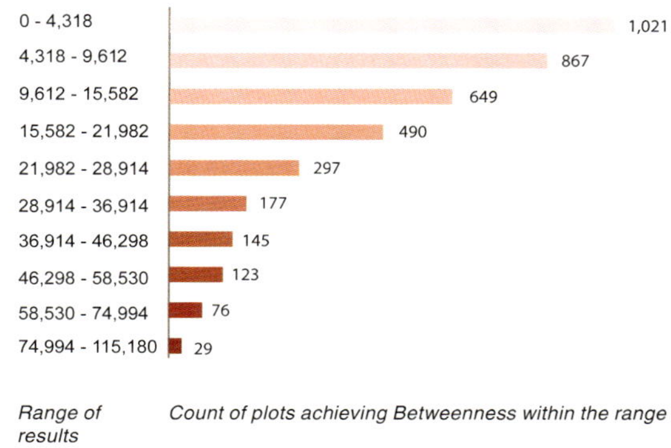

Thirty-eight percent of all segments (i.e., 1,460 out of 3,874 segments) have low Betweenness values ranging from 2,540 to 11,517. Among the categories shown in the legend, 1,021 segments have values in the range of 0 to 4,318, making this the most common value range; this range is represented by the lightest brown on the map. Very low Betweenness values ranging from 0 to 2,539 are obtained by 665 segments, which is 17% of all segments. Mid-range Betweenness values ranging from 11,518 to 20,478 are obtained by 796 segments, which is 21% of the total segments. Eight hundred and fifty-one segments have high Betweenness values (higher than 20,478 but smaller than 59,384) and 102 segments have very high Betweenness values (higher than 59,383). The average Betweenness value in Al Satwa is 15,022 (higher than 11,517 but smaller than 20,479), while the median is 9,996, indicating mid-range Betweenness at an 800 m radius.

FIG. 13.4

Straightness

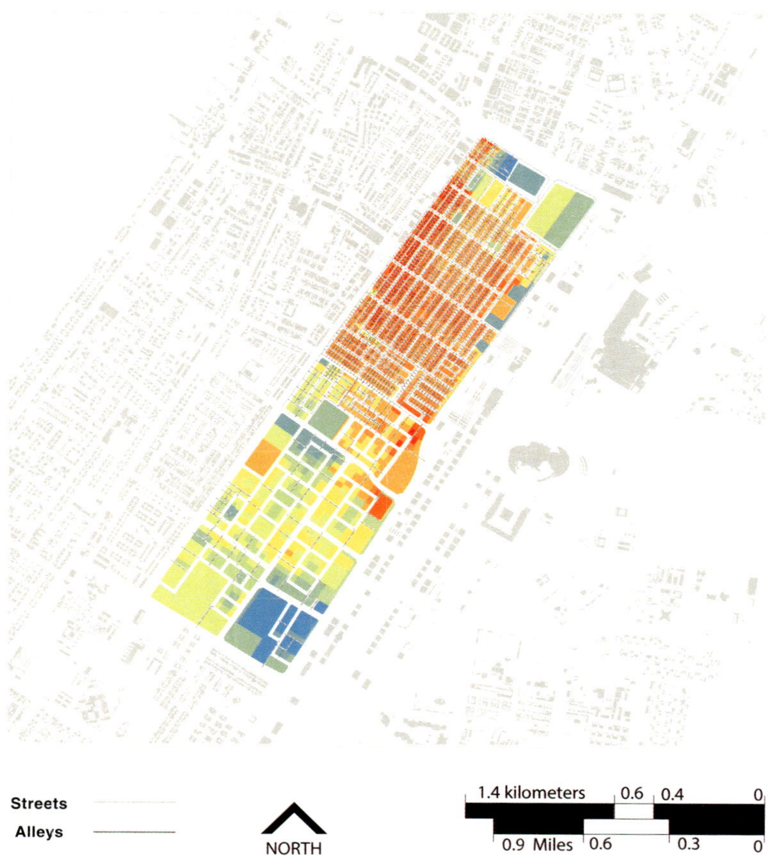

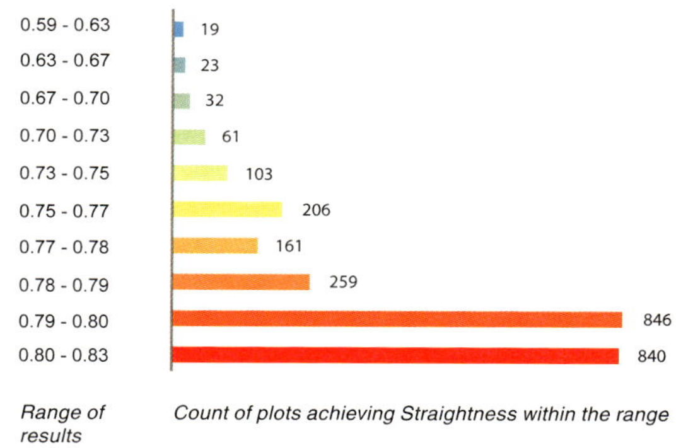

The warmer colors (greenish-yellow to red) represent Straightness values higher than 0.72, while the cooler colors (light green to dark blue) correspond to Straightness values lower than 0.73. The majority of plots, corresponding to 58% (or 1,472 out of 2,550 plots) have Straightness values ranging from 0.75 to 0.80. Among the categories shown in the legend, 846 plots have values in the range of 0.79 to 0.80, making this the most common value range; this range is represented by orange on the map. On average, at an 800 m radius, all plots in Al Satwa are 79% as straight as a straight line.

Scenario 2: Streets + Alleys — 1,600 m Radius

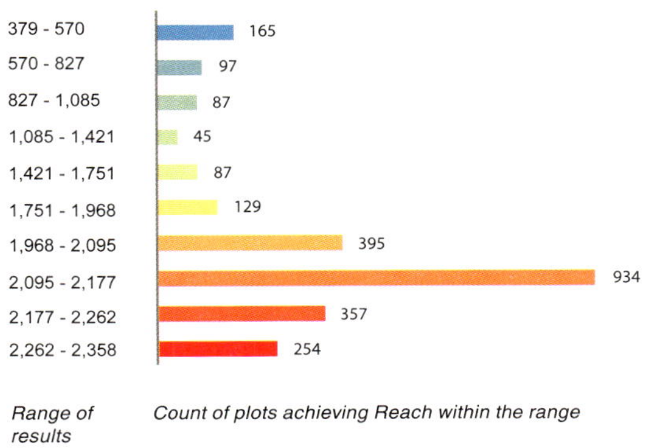

The warmer colors (i.e., greenish-yellow to red) represent a Reach value of 1,421 or more, while the cooler colors (i.e., light green to dark blue) correspond to a Reach value of 1,420 or less. The majority of plots (i.e., 1,545 out of 2,550), corresponding to 61% of all plots, have Reach values of more than 2,094. Among the categories shown in the legend, 37% of the total plots can reach 2,095 to 2,176 other plots within 20 minutes of walking. On average, each plot in Al Satwa can access at least 1,903 plots within a distance of 1,600 m.

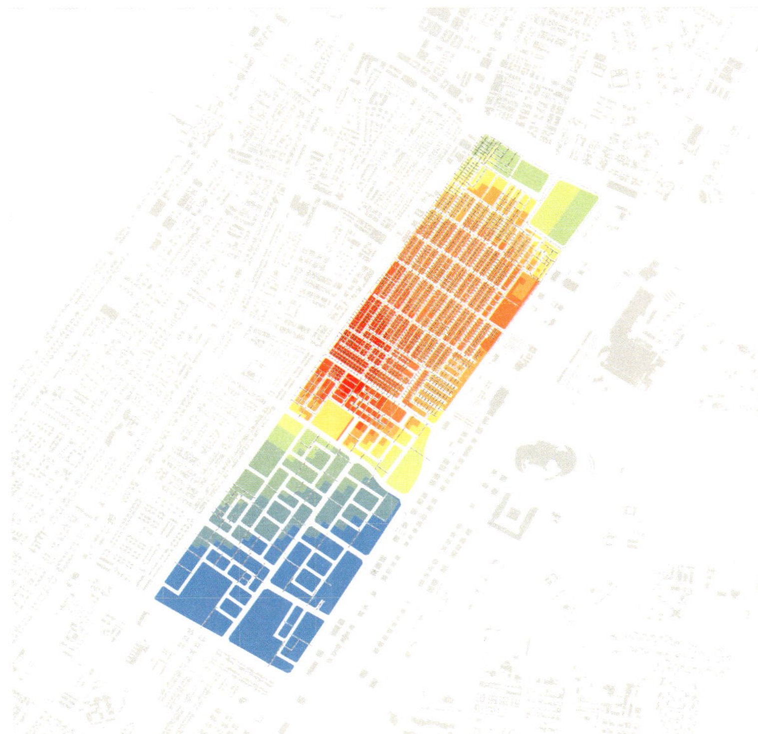

FIG. 14.1
Reach

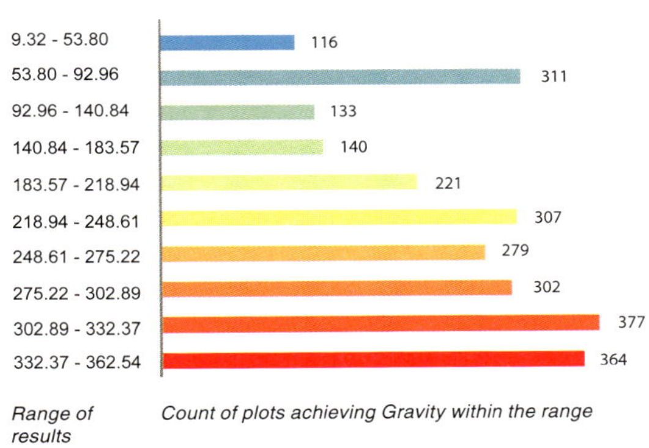

The warmer colors (i.e., greenish-yellow to red) represent Gravity values of more than 183.56, while the cooler colors (i.e., light green to dark blue) correspond to Gravity values of less than 183.57. Fifty-two percent of all plots (i.e., 1,322 out of 2,550) have Gravity values of more than 248.60. Among the categories shown in the legend, 377 plots, or 15% of the total plots, can reach 302.89 to 332.37 plots, making this the most common range; this range is represented by dark orange on the map. On average, each plot can reach 231 other plots when spatial impedance or distance decay effect is taken into consideration.

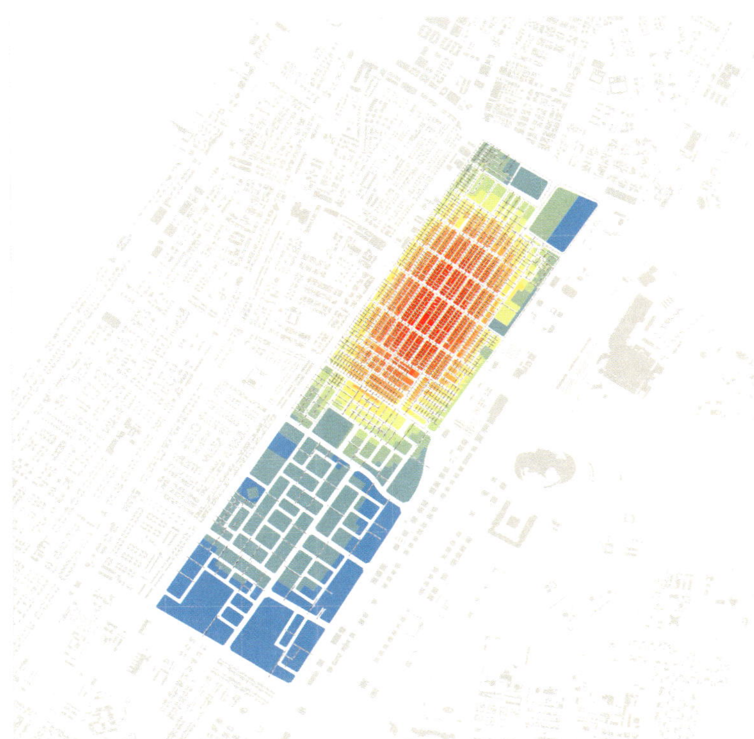

FIG. 14.2
Gravity

Scenario 2: Streets + Alleys — 1,600 m Radius

FIG. 14.3
Betweenness

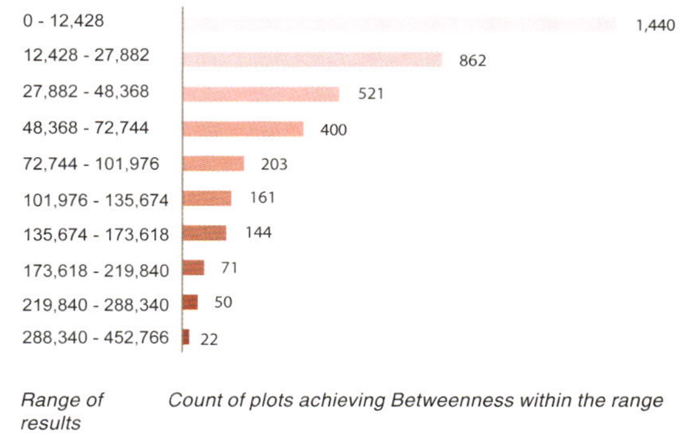

The majority of segments, corresponding to 83% (i.e., 3,232 out of 3,874 segments), have very low Betweenness values ranging from 0 to 73,682. Among the categories shown in the legend, 1,440 segments have values in the range of 0 to 12,428, making this the most common value range; this range is represented by the lightest brown on the map. Low Betweenness values ranging from 73,683 to 123,568 are obtained by 296 segments, which is 8% of all segments. Mid-range Betweenness values ranging from 123,569 to 179,444 are obtained by 217 segments, which is 6% of the total segments. Eighty-nine segments have high Betweenness values (from 179,445 to 251,415) and 40 segments have very high Betweenness values (higher than 251,415). The average Betweenness value in Al Satwa is 41,387 (smaller than 73,683), while the median is 19,822, indicating very low Betweenness at a 1,600 m radius.

FIG. 14.4
Straightness

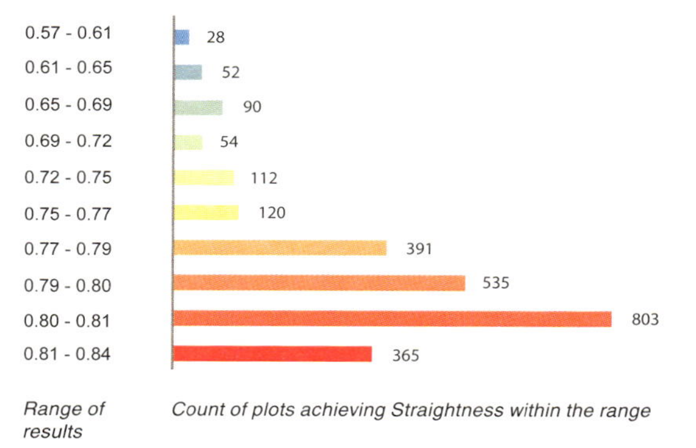

The warmer colors (greenish-yellow to red) represent Straightness values higher than 0.71, while the cooler colors (light green to dark blue) correspond to Straightness values lower than 0.72. The majority of plots, corresponding to 52% (or 1,338 out of 2,550 plots) have Straightness values ranging from 0.79 to 0.81. Among the categories shown in the legend, 803 plots have values in the range of 0.80 to 0.81, making this the most common value range; this range is represented by dark orange on the map. On average, at a 1,600 m radius, all plots in Al Satwa are 78% as straight as a straight line.

Centrality Analysis: Sample Scale

Sample 01

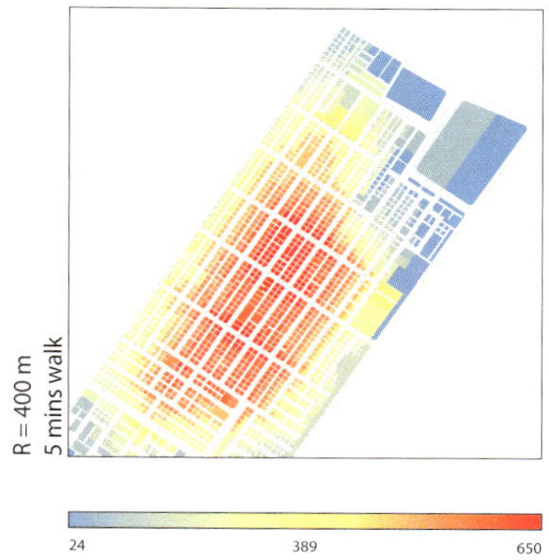

Reach (Radius = 400 m)
The maximum number of plots that can be reached within 5 minutes walking distance is 650 plots.
The average Reach of the sample is 389 plots.

Summary of Reach results
Minimum: 24
Maximum: 650
Mean: 389
Median: 400

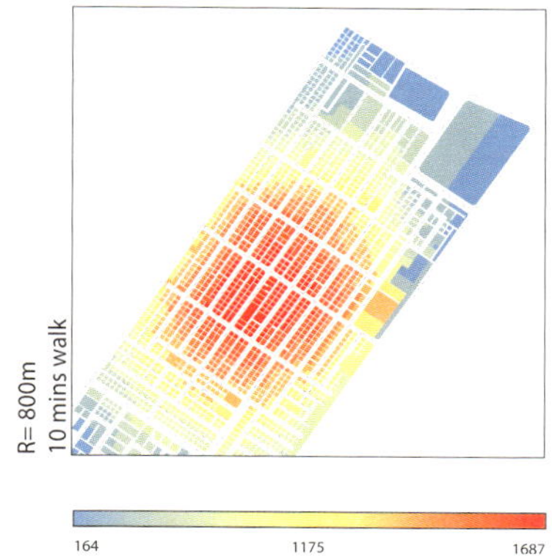

Reach (Radius = 800 m)
The maximum number of plots that can be reached within 10 minutes walking distance is 1,687 plots.
The average Reach of the sample is 1,175 plots.

Summary of Reach results
Minimum: 164
Maximum: 1,687
Mean: 1,175
Median: 1,218

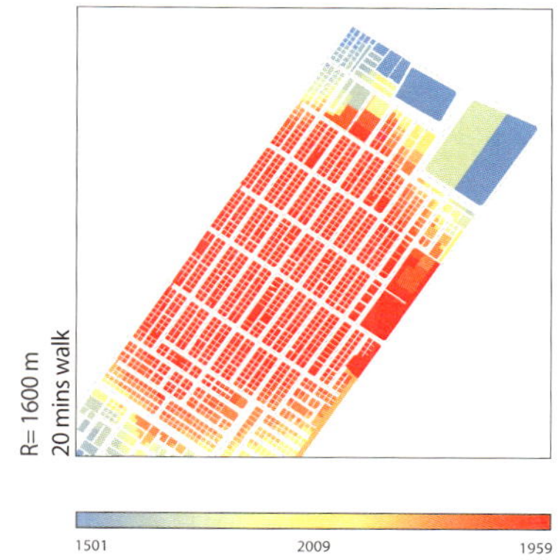

Reach (Radius = 1600 m)
The maximum number of plots that can be reached within 20 minutes walking distance is 2,009 plots.
The average Reach of the sample is 1,959 plots.

Summary of Reach results
Minimum: 1,501
Maximum: 2,009
Mean: 1,959
Median: 2,007

FIG. 15.1
Reach
Scenario 1: Streets only

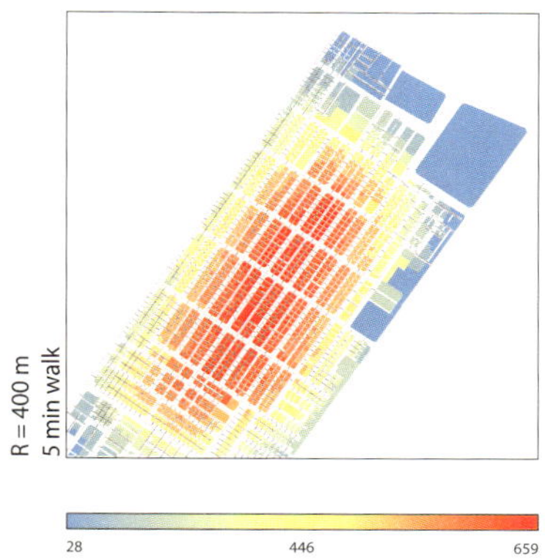

Reach (Radius = 400 m)
The maximum number of plots that can be reached within 5 minutes walking distance is 659 plots.
The average Reach of the sample is 446 plots.

Summary of Reach results
Minimum: 28
Maximum: 659
Mean: 446
Median: 454

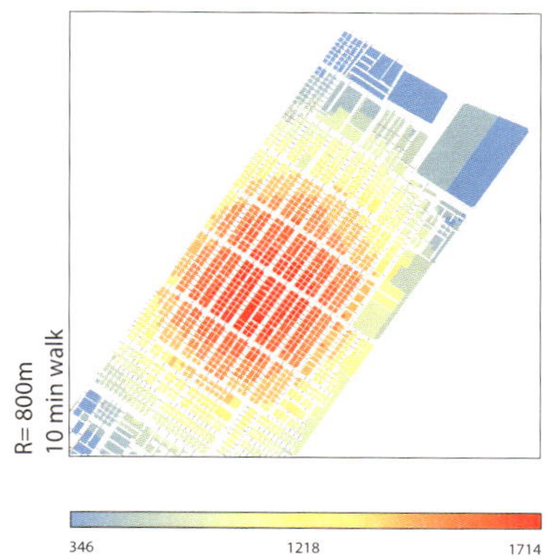

Reach (Radius = 800 m)
The maximum number of plots that can be reached within 10 minutes walking distance is 1,714 plots.
The average Reach of the sample is 1,218 plots.

Summary of Reach results
Minimum: 346
Maximum: 1,714
Mean: 1,218
Median: 1,250

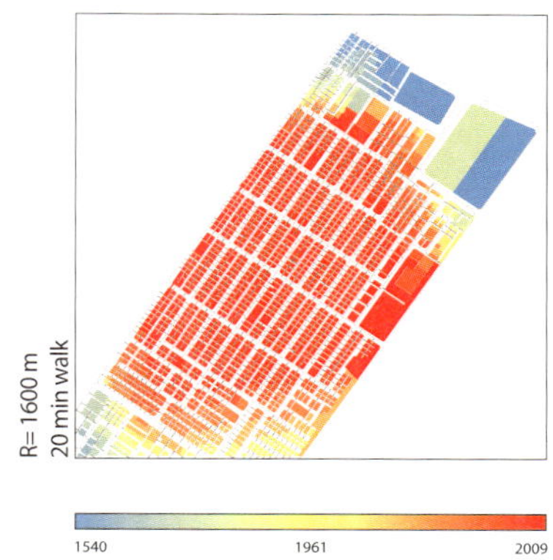

Reach (Radius = 1600 m)
The maximum number of plots that can be reached within 20 minutes walking distance is 2,009 plots.
The average Reach of the sample is 1,961 plots.

Summary of Reach results
Minimum: 1,540
Maximum: 2,009
Mean: 1,961
Median: 2,008

FIG. 15.2
Reach
Scenario 2: Streets + Alleys

At a 400 m radius, the plots with high Reach values ranging from 389 to 650 concentrate at and around the center of the sample. At an 800 m radius, high Reach values continues to accumulate at the center and forms one prominent cluster. Reach value increases for all plots and the maximum value of 1,687 is obtained by many plots at the center. At a 1,600 m radius, all plots have a Reach value greater than 1,500. With the introduction of alleys, at a 400 m radius, the concentration of high Reach values becomes stronger and clearer around the central area of the sample. At an 800 m radius, high Reach values ranging from 1,218 to 1,714 continues to be visible at the center. Similar to the case without alleys, at a 1,600 m radius, all plots have a Reach value greater than 1,539. A majority of plots have value greater than 1,960, while only a handful of plots located at the sample corners have lesser values.

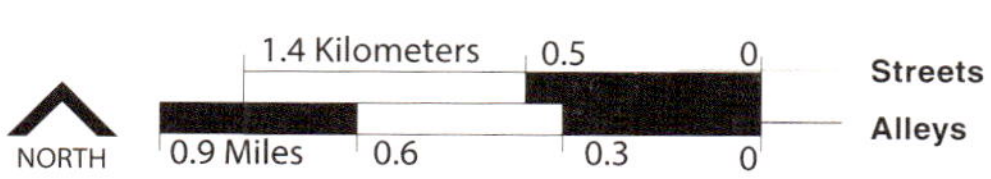

Sample 01

FIG. 15.3
Gravity
Scenario 1: Streets only

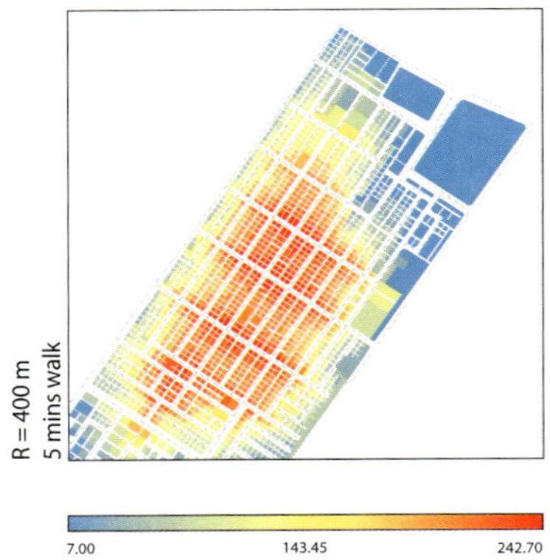

Gravity (Radius = 400 m)
The maximum number of plots that can be reached within 5 minutes walking distance with the distance decay effect is 242.70 plots. The average Gravity of the sample is 143.45 plots.

Summary of Gravity results
Minimum: 7.00
Maximum: 242.70
Mean: 143.45
Median: 149.26

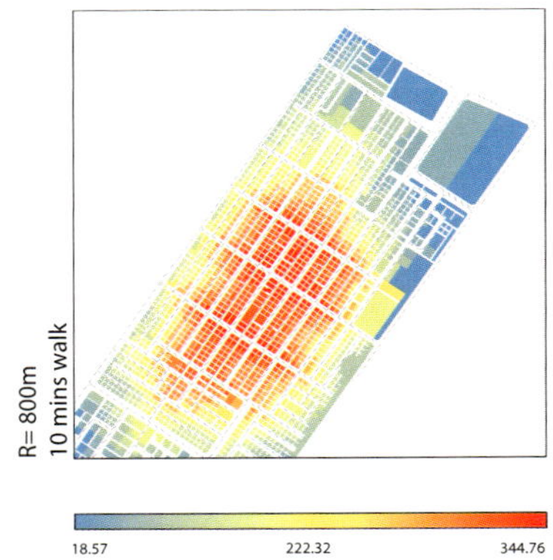

Gravity (Radius = 800 m)
The maximum number of plots that can be reached within 10 minutes walking distance with the distance decay effect is 344.76 plots. The average Gravity of the sample is 222.32 plots.

Summary of Gravity results
Minimum: 18.57
Maximum: 344.76
Mean: 222.32
Median: 227.14

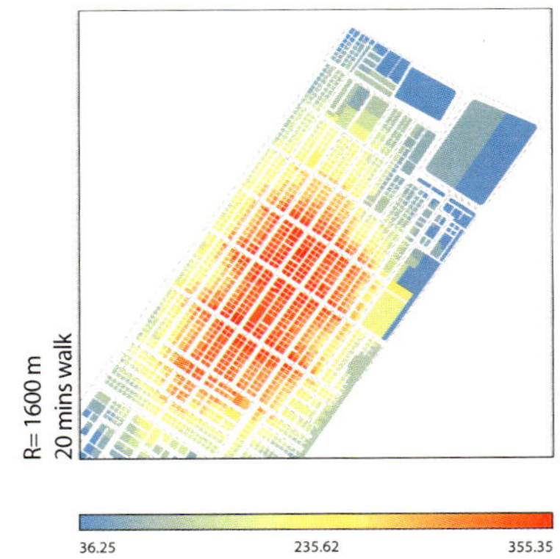

Gravity (Radius = 1600 m)
The maximum number of plots that can be reached within 20 minutes walking distance with the distance decay effect is 355.35 plots. The average Gravity of the sample is 235.62 plots.

Summary of Gravity results
Minimum: 36.25
Maximum: 355.35
Mean: 235.62
Median: 241.60

FIG. 15.4
Gravity
Scenario 2: Streets + Alleys

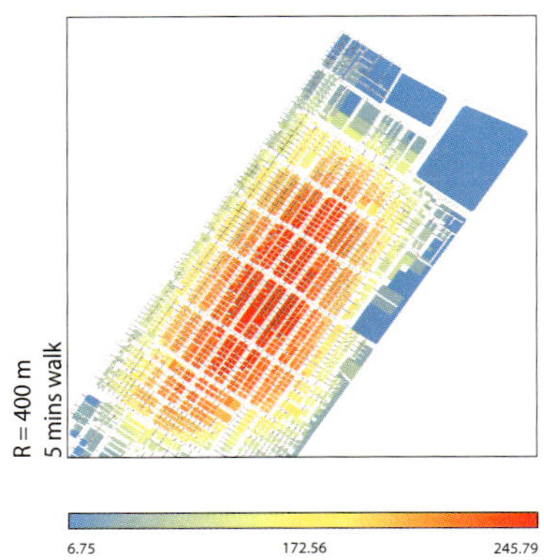

Gravity (Radius = 400 m)
The maximum number of plots that can be reached within 5 minutes walking distance with the distance decay effect is 245.79 plots. The average Gravity of the sample is 172.56 plots.

Summary of Gravity results
Minimum: 6.75
Maximum: 245.79
Mean: 172.56
Median: 178.26

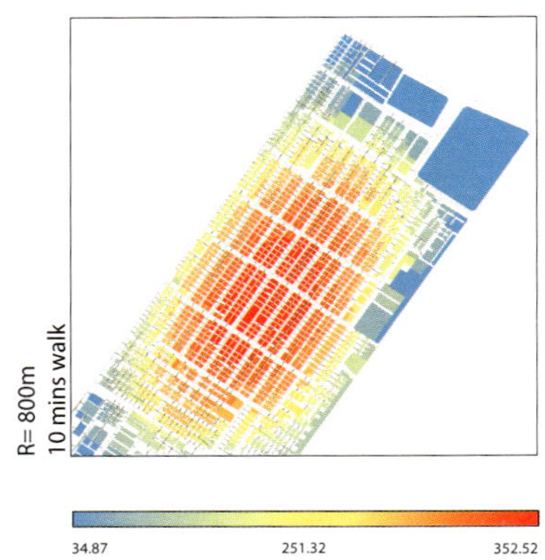

Gravity (Radius = 800 m)
The maximum number of plots that can be reached within 10 minutes walking distance with the distance decay effect is 352.52 plots. The average Gravity of the sample is 251.32 plots.

Summary of Gravity results
Minimum: 34.87
Maximum: 352.52
Mean: 251.32
Median: 257.91

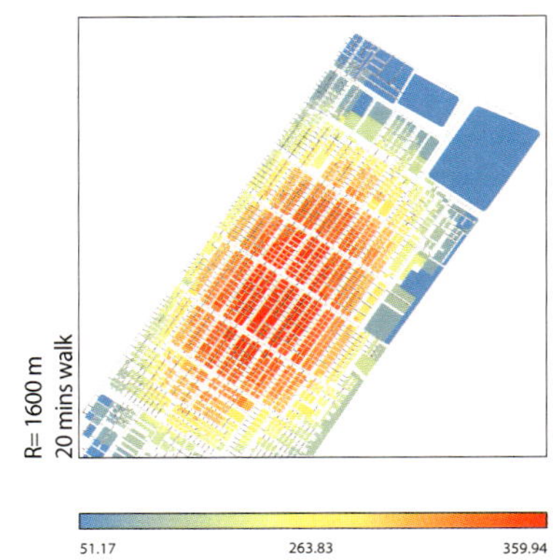

Gravity (Radius = 1600 m)
The maximum number of plots that can be reached within 20 minutes walking distance with the distance decay effect is 359.94 plots. The average Gravity of the sample is 263.83 plots.

Summary of Gravity results
Minimum: 51.17
Maximum: 359.94
Mean: 263.83
Median: 270.73

At a 400 m radius, high Gravity values ranging from 143.45 to 242.70 are obtained by plots located at and around the center of the sample. At 800 m and 1,600 m radii, high Gravity values continues to accumulate at the center where the values range from 222.32 to 355.35. With the introduction of alleys, at a 400 m radius, Gravity values improve for all plots except few plots at the corners. At 800 m and 1,600 m radii, high values continue to become even more concentrated around the center of the sample. The highest Gravity values of 352.52 and 359.94 are obtained at 800 m and 1,600 m radii respectively. The distribution of Gravity values does not change significantly when radius is changed; however, the values are improved for all plots when the radius increases.

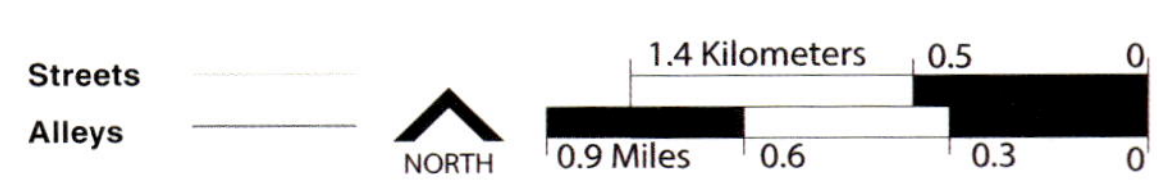

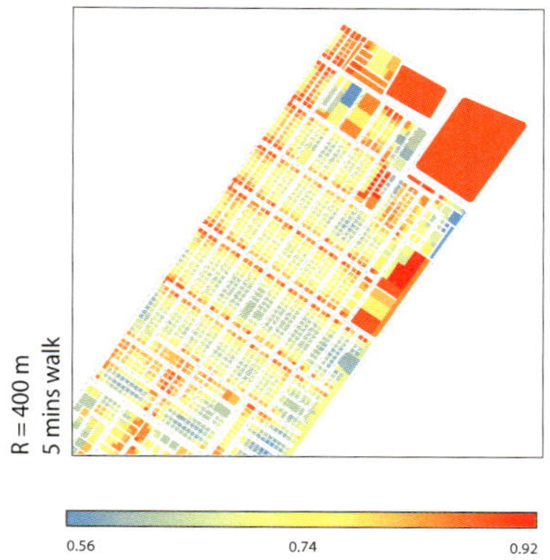

Straightness (Normalized Values, Radius = 400 m)
Plots withing 5 minutes walking distance have access to streets with an average Straightness value of 0.74

Summary of Straighness results
Minimum: 0.56
Maximum: 0.92
Mean: 0.74
Median: 0.74

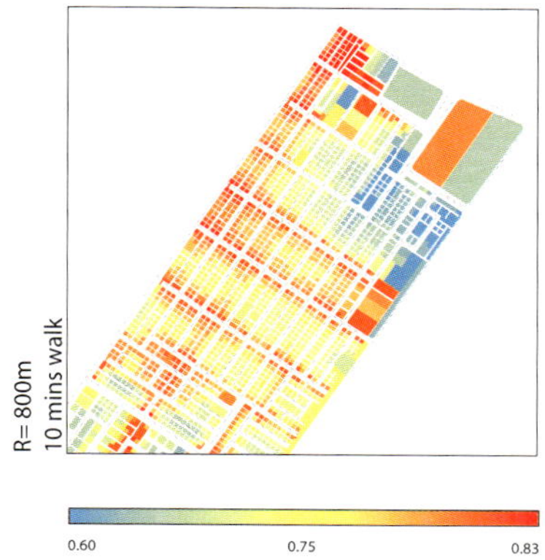

Straightness (Normalized Values, Radius = 800 m)
Plots withing 10 minutes walking distance have access to streets with an average Straightness value of 0.75

Summary of Straighness results
Minimum: 0.60
Maximum: 0.83
Mean: 0.75
Median: 0.76

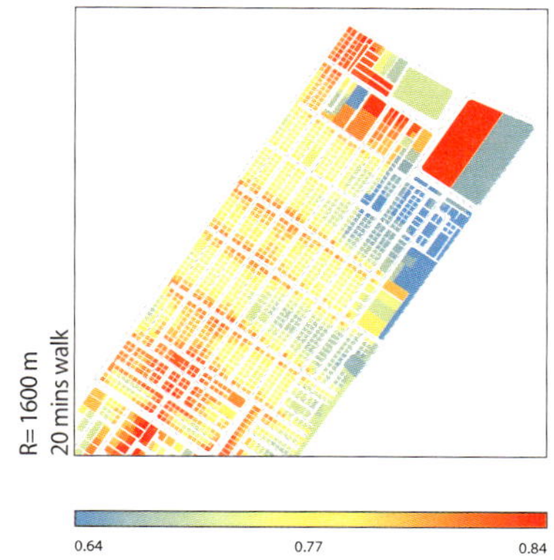

Straightness (Normalized Values, Radius = 1600 m)
Plots withing 20 minutes walking distance have access to streets with an average Straightness value of 0.77

Summary of Straighness results
Minimum: 0.64
Maximum: 0.77
Mean: 0.84
Median: 0.77

FIG. 15.5
Straightness
Scenario 1: Streets only

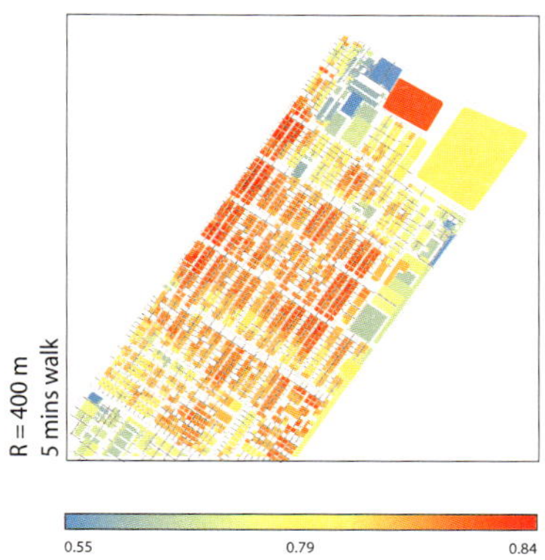

Straightness (Normalized Values, Radius = 400 m)
lots withing 5 minutes walking distance have access to streets with an average Straightness value of 0.79

Summary of Straightness results
Minimum: 0.55
Maximum: 0.84
Mean: 0.79
Median: 0.80

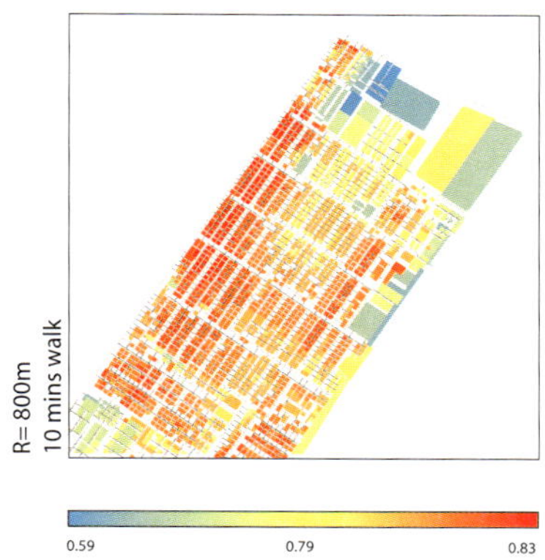

Straightness (Normalized Values, Radius = 800 m)
lots withing 10 minutes walking distance have access to streets with an average Straightness value of 0.79

Summary of Straightness results
Minimum: 0.59
Maximum: 0.83
Mean: 0.79
Median: 0.80

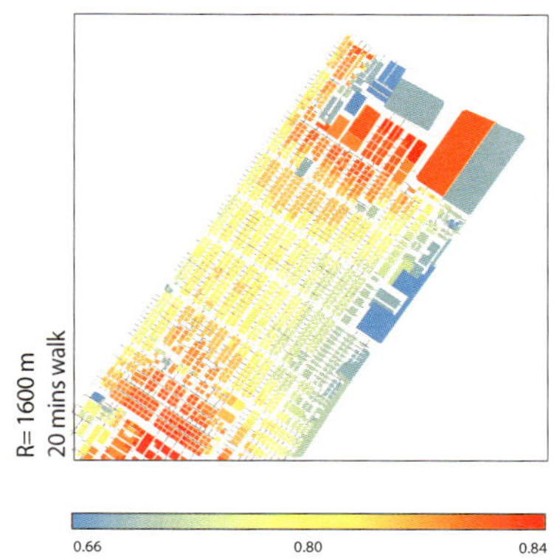

Straightness (Normalized Values, Radius = 1600 m)
Plots withing 20 minutes walking distance have access to streets with an average Straightness value of 0.80

Summary of Straightness results
Minimum: 0.66
Maximum: 0.84
Mean: 0.80
Median: 0.80

FIG. 15.6
Straightness
Scenario 2: Streets + Alleys

At a 400 m radius, high Straightness values (0.75 to 1.00) are obtained by plots along the longer internal streets that connect to the collector street at top. At an 800 m radius, high Straightness values become even more concentrated towards the top right part of the sample. At a 1,600 m radius, Straightness value increases for most plots and the maximum value increases from 0.83 at 800 m to 0.84. With the introduction of alleys, at 400 m, high Straightness values (0.75 to 1.00) are obtained by a great majority of plots concentrated around the center, near the longer internal streets. At 800 m, a prominent cluster of high values appears on the top side adjacent to the collector street. At a 1,600 m radius, high Straightness values shift and form two separate clusters at the upper and lower parts of the sample. The Straightness value increases slightly for all plots when the radius increases.

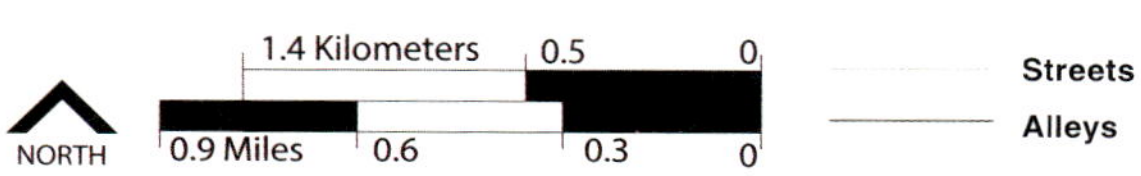

Sample 02

FIG. 16.1
Reach
Scenario 1: Streets only

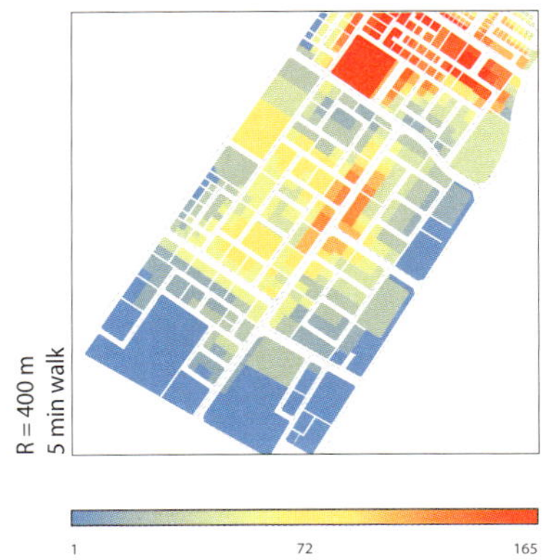

Reach (Radius = 400 m)
The maximum number of plots that can be reached within 5 minutes walking distance is 165 plots.
The average Reach of the sample is 72 plots.

Summary of Reach results
Minimum: 1
Maximum: 165
Mean: 72
Median: 69

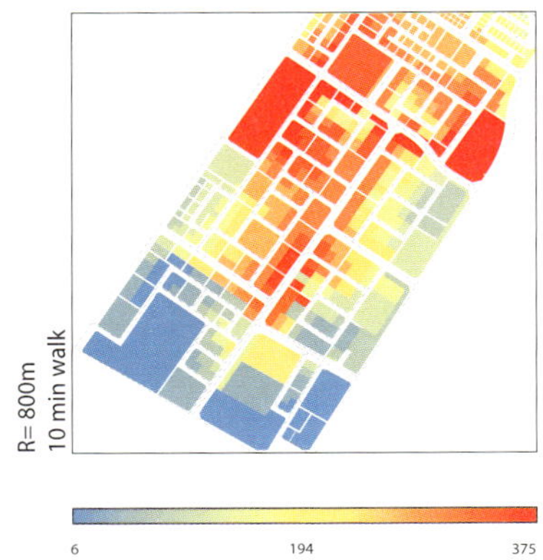

Reach (Radius = 800 m)
The maximum number of plots that can be reached within 10 minutes walking distance is 375 plots.
The average Reach of the sample is 194 plots.

Summary of Reach results
Minimum: 6
Maximum: 375
Mean: 194
Median: 215

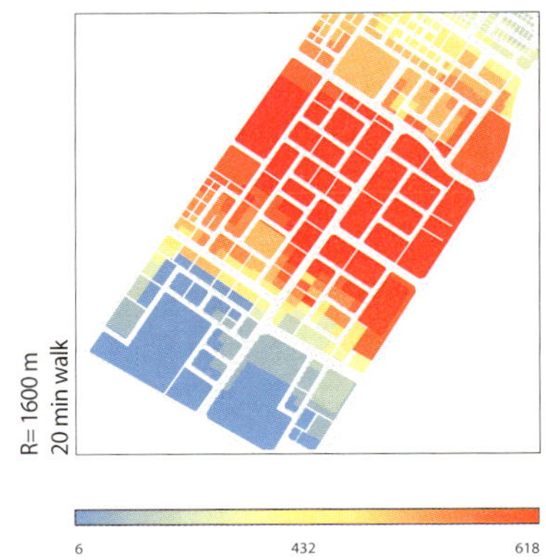

Reach (Radius = 1600 m)
The maximum number of plots that can be reached within 20 minutes walking distance is 618 plots.
The average Reach of the sample is 432 plots.

Summary of Reach results
Minimum: 6
Maximum: 618
Mean: 432
Median: 469

FIG. 16.2
Reach
Scenario 2: Streets + Alleys

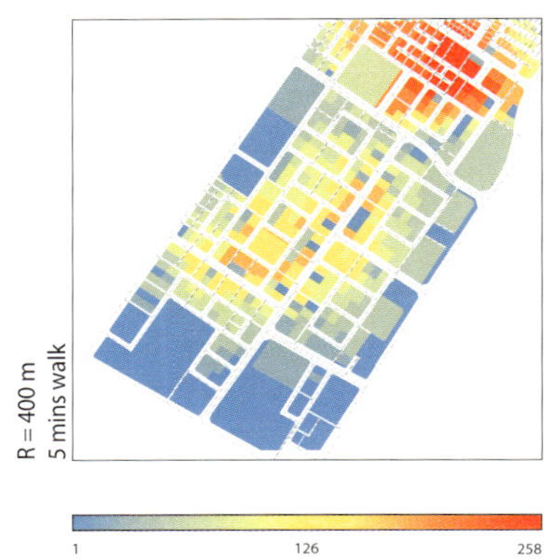

Reach (Radius = 400 m)
The maximum number of plots that can be reached within 5 minutes walking distance is 258 plots.
The average Reach of the sample is 126 plots.

Summary of Reach results
Minimum: 1
Maximum: 258
Mean: 126
Median: 121

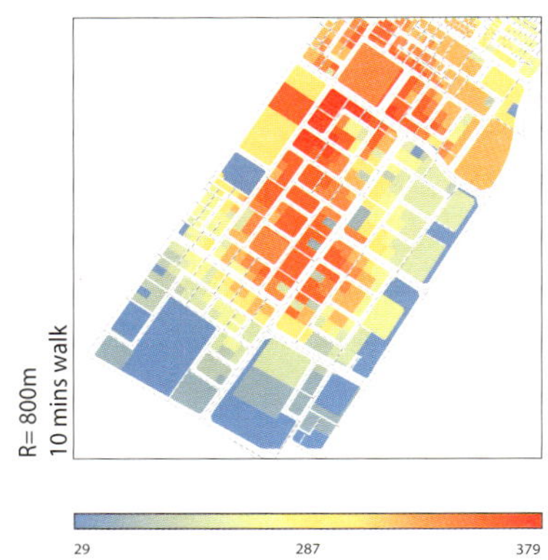

Reach (Radius = 800 m)
The maximum number of plots that can be reached within 10 minutes walking distance is 379 plots.
The average Reach of the sample is 287 plots.

Summary of Reach results
Minimum: 29
Maximum: 379
Mean: 287
Median: 306

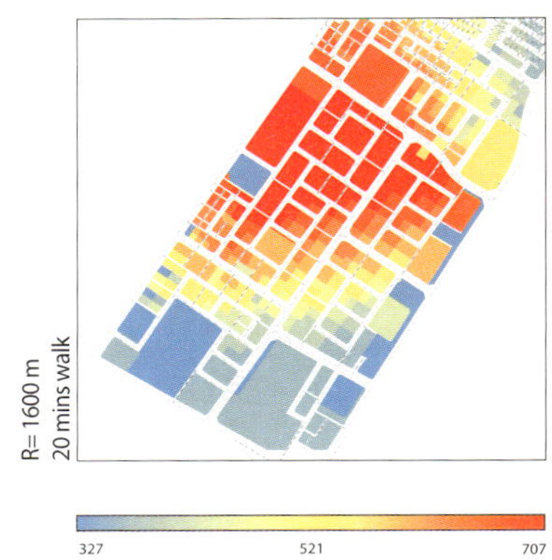

Reach (Radius = 1600 m)
The maximum number of plots that can be reached within 20 minutes walking distance is 707 plots.
The average Reach of the sample is 521 plots.

Summary of Reach results
Minimum: 327
Maximum: 707
Mean: 521
Median: 521

At a 400 m radius, the plots with high Reach values ranging from 72 to 165 concentrate at the upper side of the sample where the plots are smaller and lie in close proximity to each other as compared to other plots in the lower part. At an 800 m radius, high Reach values extend towards the center of the sample. Reach value increases considerably for all plots and the maximum value of 375 are obtained by some plots located near the intersections of collector streets. At a 1,600 m radius, all plots have Reach values greater than 5. A single prominent cluster is formed at the center where all plots have maximum Reach value of 618. With the introduction of alleys, at a 400 m radius, Reach value increases slightly for all plots. At an 800 m radius, high Reach values ranging from 287 to 379 are visible at the center. At a 1,600 m radius, high Reach values continue to become even more concentrated around the center, although it is more prominent towards the upper side of the sample.

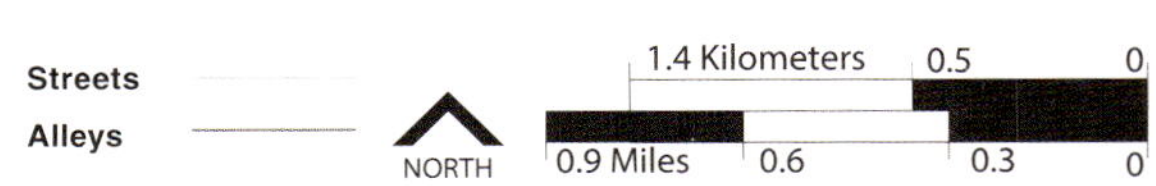

FIG. 16.3

Gravity

Scenario 1: Streets only

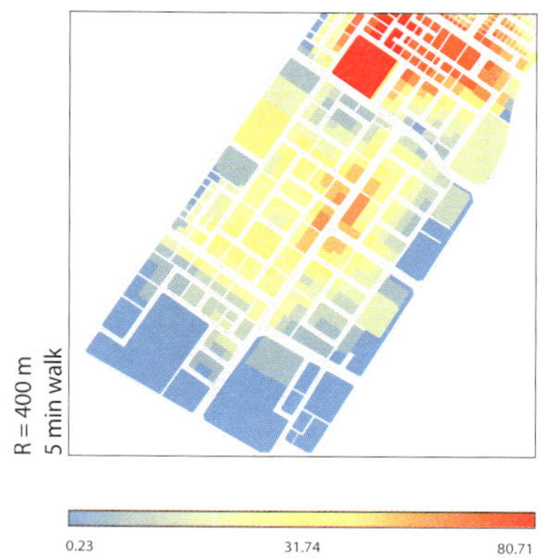

Gravity (Radius = 400 m)

The maximum number of plots that can be reached within 5 minutes walking distance with the distance decay effect is 80.71 plots. The average Gravity of the sample is 31.74 plots.

Summary of Gravity results
Minimum: 0.23
Maximum: 80.71
Mean: 31.97
Median: 29.88

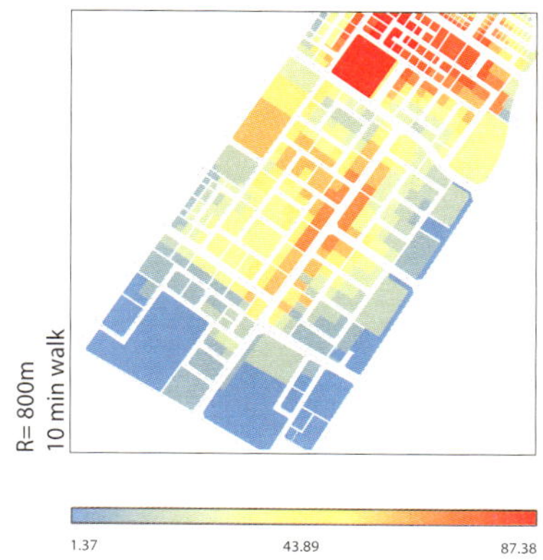

Gravity (Radius = 800 m)

The maximum number of plots that can be reached within 10 minutes walking distance with the distance decay effect is 87.38 plots. The average Gravity of the sample is 43.89 plots.

Summary of Gravity results
Minimum: 1.37
Maximum: 87.38
Mean: 43.89
Median: 45.61

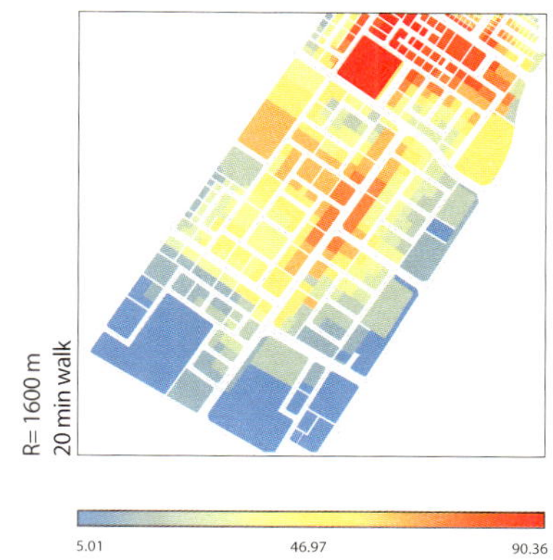

Gravity (Radius = 1600 m)

The maximum number of plots that can be reached within 20 minutes walking distance with the distance decay effect is 90.36 plots. The average Gravity of the sample is 46.97 plots.

Summary of Gravity results
Minimum: 5.01
Maximum: 90.36
Mean: 46.97
Median: 49.54

FIG. 16.4

Gravity

Scenario 2: Streets + Alleys

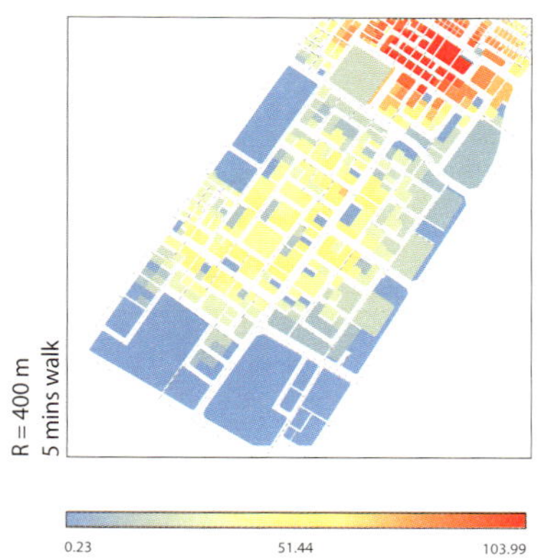

Gravity (Radius = 400 m)

The maximum number of plots that can be reached within 5 minutes walking distance with the distance decay effect is 103.99 plots. The average Gravity of the sample is 51.44 plots.

Summary of Gravity results
Minimum: 0.23
Maximum: 103.99
Mean: 51.44

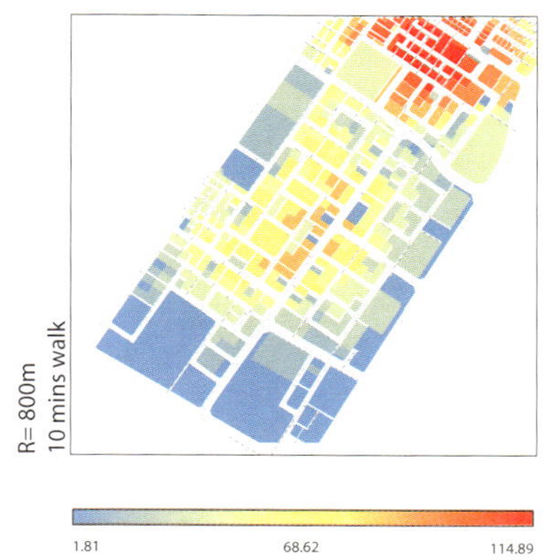

Gravity (Radius = 800 m)

The maximum number of plots that can be reached within 10 minutes walking distance with the distance decay effect is 114.89 plots. The average Gravity of the sample is 68.62 plots.

Summary of Gravity results
Minimum: 1.81
Maximum: 114.89
Mean: 68.62

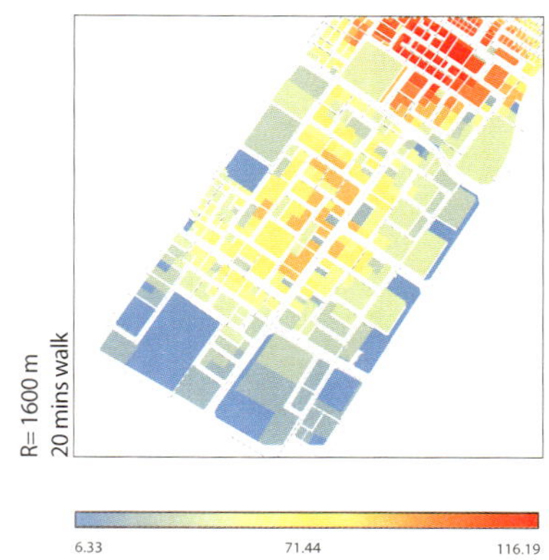

Gravity (Radius = 1600 m)

The maximum number of plots that can be reached within 20 minutes walking distance with the distance decay effect is 116.19 plots. The average Gravity of the sample is 71.44 plots.

Summary of Gravity results
Minimum: 6.33
Maximum: 116.19
Mean: 71.44

At a 400 m radius, high Gravity values ranging from 31.74 to 80.71 are found at the upper side of the sample where the plots are smaller and lie in close proximity to each other as compared to other plots in the lower part. At 800 m and 1,600 m radii, high Gravity values also appear at the center where the values range from 43.89 to 90.36. With the introduction of alleys, at a 400 m radius, Gravity continues to concentrate at the same spots on the upper side. At 800 m and 1,600 m radii, high values are also obtained by few plots at the center of the sample. The highest Gravity values of 114.89 and 116.19 are obtained at 800 m and 1,600 m radii respectively. The distribution of Gravity values does not change when the radius is changed; however, the values are improved for all plots when the radius increases.

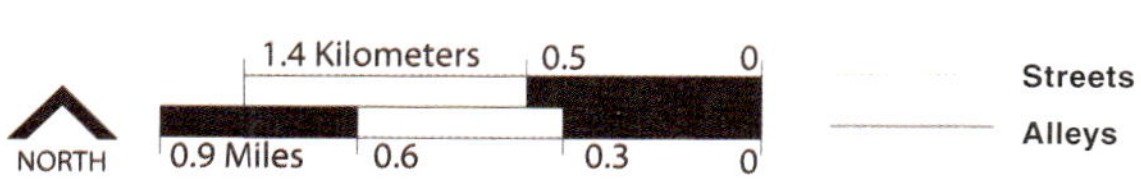

Sample 02

FIG. 16.5
Straightness
Scenario 1: Streets only

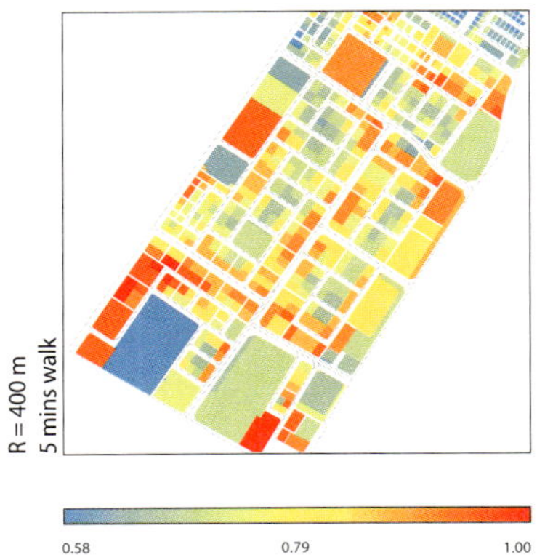

Straightness (Normalized Values, Radius = 400 m)
Plots withing 5 minutes walking distance have access to streets with an average Straightness value of 0.79

Summary of Straighness results
Minimum: 0.58
Maximum: 1.00
Mean: 0.79
Median: 0.77

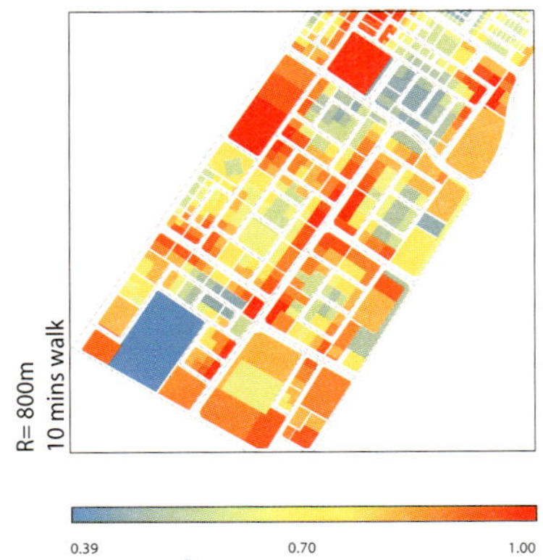

Straightness (Normalized Values, Radius = 800 m)
Plots withing 10 minutes walking distance have access to streets with an average Straightness value of 0.70

Summary of Straighness results
Minimum: 0.39
Maximum: 1.00
Mean: 0.70
Median: 0.69

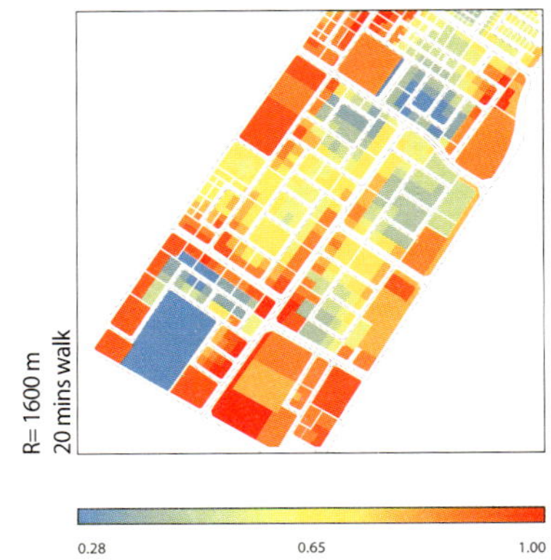

Straightness (Normalized Values, Radius = 1600 m)
Plots withing 20 minutes distance have access to streets with an average Straightness value of 0.65

Summary of Straighness results
Minimum: 0.28
Maximum: 1.00
Mean: 0.65
Median: 0.62

FIG. 16.6
Straightness
Scenario 2: Streets + Alleys

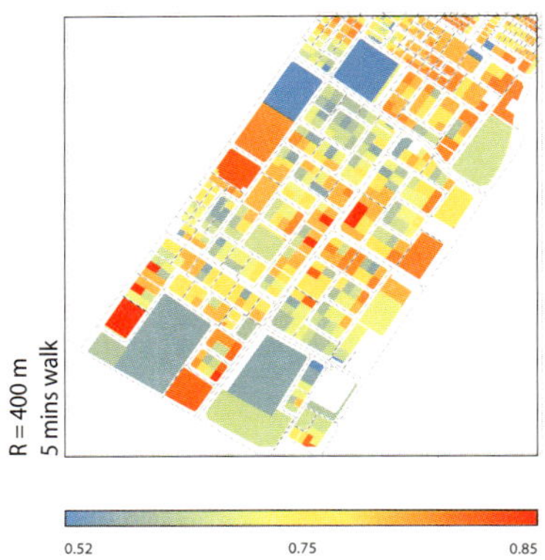

Straightness (Normalized Values, Radius = 400 m)
Plots withing 5 minutes walking distance have access to streets with an average Straightness value of 0.75

Summary of Straighness results
Minimum: 0.52
Maximum: 0.85
Mean: 0.75
Median: 0.75

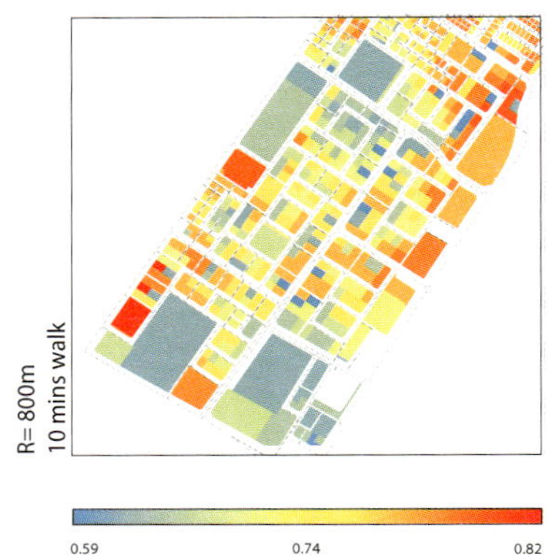

Straightness (Normalized Values, Radius = 800 m)
Plots withing 10 minutes walking distance have access to streets with an average Straightness value of 0.74

Summary of Straighness results
Minimum: 0.59
Maximum: 0.82
Mean: 0.74
Median: 0.75

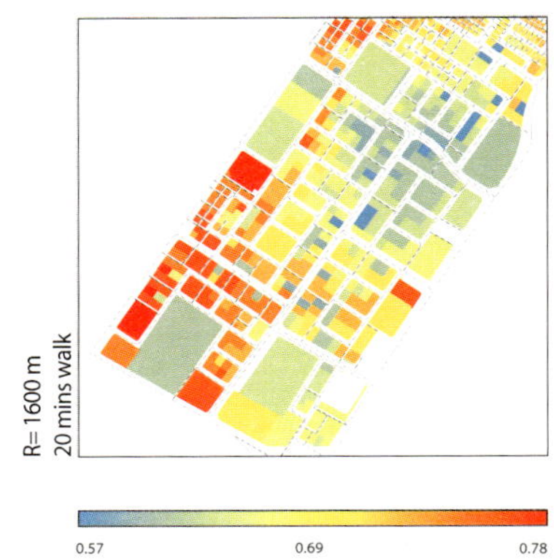

Straightness (Normalized Values, Radius = 1600 m)
Plots withing 20 minutes walking distance have access to streets with an average Straightness value of 0.69

Summary of Straighness results
Minimum: 0.57
Maximum: 0.78
Mean: 0.69
Median: 0.68

At a 400 m radius, high Straightness values (0.75 to 1.00) are obtained by some plots lying adjacent to the longer internal streets and the collector street located at the top of the sample. At an 800 m radius, high Straightness values become even more concentrated along the centrally-located internal street, and also near the collector street on the top side. At a 1,600 m radius, Straightness value slightly increases for all plots while maintaining the same distribution. With the introduction of alleys, at 400 m and 800 m radii, high Straightness values (0.75 to 1.00) are distributed evenly without a discernable pattern. At a 1,600 m radius, high Straightness values concentrate near the arterial street at the bottom left corner of the sample.

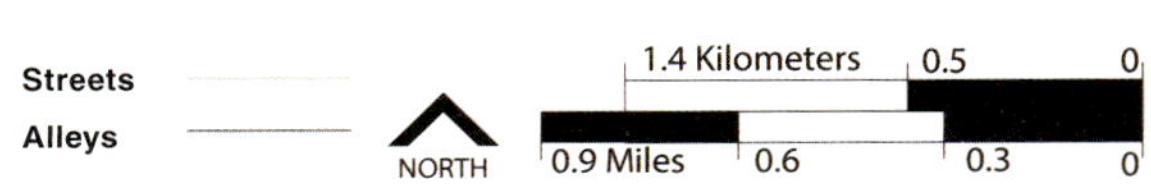

Summary of Centrality Results

Neighborhood

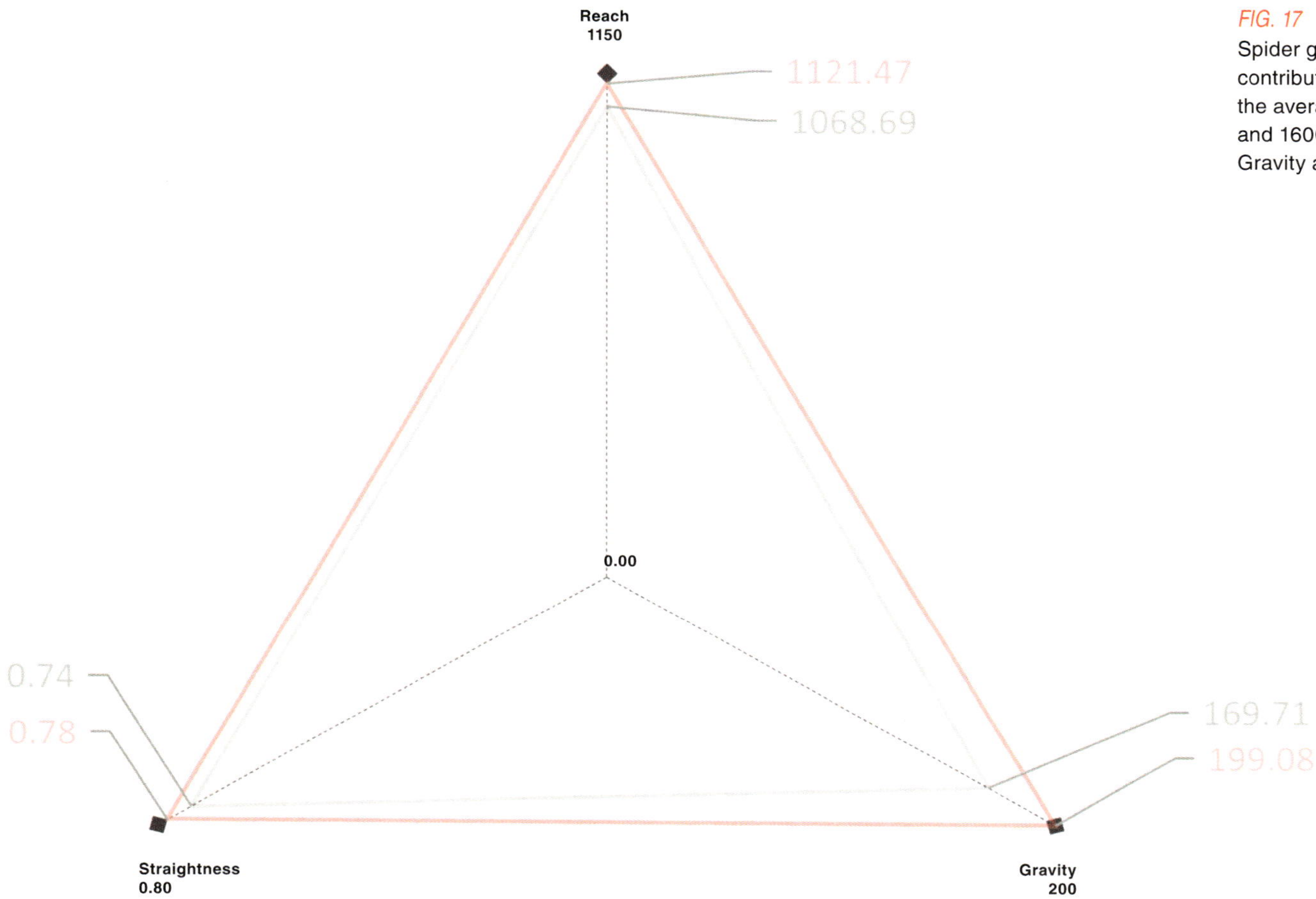

FIG. 17
Spider graphs showing the contribution of alleyways to the averages of 400m, 800m, and 1600m scales of Reach, Gravity and Straightness

Sample 01

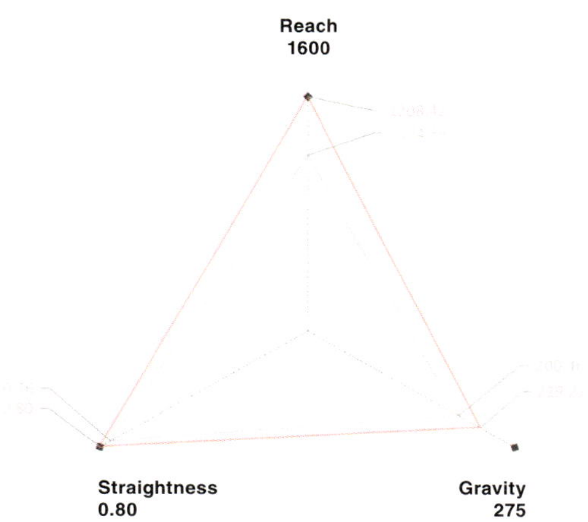

Sample 02

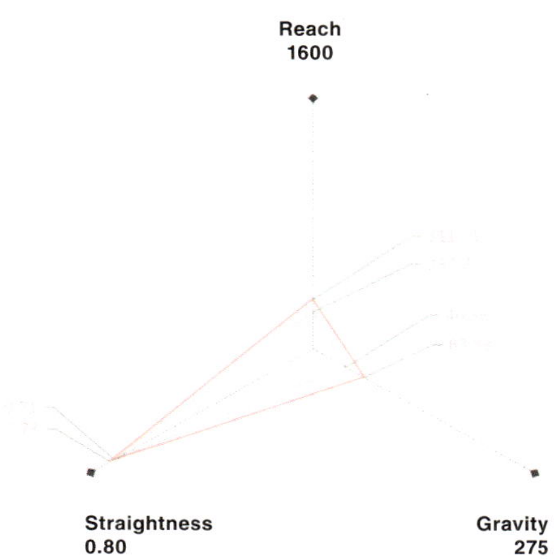

Neighborhood Scale

FIG. 18

Histograms showing the distribution of centrality values (Reach, Gravity, and Straightness) among plots with and without alleys at three different scales 400m, 800m, and 1600m. The X axis is for the centrality metric values, while the Y axis is for the percentage of plots achieving a centrality value denoted on the X axis.

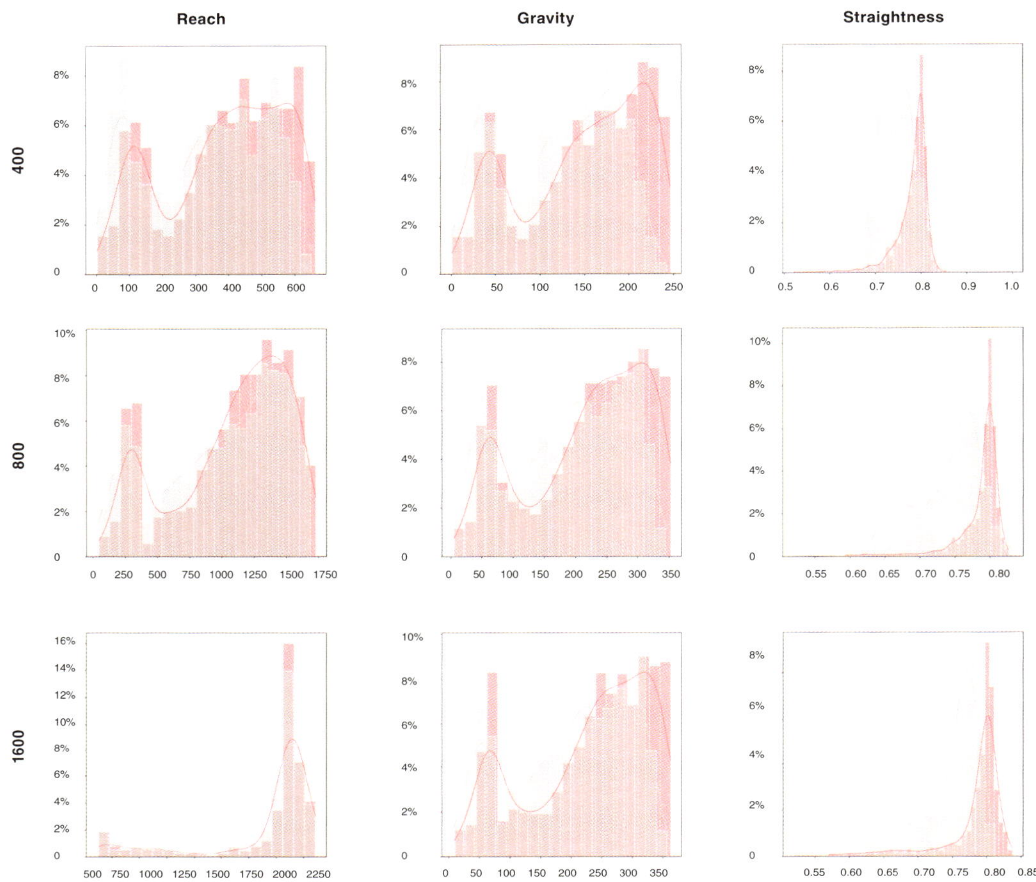

TABLE. 1

Neighborhood scale centrality values

UNA		Radius	Min	Max	Avg
Scenario 1: Streets only	Reach	400	1	649	325
		800	35	1683	1003
		1600	367	2353	1878
	Gravity	400	0.23	242.51	120.24
		800	3.19	343.92	187.88
		1600	6.54	356.06	201.01
	Straightness	400	0.57	1.00	0.75
		800	0.52	0.83	0.74
		1600	0.52	0.81	0.74

UNA		Radius	Min	Max	Avg
Scenario 2: Streets + Alleys	Reach	400	3	661	385
		800	45	1726	1077
		1600	379	2358	1903
	Gravity	400	0.77	246.61	148.19
		800	5.17	352.62	218.30
		1600	9.32	362.54	230.76
	Straightness	400	0.52	0.86	0.78
		800	0.59	0.83	0.79
		1600	0.57	0.84	0.78

Sample Scale — Sample 01

FIG. 19

Histograms showing the distribution of centrality values (Reach, Gravity, and Straightness) among plots with and without alleys at three different scales 400m, 800m, and 1600m. The X axis is for the centrality metric values, while the Y axis is for the percentage of plots achieving a centrality value denoted on the X axis.

UNA		Radius	Min	Max	Avg
Scenario 1: Streets only	Reach	400	24	650	389
		800	164	1687	1175
		1600	1501	2009	1959
	Gravity	400	7.00	242.70	143.45
		800	18.57	344.76	222.31
		1600	36.25	355.35	235.62
	Straightness	400	0.56	0.92	0.74
		800	0.60	0.83	0.75
		1600	0.64	0.84	0.77

UNA		Radius	Min	Max	Avg
Scenario 2: Streets + Alleys	Reach	400	28	659	446
		800	346	1714	1218
		1600	1540	2009	1961
	Gravity	400	6.75	245.79	172.55
		800	34.87	352.52	251.32
		1600	51.17	359.94	263.83
	Straightness	400	0.55	0.84	0.79
		800	0.59	0.83	0.79
		1600	0.66	0.84	0.80

TABLE. 2

Sample 01 centrality values

Sample Scale — Sample 02

FIG. 20

Histograms showing the distribution of centrality values (Reach, Gravity, and Straightness) among plots with and without alleys at three different scales 400m, 800m, and 1600m.The X axis is for the centrality metric values, while the Y axis is for the percentage of plots achieving a centrality value denoted on the X axis.

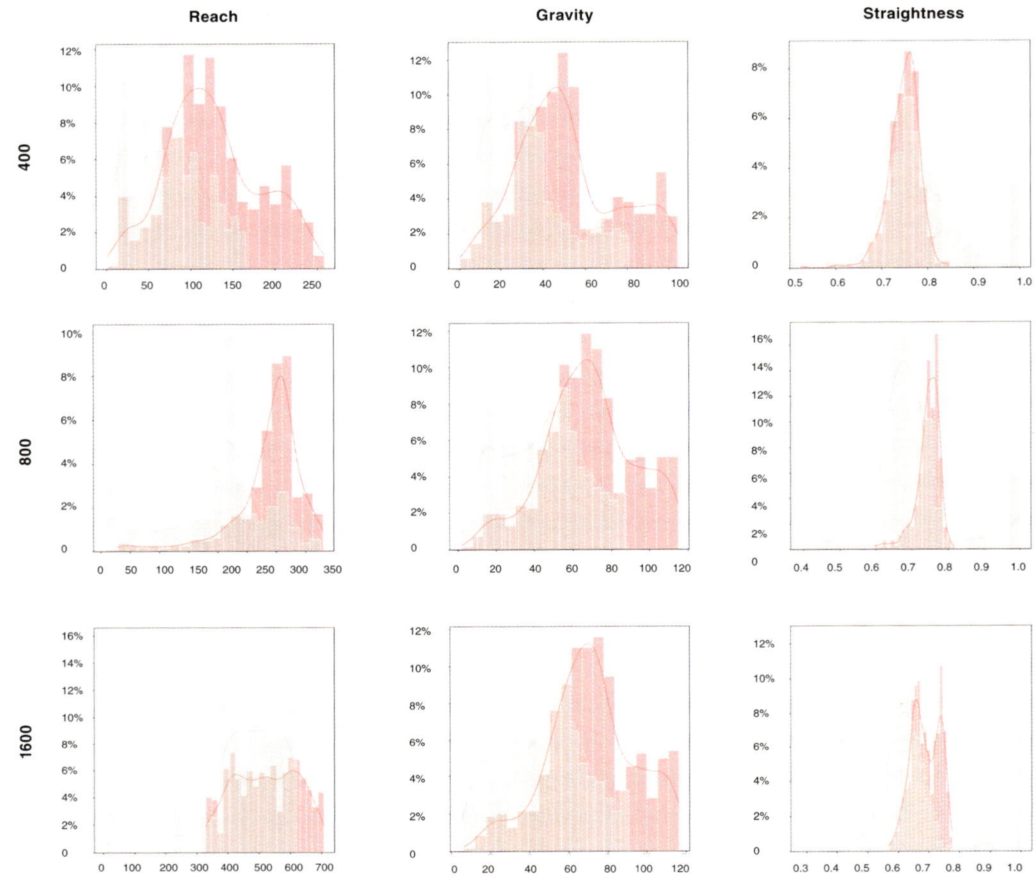

TABLE. 3

Sample 02 centrality values

UNA		Radius	Min	Max	Avg
Scenario 1: Streets only	Reach	400	1	165	72
		800	6	375	194
		1600	6	618	432
	Gravity	400	0.23	80.71	31.75
		800	1.37	87.38	43.88
		1600	5.01	90.36	46.96
	Straightness	400	0.58	1.00	0.79
		800	0.39	1.00	0.70
		1600	0.28	1.00	0.65

UNA		Radius	Min	Max	Avg
Scenario 2: Streets + Alleys	Reach	400	1	258	126
		800	29	379	287
		1600	327	707	521
	Gravity	400	0.23	103.99	51.44
		800	1.81	114.89	68.62
		1600	6.33	116.19	71.44
	Straightness	400	0.52	0.85	0.75
		800	0.59	0.82	0.74
		1600	0.57	0.78	0.69

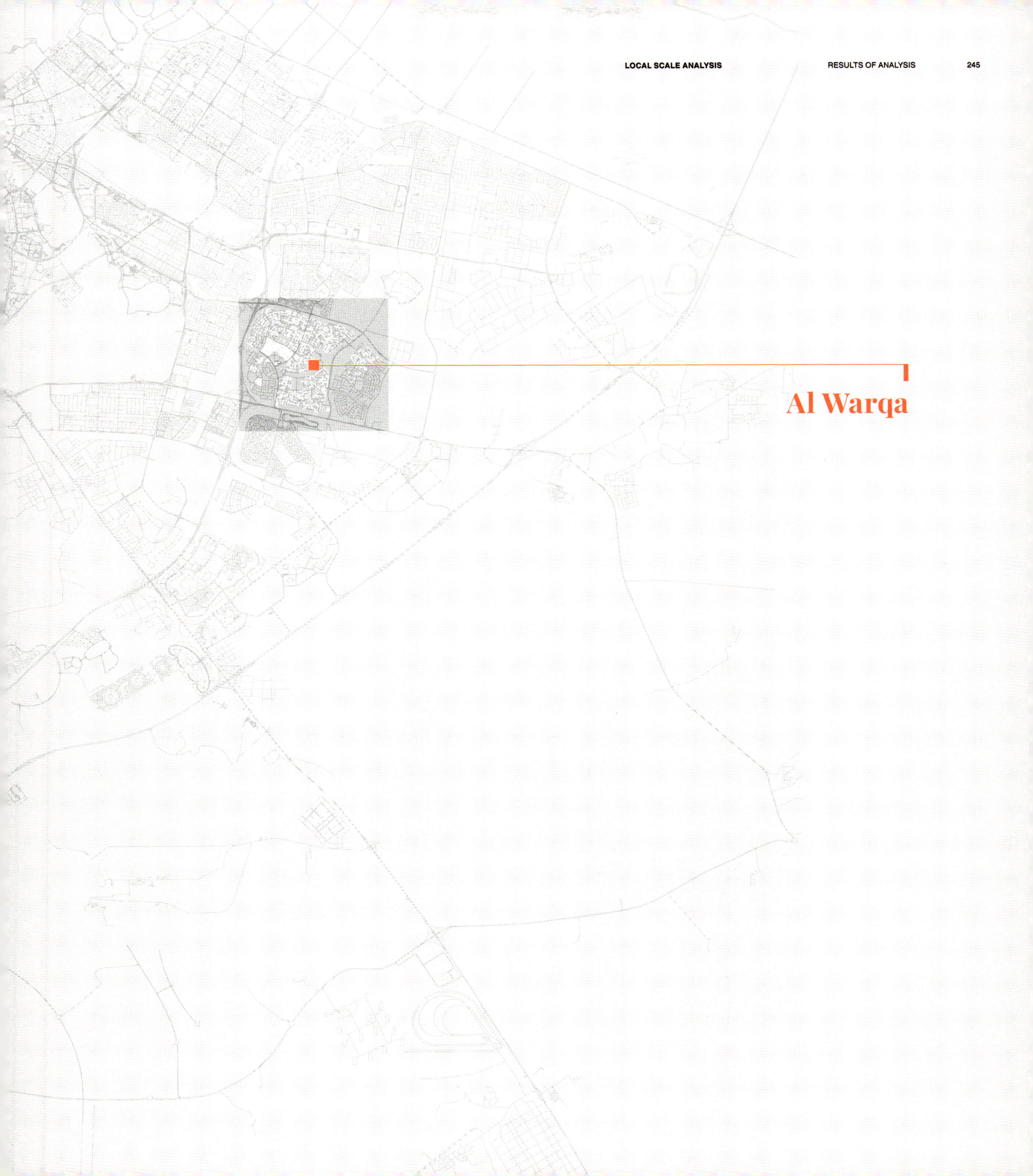
Al Warqa

Al Warqa

FIG. 1
Al Warqa skyline

FIG. 2
Low rise housing units in Al Warqa

FIG. 3
A photo montage with different views of Al Warqa

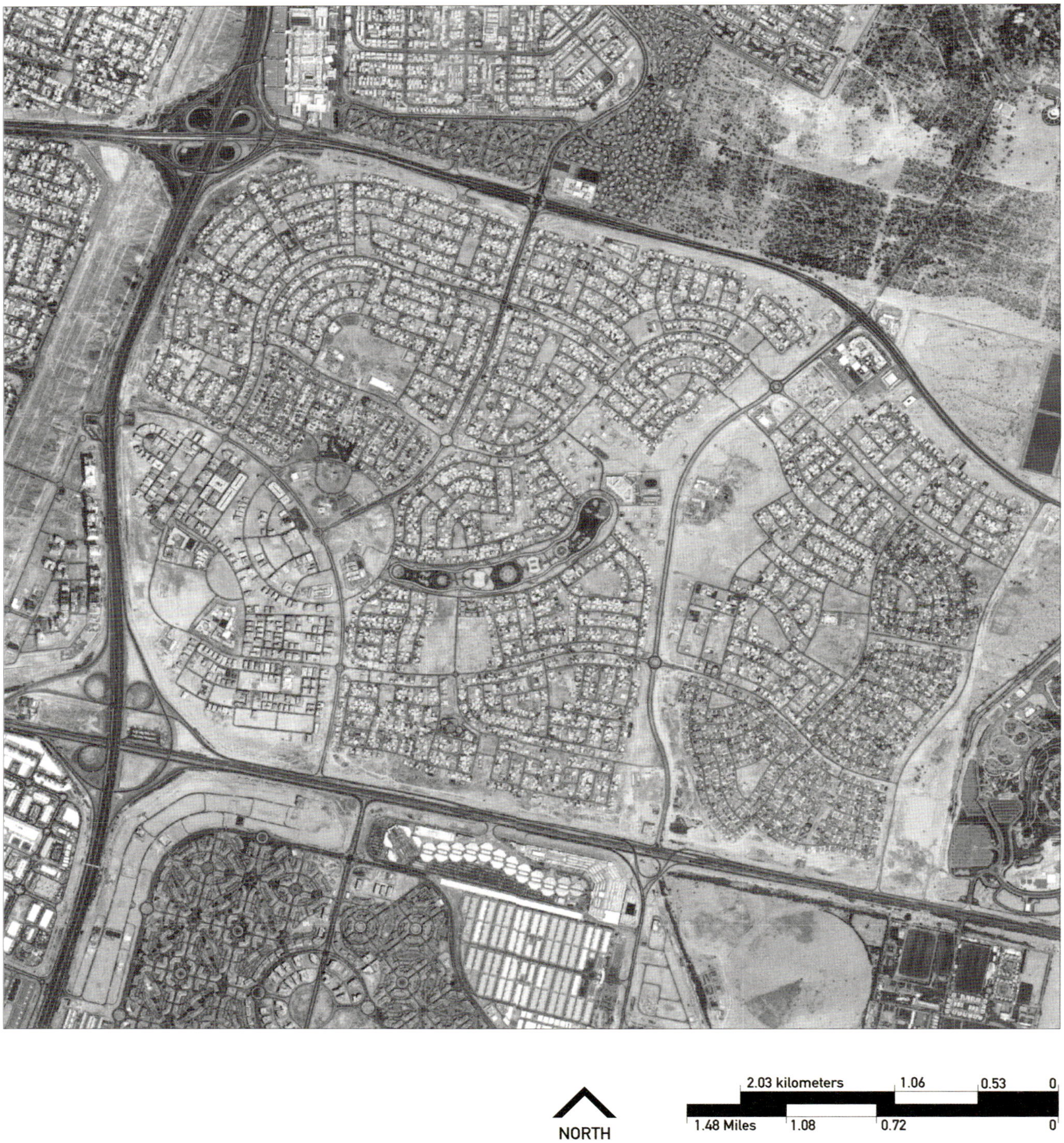

FIG. 4
Aerial image showing Al Warqa (Esri & USGS, 2021)

Morphological Analysis

Neighborhood Scale

Residential= 5,977 Plots
Non-residential= 922 Plots

Plots/Buildings:

- Total area = 1,608 Hectares
- Total plots = 6,899 Plots
- Total buildings = 2,819 Buildings
- Average plot density = 4.29 Plots/Hectare
- Average building density = 1.75 Buildings/Hectare
- Average plot area = 0.15 Hectare
- Average population density = 8.17 Population/Hectare

FIG. 5.1
Residential/ non-residential classification

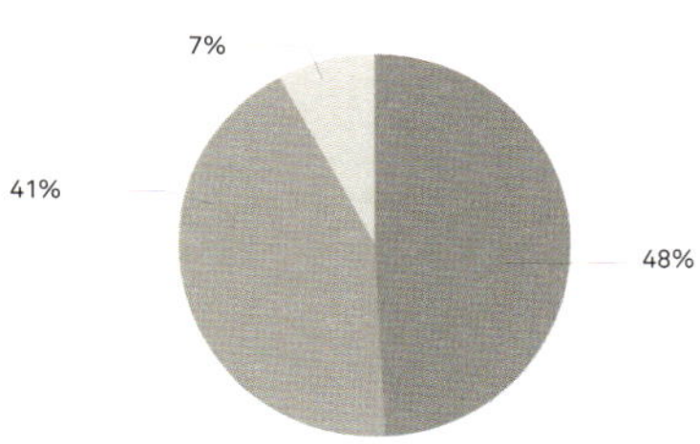

Low-rise (1-4) = 1,365 Buildings
Mid-rise (4-10)= 1,183 Buildings
High-rise (+10)= 215 Buildings

FIG. 5.2
Buildings height classification

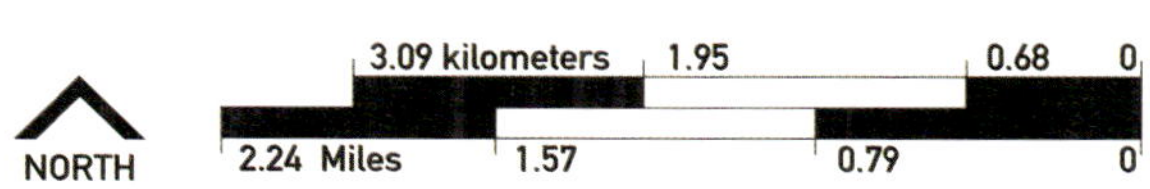

FIG. 5.3
Population density

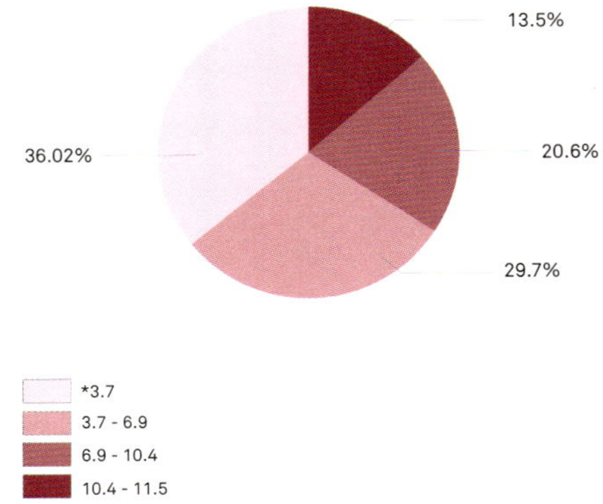

*Population per hectare.

FIG. 5.4
Land use classification

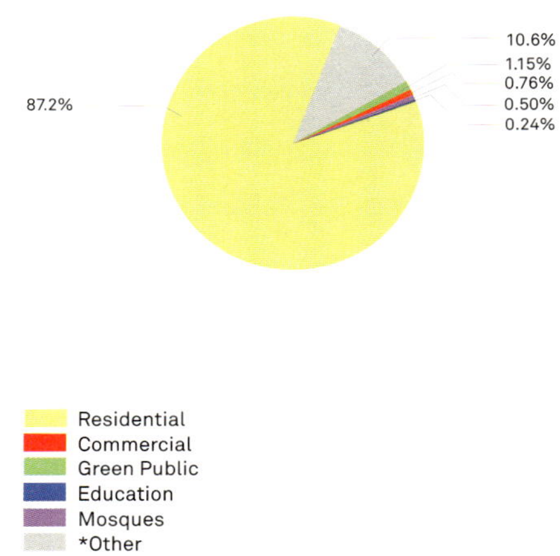

* Other land uses include: Health Care, Municipal/Goverment Facilities, Beaches, Public Library, Community Center, Utilities, Wedding hall, and Graveyard.

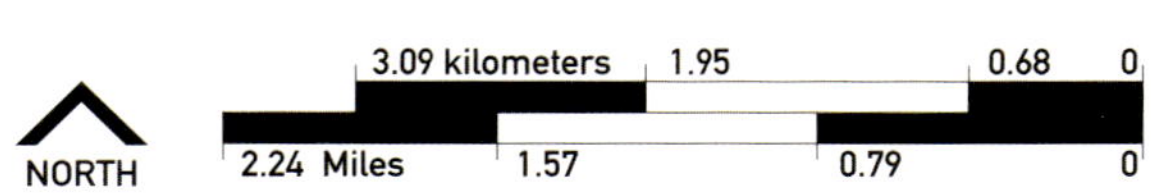

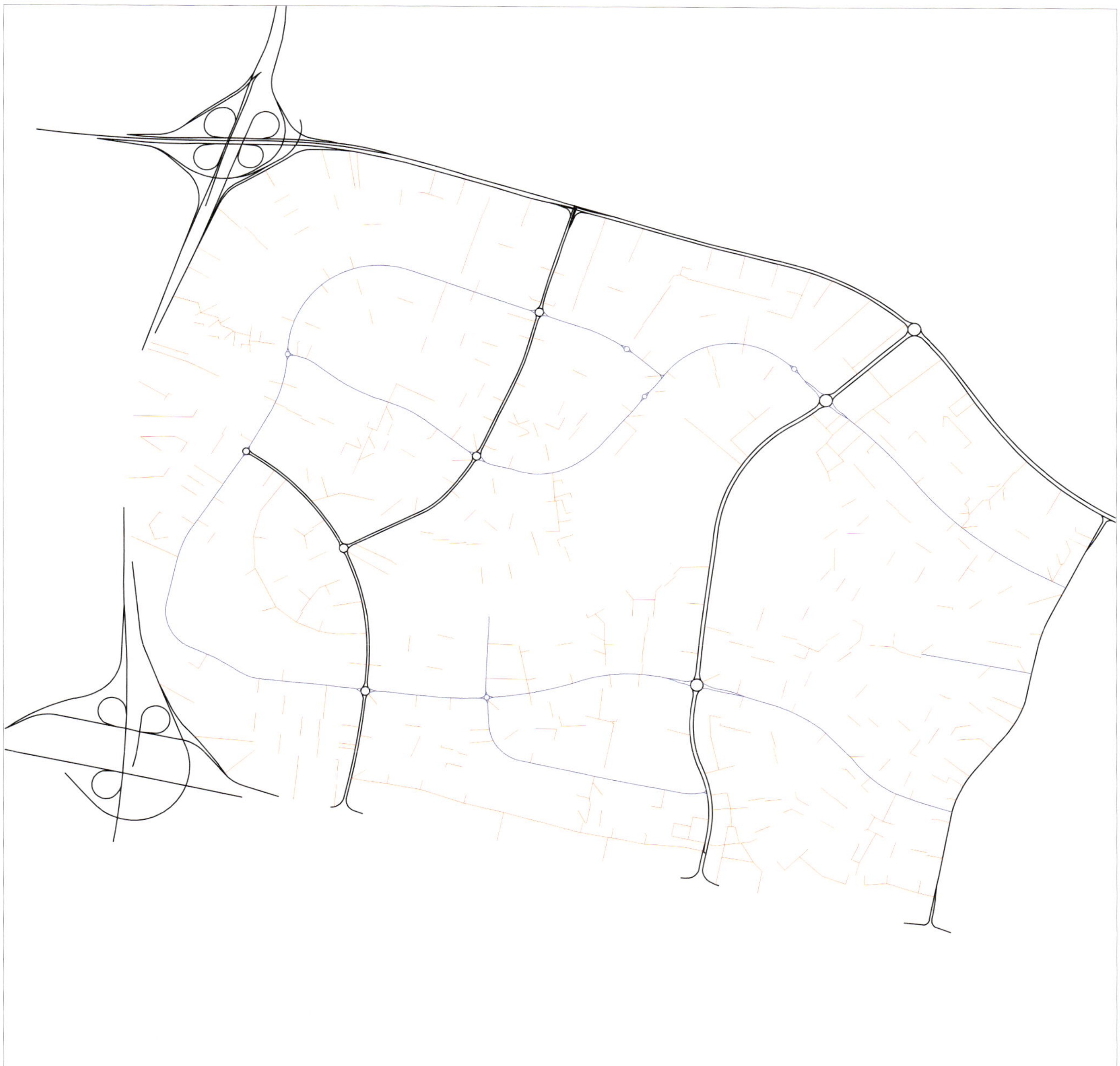

FIG. 5.5
Map showing network classification in Al Warqa

Streets:

- Street length = 260.92 km
- Street density = 0.16 km/Hectare
- Street intersections = 1,160 Intersections
- Street intersections density = 0.72 Intersection/Hectare

Alleys:

- Alley length = 58.81 km
- Alley density = 0.04 km/Hectare
- Alley intersections = 86 Intersections
- Alley intersections density = 0.03 Intersection/Hectare

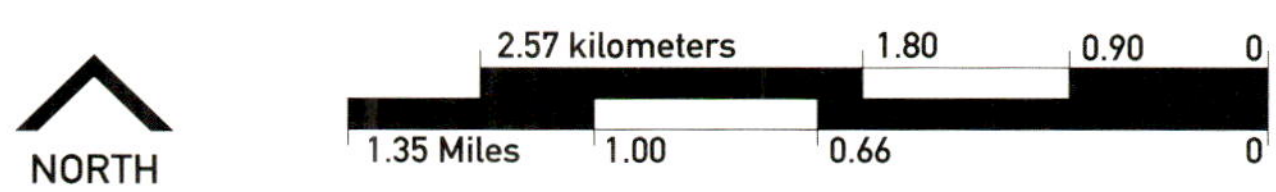

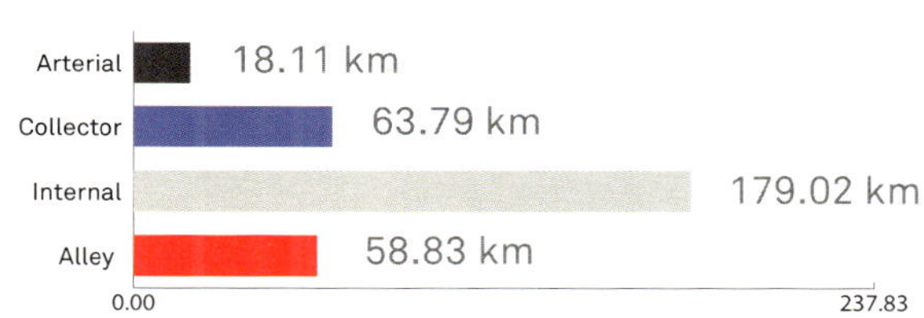

FIG. 6
Map showing Al Warqa with the location of the selected samples. Each sample has an area of 1 square mile.

Morphological Analysis

Sample Scale — Sample 01

Residential= 1,305 Plots
Non-residential= 69 Plots

Plots/Buildings:

- Total area = 256 Hectares
- Total plots = 1,374 Plots
- Total buildings = 1,070 Buildings
- Average plot area = 0.13 Hectare
- Average plot density = 5.73 Plots/Hectare

FIG. 7.1
Residential/non-residential classification

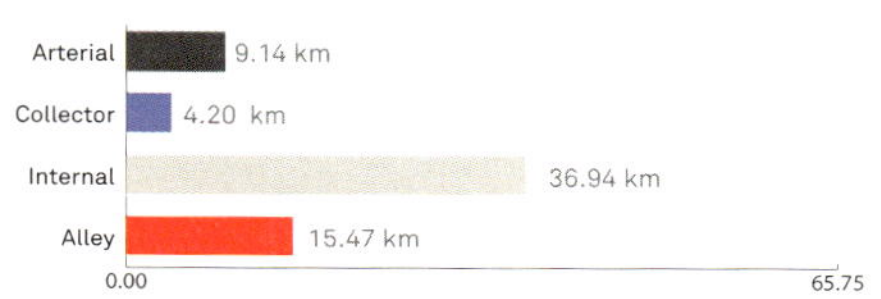

Streets:

- Street length = 50.28 km
- Street density = 0.26 km/Hectare
- Street intersections = 173 Intersections
- Street intersections density = 0.68 Intersection/Hectare

Alleys:

- Alley length = 15.47 km
- Alley density = 0.06 km/Hectare
- Alley intersections = 27 Intersections
- Alley intersections density = 0.11 Intersection/Hectare

FIG. 7.2
Network classification

Residential
Commercial
Education
Green Public
Mosques
*Other

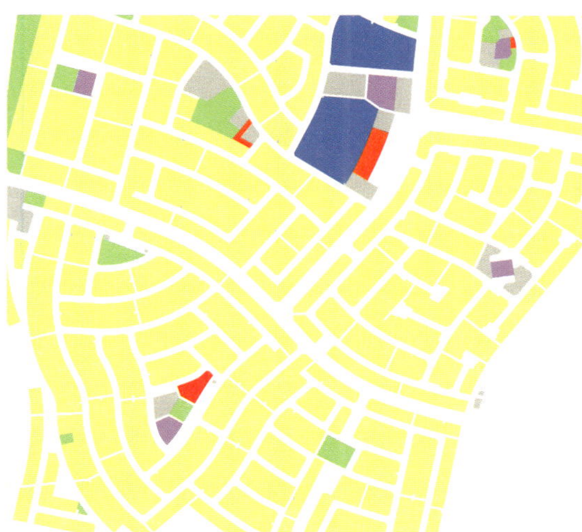

FIG. 7.3
Land use classification

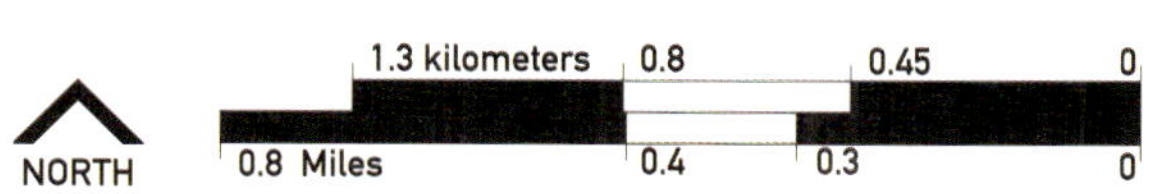

Sample Scale — Sample 02

FIG. 8.1
Residential/non-residential classification

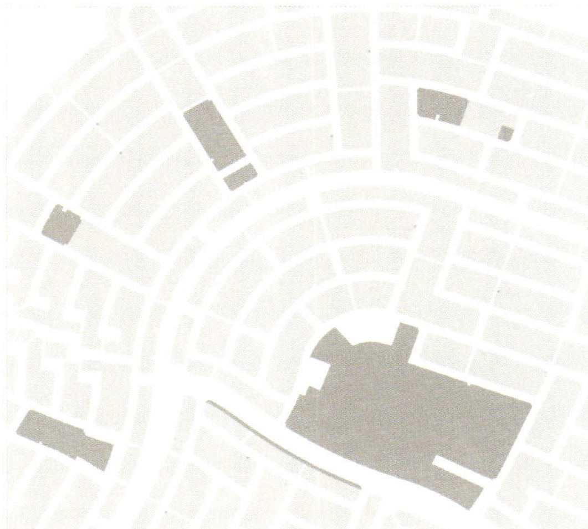

Residential= 1,252 Plots
Non-residential= 50 Plots

Plots/Buildings:

- Total area = 256 Hectares
- Total plots = 1,302 Plots
- Total buildings = 1,296 Buildings
- Average plot area = 0.14 Hectare
- Average plot density = 5.09 Plots/Hectare

FIG. 8.2
Network classification

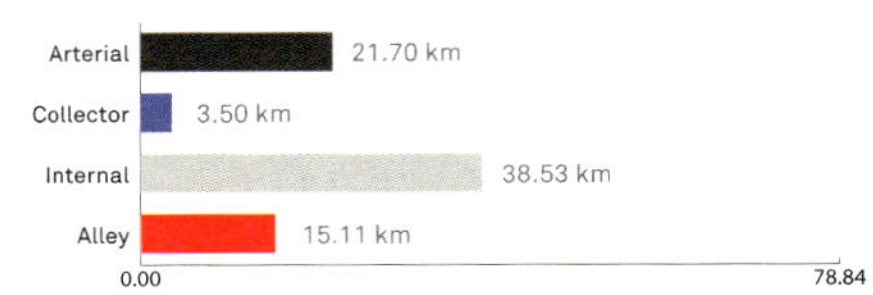

Streets:

- Street length = 63.73 km
- Street density = 0.25 km/Hectare
- Street intersections = 320 Intersections
- Street intersections density = 1.25 Intersections/Hectare

Alleys:

- Alley length = 15.11 km
- Alley density = 0.06 km/Hectare
- Alley intersections = 36 Intersections
- Alley intersections density = 0.14 Intersection/Hectare

FIG. 8.3
Land use classification

Residential
Commercial
Education
Green Public
Mosques
*Other

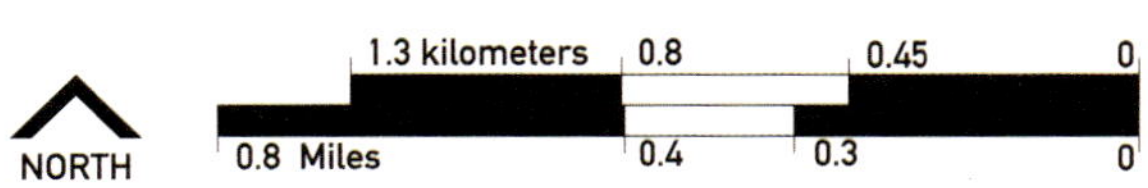

Centrality Analysis: Neighborhood Scale

Scenario 1: Streets only — 400 m Radius

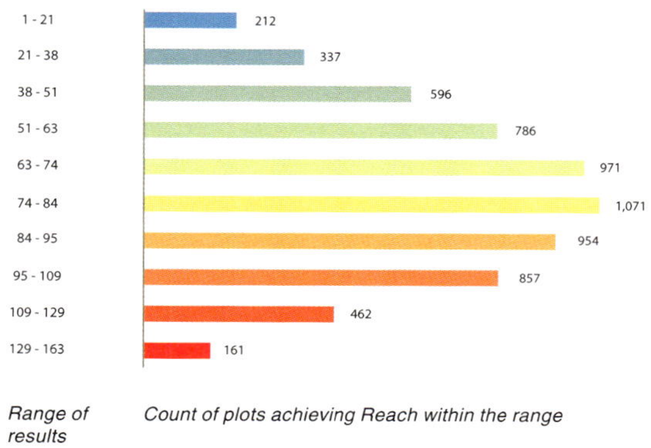

The warmer colors (i.e., greenish-yellow to red) represent a Reach value of 63 or more, while the cooler colors (i.e., light green to dark blue) correspond to a Reach value of 62 or less. The majority of plots (i.e., 3,505 out of 6,407), corresponding to 55% of all plots, have Reach values of more than 73. Among the categories shown in the legend, 17% of the total plots can reach 74 to 84 other plots within 5 minutes of walking. On average, each plot in Al Warqa can access at least 75 plots within a distance of 400 m.

FIG. 9.1
Reach

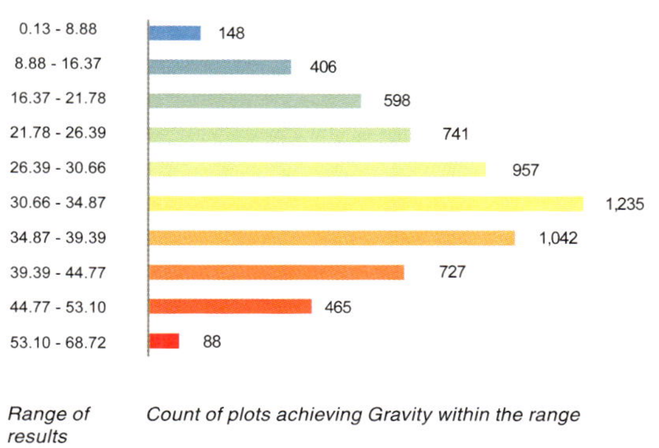

The warmer colors (i.e., greenish-yellow to red) represent Gravity values greater than 26.38, while the cooler colors (i.e., light green to dark blue) correspond to Gravity values lower than 26.39. Fifty-six percent of all plots (i.e., 3,557 out of 6,407) have Gravity values of more than 30.65. Among the categories shown in the legend, 1,235 plots, or 19% of the total plots, can reach 30.66 to 34.87 plots, making this the most common range; this range is represented by yellow on the map. On average, each plot can reach 31 other plots when spatial impedance or distance decay effect is taken into consideration.

FIG. 9.2
Gravity

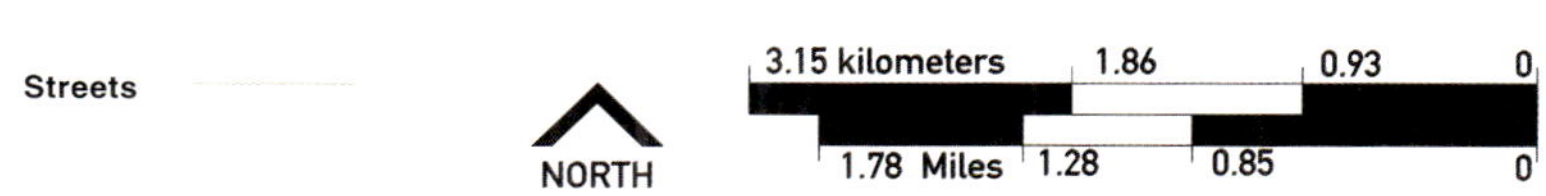

Scenario 1: Streets only — 400 m Radius

FIG. 9.3
Betweenness

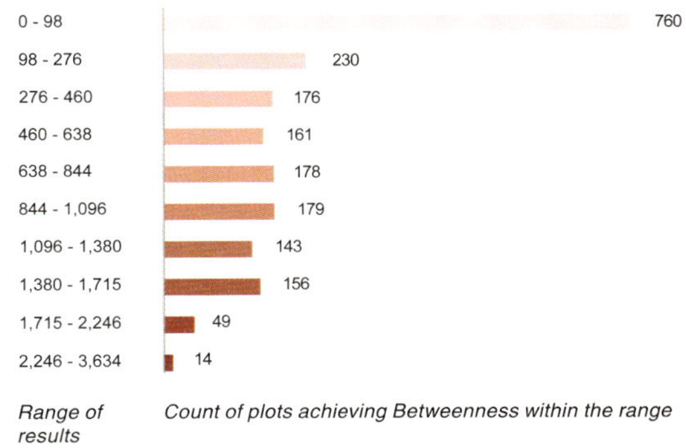

The majority of segments, corresponding to 74% (i.e., 1,516 out of 2,046 segments), have low Betweenness values ranging from 0 to 864. Among the categories shown in the legend, 760 segments have values in the range of 0 to 98 making this the most common value range; this range is represented by the lightest brown on the map. Mid-range Betweenness values ranging from 865 to 6,702 are obtained by 530 segments, which is 26% of all segments. There are no segments with high Betweenness values (higher than 6,702). The average Betweenness value in Al Warqa is 516 (smaller than 865), while the median is 330, indicating low Betweenness at a 400 m radius.

FIG. 9.4
Straightness

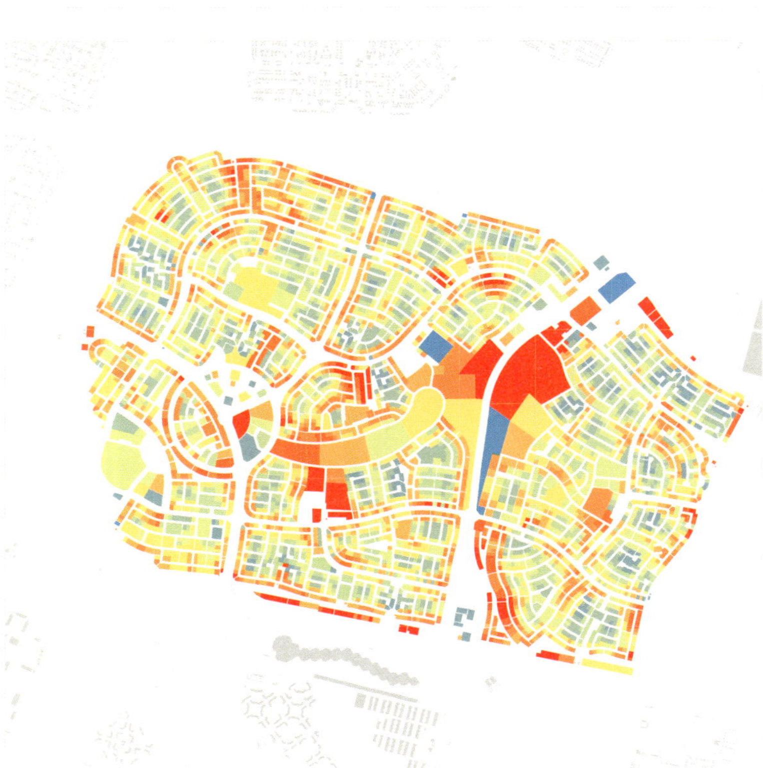

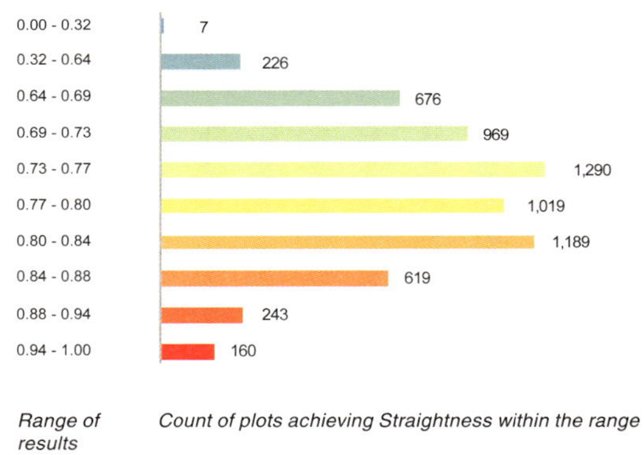

The warmer colors (greenish-yellow to red) represent Straightness values higher than 0.72, while the cooler colors (light green to dark blue) correspond to Straightness values lower than 0.73. The majority of plots, corresponding to 70% (or 4,476 out of 6,407 plots) have Straightness values ranging from 0.69 to 0.84. Among the categories shown in the legend, 1,290 plots have values in the range of 0.73 to 0.77 making this the most common value range; this range is represented by greenish-yellow on the map. On average, at a 400 m radius, all plots in Al Warqa are 77% as straight as a straight line.

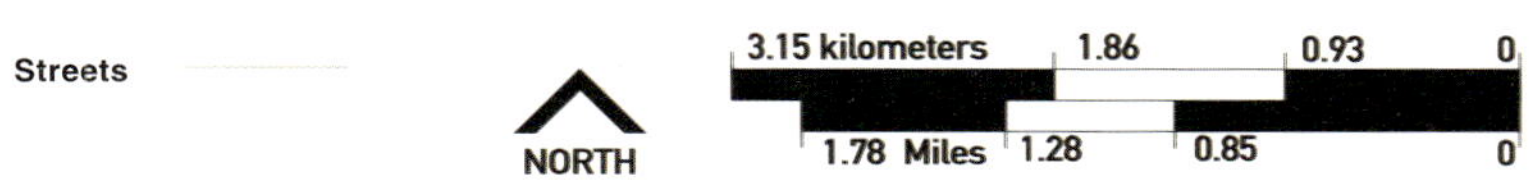

Scenario 1: Streets only — 800 m Radius

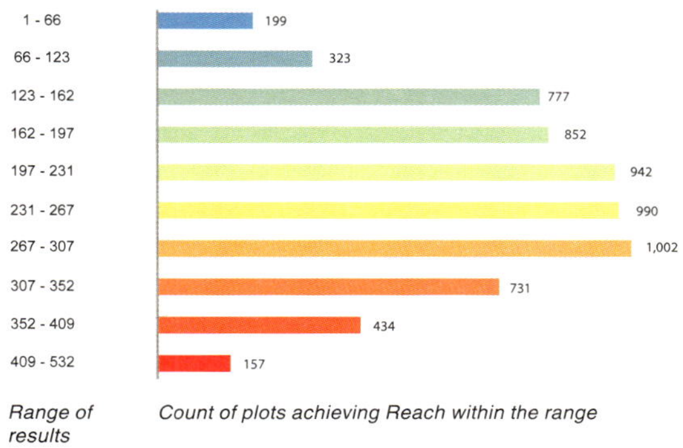

The warmer colors (i.e., greenish-yellow to red) represent a Reach value of 197 or more, while the cooler colors (i.e., light green to dark blue) correspond to a Reach value of 196 or less. Sixty-four percent of all plots (i.e., 3,596 out of 6,407) have Reach values of less than 267. Among the categories shown in the legend, 16% of all plots can reach 267 to 307 other plots within 10 minutes of walking. On average, each plot in Al Warqa can access at least 235 plots within a distance of 800 m.

FIG. 10.1
Reach

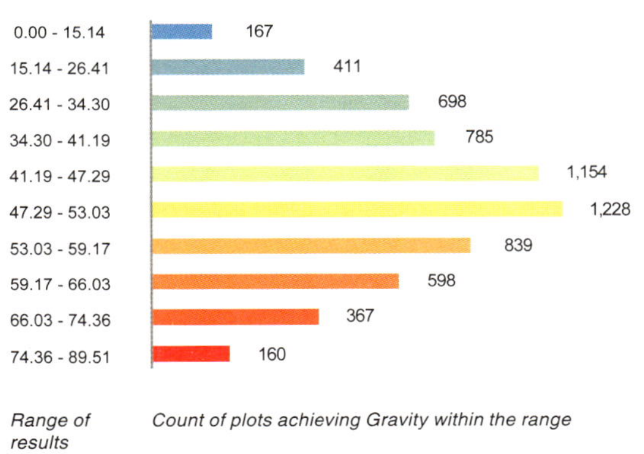

The warmer colors (i.e., greenish-yellow to red) represent Gravity values of more than 41.18, while the cooler colors (i.e., light green to dark blue) correspond to Gravity values of less than 41.19. Fifty percent of all plots (i.e., 3,192 out of 6,407) have Gravity values of more than 47.28. Among the categories shown in the legend, 1,228 plots, or 19% of the total plots, can reach 47.29 to 53.03 plots, making this the most common range; this range is represented by yellow on the map. On average, each plot can reach 46 other plots when spatial impedance or distance decay effect is taken into consideration.

FIG. 10.2
Gravity

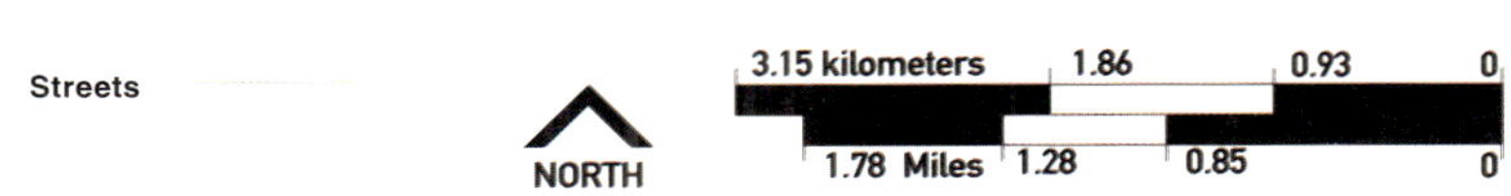

Scenario 1: Streets only — 800 m Radius

FIG. 10.3

Betweenness

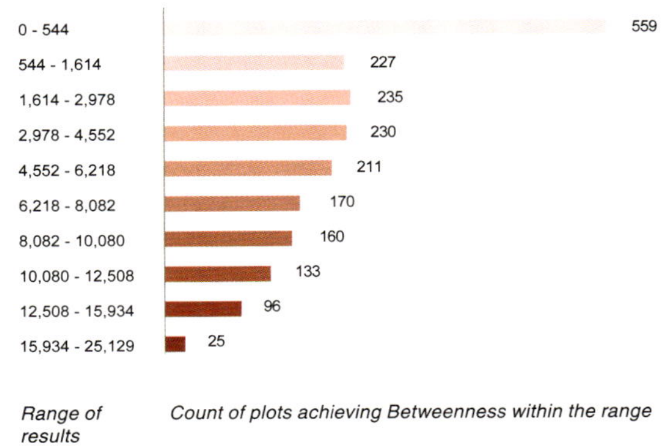

The majority of segments, corresponding to 47% (i.e., 956 out of 2,046 segments), have very low Betweenness values ranging from 0 to 2,539. Among the categories shown in the legend, 559 segments have values in the range of 0 to 544, making this the most common value range; this range is represented by the lightest brown on the map. Low Betweenness values ranging from 2,539 to 11,517 are obtained by 926 segments, which is 45% of all segments. Mid-range Betweenness values ranging from 11,518 to 20,478 are obtained by 159 segments, which is 8% of the total segments. Five segments have high Betweenness values (higher than 20,478 but smaller than 59,383) but no segments have very high Betweenness values (higher than 59,383). The average Betweenness value in Al Warqa is 4,275 (higher than 2,539 but smaller than 11,518), while the median is 3,027, indicating low Betweenness at an 800 m radius.

FIG. 10.4

Straightness

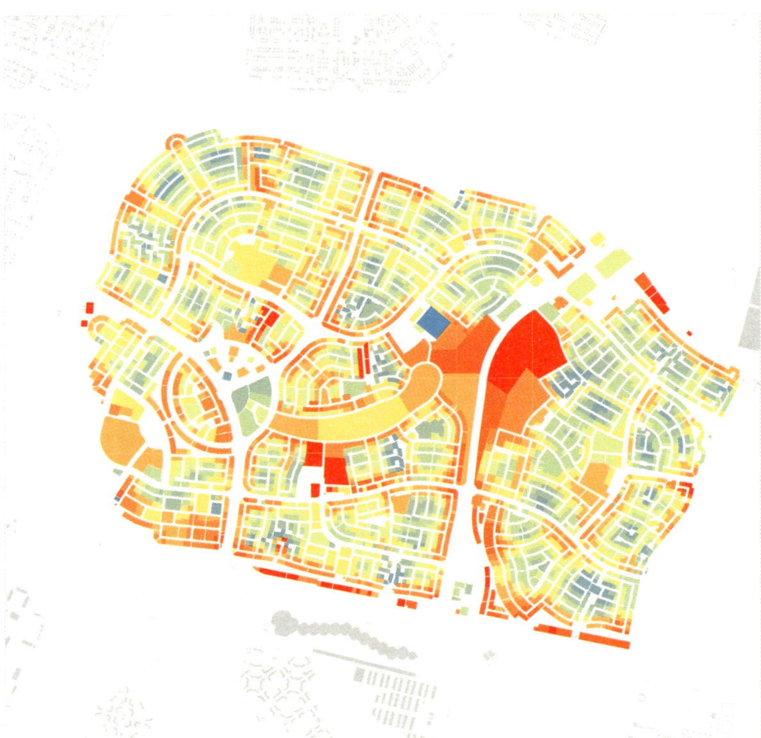

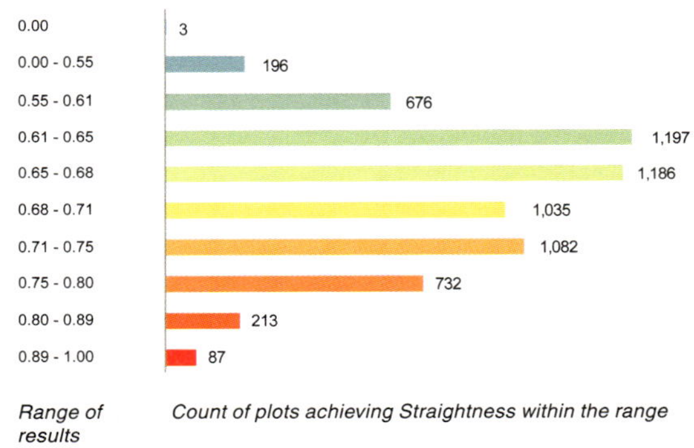

The warmer colors (greenish-yellow to red) represent Straightness values higher than 0.64, while the cooler colors (light green to dark blue) correspond to Straightness values lower than 0.65. The majority of plots, corresponding to 70% (or 4,500 out of 6,407 plots) have Straightness values ranging from 0.61 to 0.75. Among the categories shown in the legend, 1,197 plots have values in the range of 0.61 to 0.65 making this the most common value range; this range is represented by light green on the map. On average, at an 800 m radius, all plots in Al Warqa are 68% as straight as a straight line.

Scenario 1: Streets only — 1,600 m Radius

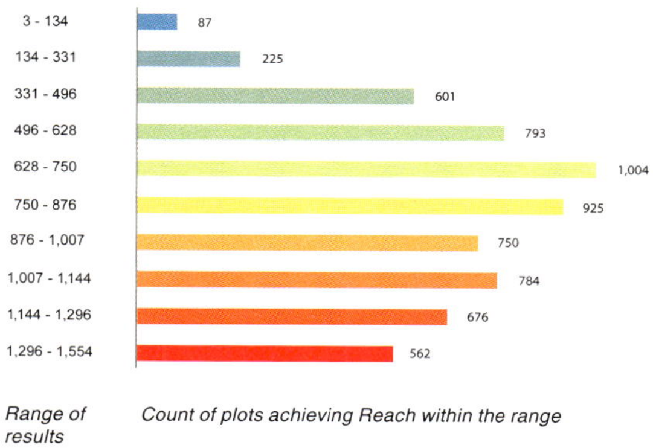

The warmer colors (i.e., greenish-yellow to red) represent Reach values of more than 627, while the cooler colors (i.e., light green to dark blue) correspond to Reach values of less than 628. The majority of plots (i.e., 3,635 out of 6,407), corresponding to 57% of all plots, have Reach values of less than 876. Among the categories shown in the legend, 16% of the total plots can reach 628 to 750 other plots within 20 minutes of walking. On average, each plot in Al Warqa can access at least 834 plots within a distance of 1,600 m.

FIG.11.1
Reach

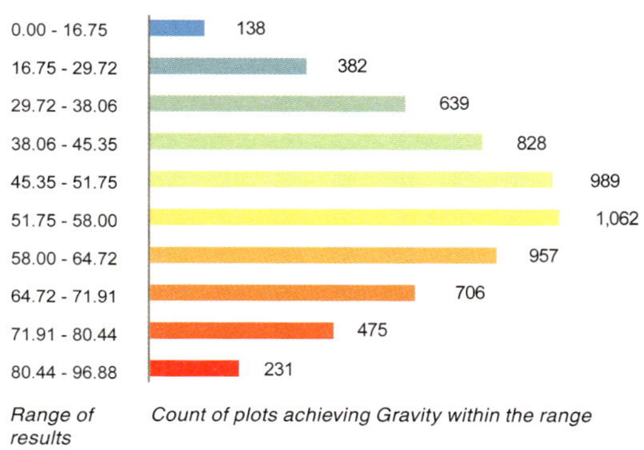

The warmer colors (i.e., greenish-yellow to red) represent Gravity values greater than 45.34, while the cooler colors (i.e., light green to dark blue) correspond to Gravity values lower than 45.35. Fifty-four percent of all plots (i.e., 3,431 out of 6,407) have Gravity values of more than 51.74. Among the categories shown in the legend, 1,062 plots, or 17% of the total plots, can reach 51.75 to 58.00 plots, making this the most common range; this range is represented by yellow on the map. On average, each plot can reach 53 other plots when spatial impedance or distance decay effect is taken into consideration.

FIG.11.2
Gravity

Streets

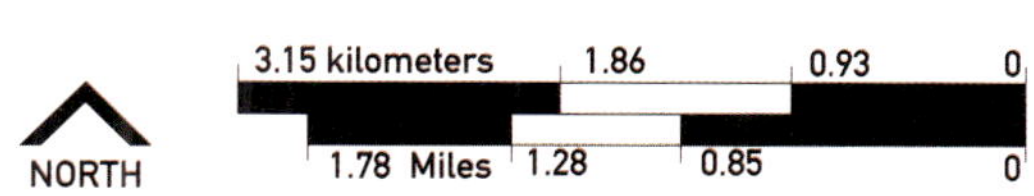

Scenario 1: Streets only — 1,600 m Radius

FIG. 11.3
Betweenness

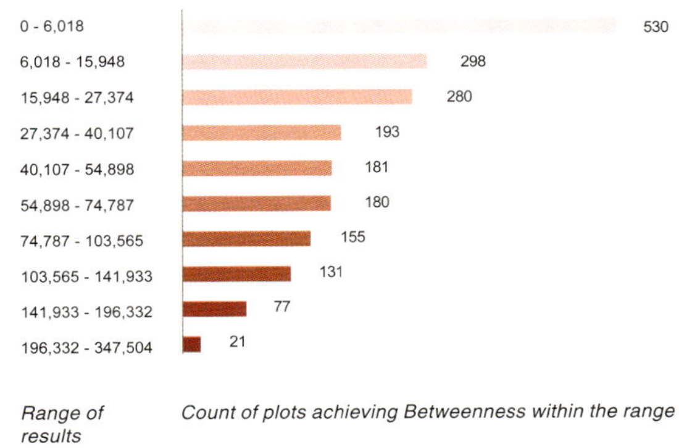

The majority of segments, corresponding to 81% (i.e., 1,659 out of 2,046 segments), have very low Betweenness values ranging from 0 to 73,682. Among the categories shown in the legend, 530 segments have values in the range of 0 to 6,018, making this the most common value range; this range is represented by the lightest brown on the map. Low Betweenness values ranging from 73,683 to 123,568 are obtained by 228 segments, which is 11% of all segments. There are 122 segments that have mid-range Betweenness values (from 123,569 to 179,444) and 30 segments that have high Betweenness values (from 179,444 to 251,415). Seven segments have very high Betweenness values that are greater than 251,415. The average Betweenness value in Jumeirah is 40,867 (smaller than 73,683), while the median is 23,444, indicating very low Betweenness at a 1,600 m radius.

FIG. 11.4
Straightness

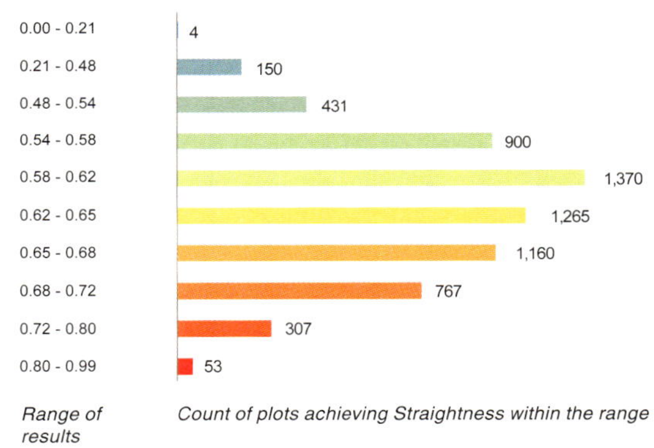

The warmer colors (greenish-yellow to red) represent Straightness values higher than 0.57, while the cooler colors (light green to dark blue) correspond to Straightness values lower than 0.58. The majority of plots, corresponding to 59% (or 3,795 out of 6,407 plots) have Straightness values ranging from 0.58 to 0.68. Among the categories shown in the legend, 1,370 plots have values in the range of 0.58 to 0.62 making this the most common value range; this range is represented by greenish-yellow on the map. On average, at a 1,600 m radius, all plots in Al Warqa are 62% as straight as a straight line.

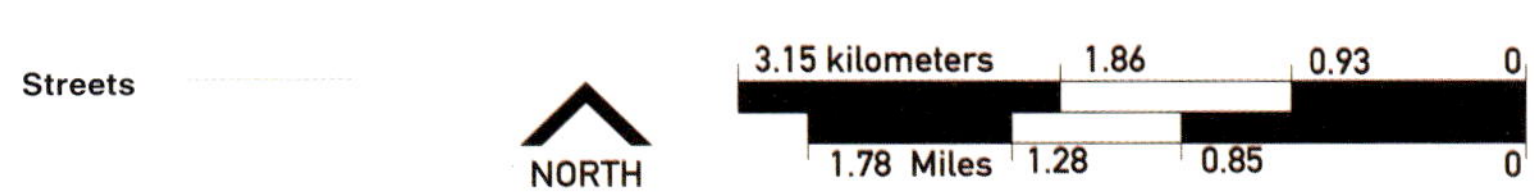

Centrality Analysis: Neighborhood Scale

Scenario 2: Streets + Alleys — 400 m Radius

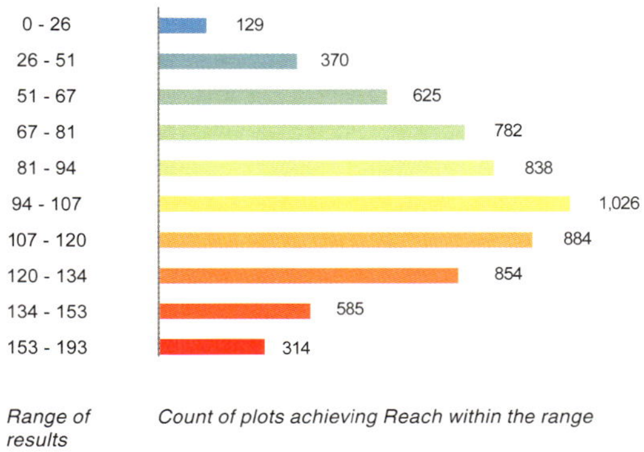

The warmer colors (i.e., greenish-yellow to red) represent a Reach value of 82 or more, while the cooler colors (i.e., light green to dark blue) correspond to a Reach value of 81 or less. Fifty-seven percent of all plots (i.e., 3,663 out of 6,407) have Reach values of more than 93. Among the categories shown in the legend, 16% of the total plots can reach 94 to 107 other plots within 5 minutes of walking. On average, each plot in Al Warqa can access at least 98 plots within a distance of 400 m.

FIG. 12.1
Reach

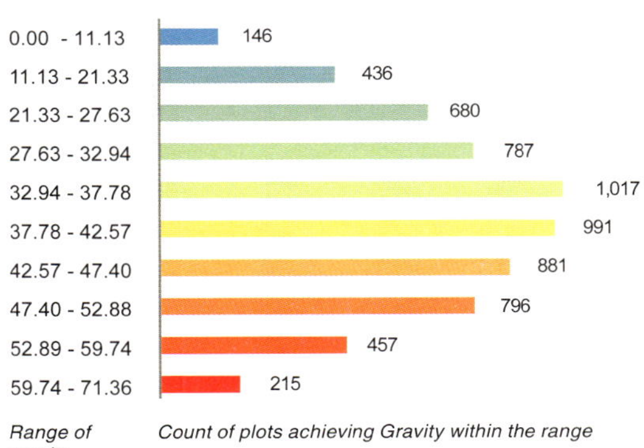

The warmer colors (i.e., greenish-yellow to red) represent Gravity values greater than 32.93, while the cooler colors (i.e., light green to dark blue) correspond to Gravity values lower than 32.94. Fifty-two percent of all plots (i.e., 3,340 out of 6,407) have Gravity values of more than 37.77. Among the categories shown in the legend, 1,017 plots, or 16% of the total plots, can reach 32.94 to 37.78 plots, making this the most common range; this range is represented by greenish-yellow on the map. On average, each plot can reach 38 other plots when spatial impedance or distance decay effect is taken into consideration.

FIG. 12.2
Gravity

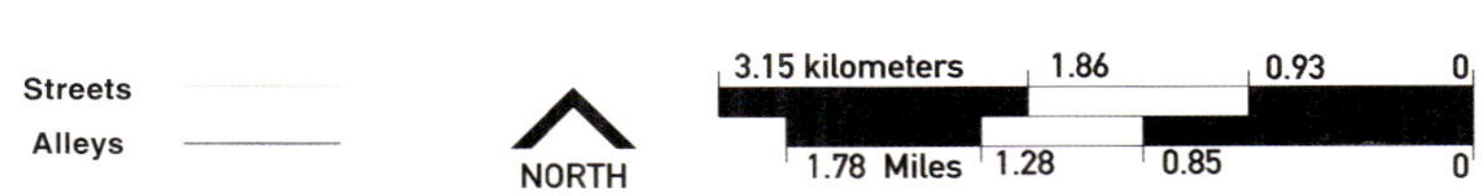

Scenario 2: Streets + Alleys — 400 m Radius

FIG. 12.3
Betweenness

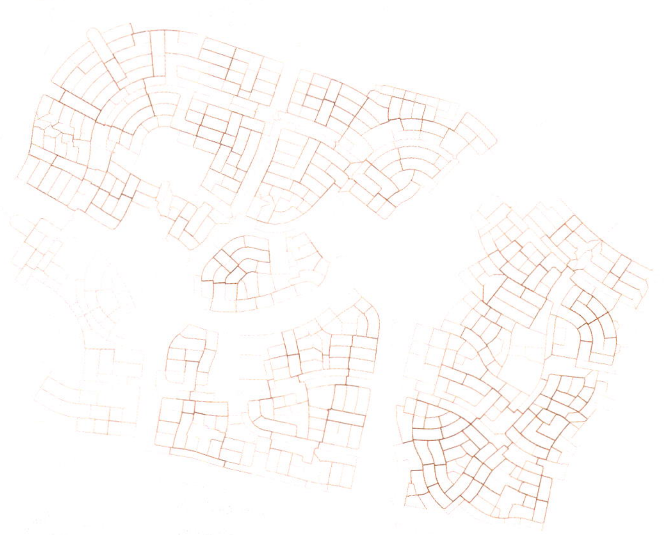

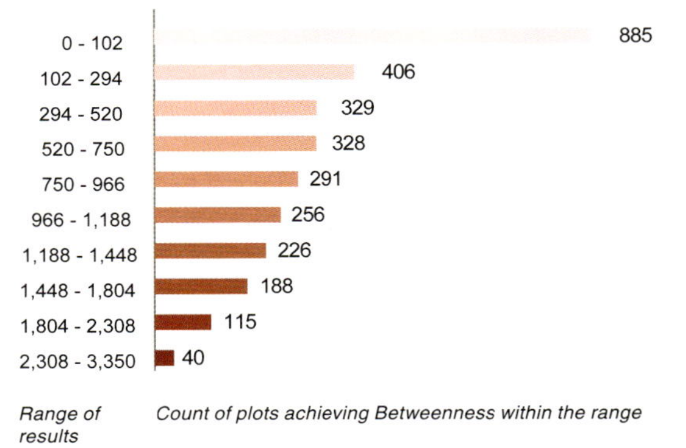

The majority of segments, corresponding to 69% (i.e., 2,109 out of 3,064 segments), have low Betweenness values ranging from 0 to 864. Among the categories shown in the legend, 885 segments have values in the range of 0 to 102 making this the most common value range; this range is represented by the lightest brown on the map. Mid-range Betweenness values ranging from 865 to 6,702 are obtained by 955 segments, which is 31% of all segments. There are no segments with high Betweenness values (higher than 6,702). The average Betweenness value in Al Warqa is 617 (smaller than 865), while the median is 447, indicating low Betweenness at a 400 m radius.

FIG. 12.4
Straightness

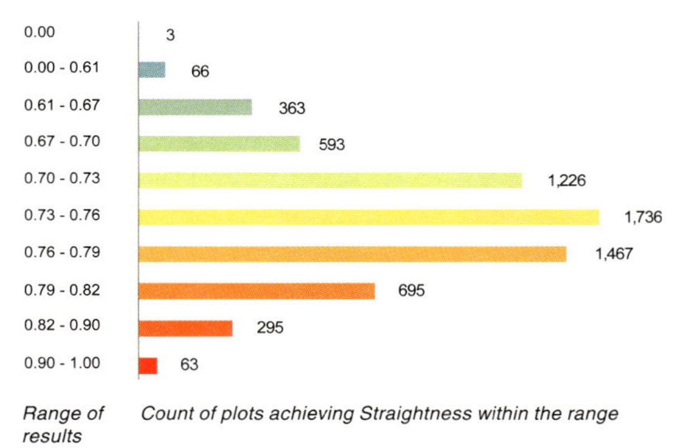

The warmer colors (greenish-yellow to red) represent Straightness values higher than 0.70, while the cooler colors (light green to dark blue) correspond to Straightness values lower than 0.71. The majority of plots, corresponding to 68% (or 4,329 out of 6,407 plots) have Straightness values ranging from 0.70 to 0.79. Among the categories shown in the legend, 1,736 plots have values in the range of 0.73 to 0.76 making this the most common value range; this range is represented by yellow on the map. On average, at a 400 m radius, all plots in Al Warqa are 75% as straight as a straight line.

Scenario 2: Streets + Alleys — 800 m Radius

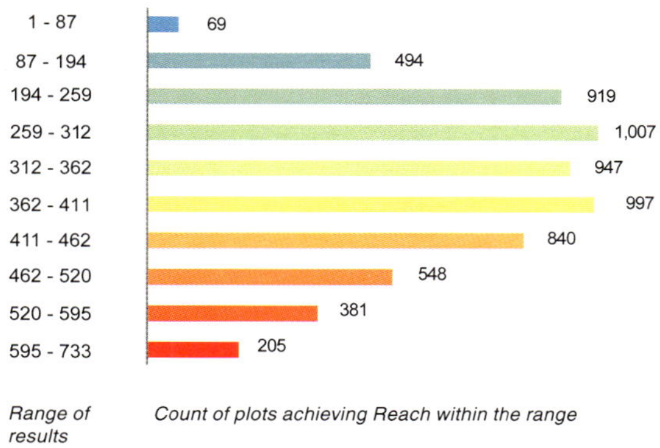

The warmer colors (i.e., greenish-yellow to red) represent a Reach value of 312 or more, while the cooler colors (i.e., light green to dark blue) correspond to a Reach value of 311 or less. The majority of plots (i.e., 3,436 out of 6,407), corresponding to 54% of all plots, have Reach values of less than 362. Among the categories shown in the legend, 16% of the total plots can reach 259 to 312 other plots within 10 minutes of walking. On average, each plot in Al Warqa can access at least 352 plots within a distance of 800 m.

FIG. 13.1
Reach

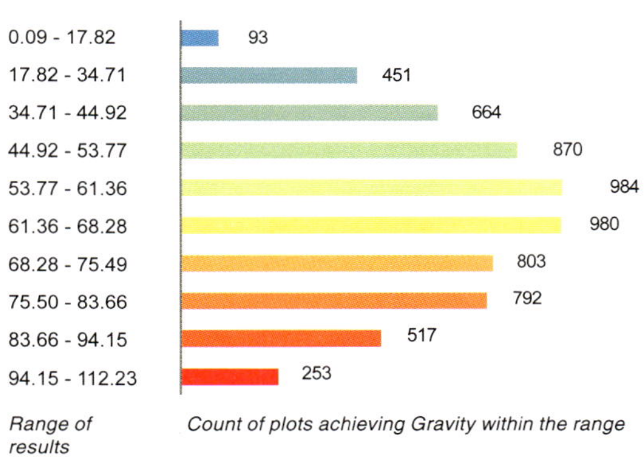

The warmer colors (i.e., greenish-yellow to red) represent Gravity values greater than 53.76, while the cooler colors (i.e., light green to dark blue) correspond to Gravity values lower than 53.77. Sixty-three percent of all plots (i.e., 4,042 out of 6,407) have Gravity values of less than 68.28. Among the categories shown in the legend, 984 plots, or 15% of the total plots, can reach 53.77 to 61.36 plots, making this the most common range; this range is represented by greenish-yellow on the map. On average, each plot can reach 62 other plots when spatial impedance or distance decay effect is taken into consideration.

FIG. 13.2
Gravity

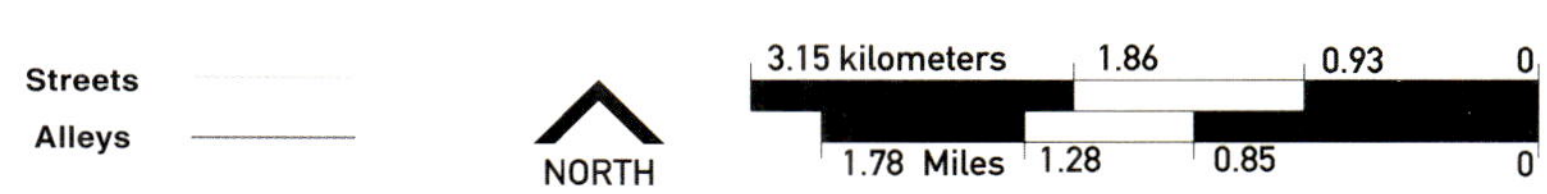

Scenario 2: Streets + Alleys — 800 m Radius

FIG. 13.3
Betweenness

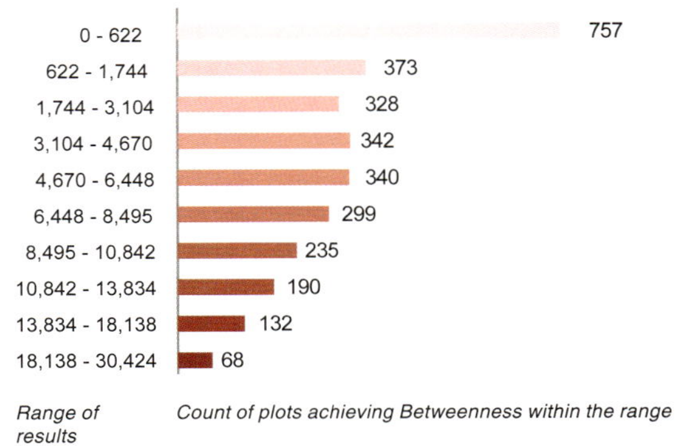

The majority of segments, corresponding to 44% (i.e., 1,351 out of 3,064 segments), have low Betweenness values ranging from 0 to 2,539. Among the categories shown in the legend, 757 segments have values in the range of 0 to 622, making this the most common value range; this range is represented by the lightest brown on the map. Very low Betweenness values ranging from 2,539 to 11,517 are obtained by 1,378 segments, which is 45% of all segments. Mid-range Betweenness values ranging from 11,518 to 20,478 are obtained by 304 segments, which is 10% of the total segments. Thirty-one segments have high Betweenness values (higher than 20,478 but smaller than 59,383) but no segments have very high Betweenness values (higher than 59,383). The average Betweenness value in Al Warqa is 4,803 (higher than 2,539 but smaller than 11,518), while the median is 3,428, indicating low Betweenness at an 800 m radius.

FIG. 13.4
Straightness

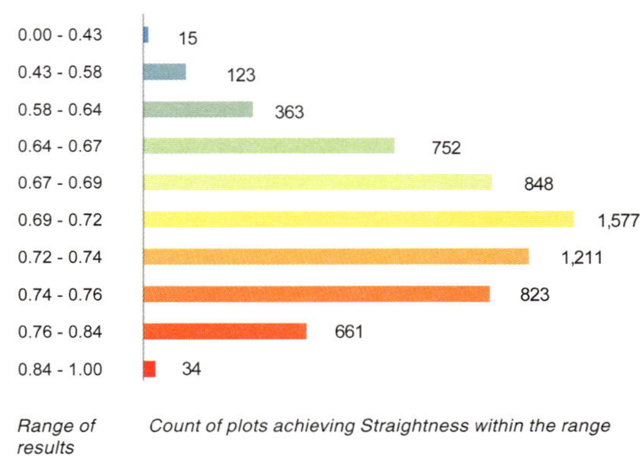

The warmer colors (greenish-yellow to red) represent Straightness values higher than 0.66, while the cooler colors (light green to dark blue) correspond to Straightness values lower than 0.67. The majority of plots, corresponding to 57% (or 3,636 out of 6,407 plots) have Straightness values ranging from 0.67 to 0.74. Among the categories shown in the legend, 1,577 plots have values in the range of 0.69 to 0.72 making this the most common value range; this range is represented by yellow on the map. On average, at an 800 m radius, all plots in Al Warqa are 71% as straight as a straight line.

Scenario 2: Streets + Alleys — 1,600 m Radius

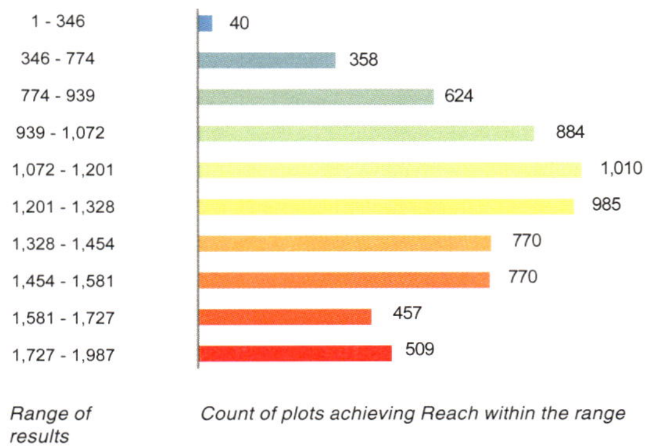

The warmer colors (i.e., greenish-yellow to red) represent a Reach value of 1,072 or more, while the cooler colors (i.e., light green to dark blue) correspond to a Reach value of 1,071 or less. The majority of plots (i.e., 3,491 out of 6,407), corresponding to 54% of all plots, have Reach values of more than 1,200. Among the categories shown in the legend, 16% of the total plots can reach 1,072 to 1,201 other plots within 20 minutes of walking. On average, each plot in Al Warqa can access at least 1,245 plots within a distance of 1,600 m.

FIG. 14.1
Reach

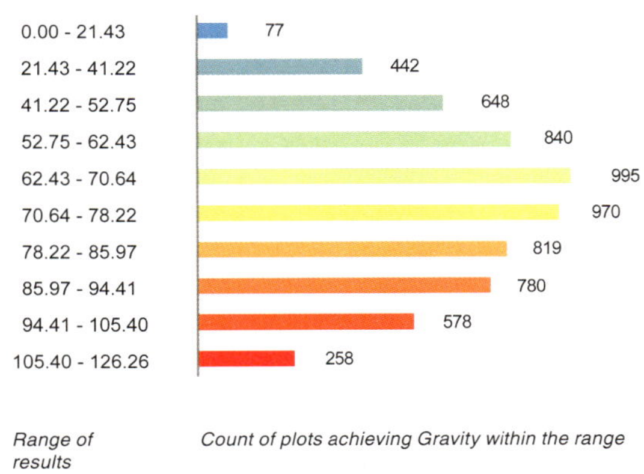

The warmer colors (i.e., greenish-yellow to red) represent Gravity values greater than 62.42, while the cooler colors (i.e., light green to dark blue) correspond to Gravity values lower than 62.43. Fifty-three percent of all plots (i.e., 3,405 out of 6,407) have Gravity values of more than 70.63. Among the categories shown in the legend, 995 plots, or 16% of the total plots, can reach 62.43 to 70.64 plots, making this the most common range; this range is represented by greenish-yellow on the map. On average, each plot can reach 71 other plots when spatial impedance or distance decay effect is taken into consideration.

FIG. 14.2
Gravity

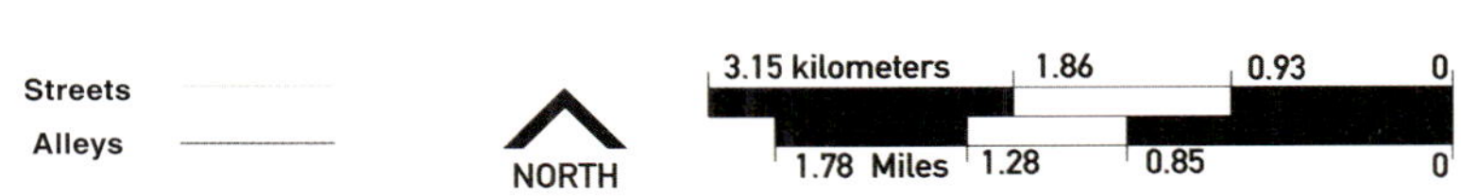

Scenario 2: Streets + Alleys — 1,600 m Radius

FIG. 14.3
Betweenness

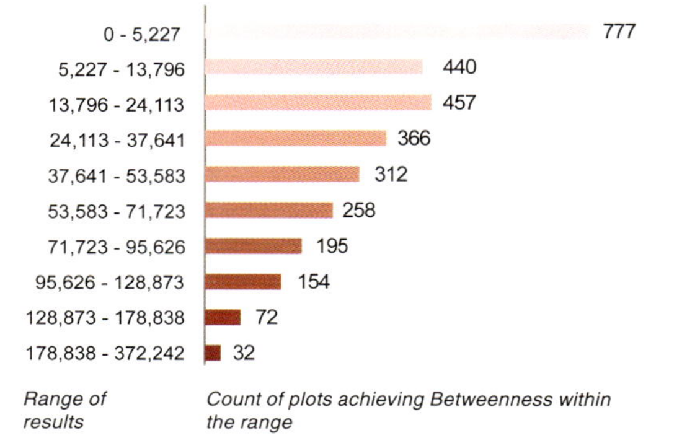

The majority of segments, corresponding to 86.06% (i.e., 2,637 out of 3,064 segments), have very low Betweenness values ranging from 0 to 73,682. Among the categories shown in the legend, 777 segments have values in the range of 0 to 5,227, making this the most common value range; this range is represented by the lightest brown on the map. Low Betweenness values ranging from 73,683 to 123,568 are obtained by 309 segments, which is 10.08% of all segments. Eighty-five segments have mid-range Betweenness values (from 123,569 to 179,444) and 27 segments that have high Betweenness values (from 179,444 to 251,415). Only 6 segments have very high Betweenness, greater than 251,415. The average Betweenness value in Al Warqa is 34,354 (smaller than 73,683), while the median is 19,951, indicating very low Betweenness at a 1,600 m radius.

FIG. 14.4
Straightness

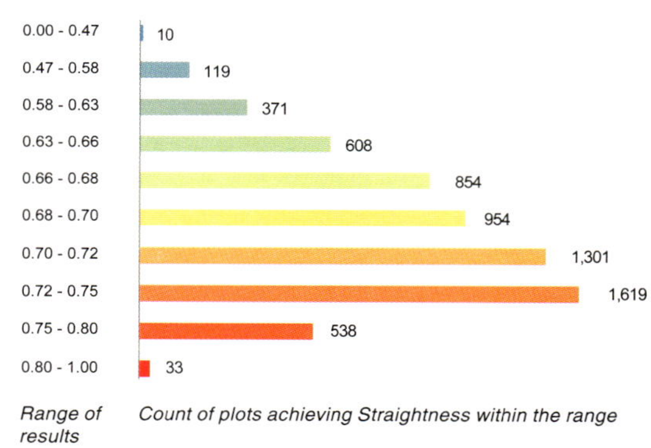

The warmer colors (greenish-yellow to red) represent Straightness values higher than 0.65, while the cooler colors (light green to dark blue) correspond to Straightness values lower than 0.66. The majority of plots, corresponding to 74% (or 4,728 out of 6,407 plots) have Straightness values ranging from 0.66 to 0.75. Among the categories shown in the legend, 1,619 plots have values in the range of 0.72 to 0.75 making this the most common value range; this range is represented by orange on the map. On average, at a 1,600 m radius, all plots in Al Warqa are 70% as straight as a straight line.

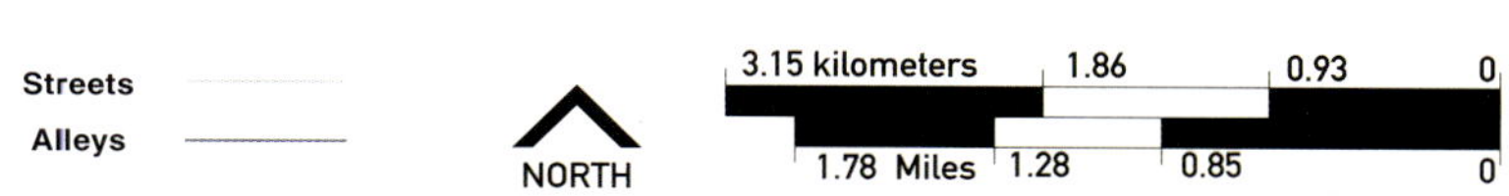

Centrality Analysis: Sample Scale

Sample 01

FIG. 15.1
Reach
Scenario 1: Streets only

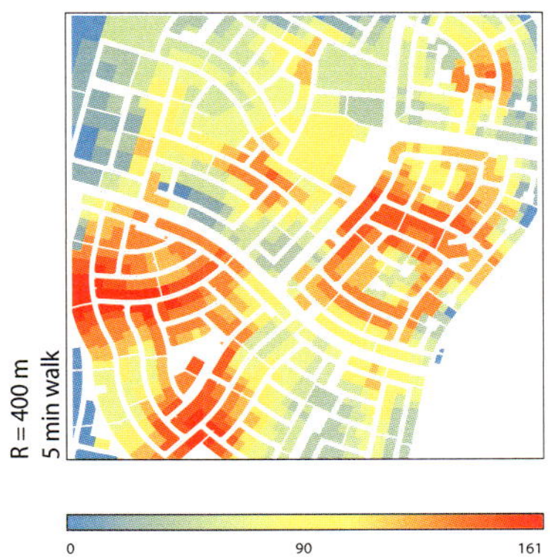

Reach (Radius = 400 m)
The maximum number of plots that can be reached within 5 min walking distance is 161 plots.
The average Reach of the sample is 89 plots.

Summary of Reach results
Minimum: 0
Maximum: 161
Mean: 89
Median: 97

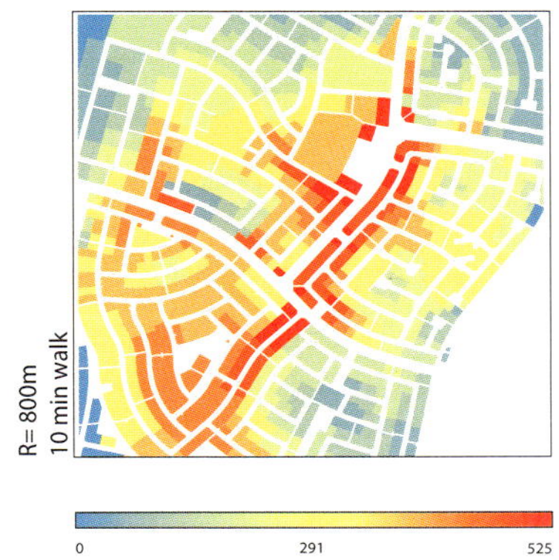

Reach (Radius = 800 m)
The maximum number of plots that can be reached within 10 min walking distance is 525 plots.
The average Reach of the sample is 291 plots.

Summary of Reach results
Minimum: 0
Maximum: 525
Mean: 291
Median: 305

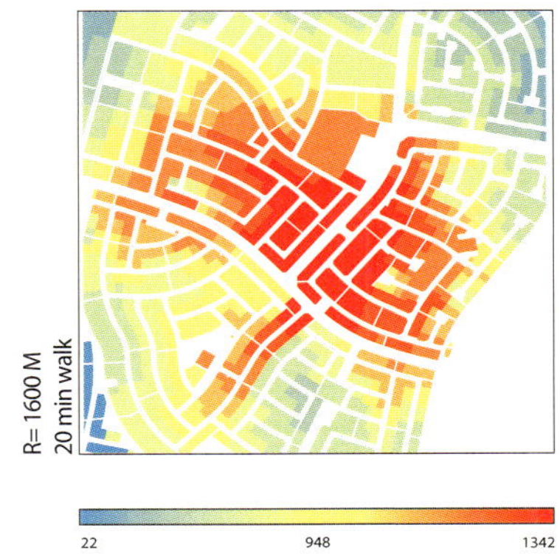

Reach (Radius = 1600 m)
The maximum number of plots that can be reached within 20 min walking distance is 1,342 plots.
The average Reach of the sample is 948 plots.

Summary of Reach results
Minimum: 22
Maximum: 1,342
Mean: 948
Median: 927

FIG. 15.2
Reach
Scenario 2: Streets + Alleys

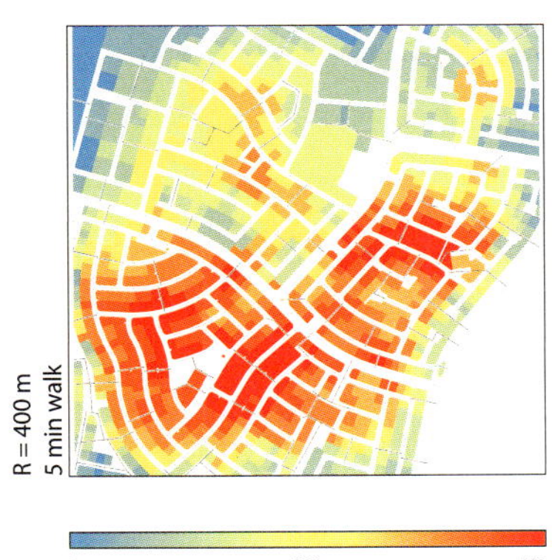

Reach (Radius = 400 m)
The maximum number of plots that can be reached within 5 min walking distance is 193 plots.
The average Reach of the sample is 120 plots.

Summary of Reach results
Minimum: 2
Maximum: 193
Mean: 120
Median: 123

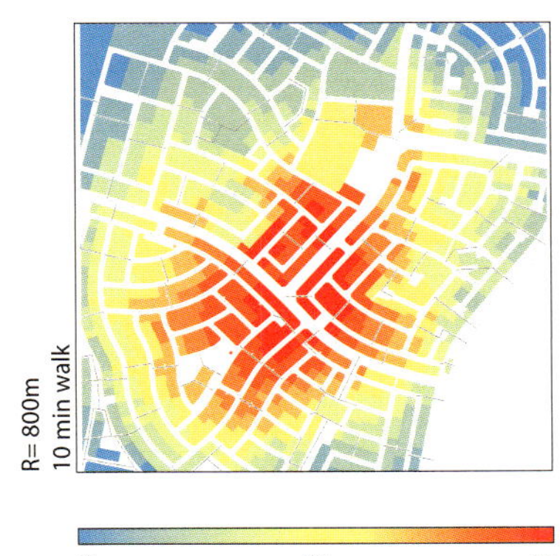

Reach (Radius = 800 m)
The maximum number of plots that can be reached within 10 min walking distance is 748 plots.
The average Reach of the sample is 422 plots.

Summary of Reach results
Minimum: 51
Maximum: 748
Mean: 423
Median: 420

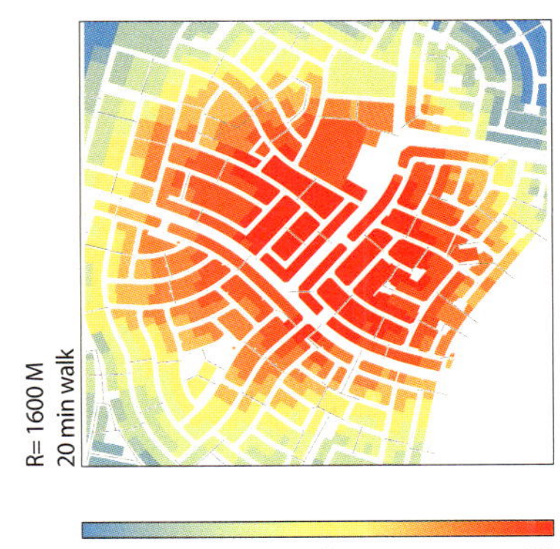

Reach (Radius = 1600 m)
The maximum number of plots that can be reached within 20 min walking distance is 1,373 plots.
The average Reach of the sample is 1,135 plots.

Summary of Reach Results
Minimum: 565
Maximum: 1,373
Mean: 1,136
Median: 1,164

At a 400 m radius, the plots with high Reach values ranging from 90 to 161 concentrate on two sides of the centrally-located collector street. At an 800 m radius, plots with high Reach values significantly appear the two collector streets that pass through the sample. At a 1,600 m radius, plots located on the upper side of the collector street have high Reach values ranging from 948 to 1,342. With the introduction of alleys, at a 400 m radius, the concentration of high Reach values becomes stronger and clearer below the centrally-located collector street, and also towards the right part of the sample. At an 800 m radius, high Reach values can be observed as one cluster at the center of the sample. At a 1,600 m radius, high Reach ranging from 1,136 to 1,373 become even more concentrated around the central area.

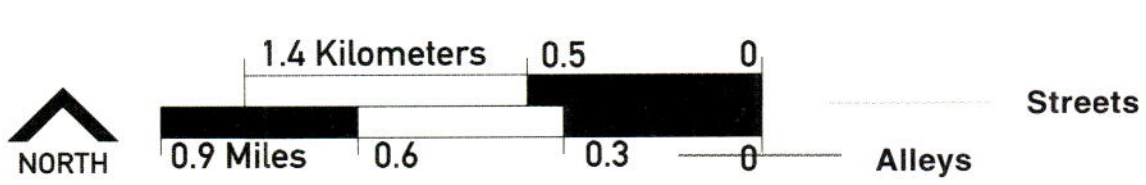

Sample 01

FIG. 15.3
Gravity
Scenario 1: Streets only

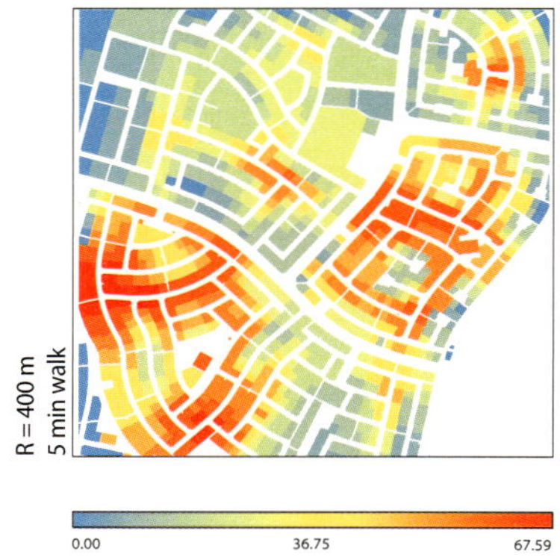

Gravity (Radius = 400 m)
The maximum number of plots that can be reached within 5 min walking distance with the distance decay effect is 67.59 plots.The average Gravity of the sample is 36.75 plots.

Summary of Gravity results
Minimum: 0.00
Maximum: 67.59
Mean: 36.75
Median: 3.17

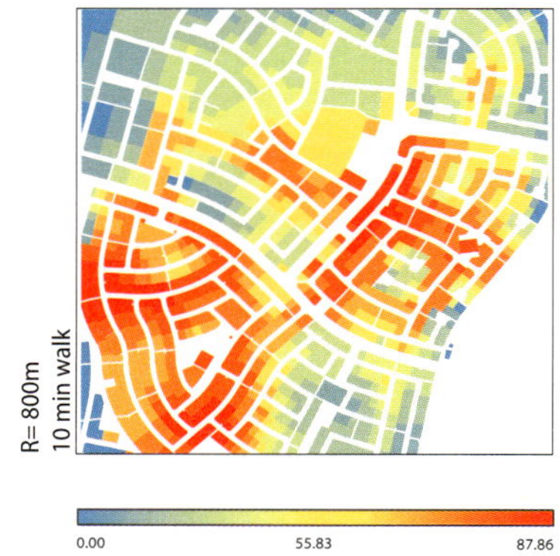

Gravity (Radius = 800 m)
The maximum number of plots that can be reached within 10 min walking distance with the distance decay effect is 87.86 plots.The average Gravity of the sample is 55.83 plots.

Summary of Gravity results
Minimum: 0.00
Maximum: 87.86
Mean: 55.83
Median: 58.39

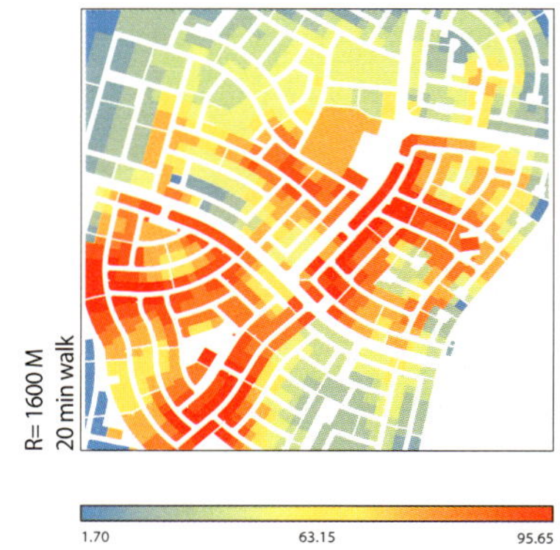

Gravity (Radius = 1600 m)
The maximum number of plots that can be reached within 20 min walking distance with the distance decay effect is 95.65 plots.The average Gravity of the sample is 63.15 plots.

Summary of Gravity results
Minimum: 1.70
Maximum: 95.65
Mean: 63.15
Median: 66.77

FIG. 15.4
Gravity
Scenario 2: Streets + Alleys

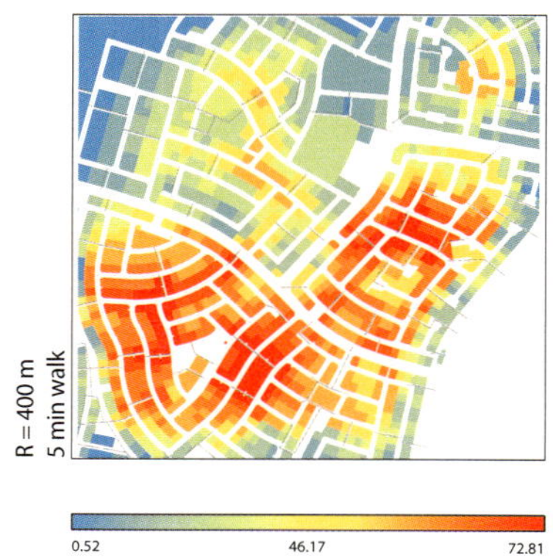

Gravity (Radius = 400 m)
The maximum number of plots that can be reached within 5 min walking distance with the distance decay effect is 72.81 plots. The average Gravity of the sample is 46 plots.

Summary of Gravity results
Minimum: 0.52
Maximum: 72.81
Mean: 46.17
Median: 47.65

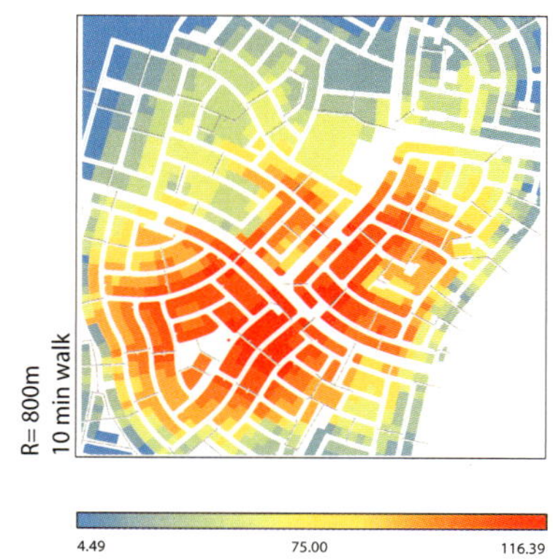

Gravity (Radius = 800 m)
The maximum number of plots that can be reached within 10 min walking distance with the distance decay effect is 116.39 plots. The average Gravity of the sample is 75.00 plots.

Summary of Gravity results
Minimum: 4.49
Maximum: 116.39
Mean: 75.00
Median: 75.53

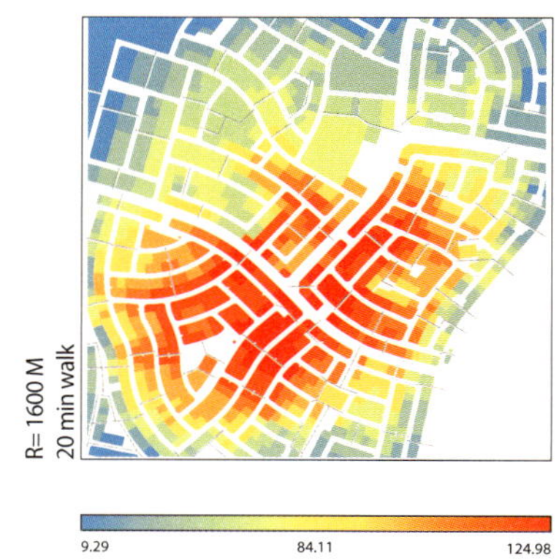

Gravity (Radius = 1600 m)
The maximum number of plots that can be reached within 20 min walking distance with the distance decay effect is 126.98 plots. The average Gravity of the sample is 84 plots.

Summary of Gravity results
Minimum: 9.29
Maximum: 124.98
Mean: 84.11
Median: 84.83

At a 400 m radius, high Gravity values ranging from 38.00 to 68.00 are found at the lower parts of the centrally-located collector streets. At 800 m and 1,600 m radii, high Gravity values ranging from 56.00 to 96.00 become even more concentrated at the same spots, and spread across the center of the sample. With the introduction of alleys, at a 400 m radius, Gravity value increases for all plots, and high values also appear below the center of the sample. At 800 m and 1,600 m radii, high values continue to become even more concentrated at the same spots. The highest Gravity values of 116.00 and 125.00 are obtained at 800 m and 1,600 m radii respectively. The distribution of Gravity values does not change notably with changing radius; however, the values are improved for all plots when the radius increases.

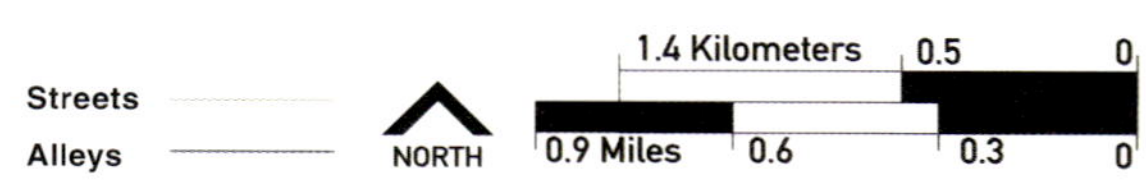

FIG. 15.5

Straightness

Scenario 1: Streets only

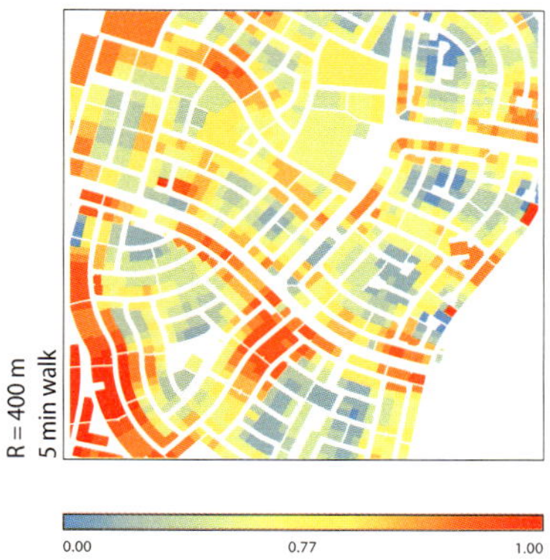

Straightness (Normalized Values, Radius = 400 m)

Plots withing 5min walking distance have access to roads with an average Straightness value of 0.77.

Summary of Straightness results
Minimum: 0.57
Maximum: 1.00
Mean: 0.77
Median: 0.76

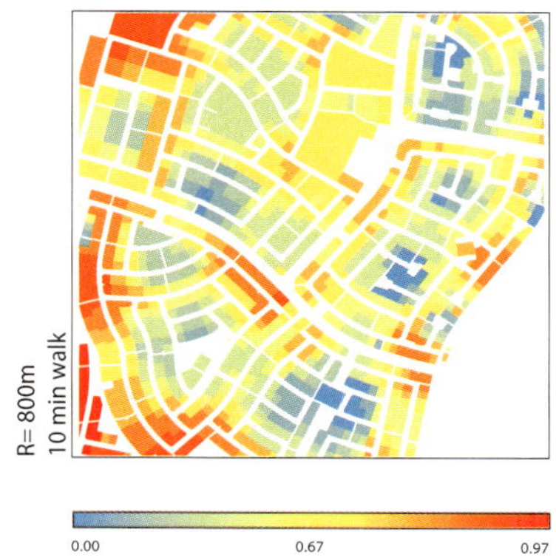

Straightness (Normalized Values, Radius = 800 m)

Plots withing 10 min walking distance have access to roads with an average Straightness value of 0.67.

Summary of Straightness results
Minimum: 0.45
Maximum: 0.97
Mean: 0.67
Median: 0.67

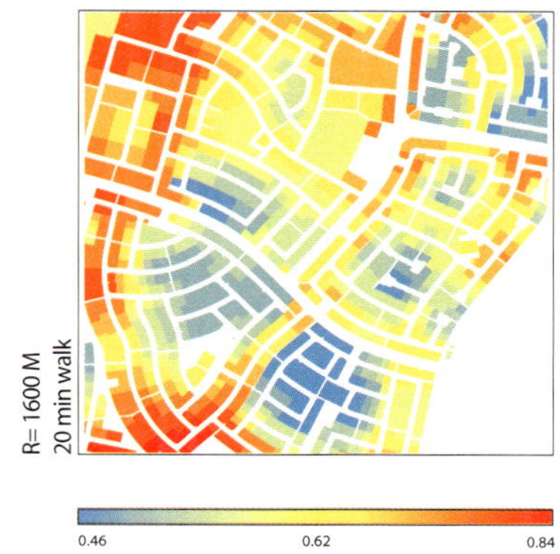

Straightness (Normalized Values, Radius = 1600 m)

Plots withing 20 min walking distance have access to roads with an average Straightness value of 0.63.

Summary of Straightness results
Minimum: 0.46
Maximum: 0.84
Mean: 0.63
Median: 0.64

FIG. 15.6

Straightness

Scenario 2: Streets + Alleys

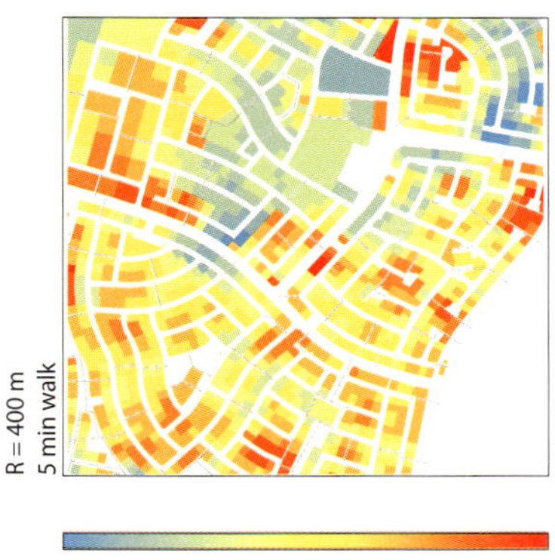

Straightness (Normalized Values, Radius = 400 m)

Plots withing 5 min walking distance have access to roads with an average Straightness value of 0.74.

Summary of Straightness results
Minimum: 0.56
Maximum:0.86
Mean: 0.74
Median: 0.75

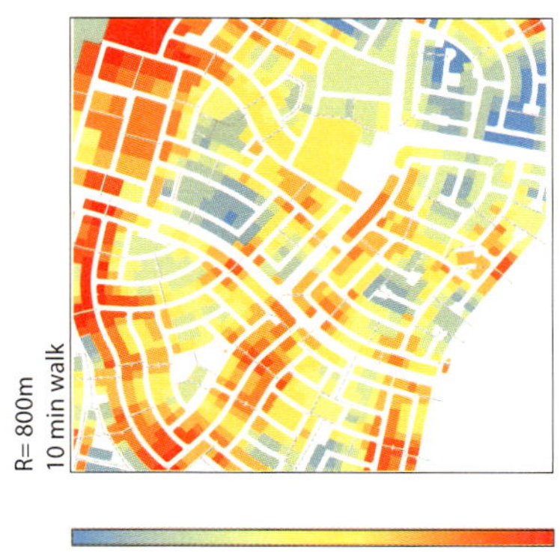

Straightness (Normalized Values, Radius = 800 m)

Plots withing 10 min walking distance have access to roads with an average Straightness value of 0.72.

Summary of Straightness results
Minimum: 0.52
Maximum: 0.82
Mean: 0.72
Median: 0.73

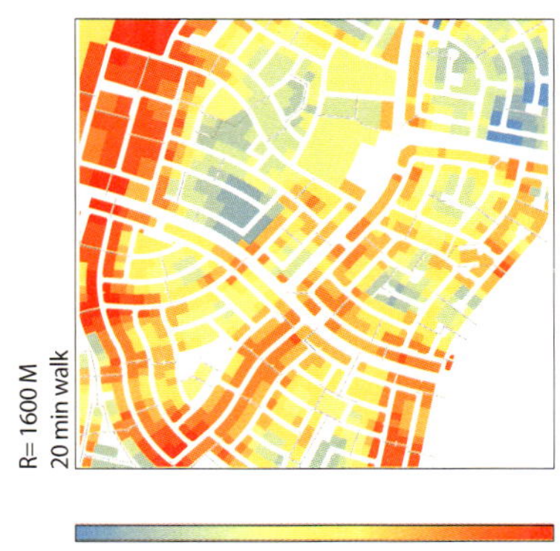

Straightness (Normalized Values, Radius = 1600 m)

Plots withing 20 min walking distance have access to roads with an average Straightness value of 0.73.

Summary of Straightness results
Minimum: 0.54
Maximum: 0.81
Mean: 0.73
Median: 0.74

At a 400 m radius, high Straightness values (0.75 to 1.00) are obtained by some plots that lie along the centrally-located collector street, and along the internal street near the bottom left corner of the sample. At an 800 m radius, the number of plots having high Straightness values is decreased. Also, the maximum Straightness value is decreased by 0.03. At a 1,600 m radius, Straightness value decreases for most plots, and the maximum value also decreases by 0.13. With the introduction of alleys, at 400 m, high Straightness values (0.75 to 0.86) are distributed evenly across the sample area, with no discernable pattern. At 800 m, high values can be observed along the internal streets near the left edge of the sample, and also along few internal streets that connect with the centrally-located collector streets. At a 1,600 m radius, high Straightness values become even more concentrated at the same spots, while the maximum Straightness value is slightly decreased by 0.01.

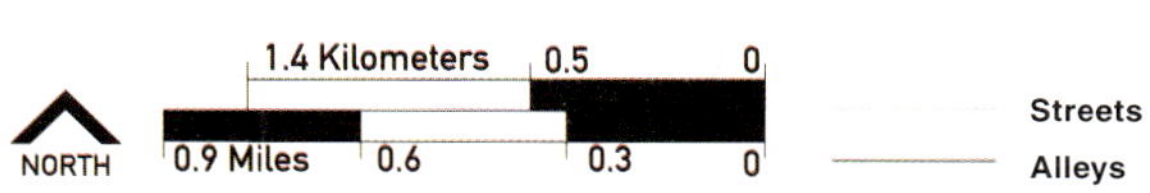

Sample 02

FIG. 16.1

Reach

Scenario 1: Streets only

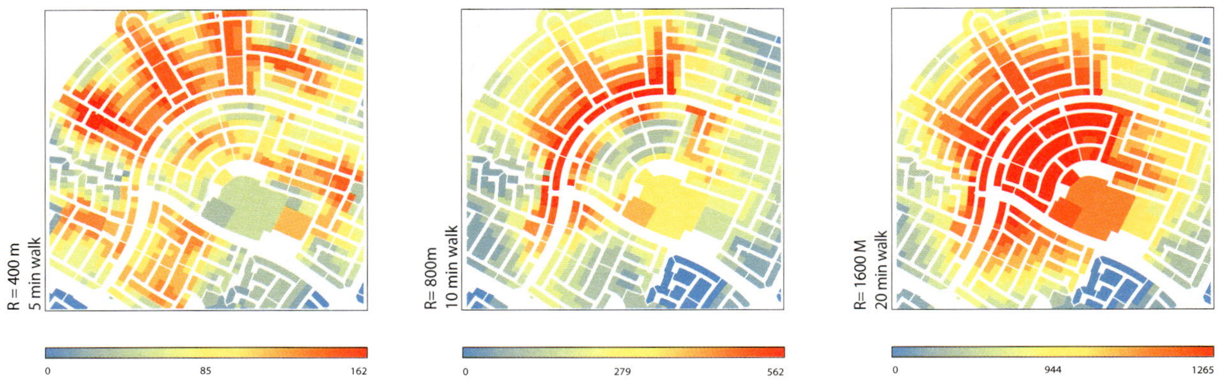

Reach (Radius = 400 m)

The maximum number of plots that can be reached within 5 min walking distance is 162 plots.
The average Reach of the sample is 89 plots.

Summary of Reach results
Minimum: 0
Maximum: 162
Mean: 89
Median: 90.0

Reach (Radius = 800 m)

The maximum number of plots that can be reached within 10 min walking distance is 562 plots.
The average Reach of the sample is 280 plots.

Summary of Reach results
Minimum: 0
Maximum: 562
Mean: 280
Median: 283.0

Reach (Radius = 1600 m)

The maximum number of plots that can be reached within 20 min walking distance is 1265 plots.
The average Reach of the sample is 944 plots.

Summary of Reach results
Minimum: 0
Maximum: 1265
Mean: 944
Median: 941

FIG. 16.2

Reach

Scenario 2: Streets + Alleys

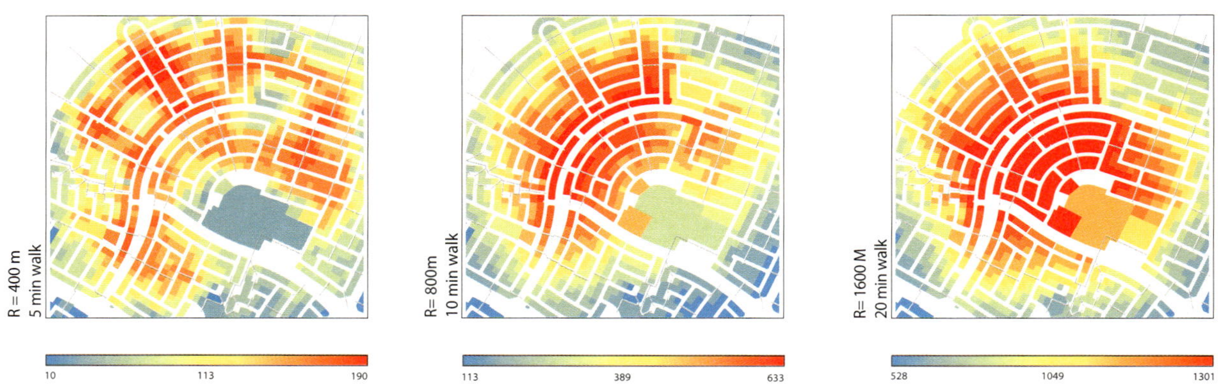

Reach (Radius = 400 m)

The maximum number of plots that can be reached within 5 min walking distance is 190 plots.
The average Reach of the sample is 113 plots.

Summary of Reach results
Minimum: 10
Maximum: 190
Mean: 113
Median: 115

Reach (Radius = 800 m)

The maximum number of plots that can be reached within 10 min walking distance is 633 plots.
The average Reach of the sample is 389 plots.

Summary of Reach results
Minimum: 113
Maximum: 633
Mean: 389
Median: 385

Reach (Radius = 1600 m)

The maximum number of plots that can be reached within 20 min walking distance is 1,301 plots.
The average Reach of the sample is 1,049 plots.

Summary of Reach Results
Minimum: 528
Maximum: 1,301
Mean: 1,049
Median: 1,040

At a 400 m radius, the plots with high Reach values ranging from 85 to 162 concentrate along few internal streets that connect to the looping collector street. At an 800 m radius, high Reach values shift towards the plots lying adjacent to the looping collector street, primarily on the upper part of the street. At a 1,600 m radius, high Reach values ranging from 944 to 1,265 are obtained by plots around the radial internal streets and also at the center of the sample. With the introduction of alleys, at a 400 m radius, high Reach values become even more concentrated along the internal streets that connect to the looping collector street, and also near the intersection of collector streets. At an 800 m radius, plots with high Reach values can be observed as one cluster along the looping collector street. Similar to the case without alleys, at a 1,600 m radius, when alleys are included in the analysis, plots with high Reach values ranging from 1,049 to 1,301 concentrate at the center of the sample.

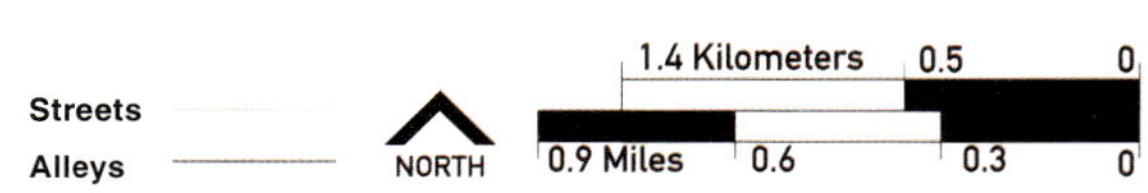

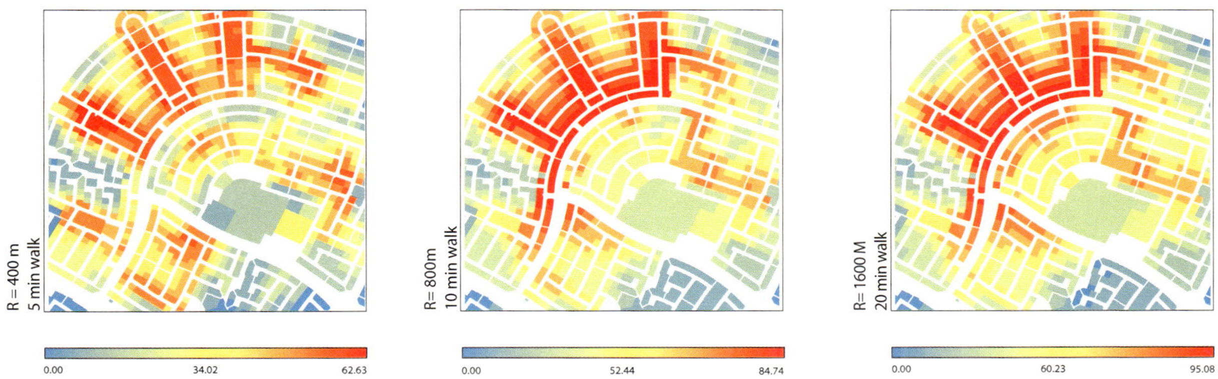

Gravity (Radius = 400 m)
The maximum number of plots that can be reached within 5 min walking distance with the distance decay effect is 62.63 plots. The average Gravity of the sample is 34.02 plots.

Summary of Gravity results
Minimum: 0.00
Maximum: 62.63
Mean: 34.02
Median: 35.01

Gravity (Radius = 800 m)
The maximum number of plots that can be reached within 10 min walking distance with the distance decay effect is 67.59 plots. The average Gravity of the sample is 52.44 plots.

Summaryof Gravity results
Minimum: 0.00
Maximum: 84.74
Mean: 52.44
Median: 52.45

Gravity (Radius = 1600 m)
The maximum number of plots that can be reached within 20 min walking distance with the distance decay effect is 67.59 plots. The average Gravity of the sample is 60 plots.

Summary of Gravity results
Minimum: 0.00
Maximum: 95.08
Mean: 60.23
Median: 61.61

FIG. 16.3
Gravity
Scenario 1: Streets only

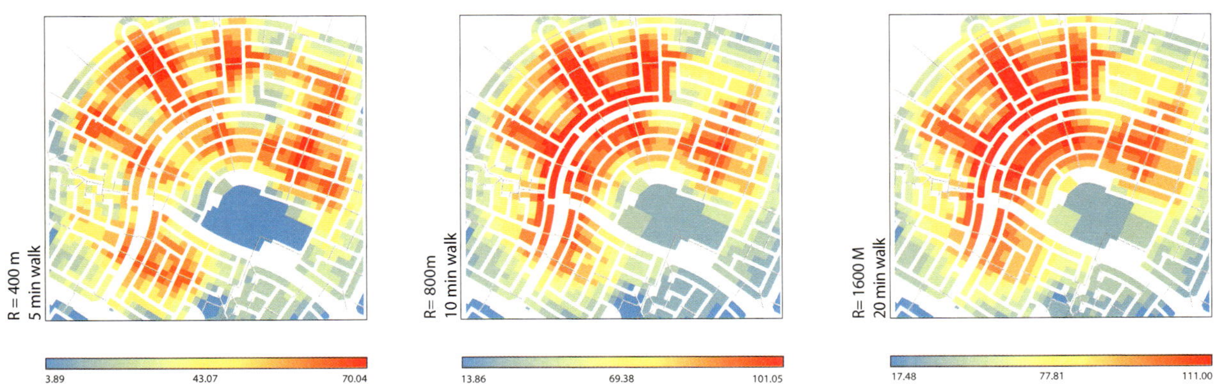

Gravity (Radius = 400 m)
The maximum number of plots that can be reached within 5 min walking distance with the distance decay effect is 70.04 plots. The average Gravity of the sample is 43.07 plots.

Summary of Gravity results
Minimum: 3.98
Maximum: 70.04
Mean: 43.07
Median: 43.98

Gravity (Radius = 800 m)
The maximum number of plots that can be reached within 10 min walking distance with the distance decay effect is 101.05 plots. The average Gravity of the sample is 69.38 plots.

Summary of Gravity results
Minimum: 13.86
Maximum: 101.05
Mean: 69.38
Median: 71.78

Gravity (Radius = 1600 m)
The maximum number of plots that can be reached within 20 min walking distance with the distance decay effect is 111.00 plots. The average Gravity of the sample is 77.81 plots.

Summary of Gravity results
Minimum: 17.48
Maximum: 111.00
Mean: 77.81
Median: 79.84

FIG. 16.4
Gravity
Scenario 2: Streets + Alleys

At a 400 m radius, high Gravity values ranging from 34.00 to 63.00 are found along few radial internal streets that connect to the looping collector street. At 800 m and 1,600 m radii, high Gravity values ranging from 52.00 to 95.00 concentrate at the same spots, and become prominent along the looping collector street. With the introduction of alleys, at a 400 m radius, high Gravity values can also be observed near the center of the sample. At 800 m and 1,600 m radii, the highest Gravity values of 101.00 and 111.00 are obtained respectively. The distribution of Gravity values does not change notably with changing radius; however, the values are improved for all plots when the radius increases.

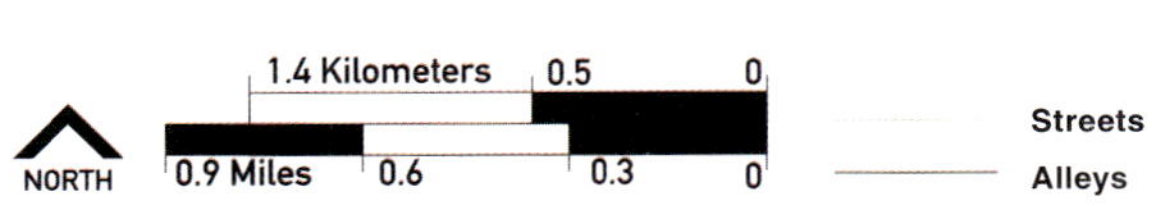

Sample 02

FIG. 16.5

Straightness

Scenario 1: Streets only

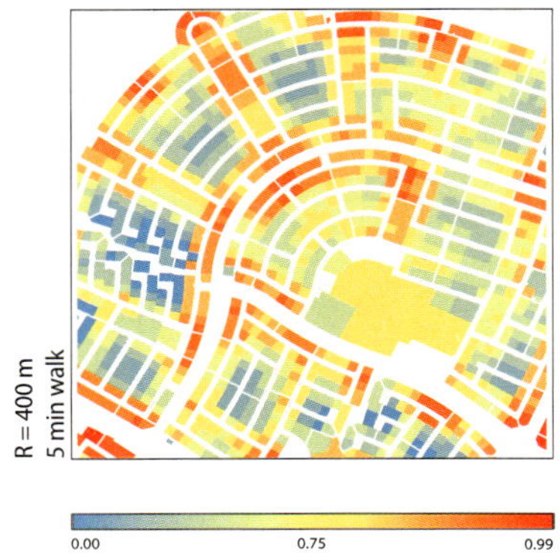

Straightness (Normalized Values, Radius = 400 m)
Plots withing 5 min walking distance have access to roads with an average Straightness value of 0.75.

Summary of Straightness results
Minimum: 0.56
Maximum: 0.99
Mean: 0.75
Median: 0.75

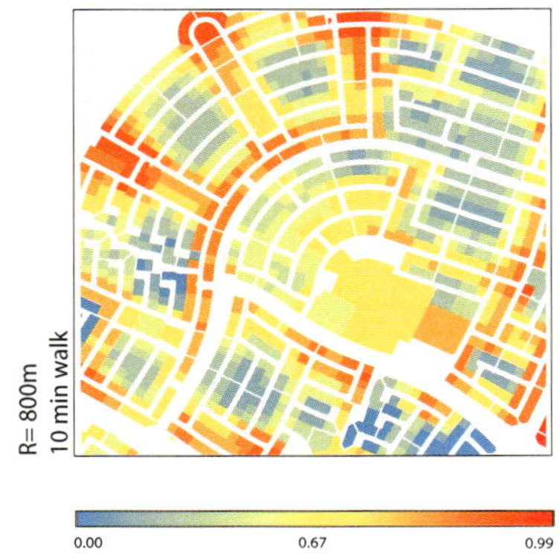

Straightness (Normalized Values, Radius = 800 m)
Plots withing 10 min walking distance have access to roads with an average Straightness value of 0.67.

Summary of Straightness results
Minimum: 0.51
Maximum: 0.99
Mean: 0.67
Median: 0.67

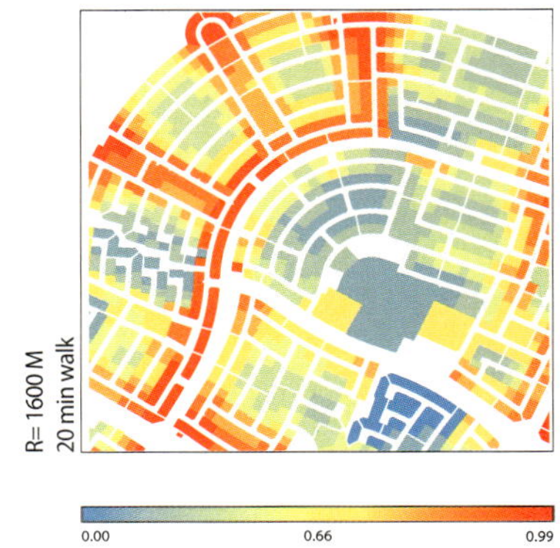

Straightness (Normalized Values, Radius = 1600 m)
Plots withing 20 min walking distance have access to roads with an average Straightness value of 0.66.

Summary of Straightness results
Minimum: 0.40
Maximum: 0.99
Mean: 0.66
Median: 0.67

FIG. 16.6

Straightness

Scenario 2: Streets + Alleys

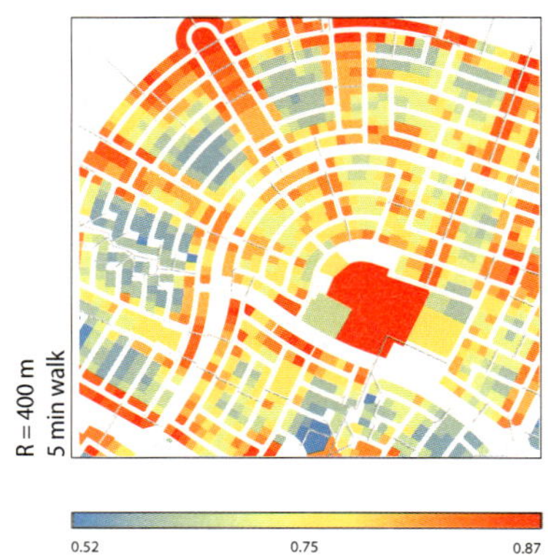

Straightness (Normalized Values, Radius = 400 m)
Plots withing 5 min walking distance have access to roads with an average Straightness value of 0.75.

Summary of Straightness results
Minimum: 0.52
Maximum: 0.87
Mean: 0.75
Median: 0.75

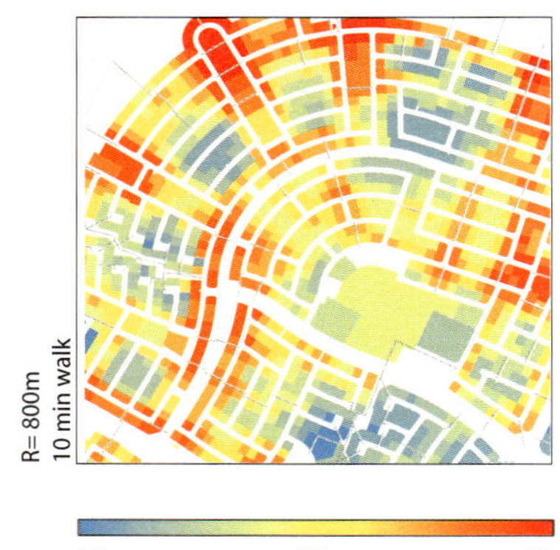

Straightness (Normalized Values, Radius = 800 m)
Plots withing 10 min walking distance have access to roads with an average Straightness value of 0.74.

Summary of Straightness results
Minimum: 0.54
Maximum: 0.84
Mean: 0.74
Median: 0.74

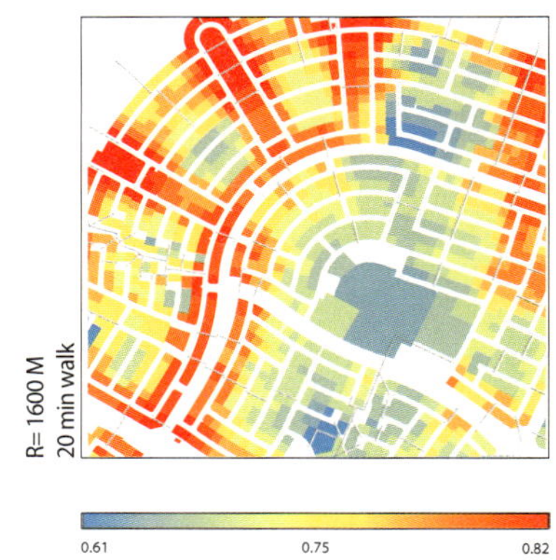

Straightness (Normalized Values, Radius = 1600 m)
Plots withing 20 min walking distance have access to roads with an average Straightness value of 0.75.

Summary of Straightness results
Minimum: 0.61
Maximum: 0.82
Mean: 0.75
Median: 0.75

At a 400 m radius, high Straightness values (0.75 to 0.99) are obtained by plots that lie along the two collector streets, and some plots near the intersections of internal streets. At an 800 m radius, high Straightness values become even more concentrated at the same spots. At a 1,600 m radius, high Straightness values continue to concentrate along the looping collector street and few internal streets that connect to it. With the introduction of alleys, at 400 m, high Straightness values (0.75 to 0.87) are obtained by plots located along the radially-oriented internal streets that connect with the looping collector street. At 800 m, high values can be also observed near the intersection of the collector streets. At a 1,600 m radius, high Straightness values become prominent along the looping collector street and few radial internal streets that connect to it.

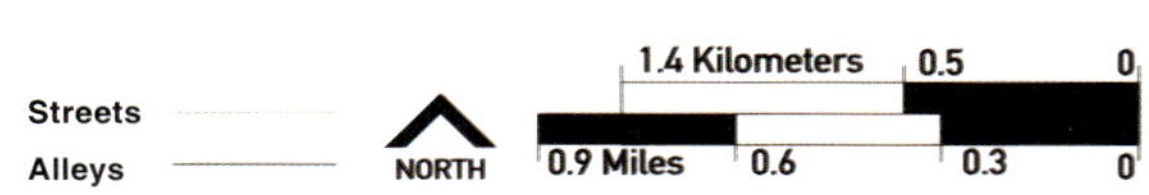

Summary of Centrality Results

Neighborhood

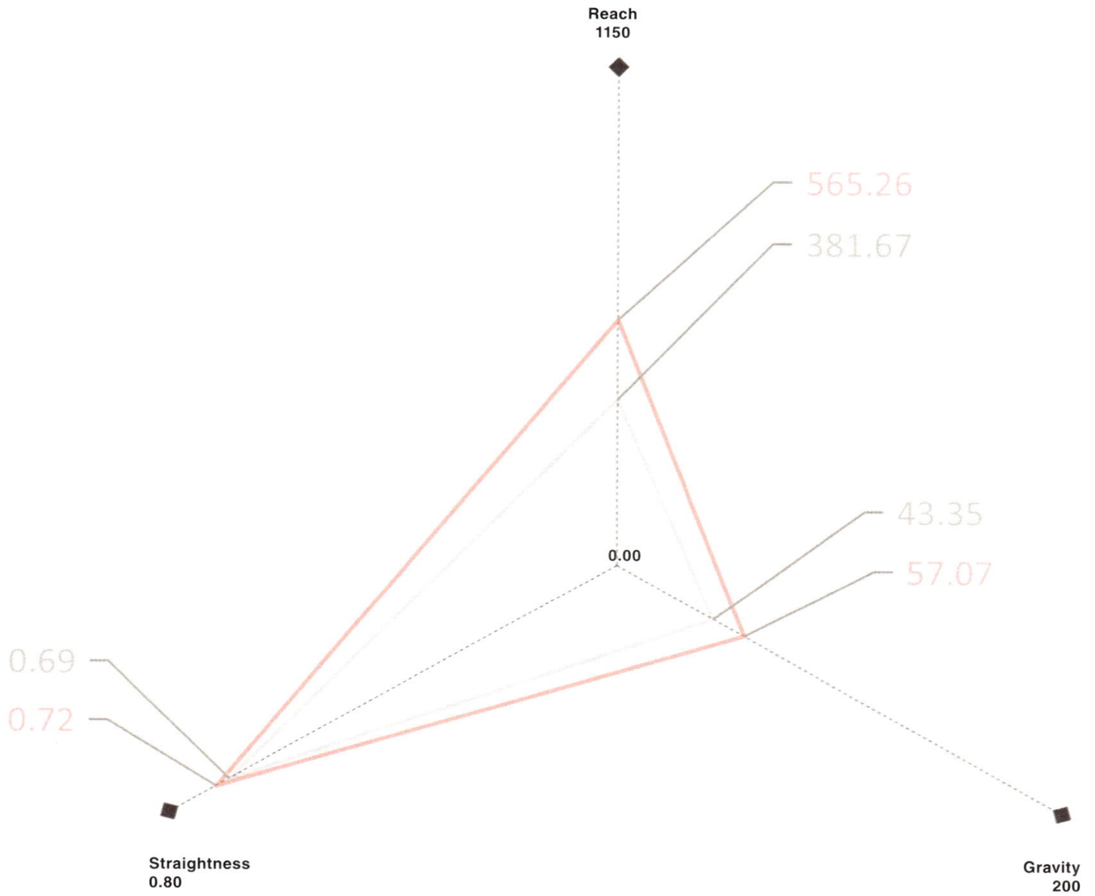

FIG. 17
Spider graphs showing the contribution of alleyways to the averages of 400m, 800m, and 1600m scales of Reach, Gravity and Straightness

Sample 01

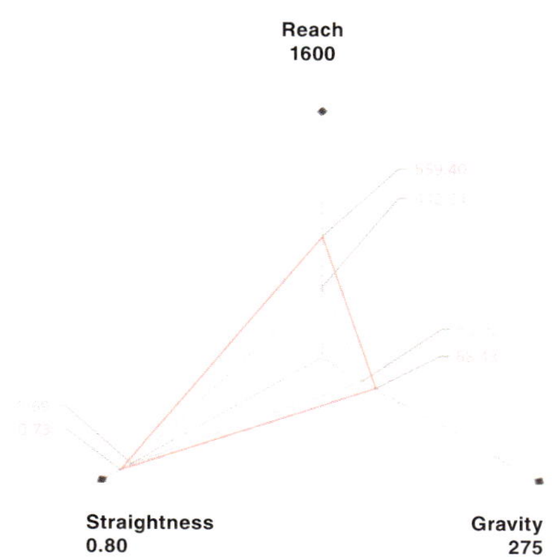

Sample 02

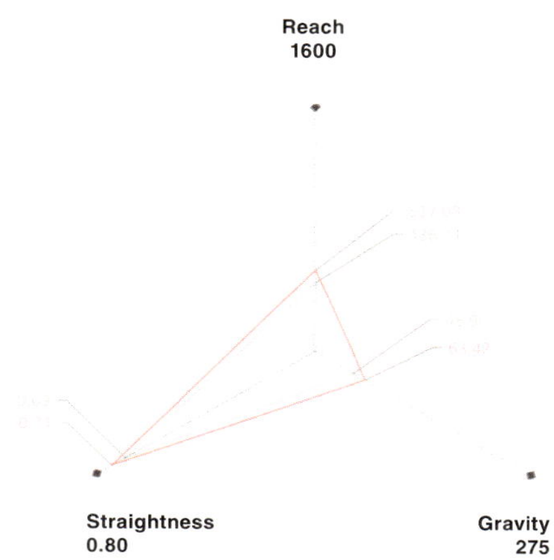

Neighborhood Scale

FIG. 18

Histograms showing the distribution of centrality values (Reach, Gravity, and Straightness) among plots with and without alleys at three different scales 400m, 800m, and 1600m. The X axis is for the centrality metric values, while the Y axis is for the percentage of plots achieving a centrality value denoted on the X axis.

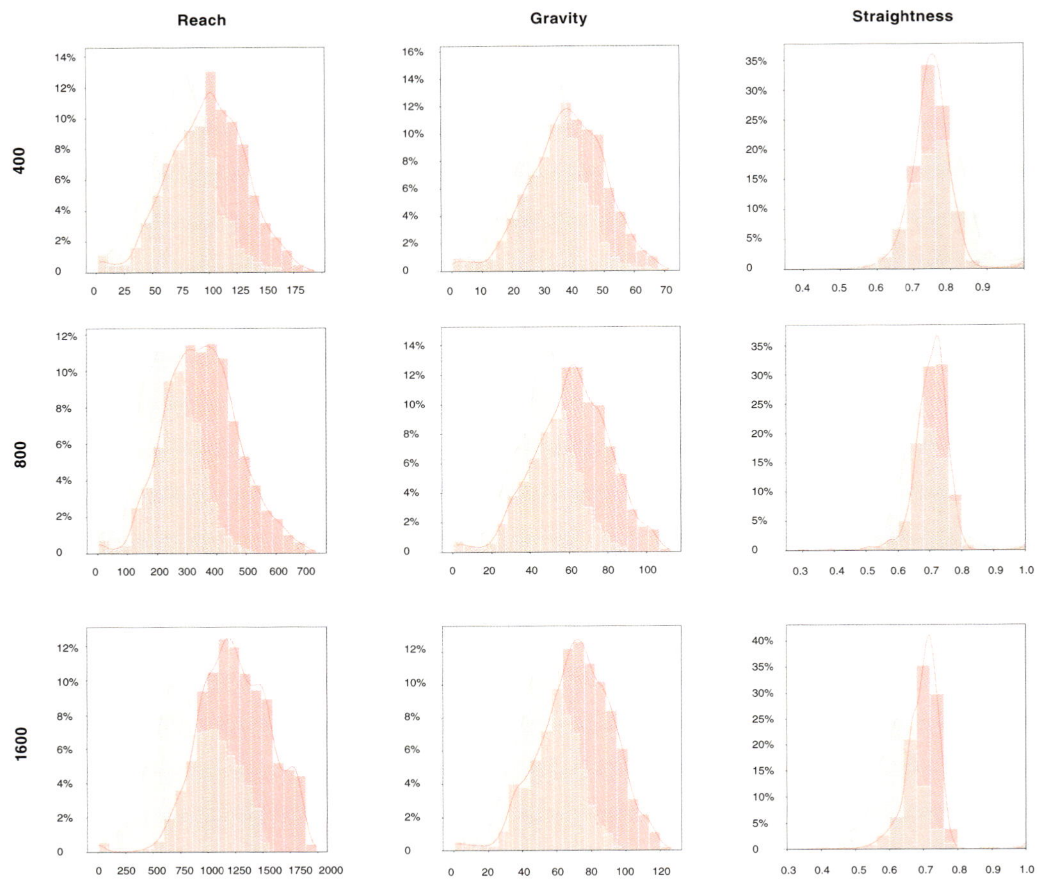

TABLE. 1

Neighborhood scale centrality values

UNA		Radius	Min	Max	Avg
Scenario 1: Streets only	Reach	400	1	163	75
		800	1	532	235
		1600	3	1554	834
	Gravity	400	0.13	68.72	31.18
		800	0.80	89.51	46.38
		1600	0.13	96.88	52.50
	Straightness	400	0.00	1.00	0.77
		800	0.00	1.00	0.68
		1600	0.00	1.00	0.62

UNA		Radius	Min	Max	Avg
Scenario 2: Streets + Alleys	Reach	400	1	193	98
		800	1	733	352
		1600	1	1987	1245
	Gravity	400	0.22	71.36	38.04
		800	0.09	112.24	61.72
		1600	0.41	126.26	71.46
	Straightness	400	0.00	1.00	0.75
		800	0.00	1.00	0.71
		1600	0.00	1.00	0.70

Sample Scale — Sample 01

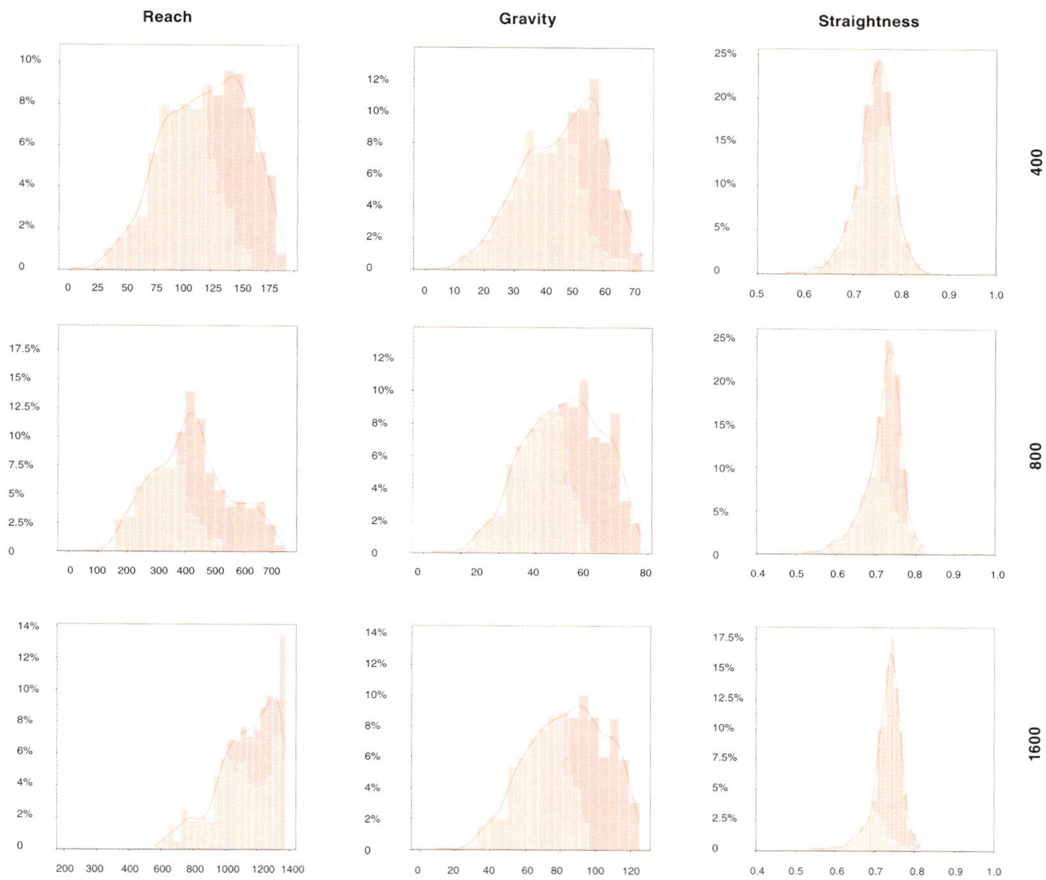

FIG. 19

Histograms showing the distribution of centrality values (Reach, Gravity, and Straightness) among plots with and without alleys at three different scales 400m, 800m, and 1600m. The X axis is for the centrality metric values, while the Y axis is for the percentage of plots achieving a centrality value denoted on the X axis.

Scenario	UNA	Radius	Min	Max	Avg
Scenario 1: Streets only	Reach	400	0	161	89
		800	0	525	291
		1600	22	1342	948
	Gravity	400	0.00	67.59	36.76
		800	0.00	87.86	55.84
		1600	1.71	95.65	63.16
	Straightness	400	0.00	1.00	0.77
		800	0.00	0.97	0.67
		1600	0.46	0.84	0.63

Scenario	UNA	Radius	Min	Max	Avg
Scenario 2: Streets + Alleys	Reach	400	2	193	120
		800	51	748	423
		1600	565	1373	1135
	Gravity	400	0.52	72.82	46.18
		800	4.49	116.40	75.00
		1600	9.29	124.99	84.12
	Straightness	400	0.56	0.86	0.74
		800	0.52	0.82	0.72
		1600	0.54	0.81	0.73

TABLE. 2

Sample 01 centrality values

Sample Scale — Sample 02

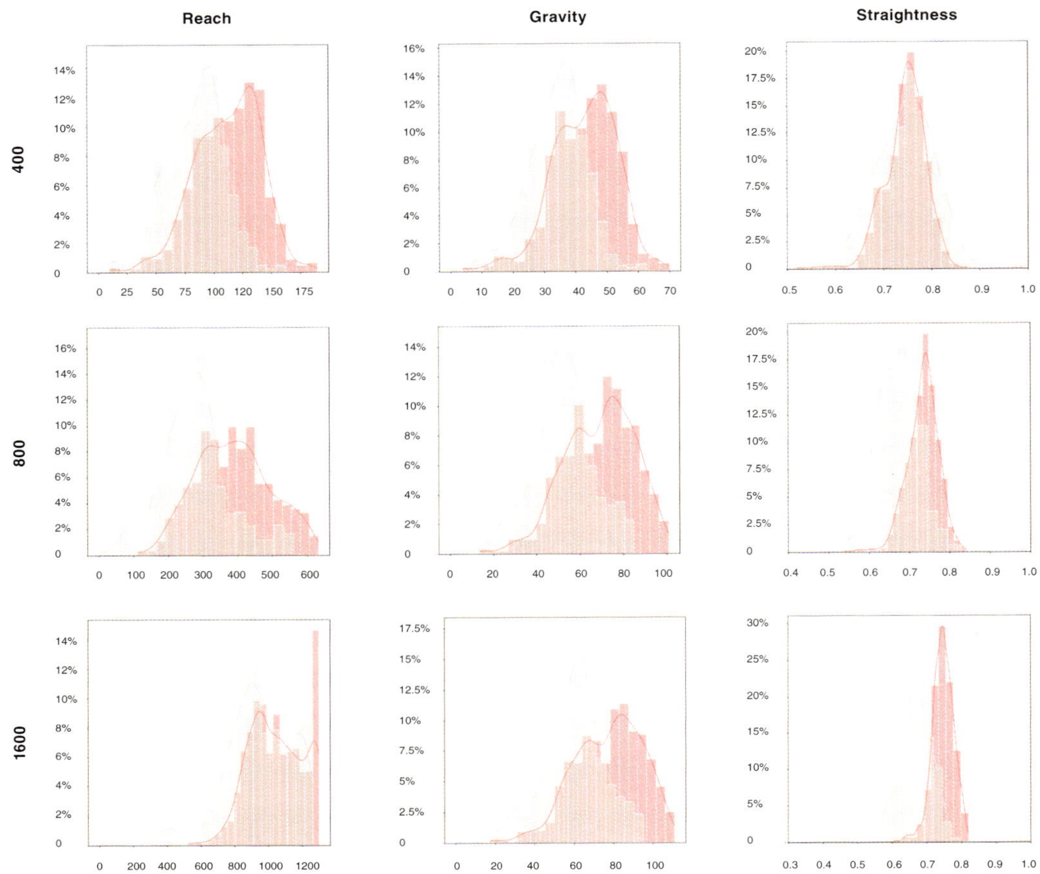

FIG. 20

Histograms showing the distribution of centrality values (Reach, Gravity, and Straightness) among plots with and without alleys at three different scales 400m, 800m, and 1600m.The X axis is for the centrality metric values, while the Y axis is for the percentage of plots achieving a centrality value denoted on the X axis.

TABLE. 3

Sample 02 centrality values

UNA		Radius	Min	Max	Avg
Scenario 2: Streets + Alleys	Reach	400	10	190	113
		800	113	633	389
		1600	528	1301	1049
	Gravity	400	3.90	70.04	43.07
		800	13.86	101.05	69.38
		1600	17.49	111.01	77.81
	Straightness	400	0.52	0.87	0.75
		800	0.54	0.84	0.74
		1600	0.61	0.82	0.75

UNA		Radius	Min	Max	Avg
Scenario 1: Streets only	Reach	400	0	162	85
		800	0	562	280
		1600	0	1265	944
	Gravity	400	0.00	62.64	34.02
		800	0.00	84.74	52.45
		1600	0.00	95.08	60.24
	Straightness	400	0.00	0.99	0.75
		800	0.00	0.99	0.67
		1600	0.00	0.99	0.66

DUBAI CREEK
AL BAHYA
WEST ISLAND

Global Scale Analysis

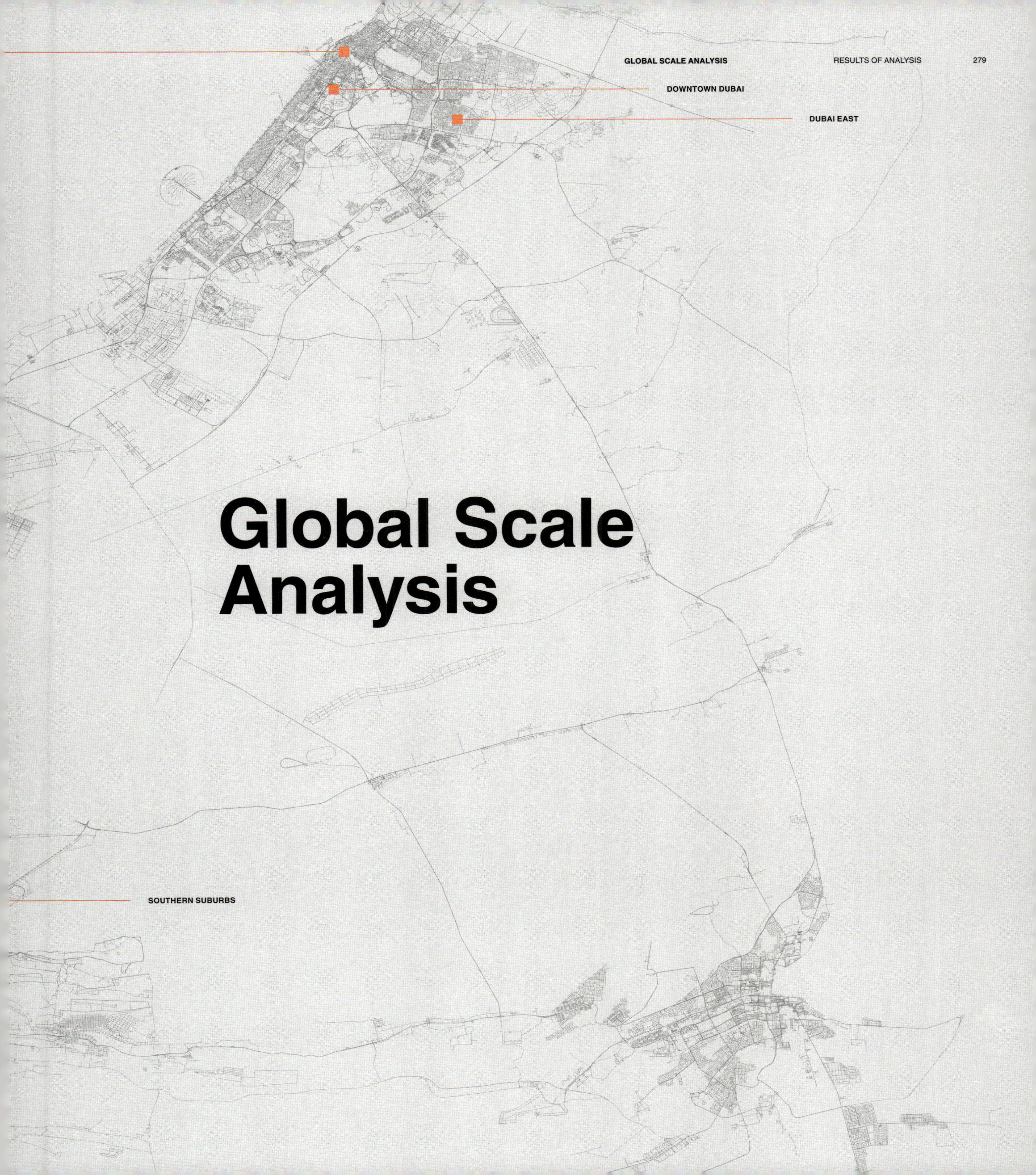

1
3

FIG. 1
Full map of Abu Dhabi showing Reach results for the selected samples

1. West Island and Vicinity
2. Al Bahya Region
3. Southern Suburbs

West Island and Vicinity

Centrality Analysis

3,000 m Radius

FIG. 2.1
Reach

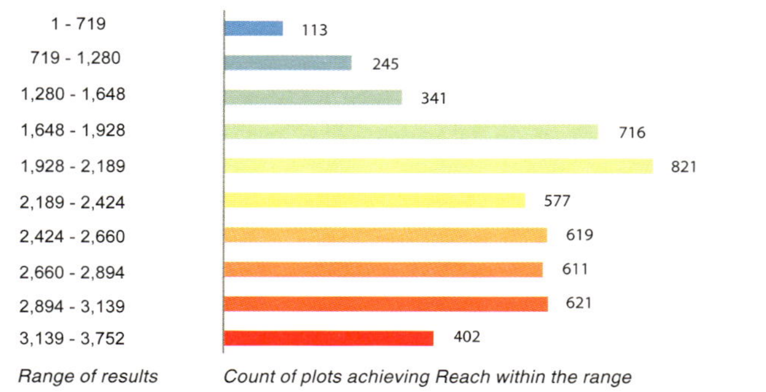

The warmer colors (greenish-yellow to red) represent Reach values of 1,928 or more, while the cooler colors (light green to dark blue) correspond to a Reach value of 1,927 or less. The majority of plots, corresponding to 56% of all plots (or 2,830 out of 5,066 plots), have Reach values ranging from 2,189 to 3,752. Among the different categories shown in the legend, 821 plots have values in the range of 1,928 to 2,189, making this the most common range; this range is represented by greenish-yellow on the map. High Reach values ranging from 2,894 to 3,752 are obtained by 1,023 plots or 20% of the total plots. These plots are located near the center of the sample, on both sides of the arterial street. Low Reach values ranging from 1 to 1,928 are obtained by 1,415 plots or 28% of the total plots. The plots are located mostly in the southwestern and the northeastern parts of the sample. On average, 2,287 plots can be reached from each plot at a radius of 3,000 m.

FIG. 2.2
Gravity

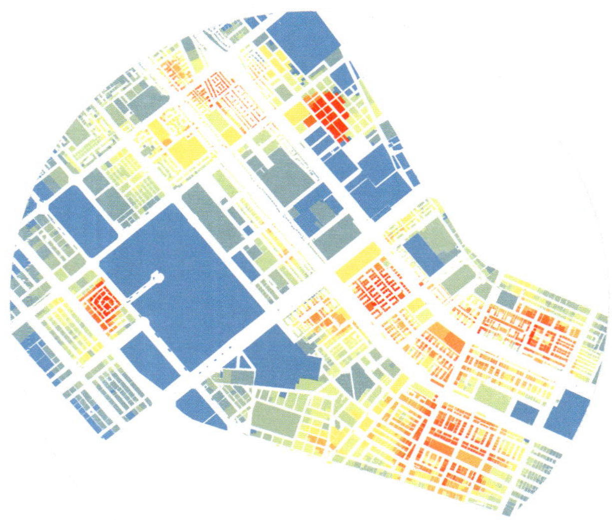

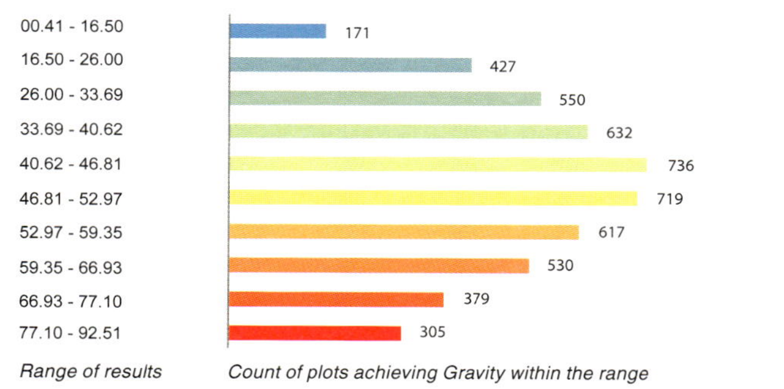

The warmer colors (greenish-yellow to red) represent Gravity values of more than 40.61, while the cooler colors (light green to dark blue) correspond to Gravity values of less than 40.62. The majority of plots, corresponding to 50% of all plots (or 2,550 out of 5,066 plots), have Gravity values ranging from 46.81 to 92.51. Among the different categories shown in the legend, 736 plots have values in the range of 40.62 to 46.81, making this the most common range; this range is represented by greenish-yellow on the map. High Gravity values ranging from 59.35 to 92.51 are obtained by 1,214 plots or 24% of the total plots. These plots are mostly located in three locations– the southeastern part, a small block in the western side, and the northeastern part of the sample. Low Gravity values ranging from 0.41 to 33.69 are obtained by 1,148 plots or 23% of the total plots. On average, at a radius of 3,000 m, 47.32 plots can be reached from each plot when the distance decay effect is taken into consideration.

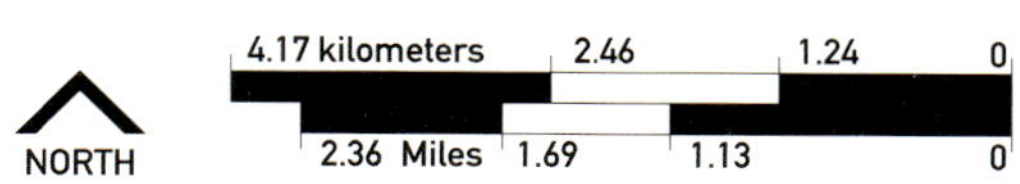

Streets

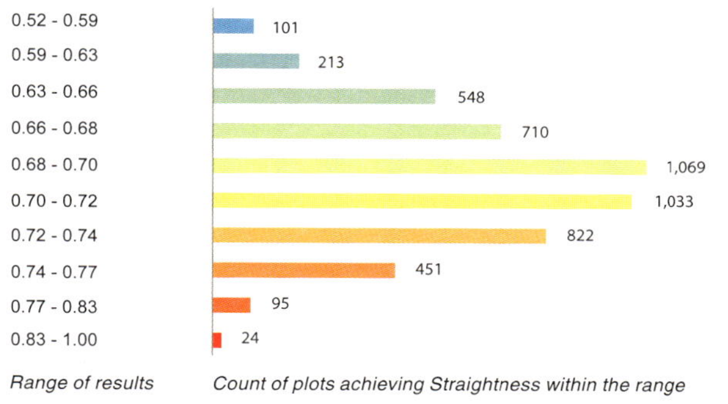

The warmer colors (greenish-yellow to red) represent Straightness values between 0.68 and 1.00, while the cooler colors (light green to dark blue) correspond to Straightness values from 0.52 to 0.68. The majority of plots, corresponding to 58% of all plots (or 2,924 out of 5,066 plots), have Straightness values ranging from 0.68 to 0.74. Among the different categories shown in the map's legend, 1,069 plots have values in the range of 0.68 to 0.70, making this the most common range; this range is represented by greenish-yellow on the map. High Straightness values (0.75 – 1.00) are located along major thoroughfares, and a prominent concentration of such plots is visible in the southeastern part of the sample. Low Straightness values are obtained by large sized plots which are located across the sample. On average, the Straightness of plots in this sample is 0.71 at a 3,000 m radius, which means that their paths to other plots are 71% as straight as a straight line.

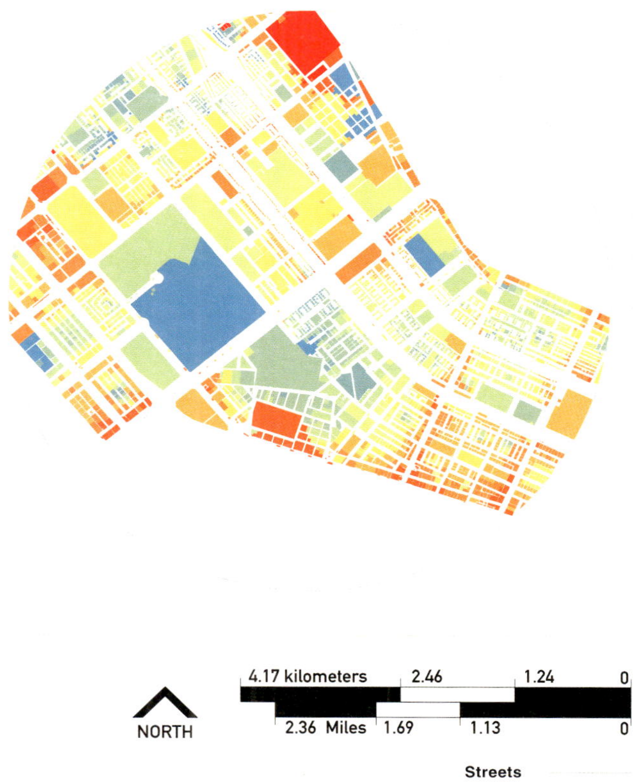

FIG. 2.3
Straightness

Al Bahya Region

Centrality Analysis

6,000 m Radius

FIG. 3.1
Reach

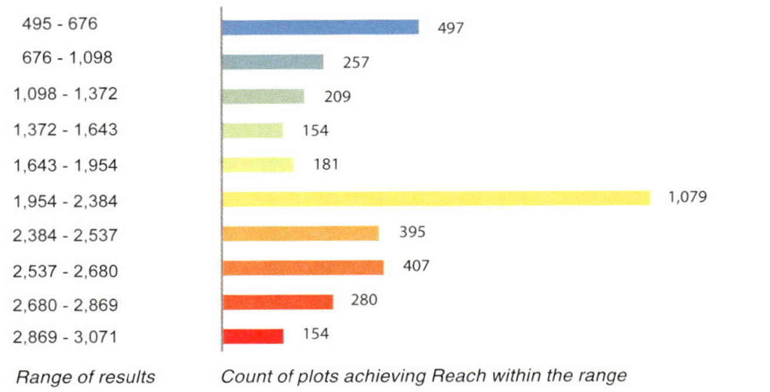

The warmer colors (greenish-yellow to red) represent Reach values of more than 1,642, while the cooler colors (light green to dark blue) correspond to Reach values of less than 1,643. The majority of plots, corresponding to 64% of all plots (or 2,315 out of 3,613 plots), have Reach values ranging from 1,954 to 3,071. Among the different categories shown in the legend, 1,079 plots have values in the range of 1,954 to 2,384, making this the most common range; this range is represented by yellow on the map. High Reach values ranging from 2,537 to 3,071 are obtained by 841 plots, or 23% of the total plots. These plots are mostly located in the western side of Al Bahya East. Low Reach values ranging from 495 to 1,372 are obtained by 963 plots, or 27% of the total plots. These plots are located in the northern and southern parts of Al Bahya West. On average, 1,956 plots can be reached from each plot at a radius of 6,000 m.

FIG. 3.2
Gravity

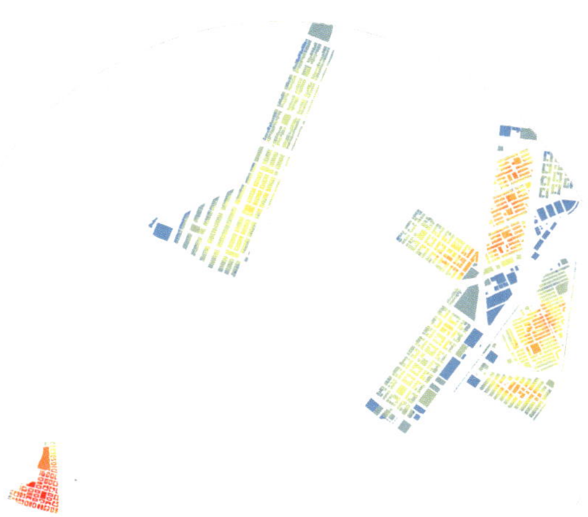

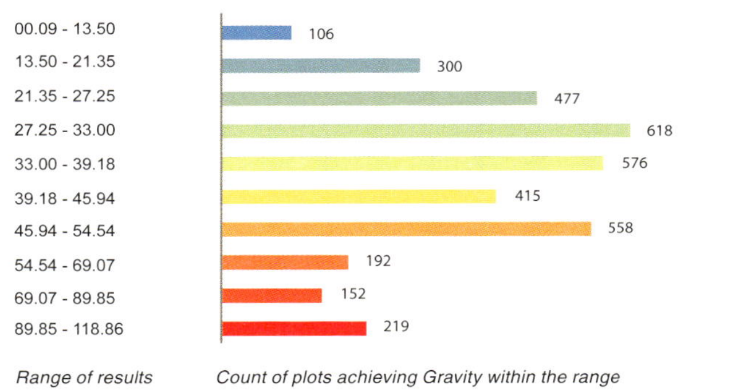

The warmer colors (greenish-yellow to red) represent Gravity values of more than 32.99, while the cooler colors (light green to dark blue) correspond to Gravity values of less than 33.00. The majority of plots, corresponding to 58% of all plots (or 2,112 out of 3,613 plots), have Gravity values ranging from 33.00 to 118.86. Among the different categories shown in the legend, 618 plots have values in the range of 27.25 to 33.00, making this the most common range; this range is represented by light green on the map. High Gravity values ranging from 54.54 to 118.86 are obtained by 563 plots, or 16% of the total plots. These plots are mostly located in Yas Island's national neighborhood. Some internally-located plots of Al Shahama also have high Gravity values. Low Gravity values ranging from 0.09 to 27.25 are obtained by 883 plots, or 24% of the total plots. These plots are located in the northern and southwestern parts of Al Bahya West and several small areas of Al Bahya East. On average, 41.03 plots can be reached from each plot when the distance decay effect is taken into consideration at a radius of 6,000 m.

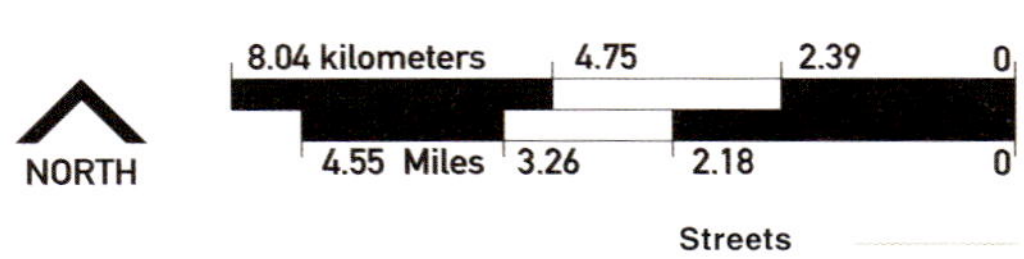

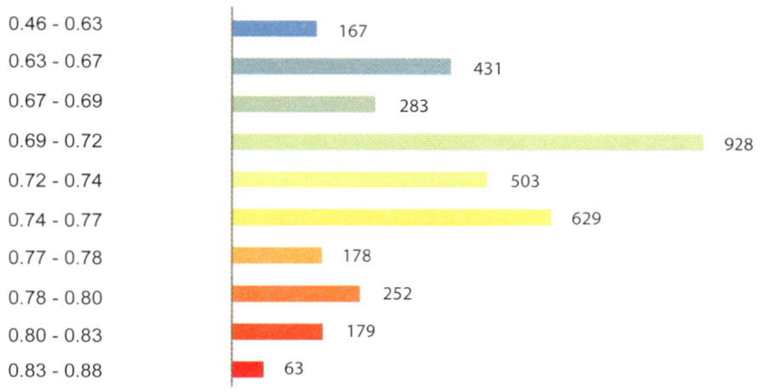

Range of results *Count of plots achieving Straightness within the range*

The warmer colors (greenish-yellow to red) represent Straightness values between 0.72 to 0.88, while the cooler colors (light green to dark blue) correspond to Straightness values from 0.46 to 0.72. The majority of plots, corresponding to 70% of all plots (or 2,521 out of 3,613 plots), have Straightness values ranging from 0.67 to 0.78. Among the different categories shown in the legend, 928 plots have values in the range of 0.69 to 0.72, making this the most common range; this range is represented by light green on the map. High Straightness values ranging from 0.78 to 0.88 are obtained by 494 plots, or 14% of the total plots. These plots are mostly located in Al Bahya West which is characterized by gridiron patterns. The southern-most tip of Al Bahya West and Yas Island also have high Straightness values. Low and medium Straightness values ranging from 0.42 to 0.74 are obtained by 2,312 plots, or 64% of the total plots. These plots are mostly located in Al Bahya East and New Shahama area, on both sides of the Abu Dhabi-Dubai highway. On average, the Straightness of plots in Al Bahya region is 0.73 at a 6,000 m radius, which means that their paths to other plots are 73% as straight as a straight line.

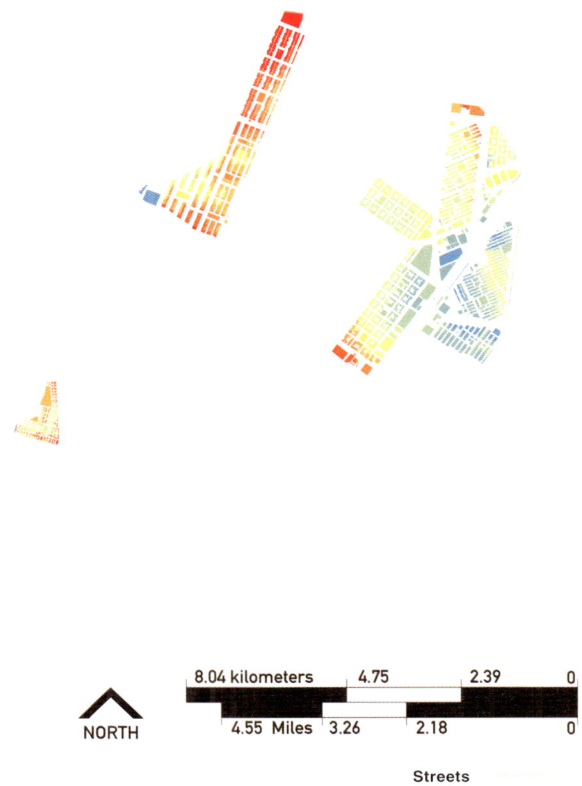

FIG. 3.3
Straightness

Southern Suburbs

Centrality Analysis

6,000 m Radius

FIG. 4.1

Reach

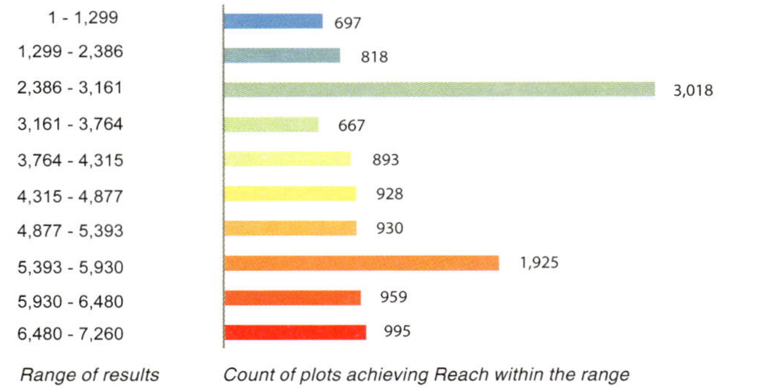

The warmer colors (greenish-yellow to red) represent Reach values of more than 3,763, while the cooler colors (light green to dark blue) correspond to a Reach value of less than 3,764. The majority of plots, corresponding to 56% of all plots (or 6,630 out of 11,830 plots), have Reach values ranging from 3,764 to 7,260. Among the different categories shown in the legend, 3,018 plots have values in the range of 2,386 to 3,161, making this the most common range; this range is represented by bluish-green on the map. High Reach values ranging from 5,930 to 7,260 are obtained by 1,954 plots, or 17% of the total plots. These plots are mostly located in the Baniyas neighborhood and Section 6 and Section 11 northeast of the Baniyas neighborhood. Low Reach values ranging from 1 to 3,161 are obtained by 4,533 plots, or 38% of the total plots. These plots are located mostly in a large portion of MBZ and Shakhbout neighborhoods. On average, 4,154 plots can be reached from each plot at a radius of 6,000 m.

FIG. 4.2

Gravity

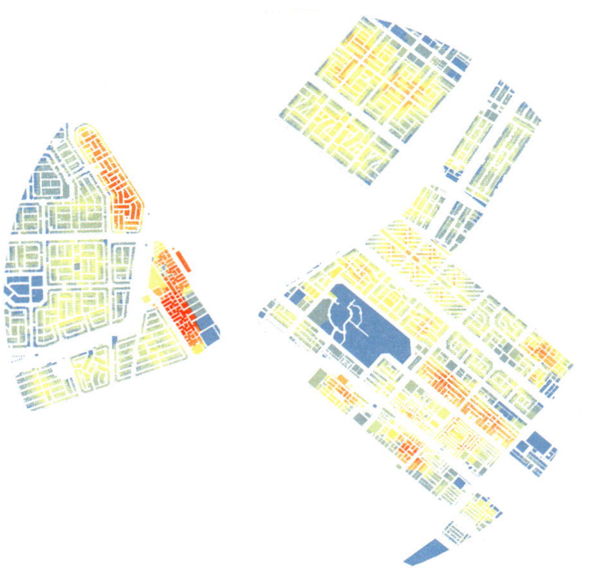

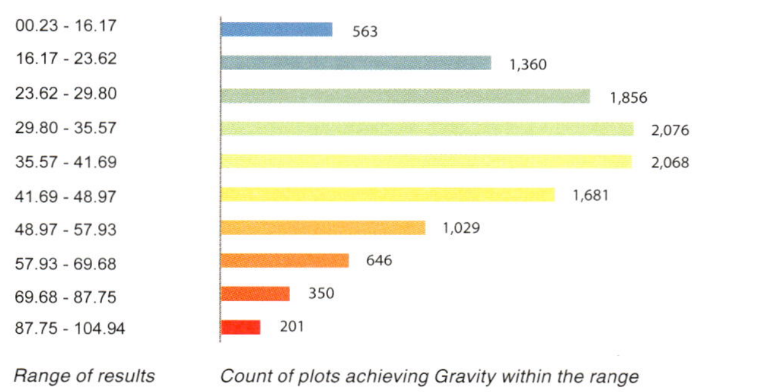

The warmer colors (greenish-yellow to red) represent Gravity values of more than 35.56, while the cooler colors (light green to dark blue) correspond to a Gravity value of less than 35.57. The majority of plots, corresponding to 51% of all plots (or 5,975 out of 11,830 plots), have Gravity values ranging from 35.57 to 104.94. Among the different categories shown in the legend, 2,076 plots have values in the range of 29.80 to 35.57, making this the most common range; this range is represented by light green on the map. High Gravity values ranging from 48.97 to 104.94 are obtained by 2,226 plots, or 19% of the total plots. These plots are mostly located in Baniyas and several small pockets in MBZ and Shakhbout neighborhoods. Low Gravity values ranging from 0.23 to 23.62 are obtained by 1,923 plots, or 16% of the total plots. These plots are located mostly in a large portion of MBZ and several small pockets of Shakhbout and Baniyas neighborhoods. On average, 37.97 plots can be reached from each plot when the distance decay effect is taken into consideration at a radius of 6,000 m.

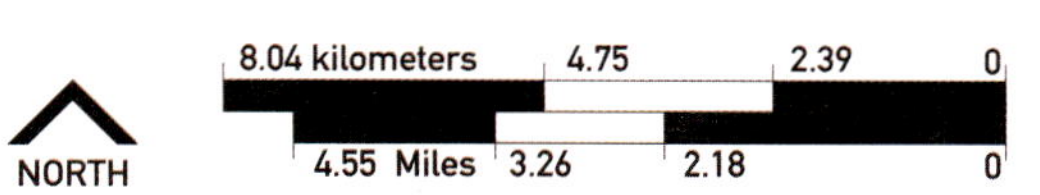

Streets

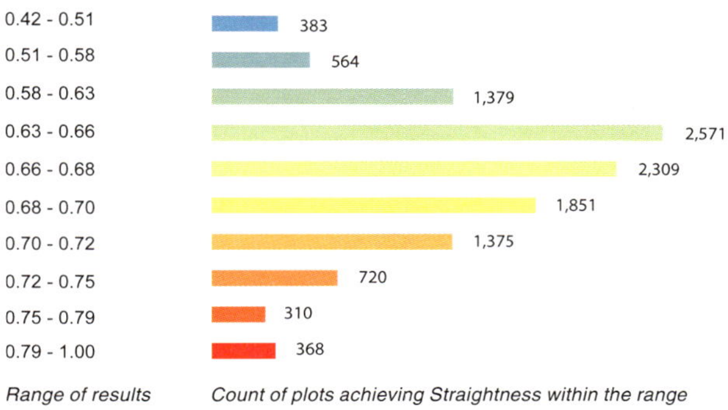

The warmer colors (greenish-yellow to red) represent Straightness values between 0.66 and 1.00, while the cooler colors (light green to dark blue) correspond to Straightness values from 0.42 to 0.66. Among the different categories shown in the legend, 2,571 plots have values in the range of 0.63 to 0.66, making this the most common range; this range is represented by light green on the map. High Straightness values ranging from 0.75 to 1.00 are obtained by 678 plots, or 6% of the total plots. These plots are majorly located in three places– on the far eastern side of MBZ, the majority of the southern part of Shakhbout, and almost all of Baniyas neighborhood. A small part of Al Shawamekh neighborhood also possesses high Straightness values. On the contrary, low and medium Straightness values ranging from 0.42 to 0.74 are obtained by 10,936 plots, or 92% of the total plots. A majority of these plots are located in the interior part of MBZ neighborhood, the southern part of Baniyas, the southeastern portion of Shakhbout, and the southern part of Al Shawamekh. On average, the Straightness of plots is 0.67 at a 6,000 m radius, which means that their paths to other plots are 67% as straight as a straight line.

FIG. 4.3
Straightness

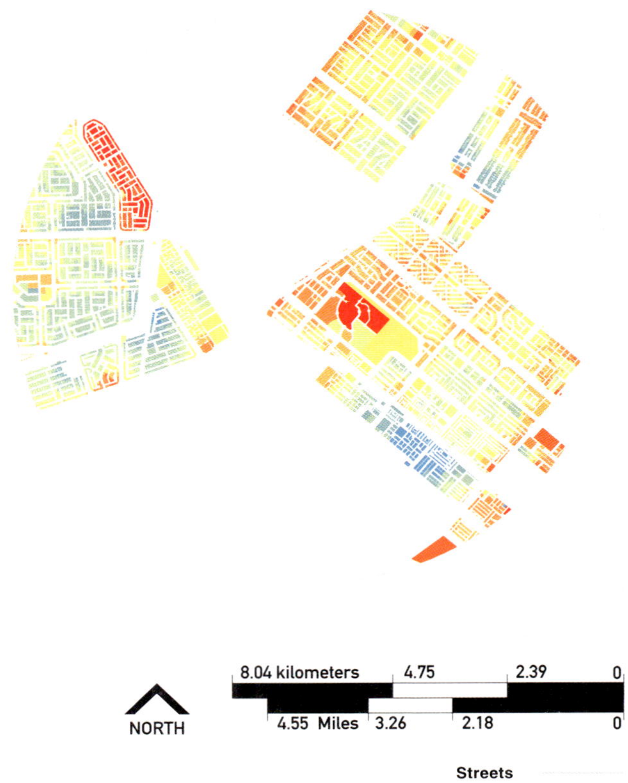

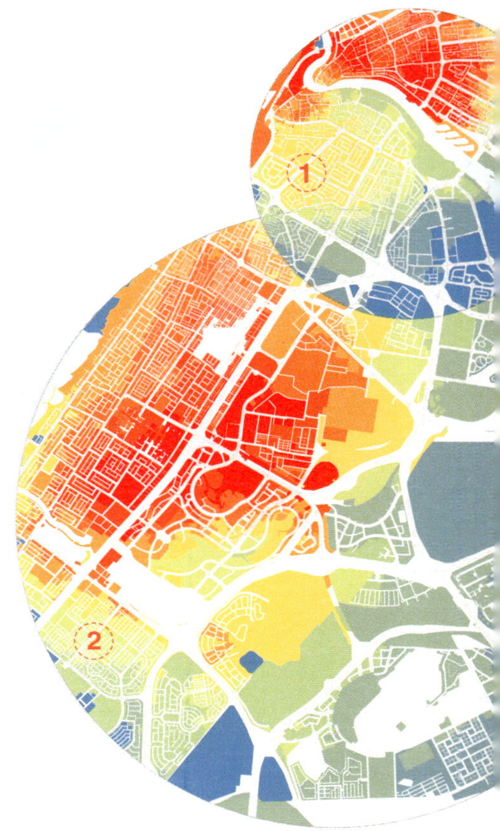
1
2

FIG. 5

Full map of Dubai showing Reach results for the selected samples

1. Dubai Creek Area
2. Downtown Dubai and Vicinity
3. Dubai East

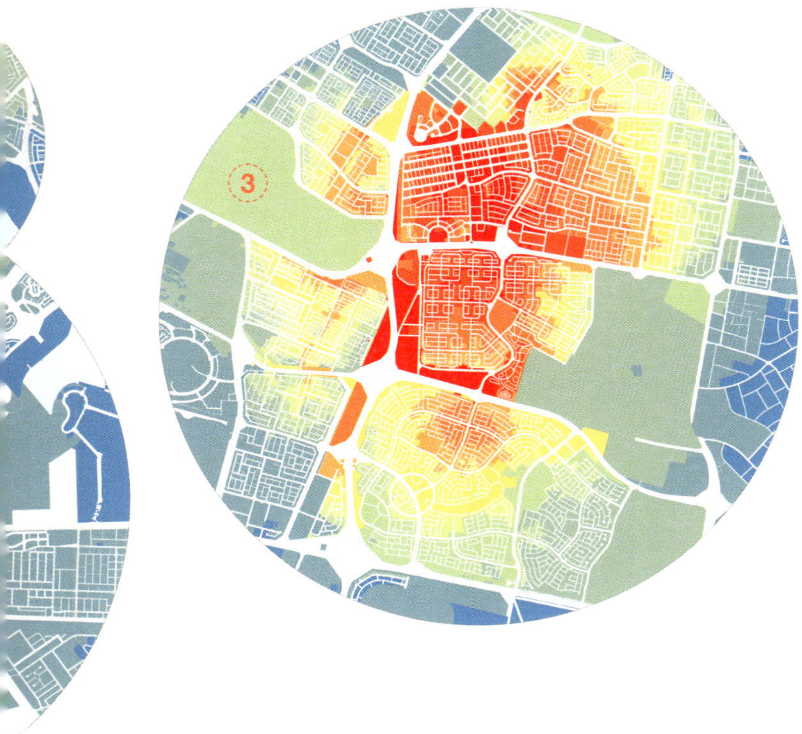

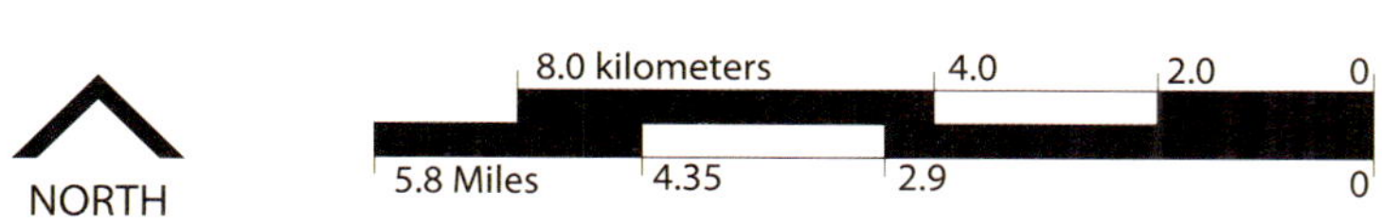

Dubai Creek Area

Centrality Analysis

3,000 m Radius

FIG. 6.1
Reach

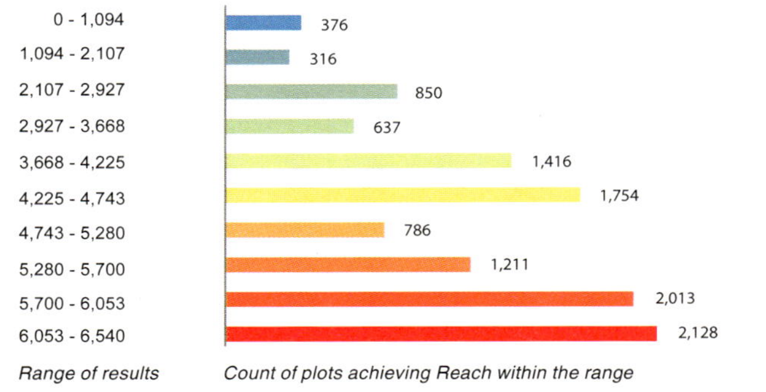

The warmer colors (greenish-yellow to red) represent Reach values of more than 3,667, while the cooler colors (light green to dark blue) correspond to Reach values of less than 3,668. The majority of plots, corresponding to 69% of all plots (or 7,892 out of 11,487 plots), have Reach values ranging from 4,225 to 6,540. Among the different categories shown in the legend, 2,128 plots have values in the range of 6,053 to 6,540, making this the most common range; this range is represented by red on the map. High Reach values ranging from 5,700 to 6,540 are obtained by 36% of the total plots. These plots are mostly located in Deira area, to the north of the creek. On the southern side of the creek also, plots located in the oldest part of Dubai (Al Fahidi fort) have high Reach values. Low Reach values ranging from 0 to 3,668 are obtained by 2,179 plots, or 19% of the total plots. The plots with low Reach values mostly concentrate in the southeastern sides of the sample. On average, there are 4,719 plots that can be reached from each plot at a radius of 3,000 m.

FIG. 6.2
Gravity

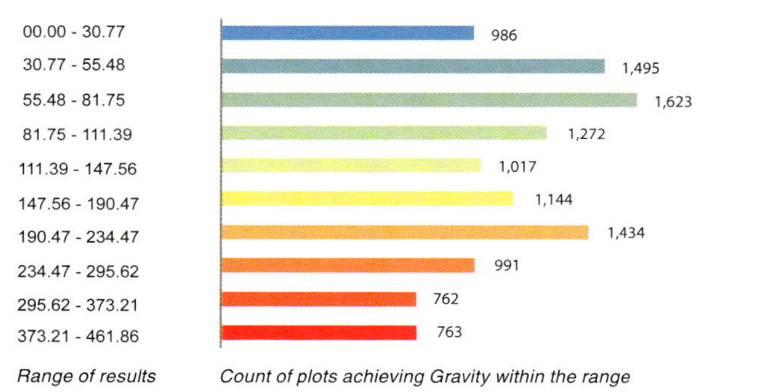

The warmer colors (greenish-yellow to red) represent Gravity values of more than 111.38, while the cooler colors (light green to dark blue) correspond to Gravity values of less than 111.39. The majority of plots, corresponding to 56% of all plots (or 6,393 out of 11,487 plots), have Gravity values ranging from 0 to 147.56. Among the different categories shown in the legend, 1,623 plots have values in the range of 55.48 to 81.75, making this the most common range; this range is represented by bluish-green on the map. High Gravity values ranging from 234.47 to 461.86 are obtained by 2,516 plots, or 22% of the total plots. These plots are located in two places– a high concentration of such plots is visible on the northern side of the creek, and the southern side in the oldest blocks of Dubai. Low Gravity values ranging from 0.00 to 55.48 are obtained by 2,481 plots, or 22% of the total plots. The plots with low Gravity values are distributed throughout the sample area, although it is more prominent on the southern side of Dubai Creek. On average, 153.62 plots can be reached from each plot when the distance decay effect is taken into consideration at a radius of 3,000 m.

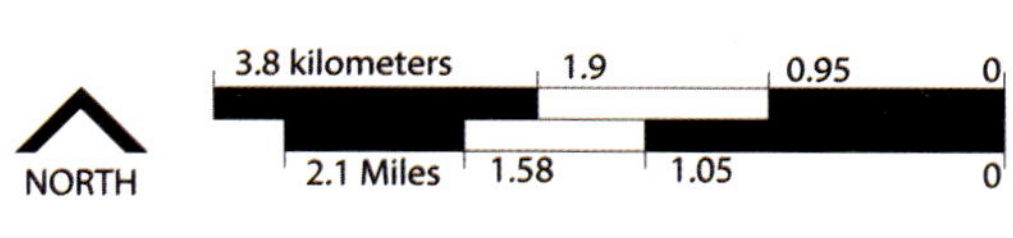

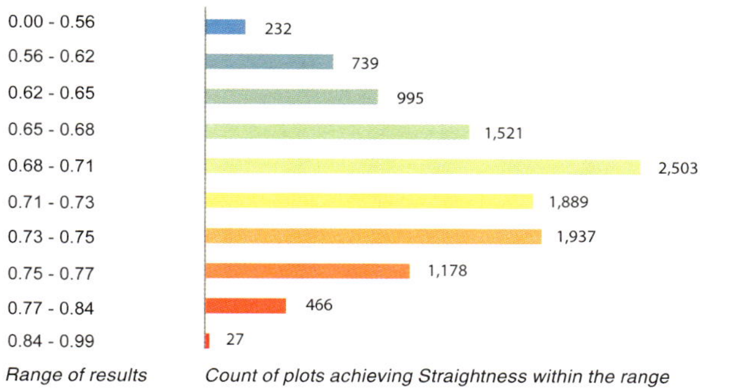

The warmer colors (greenish-yellow to red) represent Straightness values between 0.68 and 0.99, while the cooler colors (light green to dark blue) correspond to Straightness values from 0.00 to 0.68. Among the different categories shown in the map's legend, 2,503 plots have values in the range of 0.68 to 0.71, making this the most common range; this range is represented by greenish-yellow on the map. High Straightness values ranging from 0.75 to 0.99 are obtained by 1,671 plots, or 15% of the total plots. These plots are mostly located in two places– the northern bank of Dubai Creek, and the southeastern part of Dubai Creek. A large majority of plots obtain low and medium Straightness values ranging from 0.00 to 0.74 are obtained by 8,399 plots, or 73% of the total plots. These plots are mostly located on the southern bank of Dubai Creek. There are also several pockets of low Straightness values in sparsely built areas like Zabeel, and the area to the south of Dubai International Airport. On average, the Straightness of plots in the Dubai Creek area is 0.71 at a 3,000 m radius, which means that their paths to other plots are 71% as straight as a straight line.

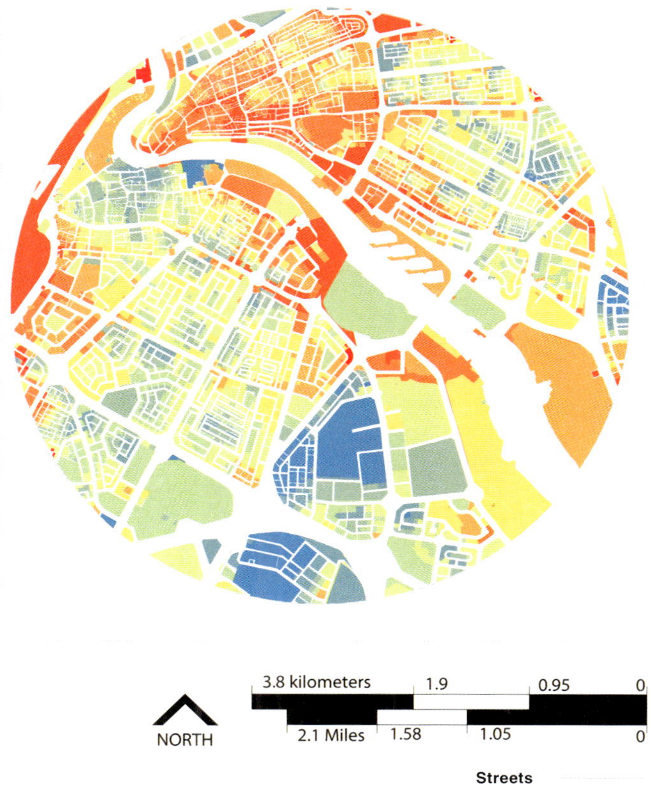

FIG. 6.3
Straightness

Downtown Dubai and Vicinity

Centrality Analysis

6,000 m Radius

FIG. 7.1

Reach

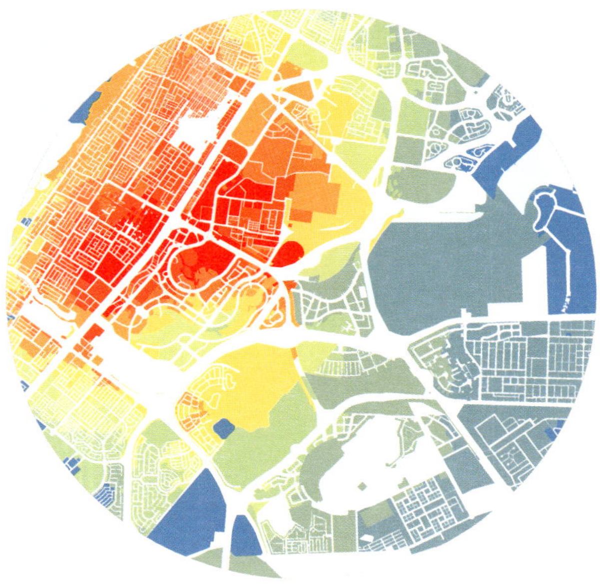

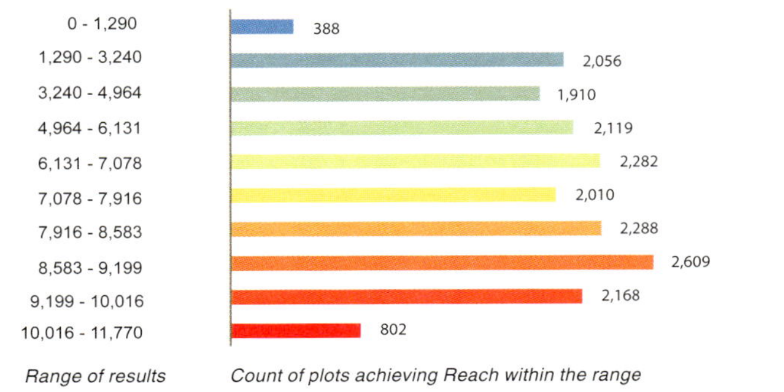

The warmer colors (greenish-yellow to red) represent Reach values of more than 6,130, while the cooler colors (light green to dark blue) correspond to a Reach value of less than 6,131. The majority of plots, corresponding to 53% of all plots (or 9,877 out of 18,632 plots), have Reach values ranging from 7,078 to 11,770. Among the different categories shown in the legend, 2,609 plots have values in the range of 8,583 to 9,199, making this the most common range; this range is represented by orange on the map. High Reach values ranging from 9,199 to 11,770 are obtained by 2,970 plots, or 16% of the total plots. These plots concentrate around the interchange of Sheikh Zayed Road, Dubai Downtown, and in neighborhoods like Za'abeel, Al Satwa, and Al Wasl. Low Reach values ranging from 0 to 3,240 are obtained by 2,444 plots, or 13% of the total plots. These plots are mostly located in the eastern and southeastern sides of the sample. On average, 6,780 plots can be reached from each plot at a radius of 6,000 m.

FIG. 7.2

Gravity

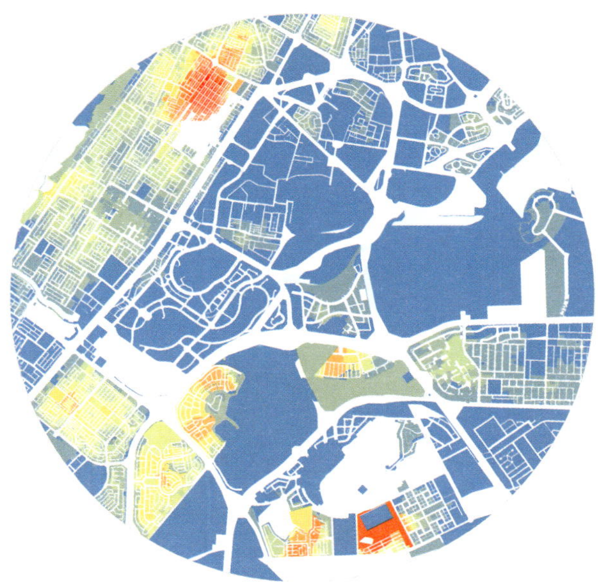

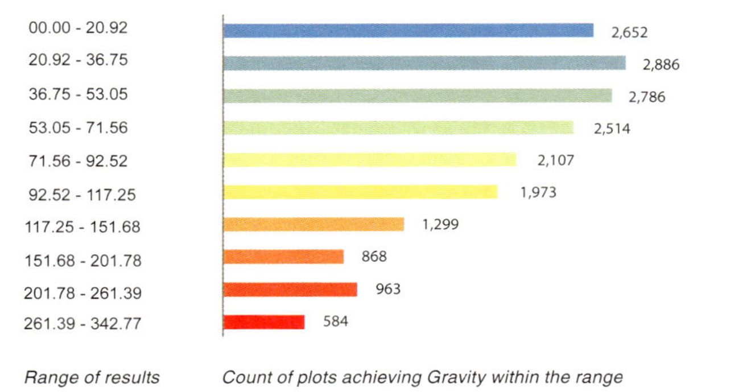

The warmer colors (greenish-yellow to red) represent Gravity values of more than 71.55, while the cooler colors (light green to dark blue) correspond to a Gravity value of less than 71.56. The majority of plots, corresponding to 69% of all plots (or 12,945 out of 18,632 plots), have Gravity values ranging from 0.00 to 92.52. Among the different categories shown in the legend, 2,886 plots have values in the range of 20.92 to 36.75, making this the most common range; this range is represented by light blue on the map. High Gravity values ranging from 117.25 to 342.77 are obtained by 3,714 plots, or 20% of the total plots. These plots are located in several places in the southern and the northwestern parts of the sample like Al Bada'a neighborhood and the southern side of Nad Al Sheba 1. Low Gravity values ranging from 0.00 to 20.92 are obtained by 2,652 plots, or 14% of the total plots. In contrast to high Gravity values, the plots with low Gravity values are distributed throughout the sample area. On average, 79.81 plots can be reached from each plot when the distance decay effect is taken into consideration at a radius of 6,000 m.

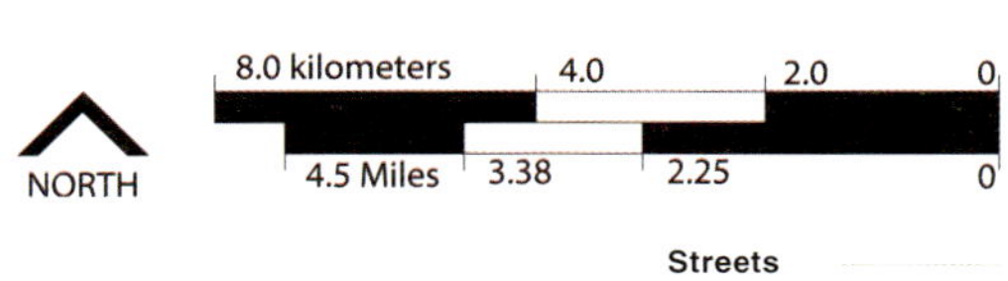

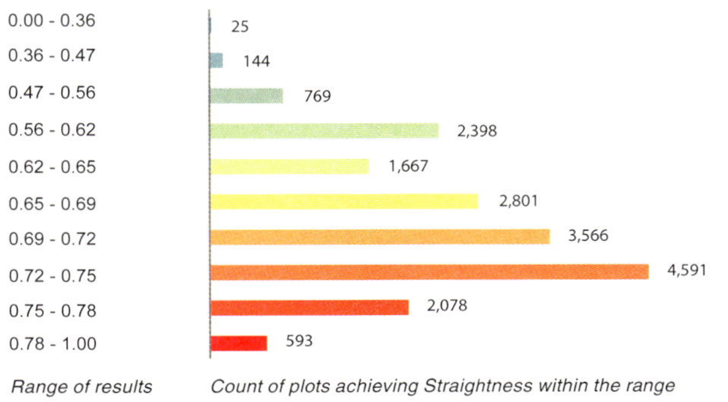

The warmer colors (greenish-yellow to red) represent Straightness values between 0.62 and 1.00, while the cooler colors (light green to dark blue) correspond to Straightness values from 0.00 to 0.62. The majority of plots, corresponding to 74% of all plots (or 13,724 out of 18,632 plots), have Straightness values ranging from 0.50 to 0.74. Among the different categories shown in the legend, 4,591 plots have values in the range of 0.72 to 0.75, making this the most common range; this range is represented by orange on the map. High Straightness values (0.75 – 1.00) are obtained by 2,671 plots, or 14% of the total plots. These plots are distributed throughout the studied area but are highly concentrated in neighborhoods like Al Satwa, Jumeirah, Al Bada'a, Al Wasl, and Umm Suqeim. Very low and low Straightness values ranging from 0.00 to 0.50 are obtained by 199 plots, or 1% of the total plots. These plots are visible in sparsely built areas like Zabeel neighborhood. There are also several pockets of low Straightness in Downtown Dubai and in the eastern and inner parts of the Jumeirah neighborhood. On average, the Straightness of plots is 0.70 at a 6,000 m radius, which means that their paths to other plots are 70% as straight as a straight line.

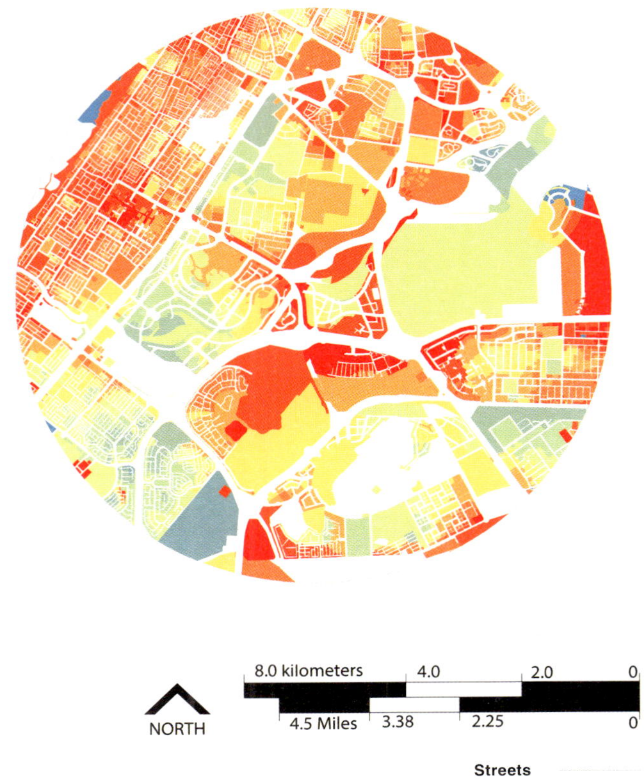

FIG. 7.3
Straightness

Dubai East

Centrality Analysis

6,000 m Radius

FIG. 8.1
Reach

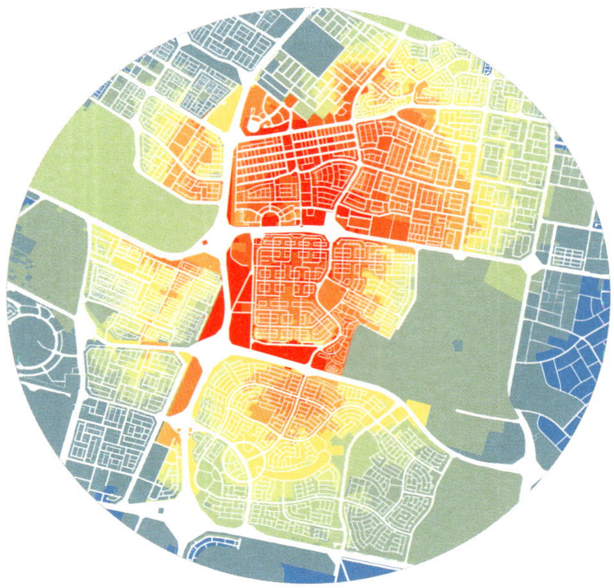

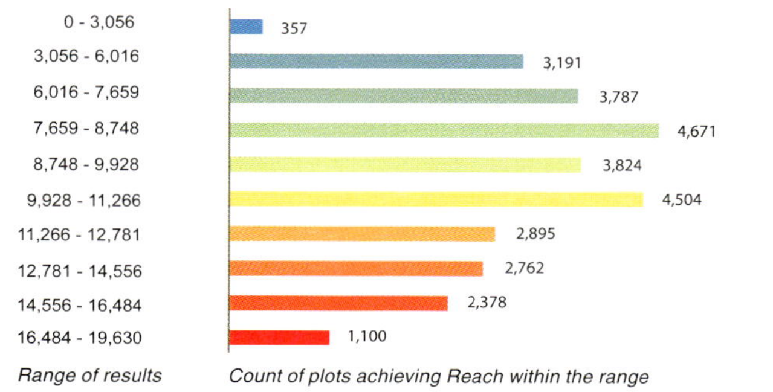

The warmer colors (greenish-yellow to red) represent Reach values of more than 8,747, while the cooler colors (light green to dark blue) correspond to a Reach value of less than 8,748. The majority of plots, corresponding to 54% of all plots (or 15,829 out of 29,470 plots), have Reach values ranging from 0 to 9,928. Among the different categories shown in the legend, 4,671 plots have values in the range of 7,659 to 8,748, making this the most common range; this range is represented by light green on the map. High Reach values ranging from 9,928 to 19,719 are obtained by 13,641 plots, or 46% of the total plots. These plots are mostly located in the central part of the sample in neighborhoods like Muhaisnah 1, Al Mizhar 1, and Al Mirdiff. Low Reach values ranging from 0 to 6,016 are obtained by 3,547 plots, or 12% of the total plots. In contrast to high Reach values, the plots with low Reach values are visible in the peripheral areas of the sample. On average, 9,936 plots can be reached from each plot at a radius of 6,000 m.

FIG. 8.2
Gravity

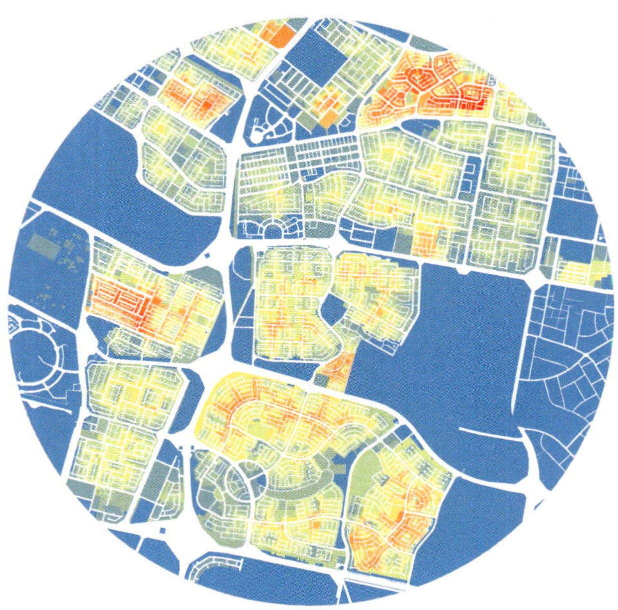

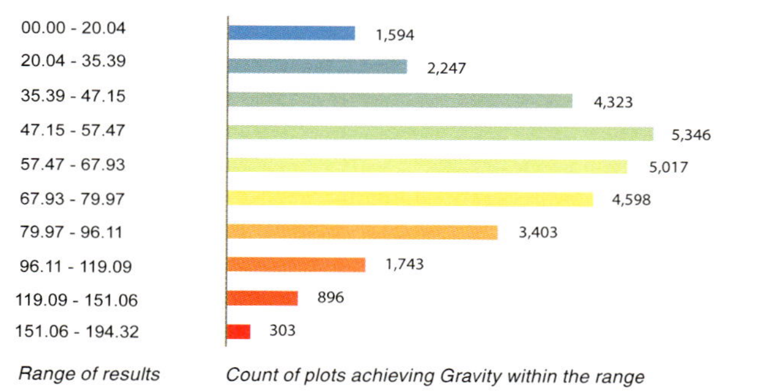

The warmer colors (greenish-yellow to red) represent Gravity values of more than 57.46, while the cooler colors (light green to dark blue) correspond to a Gravity value of less than 57.47. The majority of plots, corresponding to 63% of all plots (or 18,527 out of 29,470 plots), have Gravity values ranging from 0.00 to 67.93. Among the different categories shown in the legend, 5,346 plots have values in the range of 47.15 to 57.47, making this the most common range; this range is represented by light green on the map. High Gravity values ranging from 67.93 to 194.32 are obtained by 10,943 plots, or 37% of the total plots. These plots are located sporadically in the sample area; however, it is prominently visible in the northeastern part of the sample. Several plots with high Gravity values are also found in Al Rashidiya neighborhood, located in the western side of the sample. Low Gravity values ranging from 0.00 to 35.39 are obtained by 3,841 plots, or 13% of the total plots. In contrast to high Gravity values in the sample area, the plots with low Gravity values occupy large swaths of land in several neighborhoods like Al Qusais, Al Mizhar, and Al Muhaisnah. On average, 62.64 plots can be reached from each plot when the distance decay effect is taken into consideration at a radius of 6,000 m.

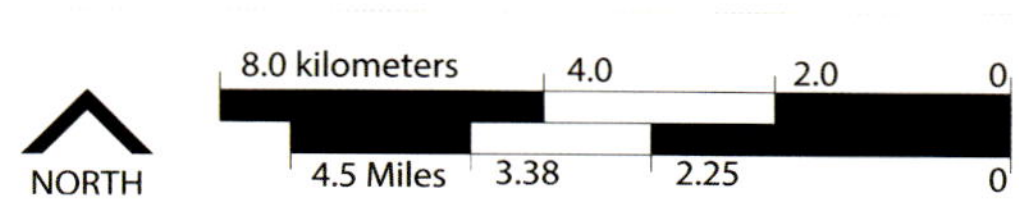

Streets

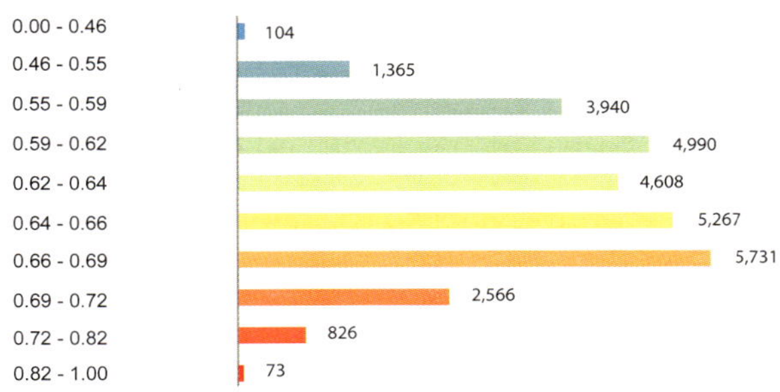

Range of results · *Count of plots achieving Straightness within the range*

The warmer colors (greenish-yellow to red) represent Straightness values between 0.62 and 1.00, while the cooler colors (light green to dark blue) correspond to Straightness values from 0.00 to 0.62. The majority of plots, corresponding to 62% of all plots (or 18,172 out of 29,470 plots), have Straightness values ranging from 0.62 to 0.72. Among the different categories shown in the legend, 5,731 plots have values in the range of 0.66 to 0.69, making this the most common range; this range is represented by light orange on the map. High Straightness values ranging from 0.75 to 1.00 are obtained by 303 plots, or 1% of the total plots. These plots are distributed throughout the studied area. One of the prominent concentrations of high Straightness values can be observed in Al Warqa neighborhood, located in the southern part of the sample. Very low and low Straightness values ranging from 0.00 to 0.50 are obtained by 137 plots, or 0.46% of the total plots. These plots are distributed throughout the sample area forming small pockets of low Straightness in sparsely built areas. On average, the Straightness of plots is 0.64 at a 6,000 m radius, which means that their paths to other plots are 64% as straight as a straight line.

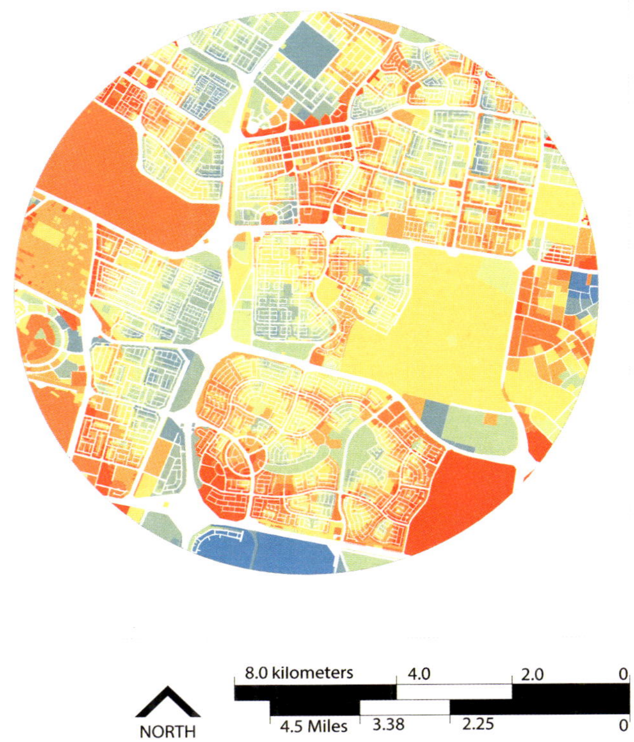

Streets

FIG. 8.3
Straightness

07 Discussion

Introduction

This section discusses the results presented in the previous chapter. For each city, findings are compared across their growth periods. A comparison is made between the neighborhoods within each city: six in Abu Dhabi and seven in Dubai. For instance, *Al Satwa*, a neighborhood in Dubai, will be compared with other neighborhoods in Dubai, such as *Creek* and *Al Warqa*. An inter-city comparison is provided in the next section. Each neighborhood has a total of 42 UNA maps that consist of 24 neighborhood scale maps and 18 sample scale maps. For both the neighborhood scale and the sample scale, four metrics—Reach, Gravity, Straightness, and Betweenness—are calculated at three different radii of analysis: 400 meters, 800 meters, and 1,600 meters, corresponding to 5-, 10-, and 15-minute walking distances. This section presents the trends and insights that are deduced from the vast number of maps and quantified figures that these analyses yield. The section is divided according to the two scenarios of analysis, namely Scenario1: Streets only and Scenario 2: Streets and alleys. Within these scenarios, for each growth phase, neighborhood-scale results are discussed first and sample-scale results are detailed second. The results are discussed in terms of the average values of Reach, Gravity, Straightness, and Betweenness obtained for the particular growth phases (i.e., Inception, Dispersion, and Redemption in Abu Dhabi and Inception, Pre-Dispersion, and Dispersion in Dubai). The results obtained for each metric at 400 meters, 800 meters, and 1600 meters are averaged to facilitate comparison between the growth phases for both neighborhood and sample scale.

Abu Dhabi

Local Scale Scenario 1: Streets Only

In Abu Dhabi, West Island is the only neighborhood belonging to the Inception phase. It is a big neighborhood that consists of more than 50 NPUs of varying sizes with an average plot density of 2.65 plots/ha. The local scale analysis is further divided into two scales - neighborhood scale, and sample scale. In neighborhood scale analysis, the average Reach, Gravity, Straightness, and Betweenness values for the Inception phase are 455, 41.33, 0.69, and 5,034, respectively. The high values obtained for all metrics can be attributed to the street intersection density of 2.52 intersections/ha and street density of 0.25 km/ha, which are the highest of all neighborhoods in Abu Dhabi. The urban form of West Island, featuring a grid system that binds the repetitive rectangular NPUs, is also responsible for these high values. The sample scale analysis of the Inception phase was conducted by taking two samples from the West Island neighborhood. The average values for Reach, Gravity, and Straightness are 385, 44.03 and 0.68, respectively. Betweenness was not analyzed at the sample scale, because the sample area of 3.2 km^2 (1.25 mile^2) is too small to show realistic variation of Betweenness values.

Neighborhoods such as *Baniyas* (segmented solar pattern), *Khalifa City* (interlocked fragmented), *Al Bahya* (grid), and *MBZ City* (looping) belong to the Dispersion phase. These neighborhoods are characterized by moderate- to low-density housing with an average plot density of 1.98 plots/ha and diverse layouts of internal streets. In neighborhood-scale analysis of this phase, a decrement in the average values for all metrics can be observed. For instance, average Reach value decreases to 244 from 455 in the Inception phase (See Figure 1). Similarly, average values for Gravity and Betweenness drop to 29.19 and 2,815, respectively (See Figures 2 and 4). One of the reasons for this decrement is the street layouts in the neighborhoods of the Dispersion phase. For instance, *MBZ City*, *Khalifa City* and *Baniyas* have looping fragmented, interlocked fragmented, and segmented solar street layouts, respectively, in contrast to the more interconnected layout of West Island of the Inception phase. Another reason for the decreasing values of UNA metrics is the sharp decrease in the street intersection density of the four neighborhoods of the Dispersion phase. For example, the average intersection density of the Inception phase at 2.52 intersections/ha is more than three times the average intersection density of the Dispersion phase at 0.54 intersections/ha. Also, average street density in the Dispersion period is 0.16 km/ha, while the Inception period's average street density is 0.25km/ha. For instance, *Al Bahya* and *MBZ City* from Dispersion phase have street densities of 0.12 and 0.14 km/ha, respectively, compared with 0.25 km/ha in *West Island* from Inception phase.

In a sample-scale analysis that was conducted by taking two samples from each neighborhood of the Dispersion phase, average values decrease for Reach and Gravity and increase for Straightness compared with the samples of the Inception phase. For instance, average Reach and Gravity values decrease from 385 to 184 and from 44.03 to 23.59, respectively. On the other hand, the average Straightness value increases from 0.68 in the Inception phase to 0.74 in the Dispersion phase.

Abu Dhabi's Redemption-phase neighborhoods include *Al Falah* (interconnected and radial) and *Yas Island* (semi-grid). However, this book only includes *Al Falah* as one of the case study neighborhoods because the *Yas Island* neighborhood is too small to perform Urban Network Analysis at all three radii (400, 800, and 1,600 m). *Al Falah* has a plot density of 3.31 plots/ha, which is greater than the plot density of *West Island* at 2.65plots/ha. In neighborhood-scale analysis, *Al Falah* performs better than West Island from the Inception phase in three UNA metrics, even though its street density of 0.13km/ha and intersection density of 0.55 intersections/ha are much lower than the densities in West Island.

Another reason for the decreasing values of UNA metrics is the sharp decrease in the street intersection density of the four neighborhoods of the Dispersion phase.

For instance, the average Reach and Gravity values for the Redemption phase are 650 and 58.63, respectively, compared with 455 and 41.33, respectively, for the Inception phase (See Figures 1 and 2). The average Straightness values for the Redemption phase at 0.75 is also higher than the corresponding value of Inception phase at 0.69 (See Figure 3). A significant increase can be observed in the average Betweenness value of 16,554, which is more than thrice the corresponding value for the Inception phase. The Redemption phase outperforms the Dispersion phase in all metrics except Straightness. For instance, the Redemption phase's average Reach value of 650 is more than double the Dispersion phase's average Reach value of 244. Similarly, the Redemption phase's average Gravity value of 58.63 is almost double the Dispersion phase's average Gravity value of 29.19. Likewise, the Redemption phase's average Betweenness value of 16,554 is almost six times the Dispersion phase's average Betweenness value of 2,815 (See Figure 4). This is because of the radial interconnected street layout of *Al Falah* as compared with the looping and fragmented layouts in Dispersion-phase neighborhoods such as *Baniyas*, *Khalifa City*, *Al Bahya*, and *MBZ City*. In addition, the higher plot density of *Al Falah* plays a crucial role, particularly for the attainment of high Reach, Gravity, and Betweenness values.

The sample scale analysis of the Redemption phase was conducted by taking two samples from *Al Falah*. The average values for Reach and Gravity are higher than those of both the Inception and Dispersion phases. For instance, the Redemption phase's average Reach value of 402 is greater than both the Inception phase average of 385 and the Dispersion phase average of 184 (See Figure 1). Similarly, the Redemption phase's average Gravity value of 51.50 is more than double the Dispersion phase's average Gravity value of 23.59. It is also greater than the Inception phase's average Gravity value of 44.03 (See Figure 2). At 0.73, the average Straightness value slightly decreases from the Dispersion phase's value of 0.74 (See Figure 3).

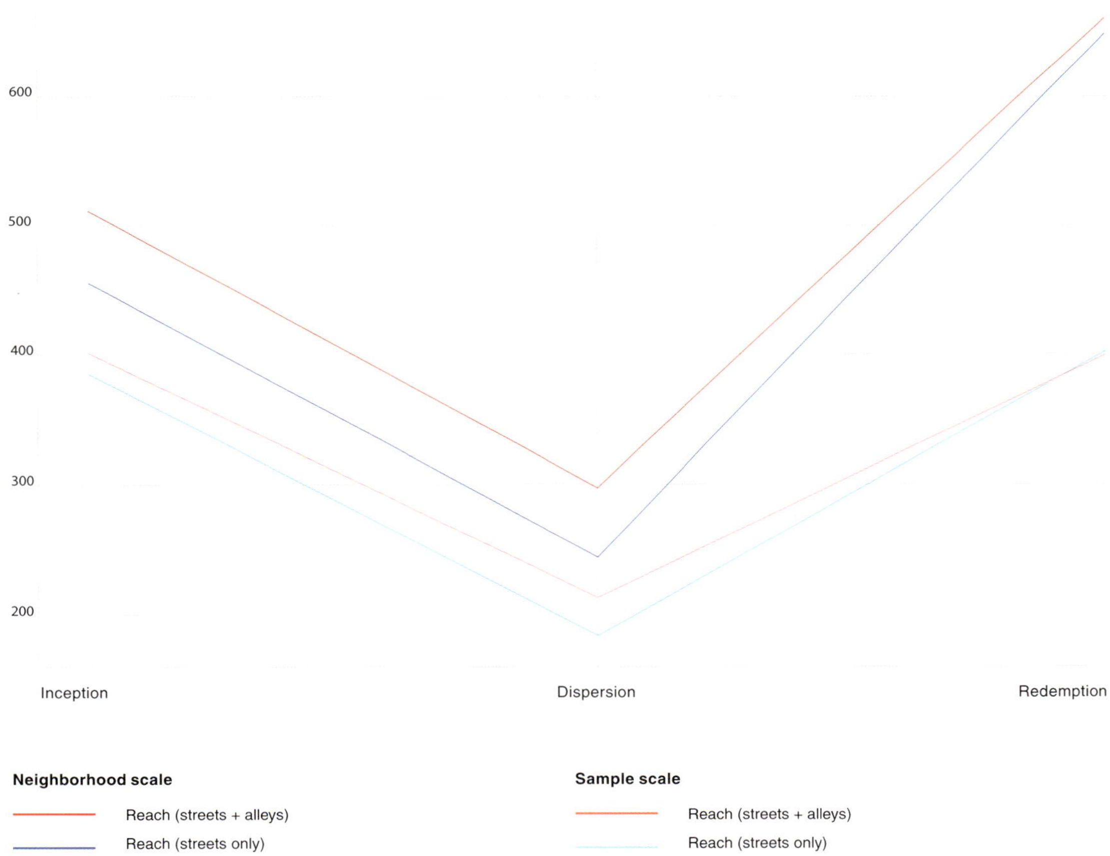

FIG. 1
Variation in Reach values in Abu Dhabi's different growth phases at both the neighborhood and the sample scale in Scenario 1: Streets only & Scenario 2: Streets + alleys).

FIG. 2
Variation in Gravity values in Abu Dhabi's different growth phases at both the neighborhood and the sample scale in Scenario 1: Streets only & Scenario 2: Streets + alleys.

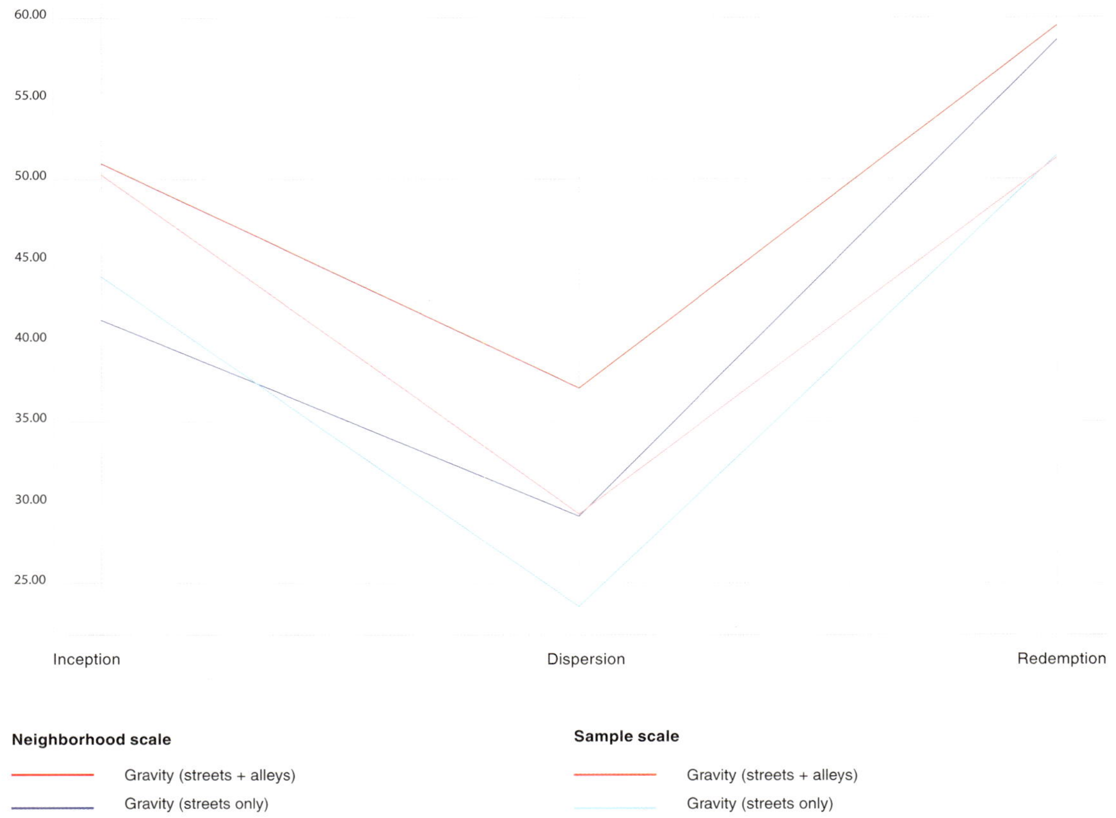

Local Scale Scenario 2: Streets + Alleys

When alleys are included in the analysis, the total network length increases significantly in the Inception phase from 853.17 km in Scenario 1 to 1,386.88 km in Scenario 2. In the Dispersion phase, the total network l ength increases from 439.91 km in Scenario 1 to 734.21 km in Scenario 2 when alleys are included. Compared with the Inception and Dispersion phases, the Redemption phase has minimal presence of alleys. Nevertheless, the total network length increases from 285.43 km in Scenario 1 to 373.87 km in Scenario 2. West Island neighborhood of the Inception phase has the most extensive presence of alleys at 533.71 km, followed by *MBZ City* of the Dispersion phase at 446.43 km. *Al Falah* neighborhood of the Redemption phase has the least extensive alley network at 88.44 km. Likewise, network density improves in all growth phases when alleys are taken into consideration: network density increases by 0.15 km/ha, 0.11 km/ha, and 0.04 km/ha in the Inception, Dispersion, and Redemption phases, respectively. In terms of alley density, *West Island* of the Inception phase has the highest value, at 0.15 km/ha, while *Al Falah* of the Redemption phase has the lowest value, at 0.04 km/ha. Neighborhoods of the Dispersion phase have varying alley densities ranging from 0.09 km/ha in *Al Bahya* to 0.14 in *Khalifa City*. The total number of intersections also increases after alleys are added to the network: it increases on average by 8,351, 5,649, and 1,007 in the Inception, Dispersion, and Redemption phases, respectively. The increase is most significant in *West Island* of the Inception phase, where the number of intersections increases by 8,351, and in *MBZ City* of the Dispersion phase, where it increases by 7,937. The smallest increase in the total number of intersections is observed in *Al Falah* of the Redemption phase, where this figure increases by 1,007.

When alleys are included in the analysis, the total network length increases significantly in the Inception phase from 853.17 km in Scenario 1 to 1,386.88 km in Scenario 2.

In the Inception phase's neighborhood-scale analysis, the inclusion of alleys results in an increase in the average values of Reach and Gravity compared with Scenario 1. The Reach value increases from 455 in Scenario 1 to 511 in Scenario 2, and the Gravity value increases from 41.33 in Scenario 1 to 51.02 in Scenario 2. There is a minor decrement in the average Straightness and Betweenness values- the Straightness value decreases from 0.69 in Scenario 1 to 0.68 in Scenario 2, and the Betweenness value decreases from 5,034 in Scenario 1 to 4,788 in Scenario 2. The decrements can be explained by the fact that when alleys are added, new shortest paths can be formed that do not always increase the straightness and betweenness of all plots. On the contrary, Reach and Gravity values always increase for all plots when alleys or any new paths are added to the existing network. This is because, unlike

Reach and Gravity, Straightness calculates route directness and Betweenness determines passerby traffic, which do not necessarily increase when the number of reachable plots increases.

The sample-scale analysis of the Inception phase was conducted by taking two samples from the *West Island* neighborhood. The average values increase for all metrics when alleys are included in the network. Compared with Scenario 1, average values of Reach, Gravity, and Straightness increase by 16, 6.30, and 0.02, respectively, in Scenario 2. The average values of Reach, Gravity, and Straightness in Scenario 1 are 385, 44.03, and 0.68, respectively, while the average values of Reach, Gravity, and Straightness in Scenario 2 are 401, 50.33, and 0.70, respectively. The best-performing sample from the Inception phase is West Island 1, which has average values of 401, 52.83, and 0.70 for Reach, Gravity, and Straightness, respectively.

In the Dispersion phase's neighborhood-scale analysis, the addition of alleyways leads to an increase in the average values of Reach, Gravity, and Straightness compared with Scenario 1. The average values of Reach, Gravity, and Straightness increase by 53, 7.91 and 0.01, respectively. For instance, in Baniyas, the average Reach value increases from 266 in Scenario 1 to 350 in Scenario 2, which is the highest increase among all Abu Dhabi neighborhoods. Similarly, the average Gravity value increases by 12.19 and by 7.73 in *Baniyas* and *Khalifa City*, respectively. Also, the average Straightness value of *Khalifa City* improve slightly by 0.02. However, the average Betweenness value decreases from 2,815 in Scenario 1 to 2,277 in Scenario 2 when alleys are added. This is due to the fact that passerby traffic measured by the Betweenness metric can decrease when new route choices appear when alleys are included in the network. Among the neighborhoods, the biggest drop in average Betweenness is observed in *Khalifa City*, where it decreases by 1,704. The average Reach value of 297 in Scenario 2 is less than the Inception phase's average Reach value of 511 (See Figure 1). Also, the average Gravity value of 37.09 is lower than the Inception phase's average Gravity value of 51.02 (See Figure 2). Similarly, the average Betweenness value of 2,277 is less than half the Inception phase's average Betweenness value of 4,788 (See Figure 4). However, the Dispersion phase's average Straightness value of 0.75 is greater than the Inception phase's average Straightness value of 0.68 (See Figure 3).

In sample-scale analysis conducted by taking two samples from each neighborhood in the Dispersion phase, average values increase for all metrics when alleys are taken into consideration. Compared with Scenario 1, average values of Reach and Gravity increase by 29 and

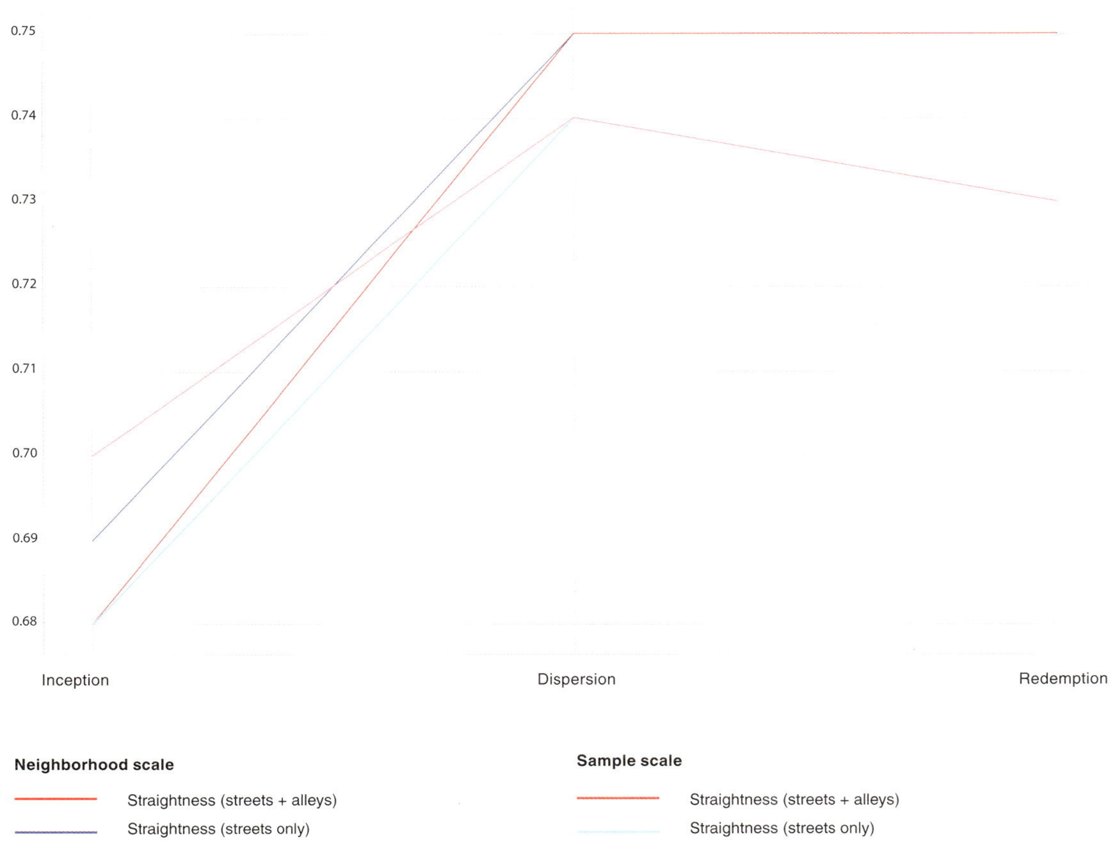

FIG. 3

Variation in Straightness values in Abu Dhabi's different growth phases at both the neighborhood and the sample scale in Scenario 1: Streets only & Scenario 2: Streets + alleys.

5.74, respectively, in Scenario 2. The average values of Reach, Gravity, and Straightness in Scenario 1 are 184, 23.59, and 0.74 respectively, while the average values of Reach, Gravity, and Straightness in Scenario 2 are 213, 29.33, and 0.74, respectively. The average Reach and Gravity values of the samples in the Inception phase are almost double the corresponding values in the Dispersion phase. For instance, average Reach is 401 in the Inception phase, while it is 213 in the Dispersion phase. Similarly, average Gravity is 50.33 in the Inception phase, compared with 29.33 in the Dispersion phase. In contrast, the Dispersion phase's samples have an average Straightness value of 0.74, which is higher than the corresponding average for the Inception phase's samples, which is 0.70 (See Figure 3). When alleys are included in the network, the best-performing sample from the Dispersion phase for Reach and Gravity is Baniyas 2 with average values of 290 and 42.07, respectively. Likewise, for Straightness, the best-performing sample from all phases is the Dispersion phase's sample *Al Bahya* 1, with an average value of 0.78.

In the Redemption phase's neighborhood-scale analysis, the average Reach value increases slightly from 650 in Scenario 1 to 662 when alleys are added to the network. The average Gravity value increases slightly (by 0.89, from 58.63 in Scenario 1 to 59.52 in Scenario 2), as the presence of alleys is minimal in *Al Falah*. This is evident from the alley density of 0.04 km/ha, as compared with 0.11 km/ha and 0.15 km/ha in the Dispersion and Inception phases, respectively. In other words, the larger part of the neighborhood does not have any alleys. The average Straightness value of 0.75 does not change due to the negligible presence of alleyways. As in the Inception and Dispersion phases, the average Betweenness value decreases, in this case from 16,554 in Scenario 1 to 10,213 in Scenario 2. And as in Scenario 1, in Scenario 2 the Redemption phase has higher Reach, Gravity, and Betweenness values than both the Inception and the Dispersion phases, although the presence of alleys is not extensive. The average Reach value of 662 is greater than the Inception and Dispersion phases' average Reach values of 511 and 297, respectively (See Figure 1). Likewise, the average Gravity value of 59.52 is greater than the Inception and Dispersion phases' average Gravity values of 51.02 and 37.09, respectively (See Figure 2). The Redemption phase's average Betweenness value of 10,213 is more than double the Inception phase's average Betweenness value of 4,788 and four times the Dispersion phase's average Betweenness value of 2,277 (See Figure 4). The average Straightness value of 0.75 is equal to the corresponding value in the Dispersion phase. However, the average Straightness of the Redemption phase is greater than Inception phase's average Straightness value of 0.68 (See Figure 3).

FIG. 4
Variation in Betweenness values in Abu Dhabi's different growth phases at the neighborhood scale in Scenario 1: Streets only & Scenario 2: Streets + alleys. Betweenness analysis is not conducted at the sample scale.

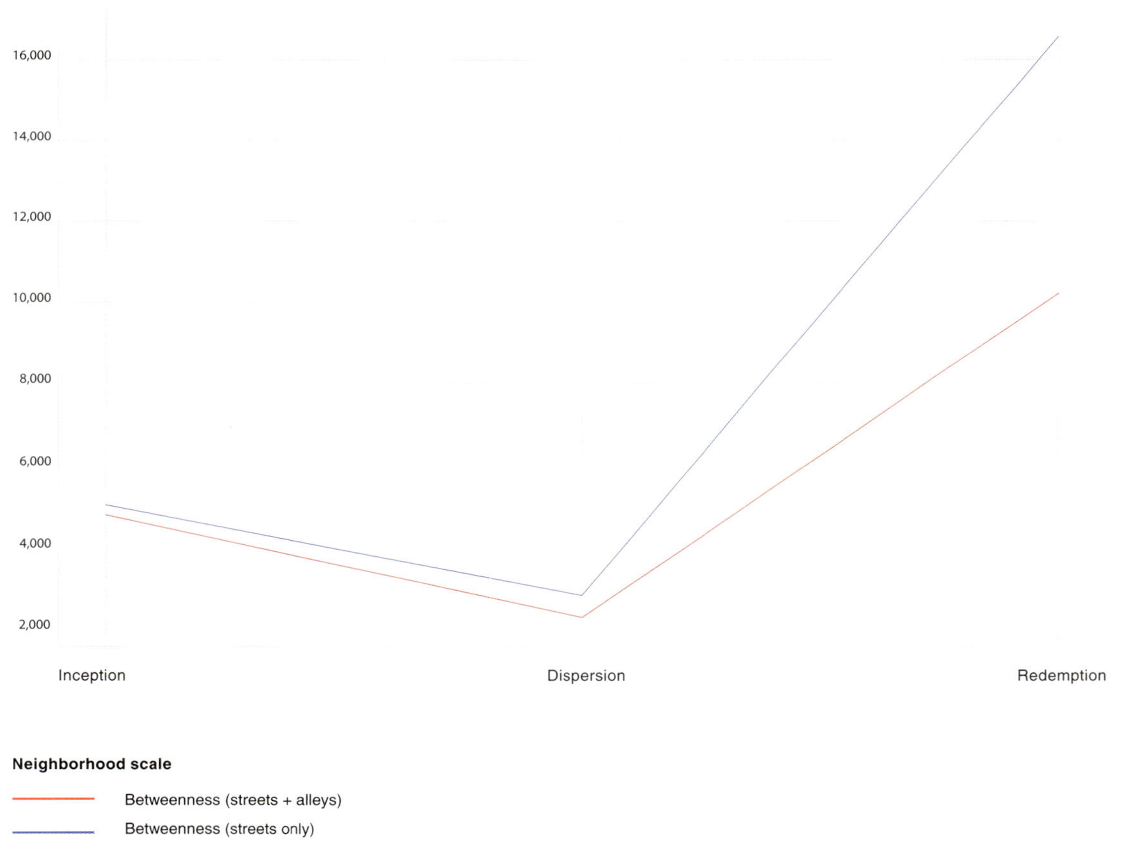

Scenario 2 of the sample-scale analysis for the Redemption phase is unavailable, because *Al Falah* (which is the only studied neighborhood of this phase) has a negligible, almost non-existent presence of alleys. Consequently, the results for Scenario 2 (streets and alleys) are not different from Scenario 1. In all cases, when the radius changes from 400 to 800 m, and from 800 to 1600 m, the Reach, Gravity, and Betweenness values always increase with the increasing radius of analysis; the Straightness metric is the only metric that does not increase.

Global Scale

Three global scale samples namely the *West Island* and vicinity, *Al Bahya* region, and Southern suburbs have been analyzed in Abu Dhabi. Three metrics namely Reach, Gravity and Straightness have been computed at 3 km radius for the global scale sample in the West Island, and at 6 km radius for other samples. Among these global scale samples, the maximum Reach value is obtained by Southern suburbs at 4,154. This sample comprises of four neighborhoods– *Mohamed Bin Zayed* (*MBZ City*) in the west, *Baniyas* in the east, and *Shakhbout* and a small part of *Al Shawamekh* in the north. The maximum Gravity value is obtained by the *West Island* and vicinity at 47.32; while the maximum Straightness value of 0.73 is obtained by *Al Bahya* region. In *West Island* and vicinity, the distribution of high Reach values indicates high level of integration between the neighborhoods located around the center of the sample area. However, the Gravity map reveals lesser integration across the neighborhoods but higher integration within the neighborhood blocks especially on the eastern part of the sample. With regard to Straightness, high values mostly accumulate on plots adjacent to the major thoroughfares.

In *Al Bahya* region, the concentration of high Reach values reveals high level of integration between the neighborhoods located on the eastern part of the sample area like *Al Bahya East* and *Al Shahama Old*. On the other hand, the Gravity map indicates lesser integration across the neighborhoods but higher integration within the neighborhood blocks especially in *Yas Island*. With regard to Straightness, high values mostly concentrate within *Al Bahya West* neighborhood, which is located in the northern part of the sample.

In Southern Suburbs, the distribution of high Reach values indicates high level of integration between the neighborhoods like *Baniyas* and *Al Shawamekh*, located in the eastern part of the sample. However, the Gravity map reveals lesser integration across the neighborhoods but higher integration among few neighborhood blocks in *MBZ City* and *Baniyas*. With regard to Straightness, high values concentrate along northeastern arterial street in *MBZ City*, along western arterial streets in *Shakbout City*, and in various blocks in western and northern part of *Baniyas* neighborhood.

Dubai

Local Scale Scenario 1: Streets Only

In Dubai, the *Creek* is the only neighborhood belonging to the Inception phase. It is an old and highly dense neighborhood with an average plot density of 11.10 plots/ha. Moreover, the neighborhood features a compact and organic street layout. In the neighborhood-scale analysis, the average Reach, Gravity, Straightness, and Betweenness values for the Inception phase were 1,117, 168.66, 0.87, and 24,168, respectively. The high values obtained for all metrics except Betweenness can be attributed to the street density of 0.19 km/ha. The *Creek* is also the densest neighborhood in Dubai with a plot density of 11.10 plots/ha. Similarly, the street intersection density of 1.72 intersections/ha is the second-highest of all neighborhoods in Dubai. The sample-scale analysis of the Inception phase was conducted by taking two samples from the *Creek* neighborhood. The average values for Reach, Gravity, and Straightness are 1,178, 180.11, and 0.71, respectively. Due to the small sample area of 1.6 km x 1.6 km, Betweenness analysis was not conducted at the sample scale.

Neighborhoods such as *Al Satwa* (interconnected) and *Al Rashidiya* (looping, fragmented, and partly semi-grid) belong to the Pre-Dispersion phase. These neighborhoods are also characterized by moderate density housing with an average plot density of 6.74 plots/ha. However, the older part of *Al Satwa* neighborhood has a high density at 9.86 plots/ha that is comparable to the *Creek* of the Inception phase. In the Pre-Dispersion phase, different street layouts can be observed, ranging from *Al Satwa's* interconnected pattern to *Rashidiya's* looping and fragmented layout. In the neighborhood-scale analysis of this phase, a decrement in the average values for all metrics except Betweenness can be observed. For instance, average Reach value decreases to 839 from 1,117 in the Inception phase (See Figure 5). Similarly, average values for Gravity and Straightness drop to 113.89 and 0.71, respectively (See Figures 6 and 7). This decrement is attributable to the change in urban morphology from compact organic in the Inception phase to a mixture of street patterns, including interconnected small blocks and looping and fragmented streets, in the Pre-Dispersion phase. The average street density of the Pre-Dispersion phase at 0.18 km/ha is slightly less than the average street density of the Inception phase at 0.19 km/ha. Also, the Inception phase's average intersection density of 1.72 intersections/ha is greater than the corresponding value for the Pre-dispersion phase, which is 1.11 intersections/ha. For instance, neighborhoods such as *Al Satwa* and *Al Rashidiya* from the Pre-Dispersion phase have street densities of 0.18 and 0.19 km/ha, respectively, as compared with 0.19 km/ha in Dubai Creek from the Inception phase.

In the Pre-Dispersion phase, different street layouts can be observed, ranging from Al Satwa's interconnected pattern to Rashidiya's looping and fragmented layout.

In the sample-scale analysis, which was conducted by taking two samples from each neighborhood of the Pre-Dispersion phase, the average value of Straightness slightly increases, while average Reach and Gravity values decreased from those of the Inception phase samples. Average Straightness values marginally increase from 0.71 to 0.72. On the other hand, average Reach and Gravity values decrease from 1,178 in the Inception phase to 635 in the Pre-Dispersion phase and from 180.11 in the Inception phase to 97.34 in the Pre-Dispersion phase, respectively.

Dubai's Dispersion-phase neighborhoods include *Al Quoz* (looping, grid, and fragmented), *Jumeirah* (fragmented with cul-de-sacs), *Al Warqa* (looping, fragmented and curvilinear), and *Al Barsha* (looping, fragmented with cul-de-sacs). These neighborhoods feature low-density housing with an average plot density of 4.14 plots/ha, which is less than the average plot densities of both the Inception and Pre-dispersion phases. Except for Straightness, the neighborhoods of the Dispersion phase perform more poorly than both prior growth phases, Inception and Pre-Dispersion. All physical attributes have much lower values in the Dispersion phase. For instance, the Dispersion phase's street-intersection density 1.08 intersections/ha is less than the Inception and Pre-Dispersion phases' street intersections densities of 1.72 and 1.42 intersections/ha, respectively.

The average neighborhood-scale Reach and Gravity values for the Dispersion phase are 429 and 49.42, respectively, compared with 1,117 and 168.66, respectively, in the Inception phase (See Figures 5 and 6). The Dispersion phase's average Straightness value of 0.70 is much lower than the Inception phase's corresponding value of 0.87 (See Figure 7). The Dispersion phase's average Betweenness value of 10,690 is less than the corresponding value of Inception phase at 24,168. Compared with the Pre-Dispersion phase, the Dispersion phase performs poorly in all metrics. For instance, the Dispersion phase's average Reach value of 408 is about half the Pre-Dispersion phase's average Reach value of 839. Similarly, the Dispersion phase's average Gravity value of 44.93 is less than half the Pre-Dispersion phase's average Gravity value of 113.89. Likewise, the Pre-dispersion phase's average Betweenness value of 29,908 is almost three times the Dispersion phase's average Betweenness value of 10,690 (See Figure 8). The low betweenness value can be attributed to the highly fragmented, looping, and curvilinear street layouts of Dispersion-phase neighborhoods such as *Jumeirah*, *Al Warqa*, and *Al Barsha* compared with Pre-Dispersion-phase neighborhoods such as *Al Satwa*, which contains interconnected small blocks. For example, *Al Satwa's* average Betweenness value is 44,337, which is about 11 times *Jumeirah's* Betweenness value of 4,044. The sample-scale analysis for the Dispersion phase

FIG. 5

Variation in Reach values in Dubai's different growth phases at both the neighborhood and the sample scale in Scenario 1: Streets only & Scenario 2: Streets + alleys.

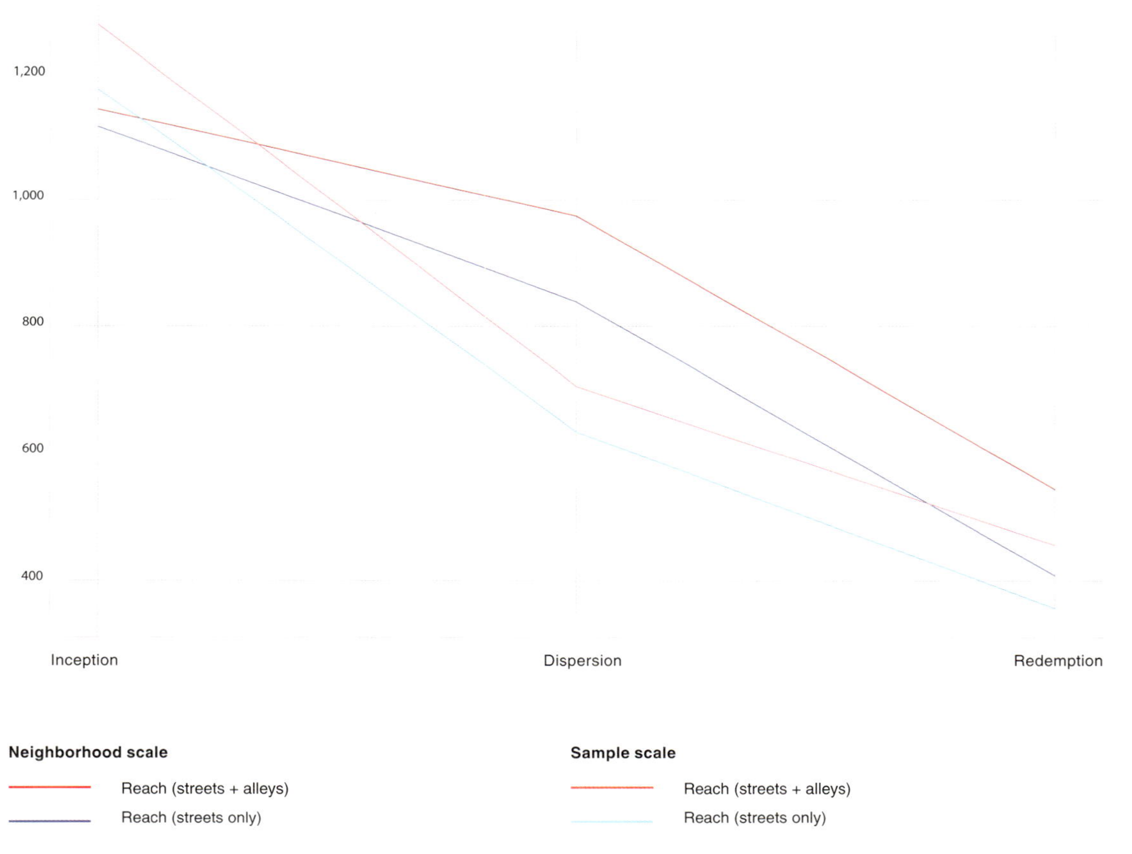

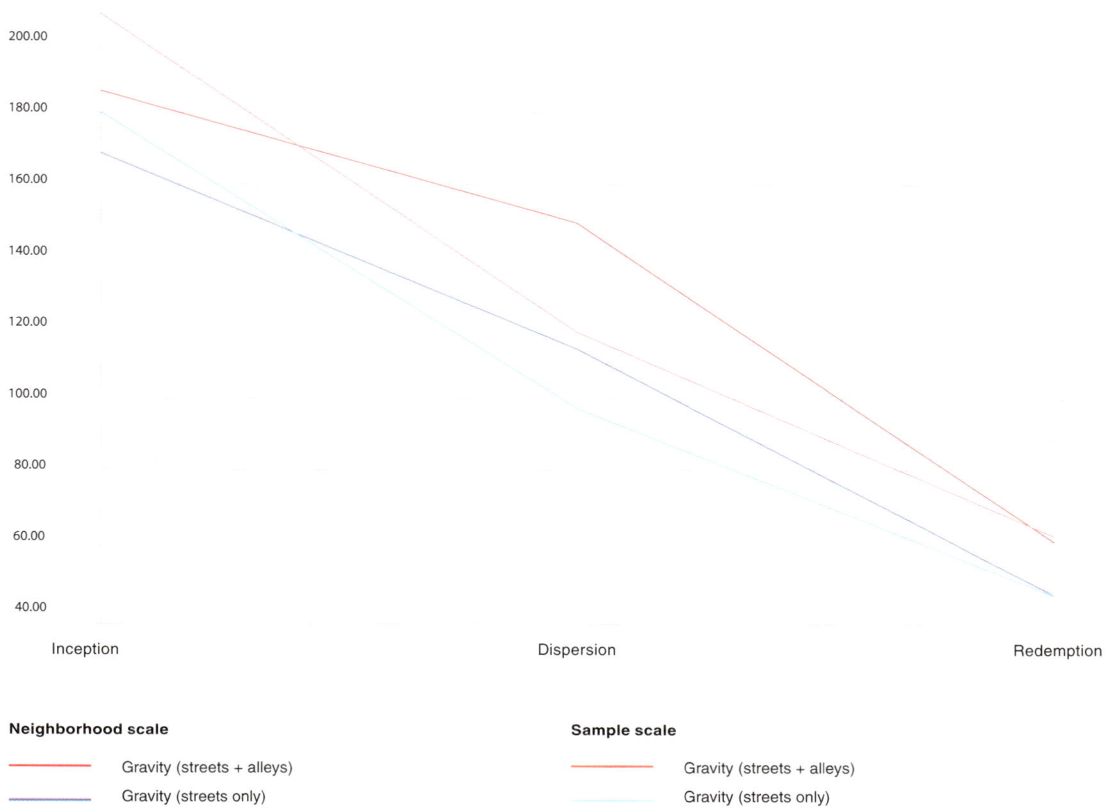

FIG. 6
Variation in Gravity values in Dubai's different growth phases at both the neighborhood and the sample scale in Scenario 1: Streets only & Scenario 2: Streets + alleys.

was conducted by taking three samples from Jumeirah, two samples from *Al Warqa* and *Al Barsha*, and one sample from *Al Quoz*. Only one sample was taken from Al Quoz, because the neighborhood area limits the possibility of taking another sample. The average values for all metrics are lower than those for both the Inception and Pre-dispersion phases. For instance, the Dispersion phase's average Reach value of 357 is much less than earlier phases' corresponding values (i.e., 1,178 in the Inception phase and 635 in the Pre-dispersion phase) (See Figure 5). Similarly, the Dispersion phase's average Gravity value of 44.85 is less than half the Pre-Dispersion phase's average Gravity value of 97.34. Likewise, it is less than one-third of Inception phase's average Gravity value of 180.11 (See Figure 6). Average Straightness also decreases in the Dispersion phase, to 0.69 from 0.71 and 0.72 in the Inception and Pre-dispersion phases, respectively (See Figure 7).

Local Scale Scenario 2: Streets + Alleys

When alleys are included in the analysis, the total network length increases considerably in the Inception phase, from 88.56 km in Scenario 1 to 130.31 km in Scenario 2. In the Pre-Dispersion phase, the total network length increases from 83.77 km to 134.67 km when alleys are included. Similarly, in the Dispersion phase, the total network length increases from 180.65 km in Scenario 1 to 220.70 km in Scenario 2. *Al Satwa* of the Pre-dispersion phase has the most extensive presence of alleys at 82.65 km, followed by *Al Warqa* and *Al Barsha* of the Dispersion phase at 58.81 km and 52.50 km, respectively. *Al Rashidiya* of the Pre-Dispersion phase has the least extensive alley network at 19.15 km. The area of *Al Rashidiya* is 387 ha, which makes it the second-smallest neighborhood after *Al Quoz* (351 ha) among the studied neighborhoods in Dubai. Likewise, network density improves in all growth phases when alleys are taken into consideration: network density increases by 0.09 km/ha, 0.10 km/ha, and 0.04 km/ha in the Inception, Pre-dispersion and Dispersion phases respectively. In terms of alleys density, *Dubai Creek* of the Inception phase has the second highest value at 0.09 km/ha, while *Jumeirah* and *Al Barsha* neighborhoods of the Dispersion phase tie for the lowest value of 0.03 km/ha. Even though *Al Warqa* of the Dispersion phase has the second-highest alley length at 58.81 km, its alley density of 0.04 km/ha is only higher than alley densities in neighborhoods like *Jumeirah* and *Al Barsha*. This is because *Al Warqa* is the biggest neighborhood in terms of area, at 1,608 ha. In contrast, *Al Rashidiya* and *Al Quoz* cover a mere 387 ha and 351 ha, respectively. Neighborhoods of the Pre-Dispersion phase have varying alley densities, ranging from 0.05 km/ha in *Al Rashidiya* to 0.16 in *Al Satwa*.

Al Satwa of the Pre-dispersion phase has the most extensive presence of alleys at 82.65 km, followed by Al Warqa and Al Barsha of the Dispersion phase at 58.81 km and 52.50 km, respectively.

FIG. 7

Variation in Straightness values in Dubai's different growth phases at both the neighborhood and the sample scale in Scenario 1: Streets only & Scenario 2: Streets + alleys.

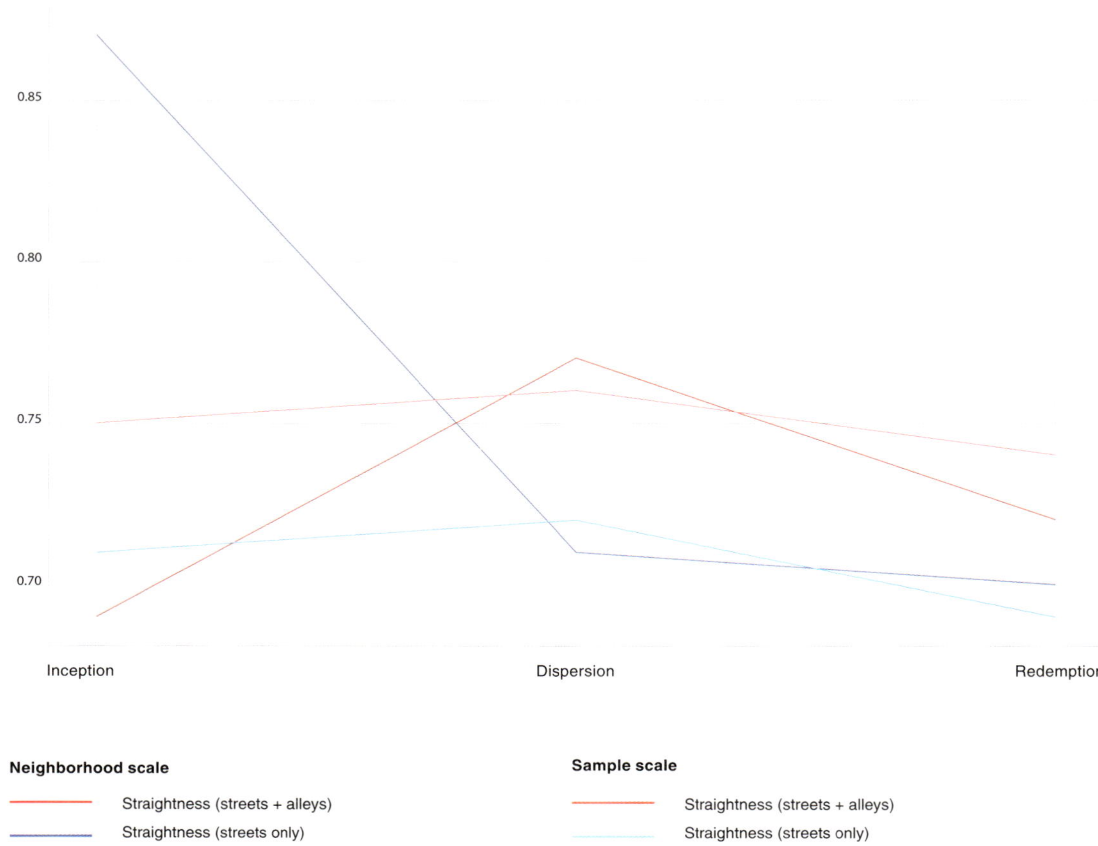

The total number of intersections also greatly increases after alleys are added to the network: this number increases by 4,228; 3,231; and 1,455 in the Inception, Pre-dispersion, and Dispersion phases, respectively. The increase is greatest in *Dubai Creek*, where the number of intersections increases by 4,228, and in *Al Satwa*, where it increases by 4,175. The smallest increase in the total number of intersections is observed in *Al Barsha* of the Dispersion phase, where it increases by 464.

In the Inception phase's neighborhood-scale analysis, the inclusion of alleys leads to an increase in the average values of Reach and Gravity as compared with Scenario 1. Average Reach increases from 1,117 in Scenario 1 to 1,145 in Scenario 2; and average Gravity increases from 168.66 in Scenario 1 to 185.95 in Scenario 2. However, the average Straightness decreases from 0.87 in Scenario 1 to 0.69 in Scenario 2. The decrement can be attributed to the fact that the street network of *Creek* is already interconnected and dense and the addition of alleys increase the network's complexity. Thus, the addition of alleys does not improve the network considerably in an organic dense layout compared with looping and fragmented networks. Average Betweenness values decrease from 24,168 in Scenario 1 to 13,843 in Scenario 2. These decrements can be explained by the fact that when alleys are added, new shortest paths can be formed that do not always increase the betweenness of all plots. In contrast, Reach and Gravity values always increase for all plots when alleys or any new paths are added to the existing network. This is because, unlike Reach and Gravity, Betweenness determines passerby traffic, which does not necessarily increase when the number of reachable plots increase.

The sample-scale analysis of the Inception phase was conducted by taking two samples from the *Dubai Creek* neighborhood. The average values increase for all metrics when alleys are added to the analysis. Compared with Scenario 1, the average values of Reach, Gravity, and Straightness increase by 102, 27.28, and 0.04 respectively in Scenario 2. The average values of Reach, Gravity and Straightness in Scenario 1 are 1,178, 180.11, and 0.71, respectively, while the average values of Reach, Gravity, and Straightness in Scenario 2 are 1,280, 207.56, and 0.75, respectively. The best-performing sample from the Inception phase is *Dubai Creek 1*, which has average values of 1,563, 275.10, and 0.76 for Reach, Gravity, and Straightness, respectively.

In the Pre-Dispersion phase's neighborhood-scale analysis, the addition of alleyways leads to an increase in the average values of Reach, Gravity and Straightness compared with Scenario 1. The average values of Reach, Gravity, and Straightness increase by 135, 35.20 and 0.06 respectively. For instance, in *Al Rashidiya*, the

The total number of intersections also greatly increases after alleys are added to the network: this number increases by 4,228; 3,231; and 1,455 in the Inception, Pre-dispersion, and Dispersion phases, respectively.

average Reach value increases from 609 in Scenario 1 to 827 in Scenario 2, which is the highest increase among all Dubai neighborhoods. Similarly, the average Gravity value notably increases by 41.02 and by 29.37 in *Al Rashidiya* and *Al Satwa*, respectively. Also, the average Straightness values of *Al Rashidiya* and *Al Satwa* improve by 0.09 and 0.04, respectively. However, the average Betweenness value decreases from 29,908 in Scenario 1 to 16,187 in Scenario 2 when alleys are added. This is due to the fact that passerby traffic measured by the Betweenness metric can decrease when new route choices appear after alleys are introduced into the network analysis. Among the neighborhoods, the biggest drop in average Betweenness is in *Al Satwa*, where it decreases by 24,584. The average Reach value of 974 is less than the Inception phase's average Reach value of 1,145 (See Figure 5). Also, the average Gravity value of 149.09 is lower than the Inception phase's average Gravity value of 185.95 (See Figure 6). In contrast, the average Betweenness value of 16,187 is higher than the corresponding value in the Inception phase at 13,843 (See Figure 8). Similarly, the Pre-Dispersion phase's average Straightness value of 0.77 is greater than the Inception phase's average Straightness value of 0.69 (See Figure 7).

The sample-scale analysis in the Pre-dispersion phase was conducted by taking two samples from each neighborhood. Compared with Scenario 1, the average values of Reach, Gravity, and Straightness increase by 70, 21.18, and 0.04, respectively, in Scenario 2. The average values of Reach, Gravity, and Straightness in Scenario 1 are 635, 97.34, and 0.72, respectively, while the average values of Reach, Gravity, and Straightness in Scenario 2 are 705, 118.52, and 0.76, respectively. The average Reach and Gravity values of the samples in the Inception phase are higher than the corresponding values for the Pre-Dispersion phase (See Figures 5 and 6). The Inception phase's average Reach value is 1,280, while the Pre-Dispersion phase's average is 705. Similarly, the Inception phase's average Gravity value is 207.56, compared with 118.52 in the Pre-dispersion phase. However, the average Straightness value of 0.75 in the Inception phase's samples is slightly less than the average Straightness value of 0.76 in the Pre-dispersion phase's samples (See Figure 7). The best-performing sample from the Pre-Dispersion phase is *Al Satwa 1* for all metrics, with average Reach, Gravity, and Straightness values of 1,208, 229.23 and 0.80, respectively.

In the Dispersion phase's neighborhood scale analysis, the average Reach value increases from 408 to 544 when alleys are added to the network. The average Gravity value also increases, from 44.93 in Scenario 1 to 59.78 in Scenario 2. Similarly, the average Straightness value increases slightly, from 0.70 to 0.72. For instance, in *Al Barsha*, the average Reach value increases from 395 in Scenario 1 to 592 in Scenario 2, which is the

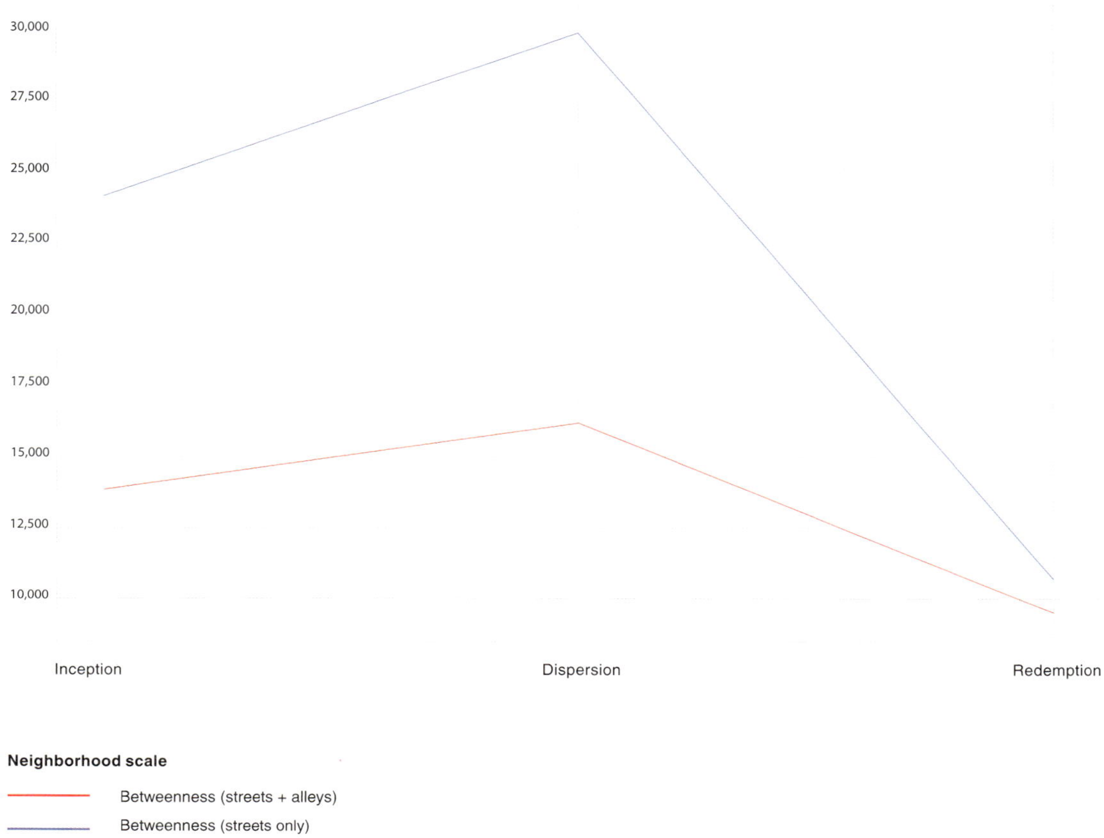

FIG. 8
Variation in Betweenness values in Dubai's different growth phases at the neighborhood scale in Scenario 1: Streets only & Scenario 2: Streets + alleys. Betweenness analysis is not conducted at the sample scale.

second highest increase among all Dubai neighborhoods (the first one being *Al Rashidiya* of the Pre-Dispersion phase). Similarly, the average Gravity value increases by 18.02 and 13.72 in *Al Barsha* and *Al Warqa*, respectively. Also, the average Straightness values of *Al Warqa* and *Al Barsha* improve by 0.03 and 0.02, respectively. As in the Inception and Pre-Dispersion phases, the average Betweenness value decreases from 10,690 in Scenario 1 to 9,487 in Scenario 2. Among the neighborhoods, the biggest drop in average Betweenness is in *Al Quoz*, where it decreases by 2,898. Compared with the Inception and Pre-dispersion phases, the Dispersion phase has lower values for all metrics when alleys are added to the analysis. The average Reach value of 544 is less than the Inception and Pre-Dispersion phase's average Reach values of 1,145 and 974, respectively (See Figure 5). Likewise, the average Gravity value of 59.78 is lower than the Inception and Pre-Dispersion phase's average Gravity values of 185.95 and 149.09, respectively (See Figure 6). The Dispersion phase's average Straightness value of 0.72 is also lower than the Pre-Dispersion phase's average Straightness value of 0.77 but higher than the Inception phase's the average Straightness value of 0.69 (See Figure 7). The average Betweenness value of 9,487 is lower than the corresponding value of Inception-phase at 13,843. However, the average Betweenness value is lower than the Pre-dispersion phase's average Betweenness value of 16,187 (See Figure 8).

The sample-scale analysis in the Dispersion phase was conducted by taking three samples from Jumeirah, two samples from *Al Warqa* and *Al Barsha*, and one sample from *Al Quoz*. The average values of Reach, Gravity, and Straightness in Scenario 1 are 357, 44.85, and 0.69, respectively, while the average values of Reach, Gravity, and Straightness in Scenario 2 are 456, 61.31, and 0.74, respectively. The average values increase for all metrics when alleys are taken into consideration. Compared with Scenario 1, average values of Reach, Gravity, and Straightness increase by 99, 16.46, and 0.05, respectively, in Scenario 2. Compared with the Inception phase's samples, the average Reach and Gravity values are about one-third in the Dispersion phase's samples. Average Reach is 1,280 in the Inception phase, while it is much lower in the Dispersion phase, at 456 (See Figure 5). The Dispersion phase's average Gravity value of 61.31 is also lower than the Inception phase's average of 207.56 (See Figure 6). Also, the average Straightness value at 0.74 is slightly less than the Inception phase's corresponding value at 0.75 (See Figure 7). Compared with the samples of the Pre-Dispersion phase, the Dispersion phase's samples have lower Reach and Gravity values. For instance, the Dispersion phase's average Reach value of 456 is lower than the Pre-Dispersion phase's average Reach value of 705 (See Figure 5). Likewise, the Dispersion phase's average Gravity value of 61.31 is almost half the Pre-Dispersion phase's corresponding value of 118.52 (See Figure 6). Similarly, the Dispersion phase's average Straightness value of 0.74 is less than the Pre-Dispersion phase's average Straightness value of 0.76 (See Figure 7). The best-performing sample from the Dispersion phase for Reach and Gravity is *Al Quoz 1*. It has average values of 610 and 76.58 for Reach and Gravity, respectively. For Straightness, *Al Barsha 1* sample has the highest value of the Dispersion-phase samples, at 0.76.

Compared with the Inception and Pre-dispersion phases, the Dispersion phase has lower values for all metrics when alleys are added to the analysis.

Global Scale

Three global scale samples namely the *Dubai Creek* area, *Downtown Dubai* and vicinity, and *Dubai East* have been analyzed. Three metrics namely Reach, Gravity and Straightness have been computed at 3 km radius for the global scale sample in *Dubai Creek*, and at 6 km radius for other samples. Among these global scale samples, the maximum Reach value is obtained by *Dubai East* at 9,936. This sample comprises of neighborhoods like *Al Rashidiya*, *Mirdif*, *Al Warqa*, *Muhaisnah*, *Al Twar*, *Al Mizhar*, *Oud Al Muteena*, and *Nadd Al Hamar*. The maximum Gravity and Straightness values are obtained by the Dubai Creek area at 153.62 and 0.71 respectively.

In *Dubai Creek*, the distribution of high Reach values indicates high level of integration between several neighborhoods located in the northern part of the *Creek*, also commonly known as *Deira*. However, the Gravity map reveals integration among a majority of old neighborhoods only, located on the northwestern part of the sample. When assessing Straightness, high values can be observed adjacent to the major thoroughfares.

In *Downtown Dubai* and vicinity, the concentration of high Reach values reveals high level of integration between the neighborhoods located on the western part of the sample area like *Al Satwa*, *Al Wasl*, *Al Bada'a*, and *Downtown Dubai*. On the other hand, the Gravity map indicates low integration among all neighborhoods except for small northern areas of *Al Satwa* and *Al Bada'a*. When analyzing Straightness, high values mostly concentrate in neighborhoods like *Al Satwa*, *Al Bada'a*, *Jumeirah*, *Al Wasl* and *Al Jafalliya*, which are located in the northwestern part of the sample.

In *Dubai East*, the distribution of high Reach values indicates high level of integration between the neighborhoods like *Mirdif*, *Muhaisnah*, and *Al Mizhar*, located around the central part of the sample. However, the Gravity map reveals lesser integration across the neighborhoods but higher integration among few neighborhood blocks in *Al Rashidiya*, *Al Qusais 3*, and *Oud Al Muteena*. When analyzing Straightness, high values concentrate in *Al Twar 2*, northern part of *Muhaisnah 1*, southwestern part of *Nadd Al Hamar*, and western parts of *Al Rashidiya* and *Al Warqa* neighborhoods.

Comparison: Abu Dhabi vs. Dubai

One of the key differences between Dubai and Abu Dhabi is the nature of their origins. While Abu Dhabi was conceptualized as a planned city from the beginning (Alawadi, Nguyen, Alrubaei and Scoppa 2021), Dubai grew organically from a fishing village to a prominent town due to pearl-trading activities and consequent immigration of businessmen from Iran and the Indian subcontinent (Alawadi, Khanal and Almulla 2018). During the 1910s, Dubai evolved from a single cluster (i.e., *Al Fahidi*) to a group of housing clusters located in close proximity to one another. Dubai was an established city long before the discovery of oil discovery, while Abu Dhabi was established after the discovery of oil. Abu Dhabi was envisioned by *Sheikh Zayed* in the early 1960s. The origins (or, more precisely, the Inception phases) of Dubai and Abu Dhabi differ significantly. However, the urban development trajectories of both cities after the oil boom, particularly during their respective Dispersion phases, are quite similar. For instance, the involvement of foreign planners to develop master plans, the construction of an extensive road network, and the adoption of a national housing policy are common to both Abu Dhabi and Dubai.

On the other hand, some distinct periods of urban growth are evident in both cities. For instance, the Pre-Dispersion growth phase is unique to Dubai, while the Redemption growth phase is peculiar to Abu Dhabi. The uniqueness of Dubai's Pre-Dispersion phase is evident from its grid typology and other morphological attributes. For example, the Pre-Dispersion phase's alley-intersection density of 1.03 intersections/ha is much higher than the corresponding value in Dubai's Dispersion phase, which is 0.07 intersections/ha. Likewise, the Pre-Dispersion plot density of 6.74 plots/ha is higher than the corresponding Dispersion-phase value of 4.14 plots/ha. Also, the Pre-Dispersion phase's street-intersection density of 1.42 intersections/ha is higher than the corresponding Dispersion-phase value of 1.08 intersections/ha. Unlike Abu Dhabi, where urban development quickly leapfrogged from the core of West Island to the suburbs on the mainland, Dubai witnessed the incremental development of early suburbs not too far from *Dubai Creek*, the old city center. In Dubai, neighborhoods such as *Al Satwa*, *Al Badaa*, and *Al Jafalliya* lie within five kilometers of the *Creek*; by contrast, Abu Dhabi's Baniyas neighborhood lies more than 30 kilometers from the *West Island*. The aforementioned neighborhoods in both cities were developed during the 1970s after their respective Inception phases (when Dubai only consisted of Dubai Creek and Abu Dhabi was limited to the *West Island*). From 2007 to 2017, while Dubai continued on the path of uncontrolled dispersion, Abu Dhabi went through a phase of Redemption. This period reflected a 'return to historicism and nostalgic urbanism' (Alawadi and Benkraouda 2018, p.10). The Redemption phase had begun with the establishment of the Urban Planning Council (UPC), and it ended with UPC's merger with the Department of Municipal Affairs in 2017 to create Department of Urban Planning and Municipalities (DPM). Then, in 2019, the Department of Municipalities and Transport (DMT) was formed by the merger of DPM and the Department of Transport (DOT). Thus, urban planning and development in Abu Dhabi has once again shifted towards the track of the Dispersion phase, which means that the policies and vision promoted by the Urban Structure Framework of the Plan Capital 2030 is being compromised.

Although the neighborhood design of the Redemption period can be lauded for adopting higher densities by introducing smaller plot sizes, smaller blocks, vernacular forms, open spaces, and courtyard-oriented designs, there are some notable criticisms to be made. First, the principles of *New Urbanism* and *Garden Suburbs* are applied naively without attuning them to Abu Dhabi's social and environmental context. Second, the implementation of community guidelines and *Estidama* principles (Abu Dhabi's version of LEED) became ineffective at fostering regional integration. The myopic vision of the regulatory codes and guidelines was unable to accommodate multiple scales of physical planning, thereby leading to the formation of segregated and alienated neighborhoods. The Redemption phase can be identified as the period of correction, when the urban planning approach in Abu Dhabi was changed from that of the prior, Dispersion phase. However, there was a notable problem of cohesion between larger-scale city planning and smaller-scale neighborhood design (Alawadi and Bekraouda 2018). As a result, Abu Dhabi continued to be an agglomeration of land uses connected by highways which still lacks a holistic urban vision.

The lack of a city-scale vision is more apparent in Dubai, where large swaths of land are developed by private developers with little consideration of the surroundings. In totality, Dubai could be described as a "vast gated community" (Davis, 2006) which appears as a yet-to-be-completed mosaic (Alawadi, Khanal and Almulla 2018). Dubai did not undergo a period of Redemption, but its growth plummeted in the wake of the Global Economic Crisis of 2008. This period continued until 2013 and brought urban development back to the city's core in the form of mixed-use infill projects. This era has also been labelled the period of demolish-rebuild gentrification (Alawadi 2014). However, with the declaration of Dubai Expo 2020 in late 2013, the city relapsed into the mode of the ever-dispersing, sprawling, and leapfrogging urban growth. Several withheld megaprojects were revived, and new, ambitious projects were announced in anticipation of the year 2020. The Dispersion phase in Dubai merely slowed down for a brief period of five years, unlike in Abu Dhabi, where the Dispersion phase reappeared only after a decade of the Redemption phase.

"This book goes beyond providing a qualitative narrative about Abu Dhabi and Dubai to offer elaborate insights

"This book goes beyond providing a qualitative narrative about Abu Dhabi and Dubai to offer elaborate insights based on the results of urban network analysis (UNA)."

based on the results of urban network analysis (UNA)." The application of Multiple Centrality Assessment (MCA) through the UNA tool has enabled us to answer the questions laid out in the introduction:

1. How do the morphological attributes of the neighborhoods change in Abu Dhabi and Dubai throughout their urban evolution?
2. Are Abu Dhabi's and Dubai's neighborhood street networks designed to promote efficiency and centrality, toward the goal of overall efficiency, at the local and global scales?
3. How can we design and plan neighborhoods in which non-motorized mobility is a viable and efficient alternative?
4. Which locations in the network are most central and conducive to development or consolidation as activity hubs if driving distances and the global scale are considered?
5. Do existing neighborhood designs integrate with one another to form coherent and accessible urban environments? If not, how could they be retrofitted to make their street systems and urban fabrics more efficient and integrated? How can additional growth be planned and designed to efficiently connect to the existing city?

For all morphological attributes except plot density, Abu Dhabi has a decreasing trend throughout its urban evolution. For example, the average values of street density, alley density, street-intersection density, and alley-intersection density decrease from the Inception phase to the Dispersion phase, and further decrease from the Dispersion phase to the Redemption phase. However, plot density increases from the Dispersion phase to the Redemption phase. Similarly, in Dubai, all morphological attributes have a clear decreasing trend except street density. The average values of other attributes, including street intersection density, alley density, alley intersection density, and plot density decrease from the Inception phase to the Pre-Dispersion phase, and further decrease from the Pre-Dispersion to the Dispersion phase. One exception is average street density, which does not change from the Pre-Dispersion to the Dispersion phase.

In Abu Dhabi, neighborhoods of the Inception and the Redemption phases are well-suited to promote efficiency, compared with the Dispersion phase's neighborhoods. In terms of centrality, the Redemption phase's neighborhoods are more suitable than neighborhoods of other phases. In Dubai, the Inception phase's neighborhoods are the most efficient in terms of both centrality and efficiency, although in terms of Betweenness, the Pre-Dispersion phase scores higher than the Inception phase.

The findings of this book provide evidence that street layout and morphological attributes such as plot density, street density, alley density, street intersection density and alley intersection density play a role in the creation of efficient neighborhoods. More specifically, a higher plot density, organic and interconnected street layouts, smaller blocks, and higher street and alley density are required to achieve greater centrality and efficiency. Non-motorized mobility is a viable and efficient option in neighborhoods that obtain high average values of UNA metrics such as Reach, Gravity, Straightness, and Betweenness in a local-scale analysis. In the present scenario, such neighborhoods include Dubai Creek and Al Satwa in Dubai, and West Island and Al Falah in Abu Dhabi. Future neighborhoods should be planned and designed by using the existing high-scoring neighborhoods as benchmarks. Before plan implementation and site construction, different neighborhood designs can be analyzed using the UNA tool. A detailed comparison at the local and global scales and at various radii can be carried out before final selection. The last chapter of this book sheds more light on specific urban planning and design strategies through its discussion and depiction of best- and worst-performing samples.

When the average values of the UNA metrics of the Abu Dhabi's and Dubai's Inception phases are compared, Dubai outperforms Abu Dhabi in all metrics. In neighborhood scale Scenario 1 (streets only), the average Reach value in Dubai is 1,117, compared with 455 in Abu Dhabi. Dubai's average Gravity value of 168.66 is four times Abu Dhabi's corresponding value of 41.33. Similarly, Dubai's average Straightness value of 0.87 is more than Abu Dhabi's corresponding value of 0.69. Also, Dubai's average Betweenness value of 24,168 is four times greater than Abu Dhabi's average Betweenness value of 5,034. Similar results are obtained in Scenario 2, when alleys are included in the network. Dubai's Inception phase has greater values for all metrics than Abu Dhabi's Inception phase. The average Reach, Gravity, Straightness, and Betweenness values in Dubai are 1,145, 185.95, 0.69, and 13,843 respectively, while the corresponding values in Abu Dhabi are 511, 51.02, 0.68, and 4,788, respectively. The notably higher values in Dubai than in Abu Dhabi can be partly explained by the considerable difference between their plot densities in their Inception phases. Dubai has a plot density of 11.10 plots/ha, while Abu Dhabi has only 2.65 plots/ha (See Table 1). Moreover, the street layout of Dubai's Inception phase is organic, unlike the super-grid layout of Abu Dhabi's corresponding growth phase. Street density is higher in Abu Dhabi, at 0.25 km/ha, compared with 0.19 km/ha in Dubai, while street intersection density is slightly higher in Abu Dhabi, at 2.52 intersections/ha, compared with Dubai's value of 1.72 intersections/ha. The alleyway density of Dubai, at 0.28 km/ha, is almost double the corresponding value for Abu Dhabi, which is 0.15 km/ha. However, the total alley length in *West Island* Abu Dhabi, at 533.71 km, is more than four times the alley length in *Dubai Creek*, which is 130.15 km. The alley intersection density of Dubai, at 0.83 alley intersections/ha, is higher than the corresponding value for Abu Dhabi, which is 0.52 alley intersections/ha.

When the two Dispersion phases in Abu Dhabi and Dubai are compared in terms of their average values of UNA metrics, Dubai outperforms Abu Dhabi in all metrics except Straightness. In Scenario 1 (streets only), the average Reach value in Dubai is 408, compared with 244 in Abu Dhabi. The average Gravity value of Dubai, at 44.93, is greater than the corresponding value for Abu Dhabi, which is 29.19. However, the average Straightness of Dubai's neighborhoods, at 0.70, is less than the corresponding value for Abu Dhabi, which is 0.75. The average Betweenness value of Dubai's neighborhoods, at 10,690 is more than thrice the average Betweenness value for Abu Dhabi's neighborhoods, at 2,815. Similar results are obtained in Scenario 2 when alleys are included in the network. Dubai's Dispersion phase has greater values for all metrics except Straightness, compared with Abu Dhabi's Dispersion phase. The average Reach, Gravity, and Betweenness values in Dubai are 544, 59.78, and 9,487 respectively; while the corresponding values in Abu Dhabi are 297, 37.09, and 2,277 respectively. However, the average Straightness of Abu Dhabi's neighborhoods, at 0.75, is greater than Dubai's corresponding value of 0.72. The higher values in Dubai compared with Abu Dhabi can be partly explained by the difference between their average plot densities in the Dispersion phase. Dubai has an average plot density of 4.14 plots/ha, while Abu Dhabi's is only 2.31 plots/ha. The comparison of global scale results also yields outcomes similar to local scale analyses. The average values of UNA metrics for Dubai are higher than Abu Dhabi except for Straightness. For instance, the average Reach of Dubai's global scale samples at 7,145 is more than double the corresponding value of Abu Dhabi's global scale samples at 2,799. Similarly, the average Gravity value of Abu Dhabi at 42.11 is less than the corresponding value of Dubai at 98.69. However, the average Straightness value of Abu Dhabi's global scale samples at 0.70 is slightly higher than the corresponding value of Dubai at 0.68. These results hint at a lower level of integration between the neighborhoods in Abu Dhabi as compared to Dubai. On the other hand, Straightness results indicate that the connectivity between neighborhoods is slightly less in Dubai's neighborhoods as compared to neighborhoods in Abu Dhabi.

Although the street density is the same in both cities, at 0.17 km/ha, the street intersection density is higher in Dubai, at 1.01 intersections/ha, compared with Abu Dhabi's street intersection density of 0.54 intersections/ha. However, Abu Dhabi has greater alleyway density, at 0.11 km/ha, compared with the corresponding value for Dubai, which is 0.04 km/ha. Likewise, the alley intersection density of Abu Dhabi, at 0.56 alley intersections/ha, is greater than the corresponding value for Dubai of 0.07 alley intersections/ha. The street layouts in both Dubai's and Abu Dhabi's Dispersion phases are predominantly looping and fragmented parallels. However, there are some peculiarities in Dubai's suburbs, for instance, a curvilinear layout in *Al Warqa* and the presence of cul-de-sacs in Al Barsha, as opposed to the monotonous, NPU-based looping and fragmented layout of Abu Dhabi's suburbs. Even though the presence of alleys in Abu Dhabi is greater than in Dubai, alleys do not make a significant contribution to efficiency and centrality. This is because other factors, such as the strategic location of alleys in the network and network layout, play equally important roles. The alleys play a crucial role in circulation networks within the superblocks in Abu Dhabi. Alleys can make networks extremely efficient for pedestrians by providing direct routes to most locations within the superblocks. However, a longer alley network does not correspond to higher network efficiency. Scoppa, Bawazir, and Alawadi (2018) have shown that optimized alley systems can increase overall network efficiency even when the total alley length is reduced in a study area. For instance, alleys should be placed strategically such that they split internal blocks in half. This finding warrants a revision of the existing practice, in which alleys are placed between each and every plot or are placed without considering their role in overall network efficiency.

	Avg. Plot Density (plots/ha)	Avg. Street Density (km/ha)	Avg. Alley Density (km/ha)	Avg. Street Intersections Density (intersections/ha)	Avg. Alley Intersections Density (intersections/ha)
Inception Abu Dhabi	2.65	0.25	0.15	2.52	0.52
Dispersion Abu Dhabi	1.98	0.16	0.11	0.54	0.56
Redemption Abu Dhabi	3.31	0.13	0.04	0.55	N/A
Inception Dubai	11.10	0.19	0.09	1.72	0.83
Pre-Dispersion Dubai	6.74	0.29	0.10	1.42	1.03
Dispersion Dubai	4.14	0.19	0.04	1.08	0.07

TABLE. 1

Comparison of the morphological attributes for Abu Dhabi's and Dubai's growth phases

References

Alawadi, Khaled. "Urban redevelopment trauma: The story of a Dubai neighbourhood." Built Environment 40, no. 3 (2014): 357-375.

Alawadi, Khaled, Asim Khanal, and Ahmed Almulla. "Land, urban form, and politics: a study on Dubai's housing landscape and rental affordability." Cities 81 (2018): 115-130.

Alawadi, Khaled, and Ouafa Benkraouda. "What happened to Abu Dhabi's urbanism? The question of regional integration." Journal of Urban Design 23, no. 3 (2018): 367-394.

Alawadi, Khaled, Ngoc Hong Nguyen, Eiman Alrubaei, and Martin Scoppa. "Streets, density, and the superblock: neighborhood planning units and street connectivity in Abu Dhabi." Journal of Urbanism: International Research on Placemaking and Urban Sustainability (2021): 1-28.

Davis, M. (2006). Fear and money in Dubai. New Left Review, 41(September/October), 47–68.

Scoppa, Martin, Khawla Bawazir, and Khaled Alawadi. "Walking the superblocks: Street layout efficiency and the sikkak system in Abu Dhabi." Sustainable Cities and Society 38 (2018): 359-369.

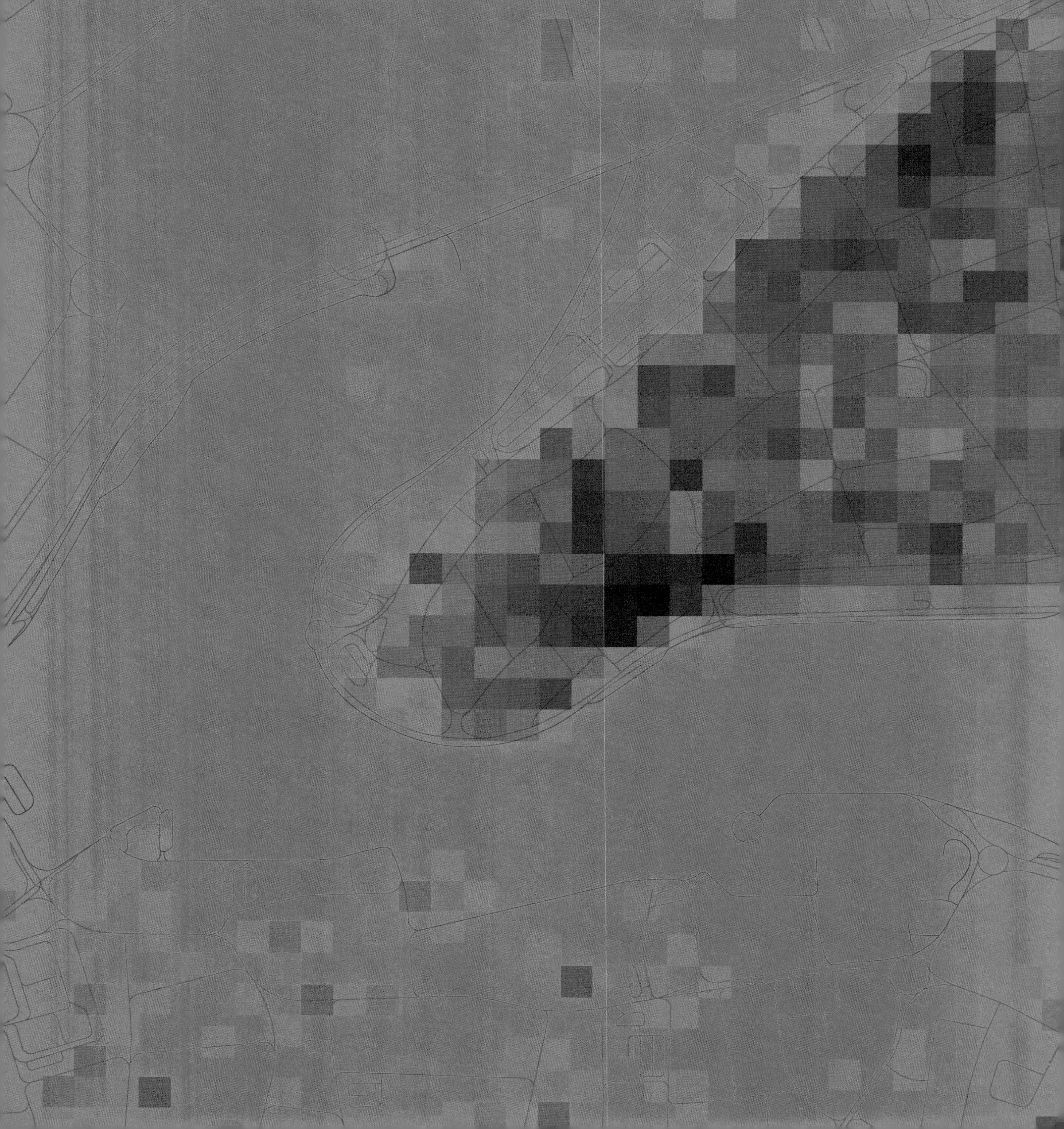

Implications for Practice

Introduction

This chapter is intended to derive design strategies that can be used as guidelines for future neighborhood development or to retrofit existing ones. After the completion of the analysis, the studied samples were ranked according to their Reach, Gravity, and Straightness results. The Reach and Gravity metrics capture the notion of accessibility, and the Straightness metric indicates efficiency. Also, the selected cases reflect the diversity of network morphology in both cities — Abu Dhabi and Dubai.

Three centrality metrics, namely Reach, Gravity, and Straightness, are considered adequate for discussing design ideals derived from the analysis results. Both Reach and Gravity are considered to be associated with plot density and network morphology. Denser neighborhoods produce higher Reach and Gravity values, because more plots can be accessed within a shorter distance. Network morphology was also found to have an impact on those metrics: gridded networks in general tended to provide accessibility to nearby plots with shorter routes. Thus, the morphological attributes and the accessibility results of the samples are correlated. The Straightness metric also helps in identifying the network morphologies with the most or least direct routes. This metric was found to be independent from the other metrics (Reach and Gravity) in terms of the performance classification. In other words, the location of high- and low-performing areas within a sample are similar for Reach and Gravity but often different for Straightness.

The UNA results of the selected samples for the three walking sheds (400, 800, and 1,600 m) have been averaged to produce centrality maps with mean values that can be used to derive conclusions (See Table 1). The average maps of the Reach metric and the Gravity metric have been further averaged into one map. This is based on the assumption that Reach maps reflect maximum possible accessibility without distance decay effects, while the Gravity maps reflect minimum accessibility due to the distance decay effect. The zones of low and high values in the maps of both metrics have been found to be of consistent patterns, and hence an averaged map between the two metrics can indicate average accessibility estimates.

It is also important to note that samples' performances have been ranked using accessibility's raw numerical results rather than percentages from the total number of plots. This approach has been used to avoid the diffusion of the effect that plot density has on accessibility. When percentages are used, samples with an efficient network morphology score higher regardless of their plot densities. Since the intention of this chapter is derive planning ideals, the role of plot density cannot be overlooked. Thus, it was decided to keep the ranking criteria based on raw numbers.

In total, 13 samples from 9 neighborhoods have been selected. Each neighborhood is discussed in terms of samples' centrality maps, morphological attributes, histograms, and analysis diagrams. The discussion starts by showing centrality maps of the selected sample/s in each neighborhood, followed by analytical diagrams, describing the network morphology and plot density, numerical attributes, and histograms. The centrality maps show the accessibility of the studied samples through the calculation of Reach and Gravity and the connectivity of the samples through the computation of Straightness. The maps are also consistent with the ones shown in earlier chapters in that they show the centrality results for the two network cases: Scenario 1 (streets only) and Scenario 2 (streets and alleys). The depiction of two scenarios helps in highlighting the impact of alleyways on centrality results. The inclusion of alleyways increases the number of intersections, as well as the total length of the network. It was also found that the layout of the alleyways and their density impact centrality metrics differently. Route continuity, connectivity of dead ends, and splitting of large blocks can have a positive impact on accessibility results. However, the types of intersections formed when the alleyways are integrated with the street network can impact the Straightness results differently. For instance, a greater presence of T-intersections reduces route directness.

The alleyways' impact can be observed visually in the Centrality maps and the histograms that follow the attributes' diagrams. Three histograms can be found for each sample: one histogram is prepared for each of the metrics, namely Reach, Gravity, and Straightness. They can be used to deduce important features about the data resulting from the analysis. For example, the histogram can show the distribution of values, the limits, and the percentages of plots achieving results above or below the median. Most importantly, they show the impact of alleyways, since the values of the two networks' scenarios (Scenario 1: Streets only and Scenario 2: Streets and alleys) are layered on top of each other. The discussion of each neighborhood is then concluded by debating key features of each sample or set of samples and their contribution to a low or high performance. Finally, a set of recommended design strategies are discussed; these strategies can inform urban planning and design decision making.

The centrality maps show the accessibility of the studied samples through the calculation of Reach and Gravity and the connectivity of the samples through the computation of Straightness.

TABLE. 1
Average Reach, average Gravity, and average Straightness for the samples in Abu Dhabi and Dubai

Abu Dhabi

Growth phase	Neighborhood	Sample no.	Scenario 1: Streets Only — Average values for Reach (R), Gravity (G) & Straightness (S)			Scenario 2: Streets + Alleys — Average values for Reach (R), Gravity (G) & Straightness (S)		
			R	G	S	R	G	S
Inception	West Island	Sample 1	380	44.43	0.67	400	52.30	0.70
		Sample 2	390	43.50	0.68	400	47.83	0.70
Dispersion	Baniyas	Sample 1	243	26.94	0.68	281	37.79	0.72
		Sample 2	248	29.29	0.67	290	42.06	0.72
	Khalifa City	Sample 1	228	26.27	0.75	256	32.91	0.77
		Sample 2	147	18.45	0.72	174	22.13	0.72
	Al Bahya	Sample 1	151	25.07	0.81	155	26.07	0.78
		Sample 2	165	21.90	0.76	190	26.30	0.75
	MBZ City	Sample 1	135	19.85	0.75	160	22.06	0.73
		Sample 2	156	20.91	0.75	197	25.28	0.75
Redemption	Al Falah	Sample 1	299	45.89	0.72	N/A	N/A	N/A
		Sample 2	505	57.16	0.74	N/A	N/A	N/A

Dubai

Growth phase	Neighborhood	Sample no.	Scenario 1: Streets Only — Average values for Reach (R), Gravity (G) & Straightness (S)			Scenario 2: Streets + Alleys — Average values for Reach (R), Gravity (G) & Straightness (S)		
			R	G	S	R	G	S
Inception	Dubai Creek	Sample 1	1488	244.77	0.73	1563	275.08	0.76
		Sample 2	868	115.77	0.68	997	140.01	0.73
Pre-Dispersion	Al Satwa	Sample 1	1174	200.46	0.76	1208	229.23	0.80
		Sample 2	233	40.86	0.71	312	63.83	0.73
	Al Rashdiya	Sample 1	413	46.27	0.68	552	69.15	0.74
		Sample 2	718	101.78	0.73	746	111.88	0.76
Dispersion	Jumeirah	Sample 1	257	48.07	0.70	290	61.01	0.75
		Sample 2	372	51.49	0.71	420	60.98	0.73
		Sample 3	206	26.10	0.69	303	38.99	0.72
	Al Quoz	Sample 1	520	58.47	0.66	610	76.58	0.71
	Al Warqa	Sample 1	443	51.92	0.69	559	68.43	0.73
		Sample 2	436	48.90	0.69	517	63.42	0.75
	Al Barsha	Sample 1	304	36.09	0.70	453	60.58	0.76
		Sample 2	314	37.73	0.71	494	60.52	0.74

Abu Dhabi

Four neighborhoods and a total of five samples have been selected from Abu Dhabi. The neighborhoods are selected to reflect diversity in network morphology. *West Island* and *Al Falah* have the highest plot densities and the highest accessibility results (See Figure 1.1). In contrast, *Al Bahya* and *MBZ City* have the lowest plot densities, which result in their also having the lowest accessibility performance.

The western part of the Abu Dhabi Island, or *West Island*, can be considered the earliest urban development in this city. *West Island* has a distinct morphology composed of several NPUs that are integrated within a semi-grid. Both samples in this neighborhood are discussed in this chapter. Results obtained from the analysis have indicated high Reach and Gravity values for the West Island samples. However, Straightness results for both samples are the lowest among all Abu Dhabi samples.

Al Falah neighborhood has a radial network morphology. The sample located in the center has relatively low Reach and Gravity values compared with the sample closer to the edge of the neighborhood. Despite having high plot densities in both samples, only Sample 2's Reach and Gravity results are considered to be high.

Al Bahya's samples are among the worst-performing samples, mainly due to the low plot density in this neighborhood. Despite having a gridiron network and alleyways, Reach and Gravity values are low. Alleyways proved to have little impact in improving accessibility and led to the reduction of Straightness. One of the samples located in *Al Bahya East* is shown in this chapter.

MBZ City has a fragmented parallel network and a relatively low density compared with the rest of the samples in Abu Dhabi. This resulted in low Reach and Gravity values and moderate Straightness values. When alleyways were included in the network analysis, they were found to have significant impact in improving accessibility values but also in reducing Straightness.

In general, certain morphological attributes have been found to contribute more to higher performances. For instance, morphological attributes such as smaller block sizes, higher street densities, greater numbers of four-way-intersections, and higher plot densities are favorable for higher performance. On the other hand, attributes that lower performance include inconsistent network morphologies (i.e., fragmented radial, fragmented looping, semi-grid), increased T-junctions upon adding alleyways to the network, discontinuous routes, and low plot densities.

West Island and Al Falah have the highest plot densities and the highest accessibility results. In contrast, Al Bahya and MBZ city have the lowest plot densities, which result in their also having the lowest accessibility performance.

Dubai

Five neighborhoods and a total of eight samples have been selected in Dubai. Neighborhoods like *Creek* and *Al Satwa* have high Reach and Gravity values, while *Al Barsha* has one of the lowest values among all Dubai neighborhoods (See Figure 1.2). *Al Warqa* and *Al Quoz* have medium to low performance levels. Each of the selected neighborhoods consists of a distinct network morphology. Hence, the discussion is inclusive of almost all the network morphologies that can be found in the city of Dubai.

Dubai Creek, recognized as the earliest urban settlement in Dubai, has a unique organic network. Both samples from *Dubai Creek* are considered for this chapter. The dense fabric of this neighborhood is used to illustrate the role of alleyways laid out in an even manner. It also shows that high plot density can lead to significantly high Reach and Gravity values. Such urban settings reflect a rich urban life where daily destinations can be accessed within reasonable walking distances, although it can be challenging for vehicles to navigate the organic layout.

Al Satwa has a gridiron network and a relatively high plot density in Sample 1. It has the second highest Reach and Gravity values and the highest Straightness value among all Dubai samples. This is different for Sample 2, which has much lower plot density. Hence, only Sample 1 is chosen for further discussion in this chapter. The high performances in Sample 1 can be credited to the network morphology, which is enhanced with an additional grid of alleyways forming continuous direct routes.

Both *Al Warqa* and *Al Barsha* are deemed low-performing samples. *Al Warqa* has looping and radially fragmented parallel network. It performs poorly in terms of Reach and Gravity and a moderately in terms of Straightness, despite having one of the highest plot densities in Dubai. The network deficiencies are slightly improved when alleys are included in the analyses. Both of this neighborhood's samples are discussed in this chapter.

Al Barsha has a looping fragmented parallel network and a medium plot density. The Reach and Gravity values indicate low performance, despite its having a better alleyway layout than *Al Warqa*. Samples in both *Al Warqa* and *Al Barsh*a have adequate Straightness results, which indicate that destinations can be accessed with considerably direct routes but at longer distances.

FIG. 1.1
West Island, Abu Dhabi, a highly performing area

FIG. 1.2
Al Satwa, Dubai, a highly performing area

WEST ISLAND
MBZ CITY

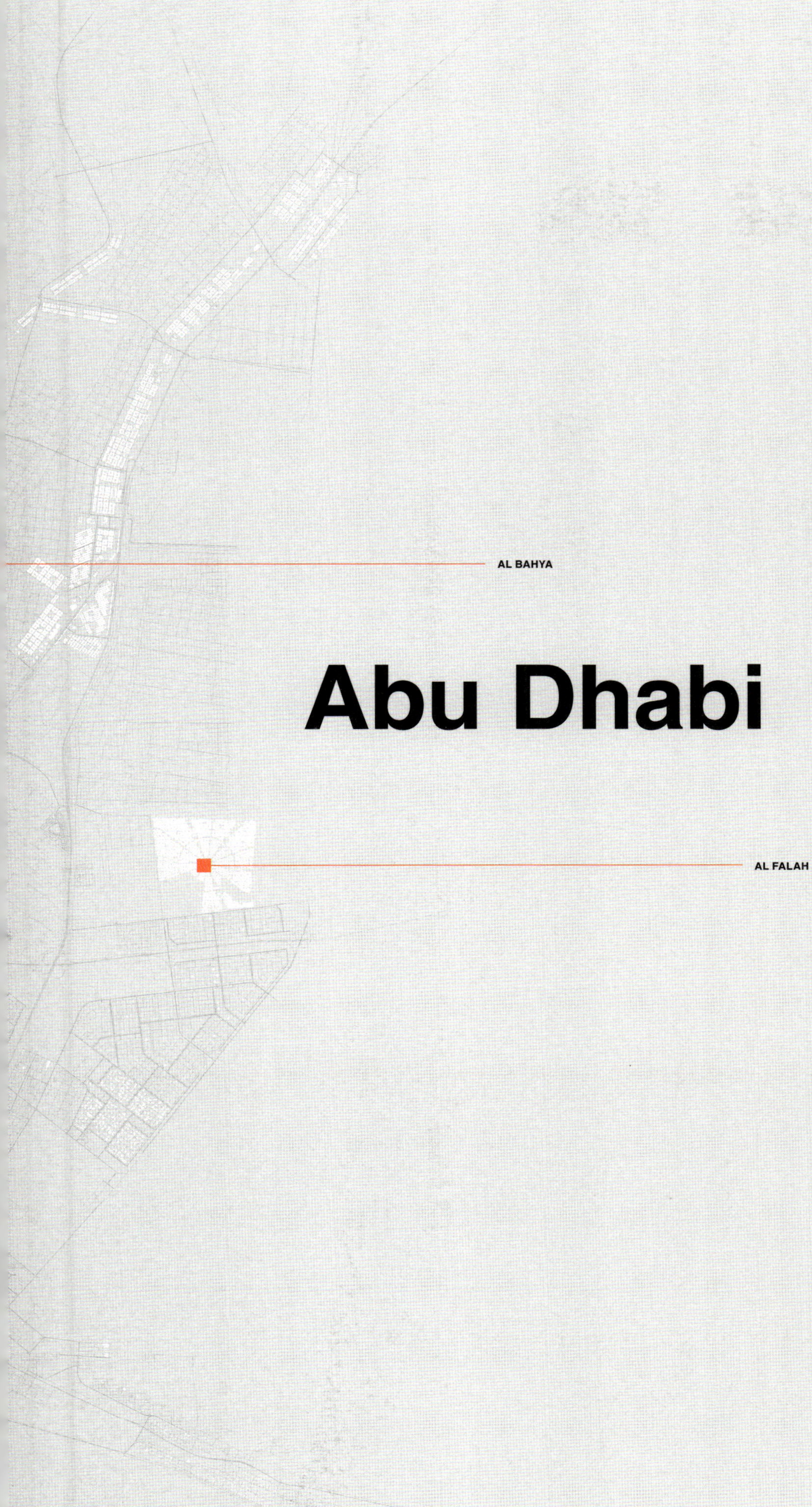

Abu Dhabi

West Island

High Performing Sample

FIG. 2.1
Sample 2 - left
Scenario 1: Streets only

FIG. 2.2
Sample 2 - right
Scenario 2: Streets + Alleys

Area	256 Hectare
Plots count	1017 plot
Plot density	3.15 plot/Ha
Streets	
Total street length	134.17 km
Street intersections	1439
Street length density	0.52 km/Ha
Street intersection density	5.62 intersections/Hectare

Network (streets + alleyways)	
Total network length	170.24 km
Total intersection	1672
Alleyways	
Alleyways length	36.07 km
Alleyways intersection	233
Alleyways length density	0.14 km/Ha
Alleyways intersection density	0.91 intersections/Hectare

Roads —— Alleyways

FIG. 2.3
Sample 2 - left
Average Reach and Gravity
Scenario 1: Streets only

FIG. 2.4
Sample 2 - right
Average Straightness
Scenario 1: Streets only

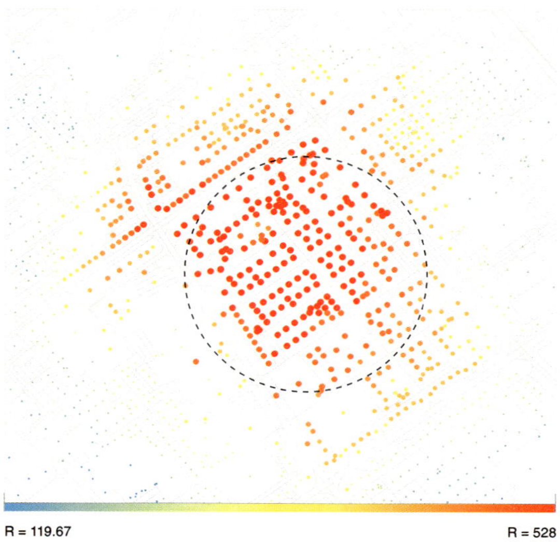

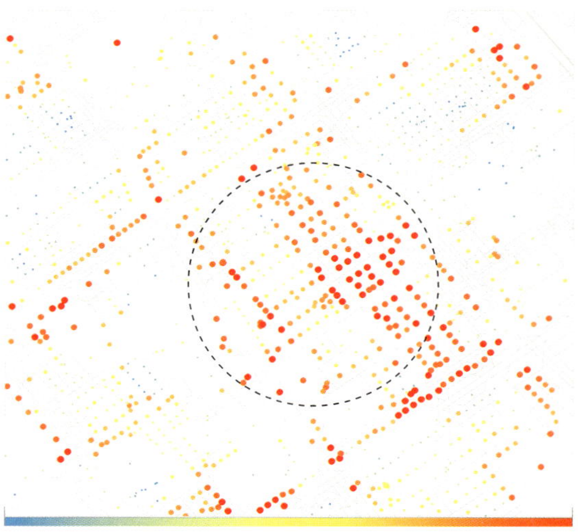

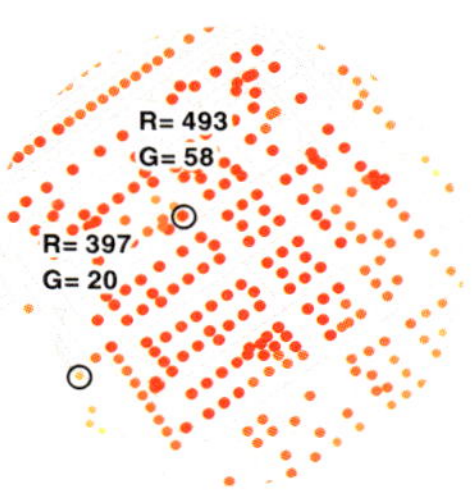

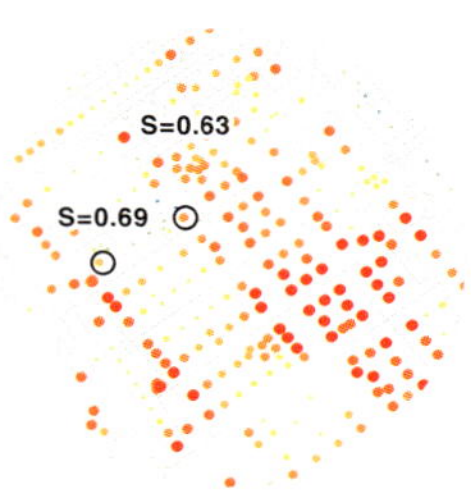

Network without alleyways
Average Reach for all plots = 379.95 plot
Average Reach percentage = 37% of the total number of plots
Average Gravity for all plots = 44.43 plot
Average Gravity percentage = 4% of the total number of plots
Average straightness = 0.67

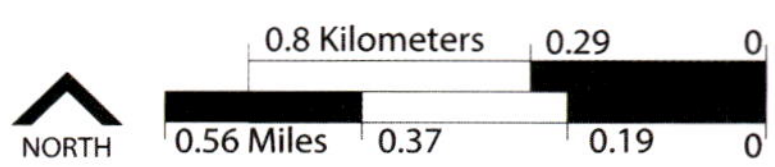

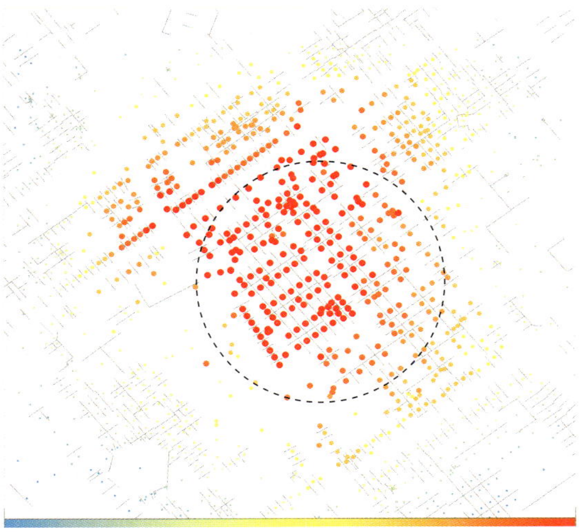

R = 120
G= 2.68

R = 539.33
G= 77.12

S= 0.51

S= 0.77

FIG. 2.5

Sample 2 - left

Average Reach and Gravity
Scenario 2: Streets + Alleys

FIG. 2.6

Sample 2 - right

Average Straightness
Scenario 2: Streets + Alleys

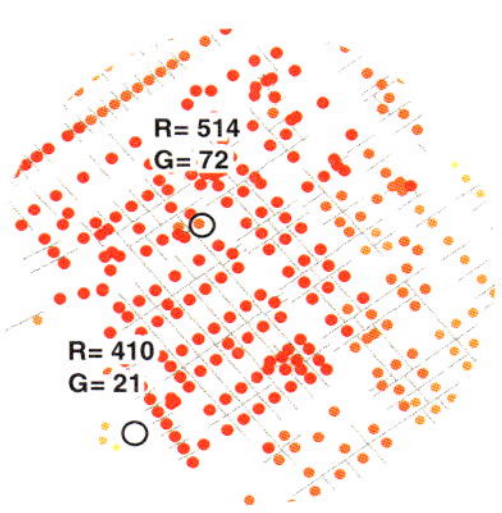

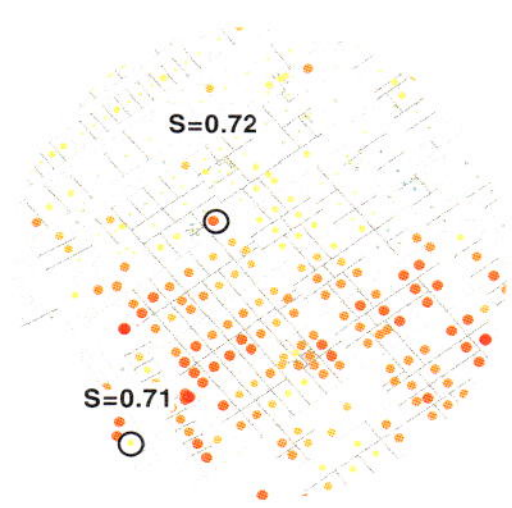

Network with alleyways

Average Reach for all plots = 400.06 plot
Average Reach percentage = 40% of the total number of plots
Average Gravity for all plots = 52.30 plot
Average Gravity percentage = 5% of the total number of plots
Average straightness = 0.70

Street —— Alleyways

Sample 1 — Average Reach

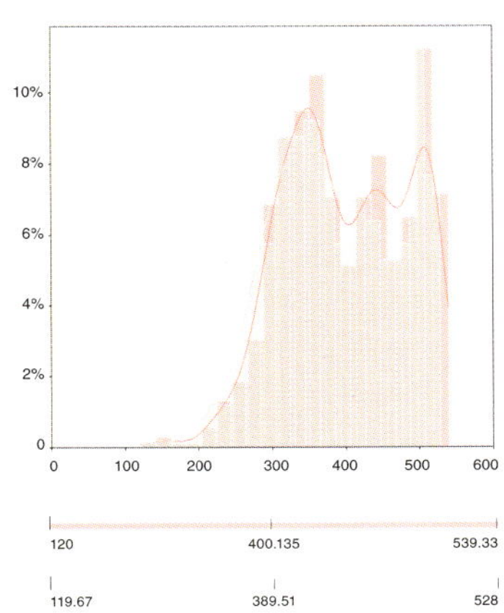

Sample 1 — Average Gravity

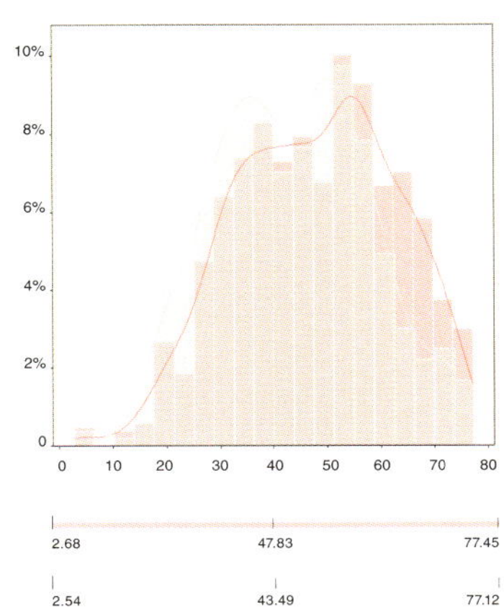

Sample 1 — Average Straightness

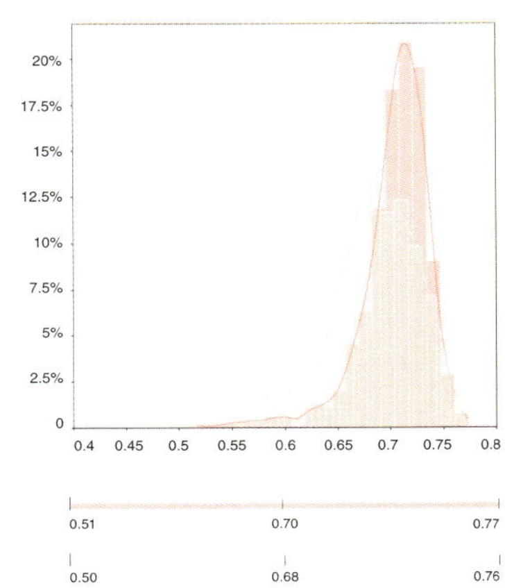

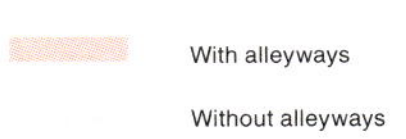

FIG. 3

Histograms showing the distribution of values for the metrics of Reach, Gravity and Straightness. Values for Straightness are bound within a theoretical range between (0,1). The values for all the three metrics are averages of three radii (400, 800, 1600).

Design Strategies

FIG. 4

Streets in West Island are semi-grid with 6.53 intersections per hectare. Alleyways reduce the average block size, improve route continuity, increase intersection density to 9.29 intersection/Ha, and enhance average Straightness values from 0.63 to 0.72. Plot densities are among the highest in the studied samples in Abu Dhabi at 3.97 plot/Ha.

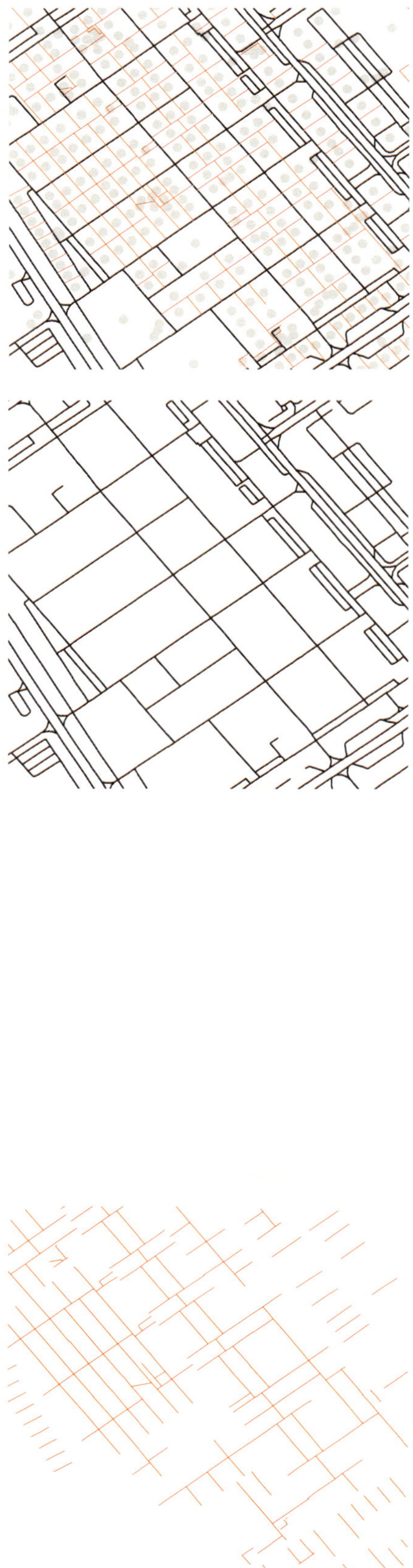

Plot Density and Network Morphology

Reach and Gravity: West Island has a semi-grid network morphology (see Figure 4). The samples have high Reach and Gravity values due to their medium plot densities, which average to 4.13 plots/Ha. When alleys are added, Reach and Gravity values improve due to the splitting of large blocks and the creation of continuous routes. This is more notable in Sample 1, where the block size decreased from 200 m x 95 m to 45 m x 40 m. However, the improvements in Reach and Gravity values are not major enough to justify adding an average of 0.29 km/Ha of alleys to the samples.

Straightness: *West Island* samples have the lowest Straightness values among all samples and medium Straightness values (0.50-0.75) according to the standard used in this book. Due to its semi-gridded layout and the combination of different network designs, the street network has many discontinuous T-junctions. The inclusion of alleys results in an increase in Straightness. This is due to both the increase in intersection density from an average of 4.33 intersections/Ha to 8.06 intersections/Ha in the samples and the evident increase in network continuity. When alleys are introduced, a majority of the intersections turn from T-junctions to four-way intersections.

Morphological Indicators for Enhancing Connectivity and Accessibility

- Street network: Grid is prioritized
- Plot density: 3.15 plots/Ha and higher is recommended.
- Alley density: At most 0.14 km/Ha. Those need to be strategically located.
- Total network intersection density: 9.29 intersections/Ha obtained high Straightness values in semi-grids; prioritize four-way intersections over T-junctions.
- Block size: Smaller block size, around 200 m x 95 m, is preferable to bigger block sizes.

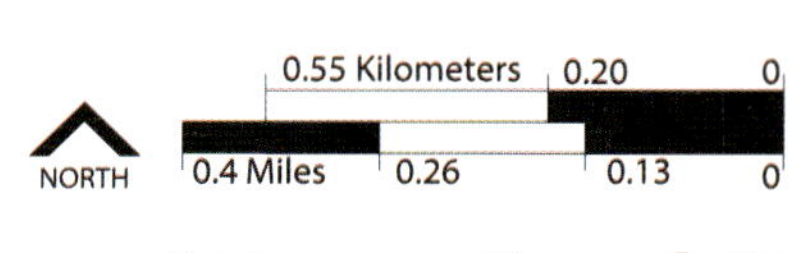

Al Falah

High Performing Sample

FIG. 5.1
Sample 2
Scenario 1: Streets only

Area	256 Hectare
Plots count	1322 plot
Plot density	5.16 plot/Ha
Streets	
Total street length	75.31 km
Street intersections	348
Street length density	0.29 km/Ha
Street intersection density	1.24 intersections/Hectare

FIG. 5.2
Sample 2 - left
Average Reach and Gravity
Scenario 1: Streets only

FIG. 5.3
Sample 2 - right
Average Straightness
Scenario 1: Streets only

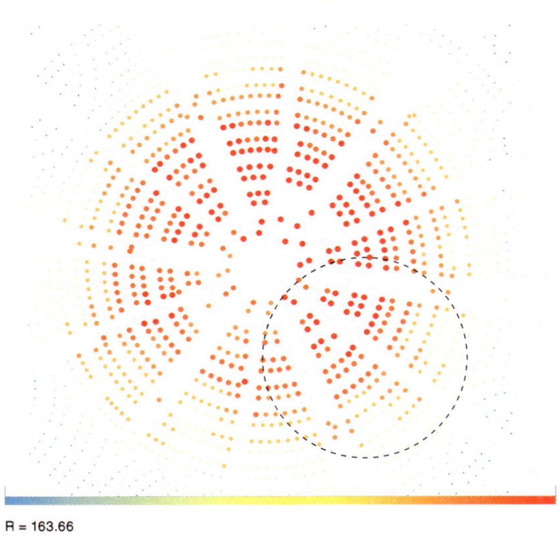

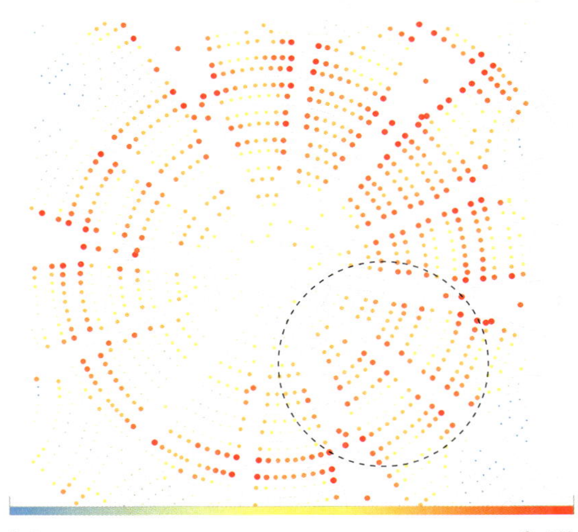

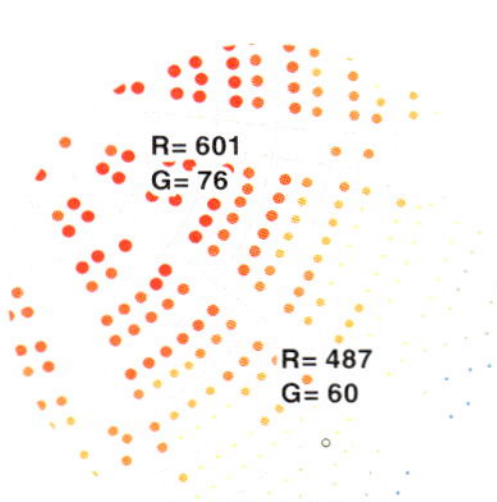

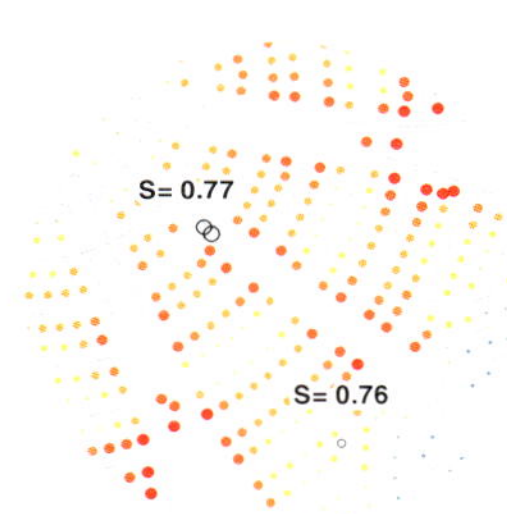

Network without alleyways
Average Reach for all plots = 504.57 plot
Average Reach percentage = 40% of the total number of plots
Average Gravity for all plots = 57.15 plot
Average Gravity percentage = 4% of the total number of plots
Average Straightness = 0.73

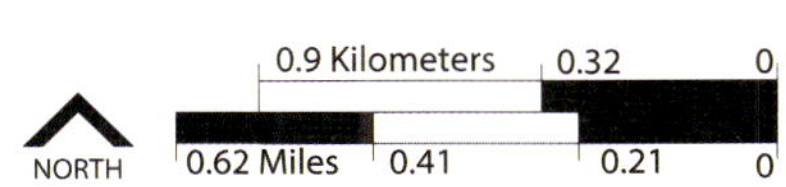

FIG. 6

Histograms showing the distribution of values for the metrics of Reach, Gravity and Straightness. Values for Straightness are bound within a theoretical range between (0,1). The values for all the three metrics are averages of three radii (400, 800, 1600).

Sample 2 — Average Reach

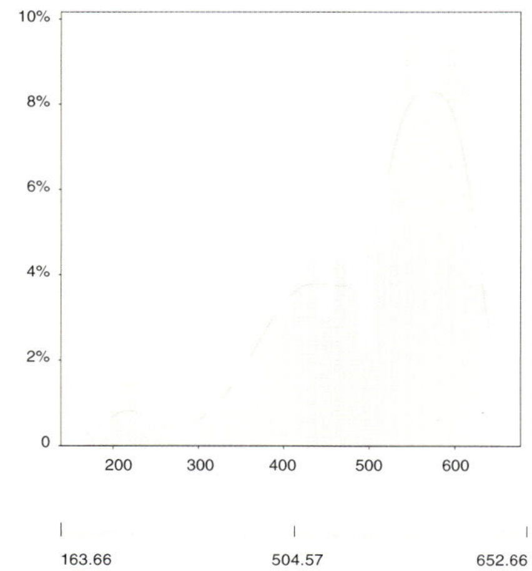

Sample 2 — Average Gravity

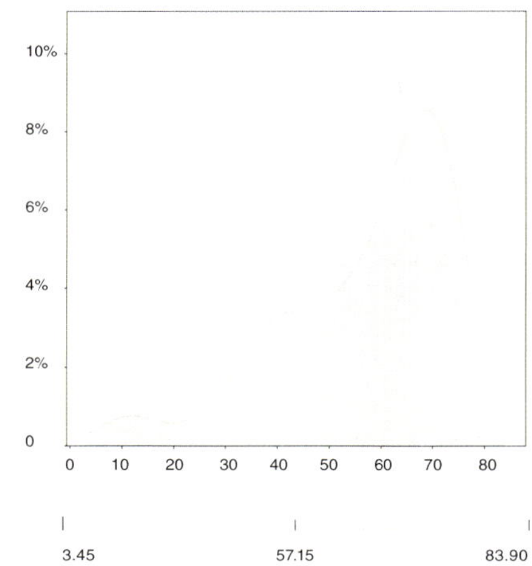

Sample 2 — Average Straightness

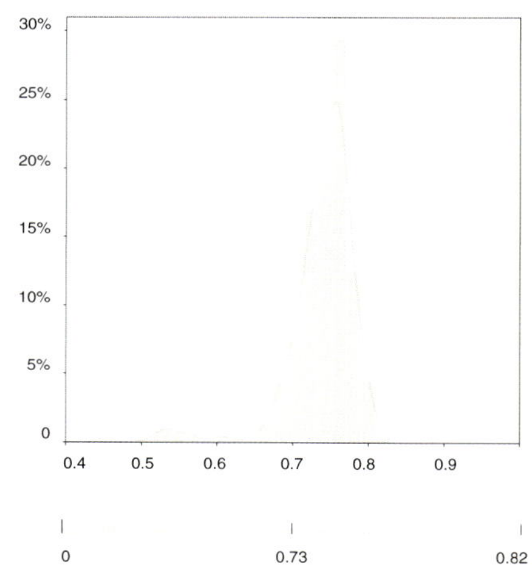

Without alleyways

Design Strategies

Plot Density and Network Morphology

Reach and Gravity: *Al Falah North* has a radial-grid network morphology (see Figure 7). The samples have high Reach and Gravity values due to their medium plot densities, which average 4.32 and 5.16 plots/Ha in samples 1 and 2, respectively. Additionally, Sample 2 performs better than Sample 1, as Sample 2 has a higher street density of 0.29 km/Ha, higher street intersection density of 1.24 intersections/Ha, and a smaller block size of 200 m x 80 m. Thus, a finer radial-grid urban grain leads to higher Reach and Gravity values. There are no alleys in Al Falah North.

Straightness: *Al Falah* has a moderate Straightness value which is higher than that of the semi-gridded samples but lower than that of the gridded samples. Al Falah's samples have Straightness values ranging from 0.50 to 0.75, which are medium values according to the standard used in this book . The radial layout in *Al Falah* does not perform well compared with the gridded network of *Al Bahya* due to the abundance of T-Junctions separating its superblocks. Additionally, *Al Falah* Sample 2 has higher Straightness values due to its high total network intersection density of 1.24 intersections/Ha, compared with 0.80 intersections/Ha in Sample 1. In this particular network, the increase in network intersections is in the form of T-Junctions rather than four-way intersections, which results in lower Straightness values.

Morphological Indicators for Enhancing Connectivity and Accessibility

- Street network: Radially fragmented parallel is not recommended.
- Plot density: 5.16 plots/Ha and higher.
- Street density: 0.29 km/Ha; higher is recommended.
- Total network intersection density: 1.24 intersections/Ha; higher is recommended; prioritize four-way intersections over T-junctions.
- Block size: 190 m x 100 m; smaller is recommended.

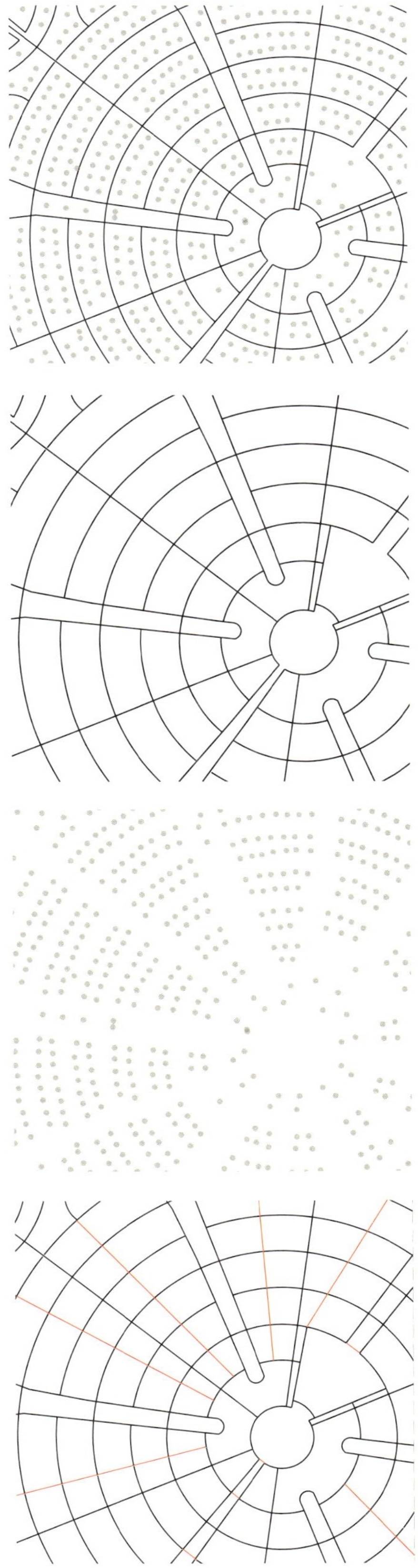

FIG. 7
Streets in Al Falah are segmented radial with 1.24 intersection/Ha. Although alleyways don't exist in this referenced sample, implementing them, strategically, would reduce the average block size, improve route continuity and average Straightness values. Plot densities are the highest in the studied samples in Abu Dhabi at 5.16 plot/Ha.

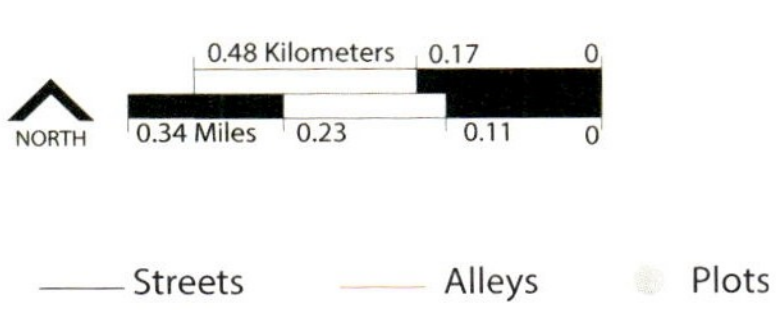

East Al Bahya

Low Performing Sample

FIG. 8.1
Sample 1 - left
Scenario 1: Streets only

FIG. 8.2
Sample 1 - right
Scenario 2: Streets + Alleys

Network (streets + alleyways)		
Total network length	297	plot
Total intersection	1.16	plot/Ha
Alleyways		
Alleyways length	28.23	km
Alleyways intersection	417	
Alleyways length density	0.11	km/Ha
Alleyways intersection density	1.62	intersections/Hectare

Area	256	Hectare
Plots count	297	plot
Plot density	1.16	plot/Ha
Streets		
Total street length	40.13	km
Street intersections	179	
Street length density	0.15	km/Ha
Street intersection density	0.55	intersections/Hectare

Roads — Alleyways

FIG. 8.3
Sample 1 - left
Average Straightness
Scenario 1: Streets only

FIG. 8.4
Sample 1 - right
Average Reach and Gravity
Scenario 1: Streets only

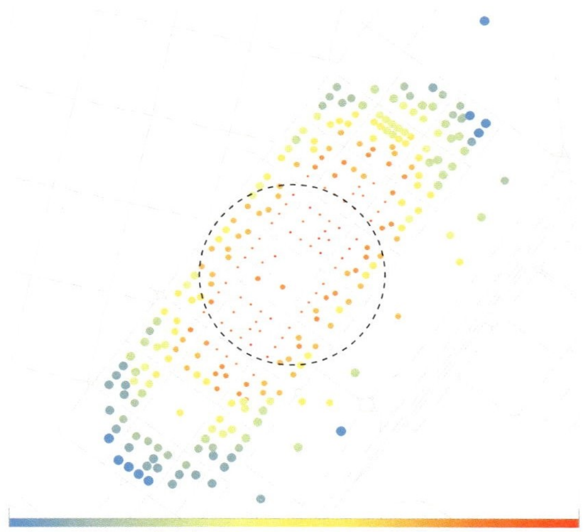

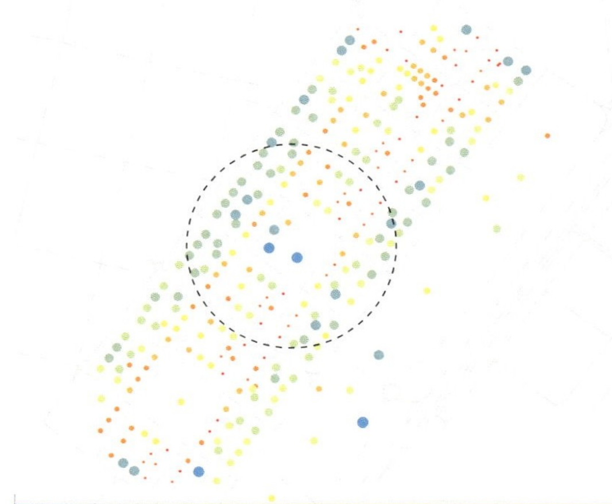

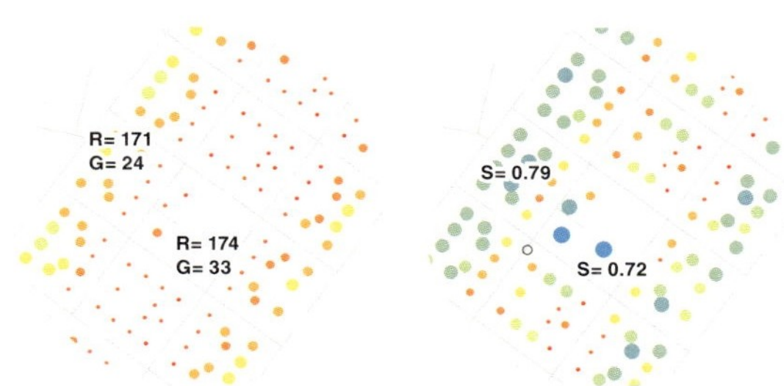

Network without alleyways
Average Reach for all plots = 165.38 plots
Average Raech percentage = 55% of the total number of plots
Average Gravity for all plots = 200.54 plots
Average Gravity percentage = 7% of the total number of plots
Average straightness = 0.76

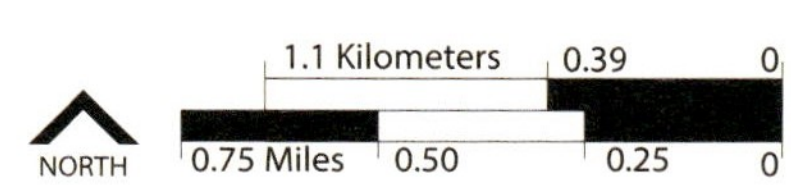

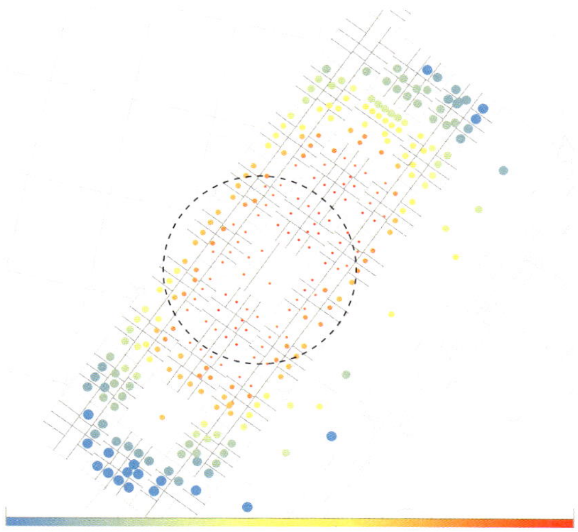

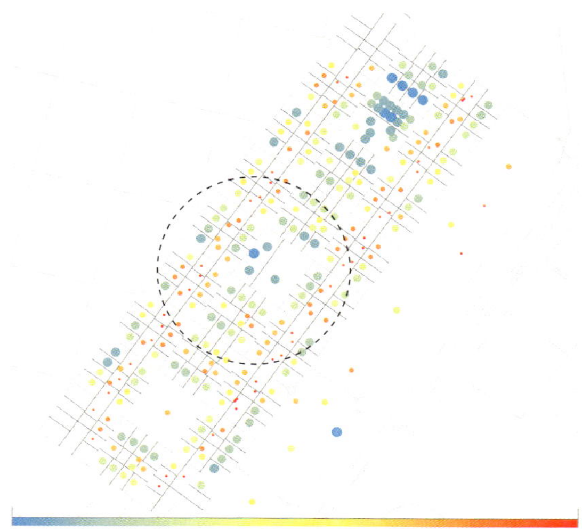

FIG. 8.5

Sample 1 - left

Average Reach and Gravity

Scenario 2: Streets + Alleys

FIG. 8.6

Sample 1 - right

Average Straightness

Scenario 2: Streets + Alleys

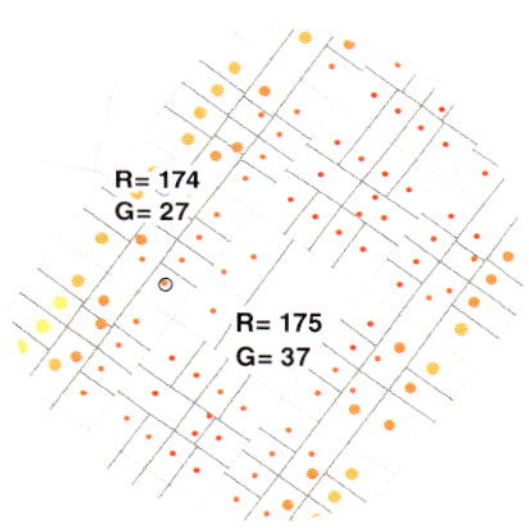

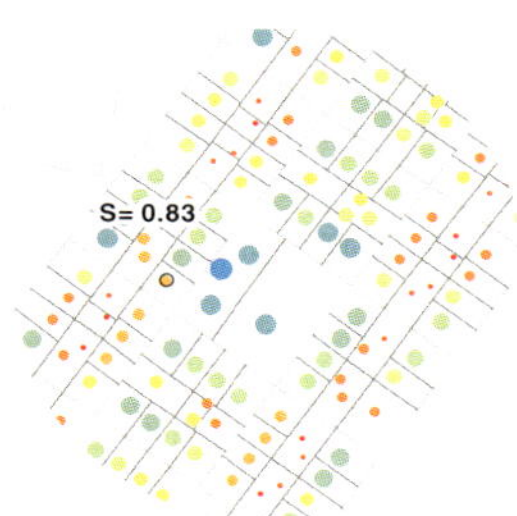

Network with alleyways

Average Reach for all plots = 190.37 plot

Average Raech percentage = 64% of the total number of plots

Average Gravity for all plots = 26.30 plots

Average Gravity percentage = 9% of the total number of plots

Average straightness = 0.74

Street ——— Alleyways

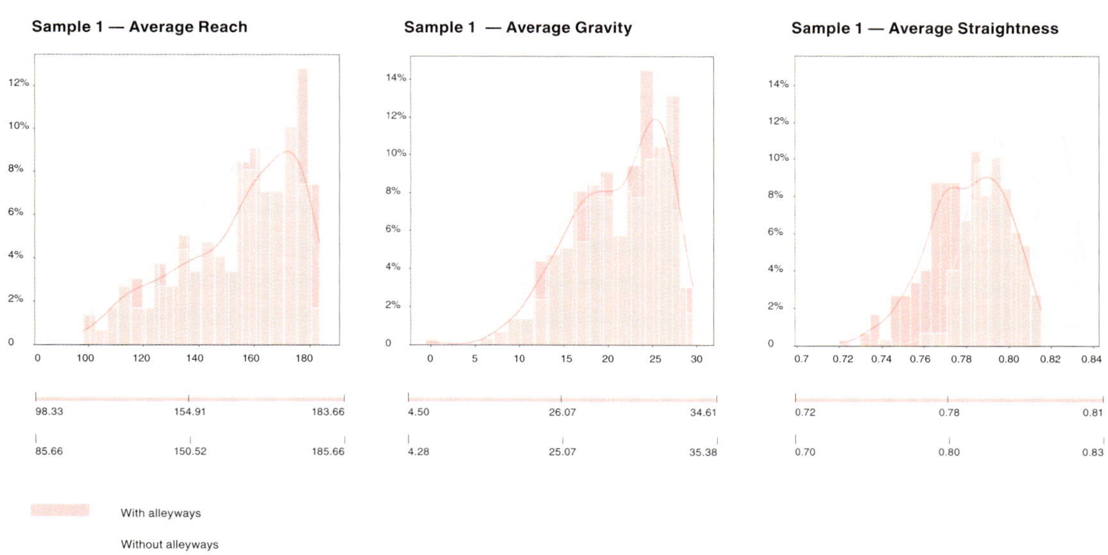

FIG. 9

Histograms showing the distribution of values for the metrics of Reach, Gravity and Straightness. Values for Straightness are bound within a theoretical range between (0,1). The values for all the three metrics are averages of three radii (400, 800, 1600).

Design Strategies

FIG. 10
Streets in Al Bahya have grid-iron typology with 0.55 intersection/Ha. Alleyways reduce the average block size and increase intersection density to 2.23 intersection/Ha; however, they fail in improving average Straightness values, which decreases from 0.80 to 0.78. Alleys have low contribution in enhancing connectivity and accessibility performances because they form T instead of 4-way junctions. This results in reduction in the average Straightness values from 0.76 to 0.75. Plot densities are the lowest among the studied samples in Abu Dhabi at 1.16 plot/Ha.

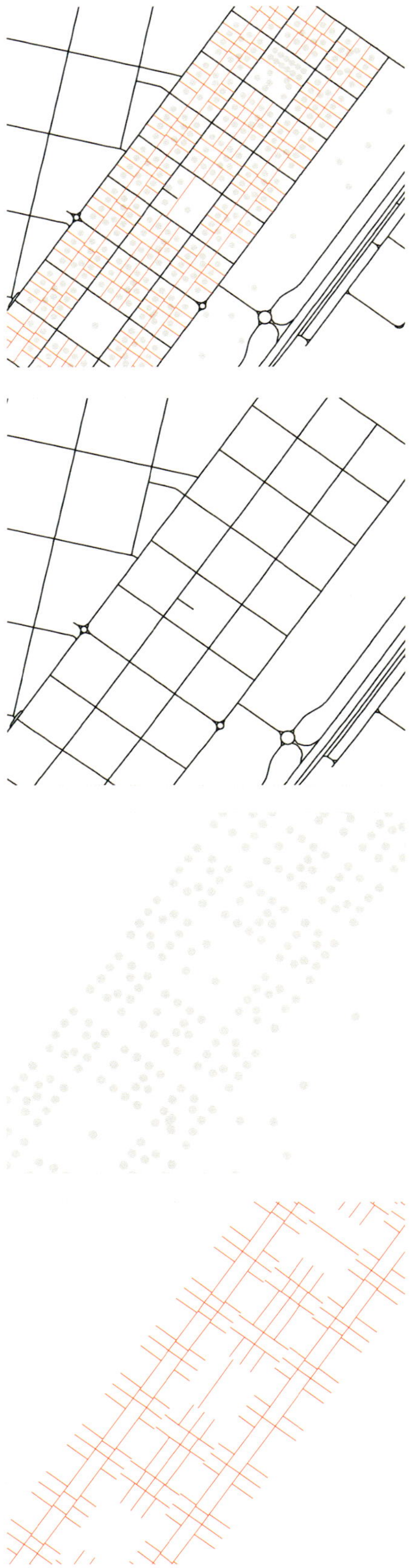

Plot Density and Network Morphology

Reach and Gravity: *Al Bahya* has a gridiron network morphology (see Figure 10). The samples have low Reach and Gravity values due to their low plot densities, which average 1.35 plots/Ha. Additionally, the block sizes in *Al Bahya* Sample 1 (*Al Bahya East*) and *Al Bahya* Sample 2 (*Al Bahya West*) are extremely large: 230 m x 215 m and 400 m x 150 m, respectively. *Al Bahya* Sample 1, which has a street density of 0.15 Km/Ha and a street intersection density of 0.55 intersections/Ha, performed better than *Al Bahya* Sample 2, which has corresponding values of 0.08 Km/Ha and 0.22 intersections/Ha, respectively. Thus, a finer gridiron urban grain leads to higher Reach and Gravity values. When alleys are introduced to this street pattern, they have only a small impact on Reach and Gravity values. Even though the block size diminishes from 230 m x 215 m to 90 m x 55 m, the plot density is too low to benefit from the addition of alleys.

Straightness: *Al Bahya's* samples have the highest Straightness values among all samples and high Straightness values ranging from 0.75 to 1.00. Due to its gridiron layout, the street network has continual four-way intersections. The addition of alleys results in a decrease in Straightness, because even though the intersection density increases, the introduced intersections include T-junctions. Consequently, the overall continuity and hence Straightness of the network is reduced.

Morphological Indicators for Enhancing Connectivity and Accessibility

- Street network: Denser grid-iron pattern; recommended but with high plot density and smaller block sizes
- Plot density: 1.16 plots/Ha is extremely low.
- Street density: 0.16 km/Ha is too low.
- Street intersection density: 0.55 intersections/Ha is too low; prioritize 4 intersections over T-junctions.
- Block size: 230 m x 215 m is too large. Shorter blocks are recommended.

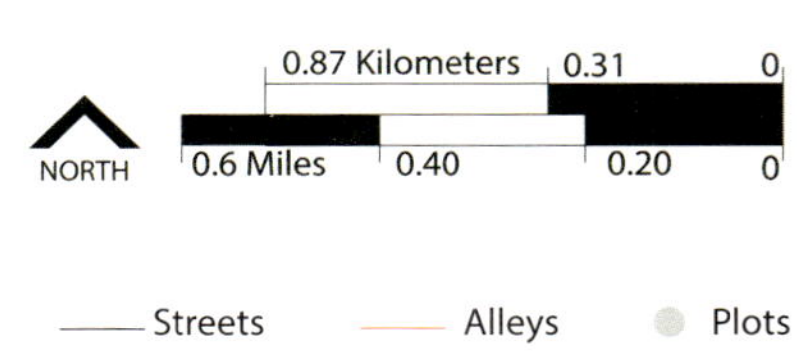

MBZ City

Low Performing Sample

FIG. 11.1
Sample 1 - left
Scenario 1: Streets only

FIG. 11.2
Sample 1 - right
Scenario 2: Streets + Alleys

Area	256 Hectare	Street intersections	212
Plots count	534 plot	Street length density	0.22 km/Ha
Plot density	2.08 plot/Ha	Street intersection density	0.82 intersections/Hectare
Network (streets + alleyways)		**Alleyways**	
Total intersection	489	Alleyways length	68.24 km
Total network length	126.25 km	Alleyways intersection	212
Streets		Alleyways length density	0.26 km/Ha
Total street length	58.01 km	Allleyways intersection density	0.82 intersections/Hectare

FIG. 11.3
Sample 2 - left
Scenario 1: Streets only

FIG. 11.4
Sample 2 - right
Scenario 2: Streets + Alleys

Area	256 Hectare	Street intersections	305
Plots count	520 plot	Street length density	0.23 km/Ha
Plot density	2.03 plot/Ha	Street intersection density	1.19 intersections/Hectare
Network (streets + alleyways)		**Alleyways**	
Total intersection	671	Alleyways length	72.24 km
Total network length	133.53 km	Alleyways intersection	366
Streets		Alleyways length density	0.28 km/Ha
Total street length	61.20 km	Allleyways intersection density	1.42 intersections/Hectare

Roads Alleyways

NORTH

0.96 Kilometers 0.34 0

0.64 Miles 0.43 0.21 0

FIG. 11.5
Sample 1 - left
Average Reach and Gravity
Scenario 1: Streets only

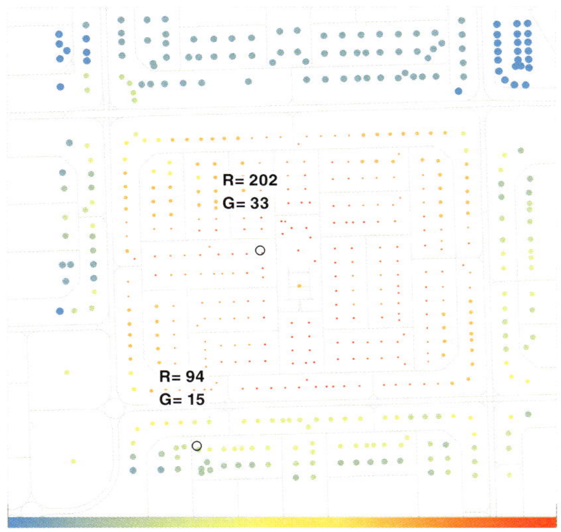

FIG. 11.6
Sample 1 - right
Average Straightness
Scenario 1: Streets only

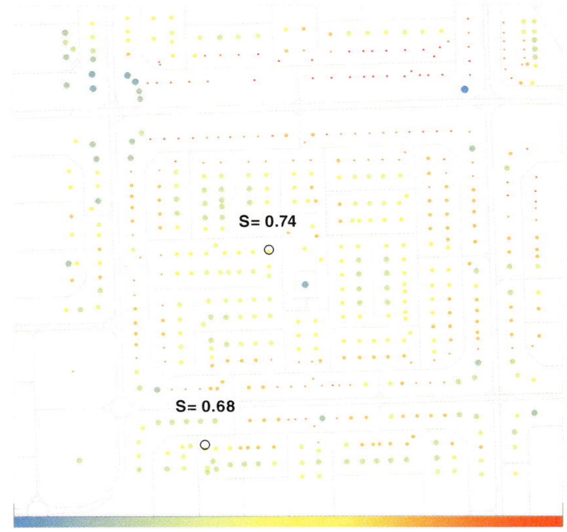

Average values without alleyways

Average Reach for all plots = 135.31 plot
Average Reach percentage = 45% of the total number of plots
Average Gravity for all plots = 19.8 plot
Average Gravity percentage = 6% of the total number of plots
Average Straightness = 0.74

FIG. 11.7
Sample 1 - left
Average Reach and Gravity
Scenario 2: Streets + Alleys

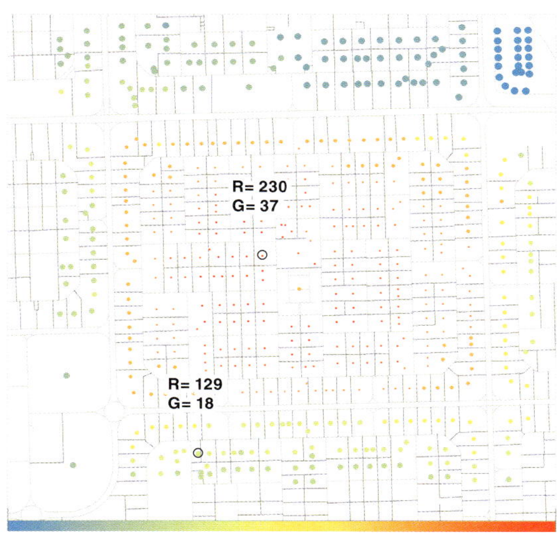

FIG. 11.8
Sample 1 - right
Average Straightness
Scenario 2: Streets + Alleys

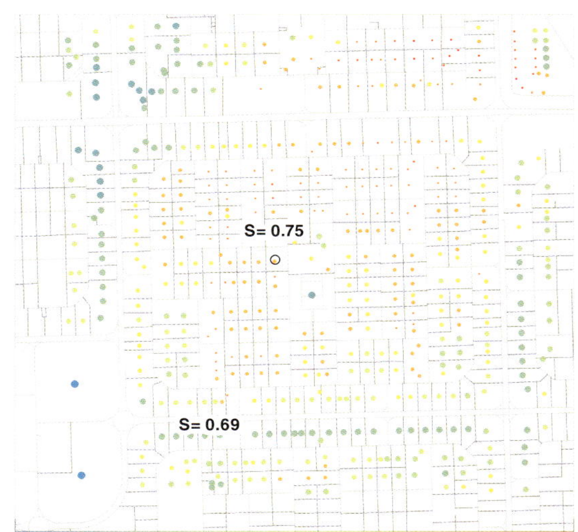

Average values with alleyways

Average Reach for all plots = 159.76 plot
Average Reach percentage = 52% of the total number of plots
Average Gravity for all plots = 22,06 plot
Average Gravity percentage = 7% of the total number of plots
Average Straightness = 0.72

Street Alleyways

NORTH

0.9 Kilometers 0.32 0
0.62 Miles 0.41 0.21 0

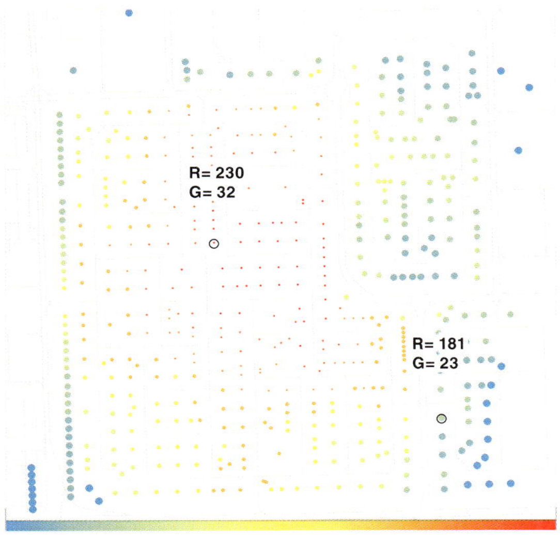

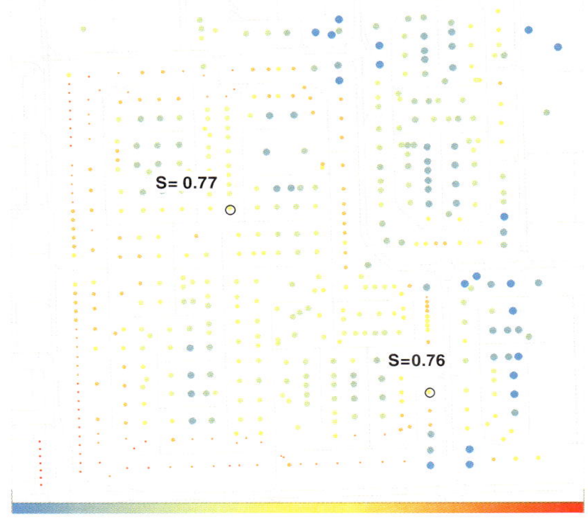

FIG. 11.9
Sample 2 - left
Average Reach and Gravity
Scenario 1: Streets only

FIG. 11.10
Sample 2 - right
Average Straightness
Scenario 1: Streets only

Average values without alleyways

Average Reach for all plots =156.28 plot
Average Reach percentage = 30% of the total number of plots
Average Gravity for all plots = 20.91 plot
Average Gravity percentage = 4% of the total number of plots
Average straightness = 0.75

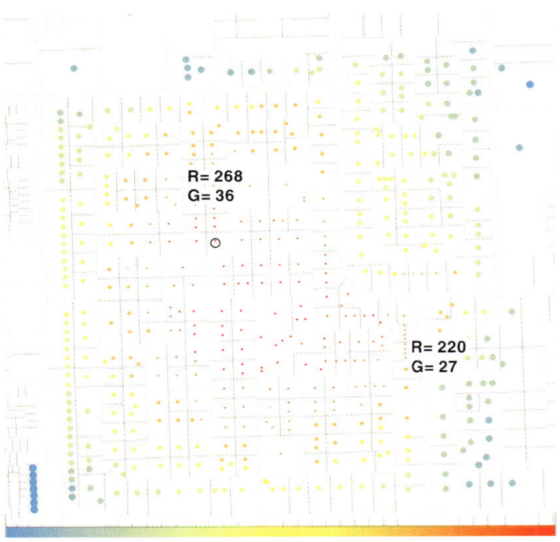

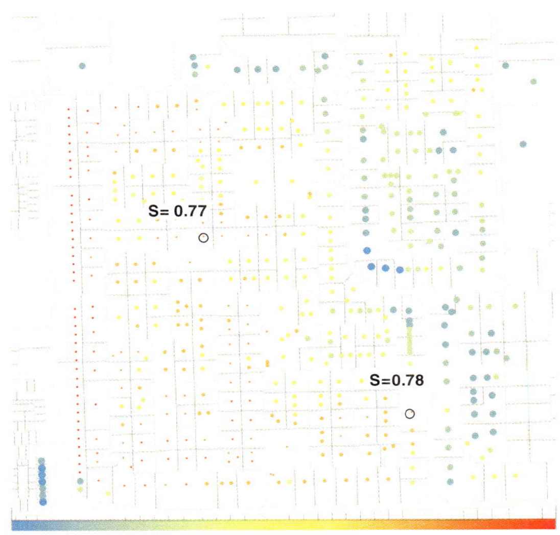

FIG. 11.11
Sample 2 - left
Average Reach and Gravity
Scenario 2: Streets + Alleys

FIG. 11.12
Sample 2 - right
Average Straightness
Scenario 2: Streets + Alleys

Average values with alleyways

Average Reach for all plots = 196.54 plot
Average Reach percentage = 38% of the total number of plots
Average Gravity for all plots = 25.2 plot
Average Gravity percentage = 5 % of the total number of plots
Average straightness = 0.75

Street ——— Alleyways

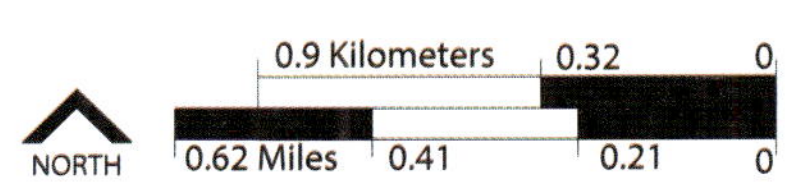

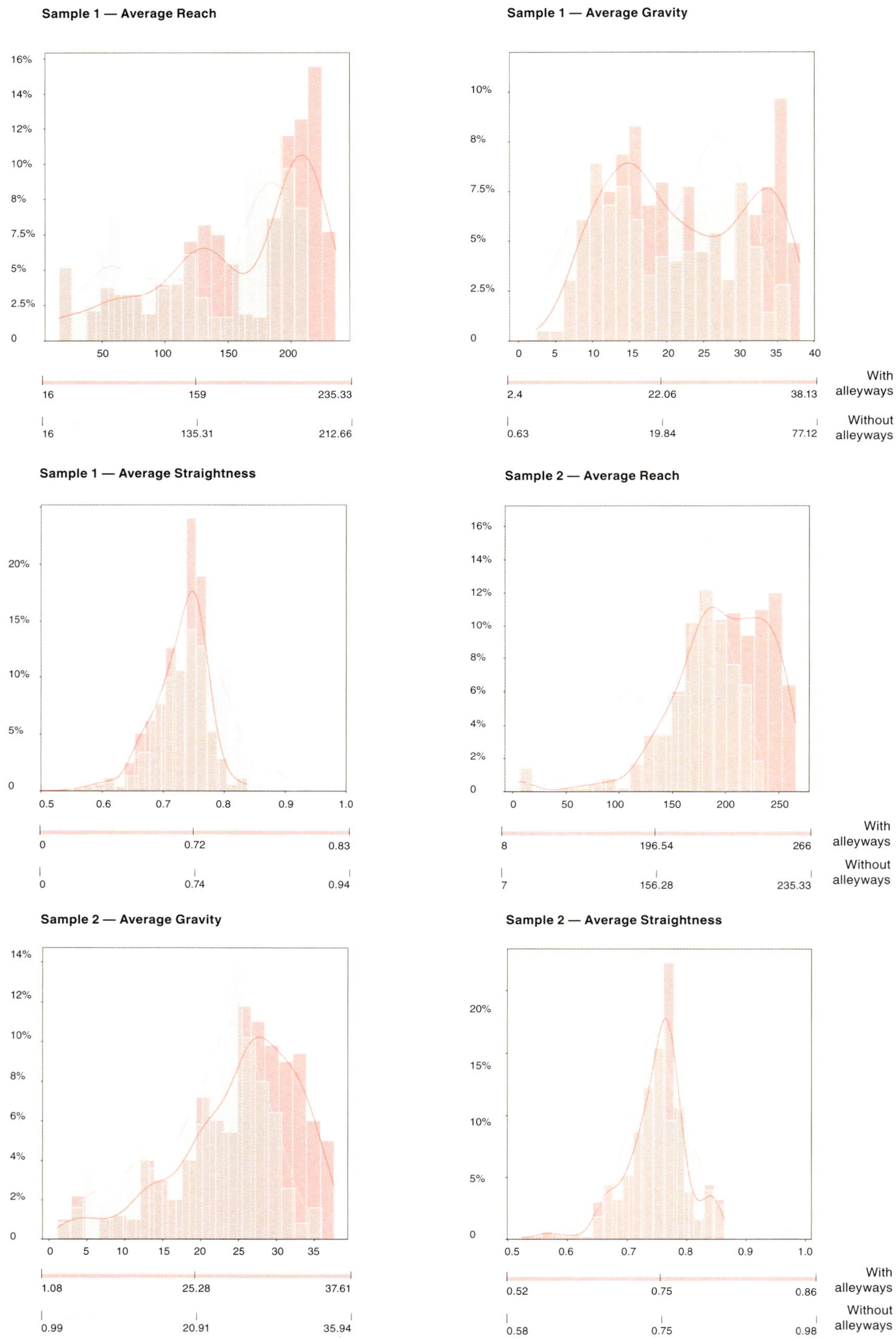

FIG. 12
Histograms showing the distribution of values for the metrics of Reach, Gravity and Straightness. Values for Straightness are bound within a theoretical range between (0,1). The values for all the three metrics are averages of three radii (400, 800, 1600).

Design Strategies

Plot Density and Network Morphology

Reach and Gravity: *MBZ City* has a looping fragmented parallel network morphology (See Figure 13). The samples have moderate Reach and Gravity values due to their low plot densities, which average 2.08 and 2.03 plots/Ha in samples 1 and 2, respectively. Sample 1 has lower Reach and Gravity values, because its street intersection density of 0.82 intersections/Ha is lower than the corresponding value of 1.19 intersections/Ha in Sample 2. This is because a higher number of intersections in a looping fragmented parallel corresponds to a higher number of T-junctions. The two samples have similar street densities (0.83 Km/Ha) and average block size (275 m x 150 m). When alleys are introduced, a considerable improvement in Reach and Gravity values can be witnessed. This is because the introduction of alleys reduces T-junctions and decreases the average block size from 275 m x 150 m to 75 m x 60 m. Thus, adding an average of 0.14 km/Ha of alleys to a looping fragmented parallel network is justifiable.

Straightness: *MBZ City's* looping fragmented parallel network has high Straightness values that range from 0.75 to 1.00. The introduction of alleys increases the total network intersection density to an average of 3.17 intersections/Ha. These alleys increase the continuity of the looping fragmented parallel network, and hence its Straightness value, by turning T-junctions into four-way intersections.

Morphological Indicators for Enhancing Connectivity and Accessibility

- Street network: Looping fragmented parallel is not recommended
- Plot density: 2.06 plots/Ha is too low; higher plot density is recommended.
- Street intersection density: More than 0.83 intersections/Ha, prioritize four-way intersections over T-junctions.
- Total network intersection density: More than 3.17 intersections/Ha, prioritize four-way intersections over T-junctions.
- Block size: 275 m x 150 m is too large, smaller is recommended.

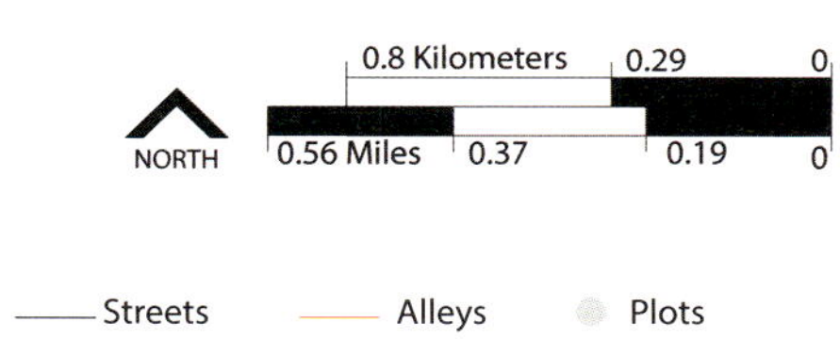

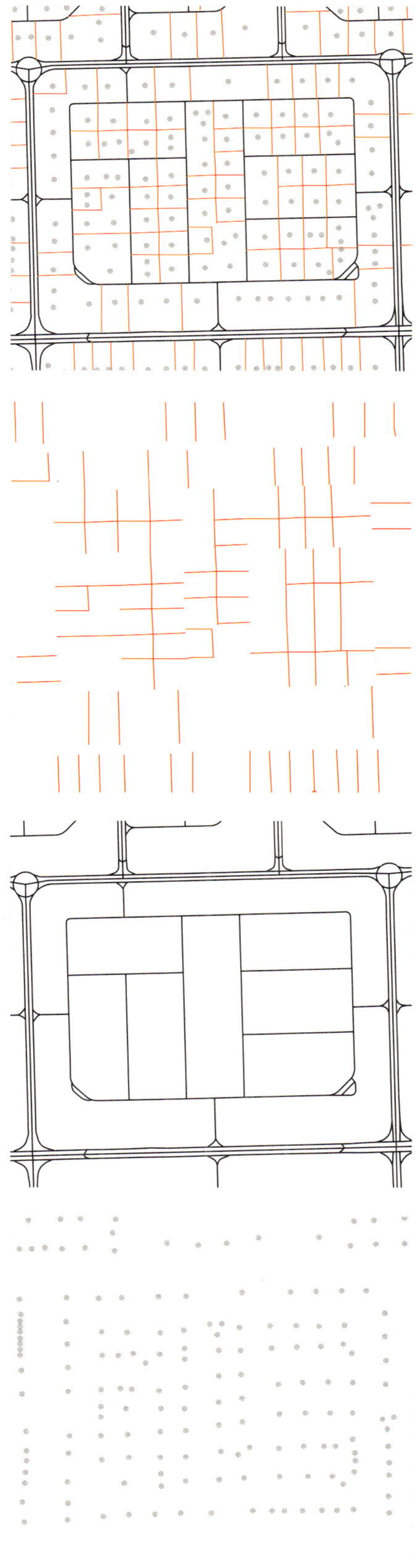

FIG. 13
Streets in MBZ city have looping and fragmented parallel typology with 0.82 and 1.19 intersection/Ha in samples 1 and 2 respectively. Alleyways reduce the average block size, increase intersection density to 1.91 and 2.62 intersection/Ha respectively, and improve route continuity. Plot densities are among the lowest in the studied samples in Abu Dhabi at 2.08 and 2.03 plot/Ha in samples 1 and 2 respectively.

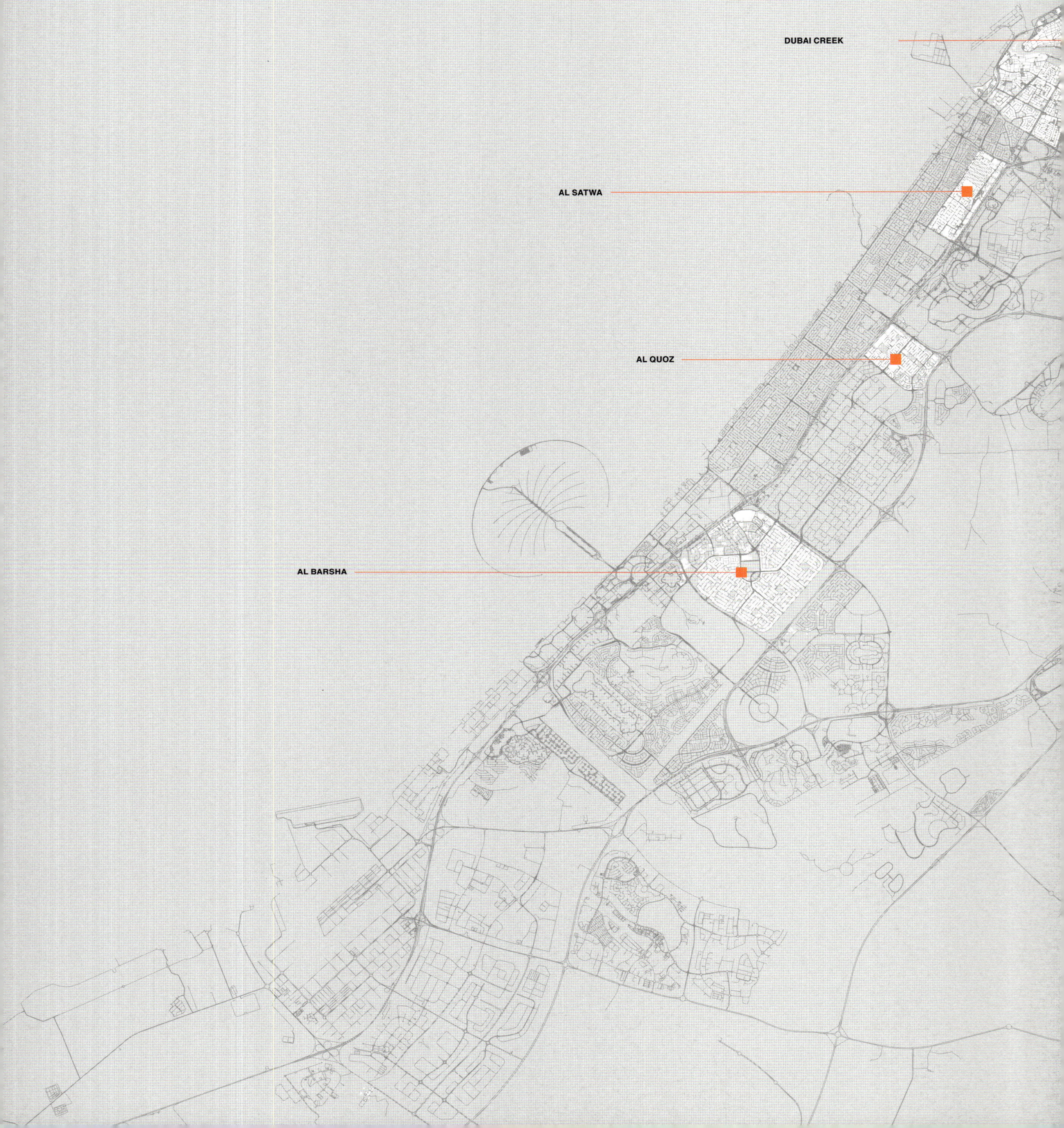
DUBAI CREEK
AL SATWA
AL QUOZ
AL BARSHA

AL WARQA
Dubai

Al Satwa

High Performing Sample

FIG. 1.1
Sample 1 - left
Scenario 1: Streets only

FIG. 1.2
Sample 1 - right
Scenario 2: Streets + Alleys

Area	256	Hectare
Plots count	1833	plot
Plot density	7.16	plot/Ha
Streets		
Total street length	106.96	km
Street intersections	755	
Street length density	0.42	km/Ha
Street intersection density	2.94	intersections/Hectare

Network (streets + alleyways)		
Total network length	211.24	km
Total intersection	2305	
Alleyways		
Alleyways length	142.28	km
Alleyways intersection	1550	
Alleyways length density	0.40	km/Ha
Alleyways intersection density	6.05	intersections/Hectare

Roads Alleyways

FIG. 1.3
Sample 1 - left
Average Reach and Gravity
Scenario 1: Streets only

FIG. 1.4
Sample 1 - right
Average Straightness
Scenario 1: Streets only

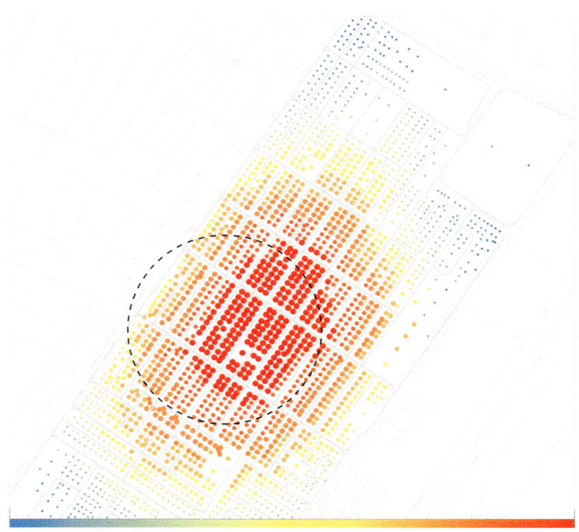

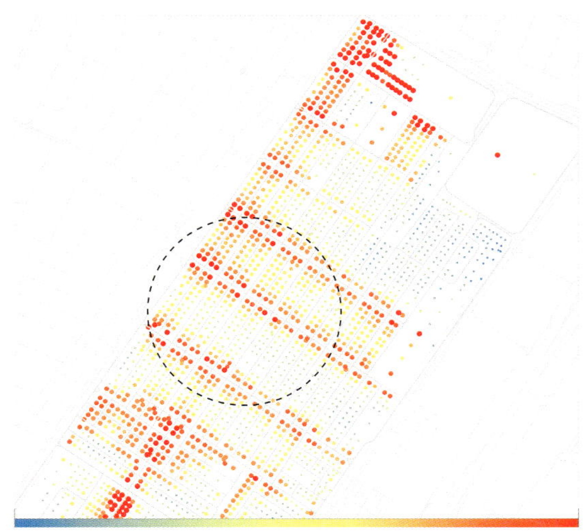

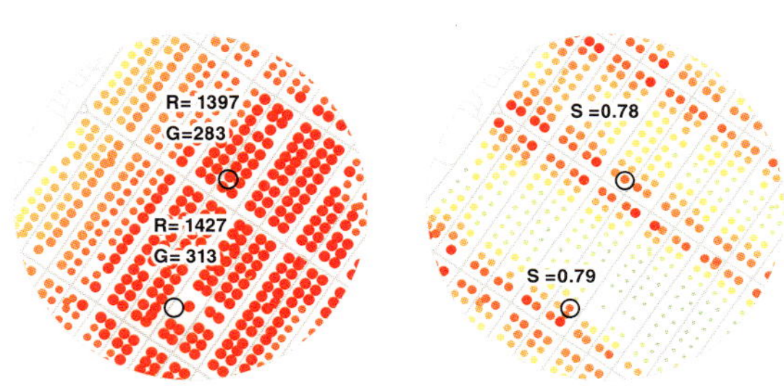

Network without alleyways
Average Reach for all plots = 1174.35 plots
Average Raech percentage = 58% of the total number of plots
Average Gravity for all plots = 200.54 plots
Average Gravity percentage = 10% of the total number of plots
Average straightness = 0.75

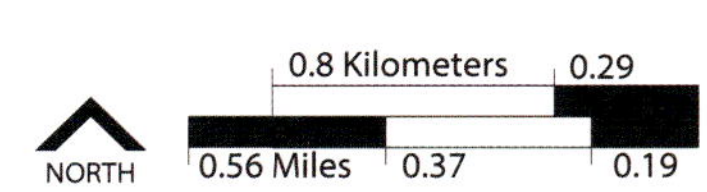

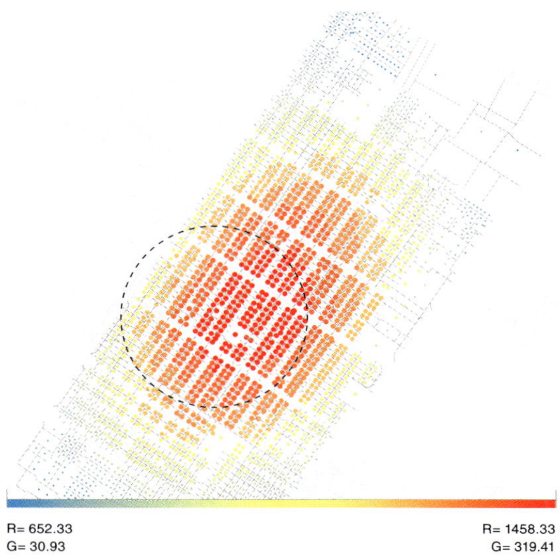

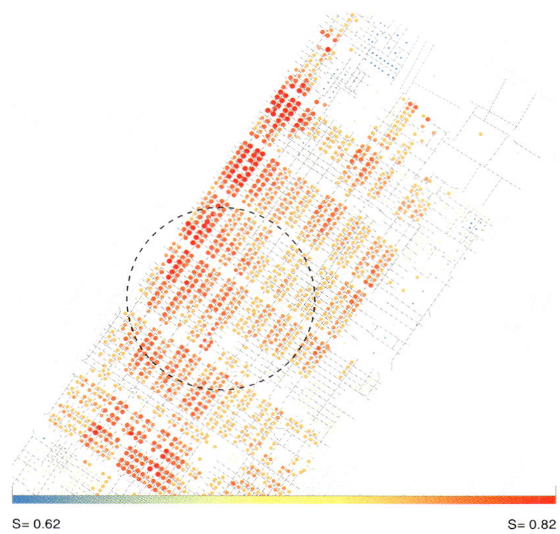

FIG. 1.5

Sample 1 - left

Average Reach and Gravity
Scenario 2: Streets + Alleys

FIG. 1.6

Sample 1 - right

Average Straightness
Scenario 2: Streets + Alleys

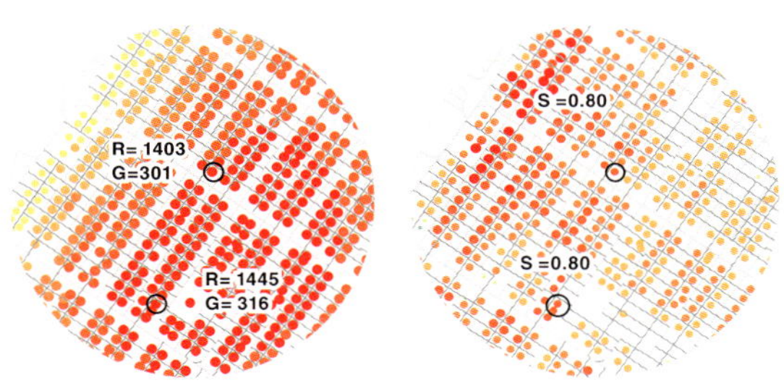

Network with alleyways

Average Reach for all plots = 1208.42 plot
Average Raech percentage = 60% of the total number of plots
Average Gravity for all plots = 229.23 plots
Average Gravity percentage = 11% of the total number of plots
Average straightness = 0.79

Street ——— Alleyways

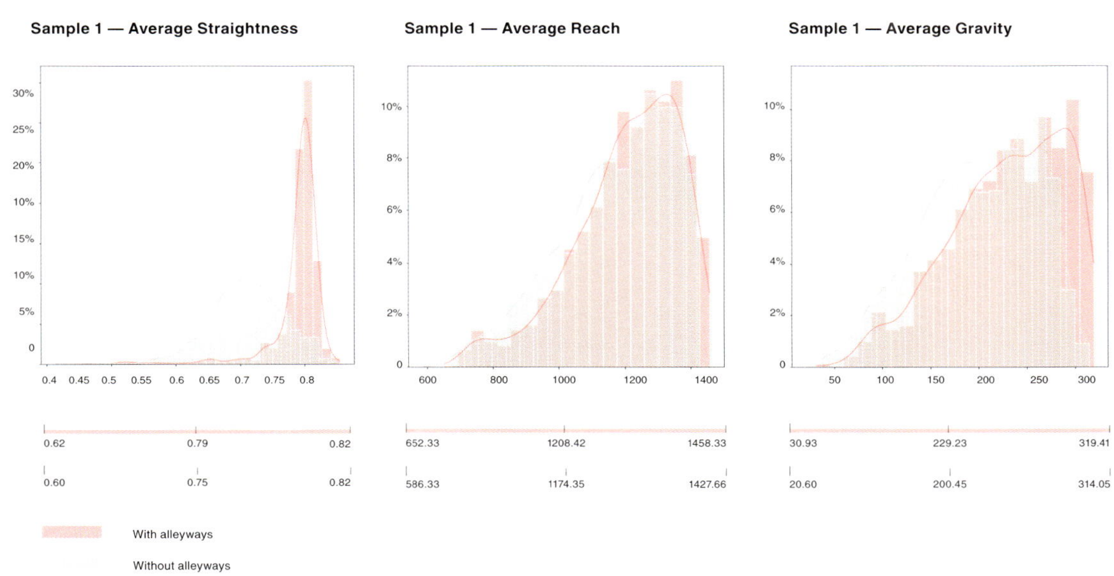

FIG. 2

Histograms showing the distribution of values for the metrics of Reach, Gravity and Straightness. Values for Straightness are bound within a theoretical range between (0,1). The values for all the three metrics are averages of three radii (400, 800, 1600).

Design Strategies

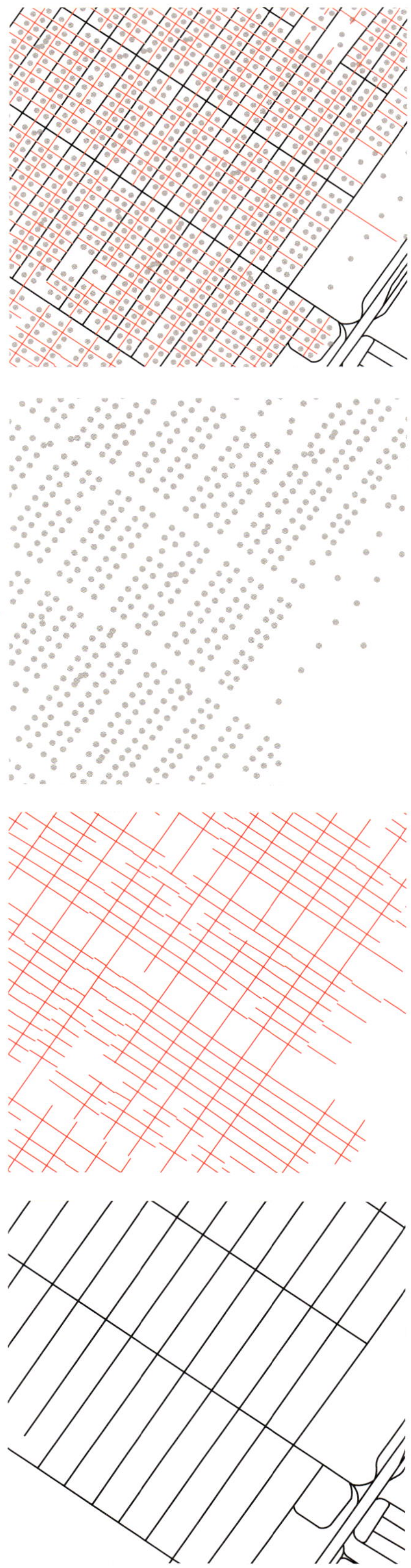

FIG. 3
Streets in Al Satwa have grid-iron topology with 5.32 intersections/Ha. Alleyways reduce the average block size, improve route continuity, increase intersection density to 9.00 intersection/Ha and improve average Straightness values from 0.75 to 0.79. Plot densities are among the highest in Dubai at 7.16 plot/Ha.

Plot Density and Network Morphology

Reach and Gravity: *Al Satwa* Sample 1 has a gridiron network morphology (See Figure 3). The sample has high Reach and Gravity values due to its high plot densities, which average 7.16 plots/Ha. *Al Satwa* Sample 1's gridiron network has a street density 0.42 Km/Ha, a street intersection density of 2.95 intersections/Ha, and a block size of 160 m x 115 m. When alleys are introduced into this street pattern, they have little impact on Reach and Gravity values. This is because the street network is already performing optimally; adding 0.12 km/Ha of alleys, which increases the total network intersection density to 6.84 intersections/Ha and reduces the block size to 30 m x 20 m, does not improve the Reach and Gravity values notably.

Straightness: *Al Satwa* Sample 1 has the highest Straightness values among all Dubai samples, ranging from 0.75 to 1.00. Due to its gridiron layout, the street network has continual four-way intersections. The addition of alleys in *Al Satwa* moderately increases the Straightness value. This is because, unlike in Al Bahya, the increase in the total network intersection density to 6.84 intersections/Ha does not introduce T-junctions, and thus the overall continuity of the network is maintained. This indicates that, while adding gridded alleys to a gridiron network is ineffective in terms of accessibility, it enhances connectivity efficiency.

Morphological Indicators for Enhancing Connectivity and Accessibility

- Street network: Gridiron pattern is recommended.
- Plot density: 7.16 plots/Ha is recommended.
- Street density: 0.42 km/Ha is recommended.
- Street intersection density: 2.95 intersections/Ha; higher is recommended.
- Block size: 160 m x 115 m and smaller is recommended.
- Alleys should only be added strategically to resolve street network deficiencies.

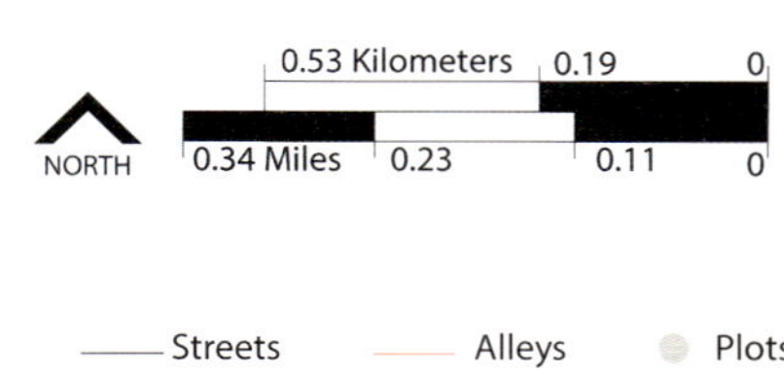

Dubai Creek

High Performing Sample

FIG. 4.1
Sample 1 - left
Scenario 1: Streets only

FIG. 4.2
Sample 1 - right
Scenario 2: Streets + Alleys

Area	256 Hectare	Street intersections	545
Plots count	2832 plot	Street length density	0.30 km/Ha
Plot density	11.06 plot/Ha	Street intersection density	2.48 intersections/Hectare
Network (streets + alleyways)		**Alleyways**	
Total intersection	1909	Alleyways length	39.45 km
Total network length	110.50 km	Alleyways intersection	1364
Streets		Alleyways length density	0.23 km/Ha
Total street length	71.05 km	Allleyways intersection density	5.32 intersections/Hectare

FIG. 4.3
Sample 2 - left
Scenario 1: Streets only

FIG. 4.4
Sample 2 - right
Scenario 2: Streets + Alleys

Area	256 Hectare	Street intersections	747
Plots count	2023 plot	Street length density	0.30 km/Ha
Plot density	7.90 plot/Ha	Street intersection density	2.91 intersections/Hectare
Network (streets + alleyways)		**Alleyways**	
Total intersection	0.58	Alleyways length	597.84 km
Total network length	149.16 km	Alleyways intersection	2128
Streets		Alleyways length density	2.33 km/Ha
Total street length	78.40 km	Allleyways intersection density	8.31 intersections/Hectare

Roads Alleyways

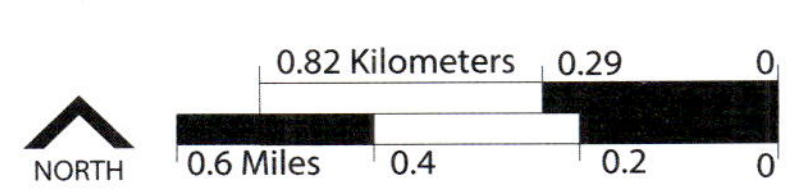

FIG. 4.5
Sample 1 - left
Average Reach and Gravity
Scenario 1: Streets only

FIG. 4.6
Sample 1 - right
Average Straightness
Scenario 1: Streets only

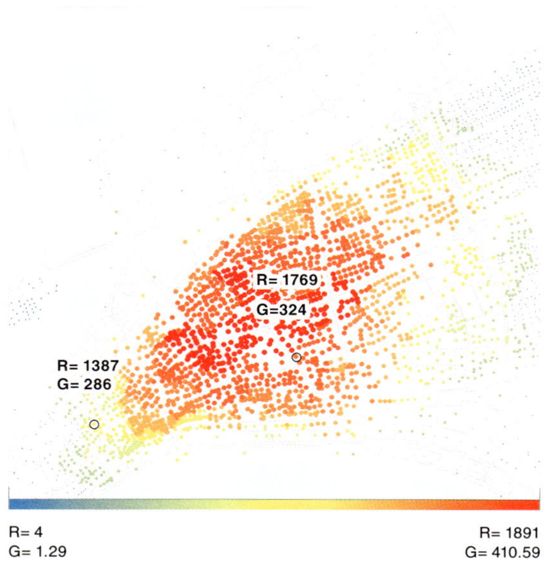

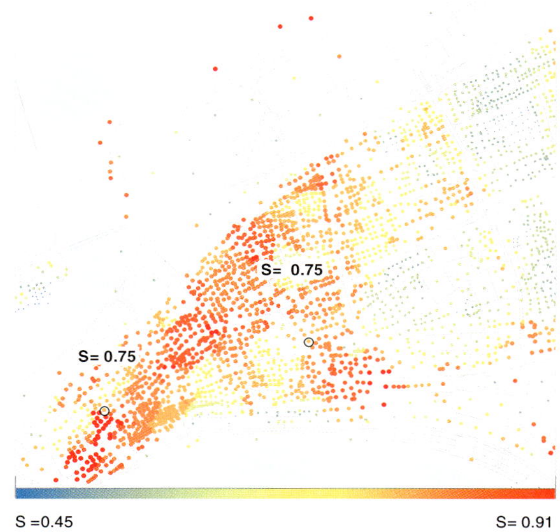

Average values without alleyways

Average Reach for all plots = 1487.96 plot
Average Reach percentage = 52% of the total number of plots
Average Gravity for all plots = 244.77 plot
Average Gravity percentage = 9% of the total number of plots
Average straightness = 0.73

FIG. 4.7
Sample 1 - left
Average Reach and Gravity
Scenario 2: Streets + Alleys

FIG. 4.8
Sample 1 - right
Average Straightness
Scenario 2: Streets + Alleys

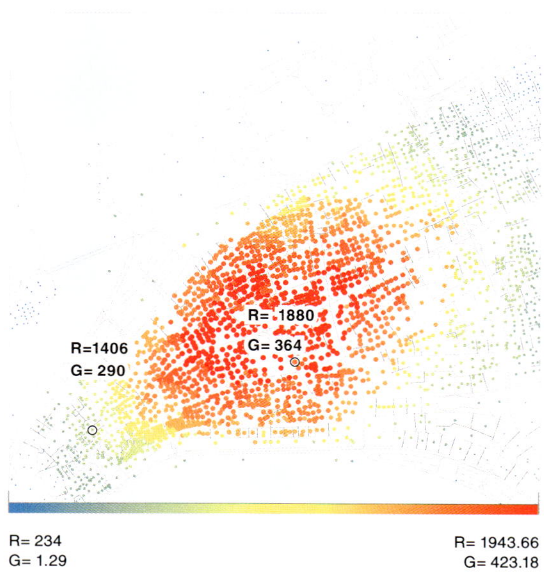

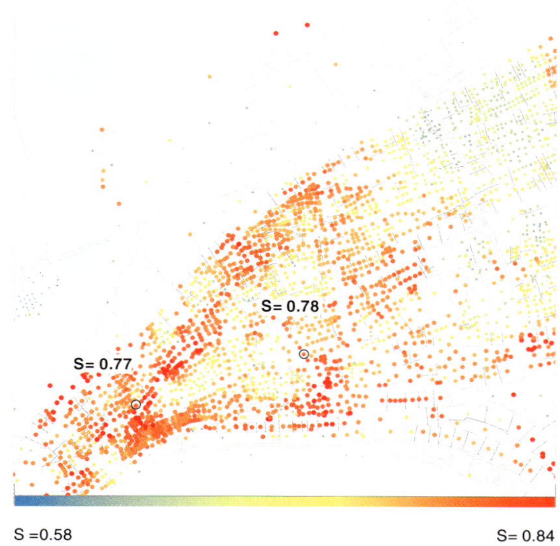

Average values with alleyways

Average Reach for all plots = 1563.39 plot
Average Reach percentage = 55% of the total number of plots
Average Gravity for all plots = 275.08 plot
Average Gravity percentage = 9.5% of the total number of plots
Average straightness = 0.76

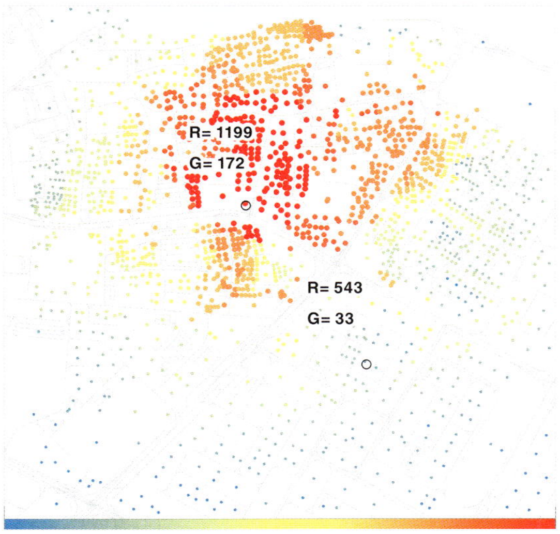

R= 0
G= 0

R= 1199.33
G= 211.01

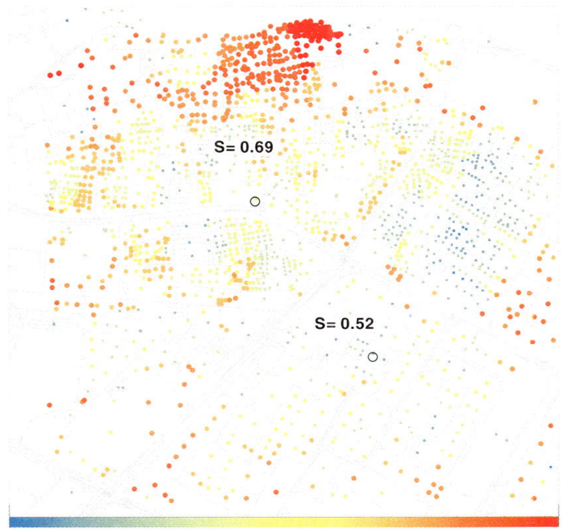

S =0.58

S= 0.98

FIG. 4.9
Sample 2 - left
Average Reach and Gravity
Scenario 1: Streets only

FIG. 4.10
Sample 2 - right
Average Straightness
Scenario 1: Streets only

Average values without alleyways

Average Reach for all plots = 867.52 plot
Average Reach percentage = 43% of the total number of plots
Average Gravity for all plots = 115.37 plot
Average Gravity percentage = 6% of the total number of plots
Average straightness = 0.68

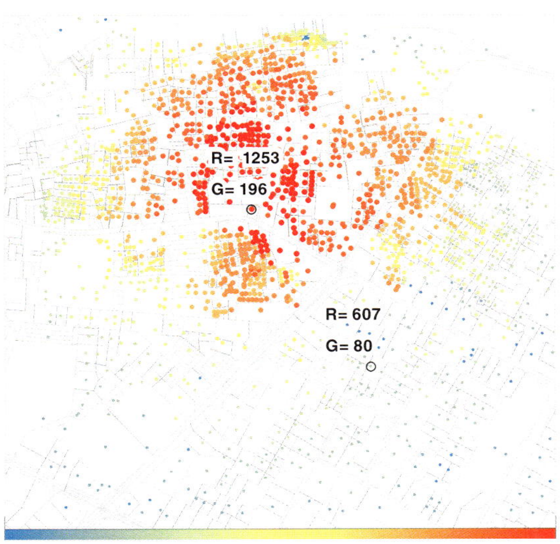

R=293
G= 7.80

R= 1277.33
G= 233.94

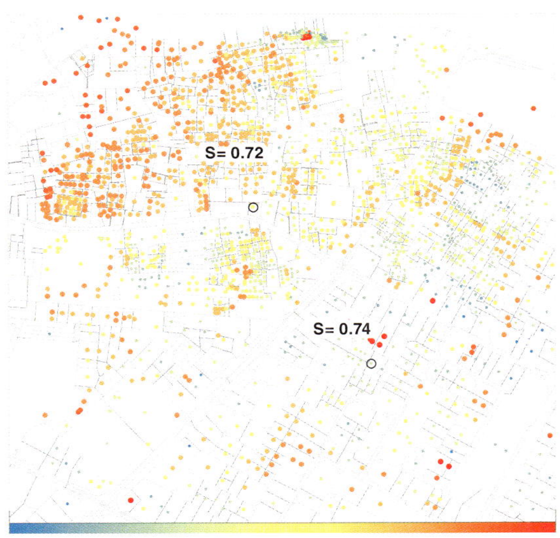

S =0.54

S= 0.81

FIG. 4.11
Sample 2 - left
Average Reach and Gravity
Scenario 2: Streets + Alleys

FIG. 4.12
Sample 2 - right
Average Straightness
Scenario 2: Streets + Alleys

Average values with alleyways

Average Reach for all plots = 997.17 plot
Average Reach percentage = 49% of the total number of plots
Average Gravity for all plots = 140 plot
Average Gravity percentage = 7% of the total number of plots
Average straightness = 0.72

Street Alleyways

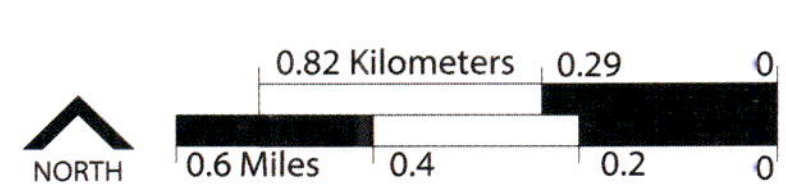

FIG. 5

Histograms showing the distribution of values for the metrics of Reach, Gravity and Straightness. Values for Straightness are bound within a theoretical range between (0,1). The values for all the three metrics are averages of three radii (400, 800, 1600).

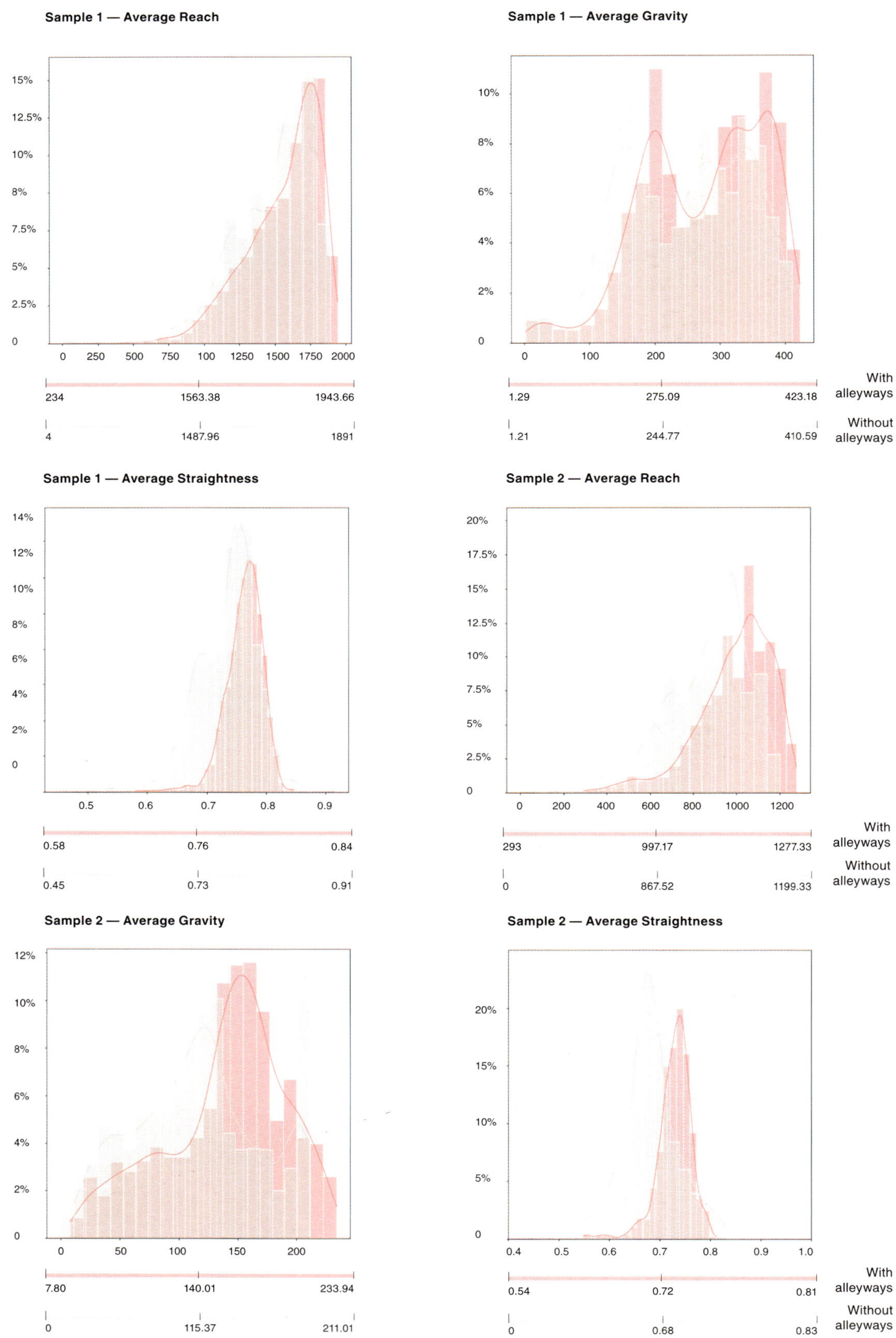

Design Strategies

Plot Density and Network Morphology

Reach and Gravity: *Dubai Creek* has an organic network morphology (See Figure 6). The samples have high Reach and Gravity values due to their high plot densities, which are 11.06 plots/Ha in Sample 1 and 7.90 plots/Ha in Sample 2. Sample 1, which has the higher plot density, performs better than Sample 2. This is despite Sample 1 having a lower street density of 0.30 Km/Ha and a lower street intersection density of 2.48 intersections/Ha. Both samples have similar average block sizes of 145 m x 90 m. This indicates that plot density has a stronger impact on Reach and Gravity values than network morphology in an organic network. When alleys are introduced, they have little impact on Reach and Gravity values. This is because the street network and street intersections densities were already high enough to maximize Reach and Gravity. Adding an average of 0.23 km/Ha of alleys, which increases the total network intersection density to around 7.79 intersections/Ha and reduces block size to an average of 60 m x 30 m, does not improve the Reach and Gravity values notably.

Straightness: *Dubai Creek* Sample 1 has moderate Straightness values, while Sample 2 has the lowest Straightness values among all the samples in Dubai. However, in terms of the standard used in this book, both samples of *Dubai Creek* have medium Straightness values ranging from 0.50 to 0.75. This shows that the Straightness of an organic network is highly variable, as it depends on the continuity of the network configuration in the sample area being investigated. Thus, this network morphology is particularly not recommended for vehicular purposes which require consistent and high Straightness values.

Morphological Indicators for Enhancing Connectivity and Accessibility

- Street network: Organic pattern is not recommended in modern planning especially when vehicular movement is dominating.
- Plot density: 11.06 plots/Ha is recommended.
- Street density: 0.30 km/Ha
- Street intersection density: 2.48 intersections/Ha and higher is recommended; prioritize four-way intersections over T-junctions
- Block size: 145 m x 90 m and smaller is recommended.

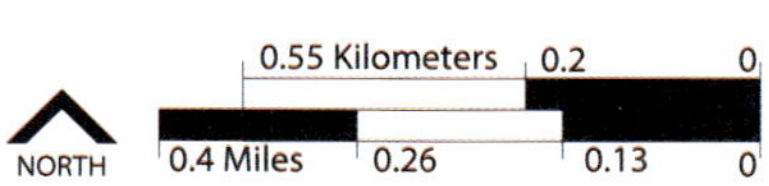

Streets Alleys Plots

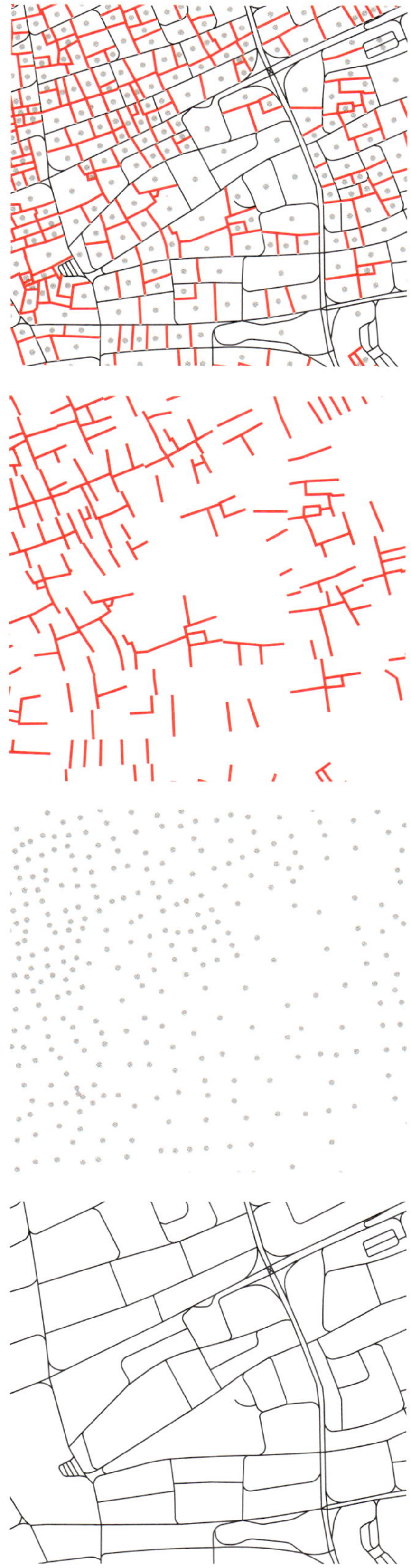

FIG. 6

Streets in the Creek have an organic typology with 2.48 and 2.91 intersection/Ha in samples 1 and 2 respectively. Alleyways reduce the average block size, increase intersection density to 7.45 and 6.82 intersection/Ha respectively, improve route continuity, and enhance average Straightness values from 0.73 to 0.76 in sample 1 and from 0.68 to 0.72 in sample 2. Plot densities are the highest in Dubai at 11.06 and 7.9 plot/Ha in samples 1 and 2 respectively.

Al Quoz

High Performing Sample

FIG. 7.1
Sample 1 - left
Scenario 1: Streets only

FIG. 7.2
Sample 1 - right
Scenario 2: Streets + Alleys

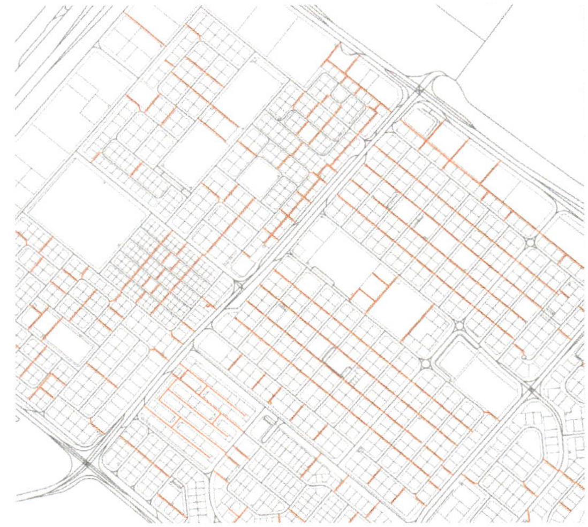

Area	256	Hectare
Plots count	1527	plot
Plot density	4.97	plot/Ha
Streets		
Total street length	70.59	km
Street intersections	493	
Street length density	0.27	km/Ha
Street intersection density	1.47	intersections/Hectare

Network (streets + alleyways)		
Total network length	89.3	km
Total intersection	546	
Alleyways		
Alleyways length	18.71	km
Alleyways intersection	53	
Alleyways length density	0.07	km/Ha
Alleyways intersection density	0.20	intersections/Hectare

Roads — Alleyways

FIG. 7.3
Sample 1 - left
Average Reach and Gravity
Scenario 1: Streets only

FIG. 7.4
Sample 1 - right
Average Straightness
Scenario 1: Streets only

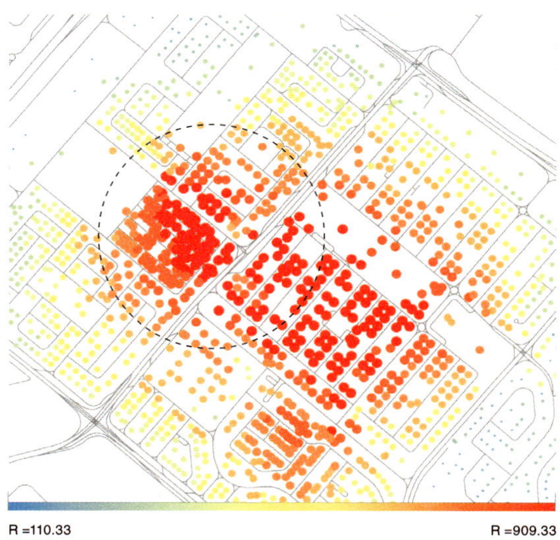

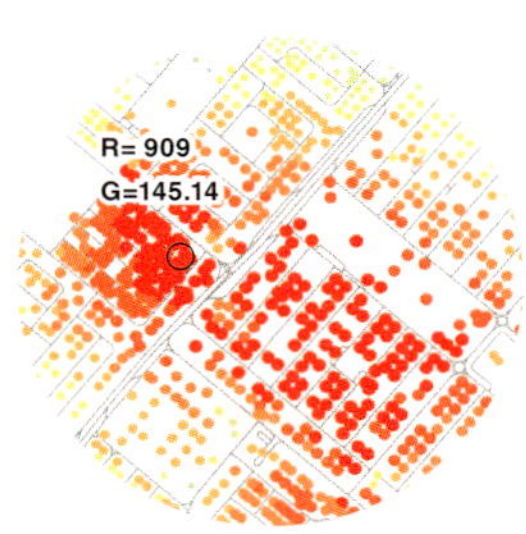

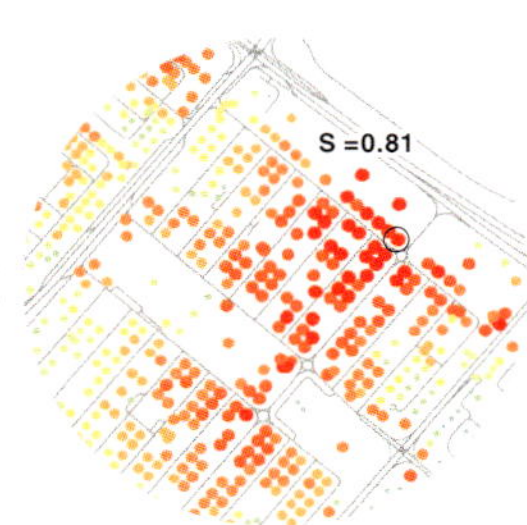

Network without alleyways
Average Reach for all plots = 654.70 plots
Average Raech percentage = 36% of the total number of plots
Average Gravity for all plots = 77.73 plots
Average Gravity percentage = 4% of the total number of plots
Average straightness = 0.72

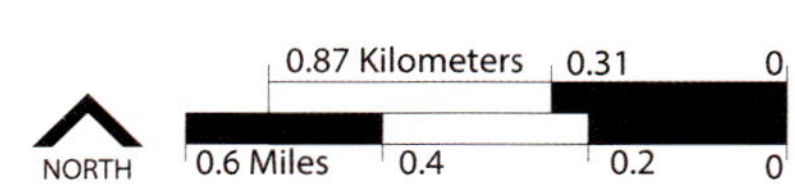

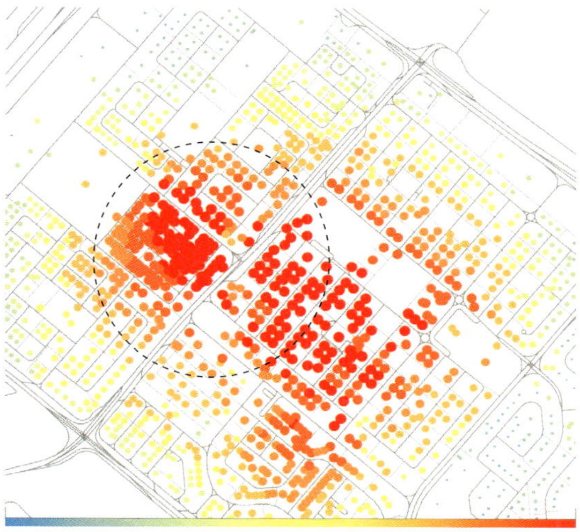

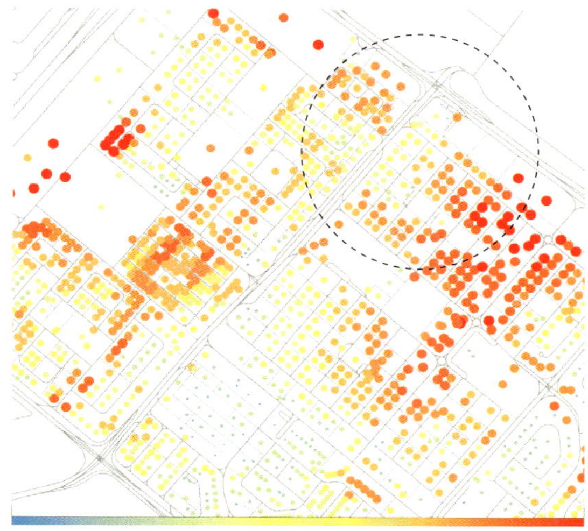

FIG. 7.5
Sample 1 - left
Average Reach and Gravity
Scenario 2: Streets + Alleys

FIG. 7.6
Sample 1 - right
Average Straightness
Scenario 2: Streets + Alleys

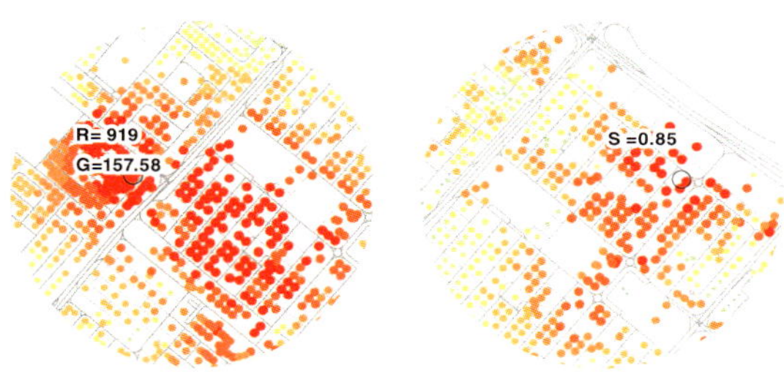

Network with alleyways
Average Reach for all plots = 659.30 plot
Average Raech percentage =36% of the total number of plots
Average Gravity for all plots = 78.22 plots
Average Gravity percentage = 4% of the total number of plots
Average straightness = 0.72

Street —— Alleyways

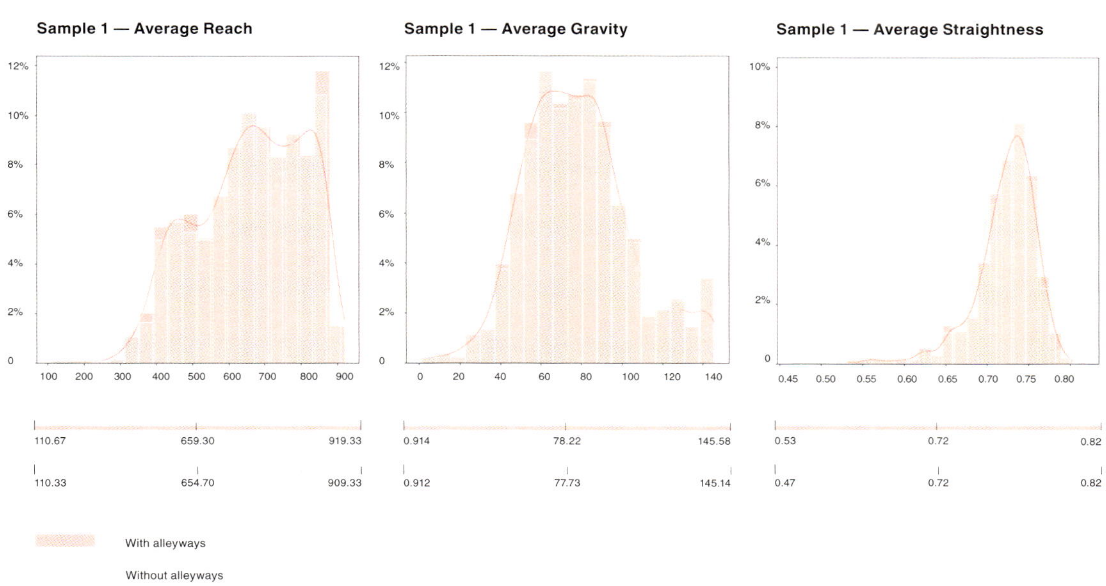

FIG. 8
Histograms showing the distribution of values for the metrics of Reach, Gravity and Straightness. Values for Straightness are bound within a theoretical range between (0,1). The values for all the three metrics are averages of three radii (400, 800, 1600).

Design Strategies

FIG. 9

Streets in Al Quoz have grid and semi-grid typology with 1.47 intersection/Ha. Alleyways reduce the average block size, improve route continuity, increase intersection density to 2.13 intersection/Ha and, enhance average Straightness values from 0.66 to 0.71. Plot densities are considered low at 4.97 plot/Ha.

Plot density and Network Morphology

Reach and Gravity: *Al Quoz* has a gridiron network morphology (See Figure 9). The sample has high Reach and Gravity values due to its high plot density at 5.96 plots/Ha. *Al Quoz's* looping and fragmented sample has a street density of 0.27 km/Ha, a street intersection density of 1.47 intersections/Ha, and a block size of 75 m x 270 m. When alleys are added to this street pattern, they have a notable impact on Reach and Gravity values. The addition of 0.07 km/Ha of alleys increases the total network intersection density to 2.73 intersections/Ha and reduces the block size to 75 m x 70 m, thereby improving the Reach and Gravity values.

Straightness: *Al Quoz* has the lowest Straightness values among all Dubai samples. Its Straightness values range from 0.50 to 0.75, which are medium values according to the standard used in this book. Due to its looping and fragmented layout, the street network has a higher presence of T-junctions and loops. The inclusion of alleys in *Al Quoz* notably increases the Straightness value from 0.66 to 0.71. This is because alleys create linear and continuous paths by connecting the fragmented street segments. The total network intersection density increases from 1.47 intersections/Ha (when only streets are considered) to 2.73 intersections/Ha.

Morphological Indicators for Enhancing Connectivity and Accessibility

- Street network: Looping and fragmented pattern is not recommended
- Plot density: 5.96 plots/Ha; higher is recommended.
- Street intersection density: 1.47 intersections/Ha; higher is recommended; prioritize four-way intersections over T-junctions.
- Block size: 75 m x 270 m and smaller is recommended.
- Alleys should only be added strategically to resolve street network deficiencies

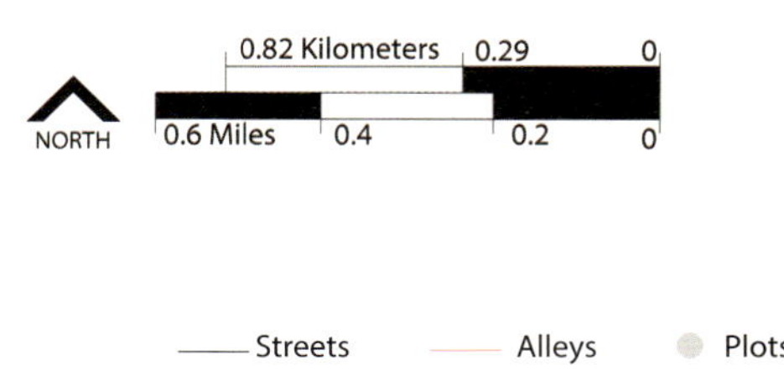

Al Warqa

Low Performing Sample

FIG. 10.1
Sample 1 - left
Scenario 1: Streets only

FIG. 10.2
Sample 1 - right
Scenario 2: Streets + Alleys

Area	256 Hectare	Street intersections	189
Plots count	1374 plot	Street length density	0.20 km/Ha
Plot density	5.86 plot/Ha	Street intersection density	0.68 intersections/Hectare
Network (streets + alleyways)		**Alleyways**	
Total intersection	375	Alleyways length	12.43 km
Total network length	66.90 km	Alleyways intersection	185
Streets		Alleyways length density	0.04 km/Ha
Total street length	53.48 km	Allleyways intersection density	0.72 intersections/Hectare

FIG. 10.3
Sample 2 - left
Scenario 1: Streets only

FIG. 10.4
Sample 2 - right
Scenario 2: Streets + Alleys

Area	256 Hectare	Street intersections	413
Plots count	1302 plot	Street length density	0.24 km/Ha
Plot density	5.08 plot/Ha	Street intersection density	1.25 intersections/Hectare
Network (streets + alleyways)		**Alleyways**	
Total intersection	525	Alleyways length	13.41 km
Total network length	76.16 km	Alleyways intersection	112
Streets		Alleyways length density	0.14 km/Ha
Total street length	63.73 km	Allleyways intersection density	0.43 intersections/Hectare

Roads — Alleyways

NORTH

0.96 Kilometers 0.34 0

0.64 Miles 0.43 0.21 0

FIG. 10.5
Sample 1 - left
Average Reach and Gravity
Scenario 1: Streets only

FIG. 10.6
Sample 1 - right
Average Straightness
Scenario 1: Streets only

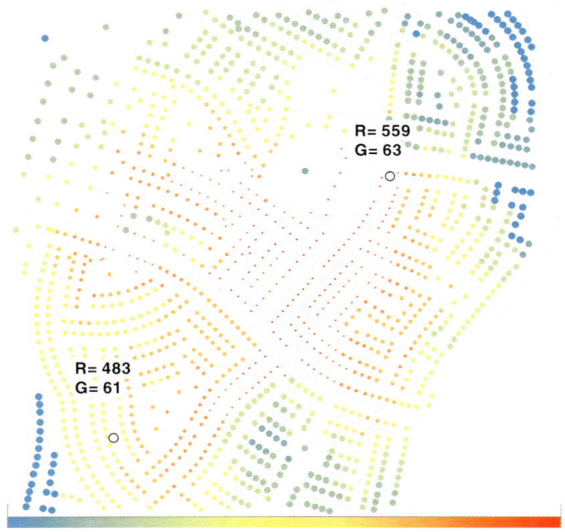

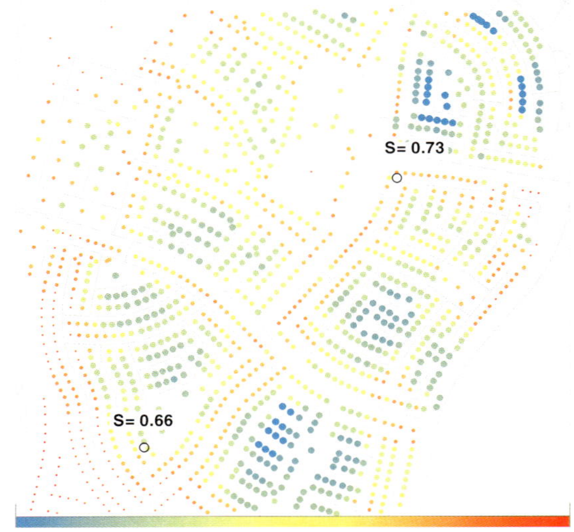

Average values without alleyways

Average Reach for all plots = 442.63 plot
Average Reach percentage = 32% of the total number of plots
Average Gravity for all plots = 51.91 plot
Average Gravity percentage = 4% of the total number of plots
Average straightness = 0.69

FIG. 10.7
Sample 1 - left
Average Reach and Gravity
Scenario 2: Streets + Alleys

FIG. 10.8
Sample 1 - right
Average Straightness
Scenario 2: Streets + Alleys

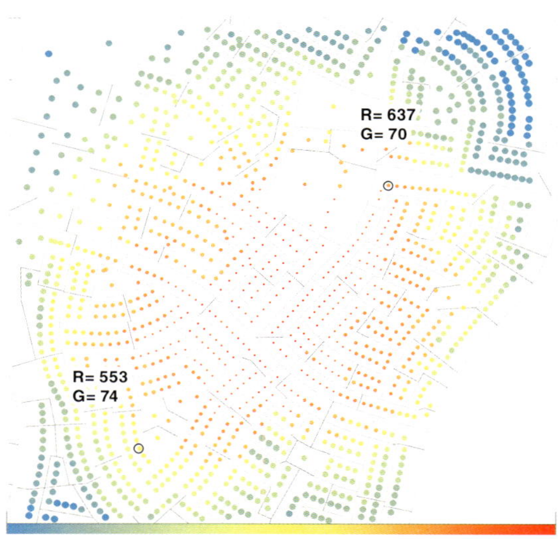

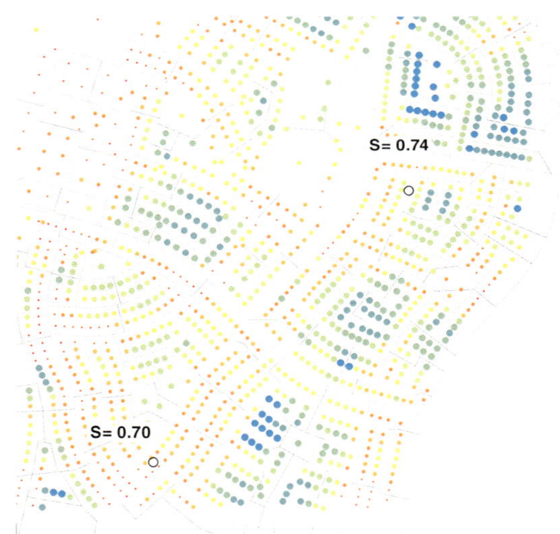

Average values with alleyways

Average Reach for all plots = 559.40 plot
Average Reach percentage = 55% of the total number of plots
Average Gravity for all plots =68.43 plot
Average Gravity percentage = 5% of the total number of plots
Average straightness = 0.73

Street — Alleyways

NORTH

0.96 Kilometers 0.34 0
0.64 Miles 0.43 0.21 0

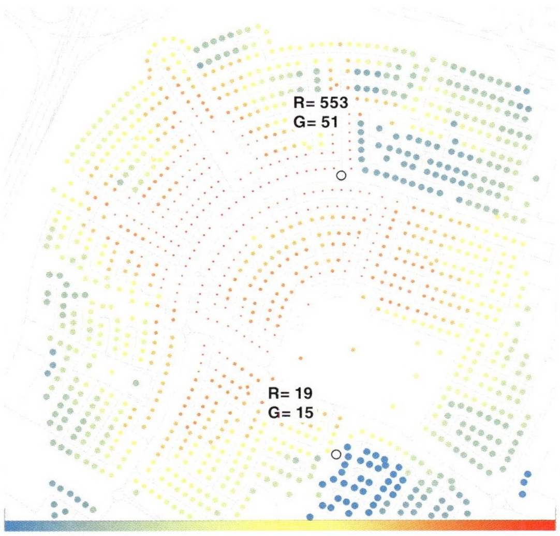

R= 0
G= 0

R= 632.66
G= 77.53

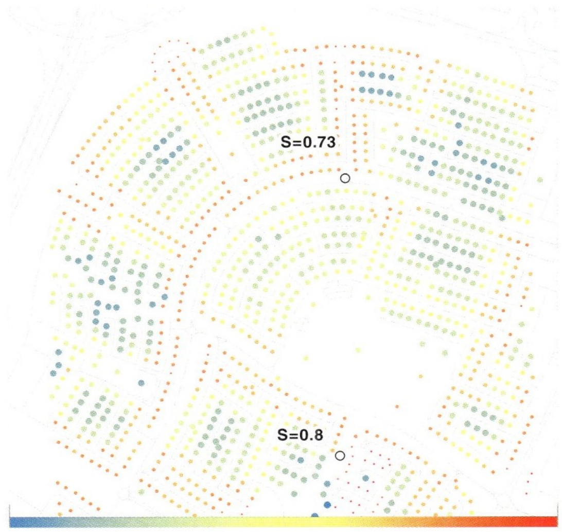

S =0

S= 0.99

FIG. 10.9
Sample 2 - left
Average Reach and Gravity
Scenario 1: Streets only

FIG. 10.10
Sample 2 - right
Average Straightness
Scenario 1: Streets only

Average values without alleyways

Average Reach for all plots = 436.34 plot
Average Reach percentage = 33% of the total number of plots
Average Gravity for all plots = 48.90 plot
Average Gravity percentage = 4% of the total number of plots
Average straightness = 0.69

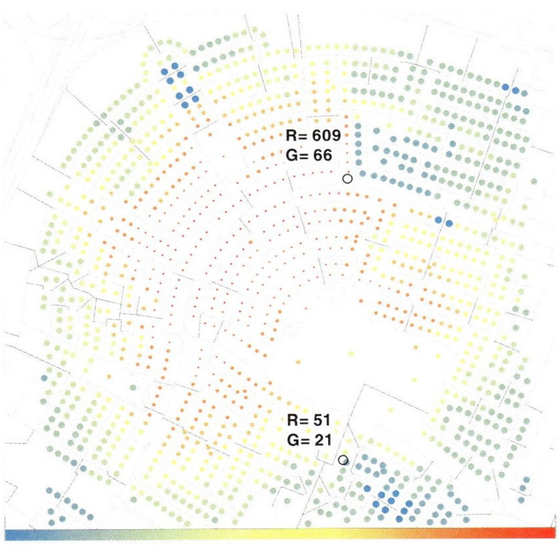

R=217.66
G= 11.7

R= 691
G= 92.26

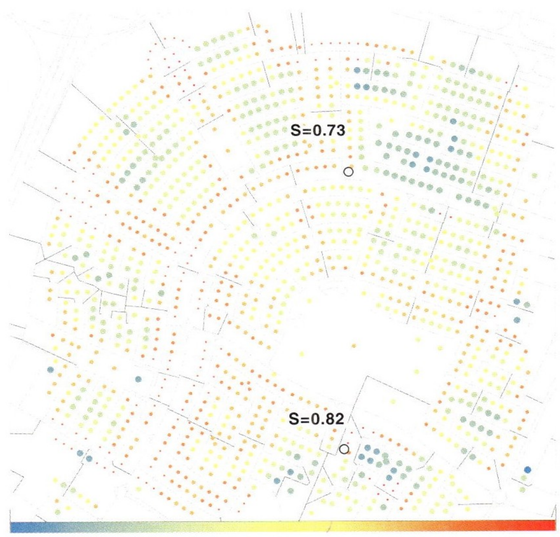

S =0.56

S= 0.84

FIG. 10.11
Sample 2 - left
Average Reach and Gravity
Scenario 2: Streets + Alleys

FIG. 10.12
Sample 2 - right
Average Straightness
Scenario 2: Streets + Alleys

Average values with alleyways

Average Reach for all plots= 517.07 plot
Average Reach percentage = 40% of the total number of plots
Average Gravity for all plots = 63.42 plot
Average Gravity percentage = 5% of the total number of plots
Average straightness = 0.74

Street —— Alleyways

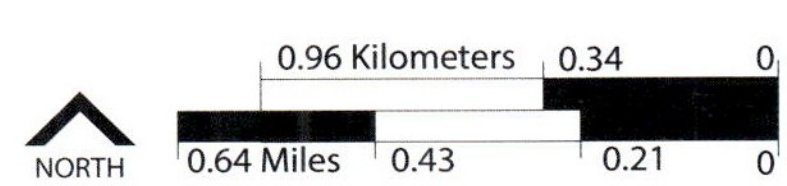

FIG. 11

Histograms showing the distribution of values for the metrics of Reach, Gravity and Straightness. Values for Straightness are bound within a theoretical range between (0,1). The values for all the three metrics are averages of three radii (400, 800, 1600).

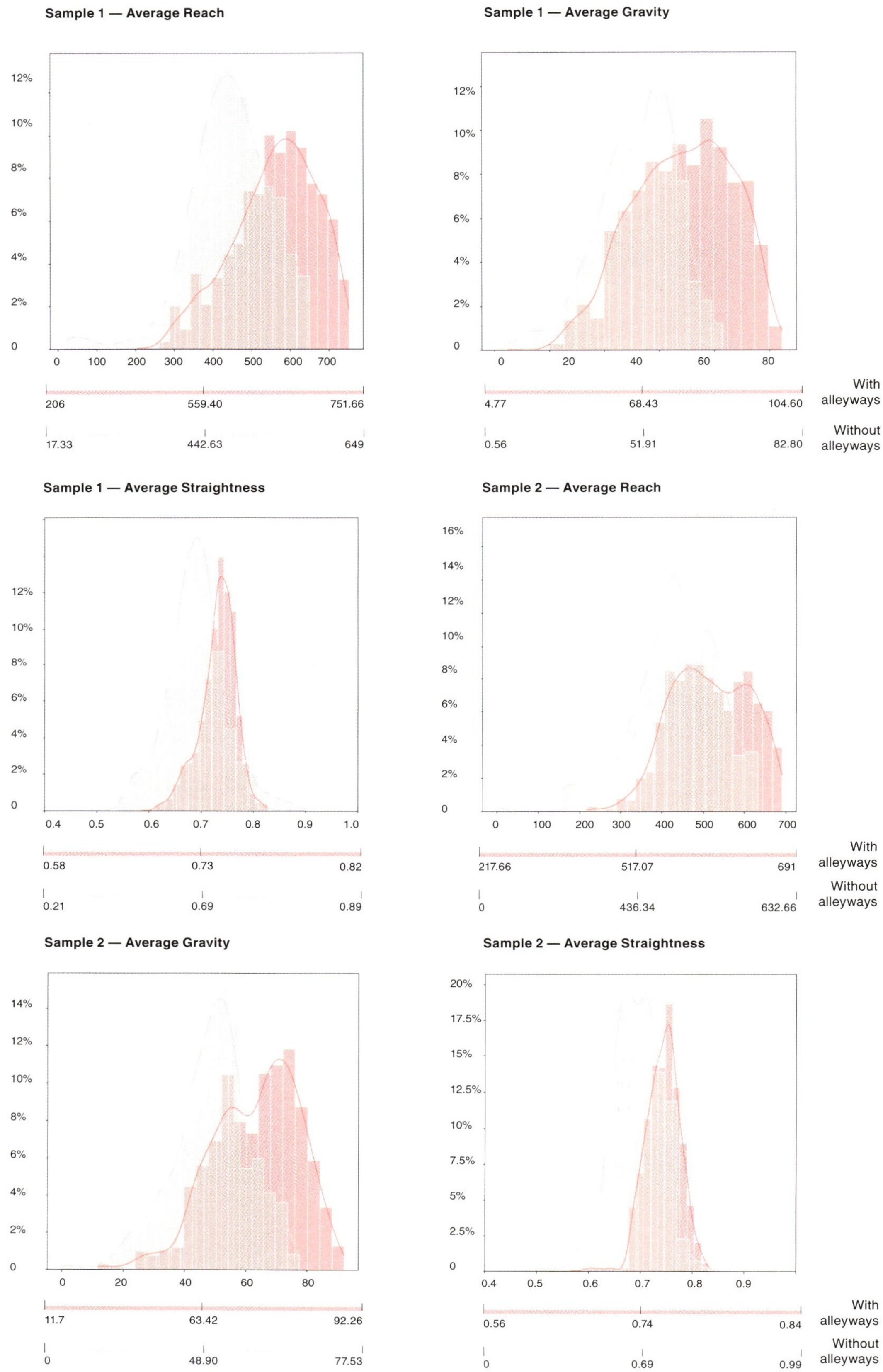

Design Strategies

Plot Density and Network Morphology

Reach and Gravity: *Al Warqa* has a fragmented parallel network morphology (See Figure 12). The samples have low Reach and Gravity values due to their radially fragmented parallel network layout. Sample 1 performs slightly better than Sample 2. This can be attributed to Sample 1 having a higher plot density of 5.37 plots/Ha and smaller blocks of 110 m x 95 m, compared with Sample 2, which has a plot density of 5.08 plots/Ha and a block size of 180 m x 90 m. Additionally, Sample 1 has a lower street intersection density of 0.68 intersections/Ha, compared with Sample 2, whose corresponding value is 1.25 intersections/Ha. Here, a lower street intersection density leads to better Reach and Gravity values compared with other Dubai samples of the Dispersion phase. This is because the samples of Al Warqa have fewer T-junctions. When alleys are added to this street pattern, they have a very high impact on Reach and Gravity values. This is more notable in Sample 2, where a higher alley density of 0.14 km/Ha results in a further increase in the total network intersection density to 1.99 intersections/Ha. These alleys turn T-junctions to four-way intersections.

Straightness: *Al Warqa* samples have medium Straightness values ranging from 0.50 to 0.75. Due to its fragmented parallel layout, the street network has multiple T-junctions. As with Reach and Gravity, the addition of alleys results in an increase in Straightness by resolving T-junctions and increasing the total network intersection density.

Morphological Indicators for Enhancing Connectivity and Accessibility

- Street network: Fragmented parallel is not recommended.
- Plot density: 5.37 plots/Ha and higher is recommended.
- Total network intersection density: 1.99 intersections/Ha is low; higher is recommended; prioritize four-way intersections over T-junctions.
- Block size: 110 m x 95 m is recommended; yet the network design should be consistent in form instead of having a combination of different network patterns.

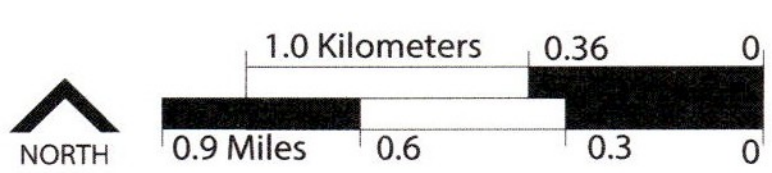

Streets Alleys Plots

FIG. 12
Streets in Al Warqa are of a looping fragmented parallel typology with 0.68 and 1.25 intersections/Ha in samples 1 and 2 respectively. Alleyways reduce the average block size, increase intersection density to 1.46 and 2.05 intersection/Ha in samples 1 and 2 respectively, improve route continuity, and enhance average Straightness values on from 0.69 to 0.73 in sample 1 and from 0.69 to 0.74 in sample 2. Plot densities are considered low at 5.37 and 5.08 plot/Ha in samples 1 and 2 respectively.

Al Barsha

Low Performing Sample

FIG. 13.1
Sample 1 - left
Scenario 1: Streets only

FIG. 13.2
Sample 1 - right
Scenario 2: Streets + Alleys

Area	256 Hectare	**Network (streets + alleyways)**	
Plots count	1197 plot	Total network length	88.84 km
Plot density	4.67 plot/Ha	Total intersection	719
Streets		**Alleyways**	
Total street length	74.89 km	Alleyways length	13.59 km
Street intersections	577	Alleyways intersection	142
Street length density	0.29 km/Ha	Alleyways length density	0.05 km/Ha
Street intersection density	1.73 intersections/Hectare	Alleyways intersection density	0.55 intersections/Hectare

FIG. 13.3
Sample 2 - left
Scenario 1: Streets only

FIG. 13.4
Sample 2 - right
Scenario 2: Streets + Alleys

Area	256 Hectare	**Network (streets + alleyways)**	
Plots count	1184 plot	Total network length	73.95 km
Plot density	4.62 plot/Ha	Total intersection	655
Streets		**Alleyways**	
Total street length		Alleyways length	11.5 km
Street intersections	393	Alleyways intersection	262
Street length density	0.24 km/Ha	Alleyways length density	0.04 km/Ha
Street intersection density	1.20 intersections/Hectare	Alleyways intersection density	1.02 intersections/Hectare

Roads — Alleyways

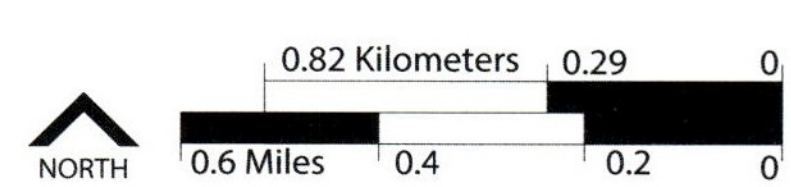

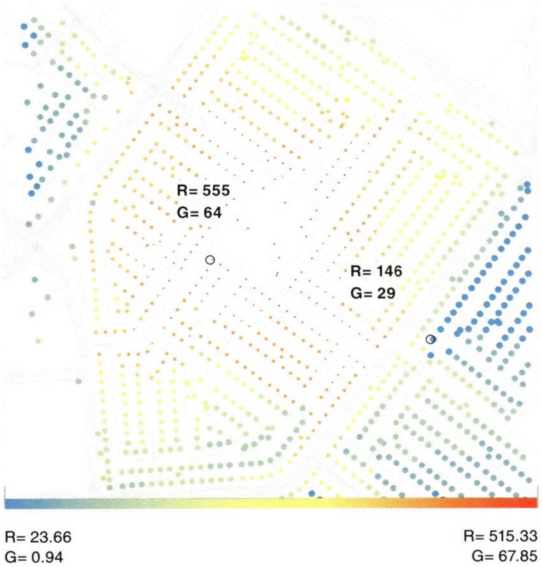

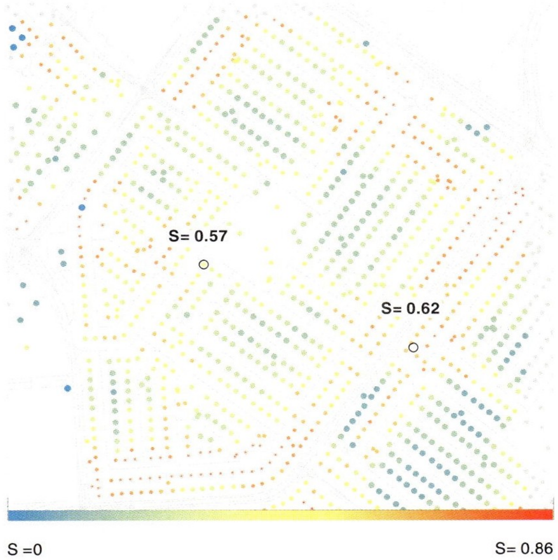

FIG. 13.5
Sample 1 - left
Average Reach and Gravity
Scenario 1: Streets only

FIG. 13.6
Sample 1 - right
Average Straightness
Scenario 1: Streets only

Average values without alleyways

Average Reach for all plots = 304.76 plot
Average Reach percentage = 26% of the total number of plots
Average Gravity for all plots = 36.19 plot
Average Gravity percentage = 3% of the total number of plots
Average straightness = 0.69

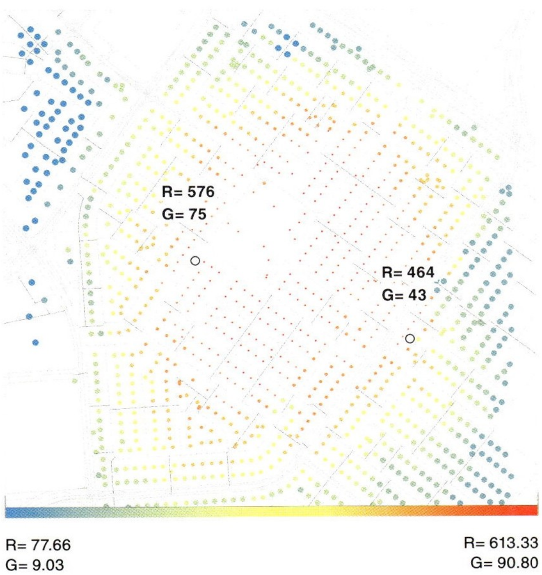

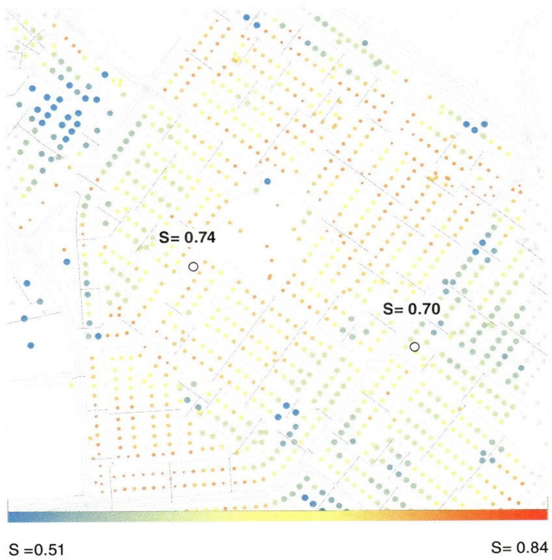

FIG. 13.7
Sample 1 - left
Average Reach and Gravity
Scenario 2: Streets + Alleys

FIG. 13.8
Sample 1 - right
Average Straightness
Scenario 2: Streets + Alleys

Average values with alleyways

Average Reach for all plots = 452.82 plot
Average Reach percentage = 38% of the total number of plots
Average Gravity for all plots = 60.58 plot
Average Gravity percentage = 5% of the total number of plots
Average straightness =0.76

FIG. 13.9
Sample 2 - left
Average Reach and Gravity
Scenario 1: Streets only

FIG. 13.10
Sample 2 - right
Average Straightness
Scenario 1: Streets only

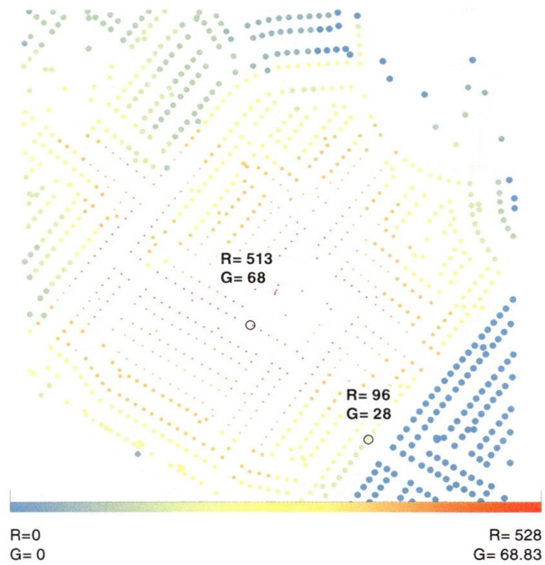

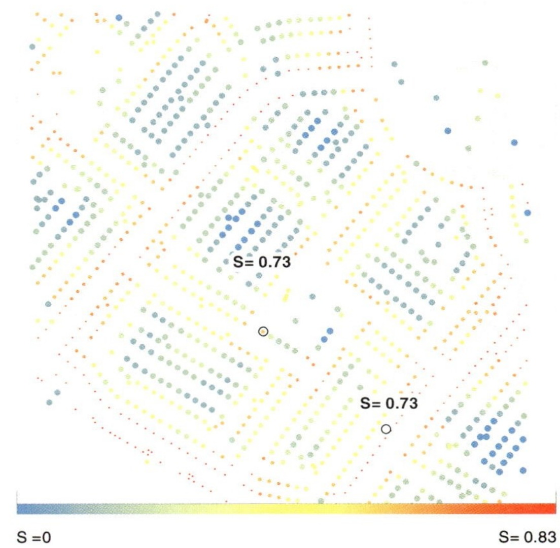

Average values without alleyways

Average Reach for all plots = 313.84 plot
Average Reach percentage = 27% of the total number of plots
Average Gravity for all plots = 37.73 plot
Average Gravity percentage = 3% of the total number of plots
Average straightness = 0.71

FIG. 13.11
Sample 2 - left
Average Reach and Gravity
Scenario 2: Streets + Alleys

FIG. 13.12
Sample 2 - right
Average Straightness
Scenario 2: Streets + Alleys

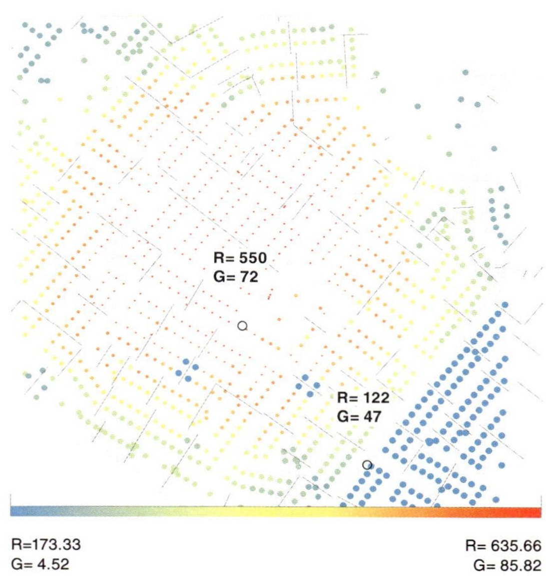

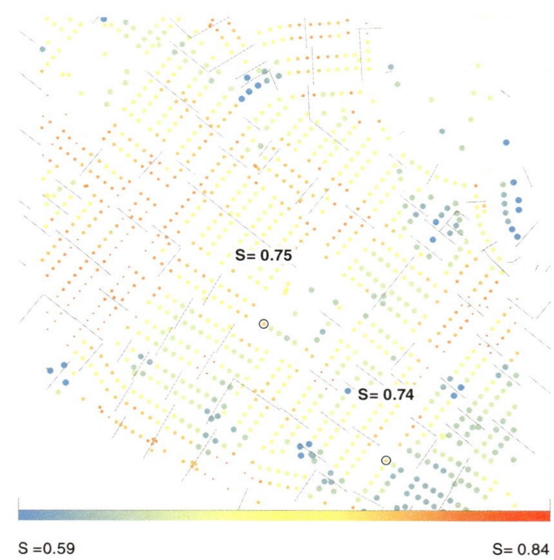

Average values with alleyways

Average Reach for all plots = 495.20 plot
Average Reach percentage = 42% of the total number of plots
Average Gravity for all plots = 60.81 plot
Average Gravity percentage = 5 % of the total number of plots
Average straightness = 0.74

Street —— Alleyways

NORTH

0.82 Kilometers 0.29 0
0.6 Miles 0.4 0.2 0

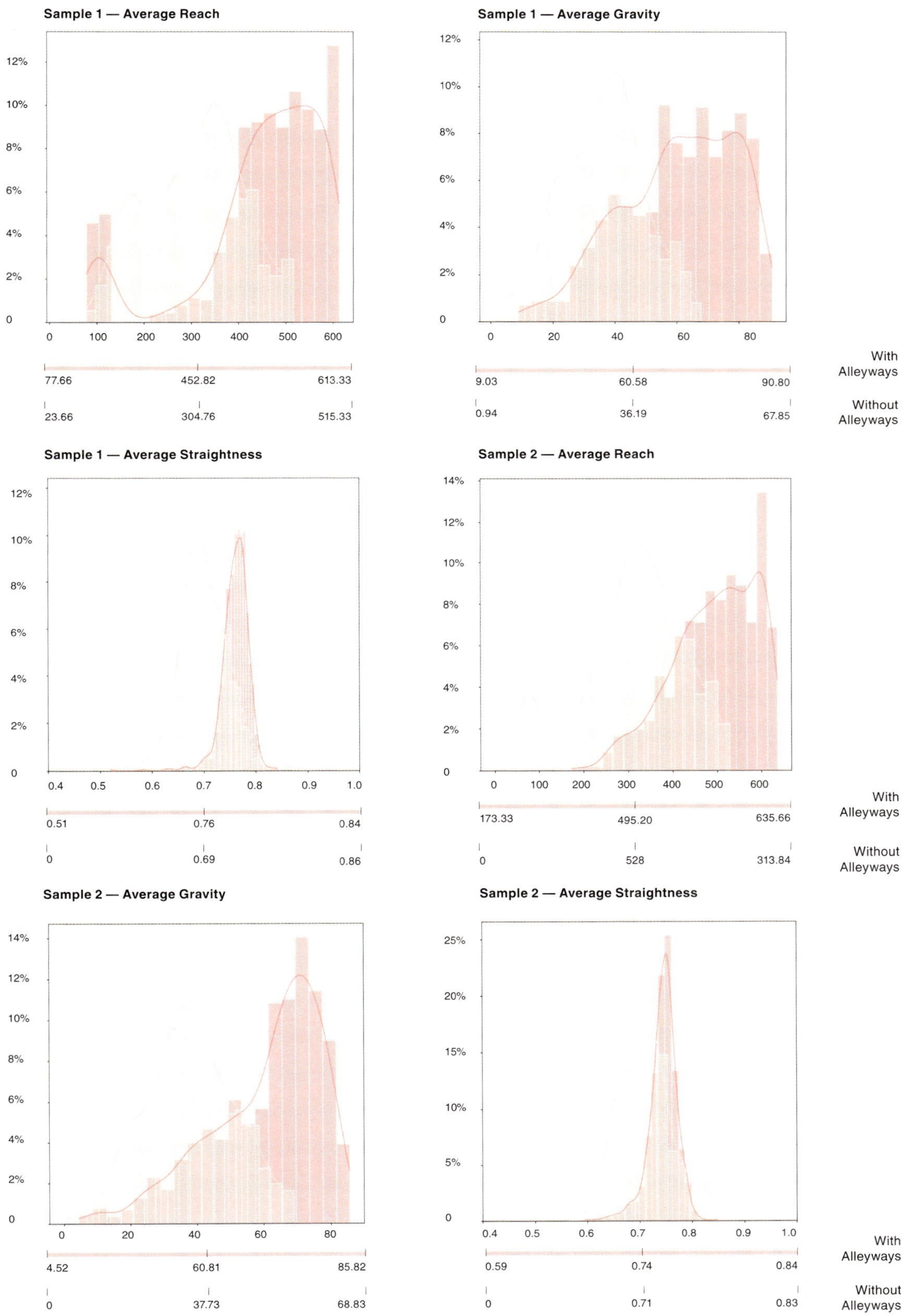

FIG. 14

Histograms showing the distribution of values for the metrics of Reach, Gravity and Straightness. Values for Straightness are bound within a theoretical range between (0,1). The values for all the three metrics are averages of three radii (400, 800, 1600).

Design Strategies

FIG. 15

Streets in Al Barsha have fragmented parallel typology with 1.73 and 1.20 intersections/Ha in samples 1 and 2 respectively. Alleyways reduce the average block size, increase intersection density to 2.80 and 2.55 intersections/Ha in samples 1 and 2 respectively, improve route continuity, and enhance average Straightness values from 0.69 to 0.76 in sample 1 and from 0.71 to 0.74 in sample 2. Plot densities are considered low at 4.67 and 4.62 plot/Ha in sample 1 and 2 respectively.

Plot Density and Network Morphology

Reach and Gravity: *Al Barsha* has a fragmented parallel network morphology (See Figure 15). The samples have low Reach and Gravity values due to their fragmented parallel network layout. The average block size in *Al Barsha* is 160 m x 100 m, and street intersection density averages 1.46 intersections/Ha. The street intersection density of Sample 1, at 1.73 intersections/Ha, is higher than the corresponding value of Sample 2, at 1.20 intersections/Ha. However, unlike the *Al Warqa* samples, the low street intersection density of *Al Barsha* Sample 2 does not result in better Reach and Gravity values. This is due to the higher presence of T-junctions in the network. When alleys are added to this street pattern, they have a very high impact on Reach and Gravity values. This is more notable in Sample 2, which has a lower total network intersection density, at 2.32 intersections/Ha, compared with 2.81 intersections/Ha in Sample 1. Hence, plot density and block size impact accessibility values more than the network morphology does.

Straightness: *Al Barsha's* samples have medium Straightness values ranging from 0.50 to 0.75. Due to its fragmented parallel layout, the street network has multiple T-junctions. The addition of alleys results in an increase in Straightness by resolving T-junctions and increasing the total network intersection density to an average of 2.56 intersections/Ha. As with Reach and Gravity, this is more notable in Sample 2, which has fewer intersections. This indicates that Straightness depends on the amount of resolved discontinuities rather than the raw density values.

Morphological Indicators for Enhancing Connectivity and Accessibility

- Street network: Fragmented parallel not recommended.
- Plot density: 4.65 or more plots/Ha is recommended.
- Street intersection density: 2.32 intersections/Ha; prioritize four-way intersections over T-junctions.
- Block size: 140 m x 100 m is recommended, but with more consistent layouts.

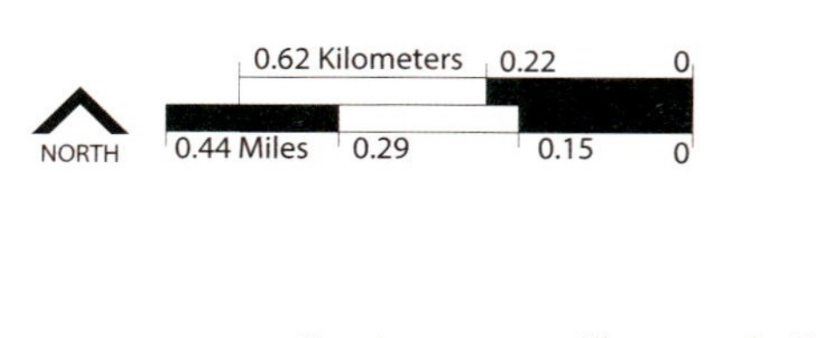

Chapter Summary

Abu Dhabi

Low Performing Samples

MBZ

Sample 1: Streets

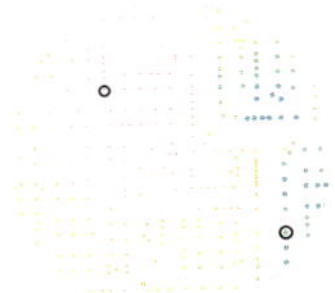
Sample 2: Streets

Sample 1: Streets + Alleys

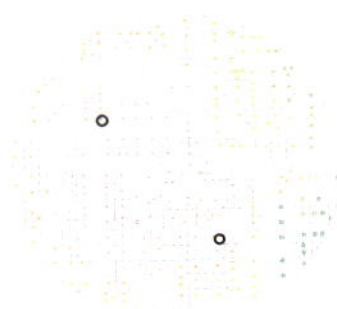
Sample 2: Streets + Alleys

Al Bahya East

Sample 1: Streets

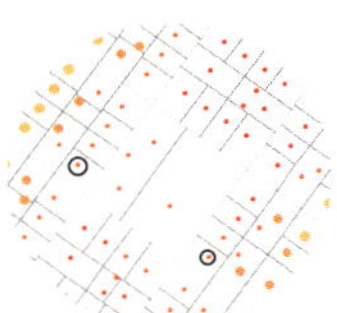
Sample 1: Streets + Alleys

Dubai

Low Performing Samples

Al Warqa

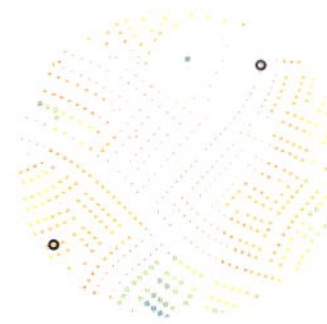
Sample 1: Streets

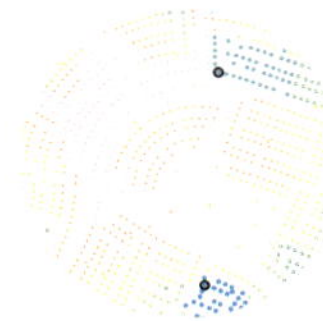
Sample 2: Streets

Sample 1: Streets + Alleys

Sample 2: Streets + Alleys

Al Barsha

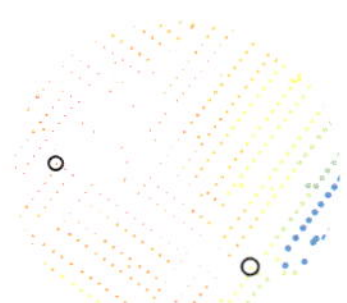
Sample 1: Streets

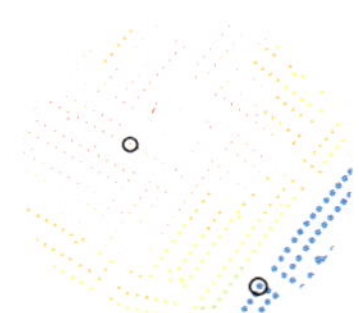
Sample 2: Streets

Sample 1: Streets + Alleys

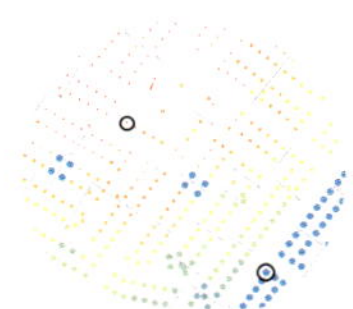
Sample 2: Streets + Alleys

FIG. 16.1
Abu Dhabi & Dubai
Low performing samples

Abu Dhabi

High Performing Samples

West Island

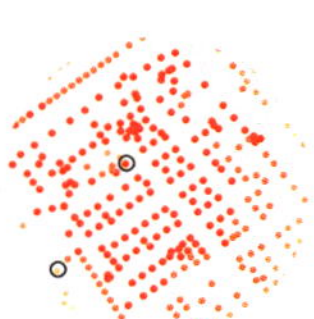
Sample 1: Streets

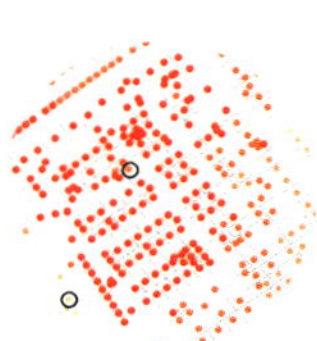
Sample 1: Streets + Alleys

Al Falah

Sample 1: Streets

Dubai

High Performing Samples

Al Satwa

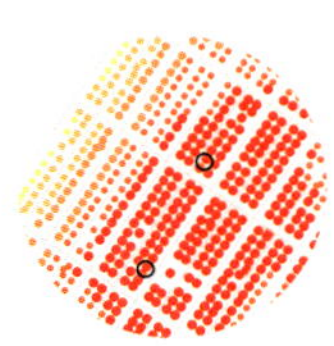
Sample 1: Streets

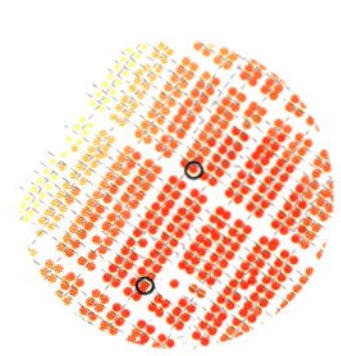
Sample 1: Streets + Alleys

Al Quoz

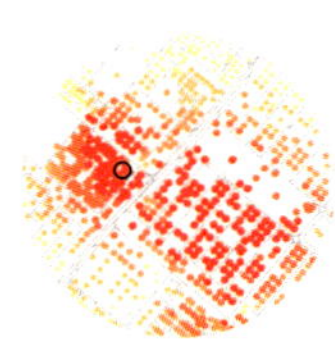
Sample 1: Streets

Sample 1: Streets + Alleys

Dubai Creek

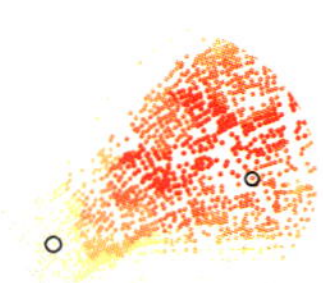
Sample 1: Streets

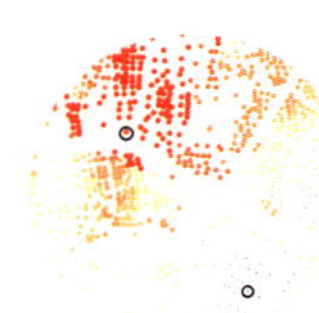
Sample 2: Streets

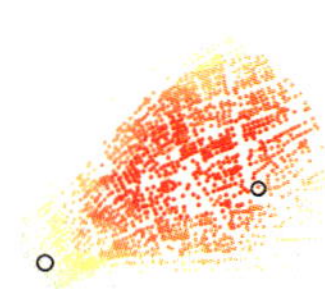
Sample 1: Streets + Alleys

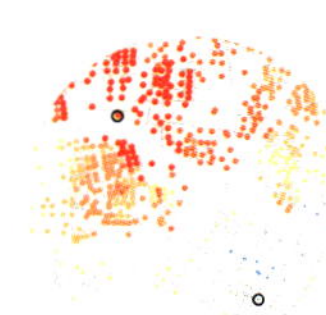
Sample 2: Streets + Alleys

FIG. 16.2
Abu Dhabi & Dubai
High performing samples

Rethinking Suburbs:
Morphological and Network Analysis Review

Published by
Actar Publishers, New York, Barcelona
www.actar.com

Author
Khaled Alawadi

Edited by
Actar Publishers

Graphic Design
Khaled Alawadi + Slash

Copy editing and proofreading
Khaled Alawadi

Printing and binding
Arlquin SL

Distribution
Actar D, Inc. New York, Barcelona.

New York
440 Park Avenue South, 17th Floor
New York, NY 10016, USA
T +1 2129662207
salesnewyork@actar-d.com

Barcelona
Roca i Batlle 2
08023 Barcelona, Spain
T +34 933 282 183
eurosales@actar-d.com

Indexing
English ISBN: 978-1-63840-107-0
Library of Congress Control Number: 2023942382

Printed inSpain
Publication date: January 2024